Information Security

FOR MANAGERS

Michael Workman, PhD
Professor, Nathan M. Bisk College of Business
Director, Security Policy Institute
Florida Institute of Technology

Daniel C. Phelps, PhD
Assistant Teaching Professor
Information Systems Program
Carnegie Mellon University in Qatar

John N. Gathegi, PhD, JD
Professor, School of Information
Courtesy Professor, School of Mass Communications
University of South Florida

JONES & BARTLETT
LEARNING

World Headquarters
Jones & Bartlett Learning
5 Wall Street
Burlington, MA 01803
978-443-5000
info@jblearning.com
www.jblearning.com

Jones & Bartlett Learning books and products are available through most bookstores and online booksellers. To contact Jones & Bartlett Learning directly, call 800-832-0034, fax 978-443-8000, or visit our website, www.jblearning.com.

Production Credits:
Publisher: Cathleen Sether
Senior Acquisitions Editor: Timothy Anderson
Senior Associate Editor: Amy Bloom
Director of Production: Amy Rose
Production Assistant: Alyssa Lawrence
Senior Marketing Manager: Andrea DeFronzo
V.P., Manufacturing and Inventory Control: Therese Connell

Composition: Laserwords Private Limited, Chennai, India
Cover Design: Scott Moden
Rights and Permissions Manager: Katherine Crighton
Rights and Photo Research Supervisor: Anna Genoese
Cover Image: © Sean Gladwell/ShutterStock, Inc.
Printing and Binding: Malloy, Inc.
Cover Printing: Malloy, Inc.

Library of Congress Cataloging-in-Publication Data
Workman, Michael D., 1957-
Information security for managers / Michael Workman, Daniel C. Phelps, and John N. Gathegi.
 p. cm.
Includes index.
ISBN-13: 978-0-7637-9301-2 (pbk.)
ISBN-10: 0-7637-9301-9 (pbk.)
1. Information technology—Security measures. 2. Computer security—Management. 3. Computer networks—Security measures. 4. Business enterprises—Security measures. I. Phelps, Daniel C. II. Gathegi, John Ng'ang'a. III. Title.
 HF5548.37.W67 2013
 658.4'78—dc23

 2011033490

6048
Printed in the United States of America
16 15 14 13 12   10 9 8 7 6 5 4 3 2 1

Contents

Preface

Welcome to *Information Security for Managers*! This textbook will provide you with an overview of conceptual and applied knowledge of information and systems security and will offer a summary overview of security concepts that are addressed in more technical detail in Jones & Bartlett Learning's Information Systems Security & Assurance series. Our goal is to provide a reference textbook suitable for computer science and information technology students in the area of what is known as *"knowledge work,"* and to introduce the concepts you may read in the series if you seek more in-depth technical knowledge. The text is also suitable for managers desiring to learn more about information security. This textbook is divided into four sections dealing with major aspects of security in which the reader needs to be familiarized: policies and procedures, technology orientation, computer and network security, and managing organizations securely. We present most of the material at a conceptual level, but, where we believe appropriate, we also delve into some of the more technical details to give the audience insights into critical security issues at the "implementation" level.

Why Study Information Security?

Security is important to managers because although information systems have improved over the years to become more effective in collecting and rendering information for human consumers, these improvements have been accompanied by increases in the frequency and sophistication of attacks against them. The impacts from attacks against companies are significant, and managers are responsible for their organizations, including security. Failures can cause significant losses to companies and to their suppliers and clients, may cost managers their jobs, and can even lead to legal liabilities that are adjudicated against them.

Unintentional and Intentional Security Failures

Examples of where the consequences of information security failures can come into play include hospital emergency rooms, rail transportation control rooms, and power grids. In hospital emergency rooms, physicians use technology to evaluate the relationships among indicators of illnesses when they review signs and symptoms, laboratory information, and results of specialized diagnostic studies or cases in order to diagnose acute patient conditions and decide on treatments. If compromised, this information could lead to severe consequences. There is a growing threat that an employee at a hospital or clinic might steal patient information and sell it on the black market for the purposes of identity theft and insurance fraud. In rail transportation control rooms, trains are electronically dispatched and switched between myriad tracks according to situational variables such as train and crew operability, and containers' contents and schedules. Compromised information can lead to catastrophes, as seen when two Burlington Northern Santa Fe (BNSF) railroad trains collided in 2010. In power grids, there are tens of thousands of different kinds of generators that must be electronically managed and monitored for electrical power output, temperature, power redirection, and unit failures, which could be compromised by attackers or disrupted simply as a cause of human or machine error.

Technologies, Time Zones, and Geography

Technologies are rapidly advancing in their capabilities, but along with these advancements come new security problems. For instance, widely available spyware software that targets mobile phones can remotely activate the phone and be used by third parties to track a person's whereabouts, read text messages from the phone, and even listen in on phone conversations. Surface computing, grid computing, cloud computing, and semantic technologies and software agents are all emerging (often called "disruptive") technologies that are being implemented well ahead of adequate security measures that might protect them. We now have to think about Software as a Service (SaaS), and we will soon have to contend with intelligent bots, called "agents," that may not only "visit" our computers to gather information and carry out instructions, but also execute instructions that are given to them, such as to make reservations through an airline or restaurant web page. Now we will have to think about the security of our technology outsourcing to various countries that may be a friend today but a foe tomorrow, and perhaps vice versa. As a case in point, consider the recent activity in Vietnam, which in a few decades has gone from a war zone to a major commercial center.

Security and Operations

In addition to protecting people and facilities, managers have the responsibility to protect the confidentiality, integrity, and availability (known as CIA) of information resources and the infrastructure that enables these attributes. There are safeguards for computer systems, networks, mobile devices, databases, and the like. However, managers need to assess the company infrastructure and the threat risks to the infrastructure. They must determine the vulnerabilities of their infrastructure to threats and determine potential exposure and probable loss in the event of an attack or disaster.

Managers need to make plans for implementing security measures and formulate contingencies in case of a security breach. They must oversee the implementations of security measures and personnel training programs and evaluate the implementations in an iterative cycle to ensure continuous vigilance and improvements. They must do all of these things in the midst of planning projects according to budgets and making their scheduled deadlines. The broad categories of tasks that managers must perform show just how much a manager's responsibilities have expanded beyond the traditional management of employee performance and asset utilization. Organizations have flattened since the 1980s, which means that managers must do more with less—and there seems to be no end in sight for this expectation.

Running daily security operations includes monitoring for and defending against security attacks. Intrusion detection systems are available to indicate attempts at finding vulnerabilities and attempts to exploit them. There are procedures that managers follow to determine how security incidents may have occurred after the fact. Managers determine corrective actions that may need to be taken, as well as how to preserve evidence. Managers are also interested in techniques and technologies that can be used to predict attacks and disasters in an effort to avoid them.

Textbook Organization

To help answer questions that many, if not most, managers have about how to stay viable in this dynamic technological world, we have developed a textbook to arm managers with answers to the most critical questions and to provide them with references to more in-depth study in areas where they may need to specialize. As such, our textbook is organized as seen in the following diagram, covering organizations and the rules of law and policies, an introduction to technologies for managers, an introduction with emphasis on security and security initiatives, and finally, a view of security operations and strategic aspects of security that may lay on the horizon:

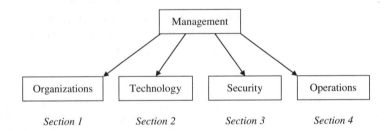

- ✓ *Section 1* introduces the legal, organizational, and informational structure of companies. This beginning frames the managerial context and discusses common constraints that confront managers in conducting their business securely.
- ✓ *Section 2* provides an orientation of technologies to a management audience. It provides a high-level summary of technical details that underlies security threats and security measures that concern managers.
- ✓ *Section 3* covers, at the conceptual level, computer, network, and information security to protect their confidentiality, integrity, and availability.
- ✓ *Section 4* explores how to monitor information and systems, handle security incidents, and manage security behaviors. This section also posits what lies on the security horizon.

Textbook Content

The field of information security is heavily published, and most of the publications are divided along either technical or administrative lines. Technical publications include resources to target security of information systems (IS) such as computers and networks aimed at implementations and implementers. Administrative publications cover policies, security models, standards, and operations aimed at regulators, auditors, and government agencies. We believe that a comprehensive information security resource for managers should introduce a broad range of topics that are not targeted at a particular security certification or a given government agency. Our position is that once managers in commercial enterprises understand security in general, they can then dive into the security domain knowledge for their industry or agency.

Given these assumptions, we introduce managers to technologies including operating systems, applications, databases, and networks, while digging into the means used to secure these systems. We introduce trends that include advances in mobile technologies, along with more traditional fixed-site systems. In addition to these technical aspects of security, we provide coverage of regulations and applicable security and employment law, but not at a level where the *forest is lost among the trees*.

In this textbook, we include coverage of these important concepts, but at a level that is appropriate for managers who oversee technology implementations and people who work with technology. We also cover security behavior in organizations because the research literature on security continues to point to the human element (sometimes called the *weakest link*) as one of the most important aspects of information security, and yet this continues to be treated sparsely in terms of what to do about this problem, especially as it relates to what is known as the *knowing–doing gap*—that is, knowing better, but not doing better. With our textbook, we present a practical and yet comprehensive publication for knowledge-work managers that includes all of these aspects.

Knowledge Scaffolding

A typical textbook is usually organized topically. Topical organization is useful for rote memorization of a topic or for referencing information later. Our approach is different. Pedagogically, we designed this textbook for academic programs in such areas as management information systems, information systems management, and information science, but it should also be applicable to management and security readership more generally and should be appealing to all those who are concerned about organizational information security. It is not written in the style of a reference manual or a guide to a particular security certification.

To that end, we utilize an incremental development method called *knowledge scaffolding*—a proven educational psychology technique for learning subject matter thoroughly. Knowledge scaffolding means that certain materials are presented in iterative chunks. A chunk is presented with other chunks to flesh out an idea, and then the ideas are presented again in different contexts (and in different chapters) to develop a deeper

and broader understanding of the topic in relation to the other topics for a holistic understanding, as well as to reinforce learning through an elaborative rehearsal process.

We chose this approach because there are plenty of reference materials generally
available for readers and students who are studying information security, including those
that are freely available on the Internet, and those resources are certainly valuable and
needed during referential lookups or general knowledge acquisition. Our goal with this
textbook is to help readers learn about managing information security from the ground
up and to reinforce the learning as they read on. This textbook is also organized to first
concentrate on general management issues and then gradually evolve into more technical
content. This should assist readers with properly framing the technical information into a
managerial perspective.

Learning Approach and Objectives

We adopt a Gestalt approach to the presentation of information in our textbook. The
essence of this approach is to create greater insight and understanding through the
presentation of "new relationships" that emerge from situating familiar information
in different contexts. This is an especially effective technique for those who bring world
experience to a learning activity and then are given a variety of frames in which to view
the information and their experiences differently.

Who Will Benefit from This Textbook?	What They Will Learn:
✓ Students of Security and Management	❑ How to use security principles in designs to improve the security of systems.
✓ Managers and Project Leads	
✓ Systems and Software Developers	❑ How to effectively manage security behaviors.
✓ Product and Technical Directors	
✓ Information Architects	❑ How to improve decision making and problem solving about security issues.
✓ Business Analysts	
✓ Human Resource Policy and Standards Coordinators	❑ How to evaluate and justify security technology selections and designs.
✓ Strategic Planners	❑ How to improve returns on security technology investments.
✓ Systems and Solutions Designers	❑ How to establish organization-wide security of information systems that align technical with business needs and goals.
✓ Technical Consultants	
✓ Information and Security Officers	
	❑ How to apply the appropriate security tools effectively.
	❑ How to plan for existing and future needs and emerging security issues.

Looking Forward

In this textbook, we want to construct a bird's-eye view of the state of the art in security management and provide a glimpse of what may lay ahead in the evolution of—or maybe even revolution in—information security. This is important because we are on the verge of a paradigm shift (to borrow Thomas Kuhn's salient term from his seminal book, *The Structure of Scientific Revolutions*). The shift is occurring on at least three levels: (1) there is an increased emphasis on understanding and managing human security behaviors, (2) there is a need to incorporate social media and new communications technology in the security rubric, and (3) there is an evolution of semantic integration and fusion systems used in security infrastructure, modeling, and prediction.

In our endeavor to provide a bird's-eye view of the state of the art, we will (1) elucidate new approaches to solving real-world information security problems, such as how to address organizational security behaviors, (2) contrast competing paradigms and approaches to security problem solving and decision making, using technology as a tool and a technique, (3) highlight promising directions, and (4) prompt constructive thought around contemporary business and technological security themes.

Additional Information About This Textbook

This textbook focuses special attention on managing information, systems, and people securely. Each chapter develops key concepts and presents issues that managers should know in order to effectively oversee their departments. Because the emphasis is on management of information resources, it provides mainly the "what" aspects of information systems and technologies, and suggests more in-depth coverage of "why" certain practices or procedures are used. It will provide some insight into features and functions of security technologies and techniques and will develop some bridge knowledge into security threats and the countermeasures that managers and security professionals use to help prevent or neutralize them. We begin our textbook with organizational considerations and then move into more technical topics. The more technical aspects of security provide a high-level view of the procedural and technological features of operations and management in an information security context. We hope you find this book a useful resource for learning, as well as a reference throughout your management and information security career.

In the chapters that follow, you will see "**In Focus**" points. These are important topics that should spark you to do some reflective thinking and suggest further research on a particularly important topic. At the end of each chapter, you will also find questions and exercises to do in a section titled "**Think About It**." The exercises will test your knowledge from your readings. There are also some extended study questions to ponder in a broader context that will require that you do some critical thinking about the materials you have read. You may need to investigate those key points using other readily available resources.

Additional Resources for Instructors

Answers to end of chapter questions and a PowerPoint Image Bank that contains key images from the text are available for instructor download at go.jblearning.com/ Workman.

Acknowledgments

The authors would like to thank the following colleagues for their valuable feedback on our textbook:

Hamid R. Arabnia, PhD, University of Georgia

William H. Bommer, PhD, California State University at Fresno

Darrell E. Burke, PhD, University of Alabama at Birmingham

Kathy Chudoba, PhD, Utah State University

Richard Ford, PhD, Florida Institute of Technology

Mike Gancarz, Vice President, Bank of America

Misook Heo, PhD, Duquesne University

Guido Hertel, PhD, University of Muenster, Germany

Peter Horn, PhD, International School of Management, France

Larry Hyde, CISSP, The Hyde Group

Ryan Long, JD, U.S. Department of Defense

E. Eugene Schultz, PhD, Late of University of California at Berkeley

Eugene H. Spafford, PhD, Purdue University

Detmar W. Straub, PhD, Georgia State University

Nikos Tsianos, PhD, University of Athens, Greece

A special thanks to E. Eugene (Gene) Schultz, who tragically passed away in October 2011.

Thank you also to the Editorial and Production teams at Jones & Bartlett Learning: Tim Anderson, Senior Acquisitions Editor; Amy Bloom, Managing Editor; Chris Will, Vice President, Professional Sales and Business Development; Alyssa Lawrence, Production Assistant; and all the Jones & Bartlett Learning staff who diligently worked with us behind the scenes.

SECTION ONE

What Should Managers Know About Security Policies and Procedures?

Introduction to Information Security

WHO CAN CONCEIVE OF AN organization that doesn't involve information and systems? Information created and used in organizations reflects all the intellectual property, competitive intelligence, business transaction records, and other strategic, tactical, and operating data for businesses and people. Regardless of industry, managers in organizations today need some understanding of how to protect these information resources, as well as their personnel. This is even more so the case if managers work in some form of "knowledge work," a term coined by Peter Drucker referring to work done primarily with information or work that develops and uses knowledge. Given the importance of information systems security in modern life, there is no escaping that we need a solid foundation in technical knowledge and a strong set of critical thinking and analytical skills to succeed in today's global knowledge work marketplace.

Chapter 1 Topics

This chapter:

- Gives an overview of technology and security behavior issues.
- Presents an overview of organizational governance.
- Discusses cyber crime, security, and costs.
- Provides a presentation of management responsibilities.
- Covers insider and outsider threats.
- Introduces assessment, planning, and evaluations and provides an overview of security attacks.

Chapter 1 Goals

When you finish this chapter, you should:

- ☐ Understand the relationships among organizational practices, technologies, and employees.
- ☐ Be familiar with the costs of cyber crime and security implementations.
- ☐ Know some of the reasons for attacks.
- ☐ Become acquainted with various security technologies.

1.1 Technological and Behavioral Security Issues

Many of the security solutions proposed in the literature have tended to ignore the fact that the problem of securing organizational systems has its grounding in human behavior. The fact remains that information security defenses have not kept pace with abusers' attempts to undermine them. Without the right skills, security decision-makers will continue with wasteful spending on ineffective or poorly implemented security technologies, protocols, procedures, and techniques. But there is a related insidious condition: Unused or poorly implemented security technologies and techniques are not sufficiently helping managers improve their security-related decisions, better solve security-related problems, make more effective plans, or take improved courses of action—leading to unbounded costs associated with lost strategic opportunities, tactical missteps, lost revenues from security breaches, and the myriad other problems that result from this waste.

Managers and security consultants are on the front lines of the problem because they assume special responsibilities for ensuring that their workforce takes precautions against violations to the security of people, organizational systems, and information resources. This has become even more crucial post-9/11 (as it has come to be known) because of growing legislation and regulation of industry. For example, terms such as "downstream liability," where companies have been held liable for unwittingly having their computer resources used for illegal purposes, have been joined by the concept of "upstream liability," where consultants might be held liable for giving advice that leads to corporate liabilities.

1.1.1 Organizational Governance

The main security management issue relative to the concept of governance is in the management of *risk*. Risk may be defined as the potential for harm or damage to be caused to people or assets from a proposed threat. We will discuss risk management in more detail later and further refine the definition, but for now keep this definition in mind so that you can frame it in your mind relative to governance. **Governance** is the use of best practices—those that are commonly accepted as "good common sense" in a particular domain of knowledge and expected relative expertise, and additionally using standards and requirements for a given industry such as regulations for the purpose of reducing risks.

Depending on the industry and the role a manager holds in the organization, it is important to realize that international work laws and regulations vary widely and that the laws that affect work are changing rapidly. In the United States, the federal Department of Labor specifies many of the public policies and regulations that affect work. This body oversees regulatory agencies such as the Occupational Safety and Health Administration, Bureau of Labor Statistics, and Worker's Compensation.

State agencies such as state departments of labor may also define work regulations, and there are regulations that affect work in a specific industry such as the National Archives and Records Administration (NARA), which has created regulations under the Federal Records Act (FRA) to prevent shredding or deleting certain kinds of email. These regulations may have implications not only for email considered to be federal records but also a range of message types in the wake of antitrust litigation and the Public Company Accounting Reform and Investor Protection Act of 2002.

Also, depending on their roles in the organization, some managers may need to know how to perform risk analyses and conduct threat and vulnerability assessments for measuring levels of security risk and producing plans for risk mitigation. These actions may include the creation of disaster preparedness, business continuity, and disaster recovery plans. (Note that we will cover these topics in more detail in subsequent chapters.) Managers may even be involved in conducting criminal forensic analyses and might be called upon to assist in the prosecution of criminal activity.

Even non-technical managers need a fundamental understanding of principles and practices used in managing information and people securely. They need to understand, at least at a cursory level, security management policies and applications, and how governance models and risk management best practices factor into implementing and managing an effective information and systems security infrastructure so that proper decisions can be made—and in gaining approvals for budgets and spending, and implementing proper and measured security controls.

1.1.2 Security, Cyber Crime, and Costs

Cyber crime statistics are difficult to come by partly because of the scope of the problem and the underreporting of incidents. Some of the best guesses, however, indicate that losses grew in the United States from roughly $378 million in the late 1990s [1, 2] to approaching $1 billion by 2009 [3]. In the late 1990s, approximately 50% of companies reported having at least one security-related incident during the year [1], but by 2008, nearly two-thirds of companies reported at least one incident in that year [4]. By 2009, nearly three-quarters of companies surveyed had had security incidents in the previous year [3].

Also, lawsuits against employers and individual actors (managers, coworkers, subordinates) are dramatically on the rise [5], along with increases in suits against outside cyber attackers and blog posters [6, 7]. Concurrent with the increase in the number of incidents and lawsuits, the costs of implementing security measures has grown steadily, reaching more than 8 percent of an average company's budget by 2006 [8], and continues climbing beyond that figure [9]. In 2003, private industry spending on information security in the United States was more than $1 billion and was more than $6.5 billion for the U.S. government. According to the Information Security Oversight Office [10] of the U.S. National Archives and Records Administration:

> The [2003] cost estimate on information security for the US government indicated a 14 percent increase over the cost estimate reported for FY 2002. For the second year in a row, industry reported an increase in its cost estimate. The total cost estimate for Government and industry for 2003 is $7.5 billion, $1 billion more than the total cost estimate for Government and industry in 2002. In particular, physical security cost estimates went up by 47 percent. All other categories noted increases: Personnel Security (1%); Professional Education, Training and Awareness (18%); Security Management, Oversight and Planning (16%); Unique Items (8%); Information Security/Classification Management (19%); and Information Technology (17%). [10]

Rapid technological changes occurring in the Internet along with new web-based technologies and social media are enabling communications in ways that are outpacing their regulation, giving rise to new issues related to "free speech" versus rights to "due process." Consequently, many companies are using what might be called ***strategic lawsuits against public participation*** (SLAPP) toward people and corporations that post negative comments about another in a public forum such as a blog or a website. The most common type of SLAPP is for defamation, but one of many alternatives has been to use tort interference against such bloggers and website posters. Although companies that file such claims hope to intimidate critics by burdening them with legal fees even if the filing party knows that the case might be dismissed at the end of a long legal battle, companies who have invested much in brand reputation are often willing to engage in this "strategic losing battle" because they know the *real* financial loser could be the critic.

Many states, especially California, have enacted some form of anti-SLAPP law to try to help neutralize frivolous lawsuits. Regardless, anyone who posts negative comments—even if it is only stated as an opinion (which is one defense against a defamation claim) should take caution. Managers should make their personnel aware that a response to their negative postings might not be in the form of a rebuttal in a blog, but rather in the form of a summons to appear in court. If the employee has made these negative posts from a company-owned system, the company as a whole may be involved in the suit—thus online governance and proper online behavior should be included in the company's policies.

On the other side of the coin relative to using a SLAPP, some "freedom of speech" proponents have criticized the tactic, but aside from the idealism of that position, the reality is that managers are responsible for protecting corporate assets that include intangible factors such as brand and corporate reputation, which affects the financial interests of the business. Thus managers have to weigh the *pros* and *cons* of striving to protect their corporate image and brand integrity through the legal system. However, it is incumbent upon management to strive to make a reasoned choice and resolve problems amicably if possible. This is one of the key pillars of risk management.

1.1.3 Management Duties, Responsibilities, and Threats

As we alluded to earlier, managers are in a vice-grip between containing costs and containing risk exposures. The tensions created by these opposing goals may force managers into certain compromises. Before making the tradeoff decisions, managers at all levels need to be both educated and informed. *Keep in mind that most management successes can be attributed to how well managers contribute to keeping the corporation profitable.* Managers carry duties and responsibilities to take prudent actions to protect their workforce and corporate assets. These responsibilities and duties encompass (among other actions) formulating and overseeing the organization policies and company practices and processes.

There are many (and the number is still growing) standards and criteria by which organizations are judged internationally [11]; we are seeing an increase in mandated regulations throughout the United States, the United Kingdom, the European Union, and all across the globe to govern organizational practices. However, even these necessary mechanisms are not sufficient to prevent security incidents. By way of analogy, as it has been said, passing a driving test and obtaining a driver's license may not be sufficient to protect one from having an automobile accident [12].

Much of the concentration in the security literature has been on dealing with outsider threats; however, a large proportion of security incidents involve insiders. We define insider attacks as *intentional computer misuse by users who are authorized to access systems and networks.* Insiders are typically employees or contractors of a corporation, although vendors, service personnel, consultants, and others may also broadly be defined as insiders [13].

Surveys indicate that current and former employees cause most of the computer attacks, that roughly 80% of those attacks were caused by internal employees, and that 89% of those attacks were done by *disgruntled employees* [14]. Detecting insider attacks can be an extremely difficult problem, but predicting them might be even more challenging. Because past behavior is a good predictor of future behavior [15], managers may examine past conduct by using pre-employment screening and background checks to help predict behaviors. However, there is always the possibility that an offender has not yet been caught, and so employers may monitor and evaluate employees continually on the job. Note that managers need to balance three "legs of the chair"—that is, (1) try to filter out anyone who is not a good fit or is a risk, (2) monitor critical behaviors for workers on the job to help prevent or intervene in deviant behavior, and (3) undertake appropriate actions in response.

1.2 Assessing and Planning

A critical managerial function is to assess the exposure of assets and strive to provide a value for those assets to the finance personnel for determining the impacts to the organization if these are lost or damaged. This can be a tedious process, and one that should be carried out by a team of qualified professionals. Also, managers have limited budgets and must prioritize their spending according to the severity and likelihood of threat risks.

The security assessment and planning functions of management may draw from guidelines, standards, and best practices. For example, the Federal Information Processing Standard (FIPS) is necessary for government systems, but may also serve as a process and criteria for commercial enterprises. As part of the E-Government Act of 2002 (Public Law 107-347), the FIPS-200 became "the second of the mandatory security standards, specifies minimum security requirements for information and information systems supporting the executive agencies of the federal government and risk-based processes for selecting the security controls necessary to satisfy the minimum security requirements" [16]. The specification defines a useful formula as follows: A security category (SC) of an information system = {(confidentiality, impact), (integrity, impact), (availability, impact)}, where the acceptable values for potential impact are low, moderate, or high. This formula hints at ways managers can categorize their information and assets and the risks to them regarding their **CIA**: *confidentiality, integrity, and availability*.

FIPS-200 subsumes FIPS-199 (Standards for Security Categorization of Federal Information and Information Systems) for risk-based processes in selecting security controls necessary to satisfy the minimum security requirements and requires assessment and planning involving activities related to (1) access controls, (2) awareness and training, (3) audit and accountability, (4) certification, accreditation, and security assessments, (5) configuration management, (6) contingency planning, (7) identification and authentication, (8) incident response, (9) security maintenance, (10) media protection, (11) security planning, (12) personnel security, (13) risk assessment, (14) systems and services acquisition, (15) system and communications protection, and (16) system and information integrity.

Rather than trying to "reinvent the wheel," using standards such as these for guidelines may help save time and money, as well as promote the development, implementation, and operation of more secure information systems, establishing reasonable levels of due diligence for information security, and facilitating a more consistent, comparable, and repeatable approach for selecting and specifying security controls for information systems that meet minimum security requirements.

1.2.1 Financial Evaluations

It is typically an important part of a manager's job to handle budgets and develop financial justifications. In security, we are interested in assessments of the value of assets and the financial impacts from losses. We use economic forecasting formulas such as annualized loss expectancy, payback period on repurchases, and others to determine the financial impacts of security incidents. However, financial assessments are best done in conjunction with the accounting and finance departments in the organization rather than having line or security managers try to figure the value of equipment and software on their own. This is because capital assets may be in various stages of depreciation or may have different net present valuations on the books than those formulated by managers.

If managers make written financial declarations, this might actually become a problem for the company because financial audits by the Internal Revenue Service (IRS), insurance companies, due diligence mergers and acquisition (M&A) teams, lending institutions, or the company's auditing firm may turn up discrepancies that might create difficulties for the company if there is a dispute down the road. We are not suggesting that managers should not use financial formulas to try to predict exposure and loss—after all, this is part of managing one's budget—but we are suggesting that managers should not make financial declarations involving asset valuation without the active and expressed involvement of the finance and accounting departments.

Because managers are often not involved in the economic transactions undertaken by the organization, another important reason managers need to involve the finance and accounting departments in assessing asset value and making financial decisions is because managers sometimes accidentally inflate the value of assets in their reporting [17–19], and these financial reports may be "rolled up" into the financial collateral of the company [20, 21]. This issue is particularly noteworthy in public companies, which fall under the Sarbanes–Oxley Act of 2002 [22] that requires that company officers (Chief Executive Officer and Chief Financial Officer) to certify and approve the integrity of their company financial reports at the risk of their own personal liabilities.

All in all, the accuracy of asset valuations such as in risk assessments is crucially important—as important as any other security measure. With the help of the finance department, financial projections and assessments act as guidelines for managers to prioritize their efforts and budget expenditures. Managers should be in a position to provide the qualitative assessments of risks and the quantitative values of new and replacement software and equipment to the finance department for determining value—but again, we emphasize that managers should not proclaim financial valuations any more than they should act as legal counsel regarding legal matters.

1.2.2 Attacks, Monitoring, and Recovery

Attacks from the outside tend to follow a predictable pattern [23]. Outsider attacks may begin with *foot printing*—a technique using technologies to determine the network infrastructure of a target such as what internet protocol (IP) addresses the company uses. They then *scan* this infrastructure to find networked services (ports), protocols, and software that the company provides, supports, and uses—as well as versions and security patch and revision levels of software—so the attacker may know what vulnerabilities can be exploited. They then use *enumeration* to find what connections and parameters specific services allow. Once this is known, they try to *infiltrate or penetrate* the targeted system, and then the attacker strives to cover his or her tracks, which means removing as much evidence as possible that the attack occurred. In the case that an attack succeeds, the management process also follows a predictable pattern of discovery, recovery, forensic analysis, preserving evidence, incident reporting, and creating a feedback loop.

In most cases, the attack process is monitored at some point [1]. Intrusion detection systems (IDS) may be computer host-based (HIDS) or network-based (NIDS). Host-based IDS such as the OSSEC (http://www.ossec.net/main) monitor a computer system by analyzing log files, checking the integrity of files to ensure they have not been tampered with, providing automated policy monitoring, and checking for illicit tools used to escalate an unauthorized user's privileges (called rootkit detection). Common network-based IDS such as Wireshark and SNORT, or commercial intrusion detection and prevention applications such as Radware, Panoscopia, or Intelligent Access Systems (AIS), can be installed on host systems or on routers or gateways to monitor protocols and ports, bandwidth utilization, packet contents, and utilizations that indicate potential threats.

> **In Focus**
>
> Statistical anomaly–based IDS determine normal network activity such as average bandwidth used at a given time and then alert an administrator when anomalies are noted (typically using a form of regression for this). Signature-based IDS are configured with and receive updates to a "signature" database (of threats). Activity is compared with these attack patterns (signatures). Important here are two concepts—false positives and false negatives. False positives occur when an IDS falsely determines some activity as "bad" and generates an alert or blocks legitimate access, when actually, it is "legitimate" activity. Statistical (anomaly) IDS is more prone to these errors than signature-based IDS. False negatives occur when the IDS fail to detect an attack. Signature IDS are more prone to false positive attacks, whereas anomaly detection is more prone to false negatives because there is no previously established attack profile (often called a first-day attack). Digital forensics is related to this and includes investigating and preserving the evidence gathered by IDS. Log files require Digital Signature (a Message Digest) to show that data have not been tampered with. A "chain of custody" must be established and proved if the evidence is to be presented in court.

How managers respond to attacks will likely include a multi-phased strategy that involves asking questions such as (1) What should managers do about identifying the attacker(s)? (2) How should they try to contain or quarantine the attack? (3) How should they eradicate an infection? (4) How do they try to recover and continue critical business operations? (5) How do they recover from an attack? and (6) What should they do to determine the lessons learned and how they should apply them to prevent similar attacks in the future?

If the organization decides to pursue legal action against an attacker, evidence must be gathered and preserved in a way admissible in a court of law. This may include retaining log files and other electronic and non-electronic records, establishing a chain of custody of these materials and proving they were not altered along the way, explaining the methods used in the investigation of the attack, and describing how the manager and/or administrator determined that a security violation was in the process of occurring or had occurred. In anticipation of this, it is important for managers to maintain records related to incidents, and the process involves multiple people including the legal department. Policies, rules, and procedures need to have been established ahead of time on how various incidents should be handled and what to do about reporting them, and managers and all personnel involved in handling security incidents need to be knowledgeable of these.

1.2.3 Reasons Why "They" Attack "Us"

Schultz [24] provided an overview of theories that try to explain why people attempt to breach security. Knowing these reasons helps managers with determining what actions to take in response. There are many different conceptual models for why people carry out attacks. One such model used by law enforcement is called the *CMO model*. The CMO model postulates that in order to commit an attack, the perpetrator must first have the capability to commit the attack such as having the skills and technologies to do so. However, having only the capability is insufficient. A perpetrator must also have a motive for the attack. Typical motives for attacks include greed and revenge. Given the capability and one or more motives, the attacker must also have an opportunity to commit the attack for it to succeed [25]. Opportunity is enhanced by factors such as remote access to target systems. However, simply having capabilities, motives, and opportunities may not be enough. To get at weaknesses that can be exploited, the attacker may need to collude with others, including those on the inside [1].

As noted by Schultz [24], Parker [26] presented an attack model similar to the CMO but with slightly different factors that included whether the attacker had sufficient skills, knowledge, and resources to succeed, and these accounted for motives ranging from computer crimes committed by insiders to outsider attacks. Tuglular and Spafford [13] took issue with the Parker model and suggested that a single model was not adequate in describing such broad outcomes. Instead, Tuglular and Spafford focused on insider attacks and argued that for an insider attack to succeed, he or she must first be able to use a given computer system with the level of authority granted to the insider, and then he or she must be able to perform some activity to harm the functions that support the organization's mission.

Building on the CMO model, Gudaitis [27] developed three-dimensional profiling (3DP). This approach focused on insider attacks and prescribed an organizationally based method for prevention. The utility of this model was twofold in that it (1) assessed an incident or attack using profiling in addition to the usual technical tools and (2) provided organizations with a way to evaluate and enhance their security processes and procedures from a human perspective as a preventive measure [1].

Some research models have formulated explanations of simple misuse of systems. Misuse in this research literature is defined as a violation of the policies established in an organization to prevent corruption of information or more malevolent actions. According to Schultz [24], insider misuse is a cumulative function of personal and organizational factors such as personality, motivation, knowledge, abilities, rights, restrictions, obligations, authority, and responsibility.

Another approach to explaining security violations has been termed a *psychodynamic driven model* as described by Shaw, Ruby, and Post [28]. This profiled the psychological makeup of convicted cyber criminals, and then categorized them as introverts and depressed people. Nevertheless, this model was limited in its explanatory power because (1) the results were drawn from convicted criminals after the fact; (2) the study was based on a small subset from a convenience (not a random) sample (the perpetrators who were caught, arrested, and convicted, as well as those who agreed to participate in the study); (3) the model included only outside attackers; and (4) the results were based exclusively on the measurement of psychological factors, even though other factors (e.g., organizational and socioeconomic factors) may have been involved [1].

Collins [29] studied the relationship between social context cues and uninhibited or abusive verbal or written behavior in online communication. This model establishes a predictive connection between the absence of social context cues and the presence of uninhibited (i.e., flaming and inappropriate language) verbal behavior, and provides some interesting insights into cyber harassment and defamation against companies and company managers. This was supported in a study by Workman [30] on factors that translate between those who cyber harass others and those who conduct cyber attacks against companies.

Finally, Morahan-Martin [31] described the general use of computers and computer behaviors across demographics, specifically focusing on gender differences. This model posited cultural and linguistic aspects of computer behavior as they relate to computer competency and Internet competency. It incorporated the notion that computer self-efficacy (competency) not only predicts computer-related behavior, but it also makes predictions about behavior online, and thus the model extends deviant or unethical computer behavior to adversarial and status-enhancing behaviors online, as demonstrated by the use of certain rhetoric [1].

These conceptual models have provided a good start in helping managers with determining meaningful measures and countermeasures to help organizations reduce the frequency and damage resulting from insider attacks. However, most do not adequately facilitate practical ways of detection, let alone prediction of insider attacks. Detection capability is desirable, but unfortunately it comes after the damage has been done. Given the potential damage that can result from insider attacks, detecting insider attacks is very important. Without understanding and control of the human element, technology alone cannot provide the level of information security needed by organizations today [24].

So what should managers do? In the chapters that follow, we will provide some important guidance regarding what managers should do, and in particular, we will give some insights into predicting current and impending attacks so managers can intervene sooner and more effectively. This is the touchstone of our textbook.

The textbook chapters that follow will stage each learning domain. First, we will present the organization context in which managers operate. We will then provide a section on technology to orient managers toward the next section on how to protect resources, technological systems, and infrastructure. We will conclude with a broad view of what managers are doing to predict attacks and what they are doing to predict attacks and ways to take appropriate actions.

Let's get started!

References

1. Schultz, E. E., & Spafford, E. H. (1999). Intrusion detection: How to utilize a still immature technology. In M. Krause and H. F. Tipton (Eds.), *Handbook of information security management*. New York, NY: Auerbach.

2. Workman, M. (2008). Fear commerce: Inflationary effects of global security initiatives. *Information Security Journal: A Global Perspective, 17,* 124–131.

3. Hernandez, H. (2010). Cyber crime wave—Who pays? *Market Times, 12,* 12–23.

4. O'Connell, K. (2008, January). Cyber fraud and online bullying affect 44% of small Irish businesses. *Internet Business Law.* Retrieved October 10, 2011, from http://www.ibls.com/internet_law_news_portal_view.aspx?s=latestnews&id=1954

5. Brenner S. W. (2010). Cybercrime and the U.S. criminal justice system. In H. Bidgoli (Ed.), *The handbook of technology management* (pp. 693–703). Hoboken, NJ: John Wiley & Sons.

6. Beadle, J. (2010). Corporate law and legal counsel: A mutually dependent relation. *The Legal Brief, 15,* 19–27.

7. Borrull, A. L., & Oppenheim, C. (2004). Legal aspects of the Web. In B. Cronin (Ed), *Annual Review of Information Science and Technology, 38* (pp. 483–548). Medford, NJ: Information Today.

8. Bartels, A. (2006, November). Global IT spending and investment forecast, 2006–2007. *Forrester Research,* pp. 4–31.

9. Bragdon, C. R. (2008). *Transportation security.* Burlington, MA: Elsevier/Butterworth-Heinemann.

10. ISOO. (2004). *The report on cost estimates for security classification activities for 2003 from the Information Security Oversight Office (ISOO).* Washington, DC: National Archives and Records Administration.

11. Straub, D. W., Goodman, S., & Baskerville, R. L. (2008). *Information security: Policy, processes, and practices.* Armonk, NY: Sharpe Books.

12. Cisco. (2009). *2009 Annual security report.* Retrieved March 19, 2011, from http://cisco.com/en/US/prod/vpndevc/annual_security_report.html

13. Tuglular, T., & Spafford, E. H. (1997). *A framework for characterization of insider computer misuse.* Unpublished colloquium presentation, Purdue University.

14. Rothfeder, J. (1996). Hacked! Are your company's files safe? *PC World, 14,* 70–74.

15. Davis, K., & Newstrom, J. W. (1989). *Human behavior at work.* New York, NY: McGraw-Hill.

16. NIST. (2006). *Minimum security requirements for federal information and information systems.* Gaithersburg, MD: FIPS Pub 200. Retrieved March 17, 2011, from http://csrc.nist.gov/publications/fips/fips200/FIPS-200-final-march.pdf

17. Aberdeen Group. (2002). *Technology forecasting consortium: 2002 user buying intentions.* Boston, MA: Aberdeen and Associates.

18. Bagozzi, R. P., Davis, F. D., & Warshaw, P. R. (1992). Development and test of a theory of technology learning and usage. *Human Relations, 45,* 659–686.

19. Morris, H. (2002, June). Analytic applications market forecast and analysis: 2001–2005, *IDC Report,* pp. 17–21.

20. Carroll, J. (2003). *Take the stress away.* Retrieved March 10, 2011, from http://proquest.umi.com/pdqweb?index=4&sid=srchmode=1&vinst=PROD&fmt=3&star

21. Venkatesh, V., Morris, M. G., & Ackerman P. L. (2000). A longitudinal field investigation of gender differences in individual technology adoption decision-making processes. *Organizational Behavior and Human Decision Processes, 83*, 33–60.

22. Sarbanes–Oxley Act of 2002, Pub.L. No. 107–204 (July 30, 2002); 116 Stat. 745 (2002).

23. Thomas, T. (2004). *Network security.* Indianapolis, IN: Cisco Press.

24. Schultz, E. E. (2002). A framework for understanding and predicting insider attacks, *Computers & Security, 21*, 526–531.

25. Bugge, B. K. (1996). *Principles of law in investigations.* Scranton, PA: Harcourt.

26. Parker, D. B. (1998). *Fighting computer crime: A new framework for protecting information.* New York, NY: John Wiley, NY: Sons.

27. Gudaitis, T. M. (1999). The missing link in information security: Three dimensional profiling. *Cyber Psychology and Behavior, 1*, 4–14.

28. Shaw, E. D., Ruby, K. G., & Post, J. M. (1998). The insider threat to information systems. *Security Awareness Bulletin, 2*, 27–46.

29. Collins, M. (1992). *Flaming: The relationship between social context cues and uninhibited verbal behavior in computer-mediated communication.* Retrieved March 17, 2011, from http://star.ucc.nau.edu/~mauri/papers/flames.html

30. Workman, M. (2010). A behaviorist perspective on corporate harassment online: Validation of a theoretical model of psychological motives. *Computers & Security, 29*, 831–839.

31. Morahan-Martin, J. (1998). Women and girls last: Females and the Internet. *Proceedings of the International Conference Research and Information Systems, Bristol: UK: IRISS'98,* 25–27.

Corporations and the Rule of Law

ET'S TAKE A QUICK high-level tour of some elements related to corporations and the rule of law to set the stage for what's to come. Because this is an introduction to legal and organizational concepts, many of the concepts presented here might be new. Rest assured that we will revisit the most important of these points in later chapters in different contexts, which should make them more relevant. Our purpose here is to simply introduce the ideas for later elaboration. Why do you suppose knowing how corporations are formed as a legal entity might matter to security? Quite simply, managers must be familiar with laws and regulations if they are going to effectively manage their organizations securely. Along with ethics, the rule of law forms the backbone of information security. We will begin this chapter by defining some terms and basic concepts, and then present an overview of some crucial legal aspects of corporations to prepare for later, when we will dive a little deeper into security-specific laws and regulations.

Chapter 2 Topics

This chapter:

- Describes how organizations are structured and how structures affect the ways in which organizations are managed and governed.
- Discusses the concept of power as the ability to influence others.
- Presents managerial responsibilities and duties, and different power bases from which managers operate.
- Provides a presentation of law and ethics, and the concept of organizational justice.
- Describes how law is involved in the enforcement of security policies.

Chapter 2 Goals

When you finish this chapter, you should:

- ❑ Understand how incorporation and power interrelate to form "corporate structures."
- ❑ Know the concepts of principals and agency, and the duties they carry.
- ❑ Be familiar with what ethics entail and how they differ from laws and regulations.
- ❑ Understand the basic elements of an enforceable security policy.

2.1 Legal Organizational Structure

As with people working in a company, a corporation is a legal entity having **rights**, is subject to legal **duties**, and is regulated by the state in which it was incorporated. Therefore, both employees and corporations have rights and duties. From a legal perspective, a right is defined as the capacity of a person or corporate entity, with the aid of law, to compel another person or corporate entity to perform or to refrain from performing an action. A duty is defined as an obligation that the law imposes on a person or corporate entity to perform an action or refrain from performing the action. Along with rights comes accountability; along with duties comes responsibility. Thus duties and rights are interdependent. A right cannot legally exist without a corresponding duty upon another.

In addition to the state's incorporation laws, corporations may also be subject to governance of commercial transactions under the **Uniform Commercial Code** (**UCC**) and by federal and even international laws. In terms of security, this is especially meaningful as it relates to employment-specific matters and regulation of industries. For example, corporations may be subject to certain regulations such as the **Health Insurance Portability and Accountability Act** (**HIPAA**) or the **Payment Care Industry Data Security Standard** (**PCI DSS**), both of which (among others) require that managers provide directives and policies for employees on the proper handling of information and computer systems in the organization [1].

2.1.1 Accountability, Responsibility, and Law

Accountability might be thought of as in the cliché *the buck stops here*, whereas **responsibility** involves a duty to perform some action; therefore, one can be held accountable but not responsible for some act. Managers are *accountable* when it comes to meeting business performance objectives. That may mean overseeing personnel who are *responsible* for maintaining the performance of applications at the levels expected by users and, from a security standpoint, for ensuring the confidentiality, integrity, and availability of information and systems—along with meeting other business objectives. In most cases, managers are accountable for actions taken by their subordinates, and are also responsible for taking actions, such as giving clear directions to them.

For example, managers may be held accountable for meeting expectations or contractual obligations for the performance of an application—contractually, this is often called a ***service-level agreement*** (**SLA**). In order to meet that agreed level of performance, administrators may need to configure the systems and networks to achieve the performance commitments. This might involve working to make sure that a network can distinguish high-priority network traffic based on the type of application or data that the network carries, which may include using policy-based routing in a TCP/IP network. As illustrated in this example, accountability and responsibility are represented by an *inverted tree*. By this, we mean that accountability and responsibility accrue as we examine bottom-up from the organizational chart.

> **In Focus**
>
> Policy-based routing is one way that telecommunications companies work to live up to their agreements. Policy-based routing was originally defined by Cisco Corp. as consisting of protocols and technologies such as creating route maps and setting type of service (TOS) in the network data packets to meet **quality of service** (**QoS**) metrics for a given payload, such as an email or text message versus streaming video.

In terms of accountability, management and governance structures of corporations are determined largely by the type of incorporation, and also by agreement of the board of directors through, for example, the articles of incorporation and bylaws, and individual contracts such as employment agreements. Types of incorporations include partnerships, limited liability corporations (LLC), subchapter "S" corporations, "C" corporations, for-profit and non-profit companies, and others.

Because a corporation is a legal entity that owes its existence to the state in which it was incorporated and is distinct from the individuals who control its operations, it holds certain liability protections for management principals. A partnership is an association of two or more people who work as co-owners of a business. Partners are personally liable for most legal violations, but the business structure has some tax advantages. A limited liability partnership is one where co-owners create a legal entity granted by statutes in the governing state. It is popular for small businesses because it offers some liability protections for the management principals. A subchapter "S" corporation allows a group of people to conduct business with the benefits of a public corporation such as liability protections, but it allows the principals to be taxed on an individual basis, similar to a partnership.

> **In Focus**
>
> Bylaws are specific legal agreements that are drawn up among the corporate principals, such as founders and/or their boards of directors.

The specific legal aspects of incorporation are beyond the scope of this textbook, but it is important to realize that management and governance are constrained to varying degrees depending on the legal structure of the organization and industry-specific regulations. It is also important to recognize that the formal or legitimate power structure within corporations is largely a function of the legal and organizational structures by which corporations are established when they are formed and reestablished as they operate. When legal violations or grievances arise, there are different classifications of law that apply, as well as venues for adjudication. Legal classifications include procedural and substantive, public and private, and civil and criminal law [2].

- Procedural law deals with the methods of remedies for violations of the law. More specifically, procedural law creates, defines, and regulates legal rights and obligations. It establishes the rules for enforcing rights and the methods for remedies in court.
- Public law comes into play when there is a breach of procedural law that deals with the rights and powers of the government in its political or sovereign capacity relative to individuals or groups. Public law consists of constitutional, administrative, and criminal law.
- Private law is the part of procedural and substantive law governing individuals and legal entities such as corporations in their relationships with one another. Private law deals with torts, contracts, sales, agency, and property.
- Civil law defines duties and what constitutes a violation or wrongdoing against an "injured" party. Civil law is part of private law.
- Criminal law defines duties and what constitutes violations or a "wrong" committed against a community or society. Criminal law is part of public law.

In Focus

The type of incorporation and the bylaws formed by corporate principals determine the legal structures and governance within organizations.

2.1.2 Roles of Corporate Trust and Regulation

Corporate officers are employees who hold a special position of trust and are accountable to a board of directors and, if the organization is a public company, to the shareholders. Among these officers are the Chief Executive Officer (CEO), who plays a key role in organizational leadership, and the Chief Financial Officer (CFO), who is responsible for the company's financial transactions. The **Sarbanes–Oxley Act of 2002**, also called SOX or, more formally, **the Public Company Accounting Reform and Investor Act of 2002**, regulates these officer roles. For example, part of the act stipulates that CEOs and CFOs must jointly issue written statements about financial transactions.

A Chief Information Officer (CIO) is responsible for enterprise information resources such as information technology and computer systems that support the enterprise goals and operations, and is typically involved in overseeing information processing and information strategy and identifying and developing the information infrastructure, including computing architecture and networking. Information security policies are usually under the control or jurisdiction of the CIO. Generally speaking, the CIO reports directly to the CEO.

The Chief Technology Officer (CTO) is similar to the CIO, but this is typically a role given in an information technology provider company. A CTO has the responsibility to oversee the technological development of the company's products. With the growing recognition of the importance of information security, and along with regulation, increasingly companies are creating the role of Chief Security Officer (CSO) or Chief Information Security Officer (CISO), whose job it is to ensure that effective policies are created and enforced.

Depending on the industry or agency, there are various regulations that may dictate certain responsibilities for these roles of trust. As indicated, the Sarbanes–Oxley Act attempts to protect investors by imposing on companies and their management specific duties to help protect the integrity of information used internally and released externally. It requires CEOs and CFOs at all public companies in the United States to certify the accuracy of their quarterly and annual financial reports (called 10-K reports), and to create internal controls for reporting and facilitating auditing. Also depending on the type of organization, information and communications related to these reports must be retained for 7 to 10 years in the United States, and companies must institute procedures to keep track of financial transactions from beginning to end and are accountable to the **Securities and Exchange Commission (SEC)** and the **Internal Revenue Service (IRS)** regarding their accuracy.

Other legislation that affects corporate officers and other roles of trust include the **Financial Services Modernization Act of 1999**, also known as the **Gramm-Leach-Bliley Act**, which requires that financial institutions ensure the security and confidentiality of customer data. These data must be stored in a secure place or medium and have protections in place to preserve the data, whether stored or in transit. There are also many federal and state regulations that may reinforce these requirements. In addition, there are industry-specific regulations. As mentioned earlier, an example is HIPAA, which stipulates medical and privacy rules and procedures in the administration of health records. Billing and the transfer of healthcare records among healthcare providers and payers require companies to retain patient information for 6 years and ensure that the data are kept confidential [1].

In Focus

Everything one does on a company computer and network (whether wired or wireless) may be monitored by something or someone, somewhere. One of the key reasons for this often has to do with laws and regulations.

2.1.3 Formal Project Undertakings

To live up to their corporate obligations, organizations undertake various approaches to implement services or technologies or develop products, all of which might be considered *projects*. For example, to determine what new security technologies might be needed, management may conduct an assessment of the organization's strengths, weaknesses, opportunities, and threats, called a SWOT analysis [3], or they may involve cross-functional teams to conduct brainstorming or utilize a total quality management approach including CMMi, Six Sigma, or a process method such as COBIT (more about these later). These approaches help managers determine what is needed, where, and when, and just as importantly, what is not needed.

Critical issues in project undertakings include determining the scope of the project. The scope element involves defining requirements, the resources and costs, and the end point for achieving the objectives of the project and meeting the requirements. Another issue that must be contended with is ***unfamiliarity***. A lack of previous experience (or precedent) with a similar undertaking usually leads to ***uncertainty*** about the scope of the undertaking. ***Complexity*** is another critical issue. Complexity is partly owing to the project scope, but in addition, it involves the degree of interdependence among tasks and among workers. The more a task depends on other tasks, and the more one team member depends on others to complete a project, the greater the complexity. A fourth set of critical issues in project undertakings is what is at ***stake***, and who the ***stakeholders*** are.

What is at stake might be thought of in terms of the amount of money invested in the project, the opportunity costs, potential revenues, or the ability to compete in the market-place, among others. Stakeholders are those who have a vested interest in the outcome, which includes all employees because the company's survival depends on successful project undertakings, but also customers, investors, and, if a public company, share-holders. However, not all members of the organization have an equal stake in a given project. Managers must determine the impact of what is at stake and give priority to those stakeholders who have most at stake (primary stakeholders).

One avenue to help managers decide these issues is to conduct a survey of primary stakeholders regarding expenditures, requirements, preferences for strategic relation-ships, and the other factors that are important to or involved in the project. For example, a question using a Likert-type scale (from 1 to 7) might be, "We should purchase our equipment from a single supplier," scaled as 1, and "We should purchase our equipment from a variety of suppliers," scaled as 7. The survey scores for each question asked of the stakeholders would be tallied for a mean score (a statistical average) and a standard deviation (a measure of dispersion or agreement).

Q1: It is most important to leverage:									
	Open Systems::	1	2	3	4	5	6	7	::Proprietary Systems
Q2: It is most important to buy from:									
	Established Vendors::	1	2	3	4	5	6	7	::Emerging Vendors
Q3: It is most important that we compete based on:									
	Lower Costs::	1	2	3	4	5	6	7	::Feature Richness
Q4: ...									

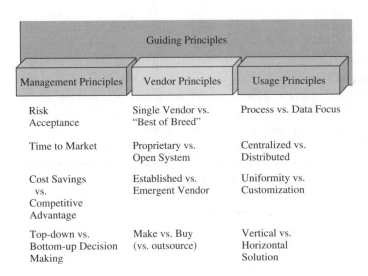

Guiding Principles		
Management Principles	Vendor Principles	Usage Principles
Risk Acceptance	Single Vendor vs. "Best of Breed"	Process vs. Data Focus
Time to Market	Proprietary vs. Open System	Centralized vs. Distributed
Cost Savings vs. Competitive Advantage	Established vs. Emergent Vendor	Uniformity vs. Customization
Top-down vs. Bottom-up Decision Making	Make vs. Buy (vs. outsource)	Vertical vs. Horizontal Solution

The mean scores on the survey questions explain where the stakeholders lean in terms of the questions; for example, a mean score of 2 on the scale related to questions about purchasing from a single or established vendor versus multiple or emerging vendors would indicate that stakeholders want to purchase equipment from a single or established vendor—perhaps due to standardization or volume buying discounts. On the other hand, a mean score of 6 would suggest that stakeholders want to purchase equipment from a variety of suppliers, perhaps to avoid being locked into a single vendor due to high costs of switching vendors, or to avoid a single point of failure, or to leverage more innovative emerging products. The standard deviation is a statistical measure of dispersion or variance; thus it tells how much agreement there is among stakeholders about these decision principles. A small standard deviation indicates strong agreement among stakeholders, but a large one indicates large disagreement, so perhaps the manager would need to get the primary stakeholders together in a meeting and discuss the issues and strive to gain greater consensus.

Based on the questions, the means, and standard deviations, managers are able to develop a guiding principles framework, and when faced with a conflict, they can refer to these principles to guide their decision. For example, say a group of stakeholders strongly favor a Linux platform whereas others strongly favor a Windows platform; if the principle is to use open systems, the choice becomes clearer to go with the Linux platform. This is not to say that the manager would always choose the Linux platform, but unless there is a compelling reason not to, the principle acts as a default or tiebreaker.

2.1.4 Power and Organizational Structure

In dealing with the critical components of a project undertaking and in gaining consensus among stakeholders, it is obvious that the abilities to communicate and influence others are critical managerial skills. However, in order to communicate and influence well, managers must understand the power distributions throughout the organization—both formal and informal. **Power** is the ability to influence someone to do something. The ability to influence someone may be accomplished through incentives, persuasion, or coercion. Thus, how power is exercised depends on the power source or base used; for example, managers have the power to reward and punish subordinates (this is called ***formal, legitimate***, or ***positional power***), whereas subordinates may have expertise (***expert power***) or charisma (***referent power***), which are forms of ***informal power*** [3].

Because power is often related to control over valued resources, the formal organizational structures offer the most recognizable sources of power. Formal organizational structures and the use of power are accomplished by means of statutory and legal perspectives. In other words, power is formally exercised through incorporation and bylaws and other agreements or, alternatively, through the delegation of authority. Nevertheless, power is often distributed through organizations in ways that go beyond the legitimate power structure.

An example of the use of informal power is when a charismatic person with less positional power is able to influence or persuade others to form a coalition against a more powerful individual on an action. This source of power is known as coming from a *referent power base*. Also, we often find in technical and knowledge work that power comes from expertise. In this case, power is inverted. Said another way, managers often rely on the expertise of individuals in the groups they oversee. Those individuals hold a valuable resource (meaning knowledge and skills) that the manager needs in order for his or her group to accomplish organizational goals. To effectively manage in those cases, managers typically exercise a combination of legitimate power—using rewards and punishments—along with using an informal referent power commonly called "leadership."

In Focus

Power, which determines influence, may come from formal or informal sources, and it may be exercised individually or through coalitions.

Organizational Structure, Principals, and Agency

We should point out that ***shareholders*** are people who purchase or are given ***stock*** in a corporation, and although they may not have an operational role in the company, they do have power to influence it. Whether a company is "private" or "public" along with the types of stock the corporation issues affect shareholder ownership and their influence in corporations. The most powerful kinds of stock are called "voting shares" because they allow shareholders to cast votes on important matters. As an example, members with voting shares may elect the board of directors for the corporation to represent their interests. In so doing, they delegate to these principals the power to manage company operations and exercise control over its resources.

We have used the term "principal" in a number of places thus far. ***Principals*** are legally vested parties in an organization who may or may not have been assigned an ***operational role***. By this we mean that some principals may simply act as corporate advisors, whereas principals with an operational role are executives who run the day-to-day operations of the company. Because they have a vested right (usually due to founding financial investments or because they are a corporate board member or officer), principals have a special say in how corporations are run. As a result, all principals hold positions of trust and confidence and are expected to devote their efforts to the benefit of the company and the shareholders. Going beyond this obligation, principals with operational duties have implied **agency**—that is, *the ability to bind the corporation to legal agreements.* Some duties and agency, however, may be further delegated to company officers and other management or staff, or even to subcontractors and independent actors.

Likewise, equity owners may or may not be principals—that is, they may simply be shareholders, and they are not necessarily agents. This may seem a little confusing at this stage, given the many variations of involvement, ownership, and power available through corporate structures. We will elaborate on these ideas later; for now, just keep in mind that legally, *agency is a consensual relationship between a principal and an authorized actor* (agent) *formed by contract or agreement,* and it is generally formed for the purpose of having the agent conduct some legitimate action on behalf of a principal. Examples of agency might be a company officer executing his or her assigned duties during the normal course of doing business, or an attorney or a consultant acting on behalf of his or her client [1].

In Focus

Directors and officers may bestow agency down through the organizational structure. This is one form of delegation.

Delegation of Responsibilities and Power

As seen, by agreement corporate principals establish the standards, activities, and responsibilities for managing the business, either by acting as advisors or by managing the business through an operational role in the company. As such, boards of directors with their votes typically appoint officers in the company who are actively involved in leading and overseeing daily company operations and executing the tactical aspects of the corporate strategy. In other words, the corporate structure dictates the formal power structure and the allocation or delegation of duties and resources.

This is typically accomplished in a corporation as follows: The board of directors has the power to manage the business of the corporation. These "directors" exercise dominion and control over the corporation, hold positions of trust and confidence, and determine the courses of operating policy. They have broad authority to delegate power to agents and to officers who hold their offices at the will of the board and who in turn hire and fire all necessary operating personnel and manage the daily transactions of the corporation [1].

Board members may function in an operational role, or they may act only as advisors, and as a voting group delegate authority to corporate officers who run the day-to-day affairs of the operation. Consequently, corporate boards select, remove, and determine the compensation of corporate officers, and furthermore (typically by a majority vote), shareholders may remove a director or an entire board of directors *with cause* by means of their voting [3]. Thus, power and the exercise of control, and the corresponding responsibilities in corporations, are not viewed strictly as a pyramid often represented in organizational charts, or even as an inverted one, but rather as a spectrum of power, rights, duties, responsibilities, and liabilities that transcend organizational structures.

2.2 Fiduciary Responsibilities

The preceding section has led us to an important legal and security concept. Principals and agents in a corporation owe to each other a **fiduciary responsibility**. A fiduciary responsibility is one that holds special duties. More specifically, a fiduciary is an actor in a position of trust and confidence such that he or she owes his or her principals the **duty of obedience**, **diligence**, and **loyalty**. This includes the duty to inform relevant parties and provide an accounting of financial and other material transactions to all the principals [2].

Diligence means that in the execution of duties, they are discharged in a manner exercised using **ordinary (or due) care** and with prudence "reasonably" expected of someone in that position who is acting in good faith, which is to say, with care taken by an ordinarily prudent person in that position given the circumstances, and in a manner one would "reasonably" believe to be in the best interest of the corporation [3]. Failure to uphold fiduciary responsibilities may expose a principal (or agent) to legal liabilities. For example, a breach of obedience might be to execute an unauthorized binding action, such as to enter into an unauthorized contract [1].

A breach of duty includes failure to use due care in acting. This can range from failure to pay attention to instruments a principal or officer signs or accedes to, or misrepresenting that a principal has a skill that one does not actually have, which is in turn relied upon by a third party in an assumption about the principal's ability to perform his or her duties. A breach of loyalty involves failures to properly inform or account to other principals regarding material matters such as sources of income and any "side work" a principal may perform. It also includes the agreement *not to compete, not to engage in conflicts of interest,* and *not to disclose confidential information* to unauthorized parties [2].

2.2.1 Fiduciary Duties and Legal Ethics

Beyond the legal dynamics explained in the previous sections regarding corporate structural relationships that comprise the legitimate or formal exercise of power, it has been argued that socially responsible behavior pays a debt owed on a moral obligation to the society that contributes to a corporation's overall success. This line of reasoning affirms that social responsibility buys goodwill, and goodwill can (albeit sometimes as an intangible factor) translate into corporate development and future success. It is from this philosophy that the terms "social contract" and "stakeholder" were derived; concepts such as **psychological contract**, **equity**, and **organizational justice** all stem from this notion of social responsibility. In this view, it is not just "stockholders" but "stakeholders" who have a legitimate right to exercise control and power in a corporation [4–6].

Working from this position, we note that ethics are codes of conduct for what constitutes "right" and "wrong." Ethics in general is a systematic effort using logical reasoning to make sense of individual, organizational, and social moral dilemmas in such a way as to determine the principles that should govern human conduct and the values they express. Unlike law, the assessments of ethics have no central authority such as a court or legislature. As such, there are no clear-cut universal ethical standards for managers to rely upon [1, 4].

Philosophically, there are different views about ethics that fall into various categories [7]. Ethical objectivism is an absolute commitment to a central authority or set of rules to guide decision making [4]. Ethical relativism asserts that individuals must judge their actions by what they perceive as right or wrong [8]. Situational ethics is the view that developing precise rules for navigating ethical dilemmas is difficult because real-life decision making is complex and ambiguous. To judge the morality of a behavior, the people judging must psychologically place themselves in the other person's situation to understand what motivated the other to choose a course of action [9]. Utilitarianism tries to view right and wrong in terms of consequences of actions. It is important to note that there are two major forms of utilitarianism, which are act- and rule-based utilitarianism [10].

Act-based utilitarianism views each act according to whether it maximizes pleasure over pain. **Rule-based utilitarianism** supports the rules that balance individual pleasures from one's own actions against the pleasure of others. Cost–benefit assessment compares the objective and subjective direct and indirect costs and benefits of an action and seeks the greatest economic efficiency at the least cost [1]. From these concepts derives the notion of **deontology**, which means a duty or obligation to perform or refrain from performing some action [2].

The rule of law generally stems from deontology, which seeks to address practical problems of utilitarianism by holding that certain underlying principles are either right or wrong regardless of the pleasure or pain involved [10]. Additionally, civil law has evolved to incorporate concepts of social ethics including egalitarianism, where persons are expected to share, in equal measure, both responsibilities and consequences. The concept of **distributive justice** developed from this ideal, which seeks equal opportunity but does not necessarily expect equal results [11].

2.2.2 Law and Ethics Intersection

There are differences between laws and ethics, as we have indicated. Laws are affected by ethical concepts, but the concepts are distinct and different. Laws are universal tenets and are codified into rules that have sanctions for disobedience. Without law, there cannot be justice. Justice has many definitions, but a common one is the fair, equitable, and impartial treatment of competing interests and desires of individuals and groups with careful regard for the common good [12]. On the other hand, ethics are generally considered to be heuristic in nature, meaning that they are "rules of thumb" to guide proper or generally acceptable human behavior [11].

For example, many people have an ethical code of conduct that would prohibit them from watching a blind person walk onto a busy road in front of a speeding car. Although failing to prevent the blind person from getting hit by the automobile lacks a legal sanction as a consequence, it may be considered wrong; yet because it is *a rule of thumb* rather than *a rule of law*, people differ in their assessments of responsible actions, such as whether to risk one's own life in the process [1].

In Focus

Whereas laws are codified rules, ethics are rules of thumb; that is, ethics are said to be heuristic. However, a branch of law allows for incorporating ethics, which is called common law, or case law, because these laws change (albeit slowly) to reflect the principles, ethics, and values of a society.

Because laws are codified into rules, they must be specific enough to determine when a law has been violated. However, because ethics are rules of thumb and involve multiple subjective views about proper actions, ethical conduct must be negotiated. There are some guiding legal principles to inform and assist in this negotiation when it comes to information security, and these are *due care*, which in this context is the careful handling of information according to the rules defined generally in security policies, and *due diligence*, which is a legal requirement that goes beyond just careful handling but also to carrying out with vigor the protection of information or performing required actions to a standard minimally defined as in a "workmanlike manner" [1, 12].

A commonly used example of an ethical violation in security involves the use of personal social security numbers as employee identifiers in light of the threat of identity theft [2]. Due care would dictate that simply because a social security number is unique does not mean that it makes a good candidate for employee identification. Employees expect that management will be concerned about their personal security, which forms the basis of a *psychological contract*, a tacit agreement about what is owed an employee such as pay or safe working conditions, based on what the employee provides, such as expertise or work effort [11]. Although ethics are rules of thumb rather than laws, attempts have been made to specify a set of maxims to govern ethical behavior in organizations. For example, as seen in **Table 2.1**, the Brookings Institution [13] produced a set of prohibitions [12].

Although such a set of maxims can be useful in general, there is a broad range of ethical considerations managers must address in the workplace. Most companies establish a behavioral policy or *code of conduct* or, even more formally, a set of *security policies*, which establish the guiding principles to govern the behavior of employees and management. These tend to address items such as privacy, publicity, and accessibility of information resources.

2.2.3 Legal and Ethical Consciousness

The function of law is to prescribe consequences for law breakers, but it can also act to deter crime. For example, in their research with computer science students, Straub, Carlson, and Jones [14] found that the threat of punishment helped to deter cheating. In particular, using general deterrence theory as a foundation, they discovered that deterrent measures, preventive measures, and deterrent severity acted as inhibitors to information security breaches and also predicted information system security effectiveness. However, the threat of punishment is not always effective in stopping information

TABLE 2.1 Examples of Breaches of Ethical Standards, Brookings Institution [13].
1. Using a computer to harm others.
2. Interfering with other people's computer work.
3. "Snooping" in other people's files.
4. Using a computer to steal.
5. Using a computer to bear false witness (i.e., lie).
6. Copying or using proprietary software without paying for it.
7. Using people's computer resource without authorization or compensation.
8. Appropriating other people's intellectual output without permission or attribution.
9. Disregard for social consequences of the program you are writing or designing.
10. Disregard for the use of a computer in ways that ensure consideration and respect for your fellow humans.

security attackers or preventing people from failing to implement important security countermeasures [15].

Relative to law, public attitudes, and behavior, there are at least two major contrasting views. One view holds that the law has to reflect societal sentiments of justice and morality, whereas the other holds that law is a vehicle to shape those sentiments and bring about social responsibility [16]. Furthermore, some researchers have shown that attitudes toward the law are part of an individual's ethical system or philosophy. From this perspective, people develop a "legal consciousness" based on their conceptions of rights, powers, duties, and related legal interactions [17]. Consequently, a person's attitude toward law is largely shaped by the person's legal socialization.

According to Fuller [18], legal socialization occurs in three main ways: (1) socialization by societal imposition, where an individual conforms to norms and customs imposed on members in order to belong, (2) socialization by state-law constraints, where an individual is willing to observe the law in order to be accepted and not punished, and (3) socialization by human interaction, where an individual perceives, respects, and participates in creating reciprocal expectations.

Tapp and Kohlberg [19] developed a moral levels classification to try to understand why people follow rules and why people should follow rules. From this classification, they developed three categories or levels. Level I was called the pre-conventional level, which consisted of people who followed rules to avoid negative consequences as well as those for whom the concept of authority was the motivating factor in their behavior. The pre-conventional level of law consciousness is therefore a reaction to the fear of punishment, and people who are classified as such seek the greatest pleasure and reward from their actions and to avoid pain and suffering to the greatest extent possible.

Tapp and Kohlberg described Level II as the conventional level, consisting of people who followed rules out of a sense of social conformity as well as those who followed rules out a sense of duty, such as to be fair to others who obeyed the law. The conventional level of law consciousness therefore involves conformance behavior to meet the expectations of a group under normative pressures such as that of peer groups, and the basis for this conformity is loyalty, affection, and trust.

The third level was labeled the post-conventional level, and this level included a category named rational-beneficial-utilitarian to reflect those who followed the rules based on logical and utilitarian considerations. That is, they followed rules as a result of weighing the consequences of their behavior rather than out of fixed obligations to obey. This level also consisted of those who followed rules out of self-defined principles independent of society. Consequently, the post-conventional law consciousness level reflects the acceptance of principles according to why things are considered "right" or "wrong." Viewed from this perspective, ethical principles are voluntary, are internalized rather than externally imposed, and stem from one's own ethical ideals, even if they question laws and values that society and others have adopted.

> **In Focus**
>
> People develop a legal and ethical consciousness independent of the rules and laws imposed by an organization or society.

2.3 Law and Enforceable Security Policies

Up to this point, we have been covering legal and ethical systems that are implemented and enacted by people typically in relation to laws, regulations, and policies. However, we should take a moment to note that security policies can also be written or codified as rules in computer software. We will consider computer-based security policies later, but in this last section of the chapter, we discuss some key considerations for creating enforceable written policies. In short, written policies address various threats with generalized rules and sanctions for violating them. A threat is defined as the anticipation of a psychological (e.g., assault), physical (e.g., battery), or sociological (e.g., theft) violation or harm to oneself or others [6].

When it comes to written policies, managers need to balance between having too much or too little specified. If there is too much specificity, several problems can occur: (1) Employees may not read them, (2) there can become contradictions in the policies that can lead to legal problems and generate a need for legal interpretations, (3) too much specificity may lead employees to refuse tasks that are not defined or are too narrowly defined, and (4) specificity in policies may actually lead to disadvantages for employers during adjudication because the policies might be too narrowly interpreted to accomplish the objective that the policy was designed to address [1].

As long as a company and its workers comply with the law, statutes, and regulations, to avoid lawsuits most organizations need only a limited number of policies to sufficiently cover important acceptable behaviors that are not otherwise common sense, commonly reasonable, or governed by the law, statutes, and regulations. Thus the number of policies management needs to create should be guided by whether there is a compelling need or regulation or statute that requires a policy, and a good policy statement is one that is general and brief but is as unambiguous as possible [20].

2.3.1 Enforceable Security Policies

For legal purposes, security policies must be both **enforced** and **enforceable**. Enforcement includes the idea that managers cannot "look the other way" or "play favorites" when a policy has been violated. Enforceability is partly a contractual matter and must meet criteria that constitute a legal agreement, and for that reason, the corporate legal and human resources departments must be involved in the drafting of security policy documents [2]. Managers should not draft security policies without having legal advice because, as with policies in general, security policies carry certain legal constraints, duties, and obligations. Some of the legal constraints fall under employment law, or corporate law, or they may be legislated or are regulatory in nature, such as those established by HIPAA for the healthcare industry. There may also be international laws to contend with.

> **In Focus**
>
> Practically speaking, security policy statements should be limited to those situations where uniform administration is necessary to avoid lawsuits [20].

Additionally, security policies may either be designed to address a broad group of people at a relatively general level, or they may need to be targeted at a group or role in an organization. In any case, from a legal standpoint, it is crucial that managers avoid creating policies that involve steps or procedures or state specifically "how to" perform tasks [1]. As indicated before, creating those kinds of policies can create problems where employees may need to deviate from the specified procedure to accomplish a goal or in case of an emergency, and that may invite a legal challenge. It is better to place procedures in a separate set of documents along with the qualification that procedures, where applicable, may need to be altered or revised [20].

Even with taking these precautions, sometimes grievances arise from the enforcement of security policies. In such cases, it is important for organizations to have systems in place to ensure **organizational procedural justice**. Procedural justice means that employees and employers deem the decision-making processes fair. There are a number of situations that lead people to perceive justice in a process. First, people want to be able to have a say or voice in any decision that might affect them. Furthermore, people want to know that managers and those with power in an organization are suspending their personal biases in their decisions and are striving to utilize objective data where possible. Finally, procedural justice is perceived when people are presented with a mechanism for correcting perceived errors or poor decisions, such as having an appeal process [6].

2.3.2 People and Policies—The Weakest Link

With the growing threats to information systems security, organizations have been looking beyond the purely technological approaches to include more behavioral controls. One example is that organizations are negatively affected by employee failures to implement discretionary security policies. An area of particular concern to managers involves policies governing information systems security behaviors that are well defined but are not obeyed. For this reason, the security literature often refers to people as the "weakest link."

To mitigate, there have been a number of recommendations in the literature, such as (1) improving the quality of security policies, (2) improving the specification of security procedures, (3) improving situational factors such as reducing workload so that security professionals have time to implement the recommend procedures, (4) creating better alignment between an organization's security goals and its practices, and (5) gaining improvements from software developers regarding the security implementations during the software development cycle [3].

A common recommendation [2] to improve information and systems security is to increase the use of *mandatory controls*. Mandatory controls are automatic security mechanisms that systems or network administrators set up, such as requiring users to change their passwords at certain intervals and generating "strong" passwords that are not found in a dictionary. However, as we shall see later, not all controls can be made mandatory—many functions must rely on *discretionary controls*, where the user is responsible for implementing a security mechanism; for example, a person might have the ability to set and change the read, write, and execute privileges on computer files that he or she creates, or change the ownership of a file from one user to another, or copy a file from one place to another. We will return to these issues in subsequent chapters and provide suggestions on how to address them.

> **In Focus**
>
> Security controls can be automated and mandatory, or they can be discretionary. A good security policy will articulate which should be used.

CHAPTER SUMMARY

In this chapter, we presented an overview of the legal and regulatory structures of an organization and how these structures relate to ethics and security policies. Along with these, concepts such as agency and authority are critical elements in managing organizations securely. Terms such as "downstream liability," where companies have been held liable for unwittingly having their resources used for illegal purposes, have been joined by the concept of "upstream liability," where organizational consultants might be held liable for giving advice that leads to corporate liabilities.

The Sarbanes–Oxley Act of 2002 regulates managerial roles. This is a vast piece of legislation that establishes rules and regulations and reporting of organizational governance

CHAPTER SUMMARY (CONTINUED)

and has significant implications for management. For example, part of the act stipulates that CEOs and CFOs must jointly issue written statements about financial transactions. We have also presented that in many if not most organizations, corporate officers hold fiduciary positions, which are special positions of trust that carry certain legal responsibilities of due care and due diligence; these officers are accountable to a board of directors and, if the organization is a public company, then also to its shareholders.

We will use this background in subsequent chapters to explain roles and responsibilities of organizational actors and to outline how managers should govern organizational information and system security for the benefit of stockholders and stakeholders. In the chapters that follow in the first section, we will discuss security standards and regulations, we will delve into more detail about security law and the implications for security policies and managers, and we will explore administrative security procedures. We will then move on to a more technical discussion of information and systems security.

THINK ABOUT IT

Topic Questions

2.1: What does procedural justice refer to?

2.2: What are the two major contrasting views about how legal attitudes are developed?

2.3: What are two primary constraints on management and organizational governance?

2.4: A requirement that goes beyond just careful handling but also to carrying out with vigor the protection of information is:

____ Due process
____ Due diligence
____ Due care
____ Obligatory duties

2.5: HIPAA is an acronym for regulations related to health care.

____ True
____ False

2.6: SOX refers to

____ Government legislation that requires public companies to shield themselves from private scrutiny
____ The Public Company Accounting Reform and Investor Act of 2002
____ A congressional act that requires public U.S. corporations to file a 10-K report
____ What government agency is in charge of investigation

2.7: Corporations are subject to the laws of state in which they are incorporated.

____ True
____ False

2.8: If organizational security policies are going to be effective, they must be:

____ Determined by the management team
____ Approved by the HR department

THINK ABOUT IT (CONTINUED)

_____ Enforceable and enforced

_____ Drawn up by an attorney

2.9: Corporations are:

_____ Formed by a management team

_____ Created by an attorney

_____ State entities and governed by the state

_____ Required to submit always and only to the Universal Commercial Code (UCC)

2.10: Deontology is:

_____ Formed by its very existence (i.e., ontological as existence)

_____ Law decided by judges such as through case law

_____ Created by an attorney

_____ The duty or obligation to perform or refrain from performing some action

Questions for Further Study

Q2.1: Should security policies specify every permissible and prohibited behavior? Why or why not?

Q2.2: What can happen if an agent breaches his/her fiduciary responsibilities?

Q2.3: Explain the key features of a "good" security policy.

Q2.4: Managers are not typically attorneys, so when laws and/or regulations are involved in managerial questions, what should managers do?

Q2.5: If a manager is questioned about his or her legal liabilities regarding a lawsuit brought about by a former employee over an issue of termination for a security breach, what should that manager do first, second, and next?

KEY CONCEPTS AND TERMS

Accountability might be thought of as in the cliché _the buck stops here._

Agency is a consensual relationship between a principal and an authorized actor (agent) formed by contract or agreement.

Discretionary controls are when the user is responsible for implementing security mechanisms.

Fiduciary responsibility is when one holds special duties. More specifically, a fiduciary is an actor in a position of trust and confidence such that he or she owes his or her principals the _duty of obedience, diligence,_ and _loyalty._ This includes the duty to inform relevant parties and provide an accounting of financial and other material transactions to all the principals.

Mandatory controls are automatic security mechanisms that systems or network administrators set up.

Policy-based routing is a technique to ensure that quality of service (QoS)-aware networks can distinguish high-priority network traffic based on the type of application and data that it carries.

Power is the ability to influence someone to do something.

Responsibility involves a duty to perform some action.

References

1. Knudsen, K. H. (2010). Cyber law. In H. Bidgoli (Ed.), *The handbook of technology management* (pp. 704–716). New York, NY: John Wiley & Sons.

2. Grama, J. L. (2011). *Legal issues in information security*. Sudbury, MA: Jones & Bartlett Learning.

3. Workman, M., Phelps, D., & Workman, J. (2008). *The management of Infosec*. Boston, MA: eAselworx Press.

4. Spinello, R. A. (2011). *Cyberethics: Morality and law in cyberspace*. Sudbury, MA: Jones & Bartelett Learning.

5. Workman, M., Bommer, W., & Straub, D. (2008). Security lapses and the omission of information security measures: An empirical test of the threat control model. *Journal of Computers in Human Behavior, 24*, 2799–2816.

6. Workman, M., Bommer, W., & Straub, D. (2009). The amplification effects of procedural justice with a threat control model of information systems security. *Journal of Behaviour and Information Technology, 28*, 563–575.

7. Mingers, J. (2011). Ethics and OR: Operationalising discourse ethics. *European Journal of Operational Research, 210*(1), 114–124.

8. Mingers, J., & Walsham, G. (2010). Toward ethical information systems: The contribution of discourse ethics. *MIS Quarterly, 34*(4), 833–844.

9. Valentine, S., & Fleischman, G. (2008). Professional ethical standards, corporate social responsibility, and the perceived role of ethics and social responsibility. *Journal of Business Ethics, 82*(4), 657–666.

10. Brenner, S. W. (2010). Cybercrime and the U. S. criminal justice system. In H. Bidgoli (Ed.), *The handbook of technology management* (pp. 693–703). Hoboken, NJ: John Wiley & Sons.

11. Baldwin, T. T., Bommer, W. H., & Rubin, R. S. (2008). *Developing management skills: What great managers know and do*. Boston, MA: McGraw-Hill/Irwin.

12. Purser, S. (2004). *A practical guide to managing information security*. Boston, MA: Artech House.

13. Brookings Institution (2006). *Computer ethics institute: The 10 commandments of ethics*. Retrieved January 13, 2010, from http://www.brook.edu/its/cei/cei_hp.htm

14. Straub, D. W., Carlson, P., & Jones, E. (1993). Deterring cheating by student programmers: A field experiment in computer security. *Journal of Management Systems, 5*, 33–48.

15. Bobek, D. D., & Hatfield, R. C. (2003). An investigation of the theory of planned behavior and the role of moral obligation in tax compliance. *Behavioral Research in Accounting, 15*, 13–39.

16. Workman, M., & Gathegi, J. (2007). Punishment and ethics deterrents: A comparative study of insider security contravention. *Journal of American Society for Information Science and Technology, 58*, 318–342.

17. Petrazhitskii, L. J. (1955). *Law and morality*. Cambridge, MA: Harvard University Press.

18. Fuller, L. L. (1977). Some presuppositions shaping the concept of socialization. In J. L. Tapp & F. J. Levine (Eds.), *Law, justice, and the individual in society: Psychological and legal issues* (pp. 89–105). New York, NY: Holt, Rinehart & Winston.

19. Tapp, J. L., & Kohlberg, L. (1977). Developing senses of law and legal justice. In J. L. Tapp & F. J. Levine (Eds.), *Law, justice, and the individual in society: Psychological and legal issues* (pp. 96–97). New York, NY: Holt, Rinehart & Winston.

20. Sovereign, K. L. (1994). *Personnel law*. Englewood Cliffs, NJ: Prentice-Hall.

Management, Security Law, and Policies

MANAGERS ARE NOT USUALLY LAWYERS; therefore, it is best to leave legal interpretations, advice, and legal procedures to the attorneys. Even those who are attorneys know the joke about a *lawyer who represents himself or herself has a fool for a client.* However, there are some aspects of security law that managers must be knowledgeable about to avoid creating legal problems for the corporation and for themselves further down the road. Main areas that are of particular interest in this regard are employment law related to security and policies, intellectual property, the use of company equipment and facilities, cyber crime and cyber law, electronic monitoring of employees, and forensic analysis and evidence preservation. In this chapter, we will present a basic orientation to these key legal issues.

Chapter 3 Topics

This chapter:

- Describes strategic security initiatives as the use of power and organizational politics to bring about broadly conceived outcomes.
- Explains security incidents from attacks or disasters.
- Illustrates the information security management life cycle (ISML) and its iterative stages.
- Covers security and employment law and security policies.
- Disscusses virtual work and related security and privacy issues.
- Explains intellectual property (IP) including trade secrets, copyrights, trademarks, and patents.
- Describes employee surveillance and privacy issues.
- Introduces forensics and the activities in collecting and preserving evidence and answering questions for legal purposes.

Chapter 3 Goals

When you finish this chapter, you should:

❑ Understand how management, security law, employment law, and policies are related.

❑ Know security-related legal aspects of mobile and remote work.

❑ Be able to identify the nature of intellectual property so that these assets can be classified for a risk assessment process.

❑ Know what is permissible regarding employee monitoring and implications for policies.

❑ Understand the basic legal aspects of forensic analysis and preservation of evidence and the *chain of custody* concept.

3.1 The Management Discipline

The functions of management include planning, organizing, directing, and controlling organizational resources [1]. Planning may be broken down into operational, tactical, and strategic levels [2]. Operational planning targets ways to gain efficiencies and cost-effectiveness in daily transactions. Tactical planning involves determining the incremental steps that are needed to achieve a strategy; strategic planning involves structured processes that lead to the realization of an envisioned future by leveraging the organization's core competencies [3–5]. How management goes about this planning divides along the lines of using processes that are scientific, formal, and structured (e.g., Semler, [6] 1997) or using techniques that involve artistry, creativity, imagination, and intuition (e.g., Stacy, 1992 [7]).

In Focus

The strategy concept has been conceptualized and defined differently by experts in the field. Some consider it to be a scientific plan for the future, others consider it to be the expedient use of resources to capitalize on major goals, and others consider it an "ability" to envision the future and inspire others to help achieve it. Michael Porter is among the most recognized experts in strategy because of his centrist views about strategy. His practical approach deals with the forces that affect decisions and corporate positioning and his use of the process of examining strengths, weaknesses, opportunities, and threats—called a SWOT analysis.

Managers organize resources by allocating their budgets and time to tasks so that they can fulfill their plans in support of organizational objectives. Organizing resources aims at the operational and tactical levels of management while keeping the strategic plan in mind [1]. The directing activity consists of clarifying goals and setting expectations with employees and superiors. The controlling activity involves conducting evaluations of business and employee performance, monitoring performance and comparing against plans, making adjustments, and creating a feedback loop for continuous organizational improvement [8].

3.1.1 Management Initiatives and Security

An initiative may simply be thought of as a project, and as with planning, initiatives may be operational, tactical, or strategic [1]. A strategic initiative is a product development or service activity that is used to gain competitive advantage [9, 10] and requires "long-term" commitment in time and resources to produce or provide [11]. Strategic initiatives therefore differ from tactics and operational initiatives in that the former is a blend of various analyses, behavioral techniques, and the use of power and organizational politics to bring about broadly conceived outcomes [12], whereas tactical initiatives are managerial actions that enact a strategy [13] and operational initiatives are the daily routines that result from management actions [8]. As such, realizing a strategy comes by way of product or service initiatives [14].

Security management comprises planning, organizing, directing, and controlling organizational resources (human and non-human) aimed specifically at securing the organization at operational, tactical, and strategic levels. Security initiatives include identifying and prioritizing business and security needs; determining the value of assets; defining, developing, overseeing, and monitoring security processes and procedures; producing and executing contingency plans; and evaluating, comparing, and selecting security technology to mitigate risks and prevent vulnerabilities from being exploited [15].

Security management may be a general management function or it or may be divided among designated security management positions; however, the management of operational, tactical, and strategic levels of security tends to ascend upward through the management echelon. For example, line managers or supervisors may oversee network and computer administrators who configure and deploy security solutions. The line managers monitor and report security threats and security needs to midlevel managers, who are usually tasked with allocating budgets and making decisions about security technologies and procedures [16].

Midlevel managers and line managers together are responsible for the implementation of the security architecture and the enforcement of security policies, and they report security and policy requirements upward to senior management. Senior managers work with the legal department and human resources to develop security policies, and they work across the organization to develop security strategies. They may also direct reviews and audits of security and ensure business continuity and/or recovery from disasters [15].

3.1.2 Information Security Management

Although managers are responsible for helping to ensure the security and well-being of employees, information security is at the core of the security management functions.

FIGURE 3.1

Information security
threats.

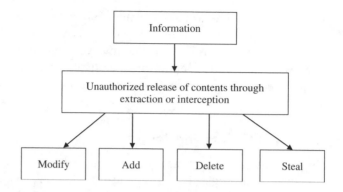

Computer security often refers to those efforts to secure computing devices such as desktops and laptops [17], whereas network security often refers to those efforts to secure the communications and data transmission infrastructure [18]. All of the efforts designed to protect computers and networks are primarily geared toward protecting the confidentiality, integrity, and availability of information. This is partially accomplished by establishing preventive and corrective measures to address unauthorized access to information that would lead to adding, deleting, modifying, or stealing. **Figure 3.1** illustrates the broad categories of threats to information security.

We have defined the concept of a threat previously, but for the purposes here relative to information security, we may view a threat as the potential for a security breach due to vulnerabilities. When vulnerabilities are exploited in attacks, the attacks can be either passive or active. A passive attack may be designed to simply steal information without the victim realizing it. An active attack may attempt to corrupt information or cause a disruption of a service or prevent access to critical information resources.

Threats may represent natural disasters, or they may represent the potential for human-induced incidents. **_Incidents_** are the realization of a disaster, such as a hurricane that obliterates an operations center or an attempted or successful attack by one or more people to bring down an operations center network. Human-induced incidents may be the result of accidental errors or intentional attacks by either company insiders (e.g., employees or contractors) or outsiders who do not work for the company. Intentional attacks aim at exploiting vulnerabilities that allow unauthorized access to information, hardware, networks, or software such as operating systems, database management systems, or applications. One classification of an intentional attack involves theft of information by identity thieves or corporate spies. **Table 3.1** provides some examples of information of interest to those who perpetrate such an attack.

To handle the threat risks, there are a variety of technologies and techniques available. For instance, access control applications coordinate who has what type of access to which resource. In this example, a systems administrator may have login access to a computer and may be authorized to read, add, and modify system configuration files, whereas non-administrators who have login access to the computer may only have permission to read them. When managers and their security assurance teams determine the threats and vulnerabilities to information resources, they assess the likelihood of attacks and the

TABLE 3.1	Examples of Information Assets

- Current customer lists: Customer information provides competitors with "competitive intelligence" about what a company is providing and to whom, which may facilitate opportunities to undermine them.
- Supplier, distributor, and contractor lists: These lists enable outsiders to determine potential vulnerabilities.
- Marketing plans: These include sales projections, statistics, pricing, forecasts, financial information, and promotional strategies, which can be exploited by a competitor.
- Research and development: This information pertains to intellectual property, strategic directions, product lines, preliminary research findings, and new product announcement dates.
- Operational information: This pertains to capacity, expansion, liquidity/working capital, austerity plans, and internal costs of doing business (i.e., profit margins).

severity of consequences from successful attacks. Managers must then weigh the threat risks (exposure) and the value of the assets against management priorities, timelines, and budgets [16].

3.1.3 Information Security Management Life Cycle

The information security management life cycle (ISML) consists of iterative stages. The stages typically include security analysis and planning, security design, security testing, security implementation, and security audit and review. Because the stages are iterative, feedback from the audits and reviews is then used the analysis and planning stage, which begins the cycle again. In the security analysis and planning stage, the assets and resources are classified according to their value, sensitivity, and exposure. Security requirements are developed according to the identified threats and vulnerabilities. Risk mitigation strategies and contingency plans are established, along with business continuity and recovery plans.

In Focus

A systems development life cycle (SDLC) is a structured set of processes used to produce a product or deliver a solution. An ISML is similar in this regard.

This stage is followed by a design stage, when security policies and procedures are created. The security design stage has a logical and a physical design aspect. The logical design involves developing the breadth and depth of the security measures that are to be implemented. The physical design involves the cost/benefit and risk assessment–based selection of technologies and techniques to be used in the implementation of information security. Depending on the technology or technique, a pre-implementation testing phase may be conducted to determine the quality and impact of the planned security measure. The security testing stage may run concurrent with or after the implementation of security measures, followed by the development of security criteria and checklists used when the confidentiality, integrity, and availability of information are audited and reviewed [15].

3.2 Security Law and Cyber Knowledge Work

Knowledge work is a term coined by Peter Drucker to describe jobs that derive their products and services from intellectual/cognitive tasks, and the Internet is often an important tool in knowledge work. Yet because information can be easily accessed and shared, this feature raises a variety of legal and security issues that managers need to consider. Among these issues are how information assets and intellectual property are used and how employees conduct their online activities, such as when posting information or comments in **newsgroups**, **blogs**, or **social media** that may affect the company. If an employee violates the law, depending on the nature of the violation, it may open a company to either civil or criminal liabilities, or both. In the United States, civil litigation seeks compensation for *injuries* to individuals or corporations, whereas the criminal justice system seeks to deter people from committing crimes and outlines punishments for those who inflict *injury* upon others [19]. Within this rubric, court decisions are called **case law**, whereas **statutes** are created from federal government and state legislation.

Statutory law may include criminal or penal law. Criminal violations of the law can be felonies, that, depending on jurisdiction, may be subdivided into four classes, where class "A" represents the most severe and class "D" represents the lesser felonies. Misdemeanors are often divided into class "A" (more severe) and class "B" (less severe). The standards of proof to determine that an offense has occurred differ between civil and criminal systems. In civil litigation, a finding of fault is based on the greater evidentiary weight (a preponderance of the evidence), whereas in criminal proceedings, guilt is decided based on the higher standard of "proof beyond a reasonable doubt" as decided by a judge or jury [20].

One of the major challenges for managers is that governments and their development of laws and legislation move slowly because, especially in the United States, there is the presumption that the slow-moving machinery of democracy promotes stability, but diffusions of technologies and organizational practices evolve and become implemented much more quickly. For instance, it has been debated (and decided differently) in many of the states in the United States as to whether a faxed signed document is an original, or a replica or copy, or nothing more than a series of "ones and zeros" that traverses a telephone line [21]. Likewise, there are different consequences and ways to adjudicate grievances depending on whether it is tried in a state or a federal jurisdiction [22]. Thus navigating these digital/cyber law issues is tricky and, in many instances, undecided. Having good security policies and well-written procedures in place is crucial in this regard.

3.2.1 Security, Employment Law, and Policies

If we are talking about security policies related to employee misconduct, we are necessarily talking about employment law. Under common law, a contract for employment for other than a definite term is generally terminable at will by either party. Accordingly, employers may dismiss their employees at will for good cause, for no cause, or even for a cause that might be considered morally reprehensible, even without being guilty of a legal wrong. However, recently, the courts have delineated a growing number of implied contract and public policy grounds for allowing suits to be brought against former employers under federal- and state-enacted rules (see *Novosel v. Nationwide Insurance Company*, 1983 [23]). There are also a growing number of tort suits [24]. A tort is defined as a breach of legal duty to exercise reasonable care that proximately causes injury or damage to another. This is a civil wrongdoing that does not arise from a breach of contract.

Because there are many international, federal, and state (or province, geographical, or local) laws that can be involved when it comes to security law, employment, and policies, when organizational policies are crafted it bears repeating that it is important to have legal guidance (such as from corporate attorneys in the legal department) along with the involvement of the human resources department [25]. Still, the implementation and enforcement of policies are often the burden of management [26], and so managers cannot afford to be ignorant of the law—and ignorance of the law is not a defense in court [27].

In Focus

Employment at will is a common-law employment doctrine that allows employers to dismiss employees without cause, and employees to quit without giving reason or notice. This contrasts with employment contracts and unionized employment.

In the United States, statutes require that an applicable regulatory agency (depending on the offense) impose penalties or fines for failure to notify employees of their rights and responsibilities [24]. Security policies therefore are an important component of this notification. Their main function, besides helping to ensure a more secure organization, is to reduce risk, and part of risk reduction is to reduce exposure to lawsuits. Because former employees are a main source of suits against companies, especially when it comes to policies and employment discharge, managers must exercise due care and due diligence in preventing problems and in handling employee misconduct and discharge issues [27]. This might include specifying what actions are worthy of immediate termination, what actions are subject to censure and/or corrective actions, and specifically excluding conduct related to policies for which there are extant laws, regulations, or statutes that could bring about a conflict in the interpretation and demand litigation to resolve or clarify by adjudication [25].

Realize that there are important differences between policies, guidelines, and procedures. Policies, in general, make clear acceptable and unacceptable actions in an organization and dictate the consequences for negligence or intentional failure to comply with communicated policies. Guidelines are rules of thumb that make suggestions about how to implement the spirit of the policies, and procedures are the detailed instructions that people must follow to implement the letter of the law intended by the policies. Policies need to delineate those actions that will result in immediate discharge from the company (and include language in the policy that states, in essence, *any violations of the law*), and those that will subject an employee to a corrective action process [25, 27].

In Focus

The main difference between a guideline and a policy is that a guideline tells management and employees what they should do about a problem. A policy tells management and employees what employee duties are and what they can expect from management as a result. As such, a policy may become a contract [24].

Regardless of whether a company is incorporated (or operates) in an "employment at will" state, it is prudent to have and to use a corrective action process when it is called for. Although technically the employment-at-will doctrine allows companies to discharge employees without cause, a company that does so without using due process (such as through a corrective action process) may open itself up to wrongful discharge suits [24, 25]. For example, most states, provinces, and districts in the United States, Canada, the United Kingdom, and several states in the European Union (EU) including France, Belgium, and the Netherlands, require a "good faith" dealing with employees [28]. Good faith means dealing honestly in one's conduct. Without proof of this basic treatment, discharged employees may file a suit based on defamation, infliction of emotional distress, malice, and bad faith dealings, or may use a discrimination defense, regardless of an employment-at-will doctrine, that a governing state may allow its incorporations [29].

Whether an employee might win the suit in a court of law is not the complete picture of the financial interests in the issue. First, litigation is expensive to the corporation, even if there are retained or corporate attorneys on staff. Second, even if the corporation wins in court, if a complaint goes to trial there could be a negative image or *bad press* conveyed. This could damage the corporation's reputation and negatively affect future recruitment of highly sought-after talent, make it more difficult to secure additional financial investments, or even negatively affect sales. A corrective action process can help to alleviate this problem.

In Focus

Corrective action is a formal process during which management and the legal and human resources departments implement steps that give employees a fair opportunity to correct counterproductive behaviors.

By ***corrective action***, the due process concept simply means notifying an employee of a deficient or negligent behavior, outlining what is required to achieve competence, giving a timeline and specific instructions to overcome the incompetence, listing the support that management is willing to offer to achieve those ends, providing a definite but reasonable timeframe for the employee to achieve competence, and naming the consequences for remission, which typically means employment discharge [25].

In Focus

An employer who tries to avoid potential discharge suits by making a work environment so hostile and onerous that the employee quits of his or her own volition may bring about a constructive discharge or harassment suit against the company, even in a state that utilizes an employment-at-will doctrine.

So how does this apply to information security, policies, and the law? Suppose you had a male employee who downloaded sexually explicit material on a company laptop, but the material did not violate child pornography laws—and a female coworker who sat next to the male employee on an airplane during a business trip saw it while he was viewing the material, and she subsequently filed a sexual harassment charge? Immediately, management has to confront what policies were established by the company for company equipment use and corporate conduct while at work or while "virtually" working.

3.2.2 Virtual Work, Security, and Privacy

Virtual work is a generic term used to describe company-sanctioned work tasks that occur away from the office. Some refer to this kind of work as telework, virtual teaming, mobile work, e-commuting, or some other moniker that essentially means doing company business outside the purview of the traditional corporate office, and it almost always means using some sort of technology and media to facilitate. As such, the technology and media "follow" the virtual worker as he or she travels or operates from a location other than the office (i.e., from a remote location). If that location happens to be a home, a hotel room, or some other "personal space," there are important intervening considerations for managers to balance relative to security and privacy. An invasion of privacy is an unjustified intrusion into another's reasonable expectation of privacy [30].

Some common intrusions that often give rise to lawsuits are public disclosure of private facts, the use of private information for the purpose of placing someone in a false or negative light in public, or misusing a person's identity or personal information for commercial gain or exploitation. In organizations, suits based on the theory of intrusion often arise from illegal searches and unauthorized electronic surveillance where the surveillance serves no business purpose or need [31]. In most organizations today, especially in knowledge work, people work not only in conventional offices, but also on the road or from home. Working from locations other than the workplace (virtual work) has major implications for security because laws and regulations governing the conventional office are being extended to home offices and virtual facilities.

More specifically, virtual work raises questions of employer liability for injuries sustained at home, or those incurred in transit between home and office, and whether these may be covered under worker's compensation, especially in cases where the employer may require employees to work away from the office. In 1999, the Occupational Safety and Health Administration (OSHA) issued an advisory letter on home-based workers, apparently requiring employer responsibility for home-based employee site safety. That letter generated so much controversy that OSHA subsequently diluted the requirement [32]. Nevertheless, employers are still required to report injuries that occur from work performed at home and to have some knowledge of employee home office environments.

Tonsing [33] noted various liability issues that virtual work creates, including jurisdictional issues involving situations where employers and employees reside in or are working in different states. This issue is commonly referred to as the "clash of laws." In the United States, litigation resulting from an Internet transaction is normally determined based on a state's "long arm" statute, which provides that a state can assert jurisdiction over a non-resident defendant who commits a tort, transacts business, or has some contact with that state [22].

Another recurring concern of employers with regard to virtual work has to do with ensuring the confidentiality of work products in the home or other environment outside the office. This can also have liability implications, where, for example, the employee is in possession of customer data or has in his or her possession employer trade secrets. Sensitive information and software assets may reside on laptop computers or mobile devices such as Blackberrys, iPhones, and so forth that can be easily lost or stolen. To highlight this point, in 2010, AvMed Health Plans Inc. reported the theft of two laptops containing unsecured social security numbers and health-related information for roughly 208,000 subscribers [34].

Conversely, there is also a personal risk for the employee, even if the employee regularly encrypts company information, because a legal "discovery" request may lead to the exposure of his or her private information encrypted using the same technologies and techniques that may reside on that computer system [28]. For these and other reasons, it is important for the protection of both employer and employee that company assets are used only for company purposes—and that employees do not use equipment such as laptops for "personal" materials or functions. This should be explicitly stated in company security policies.

A further area of concern in virtual work and security relates to the ability of management to monitor and control employee security behavior, which can run in conflict with privacy. It is generally taken for granted that employees may be under electronic surveillance in the workplace, which includes monitoring employees' computer files and email, web access, and voice mail within the ordinary course of business [35], and many employers would like to extend this surveillance ability to the remote workplace, including the home.

Although various governmental constitutions differ with regard to privacy rights, neither the Canadian Charter nor the U.S. Constitution, for example, contains provisions that explicitly define privacy rights in terms of personal information or data [18]. In the United States, the home has been an iconic bastion of privacy [36]. This may leave open the possibility for employer liabilities for certain crimes, especially in cases where managers "should have reasonably known" about them or failed to provide policies to address their prohibition in lieu of specific laws, ordinances, statutes, or regulations such as in the misuse of information and information systems [24].

Moreover, in cases where managers are not aware of, and could not reasonably foresee, illegal activities undertaken by employees, employer immunity to liabilities may be open to challenge if there is a company-required commingling of assets (software and hardware) used both in the office and at home or remote locations [27]. Next, because employees sometimes use the same home computer for both work and personal business in spite of policies prohibiting the practice [37], this raises the question of whether employers have a right to extend surveillance to the home office environment to protect their legitimate interests and take precautions from liabilities [38].

When an employee logs in to his or her employer's computer network using a home computer, the employer has the potential of accessing the employee's private files and may see what other files the employee is working on during "work time" [39]. If litigation results between the employer and employee, the employer may obtain a court order allowing it to inspect and copy an employee's home computer's storage, as happened in the Northwest Airlines case where the airline claimed employees had planned "a sick-out" in order to cripple the airline [40].

Legal and private practices at home, such as downloading explicit sexual content from the Web, may land virtual workers in trouble if the materials are stored on company-owned equipment, and there may be employer tort liabilities from unreasonable intrusions. Among the considerations are the degrees to which employees have a reasonable expectation of privacy and the presence of a legitimate business justification that overrides the privacy expectation [41].

3.3 Intellectual Property Law

Intellectual property (IP) refers to corporate proprietary information, data, trade secrets, copyrights, branding, trademarks, patents, and other materials, methods, and processes claimed as owned by a company, and thus IP is considered assets of a company. IP has value; it costs money to create it and to protect it, and the value can be diminished by someone's actions even if actual damages are hard to determine [42]. The ease with which information can be distributed over the Web has apparently contributed to common violations involving IP [43]. As part of risk assessment, IP should be classified according to type and sensitivity of the information; in managing risk, IP needs to be protected commensurately. As part of this, organizations need to develop written policies and to conduct training on the proper care and handling of IP.

3.3.1 Trade Secrets

Trade secrets consist of formulas, methods, and information that are vital to company operations. Although employees are generally under a duty of loyalty to their employers not to misappropriate trade secrets by disclosure to competitors, to help protect trade secrets, employees and outside parties to whom trade secrets are divulged are usually asked to sign non-disclosure agreements. People who violate the duty to keep trade secrets confidential commit a tort. To qualify as a tort, the offender must have had a legal duty to the injured and must have breached that duty, and damage must have been inflicted as proximate result [44]. In addition to unauthorized disclosure, trade secrets may be lost due to industrial espionage, electronic surveillance, or spying.

3.3.2 Patents

Patents are inventions to which the patent holder is granted exclusive use for a period of time by federal law (in the United States). A patent owner may profit by granting licenses to others to use the patent for fees or royalties. Unlike trade secrets that are to remain confidential, when inventors patent an invention with the Patent Office, they must describe it in such detail that it can be copied. This is so courts can determine if the invention is patentable or if an infringement has occurred. Once a patent has expired, the invention enters the public domain, where anyone can use it. There are different kinds of patents, but most patents that are related to information security are "utility" patents. To be eligible for patent as a utility, the process, machine, or composition must be novel (that is, it must not conflict with a prior pending application or previously issued patent), and it must have specific and substantial usefulness [29].

> **In Focus**
>
> 2010 *SCO v. Novell* Litigation: Following a 3-week jury trial, attorneys won a unanimous verdict for Novell in *SCO v. Novell*, a case widely watched by members of the open source software community. SCO's business model was to convince Linux users to pay license fees to SCO, based on the notion that Linux infringed certain UNIX copyrights, which SCO claimed it had acquired from Novell. Novell stated that it, not SCO, owned the UNIX copyrights, and SCO sued for slander of title, seeking damages of several hundred million dollars. Novell had earlier sought and obtained a summary judgment in the case, when the court ruled that Novell in fact owned the copyrights. SCO appealed to the Tenth Circuit, which reversed and remanded the case for a jury trial. At the conclusion of the trial, the jury unanimously agreed that Novell, not SCO, owned the copyrights, thus denying SCO's damage claims. In post-trial rulings, Judge Ted Stewart denied SCO's claims for specific performance and breach of the implied covenant of good faith and fair dealing. Judge Stewart also granted Novell judgment on its claim for declaratory judgment [45].

3.3.3 Copyrights

Copyrights are protections afforded by federal law to authors of original works. Under Section 102(a) of the Copyright Act, works include music, literature, software, semiconductor patterns and electronic programming, graphics, motion pictures and audiovisual recordings, and the like.

> **In Focus**
>
> Copyright protections do not protect an idea; they only extend to an original expression of an idea.

In most cases, copyrighted work should be registered with the Copyright Office, but this is not required in order to protect a work. For example, in some cases, simply placing a © after the copyright owner's name and the year is sufficient to create a defensible protection from infringement. Most individual copyrights hold for the lifetime of the author plus 70 years. For corporate authors, the protection extends to 95 years. There are instances where copyright protections may be limited [42]. Two such limitations are compulsory licenses and fair use. Compulsory licenses permit certain limited uses of copyrighted materials upon payment of royalties. Fair use allows reference to copyrighted materials for the purpose of criticism, comment, news reporting, teaching (including multiple copies for classroom use), scholarship, or research. Fair use is determined by (1) the purpose for which the materials were used, taking into consideration for-profit versus non-profit usage, (2) the nature of the copyrighted work, (3) the amount and proportion used in relation to protected work, and (4) the effect of the use on the market value of the copyrighted work. Owners can transfer copyrighted works to others, and under most cases when work is done for hire, there is typically an implied if not explicit ownership transfer [44].

3.4 Employee Surveillance and Privacy

To augment security, companies are increasingly using employee-monitoring (or surveillance) techniques. Recent studies found that in 1999, 67 percent of employers surveyed electronically monitored their employees, but by 2001, that number had grown to 78 percent; by 2003, 92 percent of employers surveyed indicated that they used electronic monitoring of employees. Most of the employers surveyed monitored employee web surfing, more than half reviewed email messages and examined employees' computer files, and roughly one-third tracked content, keystrokes, and time spent at the computer [46]. The majority of workplace surveillance to date has consisted primarily of electronic observation of web surfing activity, monitoring emails, and telephone call monitoring for office workers (*for quality assurance and training purposes*), and global positioning satellite (GPS) tracking of mobile workers [47]. However, the breadth and depth of surveillance is growing.

3.4.1 Video Surveillance

Fairweather [48] determined that video surveillance of employees has become commonplace in many vocations and locations. A survey by Harvey [46] showed that of companies surveyed, only 18 percent used video surveillance in 2001, but by 2005, that number had climbed to 51 percent, and 10 percent of the respondents indicated that cameras were installed specifically to track job performance. The uses of video surveillance to monitor work activity may be supported by an analogy to the "plain view" doctrine, which allows a company to monitor employees in plain sight. This position is strengthened if the company takes overt action to notify its employees of the practice [49]. Areas where video surveillance is common are in computer server rooms, accounting or bookkeeping and payroll offices, stockrooms and warehouses, and manufacturing areas.

3.4.2 Privacy and Policy

As we indicated earlier, one of the central issues in terms of surveillance initiatives concerns worker rights to their privacy versus employer rights to know what workers are doing, along with their responsibilities to report illegal activities. Laws have tended to support the rights of corporations to inspect and monitor work and workers, which arises from needs related to business emergencies and the corporation's rights over its assets and to protect its interests [50]. Employees may use email or the Web inappropriately for purposes such as disseminating harmful information, infringing on copyrighted or patented materials, harassment, corporate espionage or insider trading, or acquiring child pornography. In these instances, the courts have leaned on the principle of **_discovery_** to allow inspection, granting any party or potential party to a suit including those outside the company access to certain information such as email and backups of databases, and even to reconstruction of deleted files [51]. There are protections in place to mitigate unreasonable search and seizure, such as the Electronic Communications Privacy Act, which defines an electronic communication as:

> Any transfer of signs, signals, writing, images, sounds, data, or intelligence of any nature transmitted in whole or in part by a wire, radio, electromagnetic, photoelectronic or photooptical system that affects interstate or foreign commerce, but it does not include the radio portion of a cordless telephone communication that is transmitted between the cordless telephone handset and base unit, wireless networks, any wire or oral or video communication, any communication made through a tone-only paging device or any communication from a tracking device. [52]

The original intent of the law was to protect one from the interception of communications not otherwise subject to interception, but the U.S. Patriot Act (HR 3162) has vastly expanded the powers of government and enforcement agencies to conduct surveillance and communications interception pertaining to criminal activity [50]. From a legal perspective, the extent of an employee's expectation of privacy often turns on the nature of an intended intrusion. With the exception of personal containers, there is little reasonable expectation of privacy that attends to the work area. That is, a worker may have reasonable expectation of privacy in personal possessions such as a handbag in the office, but the law holds that employers possess a legitimate interest in the efficient operation of the workplace. One aspect of this interest is that supervisors may monitor at will that which is in plain view within an open work area, and perhaps even within a home if a home is used for teleworking [53].

With the rise of social media such as Facebook, YouTube, and MySpace, people are increasingly giving up their privacy by posting intimate and compromising photos, videos, and other information. Employers are using information posted on these sites for making hiring decisions and, in some cases, terminating employment. These sites are also sources of compromise, including dissemination of IP or defamatory postings. To help prevent company liabilities or other security issues, corporate policies need to include the protocols for appropriate online behavior that might affect the company or the company's interests [54].

3.4.3 Surveillance and Organizational Justice

The legal protections afforded employers combined with increasing technological sophistication and decreasing costs are allowing companies to monitor the actions of workers more closely than ever before [48, 55]. A concept that originated in the military, Intelligence, Surveillance, and Reconnaissance (ISR), has now made its way into the business lexicon. Software that covertly monitors computer activities and surveillance devices are being fashioned to blend into the environment by hiding them in pens, clocks, or bookends, which has a dampening effect on employee surveillance awareness regardless of employer notifications. This creates a psychological bind on employees who know they are being monitored, but the unobtrusiveness of the technology and devices make them seem innocuous [55]; moreover, the concepts of privacy and security are not simply legal matters. Privacy is an element of the psychological state of security. When people's perception of privacy is reduced, there can be deleterious consequences for work performance.

3.5 Cyber Law and Cyber Crime

Cyber law can be thought of as a collection of extensions to existing law administered under federal, state, or local law. For example, the federal cyber crime statute 18 U.S. Code § 1030, among other stipulations, makes it a crime for anyone to knowingly access a computer without authorization or exceed authorized access of systems that involve national defense or foreign relations, or any other restricted data with reason to believe that such information could result in injury to the United States, including interstate or foreign commerce. It also prohibits willfully communicating, delivering, transmitting, or in any other way allowing the protected data to be leaked to any person not entitled to receive them. This statute and others have been used to combat unauthorized intrusions into computer systems and illegal access and use of intellectual property, financial records, medical records, and fraudulent online activities. States and local municipalities also enact cyber crime laws; for example, every state in the United States prohibits unauthorized access of computer systems and theft from them or damage of them by gaining unauthorized access [19].

3.5.1 International, Federal, and State Cyber Law

As presented earlier, there are jurisdictional issues related to various crimes and civil injuries committed over the Internet. There are situations where a violation can overlap with both civil and criminal prohibitions and with international, federal, and state laws. A common example is an infringement of intellectual property such as a copyright or a patent. Conversely, there have been cases where companies have assumed that their patents were infringed upon, only to learn that their patents were filed with the United States Patent and Trademark Office but were not valid in a foreign country.

The viability of any legal complaint across national borders depends on the treaties the nations hold. For international guidance in America, the American Law Institute and the Foreign Relations Law of the United States are important resources; in Europe, check the Council of Europe's Convention on Cybercrime; and the World Trade Organization (WTO) agreement on Trade-Related Aspects of Intellectual Property Rights (TRIPS) outline rules and guidelines for conducting transactions across international borders [28].

Most of the "industrialized nations" have codified legal restrictions against the most common forms of cyber crimes, although how they are adjudicated, the penalties, and the jurisdictions are fluid and not always clear [44]. For the most part, there are prohibitions against intentionally gaining unauthorized access to ("hacking" into) computer systems to commit theft, cause damage, or commit other illegal offenses; attempting to damage or disable computer systems such as through denial of service attacks or releasing Worms or Trojans; attempting to extort money or create false identities using information gathered from intrusions or social engineering; threatening or harassing others online (cyber harassment); online stalking (cyber stalking); and misappropriating legally protected information, such as copyrighted materials [22].

3.5.2 Employee Behavior and Cyber Law

There are instances where employers may be held liable for employee conduct, both off and on the job. For example, off the job, if employees post confidential customer information or HIPAA-protected materials online, an employer may be held accountable depending on what precautions employers took to preclude such actions [27, 56]. On the job, the risk of liability is much greater. An employer will generally be held liable if an employee is negligent in his or her actions, but not necessarily for intentional violations unless the employer knew or "reasonably should have known" about them [22].

More particularly, employers may be found liable or guilty depending on the nature of the illegal actions by the employee, the employee's role in the company, and the degrees of diligence given by an employer to prevent foreseeable illegal actions. For instance, if an employer failed to take certain precautions to prevent an employee from committing a violation that leads to leakage of customer financial information or health records, employers may be made a party in the complaint [22, 44]. Or, if an employer failed to perform an appropriate background check of a job candidate where the candidate had a history of harassment and, after hiring the candidate, the employee harassed others in the office or online, the employer may be found as having contributed to the offense [27, 57].

Again, to help reduce risk, it is extremely important to have in place and have communicated policies that govern employee online behavior related to the job. Interestingly, companies are also beginning to develop policies regarding financial dealings and behaviors off the job that pertain to company interests; however, this can invite an invasion of privacy suit and so the decision about these off-the-job policies should be weighed not only with legal counsel [27], but also in risk-mitigation activities (risk of potential exposure) if no policy is established [44]. Note, however, that some legal experts advise that if an offense is already prohibited by law, then it may be best not to create a policy about that issue because it might conflict with the interpretation of the law (raising further legal challenges), and unless all reasonable precautions are taken to prevent the violation, it might make the company culpable because it implies that an action was "foreseen" by the employer [24].

Instead, some legal experts suggest that in those cases where laws are extant, policies should simply state that employees must comply with the law. This decision must be carefully decided by the company attorneys and the human resources department. Furthermore, if policies are written governing "off the job" behavior or "virtual work" behavior, companies need to ensure due care and due diligence in taking all reasonable precautions to prevent violations while simultaneously crafting measures to help ensure the protection of individual privacy [44, 47].

> **In Focus**
>
> The difference in viewpoints about the number of policies a company creates turns on the issue of whether to try to cover as many bases as possible, realizing that someone might claim that a violation not covered by policy was exempt because it was not in an "exhaustive list," or whether the minimalist approach may risk that someone might claim that management did not take sufficient steps to notify employees of what was acceptable. An attorney is in the best position to judge the lesser of the evils.

3.5.3 Corporate Espionage

In addition to threats from competitive intelligence gathering, and along with globalization and the growth of information and information value, corporate espionage has become easier and pervasive. Espionage, simply put, is a covert method of gathering information about a competitor or enemy. Espionage can lead to blackmail, extortion, defamation (character assassination), and sabotage. Techniques used to gather intelligence and commit corporate espionage can come from human intelligence (humint), signal intelligence (sigint), and image and photographic intelligence (imint).

Human intelligence may come from planted spies, from leakage of confidential information such as from picking through trash for sensitive documents (dumpster diving), and from providers of janitorial services who have access to buildings after hours. People may also reverse engineer technology to learn of trade secrets or steal proprietary information or methods. Signal intelligence is the interception of information as it moves over a communications channel, such as a telephone or a data communications network. Along with the typical video surveillance techniques, with technologies such as Google Earth, people can gather image intelligence about facilities.

Counterintelligence is the term applied to techniques used to prevent corporations from falling victim to intelligence gathering and espionage. Counterintelligence

TABLE 3.2   A Brief List of Historical Espionage *(Adapted from Casey, 1996 [58]).*
• Roman financial speculators and merchants financed and performed acts of espionage for the Roman intelligence service.
• The Celts stole the secrets for making superior chariot wheels from the Romans.
• Hannibal practiced the art of misinformation by having phoney "official" letters fall into enemy hands.
• Julius Caesar used spies to learn the weaknesses of battlefield and political opponents.
• Napoleon kept extensive background files on political rivals and suspected enemies.

attempts to prevent unauthorized disclosure of proprietary information, detect espionage attempts, and define defensive operations. Sample counterintelligence techniques include document shredding, reviews of public statements and sales presentations to ensure that no proprietary information is disclosed, and ensuring that laptop computers and mobile devices use cryptography and strong authentication (to be discussed in more detail later).

3.6 Forensics

Forensics involves all the activities in collecting and preserving evidence and answering questions for legal purposes [57]. There are many subcategories of forensics when it comes to information and computer security, which include digital forensics, computer forensics, and others. Forensics may range from a single intrusion from a hacker to systematic corporate espionage. In the latter case, a variety of forensic procedures are necessary and may uncover illicit human intelligence (humint), signal intelligence (sigint), and photographic and image intelligence (imint). For our final section of this chapter, we will address the broad and general legal aspects of forensics and evidence that managers should know about; we will return to forensic procedures and evidence gathering later, in the chapter on security operations.

3.6.1 What Constitutes Evidence?

Generally speaking, to be admissible in court, evidence must pass three tests: (1) It must be relevant to the crime or complaint, (2) it must be authentic, and (3) it must be reliable. Relevance can actually involve casting a wide net. For instance, all the data in a log may be relevant to a crime or a complaint even if the data do not come from the alleged attacker if the data provide contexts with which to interpret the crime or violation [16, 57]. Authenticity of evidence can be a much harder test to pass. For instance, because digital evidence can be altered, some form of "proof of authenticity" is required, which might include non-repudiation techniques or tracing the chain of custody of the information or materials [21]. A **chain of custody** consists of all the steps and handlers of the information or materials from origination to its delivery into proceedings. Reliability requires the "proof" that there were no errors in the generation or interpretation of the evidence—for instance, that an internet protocol (IP) address of a purported offender was not spoofed (forged) [19, 29].

3.6.2 Cyber Crime Evidence

Relative to evidence and cyber crime, there are two critical issues for managers to consider: gathering evidence and preserving evidence to present at trial. In the United States, the Fourth Amendment protects citizens from *unreasonable* searches and seizures, but a search or seizure is *reasonable* if it does not violate a presumed expectation of privacy [19, 21]. Beyond this basic facility, law enforcement and the courts must be involved in the collection of evidence for criminal prosecution and, in most cases, need a court order or a search warrant. If managers suspect criminal activity, it is important to involve the legal department and alert the relevant agencies. If the legal issues are in the nature of civil violations, the bar is set lower in terms of evidence collection and preservation because criminal law requires conviction if evidence is *beyond a reasonable doubt*, whereas in civil trials, only the lower standard of *preponderance of evidence* is needed for a favorable judgment. Nevertheless, in all cases of a suspected violation, managers need to coordinate their collection of evidence with legal counsel.

3.6.3 Cyber Law and Cyber Crime Issues

An example of a potential legal violation includes what is called cyber squatting. The U.S. Anti-Cybersquatting Consumer Protection Act (15 U.S.C. 1125) prohibits the registration of a domain name in *bad faith* (e.g., deception) by a third party. This protects those who hold a trademark or servicemark from *cyber pirates* (those who register a domain name associated with a trademark or service mark owned by another). It is important to realize that trademarks and servicemarks are given for specific uses (the codes and descriptions are available from the U.S. Patent Office website). No action should be taken unless it is clear that the use of the domain conflicts with the type of trade or service that was registered [42].

For instance, if a trademark was registered by a company called "CookiesRus" for software that installs electronic tracking cookies on a computer for marketing purposes, and a bakery registered a trademark called "CookiesRus" and wanted to register a mail order delivery service using that name, most likely there would be no conflict because these entities would have registered their trademarks or servicemarks under different trademark or service codes [21, 42]. Another example is the Communications Decency Act (47 U.S.C. 223), which stipulates that online service providers shall not be treated as publishers in terms of liability for defamatory postings made by others and may not be held liable for defamation in such cases. However, recent legal challenges may ultimately lead to changes in this stance.

CHAPTER SUMMARY

In this chapter, we presented an overview of some legal issues confronting managers who are responsible for information security. We emphasized that managers should not act in the capacity of an attorney, but we also emphasized that they cannot afford to be ignorant of the law. Most of the legal concepts we broached in this chapter will be revisited in a more applied fashion in later chapters, such as those covering topics on operations and personnel management. We discussed security management and security policies, and we covered some of the legal aspects related to mobile and remote work. We introduced the concept of intellectual property and suggested that these assets should be classified in a risk assessment process. We stated that managers should know what is permissible regarding employee monitoring and presented those implications for personnel and security policies. Finally, we gave a quick survey of cyber crime and cyber law to enable a basic understanding of the legal aspects of forensic analysis and preservation of evidence, and we introduced the chain-of-custody concept. In the next chapter, we will rely on these foundations and consider regulations and governance.

THINK ABOUT IT

Topic Questions

3.1: What are some of the key features of security management presented in this chapter?

3.2: What are some conditions mentioned in this chapter for when employers might be held liable for the actions of their employees?

3.3: Copyrights are _____, whereas patents are _____.

3.4: The Fourth Amendment provides U. S. citizens:

_____ Freedom to carry arms

_____ Freedom of speech

_____ Freedom from unreasonable searches and seizures

_____ Freedom from self-incrimination

3.5: Espionage is:

_____ Only applicable to the military and intelligence communities

_____ A covert method of gathering information about a competitor or enemy

_____ A crime that cannot be prosecuted if the perpetrators are in another country

_____ A physical action that destroys property

3.6: The agreement on Trade-Related Aspects of Intellectual Property Rights (TRIPS) is overseen by the:

_____ World Trade Organization (WTO)

_____ Securities and Exchange Commission (SEC)

_____ Internal Revenue Service (IRS)

_____ U.S. Patent Office

3.7: A chain of custody consists of all the steps and handlers of the information or materials from origination to its delivery into proceedings.

_____ True

_____ False

THINK ABOUT IT (CONTINUED)

3.8: Video surveillance is prohibited in businesses.

____ True

____ False

3.9: The U.S. Anti-Cybersquatting Consumer Protection Act (15 U.S.C. 1125) prohibits:

____ Using email to request sale of a domain name

____ Registering more than one domain name

____ People from sending SPAM

____ The registration of a domain name in bad faith

3.10: Most copyrights end with the death of the author.

____ True

____ False

Questions for Further Study

Q3.1: Contrast the U.S. First Amendment Rights with privacy protections in the European Union (EU). For example, consider the Hague Convention on Jurisdiction and Enforcement of Judgments in Civil and Commercial cases: www.hcch.net.

Q3.2: What are managerial responsibilities for protecting evidence in both criminal and civil incidents?

Q3.3: Explain where the line should be drawn between management's legal responsibilities and those that should be left to the attorneys.

Q3.4: What are some key trends and changes in cyber crime since the early 2000s?

Q3.5: Investigate the U.S. Patent Office and summarize the various codes used in trademarking.

KEY CONCEPTS AND TERMS

Defamation may result from posting false comments in newsgroups, blogs, or social media.

Discovery allows inspection access to certain information such as email by outside parties in a lawsuit.

Evidence must pass three tests to be admissible in court: (1) It must be relevant to the crime or complaint, (2) it must be

authentic, and (3) it must be reliable.

ISR stands for Intelligence (gathered information), Surveillance (observation), and Reconnaissance (scouting for information).

Management is a function that includes planning, organizing, directing, and controlling organizational resources.

Patents are inventions to which the patent holder is granted exclusive use for a period of time by federal law.

Vulnerabilities represent the potential to exploit systems and information.

References

1. Coventry, W. F., & Burstiner, I. (1977). *Management: A handbook.* Englewood Cliffs, NJ: Prentice-Hall.

2. Meredith, J. R., & Mantel, S. J. (1995). *Project management: A managerial approach.* New York, NY: John Wiley & Sons.

3. Denton, D. K., & Wisdom, B. L. (1992). Shared vision. In A. A. Thompson Jr., W. E. Fulmer, & A. J. Strickland III (Eds.), *Readings in strategic management* (pp. 52–56). Boston, MA: Irwin.

4. Hamel, G., & Prahalad, C. K. (1993, March–April). Strategy as stretch and leverage. *Harvard Business Review,* pp. 75–85.

5. Mintzberg, H. (1994, January–February). The fall and rise of strategic planning. *Harvard Business Review,* pp. 107–114.

6. Semler, S. W. (1997). Systematic agreement: A theory of organizational alignment. *Human Resource Development Quarterly, 8,* 23–39.

7. Stacy, R. D. (1992). *Managing the unknowable. Strategic boundaries between order and chaos in organizations.* San Francisco, CA: Jossey-Bass.

8. Synnott, W. R. (1987). *The information weapon: Winning customers and markets with technology.* New York, NY: John Wiley & Sons.

9. Porter, M. E. (1979). *How competitive forces shape strategy.* New York, NY: Free Press.

10. Porter, M. E. (1996, November–December). What is strategy? *Harvard Business Review,* pp. 61–78.

11. Simon, M., & Houghton, S. M. (2003). The relationship between overconfidence and the introduction of risky products: Evidence from a field study. *Academy of Management Journal, 46,* 139–149.

12. Quinn, J. B. (1992). Managing strategic change. In A. A. Thompson Jr., W. E. Fulmer, & A. J. Strickland III (Eds.), *Readings in strategic management,* 4th ed., pp. 19–42). Boston, MA: Irwin. (Reprinted from *Sloan Management Review, 21,* 3–20.

13. Greer, C. R. (1995). *Strategy and human resources. A general managerial perspective.* Englewood Cliffs, NJ: Prentice-Hall.

14. Burgleman, R. A., & Grove, A. S. (1996). Strategic dissonance. *California Management Review, 38,* 8–28.

15. Solomon, M. G., & Chapple, M. (2005). *Information security illuminated.* Sudbury, MA: Jones and Bartlett Publishers.

16. Purser, S. (2004). *A practical guide to managing information security.* Boston, MA: Artech House.

17. Newman, R. C. (2010). *Computer security: Protecting digital resources.* Sudbury, MA: Jones and Bartlett Publishers.

18. Himma, K. E. (2007). *Internet security: Hacking, counterhacking, and society.* Sudbury, MA: Jones and Bartlett Publishers.

19. Brenner, S. W. (2010). Cybercrime and the U.S. criminal justice system. In H. Bidgoli (Ed.), *The handbook of technology management* (pp. 693–703). Hoboken, NJ: John Wiley & Sons.

20. Fischer, R. J., & Green, G. (1992). *Introduction to security* (pp. 122–157). Boston, MA: Butterworth-Hienemann.

21. Keck, R. (2005). Disruptive technologies and the evolution of the law. *The Legal Brief, 23,* 22–49.

22. Knudsen, K. H. (2010). Cyber law. In H. Bidgoli (Ed.), *The handbook of technology management* (pp. 704–716). New York, NY: John Wiley & Sons.

23. *Novosel v. Nationwide Insurance Company* (1983). United States Court of appeals, Third Circuit 721 F.2d 894.

24. Sovereign, K. L. (1994). *Personnel law*. New York, NY: Prentice Hall.

25. Van Zant, K. (1991). *HR Law*. Atlanta, GA: Gerber-Alley Press.

26. Martinko, M. J., Gundlach, M. J., & Douglas, S. C. (2002). Toward an integrative theory of counterproductive workplace behavior: A causal reasoning perspective. *International Journal of Selection and Assessment, 10,* 36–50.

27. Beadle, J. (2010). Corporate law and legal counsel: A mutually dependent relation. *The Legal Brief, 15,* 19–27.

28. Spinello, R. A. (2011). *Cyberethics: Morality and law in cyberspace*. Sudbury, MA: Jones & Bartlett Learning.

29. Jenkins, J. A. (2011). *The American courts*. Sudbury, MA: Jones & Bartlett Learning.

30. Gathegi, J., & Workman, M. (2009). Virtual work. In H. Bidgoli (Ed.), *The handbook of technology management* (pp. 279–288). Hoboken, NJ: John Wiley & Sons.

31. *People v. Zelinski,* 155 Cal.Rptr. 575 (1979).

32. Swink, D. R. (2001). Telecommuter law: A new frontier in legal liability, *American Business Law Journal, 38,* 857.

33. Tonsing, M. (1999, July). Welcome to the digital danger zone: Say hello to the virtual workforce of the next millennium, *Federal Lawyer, 46,* 19.

34. Open Security Foundation (2010). *AvMed Health Plans security breach: Lost or stolen laptops*. Retrieved March 21, 2010, from http://datalossdb.org/incidents

35. Rosen, J. (2000). *The unwanted gaze: The destruction of privacy in America*. New York, NY: Random House.

36. *Commonwealth v. Brion,* 652 A.2d 287, 289 (Pa. 1994).

37. Workman, M., Bommer, W., & Straub, D. (2008). Security lapses and the omission of information security measures: An empirical test of the threat control model. *Journal of Computers in Human Behavior, 24,* 2799–2816.

38. Monitoring employee e-mail and internet usage: Avoiding the omniscient electronic sweatshop: Insights from Europe 2005. *University of Pennsylvania Journal of Labor and Employment Law,* 829.

39. Nichols, D. H. (2000). Window peeping in the workplace: A look into employee privacy in a technological era. *William Mitchell Law Review, 27,* 1587.

40. *Northwest Airlines v. Local 2000,* Civ. No. 00-08 (D. Minn. Jan. 4, 2000).

41. *Ortega v. O'Connor,* 480 U.S. 709 (1987).

42. Nydegger, C. (2010). In a legal sense or rather cents: Why nickel when you can dime your opponent to death? *The Law and Legal Strategy Review, 19,* 233–249.

43. Ryan, J. J. C. H. (2007). Plagiarism, education, and information security. *IEEE Security & Privacy, 5,* 62–65.

44. Nemeth, C. P. (2011). *Law and evidence*. Sudbury, MA: Jones & Bartlett Learning.

45. Workman, H. R., & Nydegger, R. D. (2011). *W/N scores big win in SCO v. Novell litigation*. Salt Lake City, UT: Workman and Nydegger Attorneys at Law. Retrieved June 12, 2011, from http://www.wnlaw.com

46. Harvey, C. (2007, April). The boss has new technology to spy on you. *Datamation,* pp, 1–5.

47. Himma, K. E. (2010). Legal, social, and ethical issues of the Internet. In H. Bidgoli (Ed.), *The handbook of technology management* (pp. 753–775). New York, NY: John Wiley & Sons.

48. Fairweather, B. N. (1999). Surveillance in employment: The case of teleworking. *Journal of Business Ethics, 22,* 39–49.

49. Scholz, J. T. (1997). Enforcement policy and corporate misconduct: The changing perspective of deterrence theory. *Law and Contemporary Problems, 60,* 153–268.

50. Borrull, A. L., & Oppenheim, C. (2004). Legal aspects of the Web. In B. Cronin (Ed), *Annual Review of Information Science and Technology, 38* (pp. 483–548). Medford, NJ: Information Today.

51. Bureau of Transportation Statistics. (1992). *Transportation implications of telecommuting.* Washington, DC: National Transportation Association. Retrieved July 12, 2010, from http://ntl.bts.gov/DOCS/telecommute.html

52. Losey, R. C. (1998). The electronic communications privacy act: United States Code. Orlando, FL: The Information Law Web. Retrieved July 15, 2010, from http://floridalawfirm.com/privacy.html

53. Braithwaite, J., & Drahos, P. (2000). *Global business regulation.* New York, NY: Cambride University Press.

54. Kadrich, M. (2010). Does privacy exist in the age of social networking? *ISSA Journal, 8,* 18–21.

55. Akdeniz, Y., Walker, C., & Wall, D. (2000). *The Internet, law, and society.* Harlow, UK: Pearson Publishing.

56. Milwaukee News (2009). *Nurses fired over cell phone photos of patient: Case referred to FBI for possible HIPAA violations.* Retrieved July 15, 2010, from: http://www.wisn.com/news/18796315/detail.html

57. Grama, J. L. (2011). *Legal issues in information security.* Sudbury, MA: Jones & Bartlett Learning.

58. Casey, M. S. (1996). *Corporate intelligence: Information gathering and corporate espionage.* Cambridge, MA: Harcourt Press.

Security Regulations and Governance

ECAUSE OF SECURITY BREACHES AND information leakages, an increasing number of regulations and security standards have been enacted. There are many domestic and international regulations and treaties, but in this chapter, we will simply provide an overview of some of the more sweeping ones. Many of the regulations overlap in some way, but in other cases—especially when crossing international borders—there are some that conflict with each other. We will defer detailed discussion of those and merely bring these issues to the reader's attention for further investigation. The important takeaway is that regulations and standards have important implications for managers and security, which falls under the category of "governance." Governance is the term given to the management of organizational resources according to laws, statutes, regulations, standards, and policies [1]. Governance is often called "checklist" security, for reasons that will become obvious later.

Chapter 4 Topics

This chapter:

- Presents regulations such as the Gramm-Leach-Bliley Act, and the implications these have for information and systems security.
- Provides a definition of governance and offers compliance criteria.
- Contrasts U.S. regulations with those in the United Kingdom and European Union.
- Summarizes the key points for various regulations.

Chapter 4 Goals

When you finish this chapter, you should:

- ❑ Have a working knowledge of security regulations internationally.
- ❑ Gain an introductory knowledge of security best practices and governance.
- ❑ Understand the requirements that apply to personal information.
- ❑ Be able to explain the security requirements for various types of information.

4.1 Governance and U.S. Regulations

Because of mismanagement and carelessness with important information, including information related to or managed by government entities, there are growing legislative actions and increasing regulatory controls enacted for the governance of organizations, especially those that are or deal with government agencies. Some of the regulations have targeted the protection of privacy in response to cases that have ranged from criminal front operations that were able to steal information from credit bureaus, to the loss of laptop computers that contained sensitive and unprotected employee and military data [2]. Governance therefore is, in essence, the processes by which organizations are managed according to some criteria. In the most formal sense, governance typically means conforming to regulations and/or requirements set for an agency, industry, or organization.

When many employees in the United States are asked about workplace governance, they refer to the activities of the Department of Labor and the *Occupational Safety and Health Administration* (**OSHA**). Although these are among the most visible governance bodies, there are many lesser known but equally important agencies and regulatory bodies of which managers need to be aware. Two major areas with which managers need to acquaint themselves involve standards by which regulators hold certain organizations responsible for taking or preventing certain actions and those that pertain to the development and enforcement of personnel policies and the enactment of safeguards and controls.

One example is the *Sarbanes–Oxley Act of 2002* (**SOX**) that was passed by Congress in response to several highly public corporate failures. In this legislation, all companies listed on a U.S. stock exchange must provide an assessment of their internal financial controls in their annual report. Whereas SOX specifically applies only to companies listed on a U.S. stock exchange, the United Kingdom implemented similar provisions in the *Combined Code on Corporate Governance*, and in the European Union, similar actions were taken with the **Basel II**, which also recommended the implementation of internal controls.

The implications of these regulations for information systems are that controls must be in place for systems that handle company financial information, which requires companies to pay increased attention to the information systems that store, process, and transmit that information. Although this represents a significant undertaking for private companies, the U.S. government is particularly affected. For example, the Office of Management and Budget's (OMB's) revised Circular A-123 requires federal agencies to implement internal controls similar to those found in SOX, and the Government Information Security Reform section of the National Defense Authorization of 2001 helped coordinate federal information policy with respect to information security.

In addition to laws covering financial controls, several pieces of privacy legislation have been enacted in the United States, the United Kingdom, and the European Union. Among these include the *U.S. Gramm-Leach-Bliley Act* (**GLBA**), which requires financial institutions to disclose to their customers their data-sharing policies and prohibits those institutions from selling customer information, and the *U.S. Fair and Accurate Credit Transactions Act* (**FACTA**), which requires safeguards to help prevent identity theft. The United Kingdom's Data Protection Act, the European Union's many privacy protection laws, and Canada's *Personal Information Protection and Electronic Documents Act* (**PIPEDA**) all contain requirements that affect the collection, storage, and transmission of personal information [3].

4.1.1 Gramm-Leach-Bliley Act (GLBA)

On November 12, 1999, Public Law 106-102 (GLBA, or the Financial Services Modernization Act of 1999) was approved. This act served to repeal the Glass–Steagall Act of 1933 and allowed the merging of various financial services providers; it also contained two sections that regulate the way financial institutions handle data. These sections, found under Title V of the law, include specific provisions for the privacy of customer information and for the protection against fraudulent access to customer account information.

Subtitle A: Disclosure of Nonpublic Personal Information specifically provides for protection of a customer's non-public, personal information. This section requires the financial institution to establish administrative, physical, and technical safeguards to (1) ensure the security and confidentiality of customer records and information; (2) protect against any anticipated threats or hazards to the security or integrity of such records; and (3) protect against unauthorized access to or use of such records or information that could result in substantial harm or inconvenience to any customer. Subtitle A also requires that customers be given the opportunity to "opt out" of allowing a financial institution from sharing their personal information with third parties and requires disclosure of the institution's privacy policy to the customers.

Subtitle B: Fraudulent Access to Financial Information made it a crime to attempt to obtain customer information by fraudulent means or to solicit another to do so. It gave enforcement authority primarily to the Federal Trade Commission, but also required each federal banking agency as defined in the Federal Deposit Insurance Act, the National Credit Union Administration, and the Security and Exchange Commission to prescribe regulations and guidelines for the financial institutions under their control to ensure compliance with the law. On February 1, 2001, the Interagency Guidelines Establishing Standards for Safeguarding Customer Information were published in the *Federal Register*. These guidelines were written to comply with GLBA. The stipulations are seen in **List 4.1**.

List 4.1 GLBA Mandates

(A): The board of directors or an appropriate committee of the board of each bank shall:

1. Approve the bank's written information security program; and oversee the development, implementation, and maintenance of the bank's information security program, including assigning specific responsibility for its implementation and reviewing reports from management.
2. Approve the bank's written information security program.
3. Oversee the development, implementation, and maintenance of the bank's information security program, including assigning specific responsibility for its implementation and reviewing reports from management.

(B): Each bank shall manage and control risk by:

1. Identifying reasonably foreseeable internal and external threats that could result in unauthorized disclosure, misuse, alteration, or destruction of customer information or customer information systems.
2. Assessing the likelihood and potential damage of these threats, taking into consideration the sensitivity of customer information.
3. Assessing the sufficiency of policies, procedures, customer information systems, and other arrangements in place to control risks.

(C): Each bank shall manage and control risk by:

1. Designing its information security program to control the identified risks, commensurate with the sensitivity of the information as well as the

List 4.1 GLBA Mandates (Continued)

complexity and scope of the bank's activities. Each bank must consider whether the following security measures are appropriate for the bank and, if so, adopt those measures the bank concludes are appropriate:

a. Access controls on customer information systems, including controls to authenticate and permit access only to authorized individuals and controls to prevent employees from providing customer information to unauthorized individuals who may seek to obtain this information through fraudulent means.

b. Access restrictions at physical locations containing customer information, such as buildings, computer facilities, and records storage facilities to permit access only to authorized individuals.

c. Encryption of electronic customer information, including while in transit or in storage on networks or systems to which unauthorized individuals may have access.

d. Procedures designed to ensure that customer information system modifications are consistent with the bank's information security program.

e. Dual control procedures, separation of duties, and employee background checks for employees with responsibilities for or access to customer information.

f. Monitoring systems and procedures to detect actual and attempted attacks on or intrusions into customer information systems.

g. Response programs that specify actions to be taken when the bank suspects or detects that unauthorized individuals have gained access to customer information systems, including appropriate reports to regulatory and law enforcement agencies.

h. Measures to protect against destruction, loss, or damage of customer information due to potential environmental hazards, such as fire and water damage or technological failures.

2. Training staff to implement the bank's information security program.

3. Regularly testing the key controls, systems, and procedures of the information security program. The frequency and nature of such tests should be determined by the bank's risk assessment. Tests should be conducted or reviewed by independent third parties or staff independent of those that develop or maintain the security programs.

Source: Interagency Guidelines Establishing Standards for Safeguarding Customer Information and Rescission of Year 2000 Standards for Safety and Soundness, Final Rule; *Federal Register* 66, 1 February 2001: 8616–8641.

4.1.2 U.S. Fair and Accurate Credit Transactions Act (FACTA)

In addition to the GLBA, the Fair and Accurate Credit Transactions Act of 2003 (FACTA) includes eight titles that are designed to reduce the threat of identity theft, to improve consumer access to their own credit reports and scores, to enhance the accuracy of the consumer report information, and to improve the protection of privacy related to certain privileged information that may appear in a consumer report. It provides special protections for military personnel serving on active duty and provides specific requirements related to handling reports of suspected fraud. For example, it entitles people to receive free copies of their credit reports and enables placement of fraud alerts with credit bureaus. This act also has special requirements for information systems, including requiring that only the last five digits of a credit or debit card be printed on a receipt.

From a business perspective, FACTA incorporates several provisions that require financial institutions, creditors, and other businesses that rely on consumer reports for background checks, lending, hiring, or other legitimate needs to have in place processes to detect and resolve fraud by utilizing what are called "red flags" to alert on possible fraudulent activities. These include guidelines for credit and debit card issuers to assess the validity of a change of address request. Other important implications include:

- It requires that plans include processes to identify certain signs of identity theft attempts, although the plans do not have to be uniform and may be based on a company's risk assessment of its operations.
- It requires that consumer reporting agencies and any business that uses a consumer report adopt procedures for proper document disposal.
- FACTA requires companies to conduct workplace investigations in cases of alleged employee misconduct. This investigation should be conducted by a third party the company may hire to determine (1) misconduct relating to one's employment, (2) a violation of federal, state, or local laws or regulations, or (3) a violation of any written policies established by the employer.

4.1.3 U.S. Sarbanes–Oxley Act (SOX)

After the failures of several large corporations in 2001 and 2002, Public Law 107-204, otherwise known as the Sarbanes–Oxley Act, was enacted July 30, 2002, as previously mentioned. This law consists of 11 titles that broadly seek to protect the interests of investors and further the public interest in the preparation of informative, accurate, and independent audit reports for public companies. It established in Section 101 the Public Companies Accounting Oversight Board (PCAOB) that has responsibility for creating audit standards and for overseeing public accounting firms that prepare audit reports for public companies. These standards include Auditing Standard No. 5 (AS 5), which became effective November 15, 2007. This standard established requirements for performing an audit of management's assessment of the effectiveness of internal control over financial reporting [5].

As specified in Sections 302 and 404, the CEO and CFO (or persons performing similar functions) are personally responsible for establishing and maintaining internal controls;

the controls must be designed so that they would discover any problems; the controls have been tested; and they certify that they are knowledgeable about all financial statements submitted. Because information systems play a major role in financial reporting for many if not most modern organizations, this technology must be included in the internal control matrix. Specifically related to the audit of information systems, AS 5 states, "The identification of risks and controls within IT is not a separate evaluation. Instead, it is an integral part of the top-down approach used to identify significant accounts and disclosures and their relevant assertions, and the controls to test, as well as to assess risk and allocate audit effort as described by this standard" (Section 319, p. 28).

In Focus

A main outcome of SOX is the requirement for companies to implement controls to prevent and detect fraud. SOX is far-reaching and comprehensive legislation that has major implications for management and security.

4.1.4 OMB Circular A-123 (Revised)

Much like SOX, the U.S. federal government's Office of Management and Budget (OMB) Circular A-123 defines the responsibility of management in federal departments and agencies regarding the establishment, assessment, and reporting of internal control to achieve the objectives of effective and efficient operations, reliable financial reporting, and compliance with applicable laws and regulations (OMB A-123 revised).

OMB A-123 prescribes an assessment process and annual reporting on the state of internal control in the Performance and Accountability Report, which must include a separate statement on the assurance on internal control over financial reporting, as well as a report on identified material weaknesses and corrective actions. With respect to information systems, similar to AS 5, OMB A-123 states that

Internal control also needs to be in place over information systems—general and application control. General control applies to all information systems such as the mainframe, network and end-user environments, and includes agency-wide security program planning, management, control over data center operations, system software acquisition and maintenance. Application control should be designed to ensure that transactions are properly authorized and processed accurately and that the data is valid and complete. Controls should be established at an application's interfaces to verify inputs and outputs, such as edit checks. General and application control over information systems are interrelated, both are needed to ensure complete and accurate information processing. Due to the rapid changes in information technology, controls must also adjust to remain effective. (OMB A-130 revised, Section 1)

4.1.5 Government Information Security Reform Act of 2000

Subtitle G of the National Defense Authorization for Fiscal-Year 2001 is titled: *The Government Information Security Reform Act*. This act amends Chapter 35 of title 44 of the

U.S. Code that covers federal information policy. The amendments added an entirely new subchapter specifically related to information security and, in particular, present guidelines to address controls and oversight. Although the actual legislation is quite sweeping, **List 4.2** summarizes the stipulations.

List 4.2 Subtitle G of the GIS Reform Act

1. Provide a comprehensive framework for establishing and ensuring the effectiveness of controls over information resources that support federal operations and assets.

2. Recognize the highly networked nature of the federal computing environment including the need for federal government interoperability and, in the implementation of improved security management measures, ensure that opportunities for interoperability are not adversely affected, and provide effective government-wide management and oversight of the related information security risks, including coordination of information security efforts throughout the civilian, national security, and law enforcement communities.

3. Provide for development and maintenance of minimum controls required to protect federal information and information systems.

4. Provide a mechanism for improved oversight of federal agency information security programs (PL 106-398).

The act additionally requires the Director of the Office of Management and Budget (OMB) to promulgate information security standards, to oversee the implementation of those standards, and to require agencies to (among other things) identify and provide information security protections commensurate with the risk and magnitude of the harm resulting from the unauthorized access, use, disclosure, disruption, modification, or destruction of information collected or maintained by or on behalf of an agency, or information systems used or operated by an agency or by a contractor of an agency or other organization on behalf of an agency (44 USC § 3533). As seen, each of these set of standards and criteria are far reaching and, typical of government regulation in general, the stipulations can be detailed and even tedious. We have only touched the surface here. Regulatory specialists are needed in regulated organizations to ensure compliance.

4.1.6 HIPAA and Health Insurance Reform

In 1996, Congress passed the Health Insurance Portability and Accountability Act (P.L. 104-191). With this law, Congress called for steps to improve the efficiency and effectiveness of the healthcare system by encouraging the development of a health information system through the establishment of standards and requirements for the electronic transmission of certain health information (HIPAA, Sec 261). Of particular interest is 45 C.F.R. Parts 160, 162, and 164, Standards for Privacy of Individually Identifiable Health

Information. With this rule, security standards, including administrative, physical, and technical requirements, were established to protect specific electronically held health-related information.

As seen in other regulations, these regulations also require the organization holding protected information to (1) ensure the confidentiality, integrity, and availability of all electronic protected health information the covered entity creates, receives, maintains, or transmits; (2) protect against any reasonably anticipated threats or hazards to the security or integrity of such information; (3) protect against any reasonably anticipated uses or disclosures of such information that are not permitted or required; and (4) ensure compliance with this subpart by its workforce (45 CFR Part 164.306).

Related to HIPAA is the Health Information Technology for Economic and Clinical Health Act (HITECH) of 2009. This legislation requires physical, technical, and administrative safeguards for technologies that house or transmit HIPAA-regulated data, such as patient records, and that all personnel who work with HIPAA-regulated data to be trained on HIPAA regulations and comply or face punishment. From HITECH, the government can now levy penalties on both HIPAA-regulated businesses and individuals working in the business [6].

4.2 Non-U.S. and International Governance

We have covered a number of regulations for the United States, but there are regulations to which organizations must conform if they do business in a foreign country, have headquarters in a foreign country such as with a multi-national corporation, or import/export from or to a foreign country. Some of the areas where these issues arise are in limitations on the cryptographic strength of ciphertext, which we will cover later, but in the context of this section, we are mainly interested in international laws and regulations regarding business practices and the handling of information. This topic is so vast that we cannot even scratch the surface, but we will survey a few issues and governance frameworks.

Some of the most important compliance issues involve protections of intellectual property. For example, patents or trademarks may only be valid in the United States, and not abroad. Many of the issues related to intellectual property internationally fall under the World Trade Organization (WTO) and the WTO's Trade-Related Aspects of Intellectual Property Rights (TRIPS), which, among other things, attempts to normalize international agreements or broker where there are disputes.

Given proper filings, TRIPS offers provisions to protect patents, trademarks, copyrights, and confidential information across borders and has established mechanisms for enforcement in germane or jurisdictional territories through national courts and/or administrative customs services, and for resolving disputes and obtaining settlements from WTO members [7]. In addition to these issues, there are governance frameworks that organizations may need to consider.

4.2.1 U.K. Combined Code on Corporate Governance

Similar to SOX in the United States, the United Kingdom's Combined Code on Corporate Governance (CCCG) was first issued in 1998 and began undergoing revision in 2010.

It establishes a set of standards with respect to management oversight of financial reporting. As specified in the preamble, the code is not a rigid set of rules. Instead, it is designed as a best-practice guide to governance that U.K. companies listed on the Main Market of the London Stock Exchange may use. These regulated companies must report their compliance or non-compliance in their annual reports. Unlike in the United States, non-compliance with the code is not a violation of law; rather, the code takes the view that there exists a shared responsibility between companies and shareholders regarding appropriate governance and that a "comply or explain" system is an effective alternative to proscriptive rules [8].

> **In Focus**
>
> Best practices are considered the state of the art for a given profession, field, or occupation.

4.2.2 CCCG and Turnbull Guidance

Of particular interest to managers is Section C of the CCCG: Accountability and Audit. This section covers financial reporting, internal control, and audit. Specifically, it requires the board to provide a balanced and understandable accounting of the company. It also specifies, along with the help of the Turnbull Guidance, that the effectiveness of internal controls be evaluated at least annually and include financial, operational, and compliance controls and risk management in that evaluation. Much like the U.S. SOX, FSA Rule DTS 7.2.5-R requires companies to describe the main features of the internal control and risk management systems in relation to the financial reporting process.

Section C.3, which is also covered by the Financial Reporting Council (FRC) Guidance on Audit Committees (formerly known as the Smith Guidance), establishes, among other items, an audit committee to monitor and review the integrity of the financial statements, to review internal financial controls, and to monitor the internal audit function. The Turnbull Guidance was first published in 1999 and establishes best practice for applying Section C.2 of the CCCG. It specifies the importance of internal control for an organization, the responsibilities for and elements of maintaining an effective system of internal control, and the responsibilities for reviewing the internal controls, and finally, it provides guidance on the board's statement on internal control [4].

Many organizations that have adopted the Turnbull Guidance find that it also serves as a framework for the purpose of satisfying the requirements of Section 404(a) of SOX. The FRC Guidance on Audit Committees, whose most recent update was published in 2005, establishes guidance for applying Section C.3 of the CCCG. The guidance is divided over four sections that provide information on the establishment, membership, meetings, resources, remuneration, and skills of the audit committee. It covers the relationship between the audit committee and the board, the roles and responsibilities of the audit committee with respect to financial reporting and the audit process, and communication with shareholders [9].

4.2.3 Basel II

Basel II, also known as the International Convergence of Capital Measurement and Capital Standards, is the report from the Basel Committee on Banking Supervision that, like GLBA, applies to financial organizations. Central bank leaders of the "Group of Ten" countries created the Basel Committee in 1975. This group consists of representatives from Belgium, Canada, France, Germany, Italy, Japan, Luxembourg, the Netherlands, Spain, Sweden, Switzerland, the United Kingdom, and the United States.

Basel II represents the update to the Basel I standards published in 1988 and seeks to provide standards for capital reserves related to the risk appetite of the financial institution. It consists of three pillars: Minimum Capital Requirements, Supervisory Review Process, and Market Discipline. Although Basel II may seem unrelated to information security, it requires banks to address exposure to credit, operational, and market risks. Operational risk is defined as "the risk of loss resulting from inadequate or failed internal processes, people and systems or from external events" [10]. As with SOX, the definition covers information systems associated with operations, which in financial organizations includes most of the systems utilized.

> **In Focus**
>
> Basel II is an example of an attempt to create a set of international standards—at least among cooperating members.

4.2.4 U.K. Data Protection Act

The U.K. Data Protection Act of 1998 provides protection for sensitive personal data, defined in the act as: "(a) The racial or ethnic origin of the data subject, (b) *his* political opinions, (c) *his* religious beliefs or other beliefs of a similar nature, (d) whether *he* is a member of a trade union, (e) *his* physical or mental health condition, (f) *his* sexual life, (g) the commission or alleged commission by *him* of any offence, or (h) any proceedings for any offence committed or alleged to have been committed by *him*, the disposal of such proceedings or the sentence of any court in such proceedings" (Part 1.2).

Specifically, the act applies to any system that processes data in the United Kingdom and allows individuals to be informed of any data being held that relate to them, the purpose of the processing, and to whom it may be disclosed. Additionally, it provides for remedies to the individual should he or she suffer damage for any failure to adhere to the provisions in the act. In addition to the provisions that specify notification and sensitive data, the act specifies the requirements to protect the data in Schedule 1, Part 1—the Principles. Principle 7 states that appropriate technical and organizational measures shall be taken against unauthorized or unlawful processing of personal data and against accidental loss or destruction of, or damage to, personal data [8].

The interpretation of the principles in Part 1, covered in Part 2, considers the cost of implementing any measures and requires that measures taken must ensure an appropriate level of security by addressing the harm that might result from unauthorized or unlawful processing of data, accidental loss, and the destruction or damage as mentioned in the seventh principle, and the nature of the data to be protected. The data controller must also take reasonable steps to ensure the reliability and integrity of any employee who has access to personal data.

Where processing of personal data is carried out by a "data processor" on behalf of a "data controller," the data controller must ensure that the data processor provides sufficient guarantees in regard to the technical and organizational security measures governing the processing to be carried out, and take reasonable steps to ensure compliance with those measures. The data controller is not in compliance with the seventh principle unless (a) the processing is carried out under a contract, which is made or evidenced in writing, and under which the data processor is to act only on instructions from the data controller, and (b) the contract requires the data processor to comply with obligations equivalent to those imposed on a data controller by the seventh principle.

4.2.5 European Union and Other Privacy Protections

Directive 95/46/EC of the European Parliament and of the Council of October 24, 1995, provides the foundation for the protection of personal data in the European Union (EU). The directive has two specified objectives: to protect the rights of privacy for individuals with respect to the processing of their personal data, and to provide for the free flow of personal data across member states connected with the protection of personal data. The directive is broad in scope and protections and provides for individuals to access their data, to object to the processing of data of which the individual is a subject, and for the confidentiality and security of the data. Additionally, the data that are collected must be relevant to the specified purpose for which the data were collected and not "excessive" in their amount (meaning not going beyond the scope of the specific stated purpose).

> **In Focus**
>
> Many national regulations are combining to form international regulations and laws. International law is an increasingly important area in security governance and a specialized area in law practice. Corporations that do international work need to have on staff or have retained counsel with expertise in this area.

In general, an individual must explicitly give his or her consent for the data to be collected and processed, and Article 17 of the directive specifies that each member state must implement appropriate technical and organizational measures to protect personal data against accidental or unlawful destruction or accidental loss, alteration, or unauthorized disclosure or access, in particular where the processing involves transmission of data over a network, and against all other unlawful forms of processing.

Of particular consideration is that Chapter IV of the directive specifies that transfer of personal data to third countries should only be done after ensuring that the privacy protection measures established in the third country are adequate. Because the United States utilizes a sector approach that relies on a mix of legislation, regulation, and self-regulation, the U. S. Department of Commerce established a "Safe Harbor" framework, approved by the EU in 2000, which is designed to meet the established standards and protection required by the directive so that data may be transferred to the United States [11]. Although these guidelines are fairly broad and in most cases not very explicit, the burden is on the organization to document how these objectives are being met with which specific controls.

4.2.6 Canadian PIPEDA

The Personal Information Protection and Electronic Documents Act (PIPEDA) is an act, similar to the EC directive, that provides protection of personal information held or processed by non-government firms in Canada. It specifies that an organization must receive consent and must identify and document the purpose for collecting personal information, and should that information be used for another purpose at a later point, the organization must generally first obtain a new consent from the individual to whom it applies. An organization must also limit the collection of personal data only to that sufficient to the purpose defined and must not store the data for any longer than is necessary. These directives are more protective of privacy rights than many of the enactments around the globe, but just as with recent actions in other nations, there are attempts being made to erode some of the provisions and make them more liberal in terms of information gathering and collection. Section 4.7, Principle 7, specifies the safeguards requirement for personal data. See **List 4.3**.

List 4.3   PIPEDA Section 4.7

1. Security safeguards appropriate to the sensitivity of the information shall protect personal information.

2. The security safeguards shall protect personal information against loss or theft, as well as unauthorized access, disclosure, copying, use, or modification. Organizations shall protect personal information regardless of the format in which it is held.

3. The nature of the safeguards will vary depending on the sensitivity of the information that has been collected; the amount, distribution, and format of the information; and the method of storage. A higher level of protection should safeguard more sensitive information.

4. The methods of protection should include (a) physical measures; for example, locked filing cabinets and restricted access to offices; (b) organizational measures, such as security clearances and limiting access on a "need-to-know" basis; and (c) technological measures; for example, the use of passwords and encryption.

5. Organizations shall make their employees aware of the importance of maintaining the confidentiality of personal information.

6. Care shall be used in the disposal or destruction of personal information, to prevent unauthorized parties from gaining access to the information. Additionally, organizations must designate an individual to be accountable for compliance with the legislation.

4.2.7 Asian APEC Data Privacy Subgroup

The Asia-Pacific Economic Cooperation (APEC) group was formed in 1989 with 12 members and has grown to include 21 entities with an interest in the Asia-Pacific area. The members now include Australia, Brunei Darussalam, Canada, Chile, China, Chinese Taipei, Hong Kong, Indonesia, Japan, Korea, Malaysia, Mexico, New Zealand, Papua New Guinea, Peru, the Philippines, Russia, Singapore, Thailand, the United States, and Vietnam. Under the auspices of the Electronic Commerce Steering Group, APEC published the APEC Privacy Framework in 2005. The framework was designed, much like the EC directive, to facilitate standards for the transfer of data across borders [4].

The framework covers personal information and provides requirements to notify an individual of the practices and policies related to personal information collection and disclosure; it limits collection to relevant information and specifies that personal information should be collected only with the consent of the individual. Section VII of the framework requires the safeguarding of personal information. In essence, it states that personal information controllers should protect personal information that they hold with appropriate safeguards against risks, such as loss or unauthorized access to personal information or unauthorized destruction, use, modification, or disclosure of information or other misuses. Such safeguards should be proportional to the likelihood and severity of the harm threatened, along with the sensitivity of the information and the context in which it is held, and should be subject to periodic review and reassessment.

Consistent with the other privacy regulations and frameworks, the APEC framework also provides for access to and correction of information held, accountability for complying, and when transferring the data, to obtain consent and ensure that the receiver will provide appropriate protections. Additional work on Cross Border Privacy Rules (CBPR) continued in 2009 with the endorsement of the APEC Data Privacy Pathfinder Projects Implementation Work Plan. Although not binding on the members, this plan is designed to develop a system in the APEC region that ensures accountability across borders regarding personal information for the protection of consumers while facilitating business access to the benefits of electronic commerce.

4.3 Management and Governance

To this point, we have presented a variety of national and international regulations along with some mention of various regulatory agencies. In the next chapter, we will go into some detail about management processes (risk assessment and risk management specifically) and some criteria used to help managers comply with regulations and laws, as well as to help them ensure *a well-managed organization* from a security standpoint. At this stage, we will try to bridge between those two aspects for managing securely by briefly discussing management and governance.

Earlier, we defined governance, and previously, we gave a summary of management rights and duties. Putting these two concepts together, we might say that management and governance means using policies, processes, and procedures to ensure that the organization conforms and performs according to the criteria defined for and by the organization to maintain organizational and security effectiveness. Knowing about laws and regulations as these relate to governance is important to managers in organizations where information systems are used [12]. Beyond the administrative features we have addressed thus far, also important are elements such as responsible, efficient, and effective managing of human resources and knowledge capital, which we will present later. For now, suffice it to say that management and governance strives to meet (or stay within) controls laid down as regulations, laws, guidelines, best practices, and even "good" (meaning *ethical*) advice given by stakeholders [13].

There are some categories of activities that management needs to address in order to both govern and be governed well. These include performing risk assessments; conducting audits regarding assets, policies, and procedures; doing background checks on new employees and performance evaluations of current ones; producing performance plans and communicating expectations; providing or funding training and development; conducting system and network testing and evaluation; developing contingency and remediation plans; and ensuring proper handling and reporting of incidents and continuity of operations, among other activities [6].

4.3.1 Governance and Security Programs

Earlier, we mentioned that regulations and frameworks govern actions about various aspects of information such as employee and/or customer privacy. An example we gave was the APEC framework for the Asian-Pacific rim. In actuality, security criteria by themselves are inert. They become active when management enacts programs to ensure compliance with the criteria (which includes regulations and laws). To highlight this point, the Federal Information Security Management Act (FISMA) was an attempt in the United States to consolidate laws and regulations for a variety of security issues [4].

For the most part, FISMA officially applies to U.S. government agencies and their suppliers and contractors, but in actuality, although security criteria may differ, the processes and procedures such as performing risk assessments, conducting audits, doing background checks, providing security training, and so forth can be applicable and helpful to most organizations.

In Focus

Even though it may not be required for an organization, using one or more, or a blend, of security criteria and management programs might help to improve information security, which offers many benefits that we will discuss later.

Although laws and regulations cannot be ignored and compliance is mandatory, oversight of non-regulated security programs should similarly undergo a security design, implementation, and inspection life cycle. For example, the life cycle might include an iterative process of evaluating business needs, resolving business needs with business processes, and distilling those processes into categories in which security is one and, within the security category, determining risks/vulnerabilities, determining countermeasures including their costs and cost-to-benefit metrics, implementing security controls, assessing whether the controls were effective, and then ascertaining approvals and authorizations, in which the process is repeated [14]. **List 4.4** summarizes some of these key components.

List 4.4 Key Security Criteria Components

1. Develop relevant criteria for governance.
2. Perform risk assessments.
3. Conduct random periodic audits of assets, policies, and procedures.
4. Consistently do background checks on new employees.
5. Consistently do performance evaluations of current employees.
6. Regularly do performance plans and communicate expectations.
7. Provide or adequately fund training and development on security and relevant regulations.
8. Conduct random periodic system and network testing and evaluation.
9. Develop and update contingency and remediation plans.
10. Review to ensure proper handling and reporting of incidents.
11. Prepare and audit business and operations continuity contingency plans.

4.3.2 Enactment of Security Programs

Next we will briefly introduce risk assessment and management as aspects of information security in preparation for the next chapter. Security programs begin by trying to assess risks—and because there are so many and because they are so complex, managers usually simply assign them to a quadrant in a risk matrix, for example, low, medium, or high risk on an X axis, against low, medium, or high likelihood (or exposure) on a Y axis. This yields an "impact" assessment that can be refined further and expressed in more detail. The procedure, although clearly flawed, can at least help managers prioritize which of their many security tasks they should attend to first. In relation to problem analysis:

- Problem analysis is the process of understanding real-world problems and users' needs and proposing solutions to meet those needs.
- The goal of problem analysis is to gain a better understanding, before development of solutions begins, for the target problem to be solved.
- Eventually, but not immediately, the root cause—or the problem behind the problem—needs to be determined for a final solution.

As examples of impact assessments, a low impact might be the potential loss of confidential information. To highlight this in a tangible way, the fairly recent *WikiLeaks* disclosures of U.S. State Department characterizations of foreign heads of state (such as being a "lap dog") may be embarrassing to the United States, but that specific disclosure is not likely catastrophic. Similarly, if an employee posted on his or her social media site a company assessment of a rival's technical strengths and weaknesses, this would be troubling but likewise not catastrophic unless perhaps the posting was defamatory in nature. Of more moderate concern to a corporation might be the public disclosure of a company's network topology. On the surface, this may seem benign, but in actuality, it would save an astute hacker time and energy (and possible detection) to "footprint" a target site. High impact might be a case where a hacker breaches a loosely protected database in a HIPAA-regulated company and retrieves patient histories and insurance information.

Security programs therefore need to incorporate measured and hierarchically proportionate countermeasures. The FIPS recommends the following: conducting risk assessments and analyses using structured methods, implementing access controls, offering security awareness and technical training, conducting audits and resolving these to the accountable manager, implementing configuration control (to be discussed later), performing contingency planning, using technologies that can perform identification, authentication, and authorization, having an incident reporting and response plan, and having in place (among other things) an escalation procedure for security breaches [6].

4.3.3 Analyzing the Problem and Managing IT

Security programs need to begin with analyzing the security problem. The last two decades have seen an unprecedented increase in the power of the technologies, along with an increase in the power of new security tools. Yet along with new technologies and languages are concomitant new vulnerabilities. Tools for version management, requirements management, design and analysis, defect tracking, and automated testing have helped software developers and administrators to better manage the complexity of thousands of requirements and hundreds of thousands of lines of code and security requirements. But as the productivity of the software development environment has increased, it has also become easier to exploit their weaknesses, and so security breaches continue to outpace security countermeasures installed to prevent them [15].

As we have seen, these data demonstrate that we remain challenged in our ability to truly understand and satisfy the simultaneous demands for functionality and security needs. Perhaps there is a simpler explanation for this difficulty that may represent the "problem behind the problem," but it has yet to be discovered. Because of deadlines and schedule pressures, development teams often spend too little effort in terms of understanding the real security problems, too little is known about the needs of the users and other stakeholders in relation to security, and there is information overload relative to the technological and human resources environments in most companies to effectively keep up with security threats while maintaining business competitiveness.

Managers and their teams tend to forge ahead without enough knowledge of any single aspect of these problems, often providing technological solutions based on an inadequate understanding of the issues. The resulting systems, solutions, and procedures do not fit the needs of the users or stakeholders, do not provide adequate security for the most part, and deliver less than might reasonably be expected as functional solutions. The consequences of these mismatches are often seen in the inadequacy of security solutions for the customers and for solution providers. Managers need to provide guidelines for the analysts and developers that establish specific security goals. This is the topic of our next chapter.

CHAPTER SUMMARY

In this chapter, we drew from the previous chapter foundations to consider regulations and governance. Whereas this chapter mainly provided a summary overview of regulations and criteria, later we will integrate these ideas into managerial activities. Managers need to be acquainted with regulations and laws in order to practice their craft successfully. In subsequent chapters, we will synthesize these ideas into organizational security actions and management duties and responsibilities. At this stage, we simply need to be acquainted with some of the most important governance frameworks and the major concepts.

Although there are a variety of security regulations applicable across many nations, regions, and industries, the principles and requirements for protection of data in the care of the organization are relatively standardized. Regardless of the organization, understanding the information and systems that receive, process, and store information and ensuring that adequate controls are applied to protect that information against unauthorized disclosure, modification, or transfer are fundamental to information system management. When handling personal information, particular care must be applied, and additional controls might be necessary. Understanding the laws, rules, and regulations that apply to managers is the first step to being able to make appropriate decisions with respect to the information systems under one's control.

It is also of growing importance for managers to become acquainted with international regulations, international regulatory agencies, and treaties. As cyber communications extends its reach across international borders, managers need to know what their options are and what the requirements are for conducting business securely for compliance with a given agency or compliance with established international standards. We mentioned how security procedures translate into management programs such as risk assessments, risk management, and compliance auditing. In the next chapter, we will discuss some standards that can assist in securing information systems and assets on a more local level.

THINK ABOUT IT

Topic Questions

4.1: FSA Rule DTS 7.2.5-R requires companies to describe the main features of the internal control and risk management systems in relation to the financial reporting process, similar to what U.S. regulation?

4.2: Under the GLBA, what are the basic protection aspects of Subtitle A: Disclosure of Nonpublic Personal Information?

THINK ABOUT IT (CONTINUED)

4.3: Of particular interest to managers in Section C of the Turnbull Guidance is:

_____ Confidentiality and integrity
_____ Accountability and audit
_____ Identification and authentication
_____ Protection of intellectual property

4.4: The GLBA applies to international law.

_____ True
_____ False

4.5: FACTA is a subset of criteria defined by the GLBA.

_____ True
_____ False

4.6: The CCCG applies to the:

_____ New York Stock Exchange
_____ London Stock Exchange

_____ Asian markets only
_____ All of the markets in the EU

4.7: The Personal Information Protection and Electronic Documents Act is a(n):

_____ U.S. initiative
_____ EU initiative
_____ U.K. initiative
_____ Canadian initiative

4.8: The Asia-Pacific Economic Cooperation group was formed with _____ members.

4.9: The Turnbull Guidance established _____.

4.10: Governance is in essence:

_____ Laws that managers must abide by
_____ Processes by which organizations are managed according to some criteria
_____ Government control of organizations
_____ Conformance to industry standards

Questions for Further Study

Q4.1: Describe and explain how regulations affect organizational governance as it relates to information security.

Q4.2: What are the main differences between U.S.-led regulations for maintaining privacy and those enacted in the European Union?

Q4.3: How does private legislation such as that affecting protections from identity theft interact with organizational legislation such as

that where organizations must be responsive to individual identity theft concerns?

Q4.4: What is the difference between law and regulation? Explain in terms of organizations and information security.

Q4.5: Discuss how law and treaties relate to each other.

KEY CONCEPTS AND TERMS

GLBA served to repeal the Glass–Steagall Act of 1933 and allowed the merging of various financial services providers.

OMB Circular A-123 defines the responsibility of management in federal departments and agencies regarding the

establishment, assessment, and reporting of internal control to achieve the objectives of effective and efficient operations.

Turnbull Guidance resembles the Sarbanes–Oxley Act in that the effectiveness of internal controls,

including financial, must be evaluated at least annually.

SOX is an acronym that reflects the requirement for companies to implement controls to prevent and detect fraud.

WTO attempts to create international regulations and laws.

References

1. Purser, S. (2004). *A practical guide to managing information security*. Boston, MA: Artech House.
2. DesPardes, G. (2009). *Stolen laptop contains data of 42,000 military personnel & families*. News USA, Retrieved July 17, 2010, from: http://despardes.com/?p=10987
3. Gable, J. (2006). Compliance: Where do we go from here? *Information Management Journal, 40*, 28–33.
4. Fischer, S. F. (2010). International cyberlaw. In H. Bidgoli (Ed.), *The handbook of technology management* (pp. 717–726). Hoboken, NJ: John Wiley & Sons.
5. Public Company Accounting Oversight Board. (2007). *Auditing Standard No. 5: An audit of internal control over financial reporting that is integrated with an audit of financial statements*. PCAOB Final Rule, 2007-005A. Retrieved from http://pcaobus.org/Standards/Auditing/Pages/Auditing-Standard-5.aspx
6. Grama, J. L. (2011). *Legal issues in information security*. Sudbury, MA: Jones & Bartlett Learning.
7. Gervais, D. J. (2010). International intellectual property law for technology management. In H. Bidgoli (Ed.), *The handbook of technology management* (pp. 727–737). Hoboken, NJ: John Wiley & Sons.
8. Office of Public Sector Information. (1998). The Data Protection Act of 1988, Chapter 29. Retrieved December 11, 2010, from: http://www.opsi.gov.uk/acts/acts1998/ukpga_19980029_en_1
9. Revised Turnbull Guidance. (2009). *Guide on use of Turnbull for section 404, Final Report on the 2005 Review of the Combined Code*. Combined Code June, RTG'9.
10. International Convergence of Capital Measurement and Capital Standards. (2006). *A Revised Framework Comprehensive*. June, ICCMCS'6, 144.
11. Export.gov (2000). *Safe harbor overview*. Retrieved November 11, 2010, from http://www.export.gov/safeharbor/eg_main_018236.asp
12. Appelbaum, S. H., Laconi, G. D., & Matousek, A. (2007). Positive and negative deviant workplace behaviors: Causes, impacts, and solutions. *Corporate Governance Journal, 7*(5), 586–598.
13. Mingers, J., & Walsham, G. (2010). Toward ethical information systems: The contribution of discourse ethics. *MIS Quarterly, 34*(4), 833–844.
14. Workman, M., Phelps, D., & Workman, J. (2008). *The management of Infosec*. Boston, MA: eAselworx Press.
15. Workman, M., Bommer, W. H., & Straub, D. (2008). Security lapses and the omission of information security measures: An empirical test of the threat control model, *Journal of Computers in Human Behavior, 24*, 2799–2816.

Security Programs: Risk Assessment and Management

THIS CHAPTER, SOMEWHAT LIKE THE LAST ONE, will serve as a good resource for any organizational member who is (or who might be) involved in security assessments and audits, as well as in risk management programs. In the last chapter, we introduced many regulations that require organizations to implement a risk assessment–based approach to their information system security. In an effort to meet this "due care" standard, many organizations are turning to best practices and control frameworks. Although the goal is to assist organizations with appropriate information technology (IT) governance, the increasing number of frameworks and best practices can add complexity and confusion to the process. In this chapter, we introduce security program management and the components of risk assessment and mitigation.

Although it is often tedious to keep abreast of checklist criteria for risk assessment, risk management, and regulatory and/or security compliance, it is an important task. The task is similar to the need for an accountant or bookkeeper to post a transaction in its proper place in the books, as opposed to a debit posted as a credit. Clearly, if done wrong, many problems can arise.

Chapter 5 Topics

This chapter:

- Provides an overview of risk assessment.
- Discusses some of the ways risk is determined.
- Explores risk assessment frameworks.
- Distinguishes risk management from risk assessment.
- Examines some risk management frameworks.

5.1 Risk Assessment and Management Overview

Security programs subsume risk assessments and risk management. Whereas other aspects of security programs deal with human resources or technological issues, the risk assessment and risk management aspects of a security program are administrative in nature—that is, they deal with the processes, rules, and procedures of security management. Risk assessment involves techniques to quantify and qualify the likelihood and impact of threats. To accomplish this, managers often use frameworks and technologies to identify information system assets and configurations, assess vulnerabilities to them, and survey for threats that are likely to exploit these vulnerabilities or otherwise lead to disasters. This is an important process to help managers to make informed decisions on how to best allocate their resources.

Risk management involves the enactment of security programs, and they are designed to mitigate the risks identified from the risk assessments. While the risk management process is itself administrative, it may call for the use of physical, human resource, or technological means to mitigate the risks, such as by conducting employee training to make those in operational roles more capable and to help reduce the introduction of new vulnerabilities into systems. With risk management, we are interested in minimizing the impact of exploits and disasters and in enhancing an organization's ability to deal with new vulnerabilities and risks as they arise.

These parts of the security program involve contingency planning, including continuity planning and disaster recovery planning. The objective of contingency planning is to design ways to handle the circumstances in which an organization's information systems and resources become compromised. The continuity planning aspect of this is specifically done to assist managers with ways to keep the operations up and running in case of a disaster or an exploit that results in a total outage. Disaster recovery planning involves the processes and procedures needed to make damaged systems and resources operational again. The planning falls out of the assessment processes and sets the stage for the management of risks. The complete role of a security program is to address all of the security components in an organization and provide managers with well-defined means of identifying risks and vulnerabilities and reducing them, and then monitoring for threats and rectifying them.

5.1.1 Security Program Overview

Many, if not most, organizations today depend extensively on their information systems and resources to function. As such, it has become imperative to manage information system security as a complete program with a defined scope and the support of executive leadership, and not only the responsibility of the IT department. The foundation of the security program should be a thorough understanding of the organization and the value of the information and information systems throughout the organizational echelon—the needs, goals, and priorities of the organization, and the organization's behavioral and normative culture. Within this framework, a risk assessment can be accomplished, policies can be established, and controls can be selected and implemented to ensure that the information assets and their associated systems operate effectively and efficiently. Although many organizations do this as a matter of good business practice, those that are regulated may face heavy penalties for non-compliance, and therefore management involvement and support for the security program is crucial.

Among the activities that management should be involved in include establishing priorities, valuing assets, and assigning roles and responsibilities with appropriate accountability to ensure that the information security program is effective and responsive to the needs of the organization. Once the identification and valuation of the information resources have been accomplished, specific administrative, technical, and physical controls should be established to achieve the goals of the security program.

Administrative controls are those processes, rules, and procedures that establish what should, shouldn't, can, and can't be done with the information systems and other information resources [1]. Included within this area are the definitions and implementations of policies, procedures, guidelines, and standards. Technical controls are the logical controls that define the limits of the behavior of both information systems and those who access them. Identification and authentication mechanisms, firewalls, access control lists, and associated system and application software settings are examples of technical controls. Physical controls are those controls that exist in the physical environment and include locks, removal and proper disposal of unnecessary hardware, and environmental management systems ranging from fire suppression systems to barricades [2].

5.1.2 Risk Assessment Overview

Threats can come from both internal and external sources, and they are inextricably linked to vulnerabilities inherent in any given system, and exposures of those vulnerabilities are linked to a threatening agent. Thus for our purposes now, risk is defined as the chance (or probability) of something *undesirable* happening to individuals or the organization. The concept of risk exists in the realm of uncertainty and occurs when a vulnerability, either known or unknown, has a corresponding threat associated with it.

When the concept of risk is applied to an information system, we are referring to the chance that the system will not do what we expect or need it to do. Although that is a simple definition, it really is somewhat complicated in its implementation. However, it is an extremely important concept because it establishes the foundation and goals of risk management, which are to keep the system operating in a way that we expect and in a manner that meets our needs at the lowest possible cost, regardless of whether that cost is time, effort, or financial outlay.

Risk can be accepted, mitigated or reduced, or transferred [1, 3]. Accepting a risk usually implies that the probability of the threatened risk is low or that the cost-to-benefit ratio does not warrant the concomitant investment to try to prevent the threatened risk from occurring. For example, it might not be worth spending thousands of dollars on a fail over system for a web server that hosts a minor website. Mitigation is generally the attempt to improve a situation to an acceptable level given the constraints. As an example, a manager may opt for an open source or a free virus scanner such as the *AVG-free version* for an isolated office computer that performs a minor role, but upgrade to the AVG commercial version for office computers connected by a local area network.

In Focus

Risk transference means placing the burden of a vulnerability or risk on another party, such as an insurance company.

Managers need to make both quantitative and qualitative assessments of risks to their organizations. As a generic example, risk factors may be placed into a spreadsheet and then given weights according to the risks managers might subjectively identify to various assets, systems, and services. The assigned weights given to the risks attempt to capture the potential damage that an exploit may cause if successful (see **Figure 5.1**). A tally of the threat weights can be computed to identify the greatest damage potentials. Much of what managers may decide in terms of risk probability and risk potential is a matter of judgment; others may be a statistical calculation or as computed probabilities.

5.1.3 Risk Mitigation Overview

Organizations invest in their information technology (IT) infrastructure because they believe that their investments will in some way improve their operations. Such thinking has been supported by research, which has shown that organizations that made significant investments in their IT infrastructure and resources tended to outperform those organizations that did not [4, 5]. Having a unique way of combining tangible and intangible resources, as defined by McKeen et al. [6], is called *IT capability*.

Research related to IT capability not only suggests a definitive relationship between IT investments and organizational value, but the components of IT capability are similar to those identified in best-practice and control frameworks, such as the Information Technology Infrastructure Library (ITIL) and the Control Objectives for Information and Related Technology (COBIT). Furthermore, research that has examined computer-related best practices, such as ISO 17799 and NIST Special Publication 800-53,

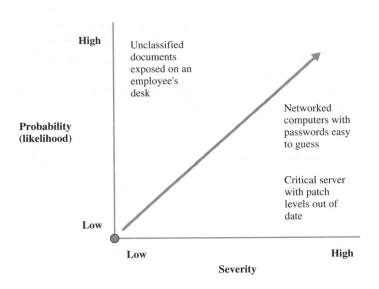

FIGURE 5.1

Risks arranged according to probability and severity.

suggests that the standards can be highly useful in mitigating risk [7]. What these best-practice and control frameworks have in common is the recognition of risk related to information systems.

As indicated earlier, risk mitigation begins with the identification of assets such as systems, software, and information, and then assessing the value of those assets. Valuations include replacement costs of equipment, loss of revenue from lost services, legal liabilities, damage to brand or reputation, and the like. In most cases, organizations log capital purchases and issue asset tags for these items. It is important that this inventory be kept current and accurate. For this purpose, audits should be regularly conducted to reconcile the asset records with the inventory and to confirm the configurations. Having a clear idea of what assets the organization has and their values, they can be matched up with the risk assessments indicating the threats and their likelihoods and severities. Managers can then plan and manage the risks accordingly [2]. Implied in these activities are the importance of risk determination and control frameworks in giving guidance to managers.

5.2 Risk Determination and Control Frameworks

There are an abundance of risk assessment, control, and risk management frameworks. Some of the prominent abbreviations that we will expand on as we go along here are ITIL, ITSM, BS15000, ISO2000x, and a few others. The **IT Infrastructure Library (ITIL)** is a set of management best practices that was developed in the United Kingdom for information systems technology and has broad support throughout Europe and Canada. **Information Technology Service Management (ITSM)** is an IT management framework that implements the components of ITIL.

The main goal of ITIL/ITSM, in terms of most management frameworks, is to enable an organization to establish and manage its IT infrastructure in the most effective and efficient manner possible. The British Standard BS 15000/ISO 2000x takes these processes and divides them over five areas called Release Processes, Control Processes, Resolution Processes, Relationship Processes, and Service Delivery Processes. These areas are then implemented and managed to improve IT delivery efficiency and effectiveness in much the same way as in ITSM.

In Focus

Many configuration frameworks are known as "checklists" in the security literature because they tend to list steps that are to be taken, and then security auditors check them off as they go down the lists to see if an organization is compliant, as we will see shortly.

5.2.1 ITIL / ITSM

ITIL/ITSM is unique in that it focuses on the provision of IT as a service. Whereas previous versions of ITIL aggregated IT processes into one of two broad areas: *Service Delivery*, which is responsible for the management of services, and *Service Support*, which relates to the effective delivery of services, version 3 has at its core Service Strategy, with Service Design, Service Transition, Service Operation, and Continuous Service Improvement defining the remainder of the service life cycle. **List 5.1** provides an overview of each area.

List 5.1 ITILv3 Areas [8]

1. Service Strategy—Defines who will receive what services and how the provision of those services will be measured. In addition, this area includes defining the value of the services offered, identifying the critical success factors associated with enacting the service strategy, and developing an understanding of the roles and responsibilities of individuals who are executing the strategy.
2. Service Design—Specifies the architecture, processes, and policies that will be used to implement the service strategy. This includes the catalog of services to be offered and the specification of the level or quality of those services, the specification of capacity and availability required to meet those service levels, and the required continuity and security management specifications. Also included in service design is a clear specification of supplier requirements. The design is pulled together into a Service Design Package (SDP).
3. Service Transition—Provides the resources required to implement the SDP. This includes managing change, configuration, product release control, and knowledge management to ensure that operations provide a known and standard level of service.

List 5.1 ITILv3 Areas [8] (Continued)

4. Service Operation—Provides the agreed-upon levels of service and handles the routine events as well as the unexpected incidents and problems. Service Operation also includes the Service Desk Function, which provides centralized customer service and serves as a focal point for collecting and managing information related to the current state of operations.
5. Continual Service Improvement—Evaluates current operations in an effort to find ways to improve them. This consists of defining what can and should be measured, collecting and analyzing data to identify variation from standards or opportunities for improvement, and planning and implementing appropriate change, and this is an ongoing process.

5.2.2 COBIT

Another popular framework is the ***Control Objectives for Information and Related Technology*** (**COBIT**). Like ITIL, COBIT defines, identifies, organizes, and links IT activities and resources to business processes to ensure that IT assets are secure, verifiable, and, in COBIT's case in particular, auditable. The framework contains 34 processes, which are organized into four major areas: planning, building, running, and monitoring (see **List 5.2**).

List 5.2 COBIT

1. Planning—covers the processes that distill down from strategic plans to tactical plans. For instance, it suggests SWOT analyses, risk assessments, and contingency planning.
2. Building—incorporates the security process life cycle, materials and requirements planning, requisitions and acquisitions, implementation, and rollouts or deployments.
3. Running—covers the operations and business processing, service and/or product delivery, and support.
4. Monitoring—covers measuring critical success factors (CSFs), collecting business alignment metrics, detecting problems, and reporting incidents, and includes a feedback loop.

Additionally, COBIT separates the framework components into control objectives with audit guidelines and control practices, activity goals for efficiency and effectiveness, and specific metrics that indicate organizational and process maturity, performance, and goal attainment.

5.2.3 ISO 27K IT Security Control Selection

Within the broader context of IT management, there are specific frameworks for IT security that enhance the generalities and, together, tend to be synergistic. The most popular among these security frameworks is the ISO 27000 family. ISO 27001/27002 (17799) are the *de facto* standards for information system security internationally. ISO 27001 provides guidelines that explain how to structure the information security management system (ISMS), analyze risks to identify suitable information security controls, and measure and improve the ISMS thereafter. It does not go into detail on implementing specific controls, but it does provide general guidance by reference to the standards.

The Information Technology Code of Practice for Information Security Management (ISO 27002) gives specific guidance in the "how" of information system security, is divided into 11 sections that broadly address information security, and provides guidelines and best practices for ensuring the security of all information assets, as seen in **List 5.3**.

> **List 5.3 ISO 27002 [9]**
>
> 1. Security Policy—The security policy section objective is to provide management direction and support for information security.
> 2. Organizing Information Security—The organizational security objectives include managing information security within the organization and maintaining the security of organizational information processing facilities and information assets accessed by third parties.

List 5.3 ISO 27002 [9] (Continued)

3. Asset Management—The asset management objectives include assigning responsibility for assets and establishing their classification related to the requirements of the organization.

4. Human Resource Security—The human resource security objectives address responsibilities before, during, and at the end of employment.

5. Physical and Environmental Security—The physical and environmental objectives address issues related to physical areas and equipment.

6. Communications and Operations Management—The communications and operations management address a variety of areas, including operational procedures, contracted service delivery, system planning and acceptance, protection against malicious code, backups, network security, media handling, exchange of information, e-commerce, and monitoring.

7. Access Control—The access control objectives include determining business requirements for access; managing users; specifying user responsibilities; controlling access on networks, operating systems, and applications; and addressing issues related to telecommuting.

8. System Acquisition, Development, and Maintenance—The system acquisition, development, and maintenance objectives include the specification of security requirements early in the acquisition or development process, ensuring the correct functional requirements of applications, cryptographic controls, file security, and technical vulnerability management.

9. Incident Management—The incident management objective specifies requirements related to reporting and management of incidents.

10. Business Continuity Management—The business continuity management objectives deal specifically with issues related to interruption of business activities.

11. Compliance—The compliance objectives include ensuring compliance with legal requirements, security policies, and standards and addressing the IT security audit process [9].

Whereas ISO 27702 provides the controls, ISO 27001, Information Security Management System Requirements, provides an approach to managing security in a well-defined and systematic way. Additionally, it provides a means for an organization to certify its adherence to the security standard. We will discuss the ISO 17799-ISO/IEC 27002 and ISO 13335 in more detail in the section on risk management, and also in the chapter on operations management.

5.2.4 NIST 800-53

Another popular framework is the Recommended Security Controls for Federal Information Systems (RSCFIS), which is also known as the U.S. National Institute of

TABLE 5.1	NIST 800-53 Revision 1, pg. 6 [10]	
CLASS	**FAMILY**	**IDENTIFIER**
Management	Risk Assessment	RA
Management	Planning	PL
Management	System and Services Acquisition	SA
Management	Certification, Accreditation, and Security Assessments	CA
Operational	Personnel Security	PS
Operational	Physical and Environmental Protection	PE
Operational	Contingency Planning	CP
Operational	Configuration Management	CM
Operational	Maintenance	MA
Operational	System and Information Integrity	SI
Operational	Media Protection	MP
Operational	Incident Response	IR
Operational	Awareness and Training	AT
Technical	Identification and Authentication	IA
Technical	Access Control	AC
Technical	Audit and Accountability	AU
Technical	System and Communications Protection	SC

Standards and Technology (NIST) Special Publication 800-53. The framework offers specific guidance in information system security management and control selection. NIST SP 800-53 outlines security controls that are based on the Federal Information Processing Standard (FIPS) 199 Standards for Security Categorization of Federal Information and Information Systems. It was designed to give guidance for organizations implementing FIPS 200, Minimum Security Requirements for Federal Information and Information Systems. NIST 800-53 organizes security controls into three classes and 17 associated families and provides guidance for establishing different groups of controls. Examples are seen in **Table 5.1**.

NIST 800-53 outlines two baseline groups of controls that are to be implemented on all information systems in an organization or unit. It also specifies system controls unique to an individual system. The partitioning of controls in this manner is both designed to be cost-efficient and to provide a central and standardized means of deployment and security assurance. The establishment of security control baselines designed to meet the organization's specific policy requirements enhances this process. In addition to establishing the baseline framework, the publication provides guidance on the process of selecting and specifying security controls to manage risk through a nine-step process. The nine steps are seen in **List 5.4**.

List 5.4 NIST 800-53

1. Categorize the information assets.
2. Select baseline controls.
3. Adjust the controls based on organizational factors.
4. Document the final set of controls.
5. Implement the controls.
6. Assess the implementation and impact of the controls.
7. Determine the risk associated with the information system.
8. Authorize system use if the risk is determined to be acceptable.
9. Monitor the controls and system for effectiveness.

5.3 Risk Management Frameworks

Risk management involves decision making according to assessments of vulnerabilities and costs. Vulnerabilities will continue to exist in complex information systems for the foreseeable future. Exposure of these vulnerabilities, whether known or unknown, can lead to loss. As such, there is an inherent risk associated with utilizing any information system. Understanding and managing risk is a key step in any information security program and is discussed in international standards ISO 17799 or ISO/IEC 27002, and ISO 13335, which are increasingly being utilized as organizational frameworks and guidelines.

In Focus

As indicated before, the concept of risk exists in the realm of uncertainty and occurs when a vulnerability, either known or unknown, has a corresponding threat associated with it, which can be accepted, mitigated or reduced, or transferred.

Risk to an information system is the chance that the system will not do what we expect or need it to do. This simple definition illustrates what we are trying to do with risk management—meaning to keep the system operating in a way that we expect and that meets our needs at the lowest possible cost. Cost is another broad term often used, but it can be thought of as expenditures. Time, effort, and money are all items covered by cost. A thorough risk analysis will allow the owner of a system to make a decision on how to manage risk. In the case of risk acceptance, if the costs associated with mitigating or transferring the risk are greater than costs associated with the risk being exploited from a cost-benefit analysis, it would be better left alone [2].

If the costs associated with the countermeasures outweigh the costs associated with the risk being exploited, then we are interested in mitigating or reducing risk. This is the most common use of information security, and any "owner" of an information system must find a balance between the costs of mitigating the risk and the costs of exploitation.

Finally, transfer of risk occurs within the model of insurance. For a given fee, another agent will accept the costs associated with exploitation of the risk.

In Focus

Nichols et al. [11] defined vulnerability as a weakness in an information system, cryptographic system, or components that could be exploited. Bace [12] divided vulnerabilities into three categories: problems in system design and development, problems in system management, and problems in allocating trust appropriately.

5.3.1 OCTAVE

OCTAVE, or the Operationally Critical Threat, Asset, and Vulnerability Evaluation methodology, was created by researchers at the Software Engineering Institute at Carnegie Mellon University to provide a structured means of helping an organization understand and conduct an information security risk assessment. The OCTAVE method is primarily qualitative and consists of eight steps divided over three phases in which an organization identifies its information assets, identifies and examines the threats and vulnerabilities associated with those assets, and develops a security strategy to address the risks identified. Although there are different OCTAVE methodologies based on the organizational need, the original OCTAVE methodology, specific phases, and process [13] are seen in **List 5.5**.

List 5.5 OCTAVE

1. Phase 1: Build asset-based threat profiles.
    Process 1: Identify senior management knowledge.
    Process 2: Identify operational area knowledge.
    Process 3: Identify staff knowledge.
    Process 4: Create threat profiles.
2. Phase 2: Identify infrastructure vulnerabilities.
    Process 5: Identify key components.
    Process 6: Evaluate selected components.
3. Phase 3: Develop security strategy and plans.
    Process 7: Conduct risk analysis.
    Process 8: Develop protection strategy.

Although it is beyond the scope of this book to cover the full OCTAVE method, an overview is appropriate. In the first step of phase 1, before the evaluation begins, the staff involved must prepare for the evaluation by securing senior management support, selecting appropriate representatives from operational and IT areas, and ensuring that everyone involved in the evaluation is appropriately trained in the method.

Once the site team is established, a meeting must be held with senior management representatives to identify current information assets, their required level of protection, known threats to the assets, and the current administrative, technical, and physical controls in place to provide security for the assets. An understanding of the operational areas to be covered by the evaluation is determined and the team conducts similar meetings with the operational managers, area staff, and finally the IT department. The information gathered from the meetings is used to construct threat profiles that are utilized in subsequent phases.

In Focus

It should be quite clear that many of the risk assessment and risk management approaches share common attributes. This means they contain core (or essential) elements related to information security, but the exact measures used in compliance depends on the company, the industry in which the company operates, or whether the organization is a government agency.

In phase 2, the site team works with the IT department (or the department in the organization responsible for information systems and information systems security) to identify and evaluate the specific information systems associated with the assets identified in phase 1. The information systems then undergo a vulnerability analysis to identify strengths and weaknesses with the technical controls established, and a summary report is completed.

In phase 3, information gathered from phases 1 and 2 is consolidated and evaluated to determine the value associated with the information assets and whether loss associated with the assets would result in a high, medium, or low impact to the organization. A similar process is conducted with the identified risks, resulting in a framework that allows the site team to develop a protection strategy, risk mitigation plans, and an action list that identifies specific short- and long-term actions to be taken to reduce or manage the identified risks.

This is reviewed with senior management, adjusted to the specific goals and needs of the organization, and finalized for implementation. In the more recent OCTAVE Allegro [14], the structured risk assessment is similar, although the steps have changed to reflect a streamlined approach, which includes the (1) establishment of risk measurement criteria, (2) development of an information asset profile, (3) identification of information asset containers, (4) identification of areas of concern, (5) identification of threat scenario, (6) identification of risks, (7) an analysis of the risks, and (8) the selection of a mitigation approach.

5.3.2 NIST 800-30

Earlier, we mentioned the NIST SP 800-53 as a risk determination and control framework. The complement to that specification is the NIST SP 800-30, which contains provisions for risk management. In addition to providing guidance for risk management in the software development life cycle (SDLC), it provides a nine-step methodology for conducting a risk assessment, identifying appropriate controls for the associated risk, mitigation strategies, and standards of practice for continuous risk evaluation and assessment. The nine steps are illustrated in **List 5.6**.

List 5.6 NIST 800-30

1. System Characterization
2. Threat Identification
3. Vulnerability Identification
4. Control Analysis
5. Likelihood Determination
6. Impact Analysis
7. Risk Determination
8. Control Recommendations
9. Results Documentation

Similar to the OCTAVE methodology, the first step in the NIST 800-30 risk management process is the definition of the scope of the project. Additionally, it is during the first step of the process that system information is collected through questionnaires, interviews, document reviews, and automated system scanning tools. This includes identification of the hardware and software, the associated data, the users, the mission and purpose of the system, and the level of importance of the data to the organization. Functional requirements, policies, controls, and system architecture are also identified and delineated in this step.

In the second step, Threat Identification, the assessment team utilizes the information gathered in step one to identify and evaluate potential threats to the IT system and operating environment. Included in this step are evaluation of potential natural threats, such as floods, earthquakes, and lightning; human threats, such as intentional and unintentional acts that cause damage to the system; and environmental threats, such as pollution and long-term power outages.

The third step, Vulnerability Identification, seeks to identify those properties of the system that could be exploited or exacerbated by the threats identified in step two. The information derived from steps two and three are combined to form Vulnerability/Threat pairs that list the vulnerability, a potential threat source, and the action the threat could engage in to exploit the vulnerability. The vulnerabilities themselves are identified through standard sources, such as vulnerability databases, scanning, audit reports, and vendor information. This can also include active vulnerability testing methods, such as "red team" or penetration testing. Any weaknesses identified in step three are used as input to step four.

In Control Analysis, the vulnerability/threat pairs are compared to existing or planned controls, and a determination is made as to the sufficiency of the management (administrative), operational (physical), and technical controls. A checklist is often utilized at this stage to compare the controls to the vulnerabilities/threat environment, and adjustments to plans are made.

In the fifth step, Likelihood Determination, a quantifier of high, medium, or low is assigned to each threat/vulnerability pair to indicate the likelihood of each individual vulnerability being exploited in the given threat environment. A high quantifier indicates that there is a great likelihood that the threat will exploit the vulnerability and that the in-place or planned controls will have little effect. A medium quantifier indicates that the threat may be significant but the controls are likely to be effective, and a low quantifier indicates that either the threat is negligible, or the controls are effective, or both.

Step six is Impact Analysis and is a determination of what the consequences of a successful exploitation of vulnerability will mean to the organization. Generally, this is described in terms of degradation to the information security triad of confidentiality, integrity, and availability with respect to each resource and again described as high, medium, or low.

The impact statements from step six feed into the Risk Determination of step seven. It is in this step that the likelihood, the impact, and the control sufficiency are utilized to create a risk-level matrix in which the assessment team generates an overall risk level for each observation. The determination of risk is a factor of the likelihood of the threat attempting exploitation and the impact to the organization should the exploit be successful. The results from this step, a quantification of risk as high, medium, or low for each threat, are the basis for step eight, Control Recommendations.

In step eight, management must be involved to make a determination as to what level of risk the organization is willing to accept for each threat. This will drive the evaluation and recommendation of specific controls, whether administrative, technical, or physical, for each threat. Step nine requires the results and underlying reasoning for decisions made in each of the prior steps to be documented in a report or briefing that can be utilized by management to make decisions on business arrangements related to the risk assessment. As discussed earlier, this may include assumption of the risk, implementation of controls to attempt to mitigate the risk, or transfer of the risk through insurance or some other means. These are not mutually exclusive areas, but may be combined in a variety of ways.

In Focus

Although we have described in some detail some of the risk assessment and management approaches, there are numerous other approaches and standards that are available. ISO/IEC 15408 provides evaluation criteria for IT security, whereas ISO/IEC 19791 provides an extension to ISO/IEC 15408 to examine the operational environment associated with systems. ISO 27000 contains a whole series and is the information system security collection of ISO standards. In addition to the ISO standards, Larsen et al. [15] evaluate a total of 17 IT governance standards and tools. There are additional ones as well.

5.3.3 Using Frameworks for Implementing Plans

Now that we have covered a variety of frameworks, we will briefly illustrate how a framework might be used in the implementation of risk mitigation plans. Risk is often represented in the function: f (risk = (threat × vulnerability)). A question managers often ask is how to translate this function into something tangible. Later in this textbook, we will go into more specifics about this, but for now, an example might be useful to show how framework criteria we have covered might be translated into risk mitigation actions. For this example, we will use OCTAVE, presented earlier, but at a simplistic level and with a single example to make it amendable for our illustration purposes. As a refresher, it involves building asset-based threat profiles, identifying infrastructure vulnerabilities, and developing a security strategy and plans.

Suppose our company had a web-based application written in JAVA, which allowed managers to track their plan to actual budgets via a login with a browser. We first need to develop a threat profile—and for this example, we will focus specifically on the login, and more specifically on password protections. Next, imagine that our system uses a mandatory access control in which users are required to change their passwords every 90 days to a randomly generated password supplied to them automatically.

Now let's say that we conducted an evaluation and found that many managers were writing down their passwords and had taped them to their keyboards because they could not remember them. From our assessment, we determined that the threat is high = 8 and the vulnerability is moderate = 5. This results in a risk factor of 40. We rated the threat as high because the password generated for logging in to the budget tracking system is the same password that is required to log in to the computer and all of the other company systems because we synchronized passwords for single sign-on purposes. If one password is compromised, all passwords are compromised, so the threat is high. However, it only applies to the local area network, so only an internal threat, such as another employee, a contractor, or a night janitorial cleaning crew would be able to use this login information; thus the vulnerability is rated medium. Let's further say that the risk of 40 is among the highest risks calculated compared to other risks we evaluated, so it requires our immediate attention.

We then interview the managers and learn that those who are doing this do not realize that a password compromise could lead to other compromises, such as an employee who wanted to look up pay and performance data to use in a scam. We then develop a security awareness program, and we develop a system that provides users with a cryptographic key phrase to remember (with hints in case they forget it) so they can log in to a system that renders their passwords over a secure channel. Although such a system could still be compromised, it substantially lowers the risk factor, and so we can then attend to higher risks.

CHAPTER SUMMARY

This chapter covered quite a bit of ground in terms of standard practices and frameworks, and we discussed security program management and the components of risk assessment and management. Compliance with these frameworks depends on the kind of operation, but more generally, establishing and governing a secure information system infrastructure depends on the needs of the organization and the costs (both social and technical) in the event of a compromise. Frameworks for risk mitigation and risk management are useful in guiding security matters regardless of whether the organization is required to comply with one or more of them.

The choices of controls should be dictated by policy or other organizational directives, and they are derived from a thorough understanding of the system, environment, and the determination of risk. Once security policy is established, secure computer and information system operations are enhanced by a mature IT management framework that considers the overall role of IT and information assets within the organization and that has reached a level of maturity in which the assets are understood, managed, and implemented in a strategic way to enhance business processes. In the last section of this textbook, we will return to these concepts in more technical terms and discuss how some of these programs are implemented.

THINK ABOUT IT

Topic Questions

5.1: What standard provides an extension to ISO/IEC 15408?

5.2: OCTAVE is primarily what type of method and has how many steps?

5.3: COBIT separates the framework components into:

_____ Stages and practices
_____ Goals and processes
_____ Control objectives and control practices
_____ Regulations and laws

5.4: Risk transference means:

_____ Patching systems so that risks are mitigated

_____ Placing the burden of risk on another party
_____ Litigating against an attacker
_____ Moving a threat from one area of a system to another

5.5: ITIL/ITSM is unique in that it focuses on the provision of information technology as a service.

_____ True
_____ False

THINK ABOUT IT (CONTINUED)

5.6: Which of the following is part of ISO 27002:

____ Build asset-based threat profiles
____ Risk = threat × vulnerability
____ Cost/benefit analysis
____ Organizing information security

5.7: ISO/IEC 19791 provides an extension to ISO/IEC 15408.

____ True
____ False

5.8: NIST SP 800-30 is a risk determination and control framework.

____ True
____ False

5.9: The first step in the NIST 800-30 risk management process is the

_____.

5.10: NIST SP 800-53 outlines security controls that are based on _____.

Questions for Further Study

Q5.1: Explain how regulations, standards, and laws affect what managers ought to do regarding security.

Q5.2: Discuss some ways (both qualitative and quantitative) that managers might assess risk.

Q5.3: What are some primary characteristics between risk assessment and risk management that managers need to consider?

Q5.4: Provide a description of one other risk management framework not discussed in this chapter.

Q5.5: Develop a short scenario on how one of the frameworks presented in this chapter could be used in a risk mitigation plan.

KEY CONCEPTS AND TERMS

Checklist is a term applied to risk assessment and risk management criteria.

Risk assessment and **risk management** deal with the processes, rules, and procedures of security management.

Risk assessment involves techniques to quantify and qualify the likelihood and impact of threats.

Risk management involves decision making according to assessments of vulnerabilities and costs.

References

1. Purser, S. (2004). *A practical guide to managing information security.* Boston, MA: Artech House.
2. Gibson, D. (2011). *Managing risk in information systems.* Boston, MA; Jones & Bartlett Learning.

3. Straub, D. W., Goodman, S., & Baskerville, R. J. (2008). *Information security: Policies, processes, and practices*. Armonk, NY: M. E. Sharpe Books.

4. Santhanam, R., & Hartono, E. (2003). Issues in linking information technology capability to firm performance. *MIS Quarterly, 27(1)*, 125–153.

5. Bharadwaj, A. S. (2000). A resource-based perspective on information technology capability and firm performance: An empirical investigation. *MIS Quarterly, 24(1)*, 169–196.

6. McKeen, J. D., Smith, H. A., & Singh, S. (2005). Developments in practive XVI: A framework for enhancing IT capabilities. *Communications of the Association for Information Systems, 15*, 661–673.

7. Ma, Q., & Pearson, J. M. (2005). ISO 17799: "Best practices" in information security management. *Communications of the Association for Information Systems, 15*, 571–593.

8. Cartlidge, A., Hanna, A., Rudd, C., Macfarlane, I., Windebank, J., & Rance, S. (2007). *An introductory overview of ITILv3*. London: The UK Chapter of the itSMF. Retrieved September 29, 2011, from http://www.itsmfi.org/content/introductory-overview-itil-v3-pdf

9. ISO/IEC 27001:2005. (2005). *Information technology—Security techniques—Information security management systems—And requirements*. Geneva, Switzerland: International Organization for Standardization.

10. NIST SP 800-53. (2005). *Information security—Recommended security controls for federal information systems*. NIST Specification 800-53. Retrieved from http://csrc.nist.gov/publications/PubsSPs.html.

11. Nichols, R. K., Ryan, D. J., & Ryan, J. J. (2000). *Defending your digital assets against hackers, crackers, spies & thieves*. New York, NY: McGraw-Hill.

12. Bace, R. G. (2000). *Intrusion detection*. Indianapolis, IN: Macmillan Technical Publishing.

13. Alberts, C., & Dorofee, A. (2003). *Managing information security risks: The OCTAVE Approach*. Boston, MA: Addison-Wesley.

14. Caralli, R. A., Stevens, J. F., Young, L. R., & Wilson, W. R. (2007). *Introducing OCTAVE Allegro: Improving the information security risk assessment process*. Pittsburgh, PA: Software Engineering Institute.

15. Larsen, M. H., Pedersen, M. K., & Andersen, K. V. (2006). *IT governance: Reviewing 17 IT governance tools and analyzing the case of novozymes A/S*. Proceedings of the 39th Hawaii International Conference on System Sciences.

Managing Organizations Securely

I N THIS CHAPTER, WE WILL devote some time to reviewing some of what we covered thus far, and then present security management concerns and cover organizational impacts, both positive and negative. In preparation for moving on to more technical content, we will visit some of the issues related to security contravention and security omission. We will distinguish between insider and outsider threats and discuss monitoring. In line with the knowledge scaffolding approach we have taken in this textbook, we will briefly summarize highlights from Section 1 to reinforce learning, and we will provide a preview of things to come.

Chapter 6 Topics

This chapter:

- Provides an overview of information architecture.
- Reviews security policies and security models and their relationships.
- Discusses security stances.
- Discusses risk management and risk assessment in relation to security countermeasures.
- Describes monitoring, information collection, and handling of incidents.
- Explains organizational impacts from monitoring.

Chapter 6 Goals

When you finish this chapter, you should:

- ❑ Be able to describe the layered aspects of information architecture and describe the relationships to information security.

- ❏ Be able to explain security management in a security policy context.
- ❏ Know what countermeasures are and how they are used.
- ❏ Understand key critical issues related to security standards and policies.
- ❏ Be able to discuss the issues related to employee monitoring and surveillance.

6.1 Security Management Overview

A primary role for managers as far as security is concerned is to provide well-defined means of identifying, monitoring, mitigating, and managing security risks. This involves oversight of members in the organization who are responsible for taking security-related actions. Viewed traditionally, it may seem as though security is only a technological problem by the concentration on techniques and technologies for creating better defenses and using criteria in performing risk analyses and the application of security countermeasures, but it is important to note that security is mainly a behavioral issue.

Along those lines, an important consideration is that businesses are dynamic, as are the environments in which they operate, and organizations are on an evolutionary path. To illustrate, organizational theory from the mid-1970s to the early 1990s saw the rise of socio-technical systems management. In this era, the importance of creativity was recognized. Organizations were viewed as strategically behaving entities, and workers were viewed as part of a larger system in which systematic alignment between inputs and outputs was seen as crucial in maintaining a well-oiled organizational machine. From the mid-1990s to the early 2000s, organizations evolved through the view of the general systems theory of management. The concept of systematic organization as a well-oiled machine was supplanted by the view of the systemic organization. Complexity, interconnectedness, and globalization generated emphasis on organizations as "*epiorganisms*"—functioning economic systems that were organic and interactive.

Since the early 2000s, we have witnessed a paradigm shift toward *reconstructivist* management view. This theory presumes that self-organizing and emergent forces shape work, and workers lead in self-development and the humanization of work, taking active roles in reconstructing organizations as parts of global societies. After several scandals, such as the one at Enron, and corporate "bailout" controversies, there has been a renewed emphasis on ethics and social responsibility; budding ethical tenants also create struggles in managing organizations securely. Incorporating all of the administrative, procedural, technological, and human resource elements of security management, we will now take a broad survey of how these interactions affect security behaviors to conclude Section 1.

6.1.1 Information and Systems Security Infrastructure

Looking back on what we have covered thus far, we understand that security management strives for the reduction of risk exposure by using the processes of threat identification, asset measurement, control, and minimization of losses associated with threats. Managers often survey and classify assets, conduct security reviews, perform risk analyses, evaluate and select information security technologies, perform cost/benefit analyses, and test security effectiveness.

This is accompanied by the development of policies, comparisons against standards, procedures, and guidelines; all of these activities help managers to ensure information CIA: confidentiality, integrity, and availability. To classify assets and information, to identify threats and vulnerabilities, and to help ensure that effective countermeasures are implemented, there are a variety of tools available to managers including information classification systems, configuration management and change controls, and employee security training. Considering all of these organizational security aspects, it is easy to see how complicated managing security can be, especially considering that a company's information systems infrastructure comprises all the resources and assets and efforts related to information and the computing facilities used by people in organizations for decision making and action taking.

We know that an organization's information and systems security infrastructure supports the organizational mission and objectives by helping to ensure CIA. Under the umbrella of information infrastructure resides information architecture, which consists of how information and systems are organized within a company and between trading partners; therefore the information architecture outlines all the facilities that must be secured. Security policies, as we have learned, are the rules used to maintain organizational security, as well as for monitoring and reporting in the case of security breaches.

Security models are methods and techniques policies might dictate, such as what privileges are allocated for which resource and to whom. Finally, countermeasures are the specific implementations or technologies used in protecting the CIA of the information architecture, and procedures are how countermeasures are carried out. **Figure 6.1** highlights these layered relationships.

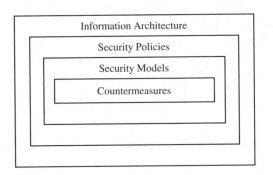

FIGURE 6.1

Layered security relationships.

6.1.2 Information Assets: Classification and Architecture

A main element in attending to information security is to know what information is maintained by the organization, where the information is located, and how the information is "classified," such as company *confidential* or *proprietary*. As previously noted, ISO/IEC 17799 and ISO/IEC 27002 are examples of classification systems and criteria. Classification is an important component in carrying out security policies, especially in relation to the rules for implementing controls that determine who has what access rights to various resources. This is necessary to ensure that only those who are authorized are able to gain the proper access. Managers can then specify in procedure manuals or other documents what technologies and techniques (countermeasures) to use to ensure this.

Architecture in a classic sense is visualized in blueprints for how a structure is organized along with its amenities or features. Information architecture similarly contains the specifications, diagrams, designs, requirements, documentation, topologies, and all the schematics that illustrate the information and computing resources used by an organization. Its function is to create and communicate the "information environment" including aesthetics, structure, and mechanics involved in organizing and facilitating information ease of use, integrity, access, and usefulness [1].

Information architecture is divided into macro- and micro-levels. For example, architecture for a web-based application on a macro-level would illustrate all of the intersections and distributions of the information storages and flows through the consumer–producer (value) chain including those among trading partners, company locations, co-locations, and agencies in which the organization corresponds such as between airlines and the Federal Aviation Administration (FAA) or banks and the Federal Reserve. On the other hand, architecture for a web-based application on a micro-level would illustrate the individual components within a system or a collection of systems. It might show how software and systems are partitioned, where the network access points are located, and which components are centralized and which are distributed; it might even specify some of the key technologies that would constrain the architecture to a type of platform or software system.

6.1.3 Security Policies and Models

As we have discussed, among the primary tools for managers are security policies. Because security policies define how information and systems assets are to be used and governed, they differ somewhat from other organizational policies. Security policies are either documents that establish the rules and punitive sanctions regarding security behaviors (for instance, they may dictate that users must change their passwords monthly) or they consist of facilities that are codified into information and communications systems that define the rules and permissions for system operations. For example, a router's security policy may permit only egress ICMP messages and deny all those that are ingress, or a host computer's security policy may prohibit files from copying themselves, or from accessing an email address book, or from making modifications to the Microsoft Windows Registry (more about these technical details in Section 6.2).

Some security policies define *security models*. For example, the Clark and Wilson model states that systems must prevent tampering from unauthorized users; that file changes must be logged; and that the integrity of data must be maintained and kept in a consistent state. A ***countermeasure*** is the specification for an implementation of a security procedure or technology to address vulnerabilities, and countermeasures are often dictated by security models. For example, if we applied the Clark and Wilson model to a human process such as "payroll," the model would specify that someone in an authorized role, such as the CFO, must approve and record the distribution of the payroll checks cut by the accounting department. A countermeasure that implements the Clark and Wilson model may include computer transaction monitors such as Tuxedo, CICS, and Open/OLTP.

The Clark and Wilson model is therefore transaction-oriented, and an electronic transaction is defined by ACID properties, for (1) atomicity—a discrete unit of work, where all of the transactions must be completed or committed to databases simultaneously, or rolled back until it can be committed, (2) consistency—where data must transition in an orderly manner from the beginning of the transaction to the end of the transaction, (3) isolation—where the transaction is self-contained and not reliant on any other transactions for its operations, and (4) durable—meaning the data remain in a consistent state until they are intentionally changed [2].

An essential concept in transactional security models such as Clark and Wilson is that operations must be ***well formed***. A well-formed transaction occurs in a specific authorized sequence, which is monitored and logged. Logging is often done to an ***audit file***, or computer program changes are typically logged to a ***change control log***. Logs allow auditors, administrators, and managers to review the transactions to ensure that only authorized and correct changes were made. Besides transaction monitors, many companies use change control applications and ***system configuration management*** (**SCM**) systems for these purposes.

6.1.4 Stances and Countermeasures

A security model may specify security ***stances***. Stances are primarily affected by the countermeasures that control the flow of information and managing what subjects (e.g., people or processes) can have what kind of access to objects (e.g., resources, data, or programs). Stances can be ***optimistic***, where that which is not explicitly denied is permitted, or ***pessimistic***, where that which is not explicitly permitted is denied. Consider, for example, that a network administrator may set a network router to permit all Internet connections unless he or she specifically creates a rule to block those named—this is an optimistic stance.

There will be combinations of stances at different points in the systems and networks in the infrastructure. For example, an optimistic security stance may be taken to allow traffic to a web server, and a pessimistic stance taken to permit only a given proxy system to access an internal domain name service (DNS). Fundamentally, in addition to resource access, stances deal with the rules that guide procedures for access rights, for instance, granting read, write, and execute permissions to an owner or creator of a file, but not to anyone else.

An example of an information flow security stance model is the Bell and LaPadula. This model (among other things) defines who is privileged to access what, in an effort to help ensure information confidentiality. In its original form, as shown in **Figure 6.2**, it was designed for the intelligence community to specify who could access information based on their security clearance levels. If we applied this model to a human process such as the production of company confidential planning documents, it would specify that no one outside the company may be given a copy of them. Technologically, we see the countermeasures implemented in computer operating systems as file system permissions and as access control lists.

Another information flow security stance model is the Biba model. This approach is similar to Bell–LaPadula, but it goes beyond addressing confidentiality by also attempting to protect the integrity of data by prohibiting unauthorized persons from making modifications to data to which they have only read access. Countermeasures using the Biba model include access controls (including biometrics; more on this later in the chapter) and authentication to ensure authorized access and to dictate that an authorized user-level process may not exceed its privileges to modify a file unless specifically granted—for example, through the Windows "Executive" security access module, or the authorized grant of escalated privileges using the "setuid" capability in the UNIX operating system, which allows a user-level program to gain access to "superuser" or "root" (administrator) operating system–level functions.

FIGURE 6.2

Illustration of the
Bell–LaPadula model.

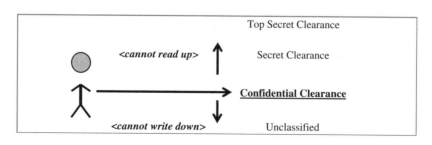

Unfortunately, as we will see later, the UNIX setuid capability can also become a source of security threats by gaining unauthorized access to privileged system functions or by illicitly escalating privileges.

As seen, then, ways to deal with threats involve implementing countermeasures. Countermeasures consist of physical, technical, administrative, and behavioral techniques. ***Physical countermeasures*** are those that have a tangible presence, such as a fireproof storage vault. ***Technical countermeasures*** are those that involve some software system or application such as a virus scanner. ***Administrative countermeasures*** are those that involve procedures, such as having employees sign non-disclosure agreements or using checklists to ensure compliance with a standard. ***Behavioral countermeasures*** are those that involve "humans in the loop," such as ensuring the administrator deletes login accounts that belonged to terminated employees [3].

6.2 Risk Assessment and Management

Obviously, information systems are critical assets in most organizations, and protecting them is essential in corporate and governmental operations, yet no system can be completely secure, and determined attackers can breach even the hardest of defenses. Managers must be prepared to define the level of risk that they are willing to accept compared to the costs associated with implementing preventive and corrective measures. As we presented in the previous chapter, *risk assessment* is an ongoing process of identifying risks and threats, whereas *risk management* is the ongoing process of implementing measures according to the costs and benefits associated with risks and security countermeasures, as well as determining containment and recovery strategies and measures for attacks when they occur.

In Chapter 5, we also presented the idea that that managers, through their administrative practices, strive to mitigate risk, or take preventive measures to reduce them. Managers also try to avoid risks by placing constraints on what people do or what they implement, where they implement countermeasures, and when, and most particularly, what not to implement. Managers may also choose to accept some level of risk because the costs or time to implement precautions are not worth the benefits. We also presented the notion of risk transference, which involves placing the onus or risk burden on another in exchange for a fee (for example, having insurance) or by exclusions in a contract, such as indemnification clauses. In this section, we will present technological countermeasures to help managers manage securely.

6.2.1 Risks and Countermeasures

We have covered some of the techniques used in the ongoing process of risk assessment, such as conducting inventories, classifying information, attempting to determine vulnerabilities, and so forth. As these functions are done, part of assessing risk includes determining how proactive versus reactive to be as an economic tradeoff when it comes to security countermeasures. To try to illustrate this idea, a manager may spend 15 percent of his or her budget to prevent access of HIPAA-regulated data (i.e., medical patient information), but perhaps he or she is willing to spend only 5 percent of his or her budget to protect sales report data, with consideration for the expenditures in mind if a security breach occurs after the fact.

Some guidelines in the security literature suggest using a formula denoted **ALE** for *annualized loss expectancy*, which is a function of the cost of a *single loss expectancy* (**SLE**), or the cost to deal with the loss of a given compromised asset, multiplied by the *annualized rate of the loss* for each potential occurrence (**ARL**) [4]. Other financial formulas that are often used include *payback periods on depreciated loss of assets* and *expected future value with time value of money for replacement costs* from a loss. However, although certainly helpful, these quantitative financial assessments overlook important qualitative components that should also be considered, such as damage to company reputation from a security breach [5]. Moreover, even the quantitative measures rely on some amount of subjectivity and guesswork.

> **In Focus**
>
> It is important that managers involve the finance and accounting departments before making financial declarations to help avoid discrepancies that may arise during an audit.

The key to determining risk is a blend of quantitative (often statistical) assessments and logical evaluations, and just plain good judgment—and managers are paid as much for their judgments as any other aspect of their job. Therefore, because countermeasures are designed to prevent a security breach and their assessed value according to the total impact, both quantitative assessments (such as ALE) and the qualitative judgments of managers (such as following normative rules) are necessary for successfully managing security.

Countermeasures are actions that implement the spirit of security policies and are designed to address vulnerabilities. Where a security policy might call for the use of *role-based access controls* (**RBAC**) for a particular business function, such as "*cut checks for payroll,*" an example of a countermeasure in computer security may be to utilize a particular *access control list* (**ACL**) maintained with a *directory service*, such as Microsoft's Active Directory. The vulnerability this may address is to prevent unauthorized access to payroll files and control who is allowed to cut checks. Or a countermeasure may call for the use of a *transaction management* system, such as Tuxedo. The vulnerability this might address is to prevent data inconsistency and preserve data integrity by ensuring a completed two-phased commit between processes and distributed databases involving an update to a hospital patient medical record (**Figure 6.3**). In this latter example, the transaction manager issues to each database a request to update (called a pre-commit); if the database can lock the data and allow the update, it will return an acknowledgment to the transaction manager. If all of the databases return positive acknowledgments, the

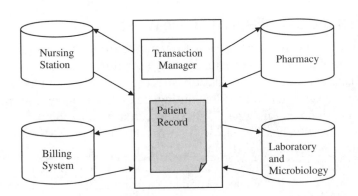

FIGURE 6.3

Two-phased commit
for a patient record.

transaction manager will commit all of the data updates simultaneously; otherwise it will do a rollback and try again.

Other countermeasures might consist of implementations of ***cryptography***—ranging from encrypting a message using *PGP* before sending it through email, to the authentication of users with Kerberos. Cryptography is also used in creating message digests (such as MD5) to ensure that there has been no tampering with data and in creating digital signatures for non-repudiation. We will explore the technical aspects involved in countermeasures in Section 6.3.

Security controls that are used in countermeasures must allow people to work efficiently and effectively; therefore, countermeasures must enable maximum control with minimum constraints. This aspect relates to ensuring resource availability to legitimate workers. Managers have to contemplate the consequences of security actions; however, in modern organizations, successful work typically means successful teamwork and open communications where information must be able to pass through organizational barriers for work to be done efficiently and effectively, and also to ensure effective security operations.

This important element was described by Sine et al. [6] as organic organizational capabilities that enable company adaptation and agility. Yet all the efforts to compartmentalize and quarantine people for security purposes work against these core organic principles. Thus, strict approaches to security such as separation of duties and compartmentalization should be confined to only those most sensitive operations, functions, and roles in the company.

In Focus

Most organizations strive to thin the boundaries between organizational units in order to improve visibility of operations and communications, and to facilitate problem solving (including solving security problems). However, certain government agencies and companies doing secure work such as Northrop Grumman, Harris Corporation, or Unisys are perhaps more inclined than an average organization to use stringent security measures in organizational controls, especially in certain departments.

6.2.2 Hoping for the Best, Planning for the Worst

Managers, of course, hope that their proactive attempts to protect the organizational resources and personnel will be successful, but they also must consider the worst-case scenarios. *Risk management*, as we have discussed, is the process that addresses threats and their associated costs and planning for contingencies. **Contingency planning** may often involve the development of "what if" disaster scenarios, and popular techniques for this range from Delphi, which is a group decision-making process in which participants provide anonymous input and ideas that are evaluated by the group—or computerized stochastic modeling, which produces statistical probabilities about possible outcomes based on information solicited from people or derived from technology queries in data mining or from expert systems.

Contingency planning includes a **disaster recovery planning** process in which alternative means of information processing and recovery (if a disaster occurs) are devised. This process produces a **business continuity plan**, which outlines how the businesses are to continue to operate in the case of a disaster—manmade or natural [4]. Managers also need to consider what to do after a disaster happens and how to recover from it.

A **recovery plan** concentrates on how to restore normal operations. These plans may include using a **disaster recovery center**, where equipment is kept and personnel are sent in such an event. There are companies such as SunGard that specifically provide these services. Another important process is **facilities management**, which incorporates procedures for dealing with disasters such as using offsite backup and storage facilities, distributed operations and monitoring centers, and *self-healing* systems.

As presented earlier, there are many standards; for example, those devised by the National Computer Security Center (NCSC), which is part of the National Security Agency (NSA), are specifically geared toward the government or makers of systems for government consumers. The NCSC conducts security evaluations and audits under the **Trusted Product Evaluation Program** (**TPEP**), which tests commercial applications against a set of security compliance criteria. In 1983, the NCSC issued the Department of Defense (DoD) **Trusted Computer System Evaluation Criteria** (**TCSEC**), which has become one of the standards for security compliance for these kinds of systems.

The TCSEC defines the concepts of **subjects** and **objects** within a security framework. Subjects fall into two categories: (1) **direct surrogates** for a user, which are applications or components that represent a human being or human action, or (2) **internal subjects**, which consist of those components or objects that provide services for other subjects, such as software applications or operating system features. Objects in this case are the instruments, applications, software, information, and other resources that subjects use or manipulate during the course of carrying out their duties. These standards rely on the notion of "trust," and *trust* from a security perspective has a specific connotation. The concept of trust in an information security context is a system that is *attack resistant* and reflects the ability of a system to protect its *information and resource integrity*. The failure of a trusted system may compromise the entire security infrastructure, and so trust is a crucial concept [7].

6.2.3 Trusted Computing Base Versus Common Criteria

Early evaluation criteria based on the notion of trust included what is commonly referred to as the orange book, which defines a **trusted computing base** (**TCB**), and attempted to establish a base level of trust. The TCB was intended to comprise the entirety of protections including the roles and actions of users for a computing system, including hardware, firmware, databases, file systems, and software, and the combination responsible for enforcing security. The TCB criteria are denoted as (1) minimal protection (class D), (2) discretionary protection (class C), (3) mandatory protection (class B), and (4) verified protection (class A).

Each of these classifications includes subcategories of trust. For example, the C1 level calls for the separation of duties, particularly in terms of users and information. Among its requirements are the identification of information and the authorizations to access it. To achieve C1, access control lists (ACLs) must be used in addition to login controls. Also, there must be insulation between user and administrative or "system" modes of operations. The C2 level extends the requirements for C1 to include a requirement for **auditing**, among other things.

In Focus

When codified into systems, security policies can dictate which actions are permitted and which ones are denied, according to roles or permissions assigned to a user. Role-based entities and permissions may also work in conjunction with a directory service. One example is a version control system that can be used to manage access to documents as well as source code. In some configurations, a directory service such as the lightweight directory access protocol, or LDAP, or the Microsoft Active Directory, can be used to manage access to information and resources.

The TCSEC orange book—at least in terms of the vernacular used in the criteria—is applicable primarily to government and military systems. Industry tends to have different needs and often has different trust requirements. For instance, the TCSEC tends to leave out criteria that are concerned with the availability of systems and specify only weak controls for integrity and authenticity actions. Moreover, the TCSEC is mainly concerned with host computers and leaves void many of the important aspects of network security—especially in the context of the Web. The **trusted network interpretation** (**TNI**), also called the **red book**, was thus devised to help compensate for some of these gaps by including criteria for local area and wide area networks.

Whereas early computer systems, such as the Digital Equipment VAX running the VMS operating system, were evaluated according to the TCSEC, globalization has forced national or regional standards bodies to cooperate on standards criteria. Consequently, the **International Standards Organization** (**ISO**) created specification **15408**, or what has become known as **Common Criteria**. The Common Criteria supplanted the TCSEC, as well as the Canadian Trusted Computer Product Evaluation Criteria (CTCPEC) and the European Information Technology Security Evaluation Criteria (ITSEC), among others.

The Common Criteria has several parts, but among the most important is the **Mutual Recognition Arrangement** (**MRA**), which is an agreement among participating countries to accept the criteria and recognize the audit results from evaluations regardless of which auditing entity (called *signatories*) performed the evaluation. U.S. signatories, such as the National Security Agency (NSA) and the National Institute of Standards and Technology (NIST), work with the *National Information Assurance Partnership* (**NIAP**) and have developed an informal standard called the *Common Criteria Evaluation and Validation Scheme* (**CCEVS**). CCEVS summarizes all the standards used by the United States in order to conform to the Common Criteria.

6.2.4 Evaluation and Certification

Systems sold to or used by government agencies are measured by various criteria (depending on the agency). In addition to the TCB and Common Criteria, there are myriad other standards and criteria that may need to be considered, as indicated in previous chapters. For commercial (non-governmental) applications, the important points for managers to know are that standards may provide some good guidelines for large organizations in terms of security assurance of systems and networks, as well as for developing security policies and conducting information assessments of risk. For instance, *ISO 13355* provides guidelines for risk management processes.

However, if an organization is a government agency, or is federally regulated, it will probably require a formal *certification* and *accreditation* (called **C&A**) as part of the overall security policy. A certification is a comprehensive evaluation of an information system and its infrastructure to ensure that it complies with federal standards, such as the *Federal Information Security Management Act* (**FISMA**). An accreditation is the result of an audit conducted by a signatory or accrediting body, such as the *National Institute of Standards and Technology* (**NIST**), which gives the "go ahead" to put into production a certified system. Signatory auditors may give one of four accreditation levels ranging from low security to high security. Auditors will use various methods depending on which agency is doing the certification and who the consumers will be [3].

Even the best-laid plans can fail, so managers spend a significant amount of time pondering and trying to balance the security risks against other important organizational needs. The problem is that there are wide-ranging risks that cannot be foreseen, and not only are they human-induced, but they also come from natural disasters such as hurricanes and floods.

In Focus

After a major hurricane hit the Florida operations center for a large transaction processing firm, engineers from the organization flew to their SunGard site in Pennsylvania, where hot standby systems were at the ready, and the company resumed operations within 24 hours of the disaster. However, one should take into account whether, in the event of a disaster, critical personnel will be able to get to these backup centers. Consider, for example, that airlines were grounded during the 9/11 attacks in the United States—how would personnel get to the standby site if one could not fly?

A difficulty presented to managers is that security technologies and infrastructure, as an overhead (non-revenue generating) cost of doing business, has grown to a sizable amount of the average company's budget. As noted earlier, security initiatives consume about 8 percent of the average company's budget. Although it is important that security countermeasures be implemented to protect against what might involve much greater financial costs related to a security breach, they need to be commensurate [8].

To highlight this escalating issue, private industry spending on information security in the United States increased to more than $1 billion and surpassed $6.5 billion in the U.S. government, and spending has continued to rise steadily [9]. That is important to note when one considers that these costs provide zero contribution to the corporate profit margin; they are pure overhead expenses to the company along with opportunity costs. Consequently, there is an entire burgeoning field in preparedness and recovery with special emphasis placed on building cost-effective "smart, sustainable, and resilient" infrastructure [10].

6.3 Monitoring and Security Policies

Because of the costs and implications of security breaches to organizations, managers are striving to be more proactive in their security implementations. Among these techniques are the creation of security and incident response teams, increasing the provision for security training, the development of policies, and the implementation of physical and electronic countermeasures. Among the latest approaches finding its way into the security arsenal is the use of employee surveillance and monitoring. Although there are benefits to this practice, there are also many issues to consider including laws and the impact on human resources and performance [11, 12].

It is one thing to put in place countermeasures to try to prevent security breaches, and another to follow up after the fact. Employee surveillance (which we will include under various forms of monitoring) is on the rise to try to intervene in the middle as behavioral conduct unfolds *real time*. Monitoring is the physical or electronic observation of someone's activities and behavior [13]—including monitoring email, observing web browsing, listening in on telephone conversations (such as for "quality assurance purposes"), and video recording employee movements and actions.

Surveillance laws and regulations differ by country, as we indicated earlier in the chapters on laws and governance. Many countries in Europe and the United Kingdom, for example, have stringent privacy laws, as noted. In the United States, privacy has been guarded under the Fourth Amendment to the Constitution, but was weakened by the Patriot Act. Moreover, privacy in a legal sense generally pertains to those places and occasions where people have an expectation of privacy, which, for the most part, excludes public places and many areas within an organization.

Generally speaking, in the United States, common law (also called case law because it is created as cases are decided) stipulates privacy torts that have been used as grounds for lawsuits against organizations, such as intrusions into seclusion, which involves invading one's private space, and public disclosure of private facts (private facts do not include public records) [14]. In the United States, there are differences among state laws in terms of what constitutes privacy; where some states such as Arizona, California, and Florida have in their constitutions a right to privacy clause, many other states do not [15].

6.3.1 Monitoring as a Policy

Managers carry special responsibilities for stewardship over personnel and organizational resources through enforcement of company policies and practices. In the execution of their stewardship, they may be involved in the gathering of information about employees such as their performance measurements compared to their objectives and other work-related activities; but also, increasingly, managers are called upon to gather information about and enforce organizational policies that include various security practices such as monitoring access to vital corporate resources [16].

To try to head off security breaches and improve prosecutorial ability, managers are implementing employee surveillance with increasing frequency. Employers generally have the right to monitor employees and their information and anything they have or do that is in "plain sight." They also have the right to monitor information stored on their assets and to determine how these assets are accessed and used. Note that there may be legal restrictions that apply to listening in on telephone conversations or monitoring information in transit from one place to another—which can be subject to wiretap laws in the United States. Nevertheless, undoubtedly, the phrase *"This call may be monitored for quality assurance and training purposes"* has been heard by anyone who has called a customer service center or a technical support department. Why do they say this? Partly, it is to notify both the caller and the customer service agent that the call might be recorded as a way to deal with restrictions from wiretap laws that prohibit such activities [15].

A survey conducted by Harvey [17] indicated that managers regularly monitored employee web surfing. More than half reviewed email messages and examined employees' computer files, and roughly one-third tracked content, keystrokes, and time spent at the computer. In addition, employers are increasingly adding video monitoring to their monitoring repertoire [18]. Of companies surveyed [17], only 18 percent of the companies used video monitoring in 2001, but by 2005, that number had climbed to 51 percent, and 10 percent of the respondents indicated that cameras were installed specifically to track job performance. Although the trend toward increased surveillance helps in prosecution *after the fact*, it has had little effect on prevention according to research [13, 19].

If a monitoring approach to security is used, it should be outlined in security and human resource policies and employment agreements; employees (and anyone who is monitored, including customers) should be notified. For legal purposes, as we stated before, security policies must be both *enforceable* and *enforced,* so there are particular elements of these legal issues to which managers must attend. Enforceability is partly a contractual matter, and for that reason, the corporate legal and human resources departments must be involved in the drafting of security policy documents regarding monitoring and surveillance, especially if security practices include telephone or video monitoring (surveillance) of employees.

6.3.2 Information Collection and Storage

Collecting information about employees has been viewed as important to perform three major functions: (1) credentialing for the purpose of allocating access rights to physical and/or virtual locations and resources, (2) the collection and distribution of data about employees, their demographics, physical characteristics (biometrics), and their travels and actions, and (3) surveillance, which is the physical or electronic observation of someone's activities and behavior. These three elements are broadly focused on identifying employees and ensuring that only authorized persons have access to only those locations and resources to which they are authorized. The storage of surveillance and monitoring information is subject to a completely separate set of laws and regulations—and those are according to industry and purpose.

Because this is a tricky and an emerging area of law, it is extremely important to have any monitoring or surveillance measures or policies examined by the human resources department and reviewed by legal counsel before they are implemented. Not only are federal and state regulations involved, there are employment laws and statutes to be considered. On the other hand, employers may be compelled by law or regulation to monitor employees and/or information. There are times when managers can be ordered to conduct surveillance of some activity by court order.

Given the range of data collected by organizations, and the many laws and regulations involved, at this point, we will raise the idea that dealing with a breach of security such as an intrusion into a computer system by a hacker may require taking certain legal steps. If a manager ends up in a situation where he or she has to be involved in litigation, or must comply with a court order served by law enforcement, he or she needs to be prepared to present admissible evidence [14]. Computer logs and email are often not admissible by themselves without ***non-repudiation*** techniques. Non-repudiation involves generating a ***message digest*** such that a sender cannot deny sending a message, and a receiver cannot deny receiving it.

Next, the *impromptu* means of monitoring that managers have to work with, such as call monitoring, are not typically disconcerting to an outsider (such as a customer), but employees often report that they feel overly scrutinized by call monitoring. Indeed, such monitoring implies that everyone is potentially guilty of a crime [20]. This can have negative effects on positive organizational behaviors such as cooperation and information sharing. However, managers can help mitigate this concern by ensuring the preservation of organizational procedural justice—which is the perceived fairness in the process and the ability to have one's concerns addressed along with having an avenue for escalation of concerns.

In Focus

Many organizations create a position called ombudsman; this person acts as a trusted intermediary between a complainant and the organization.

6.3.3 Monitoring and Organizational Justice

This point bears repeating, especially relative to surveillance: Managers should not draft security surveillance policies without legal advice. This is because, as with policies in general, security policies carry certain legal constraints and managers may even be held personally liable. Some of these constraints fall under employment law; in other cases, laws and regulations influence or determine such policies [14]. There are also laws that govern how you enforce a policy, such as how a manager (and his or her company) can monitor employees and their information.

We have suggested that enforcement of security policies needs to be offset with the concept of organizational procedural justice. Procedural justice is perceived when the process used to make the decision is deemed fair. There are a number of conditions that lead people to perceive justice in the process. First, people want to be able to have a say or voice in any decision that might affect them. Furthermore, people want to know that managers and those with power in the organization are suspending their personal biases and motivations from decisions and are relying on objective data to the greatest possible extent. Finally, procedural justice is perceived when people are presented with a mechanism for correcting perceived errors or poor decisions, such as having an appeal process.

We might consider our behavior more carefully when we know we are being recorded. In many cases, however, people do not stop and think about the many cameras that cover traffic on highways or those that are on walkways used by law enforcement to observe and record the actions of people, because these devices are blended into the landscape. However, in most cases in organizations, it is recommended (if not required) that managers inform employees of surveillance monitoring. To gain compliance with these policies, fear appeals are often used by managers as justification for conducting surveillance of employees. As technologies become cheaper, less obtrusive, and more sophisticated, there is a growing use of both overt and covert surveillance of employees, as we noted earlier. Also worth considering is that the range and the intensity of monitoring and surveillance has expanded along two axes: first, to try to determine patterns of behaviors associated with certain characteristics (some refer to this as profiling), and second, to reduce risks associated with potential harm and/or liability to individuals and companies.

D'Urso [19] reported that as many as 80 percent of organizations now routinely use some form of electronic surveillance of employees. Vehicles, cellular phones, computers, even the consumption of electricity have become tools for monitoring people and their activities. In the workplace, employers often use video, audio, and electronic surveillance; perform physical and psychological testing, including pre-employment testing, drug-testing, collecting DNA data, and conducting searches of employees and their property; and collecting, using, and disclosing workers' personal information including biometrics.

To a degree, the use of security measures and surveillance lends to employees' general perceptions of security, but there is a point at which security measures and surveillance psychologically undermine the perceptions of security as one is, or may be, increasingly placed under scrutiny, which can affect behaviors in unintended ways [21]. At a minimum, people may repress and internalize the emotional impact of the simultaneous effects of feeling under constant threat and under constant scrutiny. Studies have shown that such persistent stress conditions may lead to as much as half of all clinical diagnoses of depression, and ongoing research shows that placing people in a continuous fearful state can permanently alter the neurological circuitry in the brain that controls emotions, and this can exaggerate later responses to stress [22].

Research [23] has shown that employee monitoring can instill a feeling of distrust, and when people don't feel trusted, they in turn tend to be untrusting, which can create a climate of fear and trepidation. In addition, imposing many monitoring policies can cause a mechanistic organizational environment where people will only perform tasks that are well defined, which limits initiative and creativity and leads to information withholding and a lack of cooperation. If a manager is not careful in considering all sides and viewpoints of the surveillance spectrum, he or she might lead the organization to self-destruction; at a minimum, surveillance can lead to increased employee absenteeism, but it can also lead to legal claims against an employer for emotional distress, harassment, or duress.

In Focus

Circularly, maladaptive social coping responses lead to increased fear, which leads to increased monitoring and surveillance, further elevating maladaptive social coping responses.

6.3.4 Surveillance and Trust

Even the most ardent applied behaviorist must acknowledge that people's psychological states lead to how they behave. An important example regarding our subject matter is related to the psychological state of trust versus distrust. Trust is developed over time, and it is largely based on a consistency in meeting mutual expectations, such as keeping confidences (i.e., avoiding betrayal) and reciprocity.

In an organizational setting, this sort of trust develops between managers and employees in a rather awkward way, because managers hold reward and punishment power over their subordinates. In this manner, employees add the perception of benevolence of their managers to their perceptions that influence trust. The extent to which employee expectations of what the organization will provide and what they owe the organization in return (reciprocity) forms the basis of what is called a **_psychological contract_**. A psychological contract is maintained so long as there is trust between the parties. There are significant relationships between a psychological contract breach and negative work-related outcomes, ranging from poor performance to sabotage.

In terms of information gathering and surveillance, the psychological contract suggests that employees expect that espoused security threats by managers are real and the monitoring of their activities are justified, and that managers will act with due care and due diligence to protect the information gathered about employees and use the information for good purposes. Because the psychological contract involves trust, and because trust is influenced by perceptions of organizational justice, the mitigation for the negative effects of surveillance relies on managers ensuring procedural justice and fostering trust in the organization.

CHAPTER SUMMARY

To sum up, when people perceive that they have control over their behavior, they tend to be more responsive to internal motivations (called "endogenous" motives) such as a sense of fair play, ethics, duty, and responsibility. Conversely, when people feel that outcomes are beyond their control, they tend to be more responsive to external motivations (called "exogenous" motives) such as punishment and deterrents. Managers must have organizational treatments for dealing with security behaviors based on the different underlying motivations and factors. It is not a one-size-fits-all proposition.

The collection of employee personal information and the practices of monitoring and surveillance are growing. There can be negative psychosocial outcomes if managers are not careful with these practices—they may backfire. To help ensure that the practices are effective and serve their intended purpose, managers must maintain the sense of managerial and organizational trust that the psychological contract depends on, and this can partly be accomplished by ensuring organizational justice.

We have now defined with a broad stroke security issues and policies and described how they fit into organizations—as well as some of the ways they specify security models and some of the roles of organizational members who are responsible for security policies. We discussed how security standards might be incorporated into commercial enterprises to improve their security, but that the rigor associated with these standards needs to be carefully weighed against other organizational considerations and priorities. We then discussed how that monitoring (surveillance) may act as an important prosecutorial tool in the case of contravention, but it can also have significant consequences for dedicated and law-abiding citizens.

We have now completed Section 1. We will turn our attention to some of the more technical aspects of security. Because the Internet has become a primary means for information interchange and electronic commerce, attacks against information resources threaten the economics in modern society; thus we will devote a fair amount of our textbook to this topic. Due to the interconnection of systems within and among organizations as a matter of globalization, such attacks can be carried out not only locally, but also anonymously and from great distances. We will next review some basics about technologies, and then move into how to implement security measures for them.

THINK ABOUT IT

Topic Questions

6.1: Computer logs or emails are often not permissible in court as evidence unless they utilize what?

6.2: What is "ALE," and what is it composed of?

6.3: The defensive coping behaviors toward chronic fear appeals to buffer or neutralize anxieties can be mitigated with what?

6.4: What is a psychological contract? And how does a psychological contract affect security-related behaviors?

6.5: Employees' expectations of what the organization will provide and of what they (the employees) owe the organization is called:

_____ Procedural justice
_____ A psychological contract
_____ An obligation
_____ A best practice

6.6: Generating a message digest such that a sender cannot deny sending a message and a receiver cannot deny receiving it is called:

_____ Non-repudiation
_____ A security stance
_____ The Biba model
_____ Psychological contract

6.7: ISO 15408 is also known as:

_____ The threat control model (TCM)
_____ The orange book
_____ Trusted Computing Base
_____ Common Criteria

6.8: The physical or electronic observation of someone's activities and behavior:

_____ Is a privacy violation
_____ Is a violation of the Fourth Amendment to the Constitution
_____ Is called surveillance
_____ Is not permitted in an organization

6.9: A person who acts as a trusted intermediary between a complainant and the organization is called a(n):

_____ Ombudsman
_____ Corporate attorney
_____ Broker
_____ Moderator

6.10: Corporate monitoring of phone conversations is NEVER permitted in the United States because of wiretap laws.

_____ True
_____ False

Questions for Further Study

Q6.1: What are some ways that management in organizations use *fear appeals* to make their workforce vigilant against security threats?

Q6.2: Can you think of some ways that using fear appeals can backfire and lead to counterproductive behaviors?

Q6.3: What are some of the differences between monitoring centers, offsite storage facilities, replication centers, and disaster recovery centers? Discuss what each is used for and why the distinctions.

Q6.4: Give five examples or situations of a psychological contract.

Q6.5: How can managers protect themselves from complaints of unfairness in monitoring employees?

KEY CONCEPTS AND TERMS

Clark and Wilson is a transaction-oriented model defined by ACID properties.

Countermeasures are proactive implementations of what a policy might establish.

Information architecture is divided into macro- and micro-levels.

Organic organizational cooperation that enables company adaptation and agility

is at odds with the concept of separation of duties.

Surveillance laws and regulations differ by country, state, and local levels.

References

1. Morrogh, E. (2003). *Information architecture: An emerging 21st century profession.* Upper Saddle River, NJ: Prentice-Hall.

2. Carges, M., Belisle, D., & Workman, M. (1990). *The portable operating system interface: Distributed database transaction processing systems and the XA protocol.* IEEE Standard 1003.11 & X/Open-POSIX. Parsipanny NJ: ISO/IEC.

3. Straub, D. W., Carlson, P., & Jones, E. (1993). Deterring cheating by student programmers: A field experiment in computer security. *Journal of Management Systems, 5,* 33–48.

4. Solomon, M. G., & Chapple, M. (2005). *Information security illuminated.* Sudbury, MA: Jones and Bartlett Publishers.

5. Williams, B. R. (2009). Risk management follies. *The ISSA Journal, 7,* 6–7.

6. Sine, W. D., Mitsuhashi, H., & Kirsch, D. A. (2006). Revisiting Burns and Stalker: Formal structure and new venture performance in emerging economic sectors. *Academy of Management Journal, 49,* 121–132.

7. Tjaden, B. C. (2004). *Fundamentals of security computer systems.* Wilsonville, OR: Franklin, Beedle, & Associates.

8. Workman, M., & Gathegi, J. (2007). Punishment and ethics deterrents: A comparative study of insider security contravention. *Journal of American Society for Information Science and Technology, 58,* 318–342.

9. Workman, M. (2008). Mobility security and human behavior. In C. Bragdon (Ed.), *Transportation security* (pp. 71–95). Boston, MA: Elsevier/Butterworth-Heinemann.

10. Bragdon, C. R. (2008). *Transportation security.* Amsterdam, the Netherlands: Elsevier/Butterworth-Heinemann.

11. Hansen, K. L. (2002). Anxiety in the workplace post-September 11, 2001. *The Public Manager, 31,* 133–151.

12. Greenemeier, L. (2006, April). The fear industry. *Information Week,* pp. 35–49.

13. Workman, M. (2009). A field study of corporate employee monitoring: Attitudes, absenteeism, and the moderating influences of procedural justice perceptions. *Information and Organization, 19,* 218–232.

14. Fischer, R. J., & Green, G. (1992). *Introduction to security*. Boston, MA: Butterworth-Heinemann.

15. Grama, J. L. (2011). *Legal issues in information security*. Sudbury, MA: Jones & Bartlett Learning.

16. Thomas, T. (2004). *Network security*. Indianapolis, IN: Cisco Press.

17. Harvey, C. (2007, April). The boss has new technology to spy on you. *Datamation*, pp. 1–5.

18. Fairweather, B. N. (1999). Surveillance in employment: The case of teleworking. *Journal of Business Ethics, 22*, 39–49.

19. D'Urso, S. C. (2006). Who's watching us at work? Toward a structural-perceptual model of electronic monitoring and surveillance in organizations. *Communication Theory, 16*, 281–303.

20. Langenderfer, J., & Linnnhoff, S. (2005). The emergence of biometrics and its effect on consumers. *Journal of Consumer Affairs, 39*, 314–338.

21. Holman, D., Chissick, C., & Totterdell, P. (2002). The effects of performance monitoring on emotional labor and well-being in call centers. *Motivation and Emotion, 26*, 57–81.

22. Lee, S., & Kleiner, B. H. (2003). Electronic surveillance in the workplace. *Management Research News, 26*, 72–81.

23. Workman, M., Bommer, W., & Straub, D. (2009). The amplification effects of procedural justice with a threat control model of information systems security. *Journal of Behavior and Information Technology, 28*, 563–575.

Technology Orientation for Managers

Data, Information, and Systems

I N THE PREVIOUS SECTION, WE discussed organizational concerns and issues for security, and now we will cover more technical ones. In these next few chapters, we shall try to define terms and build up common technical knowledge so that when we cover security, sufficient technical understanding will have been developed. In other words, some of the materials in this section may not seem obviously connected to information security, but when we cover securing systems and networks, the connections should become more apparent. In this chapter, we will preview and survey some important technological concepts and define some terms so that as they come up again in subsequent topics, you will be familiar with them.

Chapter 7 Topics

This chapter:

- Discusses business strategy, operations, and tactics as they relate to information and systems.
- Explains information systems technology and software used in organizations.
- Describes data integration and middleware and the movement of information across entities.
- Explores database and data warehouse concepts and designs.
- Deals with service-oriented architecture (SOA), markup languages, and web service technology.

Chapter 7 Goals

When you finish this chapter, you should:

- ❑ Know the differences between data and information.
- ❑ Understand what information systems are and how information is shared and integrated within and among enterprises.
- ❑ Become familiar with relational database architecture and design, along with basic concepts related to information storage and retrieval.
- ❑ Be able to discuss the implementation of markup languages and service-oriented architecture in relation to information integration and the Internet.

7.1 Information Systems

When people think about information systems, most often computers come to mind. An information system (IS), however, extends to all organizational information infrastructure including networks, hard copies of documents, computer server rooms, and even physical storage vaults. The primary purpose of an information system is to facilitate the business and its mission. In this preview chapter, we will focus on (1) computer systems, (2) the networks that connect them, and (3) software applications and databases—both in terms of how they are constructed and how they are used.

Along with facilitating businesses and effectively operating in a global marketplace, managers must simultaneously consider the practicality of securing systems and information to prevent breaches or damage. Where many managers see security as an *overhead cost of doing business*, security is rather like the concept of quality—that is, although these measures may not directly affect the financial bottom line (except negatively as a financial outlay), having poor security (and quality) will indirectly affect the bottom line. For example, consider poor quality on brand reputation or a major security breach on customer trust.

Information and communications systems can be attacked from anywhere in the world nowadays, and this sometimes leaves managers with little or no recourse, unless there has been good planning followed by good actions. Although information and communications technologies can be used unethically and for dubious purposes, the technologies themselves are **value neutral**, meaning that it is up to people who apply the technologies whether to use them for good or for bad purposes. Before managers can understand how to protect their information infrastructure, they must understand important aspects of how all that works (at least at a high level). That means that before we can really appreciate each of the technological components of security concern, we need to lay some foundations—and so let's do that by developing our conceptions of the differences between data and information, which will lead into overviews of technologies and concepts that we will elaborate on in subsequent chapters in this section and discuss in more detail relative to security in the section that follows.

7.1.1 The Nature of Data and Information

Data are raw facts without much context. Examples might simply be numbers such as 16, 18, 21, 23, 30, 50, and 65. These numbers have little or no meaning in isolation, unless we add a little bit of context to these raw data such as *age = 21*. Even then, a person may only infer what this might mean—based on his or her environment, culture, or more specifically, cognitive schema (cognitive schemas are mental models and expectations one develops about the future based on past experience). Information, on the other hand, is contextually enriched data. For example, if we explained that in Florida, the legal age for consuming alcoholic beverages is age 21, but the largest consumers of alcoholic beverages are boys ages 18 to 19, we are now talking about information. Thus you can see that the main difference between data and information is that information has data, but it is contextually enriched such that it is more meaningful.

Among their core features, information systems (IS) facilitate the processes that contextually enrich data to support business functions such as marketing, finance, operations, and human resources management. IS includes applications that help with product requirements for gathering, planning, development, and testing of various IS components. For example, they may consist of supply chain management (SCM) systems, which help enterprise requirement specialists plan *just-in-time* shipping and receiving and other logistical aspects to ensure minimal cost delivery of products for on-time deliveries. IS may include customer relationship management (CRM) systems, which help the marketing and sales teams track and manage sales prospects and revenue pipelines, or IS may simply represent the underlying technological infrastructure—such as computers, operating systems, programs, and networks.

Information systems are designed to support strategic, tactical, and operational levels of information processing and decision making. Because these are so fundamental to business processes and missions, the technological functions in most organizations typically have a dedicated department, often called Operations, Technical Support, Information Technology (IT), or the Management Information Systems (MIS) department. Increasingly, organizations are adding security departments called Office of Security (OoS), or Security Assurance and Administration (SAA). These latter two types of departments specialize in planning and overseeing security operations, tactics, and strategies—and they are often overseen by a Chief Information Security Officer (CISO).

7.1.2 IS Operations, Tactics, and Strategies

Having sufficient data is important to daily business and tactical operations, which are used in the execution of organizational strategies. The important thing to note here is that information and systems security aims at maintaining business operations. There is no other reason for security other than to act as a function to help ensure that businesses are able to operate. With this in mind, let's approach some important aspects of information and systems at the operational, tactical, and strategic levels.

We pointed out earlier that data are raw numbers that describe the characteristics of an object or a transaction; for instance, a sales transaction might include the date of the sale, the description of the item, an item number such as a stock-keeping unit (SKU), quantity sold, and so forth. On the other hand, information makes the data useful. For example, information helps managers determine losses from thefts or risks associated with a sole supplier going out of business.

As illustrated, information used at the operational level is primarily associated with day-to-day events that transpire as the result of doing business; at the operational level, managers may want to know, for example, how much money was made and spent in a day, or what is left in the inventory. By contrast, information at the strategic level may involve understanding what the best-selling items are and why, what the margins are on sales items, or where the most and least profitable districts or regions are located. Collectively, information used in operational, tactical, and strategic aspects of organizational processes and decision making helps managers align plans with goals—such as in meeting sales objectives or targeted returns on investments, or maintaining just-in-time inventory stock levels to enhance profitability, finding new markets, differentiating products from competitors, and gaining advantages with buyers and suppliers over rivals [1].

In Focus

In relation to security, data and information are just like data and information for running the business—they allow managers to assess risks and threats to information and systems, and they are used in operational, tactical, and strategic security initiatives.

Depending on the nature of the data or information, and their uses, technologies organize, store, retrieve, and process data and information differently, and there are a variety of security requirements to accompany them. The basis for these stratifications falls under the rubric of information architecture. The notion of information architecture helps managers to conceptualize the areas where data, information, systems, and technologies should be applied across horizontal and vertical strata [2]. Horizontal strata are those functions that cross functional boundaries, whereas vertical strata are those that represent departments or lines of business.

Suppose that in your organization there was a compromise of data—the strata at which the data were compromised would affect different aspects of the corporation. The horizontal strata (meaning the technologies and their rendered information that facilitate all of an organization's decision making) consist of business architecture, data architecture, and communications architecture. A horizontal stratum therefore may support the operations across the entire organization, called the "*value chain.*" The vertical stratum, on the other hand, may involve the flows of the information within each of the lines of business (LOBs) at the operational, tactical, and strategic levels

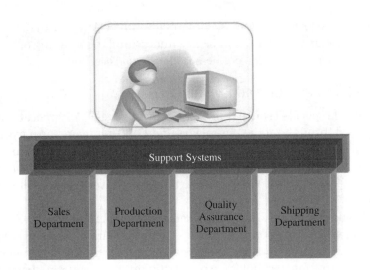

FIGURE 7.1

Line of business (LOB) integration.

(**Figure 7.1**). Consequently, some of the information is used in carrying out primary business activities, which are those that go directly toward the production and delivery of products and services, and other data and information are supportive (or secondary) in that they involve overhead and infrastructure used in the execution of the primary business activities [3].

In Focus

A critical point is that operations and tactics must be thought of holistically (sometimes called systemically) with the larger strategic mission of the organization. Relative to security, then, managers must consider the nature of information in terms of protections, and consequences in cases of security breaches.

From an information architecture perspective, security encapsulates all of the protections of information, including accidental or intentional misuse or abuse by people inside or outside the organization. Most engineers and designers in today's world understand this, but other factors, such as pressures to meet a production deadline or to stay within a budget regarding expenditures, may detract from security objectives. Beyond those competing goals, simply by virtue of the complexity of systems that involve multinational participants in a global marketplace, can be found information security risks and vulnerabilities. Although there are technological aspects of these risks that are well recognized, some major concerns are non-technical. To highlight, as is often asked in a security briefing, when someone purports that so-and-so has presented commentary on threats, trust, or credentials, the security officer may often respond: "How do *you* know?"

Realize then that data are necessary but not sufficient for making a meaningful decision. Adding context that transforms data may be useful to indicate a current operational picture of a situation into some sort of action, but to make inferences and draw upon more robust meanings, something else is needed! Most systems today help with the data-to-information transformation (along with integration of data sources), but many if not most are quite weak in helping human beings understand the meaning of the information. The term used to describe this problem is *information overload*.

7.1.3 Information Integration and Exchange

A recent IDC technical report [4] stated that there is an average of 48 applications and 14 databases deployed throughout the typical Fortune 1000 company. Even with data warehouse systems, distributed systems technologies, and various standards that have been implemented to mitigate the problem of what is commonly called *information silos*, information continues to remain isolated in departments or in vertical lines of business within enterprises.

The problem is made worse when information must traverse across enterprises and among trading partners. Among the issues encountered are (1) reduced management visibility of strategic resources, (2) redundant, inaccurate, and otherwise obsolete information, (3) increased infrastructure and technology expense to maintain the information redundancy or to build custom connections and interfaces to tap into these orphaned data sources, (4) technology limitations that preclude the full use of organizational assets, and (5) the inability to efficiently and effectively transact business with customers and trading partners.

Since the 1970s, **Electronic Data Interchange** (**EDI**) formats and standards have emerged in an effort to bring structure and order to the information integration problem. However, even with the development of EDI protocols such as X.12 and EDIFACT, each implementation has required individualized and customized work to adapt to each node in a communications network. This custom approach can be expensive, time-consuming, and static, requiring modification as the result of each change. According to IDC [4], 70 percent of the average IT department budget is devoted to data integration projects. This is because multiple standards continue to exist, and many are incompatible with one another.

Combined with nuances in nearly every business entity and application, the process of exchanging information remains extremely complex and time-consuming to implement. Recently, the Gartner Group reported that a typical enterprise devoted 35–40 percent of its development budget to programs whose sole purpose was to transfer information between different databases and legacy systems. Although a variety of solutions emerged to address the problem by providing interconnection among disparate systems, these solutions have tended to require customized modules and have required many staging points where security may be compromised. They also tend to build custom software modules that "plug in" between specific, popular commercial software applications and sometimes require system administrators to lower the security posture to permit communications among disparate communication environments.

To help integrate the data and information across organizational lines of business, or LOBs, many companies use **middleware**. As the name implies, this software intervenes between applications and system software or between two different kinds of application software so that information can be exchanged among disparate sources and systems and data types such as integers, floating point numbers, and text strings. Middleware bridges different network protocols; translates, manipulates, and formats different data types through a workflow process; and executes rules such as how to handle errors if they occur. One major class of middleware is known as **enterprise application integration** (**EAI**). EAI is specifically designed for integrating and consolidating information among the computer applications in an enterprise.

A common EAI function is to extract data from legacy applications, such as those running on a mainframe computer, with more modern systems such as distributed systems or across desktop platforms. They can also extract, translate, and load (ETL) data among different databases or allow the coexistence of two systems during a migration from one to the other by creating ways for the information to flow to each system in parallel. Some EAI systems require programming, and they use object and message *brokers* (called **object request brokers** [**ORBs**]). Other EAI do not require programming and instead use a **business process modeling language** (**BPML**) or web services in **service-oriented architecture** (**SOA**).

Enterprise resource planning (**ERP**) systems are another class of middleware, and these are used to plan and manage production "just in time" by coordinating the supply to the delivery in the production value chain. Therefore, ERP software applications help to manage product release cycles, ordering of materials, automating the purchasing process, managing inventory levels, transacting with suppliers, and tracking customer service requests and orders. **Business process management** (**BPM**) is similar to ERP, but it revolves around the business processes in the enterprise. BPM can create workflows, interface with ERP systems to trigger events or pass information among interdependent parties within the production line, and provide managers with information on how well business processes are tracking to key performance indicators (KPIs) and in meeting corporate objectives.

In Focus

It is important to realize that systems that help gather and integrate information to facilitate business functions also leave open many opportunities for security exploits at the application, storage, computer, and networking levels.

Critical information and KPIs are usually displayed on a "dashboard" or a graphical reporting system or printed with a report generator. A graphical user interface (GUI) is a visual display system. It can be a specialized monitor for showing network activity, railroad switching, or power grids, or it can display web content via a browser. GUIs provide features such as pull-down menus, buttons, scroll bars, ribbons, and mouse-driven navigation.

7.2 Databases

Software applications, for the most part, lead to the creation and/or consumption of data. If we need to store the data to be used in or across applications, the most suitable form is a database system, or **database management systems** (**DBMS**), designed to manage simultaneous access to shared data. Most modern database systems are relational, although there are others such as hierarchical and object-oriented databases. When data are stored into a database, we call this **persistence**.

A **relational database management system** (**RDBMS**) organizes data into tables that contain **keys**, so the indices remain coupled to the data that are related across tables. Tables in RDBMS are connected via **primary** and **foreign** keys. These form the linkages that preserve data relationships. When a set of data related to a transaction, such as retrieval of invoice data, is to be reconstructed from a database query, it requires a procedure called a "join" wherein criteria from all the related tables are gathered and a **result set** or a **view** is produced and returned to the software application that made the request. **Data warehouses** are similar in some respects to RDBMS, but they are used more for analytical processes than transactional ones, and so their data are structured, persisted, and retrieved differently from RDBMS.

7.2.1 Relational Databases

Relational databases contain tables of data, which are arranged into rows and columns. Rows represent a "record," whereas columns represent individual elements or concepts. Tables generally contain a primary key to uniquely identify a row and sometimes carry foreign keys, which represent keys in other tables to which a table is related. Consider **Tables 7.1** through **7.4**.

If you carefully study the tables presented, and knowing that a primary key must be unique and that there can be many foreign keys associated with it (one to many), you

TABLE 7.1   Customer Table

CUSTOMER ID (PRIMARY KEY [PK])	CUSTOMER NAME	CUSTOMER BILLING ADDRESS	ZIP CODE (FOREIGN KEY [FK])
1776	eAselworx	1221 My Street	01463
1843	Objectware	875 High Road	30004
1992	CINSec	282 Main Street	32327
2882	SPInstitute	171 Security Drive	32901

TABLE 7.2   Zip Codes Table

ZIP CODE (PK)	CITY	STATE (FOREIGN KEY [FK])
01463	Pepperell	Massachusetts
30004	Alpharetta	Georgia
32326	Crawfordville	Florida
32327	Crawfordville	Florida
32901	Melbourne	Florida
32940	Melbourne	Florida

TABLE 7.3	State Table
STATE (PK)	
Alabama	
California	
Florida	
Georgia	
Massachusetts	
Utah	

TABLE 7.4	Invoice Table		
INVOICE NUMBER (PK)	**INVOICE AMOUNT**	**INVOICE DATE**	**CUSTOMER ID (FK)**
A7543	$2,445.50	04/14/2012	1776
X2122	$3,559.60	05/01/2012	1843

can see that a customer must be uniquely identified by a customer number. The customer has a name and a billing address, which resides in a zip code (for our billing purposes, although it may be physically located in multiple jurisdictions), and the billing address is tied to a particular zip code, because these are unique also. In the zip codes table, there can be only one zip code per location (hence it is a primary key), but zip codes may span one or more cities, so we may not choose to make the city in the table a key. Consider, for example, the cities of Jacksonville, Florida, and Jacksonville, Arkansas. Cities of the same name may appear in multiple states, so we might want to allow duplicate city names even though that may seem inefficient. However, a zip code resides uniquely in a state and city, so we want to associate the zip code with the particular state we want to reference. That will allow the software to determine whether we are talking about Jacksonville, Arkansas, or Jacksonville, Florida.

The important takeaway from this slightly technical discussion is that even though a concept appears in a column more than once, structured this way, the RDBMS is smart enough to know not to duplicate the actual data—it simply creates an internal reference from one concept to an associated one—but at design time, we do it this way to make it easier for humans to visualize. This is critical to ensure a database that is efficient and to still maintain a high level of integrity maintenance in the database—and integrity is an important security concept and issue.

Next in the database configuration we have presented, when we reference a particular invoice, we can pull (like an interlocking set of chain links) all the data we need into an application. Note, though, that there are a few particulars: First, we want to minimize the frequency in which a particular concept (column) occurs. In other words, we have a state table that lists each state only once. Why should we have the state of Florida repeated over and over again in a table if we don't have to? That will only bloat our database and cause greater potential for failures. Second, we must, at all costs, try to avoid adding tables when we add new data. That can be catastrophic!

Finally, as is visible from the tables, there are inherent structures and relationships among them. Relational databases are organized (modeled) into various tables, and their relationships are called normal forms. For instance, the data, such as 30004, are given some context by naming the column "zip code." This label, along with other information, can be supplied in an RDBMS and is known as metadata (data about data). Examples include constraining how long an input can be, whether it is alphanumeric or strictly numeric, whether it has a particular format such as a date, and so on.

7.2.2 Relational Databases and Maintaining Data Integrity

Designing a relational database begins with entity-relationship modeling, which produces an ***entity-relationship diagram*** (ERD). An ERD reflects the entities (tables) and the relationships among them. An important element in the relationships is ***cardinality***, such as whether one table necessarily depends on data in another table (called mandatory), whether there might be associated data that are not essential (called optional), whether there is a one-to-one relationship between one entity and another, or whether there is a one-to-many relationship. For example, a teacher must teach (mandatory) many classes, so perhaps a teachers table would contain columns for teacher ID numbers, names, and departments, and probably has a one-to-many relationship with a classes table. The concept of a key is important in forming these relationships, as we pointed out before. A key uniquely identifies a group of data, such as a student ID number to uniquely identify a student in a students table. *Primary keys* (PK) are these sorts of indicators, but *foreign keys* (FK) are links from other tables to associate one table with the others. For example, a student ID number might be a PK in a students table and an FK in a classes table.

An important security concept in the design of relational database tables is to maintain data integrity, and the process of properly designing a relational database to protect data integrity (by removing anomalies) is called normalization [5, 6]. There are seven normal forms [7], and the higher the normal form, the more work the database does to protect the integrity of the data. However, increased normalization also tends to increase the number of tables, which can hurt the performance of the RDBMS. For this reason, most databases implement partially normalized database models [8].

In addition to normalization, another important design aspect involves what are called ***integrity constraints***. The constraints can be applied to records, tables, and relationships among tables. A DBMS can, for example, automatically check the data being stored to ensure that their data types and formatting are what the database expects. Within most RDBMSs, such as Oracle or SQLServer, data integrity may also involve using **triggers** and **stored procedures** that force the removal of linked data. Microsoft Access does not support triggers or stored procedures; however, it does have a type of trigger mechanism by a checkbox in a dialog box that says, "Enforce referential integrity." Access also allows programmers to write macros to do something similar to stored procedures.

In Focus

Integrity constraints can be set at different levels. Record-level integrity constraints can check the data type and format to ensure that only valid data are entered in the database. For example, you can set up an input mask when you design the table so that no characters other than 0–9 can be entered as a social security number. The DBMS can also automatically monitor the data change at table level using the constraints you set. A simple, automatically built constraint is "no duplicated primary keys are allowed." At this level, the DBMS will check whether deleting or modifying a record may damage the relationship among tables.

Another important aspect of maintaining integrity deals with the concept of ***concurrency***, meaning to coordinate the interactions among multiple users who are reading and writing to a database through what is called "locking." When a user updates data in a database, the data must be locked so that no other user can corrupt the data during the process. This issue leads to a question of whether to handle data integrity in a software application or in the database, or a combination of both, but data integrity must be maintained regardless. We can do almost all of the integrity management in the database by eliminating the design anomalies by increasing the normalization. However, the more normal the database, the more tables we tend to have, and consequently, more "cross-table access and locking" are needed, making for less efficient database access.

In Focus

The integrity of data must be maintained either in the database or by an application. The more normalized a database, the more it helps to ensure the integrity of the data. Databases should be normalized to at least Third Normal Form to avoid the worst types of anomalies caused by what are called transitive dependencies. For most databases (depending on the size of the database), Third Normal Form provides a straddle point, which means an optimal compromise, between integrity and efficiency. But that means that the application must filter and manage the integrity of data where that job is not given to the database—there are tradeoffs!

From a security point of view, these principles are particularly important because they deal with the issue of data integrity as we have discussed, and if we do not do good work in the design and in database housekeeping, the bad guys might be able to more easily exploit the database. Data and information are assets, no less than the computers we work on. As databases become more exposed to networking, managers and administrators need to maintain vigilance. Some protections that must be in place include using password protections, using access controls to determine to what data users have access, and defining the levels of access the users can have such as read only, adding data, adding tables, deleting tables, and so forth, as we shall discuss later under the concepts of SQL injection and other database attacks.

7.2.3 Data Warehouses

Where relational databases are used for operational and tactical transactions in the business, data warehouses are used more for strategic aspects using analytics. This is important because to thrive, companies must find ways to reduce risk and create new products to position themselves differently. They must deliberately choose a set of products or services that provide a unique mix of value at lower risk. A company can outperform its rivals only if it can establish such a difference that it can preserve. This requires a different set of technologies than those used for storing and retrieving transactional data.

To facilitate this "strategic positioning," data warehouses are used along with data mining techniques. These technologies and techniques help managers determine how to differentiate their products, find untapped markets, determine competitive threats, and determine who the "best" and "worst" customers are. These fill a critical role in strategic managerial decisions—whether regarding the business or security.

In the vernacular of a data warehouse, inbound channels are information collection points for the database system, which may come from extranets, the Internet, or other sources, and are persisted into mass storage devices. Often, data warehouse information is further extracted out into smaller databases, called "marts," by a given topic, such as "sales."

Analytic tools can then be used to scan the information by key indicators to monitor trends and detect changes in business patterns. This process may include, for example, monitoring sales and profits related to a new sales campaign. As a further example, a certain demographic may show a higher risk when the numbers of transactions involving this demographic develop large enough to become statistically significant. This, combined with information from industry partners housed in an information repository, enables companies to gain visibility of this strategic information and utilize a wide range of tools to analyze and augment their product offering, improve their positioning, and avoid marginal or high-loss customers. Analytical tools can be used to monitor the inbound channels, extracting out data in a process using extract-transform-load (ETL) techniques. ETL, using a variety of knowledge discovery methods, transforms and integrates the extracted data into useful business information.

To illustrate, suppose we have gathered data via a point-of-sales (POS) cash register and web browsing (click-stream) of our website, along with other sources, and we now want to persist all that in an operational database, such as a relational database presented earlier. That could be a problem. Instead, we aggregate all these data into a data warehouse, which in some ways resembles a relational database except that the tables are not normalized and are instead organized to store massive amounts of data by other categories such as dates, topics, or clients.

Once we have collected the data, we want to use it to help us in making effective decisions about the business (or security for that matter). Because a data warehouse primarily deals with business concepts such as customers or regulations and so on, rather than on transactional concepts such as purchases or debits and credits, we need effective ways to select the information we desire and then efficiently analyze it. To accommodate these needs, according to Inmon, Imhoff, and Sousa [9], a data warehouse then is (1) subject oriented rather than transaction oriented, (2) designed to be integrated with other systems, (3) time variant, meaning that any record in the data warehouse environment should be accurate relative to a given—specified—moment in time, (4) non-volatile, which refers to the fact that an update does not normally occur in a data warehouse during a specified timeframe; instead, updates only occur on an exception basis. When changes do occur, the time variant snapshot captures only the changes. As a series of snapshots forms, a historical record is formed. Finally, data warehouses (5) can contain both summary and detailed data, but the data are organized in a hierarchical fashion.

7.2.4 Extract-Transform-Load (ETL)

Data are loaded into a data warehouse from heterogeneous data sources, but first they must be subjected to some data transformation using "data-scrubbing tools." For example, when we surf the Web and visit a site, we may click on various links on that web page. Software watches where we click (this is called a click-stream). Software extracts that click-stream and throws away any clicks that are not on links or perhaps even just on some links, and this is called data scrubbing. The data are then indexed using some company-defined indexing scheme, based on what the company wants to know about its visitors. Perhaps the company may even deposit a text file onto a client called a "cookie" to track these electronic movements. The data are then loaded into a data warehouse.

Because of the volume of data that ends up in this warehouse, as noted earlier, sometimes companies resort to using "data marts," or smaller distributed database warehouses, which are collections of data adapted to a particular need. Data in the *marts* are subsets of data from the warehouse that have been tailored to fit the requirements of a department within a company and contain a small amount of detailed data along with summarized data.

It is important to realize that the quality of the data existing in the data warehouse must be protected and that data warehouse extraction must be well organized to enable users to make decisions quickly and effectively. Hence, data quality management is vital to the success of the data warehousing strategy and to security in particular. Extraction tools are a significant part of this. An extraction tool must be able to gain legitimate access to and extract all of the required—but only the relevant—operational data requested [10].

In Focus

Data warehouses are common and important to security because they can help managers look for patterns that might suggest information leakage or planning for sophisticated information or systems attacks.

To transform information contained in data warehouses, we may use online analytical processing (OLAP) technologies or data mining technologies. Although these differ in fundamental ways, data mining and OLAP are both used for gathering business and security intelligence. Data mining and OLAP fall into the category of decision support systems (DSS). DSS have been around for many decades, but recent advances in technology have changed what they do and how they are used. Most decision support systems offer managers or other users such as administrators "canned" (preconfigured) reports. These are basic, predefined, and formatted reports that users run to get a snapshot of current business activity. A requisite for canned reports is a well-defined business question to query against. Submitting free-form (ad hoc) questions to a database is the next logical step in the evolution of reporting. After receiving hard copy reports, business users inevitably have additional questions. OLAP thus takes various forms (slicing and dicing the data by various dimensions and, with complex multi-statement queries, producing multi-dimensional views called cubes), but the common denominator of these forms is that they provide analyses combined with relatively fast, consistent, and inter-active access to data from a variety of perspectives.

On the other hand, data mining is much more laborious. With data mining, the analytical tool identifies hypotheses from patterns that emerge, and they tell users where in the data to start the exploration process. Rather than using OLAP statements to filter out values or methodically reduce data into a concise result set, data mining uses algorithms that statistically review the relationships among data elements to determine if patterns exist. There are many kinds of data mining and analytic processes that break data into sets according to some category or grouping, including cluster analysis, which uses statistical approaches to finding patterns from massive amounts of data, and predictive modeling. We will cover these in more detail when we get to the last section of our textbook in the chapters on using data mining and predictive modeling related to security threats.

7.3 Distributed Systems and Information

Until now in this chapter, we have concentrated on data, information, and systems, in-cluding how data are transformed into information. We have also covered some high-level concepts related to storage and retrieval, and later we will get into more of the technical mechanics of these functions. At this stage, we will introduce the topic of distributed systems and present two major technical approaches that enable us to distribute systems and information. In other words, we may think of these as the means by which enterprise information integration is done and how applications such as enterprise requirements planning are enabled.

7.3.1 Globalization and Information Exchange

We know that information is shared, integrated, and stored on an enterprise level, and we also know that information is exchanged across organizations by means of various communications technologies. Thomas Friedman suggested that ***globalization*** has been behind the increases in networked and distributed systems. He defined globalization as the interweaving of markets, technology, information, and telecommunications systems in such a way that is *shrinking the world and enabling us to reach around it* [11].

According to Friedman, the world broke away from the *Cold War* system where *division* was an overarching principle, and moved in the direction of *integration*. In this new global framework, all opportunities increasingly flow from interconnections symbolized by the Web. Along these lines, we encounter the term **network effects**. Simply put, the value of a product or service increases with the number of people who use it. Here the term *network* refers to the objects (and ultimately people) that are either logically or physically connected to one another. A typical example to illustrate the concept is the telephone. If only one telephone existed, we could say that it would have virtually no value, but as we add telephones, their value increases exponentially with the number of possible connections. With email we see an even greater increase in value because theoretically everyone who has an email account can send a message to anyone they choose at the same time. Although some have taken the position that it was networking and distributed systems that fueled globalization, rather than the other way around, there is no mistaking that both are interdependent.

> **In Focus**
>
> Although email remains an important tool, social media and rich Internet applications on mobile devices are overtaking email as primary communications facilities.

Applications such as word processing programs help fuel network effects. Here the product is not physically interconnected, as is true of the telephone or email system, but the fact that a large number of people in the world use Microsoft Word increases the value of having that particular software compared to the value of owning other, less popular word processing programs. Bob Metcalfe, who was involved in the development of the network medium called **Ethernet** and who founded the 3Com company, proposed a formula to quantify the concept of *network effects*, which became known as Metcalfe's law.

> **In Focus**
>
> Metcalfe's law states that the value of a network—that is, its utility to a population—is roughly proportional to the number of users squared.

If we apply Metcalfe's law to network computing, we would say that when there is only one computer, the value stays at 1, but when there are 10 computers connected in a local area network (LAN), the value soars to 100. In other words, the benefit gains are exponential. Of course, this is only one way to illustrate the power of networking, but the concept of *network effects* is a useful way of describing some of the phenomena related to the Internet consumer market. Many networking companies cut prices below costs in the hopes that they could gain a critical mass of early adopters. Managers at these companies hoped that by attracting people to their products and services a strategic advantage would be gained. Later, if customers wanted to switch to a comparable competitor product, significant value would be lost; this is the so-called "customer lock-in" and explains why some people continue to use one operating system even when they say they would prefer to use a different one.

Network effects can play out in a number of different ways and situations. For instance, we could say that a large number of freely available web browsers such as Firefox, Opera, and Internet Explorer helped to create rich Internet content and applications because authors and publishers of information knew that they would have a large potential audience. Standards bodies such as the W3C also play a key role in determining network effects; thus, the concept of network effects provides a useful lens through which to view the diffusion of innovative technology as well as the security issues related to them.

7.3.2 Distributed Systems Architecture

At the beginning of this chapter, we presented some applications such as CRM that rely on the concept of "distributed systems." Distributed systems are applications that run on multiple computers (connected via networks) to complete a business function or transaction. A commonly recognized distributed system is a website for a large commercial enterprise such as Amazon.com. Suppose, for example, that we wanted to purchase a textbook online and we accessed a website called *www.mybooksandmusic.com* to make the purchase. It is unlikely that the textbook we want will be sitting in some warehouse that the company maintains. Instead, the company may act as an electronic storefront for publishers. The mybooksandmusic.com systems would communicate with various publisher systems to place orders on demand. It is also not likely that a single computer is handling our transaction. It is more likely that mybooksandmusic.com has myriad computers that process customer requests.

One of the more common distributed systems architectures is called an *n-tier* configuration. This means that there are multiple server computers that are connected horizontally and vertically. Using our website analogy, a horizontal connection among servers would be a collection of web servers that handle the vast number of users who want to connect to the mybooksandmusic website. These "front-end" servers would handle the display of the information and the user interaction. The front-end servers would then be connected via a network to a middle tier of systems that process the business logic, such as placing orders with the book suppliers or performing calculations such as shipping costs. The middle-tier servers connect via a network to database servers where, perhaps, catalog and customer information is stored.

The term n-tier means that the company can have many servers at each of these three horizontal layers (**Figure 7.2**). As the company's business grows, mybooksandmusic.com can simply add servers where they are needed; for example, if there are many new users who want to purchase books or music online, a server could be added to the front-end tier; if many new suppliers were added to the business, another server could be added to the middle tier, and as our data stores grow, we can add a server to the database tier. This separation of layers or tiers helps with both extensibility and security.

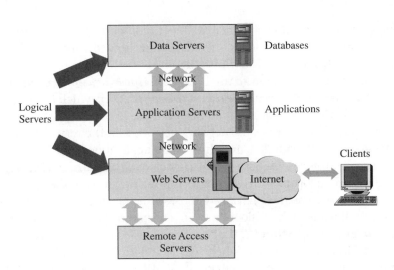

FIGURE 7.2

N-tier layered systems.

Some of the technologies that are used in distributed systems are "tightly coupled"; by that we mean they are written in technologies that require programs to coordinate through standard interfaces and share some components. An example of this would be an ***object request broker*** (**ORB**), of which there are three major ones: (1) those built on the Object Management Group's (OMG) Common Object Request Broker Architecture (CORBA), (2) the Distributed Component Object Model (DCOM) from Microsoft, and (3) the Remote Method Invocation (RMI) from Sun Microsystems/Oracle. With these distributed technologies, programmers write interfaces—which consist of data definitions and types that distributed programs expect, along with the names of functions that distributed programs can call. Programmers must also generate connector components (often called stubs and skeletons), which tell the distributed programs how to locate and communicate with each other.

An alternative to this "tightly coupled" approach is what is often called ***service-oriented architecture*** (**SOA**). A conventional description of SOA is that it is an ability to loosely couple information for disparate systems and provide services through proxy structures [12]. To try to ground this abstract idea, let's utilize some examples beginning with a question: What if a computer system needed to transact business with some other computer system in the network cloud with no prior knowledge of the other system or prearrangement for how to communicate?

In Focus

Service-oriented architecture (SOA) is a vague term, and nailing down the exact meaning is elusive. Further muddying the waters is that the term has recently intertwined with a reference for a collection of facilities called web services.

For example, suppose we offered insurance brokerage services to automobile owners and wanted to get them the best price for coverage. We would need to get quotes for them from all the available independent insurance underwriters to compare. As you might imagine, we need to first find their web services, then determine how to interact with them, and lastly determine how to secure the transmission.

One of the ways to address these issues is to use the ***eXtensible Markup Language*** (**XML**) along with the ***Web Services Description Language*** (**WSDL**), which is an XML format for describing web services as a set of endpoints for messages. Thus WSDL is basically a markup language that describes the network protocols for the services and ways to exchange messages. Specifically, it defines how client applications locate and communicate with a service provider. Trading partners or company lines of businesses that operate using different data formats can exchange WSDL directly, even though sometimes it makes more sense to use a ***registry***. A registry is a mechanism that allows for advertising services analogous to the Yellow Pages in a telephone book. The ***Universal Description and Discovery Integration*** (**UDDI**) is an XML-based registry (repository) and API that allows organizations to advertise their services on the Web. In other words, UDDI advertises services using WSDL. Companies create WSDL for their services and then register these into the repository to list their names, products, and web addresses, along with other important information such as what delivery methods to use. Client processes can simply look up the services from the registry and determine at runtime how to find and connect (bind) and exchange information with the services.

7.3.3 Markup: HTML and XML

Services and distributed systems typically depend on a flexible markup language that can be interpreted at runtime. An important feature of markup language is the ability to disengage the underlying implementation of a system from the functions performed by the system. As an example, in the ability to surf the Web with browsers, most people think of the ***Hypertext Markup Language*** (**HTML**). HTML allows a web page developer to create a display for a browser using static symbols and rules, which are used as a form of grammar by the browser program (such as Internet Explorer or Firefox). The HTML grammar is predefined by tags, such as `<p>`, which signals to the browser to start a new paragraph, the tag `<strong>`, which indicates to the browser to bold the text, and so forth. For the most part, tags used for formatting are ended using a slash, as in the following: `<strong>`**This sentence would be bold**`</strong>`. Markup such as this consists of ways for creating and manipulating information in a textual form that can be read by a standard program.

However, using a static grammar such as HTML does not afford flexibility for adaptive systems. Thus the XML was created to enable a collection of facilities and information structures to be manipulated and distributed among computer applications, between computer systems, and even over the Web. Like HTML, XML contains markup codes to describe the contents of a page or a data structure. XML is "extensible" because, unlike HTML, the markup symbols are unbounded and are user-defined; hence, XML describes the content in user-definable terms for what an XML document contains. As an example, if we placed the tag `<email>` inside the markup in an XML document, we could use the data contained between the tag and its end tag `</email>` to indicate an email address for a given record, and we could define a name attribute such as `<name>Mike</name>` as a recipient.

In Focus

The benefits of markup such as XML are that information can be processed by humans or computer programs and that the contents can be stored in a database, retained as a text file, or even displayed on a monitor or computer screen by a browser.

Now, we illustrate how XML works: A computer manufacturer might agree on a standard method to describe information about a computer, such as the computer model, a serial number, its processor speed, memory size, and peripheral options. When they want to exchange inventory information with trading partners such as customers and suppliers, they can describe the computer using XML so that the information can be passed among systems and stored in repositories without regard to the trading partners' systems and technologies.

The XML markup form of describing information even allows a mobile program called an *agent* to sift through the XML documents, similar to how a web crawler or bot might be used by Bing or Google to find relevant documents on the Web from a keyword query string. Companies can use XML to share information in a consistent way and locate specific documents or even elements within documents. An example of an XML document follows:

```xml
<?xml version="1.0" encoding="ISO-8859-1" ?>
<!-- Author: Mike -->
<automobile>
  <make>Nissan</make>
  <model>370Z</model>
  <stockno>133200353323</stockno>
  <year>2010</year>
</automobile>
```

Repeating the collections of tags is in hierarchical form in order to produce record structures, as in the following XML markup example:

```xml
<?xml version="1.0" encoding="UTF-8"?>
<books>
      <title>How To Get Rich Quick</title>
            <details="Finance genre" cost="150" unit="USD"/>
            <shelfID> HC122.345.2. </shelfID>
      <title>Information Security for Managers</title>
            <details="Security genre" cost="195" unit="USD"/>
            <shelfID> HC253.551.1. </shelfID>
</books>
```

> **In Focus**
>
> Note that XML can be displayed in a browser, passed back and forth between trading partners, or even stored (persisted) in its entirety in a database.

7.3.4 Parsing Markup

At this stage, it should be clear how information can be flexibly "marked up" into a document that can then be shared among people or computers. Realize now that we need some sort of *dictionary* to describe to people or computer translators what the tags mean and what types of data are contained in the document. For this, systems must share a markup document called a schema. Schemas (or DTD) act rather like dictionaries that match attributes defined in XML with their definitions, for example, by defining the data types: integers, strings, floating point numbers, and so on. By sharing schemas, various entities (companies, trading partners, etc.) can interpret a given XML document.

> **In Focus**
>
> The differences between a DTD and a schema are minor. The major difference is that the schema was adopted more widely as a standard data definition. They both must define the data types in the XML document and specify whether the items are mandatory or optional, along with processing parameters. It is the format of the specification that makes the major difference.

Where a browser is used to interpret HTML, a parser is used to interpret XML. There are a variety of parsers available, and there are various ways an XML document can be parsed. Two that are common are **_DOM_** (document object model) and **_SAX_** (simple access protocol interface for XML). The DOM way of parsing collects the entire XML document into memory in a tree structure, starting with the top level, or root, element. The parser then "walks down" the tree, interpreting the contents of each node in the tree structure of the XML. The SAX parser does not load an entire document in memory, but rather, it gets the contents of the XML document using calls to its **_Application Program Interface_**, or **API** (known as event parsing). Each way is used for different purposes: If information needs recursive referencing, DOM is used more often; if the data are being accessed only once, then SAX is used more often.

With the implementation of the **_Simple Object Access Protocol_** (**SOAP**), parsing and processing XML documents have become, well, simpler. SOAP is an enabling technology for XML originally developed by Microsoft. It has informational components, such as a header, that contain information that aids in exchanging and processing XML documents between applications. In addition to exchanging data among systems, XML can also be used to present information to a browser or to generate other types of documents. For this, we can use something called an XML style sheet and translator (XSLT). XSLT is used for parsing through the XML document and generating HTML for display in the browser or to render in some other fashion.

In Focus

SOAP is a formatting technology for an XML parser program to use for routing and inspecting XML documents.

7.3.5 RDF and Ontology Markup

Because XML is hierarchical in structure and therefore inefficient to process in large volume, that is, in order to gather intelligence, the W3C standards body has embarked on a revolutionary way to reorganize information in the Web, coined the "Semantic Web." Semantics is a name given to a group of technologies that evolved from XML to provide enriched and better contextualized information, thus enhancing the human ability to make meaning out of information. As such, a type of markup called **Resource Description Framework** (**RDF**) was developed to provide more relational intelligence (semantics) in web systems. In other words, RDF is based on XML, but it is an attempt to make better use of metadata (data about data) by extending the markup to form relationships among documents.

For example, using the technology of search engines, if we were going to write a research paper, we might first do a search using keywords on the topic. A typical search engine would sift through metadata looking for keywords or combinations of keywords, cross linkages, and other cues that might help match, and then we would receive back from the search engine lists of links, many of which might not be relevant. RDF, on the other hand, establishes internally defined relationships among documents by embedded **Uniform Resource Identifiers** (**URIs**), and the relationships among documents are expressed in triples: subject, verb, and object. With RDF statements, I might make assertions in separate RDF documents such as:

1. Michael is a professor.
2. Michael teaches information security for managers.
3. Michael has an office at the college of business building.

In Focus

RDF markup allows for information to be more flexibly created and linked together to increase the relevance of queries for related information.

From RDF, ontologies evolved to organize bodies of related information and provide semantic rules and context, as illustrated in the differences between these two sentences:

Wave to the crowd versus *Let's catch the next wave*. Although ontologies and ontology markup are beyond the scope of this textbook because they require an extensive understanding of programming concepts, we will briefly mention them here because they are important for managers to consider in terms of security as this technology evolves. An ontology in the context of our textbook is a controlled vocabulary in a specific knowledge domain that provides structure for representing concepts, properties, and allowable values for the concepts. As suggested, ontologies are created using a markup language, and documents are linked together with Uniform Resource Identifiers (URIs). URIs resemble URLs in that they are used by browsers to find web pages, but they differ in some subtle ways—in particular, URIs extend beyond web pages to include other media.

In Focus

There are upper and lower ontologies: Upper ontologies are nomothetic—that is, they deal with generalized concepts. Lower ontologies are ideographic—that is, they represent domain-specific relationships. Domain specific means that a doctor in a medical ontology is a physician, whereas a doctor in an educational ontology is a professor.

Because ontology markup builds on RDF, ontology markup languages include all the RDF characteristics. Just as with RDF, the predicate portion of the ontology definition is a property type for a resource, such as an attribute, relationship, or characteristic, and the object is the value of the resource property type for the specific subject. However, although RDF enables URI linkages, these are based on a relational structure, but the **Ontology Web Language** (**OWL**) and the DARPA Agent Markup Language with the **Ontology Inference Layer** (**DAML+OIL**) use RDF to form a more object-oriented markup used in organizing related bodies of information.

Ontology markup therefore establishes rules and enables inheritance features in which the constructs can form superclass–subclass relationships. For example, a disjoint relationship could be expressed such that A is a B, C is a B, but A is not C; such as, a dog is an animal, a cat is an animal, but a dog is not a cat. In the DAML+OIL markup that follows, we could assert an expression that a class `Female` is a subclass of `Animal`, but a `Female` is not a `Male` even though `Male` is also a subclass of `Animal` [13]:

```
<daml:Class rdf:ID="Female">
  <rdfs:subClassOf rdf:resource="#Animal"/>
  <daml:disjointWith rdf:resource="#Male"/>
</daml:Class>
```

7.3.6 Active Semantic Systems

Without some way to gather and utilize information stored in ontologies, these would be little more than passive *data warehouses* or, more specifically, *data marts*. However, although they consist of largely undifferentiated masses (non-normalized) snapshots of data, at least with data warehouses, statistical programs can mine patterns from them in a relatively efficient manner for making future predictions. Ontologies would be less efficient because they consist of text documents that need to be parsed before mining could take place, or before an online analytical process (OLAP) could produce meaningful multi-dimensional views of the related data.

The good news is that there are technologies to deal with this problem that have recently emerged, and some that are on the cusp. Before we get to those, let's first take stock of where we are and consider the relationships among markups because we have presented many concepts in this overview introduction. We noted that more intelligent systems need a more active type of bot or crawler that can traverse URIs and make inferences about what it "learns." The most advanced of these are called goal-directed agents. Agents (such as Aglets from IBM and those developed from the open source Cougaar framework) range widely in terms of their capabilities.

Simple utility agents have little more capability than a web search engine, but a goal-directed agent can collect information and perform evaluations, make inferences, determine deviations from a current state and an end state (goal), and even make requests of systems that the agent "visits." Consequently, with the advancement of semantic technologies, there is the classic tradeoff between functionality and security. To mitigate, agents generally work in a sandbox or a self-contained area—such as a given company's ontology—and employ a variety of security techniques such as authentication (more later).

In Focus

The Ontology Web Language (OWL) extended DAML+OIL to form what are called information models. The emergence of these new markup languages has transformed the simple attribute-value pairs of XML into representations of subject-verb-object relationships with RDF and combined with the ability to create "classes" out of these documents. They can be organized into collections of knowledge domains (ontologies) using ontology markup languages, such as OWL. It is in this evolution (called semantic fusion) that the silos of legacy data may integrate in new, more flexible ways with the corporate information infrastructure.

7.3.7 Agent Frameworks and Semantic Fusion

Agent frameworks are part of semantic fusion, which provides a different way to advertise and discover services than has existed in systems to date. Semantic fusion and agent frameworks allow users to specify parameters and program or write scripting to surf through the vast set of URI linkages for relevant information based on specific contexts within an ontology because these are usually vast expanses of information reservoirs. Using semantic persistence engines, ontologies can even be stored as subject-verb-object (triples) in databases.

In contemporary systems, information is typically drawn out of an environment and stored away in a data warehouse, where it is later examined for patterns by using various analytics, but much of the important information may have changed in the dynamic environment since the time the data were extrapolated into the closed system. This *closed-system static model* of pattern discovery is inherently limited [14]. Moreover, with data warehousing analytics, the user must provide the problem context. By way of using the Web as an analogy, the user must "drive" the search for information with the assistance of a technology such as a crawler or bot. This has widely recognized limitations.

Specifically, the Web is a sea of electronic texts and images. When we look for something of interest, unless someone provides us with a Universal Resource Locator (URL) link where we can find the relevant material, we must resort to a search engine that gathers up links for documents that are *possibly* related to our topic. We then begin a hunt from the search results, sifting through the links looking for those that might match our interests. When we find a page that seems relevant at first and begin reading through the material, we may discover that it is not what we had in mind.

With semantic fusion, advertisement and discovery of ontology models are done using agents. Agents are similar to web search engine *crawlers* or *bots*, but they have greater inferential capabilities. For example, they can evaluate information as they retrieve it. There are many types of agents depending on the roles they fulfill. Middle agents act as intermediaries or brokers among ontologies, support the flow of information across systems by assisting in locating and connecting the information providers with the information requesters, and assist in the discovery of ontology models and services based on a given description. There are a number of different types of middle agents that are useful in the development of complex distributed multi-agent systems [15].

Other types of agents include matchmakers. These do not participate in the agent-to-agent communication process; rather, they match service requests with advertisements of services or information and return matches to the requesters. Thus matchmaker agents (also called *yellow page* agents) facilitate service provisioning. There are also blackboard agents that collect requests and broker agents that coordinate both the provider and consumer processes.

Therefore, agents have a capability that enables software to "understand" (meaning evaluate) the contents of web pages, and they provide an environment in which software agents can roam from page to page and carry out sophisticated tasks on behalf of their users, including drawing inferences and making requests. With this new technology, we might advertise through a website that *We-Provide-Air-Transportation*. Agents would be able to meander from airline website to website, searching for those semantic relationships and performing tasks such as telling an airline website that "Mike-Wants-To-Make-A-Reservation" and then providing the "Amount-Mike-Will-Pay."

In Focus

Today, the Web is a passive sea of electronic data, where users have to navigate through links to find resources of interest, but the Web of tomorrow will be an active system. We haven't yet realized the range of opportunities that what the W3C is calling the Semantic Web will open up for humankind. Facilitated by software agents, we will have new ways in which we can share, work, and learn in a virtual community—but the security and privacy issues associated with this capability are profound.

CHAPTER SUMMARY

In this chapter, we covered data and information, some applications used in integrating information, and enterprise information integration, along with applications that utilize them such as customer relationship management systems. We also covered relational database concepts and introduced data warehousing. We highlighted the emergence of new markup languages and how they have transformed the simple attribute-value pairs of XML into representations of relationships with RDF and, when combined with the ability to create "classes" out of these documents, how they can be organized into collections of knowledge domains (ontologies) using ontology markup languages, such as OWL. As we shall discuss later, these technologies may also present a whole new range of security threats.

Agents, such as Cougaar and Aglets, not only have the capability to traverse from system to system to collect information similar to bots and crawlers, but they can perform evaluative and inferential logic, and they can execute instructions. We will explore these and other technologies in more detail in subsequent chapters. Once we are done, you should have a good handle on how various technologies work and techniques to help ensure that resources are reasonably secure.

THINK ABOUT IT

Topic Questions

7.1: Relational databases are designed based on what two elements?

7.2: What differentiates XML from HTML?

7.3: What does WSDL do?

7.4: The term value chain refers to the activities and departments involved in delivering a company's product or service.

____ True
____ False

7.5: Multi-dimensional views of data (cubes) are produced from queries of data warehouses by using:

____ Relational database queries
____ SQL Select * from MyData
____ Online Analytical Processing (OLAP)
____ Data mining

7.6: A "yellow pages" for WSDL is:

____ UDDI
____ An object request broker (ORB)
____ A special folder that is shared
____ SOAP

7.7: A disruptive technology is one that can change a paradigm.

____ True
____ False

7.8: A _____ links markup documents together.

7.9: In reference to technologies, the term value neutral means:

____ They nullify people's value systems.
____ It is up to people who apply technologies as to whether they are used for good or for bad purposes.
____ They are used as leverage with a customer or supplier, or over a competitor.
____ They cause people to have to personalize technologies.

7.10: Ontology markup establishes rules and enables inheritance features in which the constructs can form superclass–subclass relationships.

____ True
____ False

Questions for Further Study

Q7.1: Why has SOA become a popular method for trading information among distributed systems?

Q7.2: What are agent frameworks, and what purpose do they serve? How do they differ from web crawlers or bots?

Q7.3: What security problems might be created by using SOA?

Q7.4: What are two technologies that can be used for persistence of RDF documents?

Q7.5: Give some pros and cons to tightly coupled versus loosely coupled distributed technologies.

KEY CONCEPTS AND TERMS

Agent frameworks are part of semantic fusion.

Disruptive technology has sufficient inertia to change a paradigm.

Electronic Data Interchange (EDI) standards emerged in

an effort to bring structure and order to the information integration problem.

Normalization is the process of designing relational databases to eliminate anomalies.

Value chain consists of activities that a company performs in order to deliver its products or services.

References

1. Porter, M. E. (1979). *How competitive forces shape strategy.* New York, NY: Free Press.
2. Porter, M. E. (1996, November–December). What is strategy? *Harvard Business Review,* pp. 61–78.
3. Synnott, W. R. (1987). *The information weapon: Winning customers and markets with technology.* New York, NY: John Wiley & Sons.
4. Hendrick, S. D., Ballou, M. C., Fleming, M., Hilwa, A., & Olofson, C. W. (2011). *Worldwide application development and deployment 2011 and top 10 predictions.* Framingham, MA: International Data Group (IDC).
5. Connolly, T., & Begg, C. (2005). *Database systems: A practical approach to design, implementation and management.* New York, NY: Addison-Wesley.
6. Tillman, G. (1993). *A practical guide to logical data modeling.* New York, NY: McGraw-Hill.
7. Kroenke, D. (2002). *Database processing.* Upper Saddle River, NJ: Prentice Hall.
8. Hoechst, T., Melander, N., & Chabris, C. (1990). *A guide to Oracle.* New York, NY: McGraw-Hill.
9. Inmon, W. H., Imhoff, C., & Sousa, R. (2001). *Corporate information factory.* Boston, MA: John Wiley & Sons.
10. Webb, T., & Will, D. (1999). *Performance improvement through information management.* London, UK: Springer.
11. Friedman, T. L. (2005). *The world is flat.* New York, NY: Farrar, Straus & Giroux.
12. Workman, M. (2010). A behaviorist perspective on corporate harassment online: Validation of a theoretical model of psychological motives. *Computers & Security, 29,* 831–839.
13. Miller, E. (1998). *An introduction to resource description framework.* Retrieved July 6, 2010, from http://www.dlib.org/dlib/may98/miller/05miller.html
14. Churchman, C. W. (1971). *The design of inquiring systems: Basic concepts of systems and organization.* New York, NY: Basic Books.
15. Murray, D. (1995). Developing reactive software agents. *AI Expert, 10,* 26–29.

Programming Concepts

I N THIS CHAPTER, WE WILL briefly cover how software is designed and constructed. We will discuss important code design concepts such as coupling and cohesion, and we will present some application programming syntax and logic. Why is this important? As explained by Kaufman, Perlman, and Speciner [1], knowing how software is written helps security managers know how to observe, preserve, and curtail security incidents. We will survey some of the development tools such as computer-aided software engineering (CASE) and rapid application development (RAD) systems, as well has how these tools have evolved into component frameworks and integrated development environments.

Computer programming involves formulating instructions using both logic and mathematics (primarily algebra). In computer application programs, logic includes assignment operators, condition evaluations, ways to repeat program instructions with loops, and performing conditional and control logic (e.g., if-then-else). We will examine a few code samples in a variety of programming languages to get a glimpse later into how various programming language codes can be manipulated in security attacks or lead to unintentional security problems.

Chapter 8 Topics

This chapter:

- Explores programming logic and constructs.
- Describes software design concepts including coupling and cohesion.
- Explains interpreted and compiled programming code.
- Reviews scripting and markup.

Chapter 8 Goals

When you finish this chapter, you should:

❑ Know how logic is implemented in code at a conceptual level.

❑ Know some of the attributes of good code design for maintainability, flexibility, and security.

❑ Be familiar with some of the pros and cons of development environments.

❑ Have an understanding of programming constructs.

8.1 Program Creation

High-level languages are usually divided between ***interpreted*** and ***compiled*** languages. Compiled languages include COBOL, Pascal, "C," and C++. Interpreted languages include JavaScript and VBScript, and there are hybrid languages such JAVA and Visual Basic. All of these are considered "high-level" languages because their program instructions are written in a human-readable form called *source code*. Source code must be transformed into an executable that the computer operating system can understand. At the lowest layer of programming logic are groupings of 0s and 1s called machine language, but as you might imagine, there are differences between compiled and interpreted programs in how this transformation is done.

Interpreted code is parsed line by line and executed at the same time by an "interpreter" program. Scripts, such as JavaScript, are interpreted by a browser, for example. On the other hand, a compiled language involves an intermediate step. Before execution, a special-purpose program called a compiler scans the program. The compiler (and its linker and assembler counterparts) translates the high-level program syntax into ***executable*** machine code and produces an executable as its output. The machine code can then be loaded into memory and executed when called upon by another program or executed when initiated by a user.

8.1.1 Programming Logic and Syntax

Programming languages have different syntax, although logic is expressed in similar ways [2]. To demonstrate, the following is a simple *pseudo code* program. It tests whether a user interface collected a "YES" or a "NO" in response to a user query. If a "YES" is entered, it increments a `counter` by 1 and sends the control of the program to a function called `ProcessCodeFunction`, where it evaluates the `counter` to determine if it is less than 10. If it is, it returns the value of `counter` (whatever it is) to `ProcessInput`; otherwise, it sets `counter` to 0, and returns `counter` to `ProcessInput`, where it prints out the value. (Note that the following code example is not the "best" design. We will explain why later.)

```
Begin ProcessInput(Counter)
  Let String A = Input_Variable;
  If A = "YES" Then
        Counter = Counter + 1
        Count = Call ProcessCodeFunction (Counter)
        Printout Count
  Else If A = "NO"
        Then Terminate Program
End ProcessInput
ProcessCodeFunction (Counter)
  If Counter  < 10
        Then Return Counter
  Else
        Counter = 0
        Return Counter
End ProcessCodeFunction
```

Once the logic is understood, writing a program is a matter of writing the appropriate syntax to perform the logic. There are many programming languages and many ways to write the same logic using a given language. Ideally, programmers write the logic in a way that isolates calculations and evaluations to specific tasks in the programming code to enhance flexibility and maintainability.

In Focus

Note that in the previous code example, a better design would be to pass `Input_Variable` as a parameter into the `ProcessInput` function. Good design is an important security topic for our later discussion about cohesion and coupling.

Programming logic is implemented by assembling the programming language instructions (syntax) to form statements. A simple example is the *variable assignment*. This statement allocates memory for a variable and assigns a value to it. In most languages, this is done using a variable name, an equal sign (=), and the value or expression used in the assignment. In Visual Basic, this is done by means of the following syntax:

```
DIM <variable> AS <type>
LET <variable> = <expression>
```

The DIM statement allocates a memory of a certain <type> such as a floating point number for a <variable>. The LET keyword explicitly states that a value defined by the <expression> is to be assigned to the <variable>. The variable retains the result of the expression for future use. For expressions, most programming languages include general processing syntax such as mathematical operations using addition (+), subtraction (–), multiplication (*), and division (/). Logical operators such as AND, OR, and NOT are also part of most languages.

By putting together statements such as variable assignments and expressions, the computer can perform a wide range of behaviors and functions to complete a task. For example, in the programming languages C++, C#, "C," or JAVA, we use brackets "{" and "}" to mark the beginning and end of a logic block. With these languages, we can express if-then-else logic algebraically. For example, if the value contained in variable x is equal (denoted = =) to 2 AND (denoted &&) the value contained in variable y is equal to 4, perform some computations and assign the results to variables a and b, respectively. If x is not equal to 2, or y is not equal to 4, simply assign the value of 15 to a and assign the value of 50 to b:

```
if   (x = = 2)  && (y = = 4)
{
          a = (x + 4)  *  (y + 2);
          b = (x + 10) / (y);
}
else
{
          a = 15;
          b = 50;
}
```

Given the placement of the parentheses in the computations in the example, provided the "if" statement in the function is evaluated "true," then a should equal 36 after the computation and assignment, and b should equal 3. On the other hand, what if we had written the computations without using the parentheses (as an example)? Provided that the "if" statement is evaluated "true," then a should be equal to 20 after the assignment, and b should equal 42. This is because programming uses algebraic precedence for operators, such that multiplication (*) takes precedence over addition (+), for instance:

```
if   (x = = 2)  && (y = = 4)
{
          a = x + 4 * y + 2;
          b = x + 10 * y;
}
```

In Focus

Programming logic can be implemented differently even using the same programming language. For example, loops in "C" can be performed using `for`, `switch`, and `do-while`. The way a programmer implements the code will determine efficiency and effectiveness of the code.

8.1.2 Operations, Expressions, and Tasks

Operations are similar to a sentence in written prose in the sense that they are a complete discrete function. An operation might consist of formatting a character string (groups of letters) for output to a device. In Visual Basic, for example, there are a number of functions that convert data from numeric form into string form, and I/O operations in Visual Basic can be performed using the READ and WRITE commands. Operations also include evaluative logic, comparisons, and decisions.

Evaluations, comparisons, and decisions are often made with "if" statements in most languages, although the exact structure of the "if" statement will vary according to the language. In Visual Basic, the IF takes this form: IF <test> THEN <action>. In this case, the <test> is a comparison between two values or expressions. If the result of the test is true, the <action> will be performed. If the <test> is false, the <action> is ignored as in the following example:

```
IF A < B THEN LET C = A
```

In this case, only if the value contained in the variable A is less than B will C be given the value contained in A. We can add an ELSE to the structure to handle the condition where the evaluation of the IF statement is false. In this case, the variable C will be given the lesser of the two numbers contained in A or B.

```
IF A < B THEN LET C = A
ELSE LET C = B
```

In the languages C++, C#, JAVA, and "C," we would achieve the same result with different syntax (note that in these languages, lowercase is used by convention):

```
if (a < b)
        c = a;
else
        c = b;
```

Tasks are similar to a paragraph in written prose in the sense that they are a complete unit of work. Tasks are accomplished using subroutines and flow control logic. Subroutines are designed to implement a logic block and, in most cases, return a result to a main program. In the Pascal and "C" languages, subroutines are named and invoked by a statement that "calls" the name. Flow control refers to structures and commands that enable a sequence of instructions to be repeated (i.e., loop) or to jump to a function or subroutine.

Loops in which the number of iterations are known in Visual Basic are defined with the statements FOR and NEXT. It is also possible to define indefinite loops, where the number of repetitions is not initially known, or where the loop must be repeated until a particular condition has been met. This kind of structure may take such forms as BEGIN ...UNTIL, WHILE...DO...ENDDO, or BEGIN...WHILE...REPEAT. In the Visual Basic language, a loop may take the form seen in the next example, where <step size>

may be any real number, positive or negative. If the STEP keyword is omitted, the <step size> defaults to + 1:

```
FOR <variable name> = <start value> TO <end value>
STEP <step size>
      <sequence of instructions to repeat>
NEXT
```

The sequence of instructions within these loops may be any valid instruction, including another FOR . . . NEXT loop (called a nested loop), with one restriction. When nested FOR . . . NEXT statements are used, the inner loop must be completely contained in the outer loop. In other words, loops cannot overlap. In the Pascal language, the syntax of a loop appears in the following example:

```
FOR <index> := <start> TO <end> DO <instruction>
```

The Pascal language does not have a NEXT statement, and only the line following the FOR line will be repeated. To repeat a group of instructions, either the programmer must predefine them as a procedure (also called a function), or surround them with the BEGIN and END keywords. Alternatively, in the language "C," we use brackets; the format is seen in the following code example:

```
for ( <index> = <start>; <index> < = <end>; <index>++)
{
   <instructions to repeat>
}
```

As seen in the next example, in JAVA (or C#, C++, or "C"), we may write a "for" loop that says, start index at 0, loop while i is less than or equal to 6, and each time we loop we add 2 to the index. The first time through the loop we are at 0, the next time we are at 2, the next time 4, and the next time 6—so then terminate. Inside the loop during the first iteration, a is equal to 0, and because a is less than 10, b will be given the value of 1 because ++a increments the value of a by 1. The next time through the loop iteration, a is now 1, which is less than 10, and so in the next line b will be assigned 2, and this continues until the loop ends:

```
int a = 0, b = 0;
for ( i = 0; i < = 6; i + 2)
{
   if (a < 10)
        b = ++a;
}
```

8.2 Software Construction

Now that we have covered a little bit about syntax and logic, let's discuss design and construction concepts. Programmers work from a set of logical specifications and requirements developed by business analysts and other stakeholders, and they must transform these specifications into a physical design and, ultimately, programming code. When we set out to design a program, we may begin by thinking of the instructions in a sequential fashion. This is a bit like whenever we write instructions, say, for instance, how to bake a cake. We start with the first step (preheat oven), then the next step (mix 1 cup of milk and 2 eggs) and so on until the process is complete. But, in fact, we do not want to write code this way. In procedural programming languages such as Basic or Pascal, we take some steps, then jump to another place, take some more steps, and then return to the line of code that followed the jump and do some more steps, and then jump again.

This jumping around among various instructions in the code makes it possible to create subroutines or procedures for steps we want to call repeatedly. However, as you can imagine, the organization of the code that is to be executed is crucial to the performance and maintainability of the program. We can think of a procedure or function as a chunk of code that is executed whenever its name is called. When we set out to write code, we may start out with pseudo code. Let's say that we wanted to create a web-based application comprised of HTML pages. The pseudo code might be something like the list that follows:

1. Start of HTML page: display a page with some text and two text boxes
2. Display two labels that ask for a user name and password
3. Collect the user name from the first text box
4. Call a function, validate, and pass it the user name (branches to validate here)
5. Check to see if the validate function returned true or false
6. If false, display user name invalid and disconnect
7. Otherwise
8. Collect the user name from the second text box
9. Call the validate function and pass it the password (branches to validate here)
10. Check to see if the validate function returned true or false
11. If false, display invalid password and disconnect
12. Otherwise
13. Redirect (link to) the home page
14. Validate to see if the parameter passed to this function is alphanumeric
15. If it is, set validation true
16. If it is not, set validation false
17. Report validation parameter to control logic

18. If validation true, accept input

19. If validation false, display error

As shown in the previously illustrated steps, they are linear and sequential. We can determine logically from these steps if there are functions we may want to repeat. What do we do if we want to perform validation over and over? Do we rewrite all those lines of code? The purpose behind using functions is to preclude writing the same lines of code over and over. We write the code once and call the function or object as many times as we need.

A top-down design begins with a routine, or process, and decomposes these into stages that can be repeated. The stages then become candidates for procedures or subroutines or objects. One of the difficulties with this approach is that processes tend to be more dynamic than the data used in processes. Thus an alternative approach is to use a bottom-up or data-driven technique, and then find out how these data are used and develop the procedures to manipulate the data [3].

8.2.1 Code-Level Design: Coupling

There are many programming languages and many methods to organize code. Some languages are better for certain tasks than others, and some methods are better than others. However, there are some general design concepts that apply across languages and methods. Coupling is a design concept that deals with the ways that software modules in a design interrelate with each other [2]. Modules that are highly interdependent are said to be tightly coupled, whereas those that have low interdependence are loosely coupled. From a software engineering standpoint, developers should strive for loose coupling. Types of module coupling can be classified into six categories in which modules communicate (any given design will usually exhibit several of these characteristics) as noted in the ordinal list that follows:

1. Content (Worst)

2. Common

3. External

4. Control

5. Stamp

6. Data (Best)

Content coupling occurs when a software module makes a direct reference to the contents of another software module. This happens mainly in low-level languages such as assembly language programs, where program statements in one module may be modified by another module; changes in one module require examination of all other modules. Common (sometimes called global) coupling is an instance where a software module references a global data structure shared with another module. In this configuration, a module may have access to more data than it needs. Changes to the global data structure may require changes to all modules that share the data structure. Problems occur due to bad data in the global data structure and may be hard to track down. Other problems include those found in **List 8.1**.

List 8.1 Common Coupling Problems

1. Common coupling inhibits program readability because one must search through all the common coupled modules to understand variable usage.

2. It introduces side effects. Because each module may access the entire common area, the module may use data elements in ways not apparent in the defined interface.

3. It introduces inter-module dependencies among otherwise unrelated modules. For example, changes in a common area may require recompilation of all modules referencing that common area.

4. Common coupled modules are difficult to use and are not "re-entrant" because the modules use fixed references inside the common area.

5. Common coupled modules are difficult to use in future programs because they use fixed references inside the common area.

6. Module reusability is more complicated if the common area is a structure composed of several data elements.

7. Common coupling may supply more data to a module than it needs to do its job. This introduces the possibility of inadvertently modifying unrelated data and provides a temptation to use data not defined as part of the module interface.

8. Common coupling defeats attempts to manage and control access to data, creating security vulnerabilities.

Like common coupling, with external coupling a module references an externally declared variable also referenced in another software module. In this configuration, a module may have access to more data than it needs, and changes to the global data structure may require changes to all modules that share the data structure. Also, data corruption problems that may result can be difficult to track down (debug) and fix. It is also susceptible to security exploits designed to corrupt data or crash a system.

In control coupling, a module passes elements of control to another module. It can have subordinate modules controlling superordinate modules. A module may build into its logic a dependence on how other modules work. Each of the conditions makes it such that changes to one module may require changes to several other modules. Control coupling implies that one module "knows" something about the internal logic of another. That knowledge makes the modules highly interdependent. Changes in the operation of a module will necessarily be reflected as changes in many modules. Additionally, the usage of a function implies that the called module performs multiple functions, which undermines module cohesion. Both maintainability and extensibility are significantly decreased with control-coupled modules.

Interface coupling, or what is often called stamp coupling, is where several modules reference the same non-global data structure. With this configuration, modules share only the data they need. However, changes to the data structure may require changes to all modules that reference the data. In this situation, a module may be required to "know" something about the structure of data local to another module in order for the program to execute. Most of the time, this type of coupling is needed by programs (or objects) that are distributed across applications, or at least application boundaries. Stamp-coupled modules sometimes require changes to modules that are stamp coupled when a change is made to the interfaces or some data structures; however, stamp coupling is an improvement over common coupling because data access to individual data items is limited to interfaces and not the underlying logic, so reuse, maintainability, and security of the modules are improved.

> **In Focus**
>
> Coupling is an important concept to computer security. With common coupling, hackers can access a section of program memory space called the stack (which we will discuss in our chapter on operating systems) and, worse, attack variables used by modules in other programs than the one currently being executed.

The optimal level of coupling is data coupling, where modules pass individual data items to one another as parameters, and the parameters serve as basic data elements and thus are not part of a larger structure or elements of control. In object-oriented programming (OOP), these parameters form what is called a *signature*, and the signature is an essential aspect of a key OOP feature called *overloading*, which enables *polymorphism* (more later). In this way, modules function as *black boxes*, and their influence on other modules is limited. Testing, debugging, and maintenance are simplified compared to other coupling, and so these modules are highly independent even though they can flexibly interact interdependently. However, to make this work, data-coupled modules may still need to share an interface so that one module (or object) knows how to call another and knows what to expect as possible return values. **Table 8.1** summarizes coupling characteristics.

8.2.2 Code-Level Design: Cohesion

Module cohesion is used to measure a feature called "functional strength" of the module. In other words, cohesion defines how *single-minded* a module is in performing a task. Modules that perform a specific well-defined task are said to have high cohesion. Modules that are "scattered" rather than *single-minded* are said to have low cohesion (developers often refer to

TABLE 8.1	Coupling Characteristics		
TYPE	**ERROR RATE**	**REUSE**	**EXTENSIBILITY**
Data	Low	High	High
Stamp	Medium	Medium	Medium
Control	Medium	Medium	Medium
External	High	Low/Medium	Medium
Common	High	Low	Low
Content	High	Low	Low

this problem as spaghetti code). From a software engineering standpoint, developers should strive for developing modules that are highly cohesive [4]. Modules can be classified as possessing one of the characteristics in the list that follows:

1. Coincidental (Worst)
2. Logical
3. Temporal (or classical)
4. Procedural
5. Communicational
6. Informational
7. Functional (Best)

The spectrum formed by different cohesion types is non-linear. Low-end cohesion is much worse than mid-range cohesion, and mid-range cohesion is almost as good as high cohesion. Although we want to strive for high cohesion, mid-range cohesion is often acceptable. Coincidental cohesion results in a module that performs multiple, completely unrelated functions that have no meaningful relationship among their elements. It is not usually designed but rather is created during module changes that usually occur during maintenance cycles, or it may occur from attempts to create "modular" programs out of existing programs or to consolidate unrelated duplicate code, or it may result from attempts to break up a program because of some limitation. The following is a pseudo code example to illustrate this concept:

```
Variable A = 7
Print Line
If Variable B = 3 Then Variable C = 12
```

With logical cohesion, a module performs a set of one or more related functions each time it is invoked. From an engineering standpoint, the problem with logical cohesion is that it often results in unnecessarily complicated code that makes use of special flags or parameters. The following pseudo code demonstrates this concept:

```
Procedure General-IO (Flag, RecA)
Begin
  If (flag = 1)
       Then
                      RecA written to new master file
                      RecB set to next record in Xfile-1
                      RecC undefined
    Else If (flag = 2)
              Then
                      Use RecA as an auxiliary input flag
                      If (RecA = Null)
                      Then
                              RecB set next record in Xfile-1
                      Else
                              RecB undefined
                      RecB set to next record in Xfile-2
    Else If (flag = 3)
              Then
                      RecA set to next record in Master-2
                      RecB set to next record in Xfile-2
                      RecC set to next record in Master-1
     End
```

Logical cohesion modules have at least some relationship among their elements, but those that perform each invocation use one-to-many functions coordinated with flags to tie the logic together, violating modular design. Logical cohesion is common in programming because of the tendency to write commands according to the specific steps these kinds of programs carry out.

Temporal (also called classical) cohesion performs functions whose only relationship to each other is that they are related in time. This type of cohesion can present a problem during maintenance because modules with temporal cohesion often contain elements that are closely related to other modules in a procedure, which may frequently change, as in the pseudo code example that follows:

```
Procedure Initialize ( )
Begin
   Rewind tapeA
   Set A_Count = 0
   Rewind tapeB
   Set B_Count = 0
   Clear Items table
   Clear Totals table
```

```
    Set SW_A = "off"
    Set SW_B = "on"
End
```

With procedural cohesion, a module performs several functions that are related to a procedure. The difference between temporal and procedural cohesion is that in modules having procedural cohesion, functions performed relate to the procedure of the problem, whereas in temporal cohesion the functions are usually lumped together because they must be performed at the same time, as in the following pseudo code example:

```
Procedure ProcessIO
Begin
  Open MasterFile
  Open TransactionFile
  Open OutputFile
  Read header record from MasterFile
  Allocate storage for worktable
  Initialize worktable
  Read record from TransactionFile
  Write to OutputFile
End
```

The reason that procedural cohesion is less than ideal is that the procedural code is usually linear and not self-contained. In other words, the steps do not limit the data used in the program. Thus, procedural strength modules frequently contain multiple functions and multiple data sets, making the modules difficult to reuse. On the other hand, a communicational strength cohesion module has procedural strength but performs activities only on common data elements, as in the following pseudo code example:

```
Procedure showCustomer (integer Acct_Num)
Begin
  With Acct_Num key, Find CustomerName
  Calculate LoanBal
  Return CustomerName, LoanBal
End
```

At this level of cohesion, systems designers and programmers are able to identify required behaviors for modules or objects. Still this level of cohesion does not meet an important feature called *atomicity*. An atomic function is one that performs one very specific task, and in OOP, that task can be *overloaded* (accept varying numbers and types of values passed to the function) to achieve *polymorphism*. Polymorphism is the ability to have methods with the same name but apply to different types of objects. By way of analogy, cells in the body in one physiological system are by themselves useless unless they can interact with other cells from other physiological systems. Similarly, information cohesion represents the physical packaging together of two or more otherwise functional strength modules, but they require interaction with other systems. Informational cohesion results when a module performs a set of activities such that the output from one activity serves as input to the next, as demonstrated in the following pseudo code example:

```
Procedure Solve-Set-Eqns (parameters)
Begin
  Read Matrix-File
  Build matrix
  Add parameters to Matrix
  Invert matrix
  Solve unknowns
  Write Matrix-File
  Return unknowns
End
```

Functional strength cohesion is a module that performs a single, well-defined function with a well-defined interface (and API) for how the function is to be executed based on the desired behavior. The module name is often a good indicator of the function to be performed, and although it may call subfunctions to complete the task, all activities contribute to accomplishing the single task. Modules of this type are good for maintenance, extensibility, and testing.

Unfortunately, although these modules represent the ideal form of programming, they are the least commonly found in most programming code because their design is often only theoretical and unachievable for one of several reasons, including that (1) there are technology and language limitations, (2) these modules are completely atomic, and when modules are completely atomic, there end up being many modules, which can hurt system performance because they must interact frequently with other modules to form a complete information system, (3) there are often incompatibilities among standards or technologies, and (4) there is often a gap between the concept or ideal and the realization of the ideal in a material system such as a computer architecture (and its operating system, memory constraints, processor speed, software versions, and needs for backward software compatibility), among others [2]. The following pseudo code is an example of a procedure that received two variables, X and Y, passed to it from another procedure.

```
Procedure CalcTotals (X, Y)
Begin
  If (X > 0 and Y > 0)
        Then Let A = X * Y
  Else
     Let A = 0
  Return A
End
```

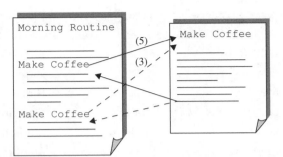

FIGURE 8.1

Calling a function/
object.

Branch to `Make Coffee` and Return

In Focus

Procedures and functions are precursors or alternative names for what are called "methods" in OOP. In both cases, a "routine" can be called and parameters passed to or received from them. In each case, the idea is to create a modular design that performs a specific task; this is called atomicity.

To illustrate, in **Figure 8.1**, a main program called `Morning Routine` can call `Make Coffee` as many times as it needs, passing in a parameter for how many cups of coffee to make. In the example in Figure 8.1, the first time `Morning Routine` calls the `Make Coffee` procedure, it passes the parameter 5, indicating 5 cups of coffee, whereas in the second call, it passes the parameter 3 to indicate to the procedure to make 3 cups.

Cohesion is important because it requires programmers to consider carefully the functions that a unit work must perform and how that function is distinguished from other functions or subroutines. It is not necessary to be able to read the source code syntax in a system to appreciate the logic the syntax is executing (although it helps). Nevertheless, in all of these cases, it is important and even essential for managers to recognize that how software is constructed can lead to either intentional or unintentional security breaches. Poor designs can leave holes in the system that have to be patched at great cost to the manufacturer and consumer, and a poor implementation can allow security exploits [3, 4]. **Table 8.2** summarizes cohesion characteristics.

In Focus

Although highly cohesive modules lead to improved maintenance and improved information security, sometimes there are good reasons why programmers may violate the rules, as previously mentioned, in terms of theory-to-practice limitations.

8.2.3 Rapid Application Development Tools

To improve productivity, techniques such as rapid prototyping and rapid application development (RAD) technologies evolved, each one bringing with it improvements in some areas and dysfunction in others. A type of RAD is computer-aided software

TABLE 8.2	Cohesion Characteristics		
TYPE	**ERROR RATE**	**REUSE**	**EXTENSIBILITY**
Functional	Low	High	High
Informational	Medium	High	High
Communicational	Low	Medium	Medium
Procedural	Low	Medium	Medium
Temporal	Medium	Low	Medium
Logical	High	Medium	Low
Coincidental	Very High	Low	Low

FIGURE 8.2

Computer-aided
software engineering
(CASE).

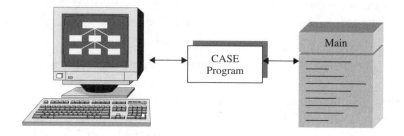

engineering (CASE), such as Unisys' LINC product. CASE applications begin with a diagram or specification of a system. Designers of the system fill out templates and forms, and graphically create diagrams of work processes and flows. From these specifications, the CASE generator produces program code to be executed (**Figure 8.2**).

Although initially promising, most of the CASE technologies lost favor partly because of limitations in the technologies and partly because of the inflexible process required for developing CASE applications. In terms of the technologies, most generated inefficient code that did not execute well. It turns out that people conceive of the processes they perform quite differently than the way an efficient program needs to be written. It also required a good understanding of the entire process before an application could be generated. Most times, designers do not fully understand a given process prior to implementation [5].

Ultimately, the design problem was simply moved from code form to graphical form, but the root problem remained. On the heels of CASE came fourth-generation languages (4GLs), such as Power Builder. These products elevated the development out of the syntax and into the logical problem domain, where requirements and functions could be more effectively addressed. They also tended to provide a rich set of tools to help automate the development process, such as form and report creations, windows and widgets, and menus. The 4GLs would then in turn generate 3GL code such as "C" or languages of some proprietary flavor.

Most of these technologies, although simpler to develop with, created other problems. In particular, the code they produced tended to be undisciplined (sometimes called spaghetti code), and they became difficult to maintain, especially if the program was complex. For most commercial applications, they inevitably proved inadequate. Nevertheless, some of the original ideas and goals of RAD and 4GL have been reinvented in smaller and more maintainable units generated by "wizards" and other "helper" tools. Many of these tools create what are called "stub" files that can be modified or included in other applications.

8.2.4 IDE, Wizards, and Toolkits

Integrated development environments (IDE) such as *Object Builder* and *Eclipse* followed the 4GL trend. Rather than code generation, they took the approach of *stub* generation and provided templates and class libraries from which to build applications. Most included integrated code debuggers, and many offered a helper, called a *wizard*, that would allow a developer to answer common software development questions, and the wizard would configure or generate some small portion of the application (stubs). This was a vast improvement over complete application generation in that it was much more flexible, efficient, and effective.

One of the main benefits of the IDE is the ability to graphically assemble a user interface (UI) by dragging objects from a palette or toolbox onto a window, and then writing the code that performs the actions when users interact with the UI. An example of this kind of IDE is Microsoft's Visual Basic (or even more so, the Microsoft .NET environment). One of the downsides of many of the IDE toolkits is that they typically embed proprietary code or require proprietary class libraries that cause organizations to become dependent on the IDE vendor. During the "open systems" era, this restriction became highly unpopular, but the basic idea of an IDE has remained tenable, and most of the newer forms of IDE have flourished.

At the heart of the IDE success is the combination of reusable objects that have been prepackaged into libraries, many of which are visual objects such as text boxes and buttons that can be integrated with the production of source code for a specific application. An integrated debugger allows for cohesive development and unit test of all the related code in the project. Once the code is completed, it is packaged up into a uniform container for distribution. This combination of reuse and loosely coupled framework makes for much more rapid development and better integration of the application and its components.

8.2.5 Native Programming Environments

Although IDEs provide a nice development environment, most also offer a native programming environment. For example, the main programming environment offered in UNIX-based systems such as Linux and MAC/OS is for the "C" programming language. The programming environment includes the *lint* syntax checker and other utilities such as *prof*, which illustrates how long programs execute in various subroutines. The "C" compiler is invoked with the "cc" command. Switches are options for the compiler and are specified on the compile command line. "C" has a two-pass compiler: the linker and loader run by default unless suppressed with a "-c" switch. Libraries of modules may be built, which can be combined to form an executable image.

Libraries can be created with the *ar* utility. The *ar* utility will place the specified source or object modules into a file library prefaced by the word "lib" and ending in ".a." The library may later be referenced with the "-l" switch on the compile line to include modules from the library into the executable. The *ranlib* utility may be run on the library to convert it into object code for the loader to increase load speed, and *dbx* is a debug utility used to find logic errors.

After the executable program is created by the compiler and debugged, the *strip* command may be run on the executable file to remove the symbol table and reduce the executable size. The symbol table is used by the *dbx* debugger. The symbol table is not needed for execution, but if the executable has been stripped, it can no longer be debugged using *dbx*. From a security standpoint, many problems are not debugged well at either the "unit" or the code level or when the code is combined into a system and tested in quality assurance (QA).

CHAPTER SUMMARY

In this chapter, we discussed programming logic, syntax, and programming design features. We provided an overview of some technologies designed to help develop applications more rapidly, along with some discussion of some of their limitations. Understanding the nature of software systems is increasingly important to managers who oversee technology and security. For example, as noted by Kaufman, Perlman, and Speciner [1], viruses may be infused into a program by replacing an instruction that causes the program to access a memory location where virus code is installed, and then the virus code often returns to the legitimate code after the virus has been executed. At this point, we have provided a foundation in several important areas that define software and have covered some syntax in various languages to ground the concepts with specific examples. We are now ready for more advanced technology topics.

THINK ABOUT IT

Topic Questions

8.1: When it comes to coupling, _____ are the best.

8.2: Why is cohesion important?

8.3: Programs can be interpreted or _____.

8.4: High-level languages are usually divided between interpreted and compiled languages.

_____ True
_____ False

8.5: In the languages, C, C++, C#, and JAVA, which symbols represent a beginning and ending of a logic block?

_____ `Begin End`
_____ `:== :==`
_____ `Start Stop`
_____ `{ }`

8.6: A compiler:

_____ Interprets program statements
_____ Translates a high-level language into executable code
_____ Ensures functional cohesion of software modules
_____ Is platform independent

THINK ABOUT IT (CONTINUED)

8.7: An external coupling of a module references an externally declared variable also referenced in another software module.

_____ True
_____ False

8.8: Programming logic can only be implemented one way in a given programming language.

_____ True
_____ False

8.9: Processes tend to be more _____ than the data used in processes:

_____ Tightly coupled
_____ Static
_____ Flexible
_____ Dynamic

8.10: Modules that are highly interdependent are said to be:

_____ Highly cohesive
_____ Loosely coupled
_____ Tightly coupled
_____ Low in cohesion

Questions for Further Study

Q8.1: How does cohesion help to improve information systems security?

Q8.2: Why has software migrated away from programming the procedural steps?

Q8.3: How might a program be written to overflow a buffer using "C"?

Q8.4: What are object libraries, and how are they used?

Q8.5: Give four pros and four cons of compiled and interpreted languages.

KEY CONCEPTS AND TERMS

Cohesion is used to measure a feature called "functional strength" of the module.

Compilers, along with linkers/loaders, create an executable program.

Coupling is a design concept that deals with the ways that software modules in a design interrelate with each other.

Interpreted code does not need to be compiled.

Programming tools have migrated from CASE and 4GLs toward using wizards and integrated development environments.

References

1. Kaufman, C., Perlman, R., & Speciner, M. (2002). _Network security: Private communication in a public world._ Upper Saddle River, NJ: Prentice Hall.

2. Workman, M. (2008). _A technology manager's guide to software._ Boston, MA: eAselworx Press.

3. Nino, J., & Hosch, F. A. (2005). *An introduction to programming and object oriented design using JAVA*. Hoboken, NJ: John Wiley & Sons.

4. Valacich, J. S., George, J. F., & Hoffer, J. A. (2004). *Essentials of systems analysis & design*. Upper Saddle River, NJ: Prentice Hall.

5. Corcho, O., Fernandez-Lopez, M., & Gomez-Perez, A. (2003). Methodologies, tools and languages. Where is their meeting point? *Data & Knowledge Engineering, 46,* 41–64.

Applications Programming

MOST SOFTWARE APPLICATIONS TODAY ARE distributed across multiple platforms and are written in an object-oriented programming language, or OOP. Also, most applications at some level interact with relational databases, often by embedding SQL statements. Because so many security threats are related to programming and scripting, such as buffer overflows and SQL injections, it is useful to know the coding behind these attacks. In this chapter, we will briefly introduce OOP concepts and present how programs interact with relational databases. We will conclude with a discussion of distributed systems.

Chapter 9 Topics

This chapter:

- Provides an overview of object-oriented (OO) concepts.
- Discusses some of the features that define OO.
- Explores how software is developed.
- Explains some SQL syntax.
- Examines distributed systems software.

Chapter 9 Goals

When you finish this chapter, you should:

- ☐ Have an understanding of OO software applications and OOP.
- ☐ Understand how OO systems interact with relational databases.
- ☐ Be able to understand basic SQL statements.
- ☐ Know the architecture of distributed systems.

9.1 Object-Oriented Software

In software applications, data are declared within a program and shared by various *coupling* means as we illustrated in the previous chapter. In legacy applications, such as those written for mainframe computers, in the worst possible situation, entire programs are coupled by means of *global variables*. A change in the value contained in the variable by one program affects another program that uses that variable, causing idiosyncratic behaviors. Even when good attempts were made to prevent this kind of interdependence, the use of pointers, such as those in the "C" language, often enabled programs to get around the design protections.

Although there remain "legacy" systems that are developed in procedure-based code, today most software is written with "object-oriented programming" (OOP). OOP has unique characteristics that differentiate it from linear or procedural programming such as that written in "C," Pascal, Fortran 77, or COBOL on mainframe computers such as the Unisys 2200 or IBM System 360 or mini-computers such as the Digital Equipment Corporation (DEC/HP) VAX 750. OOP requires software that has the ability to construct self-contained units of code that can interact with other self-contained units of code. The programming language Smalltalk epitomized OOP, but it was never widely adopted, and most OOP languages today such as C++ and JAVA are a blend of OOP and "legacy-style" programming constructs.

> **In Focus**
>
> In relation to security, OOP has created some "boundaries" between software components by "hiding" data and methods (in particular by making them "private" or "protected," as discussed later), and also has, for the most part, restricted the use of pointers that allow, for example, a virus writer to create an instruction at memory location "a" which causes the execution of virus code at memory location "b." Nevertheless, for efficiency's sake, most operating systems are not written in OOP, but are instead written in "C" and/or low-level assembler language.

Software components are made of objects that interact to achieve some purpose. Using a combination of programming and assembling components, we produce an infomation system (IS)—groups of software instructions that manipulate data and produce infomation. One way systems software organizes prewritten modules or objects is with object and component libraries. For instance, Microsoft Word allows a developer, using a programming language called VBA, to open an "object browser" that displays a library of prewritten objects such as "Font" or "Shape"; by selecting these objects from the library, the developer can customize a Word document. For example, the developer could select a Shape object and add custom curves or labels by means of programming rather than opening a Word document and creating a shape with the drawing tools. Later, we will see how this ability is one of the ways that enable people to write "malware" (malicious software such as worms and viruses).

9.1.1 Objects and Object Features

People tend to relate to the world around them in terms of objects, their forms, and their functions. For instance, when people think of a desk, they may think of its work surface and drawers in which to store things. When they think of an *accounting general ledger*, they may think of its columns for recording transactions, with a side for debits and a side for credits. Even human beings are composed of objects, having various anatomical objects such as heart, lungs, and kidneys. Objects by themselves are inert, but they become active and interact when part of a physical system. The heart pumps blood throughout the circulatory system, the lungs extract oxygen from the air we breathe, and the kidneys filter the blood and help to eliminate waste from the body [1].

As characterized by Taylor [1], the body's anatomical parts function and interact as part of the body's physiology. The cells in human bodies are organic components that maintain information in the form of proteins and chemicals. Reactions within these components enable the exchange of information among the other cells in the body. DNA in cells communicates information about how to make proteins to other cellular structures by sending mRNA messages, and the genes encompassed by the chromosomes in the DNA are turned on and off by means of these chemical messages, which determines the cell's **state** or "condition," including whether to divide into new cells or to process food proteins.

Software systems are analogous to the body's physiology. They establish the mechanisms by which information flows and functions are performed. Software systems also have an anatomy. For example, computer operating systems such as Linux (UNIX) or Microsoft Windows have a *scheduler or dispatcher*, which is a system that is responsible for switching processes in and out of the central processing unit (CPU) for execution. Word processors have a parser that interprets user input and translates the input into codes that other objects can manipulate and format. Database management systems (DBMS) have a lock manager that controls concurrent access to data in database tables.

At the most basic levels of modern software systems are software objects. As with living cells, software objects have certain essential characteristics. They have attributes that can be turned on or off, contain other information that determine objects' state or condition, have a means by which messages are passed between objects, can be aggregated into increasingly complex forms of objects, and interact to create a functioning system. Software systems today are evolving from synthetic into organic systems, where software systems are self-defining, self-renewing, and self-organizing.

In Focus

General systems theory defines the properties of self-defining, self-organizing, and self-renewing as "organic" systems, as opposed to "synthetic" systems, which do not regulate themselves or adapt [2].

Certain features define object-oriented software. Traditionally, programmers have considered three primary defining characteristics: (1) encapsulation, (2) inheritance, and (3) polymorphism [3]. ***Encapsulation*** is the embedding and "hiding" of data within an object. ***Inheritance*** is one of the facilities that enable objects to express variation through parent–child relationships. ***Polymorphism*** (meaning many forms) is another technique that facilitates variations by allowing objects to determine their behavior based on the ways parameters are passed to them from other objects [4].

Until fairly recently, the state of the art in OO technology required "tight coupling" between objects through interfaces, component frameworks (e.g., Sun/Oracle's Enterprise JavaBeans or Microsoft's .NET), or binding components (called stubs and skeletons). These were required in order for objects to exchange data and messages, but this "tight coupling" limited the ability of OO software to be easily distributed across system boundaries [5]. Again, by way of the body analogy, if cells were so specialized that they could not communicate across the body's systems, they would not be very useful. As Taylor stated, it would certainly create difficulties if only your limbs but not your lungs could make use of your blood cells, for example [1].

In Focus

An alternative to tight coupling with binding components is through the use of service-oriented architecture (SOA) and web services. These technologies create a more loosely coupled way for distributed objects to interact.

9.1.2 The Nature of Software Objects

Encapsulation has to do with the variables contained in an object, which are called ***attributes***. Encapsulation is important to protect data from direct manipulation by other objects. Language keywords—***private***, ***protected***, and ***public***—explicitly and purposefully allow or disallow access to the object's attributes. The keyword "private" is the most restrictive, allowing only the object itself to manipulate the attribute data, denying access to other objects. Beyond the benefits of improved control over the access to data within the object, this mechanism simplifies the interactions among objects by hiding the internal complexity of the functions the objects perform and also preserving many aspects of software and systems security [6].

An object can, however, request that another object make changes to its data. This is done by means of calling ***methods***, which are functions that an object performs. In this sense, methods are similar to functions in legacy programs because they can send and receive messages, that is, objects and data, but they have special characteristics that improve how objects interact. In particular, as with attributes, access to methods can be controlled using the same keywords: *public, protected,* and *private.* In addition to simplifying the interactions between objects, encapsulation also promotes reuse in the event that a programmer modifies the way an object carries out its tasks. Suppose a revenue-booking object has a group of methods to calculate revenues based on when sales are booked. Later, the accounting department wants to change the booking of revenue to when the money is received.

Without encapsulation, the change would require a major rewrite to all the code that deals with booking revenues. With encapsulation, the change is likely to be limited to a single object. All the objects in the accounting system that deal with revenue either request the revenue from the revenue-booking object or send it the revenue data for it to record and determine when it hits the books. Because all objects conform to these basic encapsulation operations, the way they are approached is consistent and dependable, and yet the ways in which the objects behave can reflect tremendous variation [4, 5].

Next, objects are assembled into hierarchies of parent–child relationships going from abstract to concrete, and they share their properties through inheritance. When people think of the concept "person," they are conceiving an abstraction, but when thinking of the person Dan, they are conceiving of a specific concrete example of a person. The concrete object is called an **instance** of a given class of objects, so Dan is an instance of person.

Objects have the ability to inherit the characteristics from their parent as indicated. For example, if there was an insurance system that needed a way to represent vehicles to insure, programmers could write an object representing the abstract concept called "vehicle" and then have various types of vehicle objects, such as automobile, motorcycle, truck, and bus, for each instance. The parent vehicle object might have chassis, engine, and wheel attributes along with the methods to set the values for these attributes, and then each instance could simply adopt or inherit these characteristics and add only their own unique attributes and methods [1, 5].

Like encapsulation, inheritance promotes reuse. A parent class (also called base class) can contain all the generalizable attributes and methods and pass them down to children objects. Suppose a conveyer belt object has a group of methods to determine the rate at which TVs move down the assembly line according to the various types of sets. If the company begins to produce flat-screen TVs, which presumably take less time to assemble, without inheritance the developers must modify all the TV code as well as the conveyer code to include these new types of TVs. With inheritance, the flat-screen TV is simply a new instance of TV that the conveyer object can read to determine how long it takes to assemble and adjust the pace accordingly [1].

Finally, a fundamental aspect of polymorphism is accomplished by means of something called **overloading**. Overloading is the ability to have methods using the same name that perform different functions depending on the **parameters** passed to the method. For example, if a programmer had written a method called payForMerchandise, and if an object called Purchase invoked *payForMerchandise* and passed the parameter `amount`, the *payForMerchandise* would treat the payment as cash, whereas if the *Purchase* object had passed the parameters, `credit card`, `expiration date`, and `amount`, then *payForMerchandise* would treat the payment as a credit card transaction. This capability precludes having to have different names for methods that perform essentially the same kind of work but with different data, as well as saving evaluation logic that would otherwise be needed in the code to determine the type of transaction to perform prior to calling the correct method [5].

9.1.3 Abstractions and Complex Data Types

If encapsulation, inheritance, and polymorphism were all there was to OO, we might conclude that only a small incremental step had taken place from the days of structured programming with procedural languages. However, contrasted with synthetic systems where functionality is essentially static and changes require the introduction of new programming, OO software has progressed to support the development of more adaptive organic systems. An organic system is self-defining, self-organizing, and self-renewing [2].

One of the major adaptive advances in OO is the ability to define complex data types. Programming languages in general support **primitive data types**, including integer, character, floating-point numbers, and so on. Yet even some of the more modern languages provide only limited capability to create user-defined data types, such as **structures** and **unions** in the "C" language [7]. In OO software, programmers can go further to create complex data types that become objects themselves. Because programmers can extend the primitive data types, they are not forced to think only in terms of the technical problem such as memory management, process creation, data storage, and the like. They can address the problem at a business level using more natural types. That is, OO programmers can perform both the lower-level computation involved in sales transactions using floating-point numbers and so on, while concurrently working with larger grained, user-defined data types such as an "invoice."

A fundamental aspect of this capability comes by way of **data abstraction**. OO programmers can create **abstract data types** by assembling primitive data types into a collection that represents a concept. An *invoice*, for example, is a concept that contains several different primitive types: integers, characters, and floating-point numbers. Even though earlier computer languages such as "C" supported data abstractions, they tended not to treat the user-defined data types the same way that they treated the primitive types, and they required special operations (such as pointer usage) to manipulate them. However, OO languages such as C++ and JAVA provide native support for data abstraction. The technology is designed to enable **new** creations dynamically and manipulate these new types of data in the same way that primitives are created and manipulated. As such, OO can be more easily extended and adapted to meet specialized needs. Because we can create new data types as objects in OO languages such as C++, programmers can perform operations on them using their methods [8].

Whereas in the languages "C" or Pascal we have to create a *string data type* out of characters, in most OO languages a "string" is an object, and as such, it has methods that can be called such as to find out how many characters the string contains. The string object is treated programmatically as a unit, unlike in a language such as "C" where we have to deal with strings character by character. Thus we see that in OO, an abstract data type is an object assembled from primitive data types, such as numbers and characters. In a system that deals with invoices, for example, we can define new data types to represent invoices directly. This new data type is created and manipulated in consistent ways with all the data types in the programming language. Just as numbers can be added, subtracted, and so on, invoices can be accumulated, collated, and paid [1, 4].

9.1.4 Object Composition

Earlier, we discussed the notion of inheritance as a means of defining objects. Objects may also have constituents aggregated into OO form, which is called *composition*. Composition is the process of combining objects into complex objects, similar to how atoms combine into molecules. How objects are designed to be composed is an important stage in the creation of OO systems [3].

When objects are conceived for a software application, the object designer strives to define *atomic* units. Atomic units are self-contained objects. For example, we might have an object called Employee. However, we would likely not have an address as one of the employee's attributes. An employee lives at an address, but he or she is not made up of an address. Therefore, we are likely to want address to be part of some other object and keep only those attributes such as name, employee ID number, and so on in our *Employee* object.

In thinking about this, however, you might recognize two distinct kinds of relationships: "*IS-A*" and "*HAS-A.*" With the property of inheritance, we can indicate that an Employee IS-A-Person, whereas an Employee HAS-An-Identification. In this latter instance, *Identification* might simply be an integer attribute defined and allocated in the Employee object, but it could also be another individual object called Identification, in which case we would be referring to composition. Writing the objects in such a way where Identification is an object has certain advantages. For example, for security purposes, we may use multiple ways of identifying an Employee that goes beyond an ID number, and perhaps includes biometric data. In this case, using a HAS-A type of relationship gives us flexibility in identification and authentication system processes.

In the case where a programmer defined an object called Recording, the relationship with another object called VideoRecording would indicate a parent–child relationship. More specifically, a *VideoRecording* is a type of *Recording*. There can be a long lineage of parent–child classes, such as Recording → VideoRecording → DVD. In this example, Recording in the relationship is called a base class, and when an object is created (constructed), all of the classes would be combined such that we would have a DVD that included all of the methods and attributes of the VideoRecording and Recording classes also.

On the other hand, the relationship between *Motor* and *Automobile* is such that an *Automobile* has a *Motor*. This is useful in the case where a make and model of automobile may have different motor options. In the HAS-A type of composition relationship, there are two kinds: *pure composition* and *aggregation*. Both are used when a whole is made up of parts, with each part being a separate object rather than an attribute or a parent or child of an object. However, with pure composition, an object belongs to one and only one other object, whereas with aggregation, an object may be part of several other objects.

From both a design and a programming standpoint, if we were referring to an *Automobile*, the type of relationship would depend on the application. For example, if we sold automobiles, a new automobile would include a motor. If we ran a junkyard instead, people may purchase parts, or even just a chassis of an automobile. Therefore, depending on our application, we might define *Motor* in either the pure composition or aggregation category. In aggregation, because an object might belong to others, if one is removed from memory, we might want the others to remain in memory so the application can continue to work with these objects. For example, suppose we had an application that processed insurance policies in which an object called Insured had policies for two other objects, Home and Automobile. If our Insured sold the automobile, we may want to remove that object from memory, but not the Insured or the Home.

> **In Focus**
>
> Composition is handled by the OOP language syntax. For example, "IS-A" relationships represent inheritance, and in the JAVA programming language, this is done using the "extends" keyword. On the other hand, "HAS-A" composition is done by instantiating a new object within an object, and this can be done in JAVA with the "new" operator.

It is important to note that composite objects do not actually "contain" other objects in the sense that one object is physically stored inside the other. Rather, composite objects have references, or pointers, to other objects [9]. That is, composite objects have data structures that contain the memory addresses of the locations for their constituent objects. In this way, any given object can be composed of any number of other objects simply by referring to them through these "connectors"—and the importance of this to computer security will become apparent later.

9.1.5 OOP and Applications

We have covered a little bit about programming syntax and discussed OOP and how these are designed. We now examine OOP from an applications point of view. Software objects in source code form are called classes, and when they are executed, they are called objects. The difference between these two is mostly vernacular, although they do have specific meanings to programmers. For example, an object implies all of the methods and attributes of its parents and composites, whereas a class may simply refer to one of these pieces. For simplicity in our discussion here, we can consider a class as the programming source code version or a diagrammed concept. To transform a class into an object, classes must be subjected to a program called a ***compiler*** that converts the human-readable source code into computer-readable executable code.

When objects are executed, they have a ***life cycle***. That is to say, when they are created, they are said to be ***instantiated***; when they are terminated, they are ***destroyed***. When an object is instantiated, it receives and allocates data structures (in the stack and on the heap—more about these later), and when the object is destroyed, these data structures are deleted and returned to queues for other objects to use. Therefore, the life cycle results from the interactions between objects. For example, a web server may instantiate a "server" object to receive a connection over a network, which in turn instantiates several children server objects to handle multiple "client" connections, and then each of these objects destroys itself when it has completed its tasks (i.e., finished providing services).

In Focus

Self-contained (virtual machine) environments such as JAVA have a process known as a "garbage collector" that is used to reclaim portions of memory that have been unallocated by a program and return the memory addresses to the native operating system's pool of memory resources. From a security standpoint, if objects aren't collected and returned soon enough, a rogue program (process thread—to be discussed later) may obtain access to them, causing a variety of security threats.

When classes are envisioned in their general forms, we design a set of parent–child classes. For example, Vehicle object may have a child class called Bus, and at runtime the Bus object is instantiated, inheriting all that which is contained in the Vehicle. We may also have many Bus objects executing at a given time, each one with different routes and stops. At design time, programmers must consider how objects will interact, that is, how they will call each other's methods. They must also consider how objects change their tasks or conditions (states), and the levels at which an object can manipulate the data.

When an object needs to execute a method that belongs to another object, how do you suppose the object knows what the names of the other object's methods are and what parameters to pass? A class, called an ***interface***, is written that contains only the names and parameters of objects, typically without any other source code. All objects that may call each other's methods share this interface at the time they are compiled. Thus when an object is executed, it can look up, like in a dictionary, the name of the methods and the parameters that are implemented by the other classes.

In Focus

Different terminology is used to mean various aspects of a class. For example, a parent class at the top of a hierarchy is usually called a base class, and depending on the design, the base class and some of its children may be called abstract classes, which mean they will not be instantiated.

As objects transition from one condition to another through their life cycles, they may not yet have finished performing the tasks required of them. They may have to go through several passes before they complete. Each time objects change from one task to another, they go through **state transitions**. By way of example, if we were driving our cars down a highway on our way home from work and we pulled up to an intersection where the light was red, the light object is in the red state. When it changes to green, it transitions from the red state to the green state. Some **event**, in this case driving over the sensory plate under the road, **triggered** the signal to transition the light from the red state to the green state, and this may recur through several intersections until we arrive home. We may think of this similarly to how objects perform.

Objects and their data also have a notion of **scope**. Scope is the point at which an object (and/or its data) is accessible by a line of code or another object. If a programmer declared a variable called "payDate" inside a class called "Payroll," it is likely *payDate* would not be accessible from a class called "JournalEntry," at least not without going through a method that the class *Payroll* provided to the *JournalEntry* class. Likewise, if a variable were declared inside a block of programming routines, once the routines had completed and exited, the variable would no longer be accessible to other blocks of routines. It would be **out of scope**.

9.2 Database Interaction

We have previously covered how relational databases are designed and have some understanding of tables, keys, and normalization, and now that we have some knowledge of OOP, we are ready to cover some fundamental ways that software interacts with relational databases. First we will present a hurdle that OO programmers have to overcome when they retrieve and store data between objects and relational databases, sometimes called an impedance mismatch—borrowing from a hardware term; then we look at some database programming syntax and Structured Query Language (SQL).

Suppose we are in charge of a health informatics department at a hospital and the software application we are implementing is written in an OOP such as JAVA or C++, but we are using an Oracle relational database to store the data. Let's say we have the following software objects: *Nurse, Physician, Administrator, Staff, Pharmacist, Pharmacy, Microbiology, Admitting, Billing, Patient,* and *Medical Record.* You now know that classes are self-contained units that have data and behaviors. When instantiated, objects are formed from the potentially many classes they inherit and of those from which they are composed. In this regard, they are large-grained structures, but they represent individual units.

Now let's say we have normalized our relational database to Third Normal Form, or 3NF. We might have tables that consist of the following: *Personnel, Medications, Location,* and *Patients.* We would probably have more tables and more objects in the real application, but this will serve to point out that our tables are not the same as our objects. For instance, we have an individual object for each kind of employee, but our table merely has personnel with a column that describes a type of employee. That is correctly done, but presents a common disparity.

It would be quite inefficient from a database point of view to have a table for each kind of employee; in fact, that would be ridiculous because it would require adding a table when a new type of employee is added. Here we have designed an economical database structure with one personnel table. Likewise, having a Personnel object would be ridiculous, because we have specific kinds of personnel, and that would leave us with orphaned attributes and non-functional methods in our Personnel object for things that would apply to one kind of employee but not another.

When we extend this problem to the domain of code, we have to determine where in the objects we will place our database (SQL) code. For example, where would the SQL go for the query to gather the Nurse object's data from the database? And then, where does the SQL go to perform an insert to write a Nurse object's data to the database? We can see that there are data elements that are not part of the Nurse object that need to go into the personnel table. This is at the core of the impedance mismatch problem [1].

We see a similar condition involving the persistence of XML, because XML is hierarchical in nature. In many ways, XML has taken us back to the old hierarchical database structure along with its limitations; however, as we previously discussed, there are new ways of marking up these structures to make them relational, with RDF, and the more object-oriented markup with an ontology markup language such as OWL or DAML+OIL. Later, we will discuss some of the critical issues these sorts of design implications have for systems development and security.

9.2.1 SQL Overview

The American National Standards Institute (ANSI) defined the **Structured Query Language (SQL)**, and they are in charge of maintaining SQL standards and publishing new standards periodically. For example, the 1992 standard is known as SQL92. In addition to SQL, the languages a typical RDBMS supports include Data Definition Language (DDL), which is used to define schemas (table structure), and Data Manipulation Language (DML), which is used for operations such as retrieval, insertion, deletion, and modification of the data. DDL and DML can either be used interactively from within the RDBMS or be embedded in a general-purpose programming language, such as C++ or Visual Basic [5].

When a programming language is used, a user-friendly user interface is often created in the application program to accept the user's queries so the end users don't have to deal with DDL or DML. The user's input is converted to DDL or DML statements and sent to the DBMS. The DBMS will process the DDL or DML statements and send the results back to the application program so the end users can see the result. SQL is both a DDL and a DML. It has statements for table creation, metadata definition, grant (access rights), query (select), insert, delete, and update data (sometimes called a CRUD model—create, retrieve, update, delete) [10].

In Focus

One of the most important (and dangerous) database commands is "grant," which allocates read, write, and create permissions to users. Also, because databases are typically accessed over a network, they need to be secured with a password, and yet many are not—creating a security hole.

A SQL query gathers data from the relational database. If more than one table is involved, the query does a "join," which gathers the data requested from the multiple tables. SQL has only one basic statement for retrieving information from a database, the SELECT statement. A basic SQL statement also contains the clauses such as FROM and WHERE. The SQL query statement is shown in the following example:

```
SELECT <a list of attributes>
FROM <a list of tables>
WHERE <condition>
```

The result of a query is called a **view**. A view is a temporary table of the query results. The reason we need to use a query or create views is that users often want to read only part of the fields and part of the records. The <a list of attributes> is where we tell the DBMS what fields we want to display. All we need to do is list those fields separated by commas, such as, SELECT SSN, LNAME, PHONE. We can use the WHERE clause to specify conditions for what records we want to display. The <condition> looks like an equation and only records that meet the condition will be included in the result. For example, if we want to display records of all the employees who are older than 62 years of age, the Where clause may appear as WHERE AGE > 62. Furthermore, we can specify one table name after the FROM keyword if the query is limited to a single table, or we can have a list of table names if the query involves fields in multiple tables; for example, a FROM clause may be as simple as FROM EMPLOYEE.

An SQL query statement must contain a SELECT clause and a FROM clause. If the WHERE clause is omitted, all the records in the database will be included in the result set. If we want to display all the fields in a table, it is not necessary to type all the field names in the SQL statement; we simply use the asterisk (*) to tell the DBMS to have all the fields included. The statement SELECT * FROM CARS generates a view with all records from the CARS table.

The spirit of the relational database design is such that we can break the data into small pieces when we store the data, and we can put the data together on the fly when we retrieve the data. SQL supports the operation of getting data from multiple tables using JOIN operations, of which there are two types: inner joins and outer joins. These are the mechanisms by which parts of multiple tables can be gathered. An inner join combines records from two tables whenever there are matching values in a common field. The basic form of an inner join is shown in the example that follows:

```
SELECT <field list>
FROM table1 INNER JOIN table2 ON field1 = field2;
```

The RDBMS needs to know which tables to JOIN. To do this, we need to put the two tables we want to join at both sides of the INNER JOIN keyword. The sequence of the table names does not affect the result. The RDBMS also needs to know on what fields we want to make the JOIN, which is represented by a statement using the ON keyword. When many records are included in a view, it is usually desirable to organize the result set records in a certain order. SQL's ORDER BY statement can help us with this. The ORDER BY clause sorts a query's resulting records on a specified field or fields in ascending or descending order, as seen in the example that follows:

```
SELECT <fieldlist>
FROM <table list>
[WHERE <criteria>]
[ORDER BY field1 [ASC | DESC ] [, field2 [ASC | DESC] ]
[,...]]]
```

> **In Focus**
>
> A major security threat is called SQL Injection. One way this attack can be perpetrated is for a hacker to insert characters into a URL line of a browser in a transaction with a web server, and then see what errors the web server reports. Unprotected systems may return what the expected SQL format should be. The attacker may then inject attack parameters in the URL to cause the web server to execute SQL statements improperly.

9.2.2 Software and RDBMS Concurrency

A single person generally accesses a database on a PC, but a commercial database needs to be accessed by many users simultaneously. For example, a credit card company's system may contain hundreds of thousands of client records. Its customer service department may hire hundreds of customer service representatives to answer the phone, all of whom need access to the data in the database. Data are often changed from their original value. For instance, when an employee receives a raise, the salary in the database contains the old values and must be updated. The update process can be summarized in three steps: read old value from the database into the computer's RAM (random access memory), calculate the new value based on the old value in RAM, and write the new value back into the database.

We can imagine a problem when two or more persons access the same record at the same time. The solution of this problem is ***locking***, which blocks other transactions from taking place while the transaction is modifying the data. Many DBMS or programming languages support various kinds of resource locking, and the locking can be applied at different levels: record level, table level, and database level. A record-level lock does not allow other transactions to read or change the record that is locked. On the other hand, other transactions can access multiple records in the same table. As imagined, record-level locking is the most common type of resource locking. Secondly, the locking, no matter at which level, can vary from exclusive lock to shared lock. No other transactions can read the record if an exclusive lock is applied. When a shared lock is added, other transactions can read the record that is being processed but cannot update the value in that record. Next, when an application requests a lock, there are two strategies that can be used.

Optimistic locking assumes that the record (or table, etc.) will be free in that no conflict will occur. Data are read and the transaction is processed, and then a check is made to see if there was a conflict. If not, the transaction completes. If there is a conflict, the process is repeated. In pessimistic locking, the assumption is made that there will be a conflict; hence a lock is first issued, and then the transaction is attempted. Optimistic locking is chosen on tables that are rarely updated, whereas pessimistic locking is used when a table is volatile. Locking falls under the rubric of what we call **concurrency** as indicated earlier. There is another aspect to concurrency as well. To understand distributed systems and client-server architecture, we need to distinguish database from application activities.

Beyond having multiple users accessing a database in a client-server configuration, imagine a case where you have multiple databases that are involved in a database transaction. For instance, let's say a patient entered the hospital to have his tonsils removed. The admitting office creates a patient record and then sends the patient to a room where he will remain until they finish the operation. A nurse comes into the room and gives the patient an injection of medication to make him sleep while they extract his tonsils. The computers for each of these "transactions" reside in different departments. Admitting is likely to have a computer where the patient record is created and kept; the nurses' station is likely to have a PC, perhaps running Windows; and the pharmacy (where the medication is dispensed) is likely to have a mini-computer, perhaps such as an HP running Linux, as examples.

It would be a disaster if the nurse or doctor were to give medication to sedate the patient, but the software could not update the pharmacy inventory file to deduct that medication. When the next patient needed it, the medication may show in the computer, but not on the shelf. What is needed is an all-or-nothing transaction. That is to say, the mainframe patient record, the nurses' station indicating what medications the patient has received, and the pharmacy inventory database containing what is in stock all need to be concurrently updated. To handle this, we need a transaction manager (sometimes called monitor), which is a software application that performs a **two-phase commit**, as we introduced before. To elaborate how two-phase commit works, let's say that transaction "A" needs to concurrently update records in multiple heterogeneous systems and databases. The sequence is described as follows:

1. Transaction manager sends the three databases a pre-commit request.
2. If the records are not locked by another application, each database sets a provisionary lock and replies to the transaction manager with an affirmative lock acknowledgment (ACK).
   a. If a record is locked, jump to step 3.
   b. Transaction manager in the second phase tells the databases to commit the transaction.
   c. The databases update their records and respond with an acknowledgment.
   d. The transaction manager signals the application and terminates the transaction.

3. Else if a record is locked in one or more of the databases by another application, a negative lock acknowledgment (NAK) is sent to the transaction manager.

   a. The transaction manager signals the application to roll back the transaction and retry later (in milliseconds).

   b. If fail on retry, check for deadly embrace (where two different applications lock a record in a multi-record update that the other needs).

In Focus

Transaction monitors such as Tuxedo and Open/OLTP enable distributed transaction processing between heterogeneous databases using a two-phase commit protocol. There are other technologies, besides a transaction manager, needed to make distributed systems work—not only do multiple databases need to coordinate, the application needs to coordinate multiple data objects that perform the database logic.

9.3 Distributed Systems

Most commercial systems are distributed, meaning they use a multi-tiered design. Applications that are distributed within an enterprise often employ "tightly coupled" client/server architecture such as those that use an ***object request broker*** (**ORB**) as we presented in the previous chapter. Others are "loosely coupled" across organizational boundaries and over the Internet using some sort of web-based technology such as markup languages and ***service-oriented architecture*** (**SOA**). These technologies are needed to allow distributed objects to find and work with each other.

Using the ORB approach, code called ***stubs*** and ***skeletons*** must be generated and distributed to communications partners. All client applications must have a *stub*, and all the servers must have a *skeleton*. These files contain the underlying networking code that allows distributed objects to communicate with each other over a network. Furthermore, servers must be located in a registry so that clients can locate them. Beyond this widely distributed architecture, systems in an enterprise often utilize a multi-tiered configuration where there are "n" number of servers deployed horizontally in a tier, as well as n-number deployed vertically. This, as you may recall, is referred to as ***n-tier architecture***.

Examples of distributed technologies in the Microsoft arena are the Common Object Model (COM) and Distributed Common Object Model (DCOM) that enable interoperability between various application objects and components. The COM architecture allows features such as Object Linking and Embedding (OLE), which is used when pasting an Excel spreadsheet into a Word document, for example; DCOM supports ActiveX controls, which enable executables to be distributed and run over the Web for ***rich and interactive Internet applications*** (**RIAs**).

Another approach to distributed systems involves service-oriented architecture (SOA). SOA is more flexible and loosely coupled than the tight coupling of objects, but sometimes they can be less secure and less efficient than those that are more tightly coupled. Usually we see SOA for applications that involve transactions among multiple trading partners, say, between a manufacturer and suppliers and distributors, whereas we usually see distributed objects in enterprise applications—those that involve a corporation's internal enterprise applications.

9.3.1 Web Applications

Most modern software implementations are web-enabled at a minimum, or they are web-based. Web-enabled applications are those that have a web interface to a server-side application. Web-based applications communicate with software on a host computer called a web server. Common web servers include Microsoft Internet Information Services (IIS), Apache Tomcat, and Caucho Resin. In a typical web application, an HTML or XML page is used for display of the content by a browser, which communicates with the web server to receive and interpret the HTML or XML over the HTTP protocol. Web pages often have visual effects embedded in the HTML pages, which could be animations in the form of Flash movies or other graphics, sound, or other animation. Increasingly, we are seeing implementations of web interfaces developed with Flash and/or FLEX (an Adobe Rich Internet Application, or RIA).

Beyond HTML, most web pages also contain scripting languages such as JavaScript and AJAX (AJAX is a JavaScript RIA). Scripts create the ability to perform rudimentary logic within a web page such as performing validation of fields such as: were data entered numeric? These things might be processed client-side, meaning by the browser, or server-side, meaning by the host server computer. Note that although client-side scripting is more immediately responsive, it is also a bigger security risk because it is susceptible to modification from a man-in-the-middle attack (which we will discuss later when we get to the network security topic).

In Focus

Important to managers also are RSS feeds, social media integration, and "smart" phone applications because these serve to blur the distinctions between business goals, systems, and processes, but they also create new security challenges. See for example Moore, Budd, & Benson, 2007 [11].

Microsoft IIS has an interface called Internet Server Application Program Interface, or ISAPI, which traps and processes HTTP messages. ISAPI can be used by various programming languages (C++, JAVA, etc.) for the request processing. Primarily, however, ISAPI is used with a Microsoft technology called Active Server Pages (or ASP—and you will notice these on the URL file because they have an extension .asp). When IIS receives an ASP page, it sends it to an ASP processor over the ISAPI interface, and then sends the response back to the client in the reverse.

ASP pages can also contain scripting, such as JavaScript, VBScript, or Perl, and the ASP processor that runs on the host server executes these. In addition, Microsoft applications often use ActiveX controls that can perform some processing in the browser. By embedding (using the OBJECT tag) within the HTML code, the ActiveX object overlays Microsoft's DCOM technology to enable programs to share information, especially through web pages. Many attackers exploit this capability to create viruses and worms.

Host servers are located using a URL, which contains a service name, a domain name, a path name, and an optional file name or it defaults to index.html. When a server sends a file to a client, it also sends a code indicating the file type. The client system interprets the code to determine which program to use to process the file. These codes are called Multipurpose Internet Mail codE (MIME). MIME was initially developed for email but has since proliferated for other uses. MIME types usually (but not always) have three-letter extensions on Windows and four on UNIX-based systems. For example, text/html is .htm, or .html; text/plain is .txt, image/gif is .gif; image/jpeg is .jpg or .jpeg; and so on.

MIME can be extended such that an application-defined type can be added to the MIME list. For instance, it is possible to create an application that has a specific MIME type code, and that code can be placed in the MIME files on clients and servers and then associated with a graphic image. When a user clicks on the image, the browser will check the MIME code and determine that it should invoke the application, which it may download from a server.

9.3.2 Web Application Processing

Web applications are request-processor services [12]. This means that servers wait to be accessed and provide services upon request, unlike client-server, which uses either a polling mechanism or an interrupt mechanism, and an exchange or handshake to determine if a client is connected. Web servers "listen" on a *port* for connections to be made from a browser. A web server is located with the name placed in the URL. The name we placed inside the URL has to be translated to an IP address by a ***domain name service* (DNS)**.

The DNS provides the IP address to the target computer, which is then used to route the information from the browser out over the Internet to the host to which we wish to connect. Because HTTP is a stateless protocol (which we will cover later), some tricks have to be performed to carry out two-way communication. When the client browser opens a connection to a web server, it sends the server an HTTP request. The server responds by sending an HTML page back to the client and closes the connection. If the communication involves processing a transaction, such as purchasing an insurance policy at an e-insurance company or purchasing an item that is placed into a shopping cart, rather than simply rendering a document in HTML, sessions and state must be managed by the web server application.

In Focus

Web applications are a special case. They use HTTP, which is a stateless protocol, even though it uses TCP underneath. When it was originally created, it was envisioned only for browsing in the Web, but now we see it for all kinds of web-based applications. It makes web applications tricky, though, because fancy footwork is needed to simulate a stateful connection.

To illustrate, let's say that the HTML document contains a control or validation for entering an insurance policyholder's name to get a quote from the web server, and it must look up the policy information from its database. There are two ways the browser can send this information, either (1) Post, to send data enclosed in the request message, or (2) Get, to send data in the URL. A program on the web server must process the information; for this example, suppose we are using a JAVA Servlet. The Servlet is a web server program that reads the Post (or Get) and collects the values from the HTML page for processing in the server. In the HTML form, let's say we have the following markup:

```
INPUT type=Text name="policyholder".
```

In the Servlet, we then have a program statement as follows:

```
request.getParameter("policyholder");.
```

The request is a JAVA object, and it has a method "getParameter." Using this object and method, a web page is able to post the "policyholder" parameter to a JAVA Servlet running in the web server. It gets the name of the policyholder to process inside a main application. At this point, the web server may typically construct a query (using a database access language like SQL or, in JAVA, JDBC) to get the policy information from the database. Once it does this, it may dynamically create an HTML page and embed this policy information inside it. Then it transmits this back to the client browser.

Suppose, however, that rather than one page to process this insurance policy, we require many pages. Because HTTP is stateless (as we indicated and will explain in more detail later), with each page, the web server addresses it as a new connection. For transactions such as these, we need a way to group multiple pages. This is done by session management, which using our example might be through one of three ways: (1) URL rewriting, which is discouraged from a security standpoint, (2) hidden form fields, which are not secure, or (3) cookies. Cookies are small pieces of text exchanged between web server and browser and passed in the HTTP header. They can be used for tracking preferences, but they are also used for identification (note that they are encrypted), and they can be used for keeping state information used in session management.

Importantly, cookies can be persistent or non-persistent. Where persistent cookies are written to a computer and used for things such as determining user preferences, in session management, non-persistent cookies (also called session variables) are passed back and forth for the life of the session (or series of connections), but they are not typically saved on the computer. This is accomplished by means of the server creating and assigning the client a unique session ID. The unique ID is passed back and forth between the client and server through the entire conversation until the connection is terminated. In our example, with each page change, the Servlet program will check the session ID by using the JAVA program statement: `HttpSession sessionID = request.getSession( )`. As long as the value of `sessionID` is as expected, the session will keep going in the logical transaction sequence. If it finds that the `sessionID` is different than expected, it may force the user to log in and begin a new session.

In Focus

Session management in web applications is complex. For transactions, there are typically three options used: URL rewriting (bad!), hidden form fields (not secure), or non-persistent cookies—otherwise known as session variables (preferred—but can be turned off in a browser).

9.3.3 JAVA Servlets

We presented the idea of a Servlet. A Servlet is a program written in the JAVA language that runs inside a web server and processes requests as we indicated. Let us now get acquainted with some of the JAVA syntax using a Servlet example. There are three common things for which Servlets are typically used (although note that there could be many more): (1) to process HTML input (e.g., with Get or Post), (2) to receive parameters and generate events, including to act as a controller to dispatch commands to middleware or other server-side components, and (3) to generate HTML dynamically to display in a browser (e.g., the results of a query).

JAVA is an object-oriented, or OO (or, more accurately, nearly OO), language. Hence, we write objects, and each object has methods that are called to perform an action. Variables inside an object are called attributes, and when passed between objects, they are called parameters. OO syntax calls objects in the following form: object.Method (parameters). As we indicated earlier, an important object contained inside a Servlet is called "request," and it has a method called getParameter. The getParameter is a method inside the request object: `request.getParameter(html_Identifier)`. The html_identifier is a name of a parameter we collected from an HTML page. If we have an HTML statement that collects a name from a text field such as `input type=Text name="Name"`, then in the HTML page we may use the Post (or Get) method to send the name to the web server. We tell the web server in this example to call the Servlet named `testServlet` to process the name as follows:

```
form name="example"  method="POST"  action="/servlet/
testServlet" onSubmit=" this.Name.optional = false;
```

Inside the Servlet, `testServlet`, we use request.getParameter to get the name to process thus: `request.getParameter("Name")`. We now have in our JAVA Servlet an attribute called `Name`, and we could store the Name value in this attribute in a database or do a lookup in the database. If we simply wanted to echo it back to the browser in an HTML page, we would write the embedded HTML markup in the JAVA Servlet code snippet that follows:

```
String n = request.getParameter("Name");
response.setContentType("text/html");
PrintWriter out = response.getWriter();
out.println("<html>");
out.println("<head><title>Name</title></head>");
out.println(<body>)
out.println(n);
out.println("</body></html>");
```

The previous snippet of code gets the value contained in the parameter Name (such as "Dan") and assigns it to string n, sets the response content type to HTML (this could also have been XML or WML), gets a PrintWriter object to write the HTML to the output response (this would be a browser), and then outputs the HTML markup statements along with the value of n, which is the name.

9.3.4 Distributed Web-Based Systems

Web applications may use some combination of mechanisms such as JAVA Servlets and JAVA Server Pages (JSP) for processing web-based transactions, but because systems are distributed, by and large those technologies alone are often not sufficient. We may need application servers and distributed technologies to make the solution complete. The extent to which we need these additional technologies will be partly driven by whether we are doing content management or transaction processing over the Web.

Content management is the display of information; an example is the CNN website, www.cnn.com. The way CNN presents information to the Web may work something like this: Reporters from around the world send their news reports as "stream data" via a computer program to a host system. The host system aggregates all of the news stream data, then tags, categorizes, and sorts the data. A computer program that acts as a screener sifts through these tagged and sorted data and forwards the data to copy editors who fix the grammar and prepare it for presentation. The data are then fed into a queue, and a workflow system collects the stories and dynamically renders the data onto the website. It is amazing how much of this process is automated. That is really the only way CNN could possibly keep its website updated with news stories coming in constantly.

Alternatively, if you have ever purchased a book online (e.g., www.amazon.com), then you interacted with a transaction processing system over the Web. The transaction processing system had to collect some information from you, such as your order and your credit card information; do some lookups in a database to see where the inventory is kept for the book; call out over its network to a credit card clearinghouse or credit card company to make sure your Mastercard or Visa can be charged; and finally post back to you the results of your transaction.

It is important to note that distributed systems need to address the issue of scalability specifically. As the load on some portion of the system increases, new platforms can be installed and the computing can be distributed across the platforms. At low volume/load, however, distributed application servers carry unnecessary overhead. However, as systems need to be distributed to scale up, programmers often turn to using application servers and Enterprise JavaBeans (EJB) because communications components of the application must be shared between clients and servers. Also, as mentioned earlier, a distributed technology such as the JAVA Remote Method Invocation (RMI) or Common Object Request Broker Architecture (CORBA) ORB, which uses stubs and skeletons, may be used for communications among distributed components.

Let's illustrate this with a look at the architecture of distributed systems and distributed objects in a practical situation. Let's say that we have a company that processes insurance transactions over the Web, such as www.insuremycar.com. A prospective customer wants to insure his or her car and goes to www.insuremycar.com in order to get a quote. Insuremycar does not underwrite insurance. Instead, they work with a variety of independent insurance brokers and underwriters, and when you request a quote, they have software that takes your information and searches these independent underwriters to get quotes and prepare insurance binders. Insuremycar is a big company with a huge number of clients.

It is doubtful we would find a single computer with its 32-bit processor running Microsoft Windows and IIS handling all those transactions. More likely, we would find dozens and dozens of computers, perhaps even running Linux or some other flavor of UNIX (such as MAC/OS), and probably with 64-bit multi-processors all clustered together using a distributed technology. When we connect to one of these servers, it would be impractical if we had to connect to the same server for each function. What we need is for all of these servers to work in lockstep no matter what server we connect to.

When a function called "issue policy binder" occurs in the transaction, this is the result of some program object (called, perhaps, policyBinder) performing some logic in response to some triggered event, such as a mouse button click. But this program object is not sitting on a single server. There are policyBinder objects on all of the middle-tier server computers in the "n-tier" architecture, where there are multiple servers at multiple layers—for example, multiple web servers, multiple application servers, and multiple database servers, connected together via networking. There will also be software to manipulate these distributed objects.

In Focus

Web applications have a specific set of unique vulnerabilities. Part of these vulnerabilities, as you will read, involves the statelessness of the protocol HTTP, along with weaknesses in some of the technologies such as the use of JavaScript or the need for ActiveX controls. These can result in security risks, especially combined with the limitation that Microsoft Windows hides file extensions; for example, readme.txt might actually be readme.txt.exe, which can execute malicious code if downloaded from a website.

CHAPTER SUMMARY

Up to this point, we have covered some major aspects of OOP software applications and programming with databases. We finished this chapter with a brief discussion of n-tier distributed architecture and distributed objects that commercial enterprise applications use. As a result of the complexity and multiple components, as you can see, applications are greatly complicated by the Web and distributed systems. We have briefly covered three basic types of distributed systems—the web server and web application approach such as with JAVA Servlets, an application server approach using the Enterprise JavaBeans (EJB), and service-oriented architecture (SOA).

Using CORBA, DCOM, or EJB, we get tighter coupling among distributed objects than with SOA and web services, but there are advantages and disadvantages with each of these that managers, programmers, administrators, and security personnel need to consider. The security techniques used in the more tightly coupled approaches are more mature than the SOA approach, along with the added benefit that they tend to live inside a more protected environment such as behind a firewall. Web-based and SOA applications are among the most exposed and complicated systems to build, but they are becoming the norm and thus need special attention. We will return to these important issues when we cover web applications security in the next section.

THINK ABOUT IT

Topic Questions

9.1: What are three primary object-oriented characteristics?

9.2: Web applications are often hosted by a web server.

_____ True
_____ False

9.3: Composition is the process of combining objects into complex objects.

_____ True
_____ False

9.4: A concrete object is called:

_____ An ORB

_____ An instance
_____ A class
_____ A stub

9.5: Software systems are analogous to the body's:

_____ Anatomy
_____ Biology
_____ Physiology
_____ Cells

9.6: Encapsulation includes using language keywords _private_, _protected_, and _public_.

_____ True
_____ False

THINK ABOUT IT (CONTINUED)

9.7: IS-A means composition.

____ True
____ False

9.8: To manage a single transaction across multiple databases, a transaction manager needs to do a:

____ Rollback
____ Concurrent update
____ SQL Select
____ Two-phase commit

9.9: Table locking falls under the rubric of what we call:

____ Transaction processing

____ Concurrency
____ Commit
____ Journaling

9.10: Using the ORB approach, code called a stub must be generated and distributed to:

____ Servers
____ Registries
____ Databases
____ Clients

Questions for Further Study

Q9.1: How do web servers such as Tomcat differ from application servers WebLogic (AquaLogic)?

Q9.2: What special considerations do systems designers need to take into account with tightly coupled versus loosely coupled distributed technologies?

Q9.3: What technologies has OO enabled in terms of rapid software development?

Q9.4: What have web services introduced as far as distributed computing flexibility?

Q9.5: Explain the concept of impedance mismatch in terms of OO-to-relational database.

KEY CONCEPTS AND TERMS

Composition can be pure or aggregate.

Overloading is the ability to have methods using the same name that perform different functions depending on the parameters passed to the method.

Servlets are JAVA web server programs that process requests and send responses.

Structured Query Language (SQL) is used to store data in and retrieve data from a relational database.

Web-based applications use the stateless HTTP protocol.

References

1. Taylor, D. A. (1990). *Object-oriented technology: A manager's guide.* Alameda, CA: Servio Press.

2. Skyttner, L. (1996). *General systems theory: An introduction*. London, UK: Macmillan Press.

3. Booch, G. (1996). *Object solutions: Managing the object-oriented project*. Santa Clara, CA: Addison-Wesley.

4. Coad, P., & Nicola, J. (1993). *Object-oriented programming*. Englewood Cliffs, NJ: Prentice Hall.

5. Rao, B. R. (1993). *C++ and the OOP paradigm*. New York, NY: McGraw-Hill.

6. Coplien, J. O. (1992). *Advanced C++: Programming styles and idioms*. Reading, MA: Addison-Wesley.

7. Deitel, H. M., & Deitel, P. J. (1994). *C how to program*. Englewood Cliffs, NJ: Prentice Hall.

8. Ellis, M. A., & Stroustrup, B. (1990). *The annotated C++ reference manual*. Reading, MA: Addison-Wesley.

9. Corcho, O., Fernandez-Lopez, M., & Gomez-Perez, A. (2003). Methodologies, tools and languages. Where is their meeting point? *Data & Knowledge Engineering, 46*, 41–64.

10. Kronke, D. M. (2002). *Database processing: Fundamentals, design, and implementation*. Upper Saddle River, NJ: Pearson/Prentice Hall.

11. Moore, D., Budd, R., & Benson, E. (2007). *Rich Internet applications, AJAX and beyond*. Indianapolis, IN: WROX/Wiley Publishing.

12. Murach, J., & Steelman, A. (2007). *Java SE 6*. Fresno, CA: Murach Publishing.

Computer Operating Systems

WE HAVE COVERED SOME OF THE BASIC concepts about information systems, databases, and programming. Now in this chapter, we will summarize functions of general-purpose computer operating systems. Rather than simply provide a user's view, we will delve into some operating systems' internal functions and data structures by examining *Microsoft Windows* and *UNIX-based* operating systems, such as Linux, FreeBSD, and MAC/OS, as reference examples. This will provide a conceptual perspective to set the stage for the chapter on host computer security in the next section. We will begin with a view into digital logic and move on to how operating systems work with computer hardware and mediate user activities.

Chapter 10 Topics

This chapter:

- Briefly presents what operating systems do.
- Covers digital architecture and logic.
- Explores how hardware and operating systems interact.
- Helps you to become familiar with data structures and algorithms.
- Examines how user actions translate through Linux (UNIX) and Windows operating systems.

Chapter 10 Goals

When you finish this chapter, you should:

- ❏ Have a basic understanding of how hardware and the operating system work together.
- ❏ Have an understanding of what processes and threads are and how they are managed.
- ❏ Know how a process scheduler works.
- ❏ Understand interprocess communications.
- ❏ Be able to explain memory management techniques.
- ❏ Have a grasp of file systems and file management.
- ❏ Know about I/O and the interaction with hardware and drivers.

10.1 Operating Systems: An Introduction

You are probably used to working with computers but perhaps you may not think about how they work. Let's briefly discuss this before we move into what operating systems are and what they do. Note that there are many types of software systems and applications. At the highest level, such as Microsoft Word, we know this as a "software tool," but it is written in a programming language. When we launch Word, it also launches several software components such as something called COM (Common Object Model) that allows Word to exchange information (through an interface called Object Linking and Embedding [OLE]) with other applications. If you have ever copied an Excel spreadsheet and pasted it in a Word document, you have experienced COM/OLE at work. The key point is that neither program applications nor hardware would work without an operating system (OS).

10.1.1 Systems and Software

We have already considered programming, but imagine the programming that goes into creating applications such as Microsoft Word. You may already know that you can customize Word by extending it with programming code. For example, if you added the "Developer" tab to your Word application, you could bring up the "development environment." At this point, you could actually program embedded code into your Word document using Visual Basic. So you get the idea that Visual Basic is a high-level language, like C++, and is used for writing applications, for example, when Visual Basic is embedded in Word. (There are many other high-level languages, as we have noted earlier, besides Visual Basic, such as COBOL, Fortran77, and Pascal.) With a little more coding work, this code could create a message that says "Hello" when you open a document:

```
Private Sub Document_New()
   Dim A As String
   Let A = "Hello"
   MsgBox (A)
End Sub
```

Where high-level programming languages, such as Visual Basic, are useful for writing applications, they are not very useful for writing operating systems. Operating systems must work quickly and be able to communicate directly with the hardware components. Operating systems also must "execute" these high-level programs such as Word.

It is important to realize then that systems are made up of software. A system needs more than just a Microsoft Word application to run; it needs to interact with other software—and much of the interaction is in the form of what we call a client and a server. Most people associate a client and server with the Web, and although that is certainly true, the Microsoft Word editor is a client to the Word server. The server executes when you launch Word and open a document. You can see that software is a broad classification for any type of constructed statements that perform some computerized function; as such, software falls into different categories. Systems software is usually associated with computer operating systems such as Microsoft Windows or Linux, but it could also be software that makes network routers function or that controls certain devices. There are finer classifications of operating systems such as "real time" or "near real time" systems that monitor devices such as process controllers, air traffic control systems, or certain kinds of robotics.

Consequently, applications software consists mainly of the kinds of programs that users interface with to perform some function; for example, Microsoft Word is used to write documents, or a customer relationship management (CRM) application might be used to help track and manage client activity, or an inventory control system or accounting system might be used for business types of tasks, which we have previously mentioned.

Another important class of software involves what is often called middleware. As the name implies, this software intervenes between application and system software or between two different kinds of application software so that information can be exchanged among disparate sources and systems. Middleware can usually bridge between different network protocols, translate, manipulate, and format different data types, and execute rules such as what to do if an error occurs in a translation. A major class of middleware is known as enterprise application integration (EAI) software. EAI is focused on integrating and consolidating information among the computer applications in an enterprise. One common EAI use is to extract data from legacy applications, running on a mainframe computer, and load the data onto more modern systems such as distributed or desktop computers. It can also extract, translate, and load data among different databases, or allow for two systems to exist during a migration by creating ways for the information to flow to each system in parallel.

There are other systems as well, such as enterprise resource planning (ERP) systems used to plan and manage production "just in time" by coordinating the materials through the delivery chain, and business process management (BPM), which is similar to ERP, but it revolves around the business functions in an enterprise. These types of applications usually have a graphical user interface (GUI). A GUI is a visual display of some sort; for example, it can be a specialized monitor for showing network activity, railroads, or power grids, or it can display web content via a browser. The idea of GUI grew from the lumbering interaction that most people were subjected to with textual interfaces such as the UNIX shell or DOS window. GUIs provide features such as pull-down menus, buttons, scroll bars, "hot" images, and mouse-driven navigation—the features that most people associate with human–computer interaction.

Although we gave a list of sample applications you may already be familiar with, there are also programs for specialized scientific functions that OS perform such as running a nuclear plant or performing statistical analyses on data. Software exists for vertical applications such as banking, retailing, manufacturing, and logistical systems. There are utility programs used for doing system maintenance, backups, or automating manual functions. There are programs that are designed to work over the Web, such as to allow you to purchase a book online, and even database management systems that hold data are software applications. The lists in these categories are endless!

10.1.2 What Do OS Do?

In Microsoft Windows, people first see their desktop displaying frequently used program icons on it (**Figure 10.1**). Clicking on an icon (which is an image that has an associated link to a program) will cause the selected program to execute. This interaction between user, display, and program execution is what we call the "user view" of the system. Sometimes people relate to their computers by means of their user views—and mainly their GUI. This is often Windows Explorer, or sometimes could be a command window. However, the user view of the system and the user interfaces that these provide are not part of the OS, per se; these are support services that use the OS and vice versa.

As we will present later, the main part of an OS is called the kernel. The kernel is responsible for interacting with hardware devices, managing the data loaded into random access memory (RAM) or on the hard disk drive, loading programs into the central processing unit (CPU) for execution, and the like. Depending on whether you use a Microsoft Windows system or a MAC/OS, Linux, or some flavor of UNIX, the kernel will play a smaller or larger role in what the OS does in terms of these responsibilities. For instance, the Windows kernel plays a smaller role and relies more on "subsystems" than do UNIX-based system such as Linux or MAC/OS.

Overall, the OS can be thought of as consisting of programming code and sets of data structures. The programming code is written in a low-level language such as "C" or assembly language, and the data structures are often linked lists or queues (more shortly). Most OS are also "event-driven," meaning that when a user types on a keyboard or clicks on

FIGURE 10.1
Windows desktop.

something with the mouse, or when a storage place in memory becomes full, or when the CPU is ready to execute a new program, a type of signal or event is generated, which causes the OS to notice the event and respond to it. Because many people can use a computer at the same time, and many programs are running at the same time on a computer, the orchestration of these events and the execution of responses are very complex.

From a user perspective, we may see programs in a directory or folder with an ".exe" extension. These executable files lie dormant until a user or another program invokes them. When the program is invoked, it becomes a "process," which means that the OS allocates memory and sets aside various data structures for the program to run. The process is divided into parts, where some of the parts are only accessible by specific OS processes and other parts may be accessible by a user—a browser is a good example of this. Once the data structures have been created and memory allocations have been done by the OS, the process is placed in a queue until its turn comes to be executed by the CPU. In Windows, there are also ".dll" files (**Figure 10.2**). These are dynamically linked library files used by executable programs; in a sense, they too are executable, but not on their own.

10.1.3 Windows and UNIX (Linux)

Generally speaking, most people are familiar with Microsoft Windows—at least some version or another. However, there have been many changes to the Windows operating system over the recent years, and there seems no end to it either. We are going to cover some of the varieties of Windows ranging from XP to Version 7 and beyond, but in modern times, most of us have already grown familiar with Microsoft Vista or XP versions of Windows. However, Vista created new paradigms to deal with compared to previous versions, along with some unintuitive behaviors in associated applications. This was especially the case in Microsoft applications associated with the OS release, such as its Office 2007 suite, in which new features were added and others were moved around into

DLLs and
components.

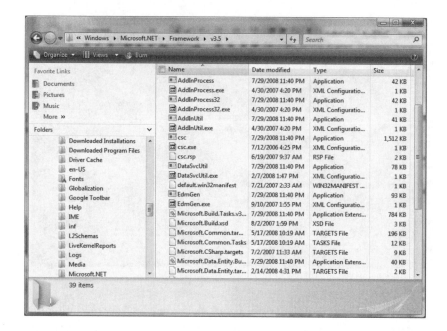

different locations in a seemingly bewildering and random fashion. Windows version 7 attempted to compensate for some of those quirks and also attended to some of the persistent security flaws in Windows; in the process, it grew to look a little more like a MAC/OS type of operating system than what we were familiar with as Windows users.

> **In Focus**
>
> People grow accustomed to predicting their environments and pay attention mainly to anomalies, such as in new user interfaces and functions. When these change, there are not only new features to learn, but changes that can "fool" people into doing the wrong thing from a security perspective. Linux and other UNIX-based systems such as MAC/OS have presented a much more consistent "look and feel" by introducing incremental changes to the user interfaces rather than radical ones.

Microsoft Windows is a proprietary system, so the code and internals are a partially guarded trade secret. However, there are some published aspects of the OS that can be presented, and many internal parts of it can be inferred as we will describe later. Dave Cutler was the chief architect of the modern Windows OS (beginning with Windows NT). Before joining Microsoft, Cutler designed the Digital Equipment Corporation's VMS OS, and he (and others) wrote many publications about VMS internals [1]. Although Cutler had a limited hardware platform to work with at the time he joined Microsoft (compared to the more robust DEC VAX mini-computer), there were hints given, for instance, that the new Windows NT architecture was a vastly scaled down version of many of the VMS concepts. At the base level, we need to understand some specific aspects of hardware–OS interaction and digital logic to appreciate how computer security is maintained or compromised.

10.2 Digital Architecture

Thus far, we have introduced the notion of how users interact with computers and, more specifically, an operating system, but how do operating systems interact with hardware? This matters because anyone who works in security must realize the entire chain of events from a user to the hardware. For example, how does a person in Beijing, China, cause a computer to crash in Sophia Antipolis, France, or in Toronto, Canada? To understand this, we must start from the ground up! At its most basic level, computers work with binary codes: bits of 1s and 0s. Groups of bits create patterns that are translated into the numbers and characters human beings recognize and vice versa. This scheme allows, for example, a programmer to write a statement that says, "if (a)," which says that if a number represented by variable "a" is any number other than 0, the result is true; otherwise, the result is false. Constructs such as "if (a)" are used to make decisions in program logic, and computer logic uses binary mathematics to represent varying electrical charges in solid-state circuitry. Binary logic, as you know, uses two digits: 0 and 1. Although a 0 may be associated with a lower voltage and a 1 with higher voltage, let's assume that in most computer systems, a 0 represents a negative physical charge and a 1 represents a positive physical charge, and these charges indicate false and true, respectively. How this binary logic is converted between higher-level coding and interpreted by various components is complex, so we will only provide a basic "functional-level" overview.

10.2.1 Hardware Components

The central processing unit (or CPU) executes the instructions for software applications running at any given time. Software components that communicate directly with the CPU are part of the **operating system** (**OS**). The OS must have functions that enable users to enter commands and translate those into codes to be executed by the CPU.

A **device driver** controls the devices (disk drives, user interfaces, and other hardware devices) and manages the hardware interaction for the OS, and a **scheduler** (or **dispatcher**) determines the order that applications are queued to run by the CPU. The CPU is actually composed of a highly dense circuitry, part of which contains a component called the arithmetic logic unit (ALU) that performs computations. Central processors also tend to work with either 32 or 64 bits at time.

Besides their "bit width," CPUs are also known by the number of their "cores." A core is a processor that reads and writes instructions, so a single-core processor can handle only one process instruction at a time. However, multi-core processors are now commonplace. These can do reading and writing of instructions in parallel, depending on their number of cores—dual core are two cores, for instance, whereas quad core are four cores—integrated into a single CPU chip.

Random access memory (**RAM**) consists of integrated circuitry that stores information being accessed by the operating system. When the computer is turned off, anything kept in RAM is lost; thus RAM is said to be ***volatile***. A ***memory manager*** controls the data structures in memory. Data are also stored in the computer's ***persistent*** memory such as hard disk drives, flash drives, or tape drives. Here, information is magnetically stored and remains even when the power is turned off; hence the name *persistent storage*.

Components such as a hard disk drive communicate with the CPU by means of an intermediary component called a ***controller board***. This circuitry handles the exchange of information between RAM, CPU, and other devices. There are controllers (and device drivers) for each hardware component—for instance, hard disk controller, monitor controller, and DVD controller. All of these devices are joined by an electronic pathway called a logic ***bus***, or simply bus. The bus consists of the circuitry by which information is shared among the devices: controllers, RAM, CPU, and other hardware.

There may be a separate bus for high-speed devices, or even between the CPU and a static form of memory called ***cache***. Contained on each one of the circuit boards are logic gate chips. Gates manage the logic flow within and among computer devices and circuitry. Other circuitry one will see on a schematic include resistors and transistors that control the flow of electricity through the circuit board, "buffers" and "registers" that temporarily hold information, amplifiers, relays, and a varied number of other types of circuit.

10.2.2 Binary Logic and Computer Hardware

When information is input into a computer, the CPU translates the binary codes into digits as indicated. The codes are then stored in a variety of circuit chips as groups of electrical charges represented as binary bits. Groups of bits create patterns that are translated into the numbers and characters people recognize. These bits are manipulated by the silicon components inside computers to perform specific roles. Logic gates and other components carry out the commands issued by the programming software. Some of the logic functions are AND, OR, NOT, NAND, and NOR. If we were to look at a computer circuit board diagram, called a schematic, we would see the symbols shown in **Figure 10.3**.

> **In Focus**
>
> Understanding logic such as AND, OR, and XOR is important in security—for example, creating subnetworks uses logical AND, and cryptographic ciphers use XOR, as we shall see later.

Inside the circuitry represented by these symbols, electrical current is passed (true) or prevented (false) based on the type of logic these symbols perform. The lines at the back of these symbols represent incoming electrical pathways, and the line coming out

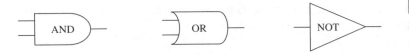

FIGURE 10.3

Schematic representations of logic gates.

is the resulting electrical pathway. We can illustrate the logic using truth tables. In truth tables, a 0 represents false or off, and a 1 represents true or on. The truth table for AND in **Table 10.1** indicates that when both incoming pathways (labeled A and B) are true (1), then the output (labeled C) is true (1); otherwise the output is false. In other words, it is only when electrical current is present on both incoming pathways that the AND gate will allow current to pass out of the gate.

Now consider the truth table for the OR gate as seen in **Table 10.2**. Unlike the AND gate, the OR gate allows true (1) for an output when only one (or both) incoming pathway(s) is (are) true (1); otherwise, if both pathways are false (0), the output is false (0).

Next, let's consider the NOT gate in **Table 10.3**. Notice that the NOT gate has only one incoming pathway (denoted A) and so its purpose is to invert the logic to the output (denoted B). Said another way, NOT simply converts true to false and false to true. As seen in the table, if the input is 1 (true), NOT will change the output to 0 (false); otherwise, if the input is 0 (false), NOT will change the output to 1 (true). Note that some gates may

TABLE 10.1 AND Truth Table

AND	A	B	C
	0	0	0 (if A and B are 0, then C = 0)
	0	1	0 (because only B is 1, then C = 0)
	1	0	0 (because only A is 1, then C = 0)
	1	1	1 (A and B are 1, so C = 1)

TABLE 10.2 OR Truth Table

OR	A	B	C
	0	0	0 (if A or B is 1, C = 1, else C = 0)
	0	1	1 (because B = 1, then C = 1)
	1	0	1 (because A = 1, then C = 1)
	1	1	1 (because A = 1, B = 1, then C = 1)

TABLE 10.3 NOT Truth Table

NOT	A	B
	1	0 (invert A to B)
	0	1

work with positive or negative electrical charges rather than the presence or absence of electrical current (depending on the hardware device).

10.2.3 Hardware Logic and Software Instructions

The CPU, memory, and other hardware devices could not function without logic components and the software to interact with them, and the OS provides the software components that make the hardware work. For example, registers are storages places for instructions. Operating systems also use **buffers**, which store data temporarily until the data can be processed by the OS. The OS manages various queues and data structures, such as the "stack" and "heap" where a program's variables and parameters are stored. You may have heard of buffer or stack overflows; they are related to programming problems and some common security attacks, which we will cover later.

> **In Focus**
>
> Buffer overflows are a major security threat. Understanding how systems buffer data is fundamental to knowing what this threat means and how to deal with the threat.

Modern operating systems (e.g., Linux and Windows) use a layered architecture. Each layer communicates with the layer above and below it, and it is the OS that coordinates these layers as each carry out specialized functions. Depending on the type of computer, the CPU may utilize either a CISC (complex instruction set computer) or RISC (reduced instruction set computer) instruction set. A CPU can perform more work with CISC during one instruction cycle, but it cannot execute instruction cycles as fast as when RISC is used.

> **In Focus**
>
> The discussion of MIPS and processor speed you may have heard about is a distraction. It takes more RISC instructions to perform a single CISC instruction, even though it may execute RISC more quickly [1].

Software subsystems link into the OS to provide ancillary or intermediary functions to application programs. In this layered scheme, there are user processes and system processes that represent executing programs. User processes are those generally initiated by an end user, whereas a system process is generally initiated by the OS either as the result of another OS process or on behalf of a user process in the form of what is known as a *system call* (more later). In any case, a process begins its life as source code, and there are many kinds of programming source code languages such as COBOL, "C," C++, C#, and JAVA.

Source code is not executable by the computer, as we learned earlier. It requires a compiler to transform the source code into RISC or CISC assembly language instructions.

The compiler has a companion program called an assembler (along with a linker/loader) that transforms the assembly language into machine instructions—a low-level nomenclature that ultimately ends up as patterns of 1s and 0s—as we discussed earlier. At this stage, programs become executable, but they reside on hard disk until there is a request for the program to run, at which time the program executable becomes a process, which is managed by the operating system.

10.3 UNIX-Based Operating System Functions

A UNIX-based operating system includes *Linux*, *Free BSD*, and *MAC/OS*. Although each has diverged in terms of feature function, the cores of their systems remain consistently UNIX. The kernel is the central component of a UNIX-based OS, and it consists of the computer's main set of "privileged" functions (**List 10.1**). The primary set of functions in a general-purpose kernel consists of the following [2]:

List 10.1

1. A *memory manager* that determines when and how memory is allocated to processes and what to do when memory fills up; this contains a subsystem called the *pager/swapper* that moves processes (or portions of processes called pages) from RAM onto a storage space on a hard disk drive called the "swap partition" when RAM becomes full.

2. A *process scheduler* that determines when and for how long a process can be executed by the CPU.

3. A *file system manager* that organizes collections of data on storage devices and provides an interface for accessing data.

4. *Interprocess communications* (**IPC**) facilities that handle the various communications between processes or threads.

5. An *I/O manager* that services input and output requests from hardware.

10.3.1 OS Features

As with most modern operating systems, the UNIX-based (Linux, Free BSD, MAC/OS [hereafter UNIX-based]) kernel is a multi-user, multi-tasking, multi-processing system. It performs process scheduling, process management, memory management, and hardware control. The multi-user capability enables concurrency among users, and the multi-tasking capability allows multiple processes and threads per user to execute. Multiprocessing allows many CPUs to cooperatively execute processes simultaneously [3]. Although most UNIX-based systems provide a GUI such as Gnome, GIMP,

X/Windows, or Motif [4], unlike Microsoft Windows, unless through a virtual machine, the interaction with the UNIX-based OS is usually through a command line interface called the ***shell***.

In Focus

Note that the latest trend in OS is what is called a virtual machine. For example, VMWare has a client that allows a user to interact with user applications provided by a VMWare server. The VMWare client appears to be a desktop set of applications, and these interact with a virtual server. When interacting with a system in this way, one may never "see" a primitive "window" prompt.

Windowing capability in UNIX-based systems is provided by layered subsystems, such as X/Windows, Motif, Gnome, and GIMP, but these are not part of the operating system. They are, in fact, program libraries and programs that the OS can use for display. In UNIX-based operating systems, such as Linux, a special privileged user account is called "root" or "superuser." The root login has special permissions to allow system administration and restricted command operation, allowing superusers to bypass file protections and perform functions that are not generally available to other users. (The Windows operating system equivalent to UNIX *superuser* is the *supervisor* mode.)

In Focus

Applications may make system calls to gain privileged functions, whether performed by a command or executed via a program. Programs can also perform privileged functions by having a superuser set a flag on an executable file, called setuid. This allows user functions to directly execute privileged operations.

10.3.2 UNIX-Based (Including Linux and MAC/OS) Processes

After a programmer has written instructions and compiled them, the program is ready to run (we see these as .exe files in a directory listing). A process is therefore an executing program. Processes that create other processes are called parent processes, and the created processes are called child processes. Because processes populate data structures and occupy memory, sometimes small tasks can be accomplished more efficiently using "light-weight" processes or threads. Threads share some of the data structures with their parent processes, so they can only be used for special purposes.

Programs are identified by the user login name and a user identification code (UID), both of which are stored in the UNIX "*passwd*" file. When a program is executed, these identification numbers are stored in the data structures that are created for the process. A process is also assigned a unique process identification number (PID) by the OS as well as a parent process identifier (PPID) for the process that created it. These PID and PPID are used to identify each other for interprocess communications (IPC).

> **In Focus**
>
> In Windows, most processes are peers, and so the concept of a pure parent and child relationship is rare. Windows processes, however, do often spawn threads.

Programmers initiate IPC by writing instructions using an application program interface (API). An API is a standard set of codes that a program calls to send a message to another program. This is usually a user-level call—where one program makes a function (method) call to another program written as part of an application. However, when an application wants to invoke an OS function, it makes a *system call* through an API provided by the OS. For example, if we escaped out of our GUI to a command line interface (UNIX shell) and we typed a command such as *ls*, a directory listing output would be generated by the *ls* process, which is spawned by the shell. If we were to look at the UNIX shell source code, we would see a program statement (written in the "C" language) that invokes a process (in this example, "ls") using the **system call** "fork." The *fork* system call in the shell makes a request of the kernel to create (fork) the "ls" child process.

> **In Focus**
>
> A signal is an IPC that operates as a type of software interrupt. There are a variety of signals, but one that is familiar in UNIX is "kill" (or sighup), where one process (usually the parent) tells another process (usually the child) to terminate.

An External View of UNIX Processes

In the Windows OS, processes can be seen by simultaneously pressing the <ctrl><alt><delete> keys. This brings up the Windows Task Manager, from which processes can be viewed by choosing the Processes tab. Processes in UNIX are usually viewed from the command prompt using the UNIX command *ps*. For example, the command *ps –al* will display processes and their status, where the "*a*" is an option (also called a switch) used to display *all* processes, and the "*l*" is an option to display a full (long) listing of processes and their details.

> **In Focus**
>
> In Windows, to view "all," you must have administrator privileges and select the "show processes from all users" button.

Processes normally run in the foreground, that is, interactively with the user, but they may be made to run in the background, where output continues to be reported to the standard output, which is usually the monitor's screen or window. This leaves standard input (the user interface by default) free for other interaction. Processes that run in the background, which are called ***daemons***, operate like processes running in the foreground with the exception that the process identification number associated with it (the PID) is reported to the standard output for status and termination by the *ps* and *kill* commands in UNIX. The *shell* will then continue to accept standard input from the user interface and does not wait for the processing to complete.

To highlight with an example, note the command prompt denoted "#" and that background processes are invoked with the "&" at the end of the command line. The following example shows a program compiler executed for a program called tst.c that will produce an output file called test.exe in the background using the &. Notice that it reports a unique process identifier (19823) back to the user interface, and the user can continue to execute other commands while the compilation is in process.

In this example, after the compiler was invoked in the background, the user then executed a sort of the contents from one file and sent the sorted output to another file (using the redirection or > symbol), and this too was done in the background. The user instructed that the contents of "dfile" be sent to the soft program through redirection (<) and the output of that file be sorted and sent to a file named "sorted" (>), also in the background (&). This too received a unique process identification code: 27482. At the UNIX command line, if we executed the ps command, we would see the following, where STAT reflects running in the background (d) or in the foreground (r) and the device that invoked the command:

```
# cc -O -o test tst.c &
19823
# sort tfile > sfile &
19824
# sort < dfile > sorted &
27482
# ps
PID        STAT      TTY          TIME        COMMAND
27482      d         co           0:02        sort
27486      r         co           0:02        ps
```

Process and Memory Management

The memory manager is responsible for handling the data structures and managing the available RAM. Remember that data structures are little more than data (or variables containing values) that are stored at specific memory addresses. The memory manager must ensure that proper data are stored in proper locations and that there are no overlaps or that data that have been unreferenced (deallocated) are returned to reassignment and reuse by other processes.

The memory manager also attempts to load all the processes and threads and their data structures into RAM because all processes and their data structures have to be resident in memory for the CPU to execute them. For processes, there are two classifications of data structures: user data structures (specifically the *user structure*) and *kernel data* structures (i.e., the *proc structure*). User data structures contain information a process uses, such as indexes and descriptors for open files and their permissions. Kernel data structures are used by the OS to manage the user data structures [5].

A program's "process" memory is divided into four logical segments: (1) the program text segment, (2) the data segment, (3) block segment space, and (4) the stack segment. These segments are managed by the operating system as part of a user structure. The user structure contains system information about the state of the process such as system calls pending and files open and being accessed. The text segment contains the code portion of a program and associated registers. The data segment contains variables and pre-initialized data. The block storage space (or bss) contains the "heap" for storage allocation for uninitialized data. The stack is used for automatic variables and for passing parameters. These segments are decomposed from this logical grouping into virtual address groupings managed by the kernel, as seen in **Figure 10.4**.

Many processes are "shared text," meaning they each use the same text region simultaneously with other processes. Examples are the shell, editors, and compilers. When an editor is invoked, for example, its text region is the same as the other editors being executed on the system so programs may logically contain a text segment, although physically, they reside in separate address spaces. In other words, processes may share (reside in) the same set of virtual addresses but not the same physical addresses (more later).

In Focus

Virtual memory includes a swap partition on disk to enable greater memory capacity than provided with RAM only.

Processes and their data structures sit idle in queues while they wait for an execution time slice (quantum) from the CPU, which is handled by the kernel's scheduler. If RAM becomes full while they are in this *wait state*, the user data structures (with the exception of the text data structure) can be moved to disk to the *swap partition*, whereas the kernel data structures (and text structure) for the process must remain resident in memory. This is because the kernel data structures that remain in memory are needed by the ***pager/ swapper*** (or dispatcher in Windows) to locate and retrieve the user data structures from the swap partition when the CPU calls for that process to execute.

UNIX-based systems such as Linux and MAC/OS (like Windows) support demand paging ***virtual memory***—where only portions of processes are required to be "paged" out to the swap partition when memory becomes full. This feature allows memory storage to be greater than the physical RAM in the system, and it improves OS performance by shortening the storage and retrieval time when the pieces have to be written to disk or brought back into memory.

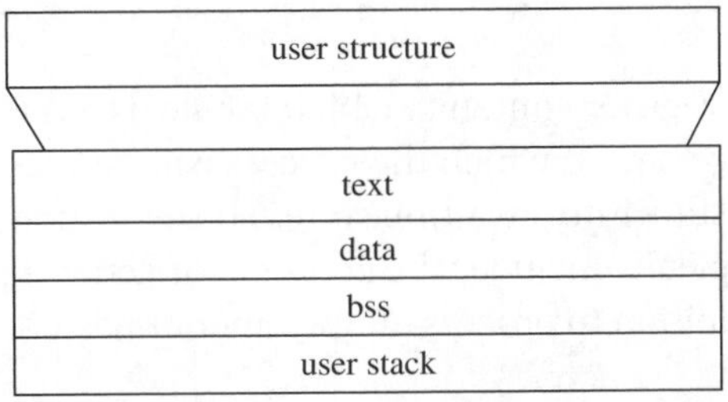

```
┌──────────────────────────────┐
│        user structure        │
└──────────────────────────────┘
┌──────────────────────────────┐
│             text             │
├──────────────────────────────┤
│             data             │
├──────────────────────────────┤
│             bss              │
├──────────────────────────────┤
│          user stack          │
└──────────────────────────────┘
```

FIGURE 10.4

Memory segmentation and data structures.

When a process terminates either voluntarily or as initiated by the OS, the OS frees up the process's memory and other resources and data structures, removes the process from the process table (*proc table*), and makes its memory and other resources available to other processes. Sometimes an error may cause a parent process to terminate before its children processes exit, making them orphans. In those cases, some data structures may be left in memory, and the children processes (called *zombies* in UNIX or *rogues* in Windows) will need to have their data structures removed. UNIX has a process called *init* that "adopts" these orphaned processes and does this "cleanup" work [6, 7].

Process Control and Scheduling

Process management and memory management are closely related in the UNIX OS. Processes that are created require the allocation of memory, and process components must be relocated between memory segments. The CPU must also have a way for processes to be scheduled for execution. The scheduler identifies "runnable" processes waiting in queue, selects them based on priority, and allocates a quantum of CPU time.

Data structures called the **process control block** (**PCB**) contain information about processes needed by the scheduler, such as the process identifier (PID), process state (e.g., running, which means executing in the CPU, ready to run, or blocked in a wait state), a program counter (values that determine which instruction of the process should execute next), a CPU scheduling priority, credentials (data that determines the resources this process can access), a pointer to the process creator (parent process), pointers to processes created (children), pointers to locate the process data and instructions in memory, and pointers to allocated resources (such as files on disk).

The PCB also stores the register contents, which is called the *execution context*. This is information about the processor on which the process was last running when it transitioned out of the running state into a waiting state. The execution context of a process is computer specific but typically includes the contents of general-purpose registers that contain process data, in addition to process management registers such as those that store pointers to a process's address space. This enables the OS to restore a process execution context when the process returns to a running state. When a process transitions from one state to another, the OS must update information in the PCB for that process. The OS maintains pointers to each process PCB in a system-wide or per-user process table (the *proc table*) so that it can access the PCB quickly.

Processes fall into two categories: ***system processes*** and ***user processes***. System (or kernel) processes always take precedence over user processes in their execution order. User processes started after logging in receive default execution priorities by the kernel, which subsequently degrade as the processes use the CPU. The UNIX scheduler is a "fair" scheduler, designed for time sharing, and the only control a user has over process scheduling priority is through the use of system calls *nice* and *renice*. A user may only decrease his or her process priority (i.e., to be nice), not increase it. On the other hand, the computer system administrator, or superuser (root) in UNIX, may temporarily increase a process priority. Eventually, however, as the process receives CPU time, it begins again to degrade in priority according to its status and whether it is a kernel versus a user process [5].

In Focus

The scheduler will pick a process to execute by taking into account the following rules: (1) kernel processes run before user processes, (2) short processes run before longer ones, and (3) processes that have waited for a long time run before those that recently ran.

Process priorities can range from 0 to 127, with lower numbers having higher priorities in UNIX. The user process priority is a combination of a value called *PUSER* maintained for a process, which is initially set to 50 (best ever priority), plus the *nice* value, plus CPU time used. Based on CPU time used, the process priority number is increased, giving it a lower priority, every 1/100 of a CPU second. Processes with better priority (i.e., < 50) are reserved for system processes such as daemons and user processes performing I/O. As processes go through their life cycles, they may be transitioned in and out of the queue depending on their state and regardless of their priority. In other words, even a high-priority process may be transitioned out of the CPU and back into the queue if it becomes blocked (e.g., waiting for an event to occur).

In Focus

Processes in a zombie state have exited and are waiting to be cleaned up (e.g., deallocation of memory, stack, tables). While in a zombie state, the process cleans up the data structures that have been allocated by it before exiting, although some data structures will be left behind in memory. The parent process must then clean up what remains of the process data structures left in memory. If the parent process terminates before the child does, the UNIX system init process will assume the role of the parent, adopt orphaned children, and do the cleanup work. The init process is a system process that is created at boot time.

10.3.3 The UNIX-Based File System

In most cases, people relate either to files in directories or folders, or data in a database. Whereas in Windows, file elements are managed via a file bitmap scheme, in UNIX, a *file* can be a container or an executable program. A file has a name and an owner, and permissions are given to others to read, modify, or execute its contents. The routines responsible for creating, protecting, and providing access to files are known collectively as the UNIX file system. The manner in which data are stored on a particular device is called the *file structure*, which has both a physical and a logical structure. The physical structure of the file determines how bits that represent data are arranged on storage surfaces such as a disk and is largely managed by the hardware controller for a device. The logical structure determines how data are maintained, accessed, and presented to a user, largely managed by a device driver [8].

In Focus

The file system software and device drivers share in the responsibility of maintaining, accessing, and presenting data to users from the software standpoint. The controllers and disk and tape drive hardware share in the responsibility for storing and accessing the information from the hardware standpoint.

UNIX File Management

The smallest addressable unit of data on UNIX is a *byte*. Because of its size, the *byte* is not a convenient unit for either the storage of information or its transfer between the main memory of the computer and the disk and tape devices it supports. Instead, bytes are packed into larger units called *blocks* to form files. The UNIX OS provides for the methods of keeping data, protecting the data, and accessing the information on a per-file basis, but there is no standard record organization and no standard record access method. Instead, the information is stored in the file on a byte-by-byte basis, and record management must be accomplished by user routines and database management systems that are not by the OS.

Because UNIX was created before databases became commonplace, only some rudimentary database functionality was incorporated into the file system architecture. For example, the UNIX system provides the system calls *flock* and *lockf* for file and data locking, but user file access programs must manage these system calls. A file may contain program source code, data, compiled and executable code, or other types of information. There are four main types of files, seen in **List 10.2**.

UNIX File Protections

Files have protections to prevent access by unauthorized users, although the system administrator (superuser) on UNIX may bypass these protections. Note also that whereas Windows has four levels of file protections, the native UNIX file system has only three, as seen in **Figure 10.5**.

In UNIX-based systems such as Linux, because files can be executable (i.e., a program), processes become associated with a user based on login information and the file

---

List 10.2 UNIX File Types

- Text (ASCII files): Consists of text lines, usually created with an editor.

- Binary Files: Usually fixed-size records, containing any byte values, mostly used by compilers, assemblers, and linkers, for objects and executables.

- Directory Files: A logically hierarchical table of contents that contains a list of names of other files and directory files, along with their associated index numbers called inodes that uniquely identify the files and tell UNIX where the files are found.

- Special Files: Descriptors for devices such as disks, tapes, and monitors (also called terminals or ttys in UNIX).

FIGURE 10.5

UNIX file protections.

```
Protection      File Meaning        Directory Meaning       Where <c> is:
  read (r)       may read file       may list (ls) contents  -  file
  write (w)      may add or delete   may create or remove    d  directory
  execute (x)    may run program     may use (cd) in path    b  block file
             | owner | group | public |                      c  character file
             -------------------------------------           l  linked file
    <c>      |r| w|x|r| w|x|r| w|x|                           s  socket end point
```

ownership given to the file. The user identification number (UID) associated with the login name is compared to that of the file to determine accessibility. In other words, the file protections specify whether a given UID has proper authority to access a file (along with the type of access). The creator of a file or directory is the owner unless the ownership is manually changed with the *chown* utility.

A group number is also assigned to the file. This number would be the same for users sharing common information or data, such as members of the same development project, cost center, organization, or division. Thus as indicated, file protections consist of read, write, and execute, and they are specified for a user (owner), a group, or public access. Protections may be set using the *chmod* command and an octal number, or code, by the owner or superuser. A dash, "-", in place of a protection letter indicates that the permission to perform that operation is denied. Let's consider an example, seen in **Figure 10.6**.

Note that the permissions are shown in octal codes and are displayed r (read), w (write), and x (execute). Execute permissions on program files makes sense; execute on a directory is unique. It refers to allowing others to view the contents of a directory. The fourth bit (to

FIGURE 10.6

UNIX permission bits.

Application	Owner	Group	Public	Octal
Public data	r w -	r w -	r w -	0666
Private data	r w -	- - -	- - -	0600
Public directory	r w x	r w x	r w x	0777
Public/read	r w x	r - x	r - x	0755

the left), is used for special flags and is useful for executable files only. If the flag is set to 1, for example 1755, this is known as the sticky bit. The sticky bit is used to maintain swap space for a process after the process terminates. Without the sticky bit set, swap space is unallocated when the process exits. Programs that are executed frequently may have their sticky bit set to improve startup performance, but this can create other problems (such as taking up swap space) [7].

In Focus

In UNIX, files and directories are organized in a tree structure. The parent of all directories is called the root directory. The search path determines where the OS looks for files. The "." refers to the current working directory, whereas ".." refers to its parent directory.

If the flag bit is set to 2, the file may have the group ID (GID) set on execution. This allows a program to access files using the *setgid* system call. If a file belongs to a different group than the one the process belongs to, and if file protections do not allow group access, the *setgid* allows access to a file that would normally require superuser privileges. If the flag bit is set to 4, the file may have the user ID (UID) set on execution. This allows a program to access files using the *setuid* system call. If a file belongs to a different user other than the process, and if file protections do not allow public access, *setuid* likewise allows a user access that would normally require superuser privileges. All of these permission-setting capabilities in UNIX are convenient for users and administrators, but they are weakly protected, and they are particularly vulnerable to exploits. We will illustrate with a command sequence:

```
# ls -l  file.c
- rwxr - xr- -        1      mike    510    apr 14  01:00    file.c
# chmod 777 file.c
# ls -l file.c
- rwxrwxrwx          1      mike    510    apr 14  01:00    file.c
# chmod o-w file.c
# ls -l file.c
- r - xrwxrwx        1      mike    510    apr 14  01:00    file.c
# chmod -w file.c
# ls -l file.c
- r - xr - xr - x    1      mike    510    apr 14  01:00    file.c
#chmod o+w,g+w file.c
# ls -l file.c
- rwxrwxr - x        1      mike    510    apr 14  01:00    file.c
```

The illustration we presented shows file protections or permissions as r, w, x, or a—if permissions are not granted, for user, group, and the world. By default, the flag bit on files is set to 0 when a file is created, but this can be changed by the superuser to be 1 (sticky bit), 2 (set group id), 4 (set user id), or 7 (set all flags on). As with files, the *ls* command with the *-ld* option will list the protections associated with the current working directory.

When a user creates a file, the ownership of the file is by default assigned to the user. There are times when it is useful to change the ownership of a file to another user or its permissions. The *chmod* command is used to change the default protections for a file or directory, and the *chown* command may be used to change the owner of a file, as seen in the command sequence that follows:

```
# chown keith file.c
# ls -l file.c
- rwxrwxr - x        1      keith 510    apr 14  01:00     file.c
```

One way an administrator can implement file protections on some UNIX-based platforms, such as Linux, is to ensure that common files cannot be overwritten or changed. This is done by setting the *immutable* flag when logged in as *superuser*. One becomes superuser by logging into the system with the login name "root" or by typing "su" after logging in and supplying the appropriate password. The immutable flag prevents files from being changed, renamed, deleted, or linked to another file. The *chattr* command is used to set the immutable flag on files, as follows:

```
chattr +i <file>: sets the immutable flag.
chattr -i <file>: unsets the immutable flag.
lsattr <file>: displays attributes set on a file.
```

In Focus

It is important to realize from a security standpoint that once someone has superuser (root) access, they may create setuid files that can allow superuser access even after the superuser password has been changed.

Files may have links from one file to another. A link is created using the *ln* command, and these can be seen by an increase in the link count on the linked file. Linking files makes it possible for users to share a single file without having to copy it or require a reference to the file via the absolute file name. Links can be convenient, but they also present a variety of security risks. Note that there are two types of links: hard links and symbolic links.

Hard links make it possible for a user to remove a link to a file, thus removing the file for him or herself without removing the file altogether, and this is done with the *rm* command. When the link count becomes 0, the file goes away and the disk space is then unallocated, making the space available for reuse by other files. **Symbolic links** work similarly but may be established for files or directories on another device or file system. In order to remove a file (remove link) on a file that a user does not own, the user must have "write" privileges. If the user does not own the file but is in the same group as the owner, "write" privileges are required for the group. If the user is not the owner of the file and is not in the same group as the owner, write protection is required for public access. If the user is the owner of the file but does not have write protections, when the user attempts to remove the file, the system will prompt for an override of the protection set on the file.

10.3.4 Disk Memory Management

In memory, among other things, the kernel data structures are allocated to locate data stored on the disk drive, and the ***file system manager*** is responsible for the organization of data on disk. It is important that we point out that just as Windows has different file systems (e.g., FAT, NTFS) UNIX also has different file systems. To highlight this, we will contrast the native file systems on BSD UNIX with UNIX System V. In both UNIX file systems, data are organized on disk in logically localized regions. This is done in order to reduce searching of the file system for related information. The first block located on disk is called the ***boot block***, and this maintains the necessary information for the system to organize itself when the system comes up, such as how to determine where to find the kernel.

The next logically contiguous segment maintains the block called the super block. Static information about the UNIX file system is stored in the ***super block***, such as disk block size, data fragment size, and disk layout policy—or the physical configuration of the data into their sectors and within concentric circles called cylinders. It is beyond this configuration where there is a departure between the various native file systems on UNIX. Note that the term "native" is used because there are other file systems for UNIX such as the "Andrew" file system, which is more resilient and secure than native UNIX ones.

> ### In Focus
>
> On UNIX-BSD systems, cylinder group maps contain replicated dynamic segments of information such as arrays used in allocation of files and data space. Note, however, that on System V UNIX file systems, the dynamic information is kept only in the super block and is not replicated, making that file system more "fragile." On BSD systems, cylinder group maps maintain information about logically contiguous segments of information related to a group of files called cylinder groups.

Whether text, binary, directory, or device (*special*) file, each has a structure called an inode. The inodes are numbered, and they contain important information depending upon the file type. For example, text and data file inodes contain data such as the size of the file, the date it was created, protections, ownership, and pointers to blocks of data held by the file. Directory file inodes include data such as a list of inode numbers and file names located immediately below the directory in the directory tree. The file system maintains information about inodes in the "ilist" (**Figure 10.7**).

The inodes that are available to be allocated to a file are maintained in a "free inode list." A small number of addresses of free inodes in the free inode list are cached in a "free inode array" for quick access. On BSD UNIX file systems, the free inode array is kept in the cylinder group maps. On System V UNIX file systems, the free inode array is kept in the super block.

UNIX works with two copies of active inodes. One copy resides on disk, whereas another is kept in memory for efficiency. The inodes in memory are kept in the ***in-core inode*** table, and disk copies of inodes are updated from in-core copies. In memory, in-core inodes contain additional chaining pointers (forward and backward), which are not present in the inode copy on disk [5].

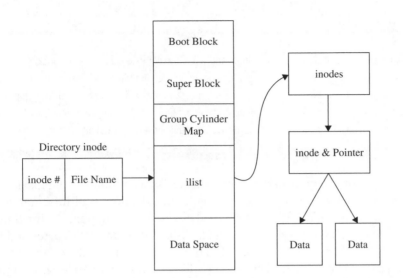

FIGURE 10.7

File pointers and ilist structures.

In addition to file type, file protections, and file creation information, the kernel keeps track of pointers to the associated data blocks in various "ilist" data structures (**Figure 10.8**). As files are created, added to, or deleted, the inodes and data associated with them are relocated from list to list. For increased speed of file access, the most recently used (active) inodes are buffered and hash indexed within kernel memory to prevent having to read the inode table on disk each time the file is accessed. Data blocks are also buffered in memory; thus the lists are constantly in flux, and if the system crashes or is improperly shut down, the inode tables can become corrupted.

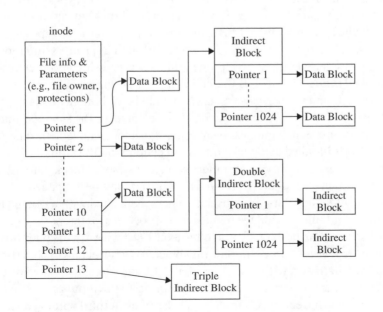

FIGURE 10.8

Inode data structures.

In Focus

An orderly shutdown in UNIX is crucial to flush the buffers and write out all the temporary data to disk. This is referred to as a fragile file system because if the computer is shut down without clearing the buffers first, using the shutdown command, this buffered information will be lost and can cause corruption of the file system. The UNIX fsck program is run to repair the file system. Attackers know this vulnerability, and if they can determine a system is UNIX-based, including Linux, MAC/OS, FreeBSD, they can exploit this by using a denial of service (DoS) attack.

Data blocks are groups of information held by a file. Data are handled in blocks both on disk and in memory for efficiency in dealing with related amounts of information. Each file system has a basic block size, determined by the system manager at the time the file system is created. On BSD file systems, data blocks are generally 4096 bytes and have fragments, usually 1024 bytes. If less than a full block is written to disk, a fragment is written so as not to waste disk space. On System V file systems, there are no fragments; there are only data blocks consisting usually of 1024 bytes. BSD file systems are called "fast file systems" because of this grouping of information into cylinder groups and because of the organization of data blocks and fragments. The fast file system will store fragments of data until it is opportune to copy fragments to full blocks. For this scheme to work efficiently, the disk must retain about 10 percent free space [1, 6].

10.3.5 UNIX System Input–Output (I/O) and Device Drivers

Input–output, or I/O, are all the facilities that pass data bits between devices. For the most part, I/O means sending grouped bits of data from one process and device to another, but the grouped sizes depend on the hardware used. There are two major types of I/O devices in UNIX: *block devices* and *character devices*. Block devices are those that can transfer blocks of data rather than bytes, such as disks, USB drives, and tapes. Character-type devices are those that transfer data bytes (character by character) such as printers and monitors (called terminals or ttys in UNIX). The grouping of data for processing is known as ***buffering*** or "***cooked mode***" in UNIX. Buffered I/O in UNIX is queued in a buffer cache in kernel memory rather than on a per-process basis. Data in block buffers are flushed by the kernel every 30 seconds unless the *fsync* system call is executed, or the *sync* command is typed at the command line, which queues the memory flush for a convenient (lazy) cycle. Block device buffering is handled using four queues depending on the kinds of data they hold: (1) BQ_locked is used for permanent buffers such as disk super block data, (2) BQ_lru is used for active data such as data blocks related to files that have been opened, (3) BQ_age is used for non-useful data (free data, such as data blocks associated with a deleted file), and (4) BQ_empty is used for buffers available to allocate to processes for temporary storage.

In addition to buffered I/O, both block and character I/O device drivers offer non-buffered I/O, called "***raw mode***" in UNIX. For raw block I/O, characters bypass the internal buffering mechanisms; with raw character I/O, characters are passed directly from a set of data structures in what is called the *raw queue* to the input process without any manipulation of the characters. Character I/O also offers a third option called *cbreak*, or "***half-cooked***" mode. In the cbreak mode, there are some limited character manipulations possible, which are performed within the device driver itself. That is, in cbreak mode, characters are sent to the process as soon as they are typed with little manipulation except that characters are echoed, and interrupt, parity, and delays are managed by the driver; however, there is no processing of erase, terminate (kill), or end-of-text characters. Character buffers are flushed by a program calling the *fflush* subroutine on output, or with a new-line character (<return>) on input.

Device files in UNIX are called "special" files, and special files differ depending on how they interact with the OS and their device drivers. One of the unique attributes of the UNIX system is this ability to have devices appear as files causing the file system and the I/O subsystem to overlap significantly. There are many data structures associated with files and I/O. An example is the "open file table" that contains file descriptors of the information needed to access an underlying file object. The file system and I/O subsystem have components partially contained in the user data structures and partially maintained by the kernel, and the data that are passed between processes must be stored while waiting to be processed.

Special files can be seen from the command prompt with the *ls* command of the /dev directory, but the listing displays special file characteristics. The listing shows leading characters (b or c) that indicate whether the special file is a block or character mode file. Other file attributes are also shown, such as the creation date and the type of device, along with major and minor device numbers. The major device number is an index to a table in the kernel code called the *device switch table*, used to access the associated device driver for that device. The device switch table is divided into block and character device tables called the *bdevsw* and *cdevsw*, respectively.

The minor device number associated with the file is passed into the driver to determine a device type or function. The meaning of the minor device number differs from device to device depending on the type; for example, the minor device number on a UNIX monitor or terminal (called *tty*) device generally represents a port number, whereas on tape devices, it directs the driver to rewind or not rewind the tape. In other words, the minor device numbers serve as an index or an entry point into the device driver for performing specific actions, such as to get data from a buffer or put data in a queue.

In Focus

In the UNIX file system, there are device files (special files) that designate device types. Files that are raw block devices have names that are preceded with "r"—for example, "rra0." Special files for cooked block devices are not preceded by an "r"—for example, "ra0." Raw I/O for character devices is set with the raw flag from a command called stty, or using the cbreak option, which is also set using stty.

The entire function of a driver is to get and send data to and from some device. In addition, the driver may check to ensure that the data are good using parity or cyclic redundancy checks. When the computer boots up, the device driver has what is called a *probe* routine that initializes the devices and announces to the computer's bus that the devices are ready, including specifying the interrupt level for the device by setting binary bits in what is called an *interrupt mask*. As data are sent back and forth from devices and processes in the system, all the processes that read and write data make calls to the driver's "open" function. When all communications have ceased, the last process running makes a call to the driver's "close" function, which cleans up the queues and signals the I/O process termination [8].

Disk device drivers are responsible for handling I/O between RAM (and also static cache memory) and the disk drive. The driver must determine what data segments (called sectors) are already allocated and what segments are available for storing new data. This process is called a storage allocation policy or strategy. Although logically, strategies for writing data to a disk drive may follow a *first fit* or a *best fit* or other type of procedure, on disk the data are written to cylinders (the concentric rings on a disk platter) in groupings according to the amount of data and based on the rotation speed of the disk for reading and writing optimization by the hardware, and this is handled by the disk device driver. The first fit strategy takes a block of data and writes it to the first available location. Although this strategy is quicker than best fit at the initial storage of data, the retrieval of the data is slower than best fit because the data are scattered around the disk. Thus first fit is best at storage time, whereas best fit is faster at retrieval time because the data are more logically contiguous.

Input from monitors (called terminals or ttys in UNIX) uses serial communications. On the computer's communications circuit board resides a universal receiver-transmitter, or UART. This hardware chip gathers data from and places data into a buffer. These buffers are read and written character by character by the tty device driver. In UNIX, there are two levels of tty driver, the line switch driver and line discipline driver. The driver is also divided into a top half and a bottom half. The line switch driver essentially handles the control of the conversation, and it takes the data and sets the bits for invoking hardware interrupts. The line discipline driver reads and writes the data in and out of the buffer queues. Using the system call *ioctl*, the line switch driver (*linesw*) calls the line discipline to set the device controls, such as data transmission rates and parity checking. The *ttread* and *ttwrite* and *ttinterrupt* functions are then used by the driver to coordinate the reading and writing from the various queues.

As we have presented, character mode devices store characters in a queue called the *raw queue*. When a line of characters is terminated with the <return> key, the device driver copies the raw queue data (handling deletes and escapes) into the *canonical queue*. The canonical queue is a staging area for data so that the driver can pass "clean" data to a receiving process. On output from a process, the characters are stored in a "Cblock," which does not need character processing. The Cblock is a block contained in a linked list called the ***clist***. Cblocks are allocated dynamically in the clist as output from a process increases until it can be passed by the device driver to the device (see Workman [8] for examples).

10.4 Microsoft Windows Operating System

By now, we know that Microsoft changes operating system versions frequently, but in spite of their many versions and changes, a major shift occurred when Microsoft hired Dave Cutler away from Digital Equipment Corporation (DEC) to design a version of DEC's operating system written for their PDP and then later their VAX mini-mainframe systems for a PC, which we now have come to call Windows NT [5]. The Microsoft Windows derivatives such as XP, Vista, and Windows V.7 all stem from this change. As a result, Windows has had to evolve from a PC (MS-DOS) operating system into a commercially capable system akin to the DEC (now HP) mini-mainframe operating system (Open/VMS). Windows, like UNIX, was designed to be a general-purpose computer and network OS. Over the years, it has developed along the Windows NT architecture (for example, witness Windows FAT file system compared to NTFS). The main goal for a general-purpose OS is to make many complex computing tasks easy for the user. It also takes a lot of burden off the application software by coordinating different devices and getting rid of repetitive functions that each software program has to go through. Windows shares many features with the Digital Equipment (now HP) VMS operating system [1], but also offers some of the design features of MAC/Linux/UNIX.

10.4.1 Windows as a Reference Example

Windows was developed to focus on ease-of-use computing for home and small office computer users. It has evolved to provide many network operating systems (NOS) capabilities, so it has become popular for that dual-purpose role. There has been an evolution toward using general-purpose OS, such as Windows, as NOS because of Window's low-cost, multi-use, multi-threaded, and multi-tasking capabilities (especially beginning with Windows Version 7). Multi-tasking means that a computer can handle several programs at the same time, and multi-threaded multi-tasking takes this concept further by breaking down a program into smaller threads that manage tasks on a finer-grained scale for efficiency.

In Focus

Unlike DEC/HP OpenVMS, which automatically names file versions, UNIX and Windows write over files unless specifically requested otherwise.

The rapid escalation toward dual-purpose systems was fueled by Windows servers, especially with Windows Server 2003 and 2008, given the ability to serve as domain controllers; however, Windows has gradually expanded server capabilities with each new server release. Also, Windows has offered a roaming user profile, which has allowed users to log in from any networked computer in the same Windows environment to display the same desktop and retain the settings saved by the user. Moreover, Windows supports the industry standard TCP/IP protocols including DNS and DHCP, and it has added its own network resource naming and discovery tools such as WINS (Windows Internet Naming Service).

Windows also provides extensive event and account logging facilities, which feeds information into a report-generation program. It supports all levels of redundant array (RAID) disks for backup and restore. Microsoft's domain architecture has become a convenient way to organize network resources. By using the domain structure, Windows allows users to access one account and have one password to access network resources scattered around in multiple servers. Once a server is set up, we have a choice among primary domain controller, backup domain controller (BDC), and stand-alone server in terms of the server's role in the network [3].

Let's quickly survey the Windows architecture, subsystems, and executive managers. At the base layer of the Windows system is the hardware abstraction layer, or HAL. This exports a virtual interface to the rest of the Windows system to enable dynamic software configurations on top of hardware. In other words, it enables software to interact more flexibly with the underlying hardware by hiding the hardware specifics from the software [9].

Examine **Figure 10.9**. Notice that the ***executive*** consists of a group of services that support the subsystems, and it acts as a critical divide between user functions and kernel functions. ***Integral subsystems*** support basic OS services through the executive. Key integral subsystems are the security service, the workstation, and server services. ***Environment subsystems*** execute in user mode and provide functions through its API. Win32 is the most fundamental of these, providing the interface for operating system services, GUI capabilities, and functions to control the I/O. The login process is handled by the Win32 subsystem called the ***graphical identification and authentication dynamic-link library*** (**GINA**), which creates the initial process and its context for a user, known as the user desktop [2, 10, 11].

In Windows, kernel drivers and the microkernel work as intermediaries for hardware and OS functions. A microkernel is a design approach where only limited system functions are performed by the kernel [8] and most of the OS work is parceled out to subsystems or "managers" [9]. The ***object manager*** in Windows intermediates access to system resources. All resources are therefore abstracted as objects. The ***I/O manager*** controls the I/O system calls from applications and services in user memory space, intermediating between them and the I/O device drivers. The ***IPC manager*** handles the communication between the environment subsystems and servers running in the executive, which consist of all the "privileged" subsystems and managers [7].

The ***virtual memory manager*** is similar to the virtual memory manager in the UNIX operating system, enabling the use of disk caches as auxiliary system memory. The ***process manager*** handles process and thread creation and termination. The ***PnP manager*** handles plug-and-play features (i.e., hardware support) mostly at boot time, or when a new device is added to the system, and the ***power manager*** controls power-related events and interrupts, and assists in an orderly system shutdown. The ***security reference monitor*** makes access control decisions and manages what parts of processes

FIGURE 10.9

Windows architecture.

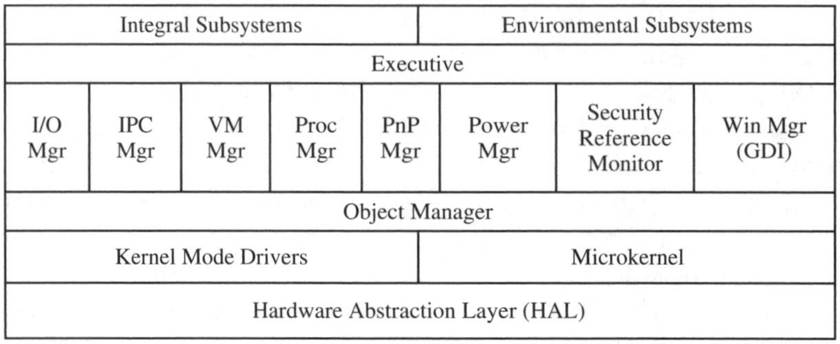

Integral Subsystems					Environmental Subsystems		
Executive							
I/O Mgr	IPC Mgr	VM Mgr	Proc Mgr	PnP Mgr	Power Mgr	Security Reference Monitor	Win Mgr (GDI)
Object Manager							
Kernel Mode Drivers				Microkernel			
Hardware Abstraction Layer (HAL)							

or threads run in protected kernel mode, and the ***Windows manager*** deals with graphical display devices and communications.

In Focus

Windows memory management is handled by the virtual memory manager (VMM), which employs a "lazy allocation policy." This is a method of postponing the allocation of pages and page table entries in memory until they are flushed to disk at a convenient time for the OS.

10.4.2 Windows Microkernel, Memory, and I/O Management

In the UNIX OS (and its derivatives: Linux, FreeBSD, MAC/OS, and others), the kernel plays a significant role in the intermediation of user and system processes. In Windows, however, the kernel plays a more specialized role; hence it is called a ***microkernel***. The Windows microkernel mainly facilitates the transactions between the executive and the subsystems and assumes four primary functions: (1) process/thread scheduling, (2) interrupt and exception handling, (3) low-level processor synchronization for symmetric multiprocessing, and (4) restoration of the system context after a system crash. Like UNIX, the kernel is never preempted or swapped out of memory, and like the UNIX scheduler, the Windows dispatcher manages process and thread queuing for execution by the CPU. Unlike the UNIX "fair" round-robin scheduler, Windows uses a 32-level prioritization, allowing a much greater level of granularity in scheduling [11].

Like UNIX, Windows is a multi-tasking OS. Each process has its own set of code, data, system resources, and state. Resources include virtual address space, files, and synchronization objects through callable application program interfaces (API). These subsystems send messages among processes by passing the messages through the executive where security checking is performed to ensure that subsystem processes do not interfere with each other. As with UNIX, Windows programs are essentially networked in terms of how they communicate, even if they are not passing data over a network. By that, we mean that the OS uses network-style interprocess communications; networking IPC mechanisms are all built into how the OS and processes work together.

A similar technique to the UNIX I/O "signal" implementation is the exception handling mechanism in Windows, which manages events such as the termination of a process by the user. In cases where errors are thrown, such as from an invalid memory access, the OS uses the structured exception handler. In the Windows vernacular, daemon processes are services, which are generally long-running user mode applications that start when the system is booted and continue running across user sessions. In Windows, much of the IPC occurs through an "object model" and as indicated; this is the part of the operating system that is related to the allocation and operation of system resources. In Windows, the term ***protected*** indicates processes that run in a *separate virtual memory address space* from other processes. As with UNIX-based systems, Windows has user and kernel (or supervisor) modes of operation. The user mode includes applications such as those designated Win32, along with protected subsystems.

Also, as with the system-level processes on UNIX, kernel mode processes have special privileges that enable access to protected memory addresses, including those occupied by user processes. The kernel mode of Windows contains the executive as well as the system kernel. The purpose of the executive is to export generic services for protected subsystems to call to obtain OS services such as file operations, I/O, and synchronization services. This partitioning of the protected subsystems and the executive enables the kernel to control how the operating system uses the CPU, performs scheduling and multi-processor synchronization, and exports objects to applications.

In Focus

Windows takes a different approach than UNIX for file I/O. Rather than using linked lists for files and file I/O, Windows uses what is called a cluster map.

In addition to processes, for performance reasons, Windows natively supports light-weight processes or threads, which share some of the data structures with its siblings. Windows also supports even smaller process fragments called fibers, also known as lightweight threads. Fibers are run from a thread and share the same memory and process contexts and data structures. Fibers are usually used in applications that serve a large number of users, such as database systems. Unlike UNIX, Windows processes are not generally formed of parent/child relationships. The process creation passes a type of pointer called a ***process handle*** and an identifier to the process it spawns. Thus, the operating system treats processes as peers [9].

In Focus

The Windows master file table (MFT) is compared to the UNIX file system management inode data structures. The MFT stores information about files on a disk including file names, file permissions, and the size of the files (in fixed-size blocks). In Windows, the I/O strategy is determined when the master boot record is read, which reads a configuration file; thus, the disk layout policy is determined by the configuration file read when the computer is booted. The device driver then uses the strategy for appropriately laying down and reading the data, and all this happens in kernel (protected) mode.

10.4.3 Windows Processes and Security Management

As the name implies, the ***service control manager*** (**SCM**) in Windows is responsible for service management. The security context of a process determines the capabilities of the service. Most services run as a local system account that has elevated access rights on the local host but has no privileges on the network domain. If a service needs to access network resources, it must run as a domain user with sufficient privileges to perform the required tasks. As we will discuss in more detail when we get to the chapter on host security, Windows has four main security components: (1) executive or kernel mode, (2) protected servers (user mode), (3) network subsystem (both kernel and user modes), and (4) administrator tools (user mode). Each process has a table of object handles that enable a process to access system resources maintained by the object manager. A handle is software reference to a memory address. Each handle describes the type of access the process has to the object (read, write, etc.).

The ***object manager*** ensures that access is only granted if compatible with the handle. When a process requests a resource for the first time, the object manager asks the security reference monitor to decide if the process may acquire a handle to it. Subsequent accesses to the same resource will not involve the security reference monitor because a handle granting the type of access will be already available in the process handle table. Processes are themselves objects in the system. A process essentially contains a handle table containing all objects to which it has access, process virtual, private address space, an associated space in the physical memory, and a list of threads. Because processes are objects in Windows, they can be accessed directly (if a handle to them exists), and each thread has its own execution context, including registers and stack pointers [7].

10.4.4 Microsoft Registry

The Windows Registry is a configuration database that maintains information about applications, users, and hardware on a system (**Figure 10.10**). The Registry uses registry keys, called HKEY, to denote an entry in the configuration database. There are HKEY entries for each component, listed under a root node such as HKEY_LOCAL_MACHINE, which is the root of configuration components for a local system. The ***configuration manager*** is the part of the executive that is responsible for maintaining

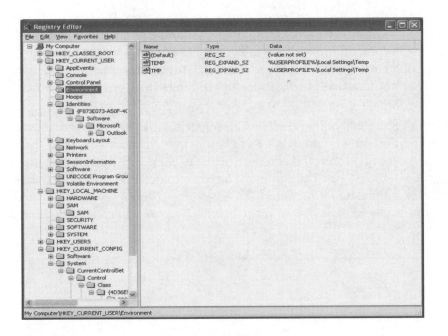

FIGURE 10.10

Regeidt view of registry.

the Registry. Software ranging from device drivers to user applications use the Registry for locating executables and coordinating IPC and for keeping track of information such as user preferences. The Registry provides a convenient, centralized store of configuration information, but it is a source of host computer threats, which we will examine later in the chapter on computer security.

CHAPTER SUMMARY

In the late 1980s and early 1990s, there were four main CPU competitors: Motorola, Intel, National Semiconductor, and Digital Equipment Corporation. The competitive nature of "micro-processing" eliminated a couple of them [5]. Creating software to operate high-demand operating systems to make these CPUs work properly further complicated matters. (Old timers call this the RISC versus CISC wars). Two variants emerged from the rubble: Windows and UNIX (including strains such as Linux and MAC/OS).

We have now covered operating systems concepts and using UNIX and Windows examples, and we have seen that modern operating systems are layered and modular. UNIX is portable to a variety of hardware platforms, although there are still differences between UNIX versions and various platforms (for example, between MAC/OS, Linux, and Free BSD). Windows, on the other hand, is a single-source OS from Microsoft that runs on a few (mostly Intel or Advanced Microdevices [AMD]) platforms. The trend for operating systems is toward smaller, more specialized "microkernels" such as seen in Windows.

We learned that UNIX and Windows are virtual memory systems. With virtual memory, a partition on the disk drive is set aside for temporary storage of process and thread data structures if RAM becomes full. Processes are divided into memory pages split into text, data, and stack segments. User process (and thread) data structures are maintained separately from kernel data structures. If memory becomes full, the pager/swapper will begin moving pages to the swap partition on disk.

We also learned that the scheduler is responsible for switching runnable processes from the run queue into the CPU for execution. In so doing, the scheduler scans the "proc table" to find runnable processes. If a process is idle (i.e., marked "sleeping"), it is blocked waiting for an event. If a process is a zombie, it has terminated and is waiting to have its data structures cleaned out of memory. These basic functions must be performed (regardless of what they are called) by almost any OS. Now we will turn our attention to networks and networking.

THINK ABOUT IT

Topic Questions

10.1: What does RISC stand for?

10.2: What does a process scheduler do?

10.3: What does a memory manager do?

10.4: Processes are divided into what two types?

10.5: A device driver controls the devices (disk drives, user interfaces, and other hardware devices) and manages the hardware interaction for the:

_____ Computer hardware
_____ Operating system
_____ Bus controller
_____ Main static memory

10.6: A memory manager controls the data structures in memory.

_____ True
_____ False

10.7: CISC stands for:

_____ Complicated InstructionS for Computer
_____ Complex Instruction Set Computer
_____ Component InStruction Controller
_____ Conversion Instructions for Systems Components

10.8: A general OS consists of the following subsystems or functions:

(a) _____
(b) _____
(c) _____
(d) _____
(e) _____

10.9: The object manager ensures that access is only granted if compatible with the handle.

_____ True
_____ False

10.10: Windows NT was one of the first clean breaks from the MS-DOS past.

_____ True
_____ False

Questions for Further Study

Q10.1: Why is layering a good approach to operating system design?

Q10.2: How are files allocated and managed in a UNIX system?

Q10.3: What are inodes and data blocks, and how do they relate to each other?

Q10.4: Compare the UNIX inode data structures with the Windows file (bit) map.

Q10.5: Explain how operating systems and host computer security might be related. Give five examples.

KEY CONCEPTS AND TERMS

A **bus** is an electronic pathway among devices.

Daemons are processes that operate like processes running in the foreground with the exception that the process

identification is reported and the user can continue working.

Device drivers signal the CPU for control of how the device interrupts and data are processed.

File system manager is a component responsible for the organization of data on disk.

Virtual memory allows address space greater than physical space.

References

1. Kenah, L. J., & Bate, S. F. (1984). *VAX/VMS internals and data structures*. Boston, MA: Digital Press.
2. Harris, J. A. (2002). *Operating systems*. New York, NY: McGraw-Hill.
3. Elmarsi, R., Carrick, A. G., & Levine, D. (2010). *Operating systems: A spiral approach*. New York, NY: McGraw-Hill.
4. Gancarz, M. (2003). *The Linux and Unix philosophy*. Amsterdam, the Netherlands: Elsevier.
5. Workman, M., & Coleman, M. (1990). *The Ultrix operating system: Internal OS workings for the DECStart program*. Boston, MA: Digital Press.
6. Leffler, S. J., McKusick, M. K., Karels, M. J., & Quarterman, J. S. (1989). *The design and implementation of the 4.3BSD UNIX operating system*. Reading, MA: Addison-Wesley.
7. Deitel, H. M., Dietel, P. J., & Choffnes, D. R. (2004). *Operating systems*. Upper Saddle River, NJ: Pearson/Prentice Hall.
8. Workman, M. (1989). *The DECStart and the Ultrix operating system: DEC Ultrix and its internal processing*. Maynard, MA: Digital Press.
9. Silberschatz, A., Galvin, P. B., & Gagne, G. (2007). *Operating systems concepts with JAVA*. New York, NY: John Wiley & Sons.
10. de Medeiros, B. (2005). *Windows security: A synopsis on host protection, 59*, 23–30. Tallahassee: Florida State University Press.
11. Tanenbaum, A. S. (2008). *Modern operating systems*. Upper Saddle River, NJ: Pearson/Prentice Hall.

Networks and Addressing

G ENERALLY SPEAKING, PEOPLE THINK ABOUT networking in terms of either the connection from one system to another or the service they use to communicate, such as email or browsing the Web. They tend not to think about the underlying protocols such as X.400 or SMTP used for email, or the simple network management protocol (SNMP) used in managing networks, or the types of network protocols used in the connectivity such as asynchronous transfer mode (ATM), switched multimegabit data service (SMDS), or Frame Relay. In this chapter, we will cover networking basics, emphasizing the TCP/IP (Version 4, or IPv4, and Version 6, or IPv6) family of networks, and we will discuss network addressing and architecture. In the next chapter, we will go into network protocols in more detail. At this point, we will simply introduce some basic concepts.

Chapter 11 Topics

This chapter:

- Compares the ISO/OSI reference model with the TCP/IP protocols suite.
- Covers at the functional layer what various protocols in the TCP/IP suite do.
- Discusses networking at the connection level.
- Reviews physical and logical addressing and presents the concept of creating subnetworks.

Chapter 11 Goals

When you finish this chapter, you should:

- ❏ Know how computers connect to a network.
- ❏ Be able to explain the role of network layers, especially at the link layer.
- ❏ Be able to discuss the differences and similarities between OSI and TCP/IP.
- ❏ Be able to describe how networks are addressed at a conceptual level.
- ❏ Understand what is meant by network architecture.

11.1 The ISO/OSI and TCP/IP

Ensuring the security of a standalone computer can be difficult, but when a computer is connected to a network, the complexity (and security risks) escalates exponentially. In this chapter, we will begin introducing networking concepts. We will start with communications and protocols. Consider that just as with human conversations where communication is difficult when two people speak different languages, two networked hosts cannot communicate if they speak different protocols. The need for standardization and interoperability has long been apparent. The ***International Standards Organization*** (**ISO**) formed a committee in 1977 to develop a network specification known as the ***Open System Interconnection*** (**OSI**). The first draft of the standard was finalized in 1984 but was never implemented, and thus TCP/IP has supplanted the OSI [1]. However, the OSI model continues to serve as a reference model for protocol functions.

The ISO/OSI model presents ***seven layers*** to describe the data flows through a network protocol stack. At the top of the model is the application layer; these are protocols for user programs such as email user agents (for example, Outlook), Web browsers, and other user programs. At the bottom of the model is where the physical layer is represented; it consists of the network media—for instance, copper or fiber cable—which make the actual connection between computers. The main philosophy behind the layered architecture was something along the lines of "divide and conquer." Moving data from one computer to another computer is a complex problem, and by breaking this huge task into smaller functions we can look at each task more closely and can come up with a rather well-defined solution.

The layered approach also allows standardization of interfaces because the tasks are narrowly defined such that when an application sends information from one computer to another, the data travel down through the protocol stack on the sending computer, across the network, and then up through the protocol stack on the receiving computer. At the sending computer, header information is attached as the data are constructed, encapsulated, and passed down the stack. The headers contain information such as the address of the sending and receiving computers, encryption method, and other information that can be used by the receiving computer to correctly identify where the data came from and how to unpack, sort, interpret, and deliver the message to the proper recipient.

As mentioned, the ISO/OSI has remained primarily a reference model rather than a network implementation, and so the ***Transmission Control Protocol/Internet Protocol*** (**TCP/IP**) has been adopted as the *de facto* standard used in networks ranging from LANs to the Internet. TCP/IP evolved because the need and technology outpaced the development of the OSI standard specifications. Although the OSI and TCP/IP share many features, there are also a number of differences. For instance, TCP/IP combines a number of OSI top-level layers into one layer.

In Focus

When discussing protocols in a network sense, it is important to realize that there are stack protocols and routing protocols (and other types of protocols as well). Stack protocols share network data on a given machine such as in the TCP/IP network stack, whereas routing protocols share information between network devices in a network such as with an exterior gateway protocol. We will be covering both of these types of protocols, but keep the distinction in mind when you read because they can easily become jumbled up because in many ways, they must work in concert.

The Internet sometimes is viewed as an amorphous cloud with no overall control. There have been many attempts to provide some governance of this important resource, but key entities remain largely a loose confederation. Still, one influential organization is the **Internet Activities Board** (**IAB**). The board was first established in 1983 to ensure that important technology advances were promoted and the Internet standards were made widely available. An IAB subgroup that deals with the research promotion is called the **Internet Research Task Force** (**IRTF**), and the **Internet Engineering Steering Group** (**IESG**) is a subgroup within the **Internet Engineering Task Force** (**IETF**), which reviews and selects Internet standards.

People who want to submit ideas for Internet standards can do so by sending a proposal to the steering group. These submissions are called the *Internet drafts*. The steering group meets and reviews the technical and other merits of the drafts periodically. Most of the proposals do not make it into the official standards and fall into the "do not publish" category. The proposals that are adopted by the steering group are officially recognized and are assigned an **RFC** (**Request for Comment**) designation. There are many Internet standards, but the majority of RFCs are either updates or revisions to existing standards.

11.1.1 Layered Architecture

Both the OSI reference model and the TCP/IP protocols use a layering (or stack) approach as indicated (**Figure 11.1**). The top **application** layer is the one that people usually relate to most because the main function of the application layer is to provide a user interface for user interaction. Applications such as email, databases, file transfers (e.g., FTP), and browsers are examples of programs that use the application layer. The next layer is the **presentation** layer, which is a critical point for network data manipulation, such as compression and application layer encryption processes. We can think about this layer as the packaging layer.

When two computers communicate with each other, they need to establish some kind of connection, or what is called a **session**. Examples of the session layer protocol are NetBIOS, developed by IBM, which was an attempt to provide primitive network

TCP/IP and OSI
layers compared.

TCP/IP		OSI
Applications and Services		Applications and Services
		Presentation
		Session
TCP UDP		Transport
IP		Network
Data Link		Data Link
Physical		Physical

capabilities to stand-alone PCs, and **remote procedure calls** (**RPC**) that enable a client computer to invoke a program on a server computer. The **transport** layer has to do with getting and delivering data for a session. Roughly speaking, there are two types of data transport: one that provides a **reliable** connection and the other that is a **best effort** delivery system. As an illustration, an application such as a chat program needs to have a "reliable connection" so that the communications between one chat client and another can alternate in a seamless way [2].

> **In Focus**
>
> TCP/IP collapses several of the OSI top layers into one layer. The primary reason for this was to achieve network transmission efficiency. Although TCP/IP does not cleanly discriminate these top layers, the basic functions described by OSI must still be performed.

The **network** layer deals with routing of data through a network. Routing involves sending data packets to a destination address through the best available path. It is at the transport and network layers where the issue of **multiplexing** is addressed. Multiplexing is the ability to send multiple types of data or signals over a single line or connection. This increases the efficiency of data communication. The **data link** layer involves how the physical connections between systems are identified and the information associated with them communicated over a physical medium—wire, fiber, or airwaves [2, 3].

11.1.2 Inter-Networking

By now you know that the Internet consists of a vast set of computer interconnections using computers called **routers**. Routers typically use IP for transporting various **data packets** (also called **datagrams**) among computers. You should also know that the Web is a way that the Internet is used. Specifically, it consists of a set of technologies that (logically) reside *at the application layer* of the Internet using **HTTP** (**Hypertext Transfer**

Protocol). You may also be familiar with Telnet, FTP (File Transfer Protocol), DHCP (Dynamic Host Configuration Protocol), and DNS (Domain Name Service). These are all examples of programs and protocols included in, or that support, the TCP/IP suite.

Although these protocols may be most familiar, note that there are network protocols used such as Asynchronous Transfer Mode (ATM), Fiber Distributed Data Interconnect (FDDI), X.25, and Frame Relay. Our focus in this textbook is on the TCP/IP suite because TCP/IP is the *de facto* protocol in the Internet and is used in most local area networks, but it is important to know that large organizations and telecommunications companies are likely to utilize a variety of network protocols that need to be secured.

Network protocols are defined by standards specified in what are called Request for Comment, or RFC. For example, the **RFC 822** defines the message format for email. RFC specifications define the ways the various protocols work such that each has well-defined interfaces and clearly articulated behavior to enable global interconnections. Where TCP/IP defines a suite of protocols for communicating over networks, **Ethernet** is a medium that governs one of the physical aspects of how computers are connected and how they send data over a wire or through the airwaves. Since its development in the 1970s, Ethernet technologies have evolved over the years and provide the basis for most high-performing networking systems, especially for local area networks.

A major competitor to Ethernet is the **Asynchronous Transmission Mode**, or **ATM**, as mentioned. ATM had strong appeal because it was a circuit-switched and cell-based technology that can prioritize and guarantee delivery of different types of transmission—for example, data versus voice versus video. Because video in particular is sensitive to network delays (called **latency**), this led to some initial deployments in major organizations. Also, ATM initially provided a higher-speed bandwidth compared to Ethernet. In many government and telecommunications organizations, ATM continues to be a popular network solution because of its circuit-based, connection-oriented dependable delivery and strong security capabilities; however, over time, interest in ATM has waned in most commercial organizations.

The reasons for this are that ATM technology has been much costlier than Ethernet. Switching to an ATM environment from Ethernet has required the replacement of existing network infrastructure, including all the devices and cables. Next, TCP/IP has implemented "policy-based routing" such as with Cisco's Multi Protocol Label Switching (MPLS) protocol, which enables certain types of network traffic (e.g., video and voice) to receive priority routing to reduce their latency. Finally, the transmission speed of Ethernet technology has since evolved quite rapidly (going well into many gigabits per second), which now surpasses ATM performance.

11.1.3 Packet and Circuit Switching

Networks are composed of **network nodes** or **hosts** and **network links**. Network nodes and hosts are usually interchangeable; they refer to computers, or sometimes hardware devices, that are connected by means of network medium or links such as copper cables, fiber optics, or airwaves (wireless), as mentioned. One of the ways to establish links among network nodes is to have every node linked to every other node on the network, but this approach is not practical. Alternatively, we can place devices called **switches** and/or routers around the network and establish links through them rather than at the node level. This was patterned after how telephone companies built their infrastructure.

> **In Focus**
>
> In the beginning, the switching function was done by human operators sitting in front of a switching panel. Now all of this is accomplished through sophisticated machinery, but the idea is the same. We make the link only when there is a communications need.

The collection of linkage devices—switches or routers—is commonly referred to as the *cloud*. The cloud represents a placeholder of an interconnected network, regardless of the underlying networking technologies used. A **switched** network is a configuration where most of the links are established through routing devices rather than point-to-point links. There are numerous types of switched networks; the two most common are **circuit-switched** (as indicated earlier with ATM) and **packet-switched**. The circuit-switching system is most commonly associated with the telephone system, whereas the packet-switching system is the dominant model for data networking, including the Internet. Thus the TCP/IP protocol suite is a packet-switching technology.

In a packet-switched network, information is broken into units (packets or datagrams) and multiplexed onto some form of transport or transmission *fabric*. The fabric may connect intranets or **local area networks** (**LAN**), extranets, campuses, or cities with **metropolitan area networks** (**MAN**), or over the Internet **wide area network** (**WAN**). In a packet-switching model, the links are shared between nodes—they are not dedicated. It is possible that different packets of the same message can travel different routes to the destination.

Once all the pieces of packets arrive at the destination, they are reassembled into the original message. This type of transmission is sometimes called **store and forward** because each node in the packet-switching network first receives a packet over some link, stores the packet in its internal memory, and then forwards the packet to the next node. In a circuit-switching model such as ATM, when a link is established, it has a dedicated link between nodes, and it allows the nodes to send chunks (called cells) of data across the link for the duration of the connection.

11.1.4 Network Topologies

Network topologies have to do with actual layouts of a network; that is, how computers are physically connected to one another. There are three major types of network topology for local area networks (LAN): **bus**, **ring**, and **star**, and many more variations of those, including what is called a mesh. Each network topology entails a particular network media type and media access method. Note that selection of a certain network topology binds one to a set of choices available for that topology.

Media access methods have to do with how networked computers gain access to the network. One way to do that is to have a central administrator that acts as sort of a traffic cop responsible for all the inbound and outbound traffic through a network cloud (often referred to as ***ingress*** and ***egress***, respectively). When a network request (query) is performed, it has ***contention*** with other networked devices, which means computers gain access to a network link upon demand whenever the link is available; otherwise, it has to wait. Of course, the fallout of this method is that there are cases where more than one computer tries to send data on the network at a time, which leads to a ***collision***. Finally, we can have the computers pass a special kind of electronic baton called a ***token*** and let them send data only when they have possession of the (electronic) token.

In a *bus* topology, all computers are strung together by a wire, such as Ethernet. To prevent data from bouncing back when it reaches one end of a cable, a special device called a ***terminator*** is connected on each end of the cable to absorb the signal. Bus topology typically uses copper wires, and they tend to go a lot farther than the typical twisted pair of cables found in telephone lines. Most early networks were built around bus network topology because of its simplicity, but this topology proved to be not quite as scalable as desired. It can also be difficult to detect network problems because we must check each network link—something similar to trying to determine which light in a series on the Christmas tree light string might be causing the entire lighting string to fail.

Also because of the way the computers are connected, increased network traffic can result in a significant performance downgrade because the network "broadcasts" data. In addition to the collisions among network packets that result, the broadcast data are received by both intended and unintended recipients. Although unintended recipient systems are supposed to discard the data, data can be intercepted with a network monitor or a host data capture program, commonly called a network monitor or network sniffer.

A second type of topology is called ***ring*** because all computers are connected in a loop. We can think of this as a democratic version of the network topology because the ring topology works as if we share a postal worker who delivers and collects mail for a neighborhood. In this scenario, every household has equal access to that mail carrier. You can send messages only when the messenger comes to your home. This is essentially how ring topology works, but rather than visiting a household mailbox, the messenger uses a computer-generated token.

As indicated previously, a token is a small data packet that is constantly passed around the ring network. Only when a system has the token can it transmit data. Because computers form a loop in this topology, there is no need to have a terminator, as is the case in the bus network. However, just as with the bus network, any failure of even one network connection can bring the entire network down, and installing even one additional computer will temporarily halt the functioning of the network; but note that FDDI (Fiber Distributed Data Interchange) utilizes a second ring to help alleviate these problems.

Many of today's network installations are based on the ***star*** topology, where a central switch connects the computers. When a computer sends a signal, it travels into the switch and then out to all other computers connected to it. There are two types of switches: *passive* and *active*. Passive switches simply pass the signal; they are used primarily for small networks. Active switches have more "intelligence" in managing data and are therefore more suitable for larger networks.

Next, one of the things to understand about the star topology is that only one computer can transmit data at a time, similar to the ring topology. Intelligent switches are useful in helping to ensure timely management of data transmission. Once the data are directed from the switch, each computer connected to it will receive the data packets and must examine the destination address of each packet. If the data are addressed to the computer, further processing will occur on that computer. If the data are sent to another computer, they are simply ignored (discarded).

The star topology is useful because it allows for a more structured network design. Unlike the bus and ring topologies, failure of a single computer will not stop data traffic among other computers. Although failure of a switch may bring down an entire network, that is quite unlikely because most network devices nowadays are of high quality, and unlike computers, they are simple devices focused on a simple task. Consequently, in the star topology, it is much easier to add or remove computers because that does not affect the functioning of other computers, and it has mitigated the difficulty in troubleshooting network problems.

In Focus

Bus, ring, and star are the main types of network topologies. In reality, you should expect to see many variations of these meshed topologies.

11.2 Devices and Addressing

For packets to arrive at their intended destinations, they need to be addressed. More specifically, each node and device needs to have at least one a unique address so they can be identified. Addresses may be specified in decimal, binary, octal, and hexadecimal notation. This is because there are both practical and physical limitations in the various devices and protocols used for addressing. Managers and administrators need to be familiar with each of these numbering systems.

At the physical layer, computers communicate with other devices using a communications medium that includes at least one network interface card (NIC) per computer and the network wiring or cable or wireless network gear. Each NIC carries a *media access control* (**MAC**) address hard-coded into it, which serves as a unique identifier. Each computer then sends messages to others by knowing this hard-coded address. The problem with this hard-coded address is that it does not lend itself to the flexibility needed for highly distributed networking configurations, such as a WAN or the Internet. To solve this difficulty, a logical addressing scheme was created for the Internet Protocol (IP) at the network layer, and unlike the physical addressing approach, it allows for flexibility and extensibility because the numbers can be "assigned" in software.

In Focus

The IEEE standards organization assigns a block of MAC addresses to each manufacturer of network cards to help ensure that each card is unique. MAC addresses are hard-coded into the network cards. MAC addresses are used by computers to uniquely identify themselves on a network at the bottom layer of the communications protocol stack—or frame layer.

In Version 4 of the Internet Protocol, addressing uses a 32-bit scheme and each address can be broken down to two parts: network address and host address. The network address part tells us what organization, institution, or department a host belongs to, and the host address portion tells the unique name for the host in that organization. A separate piece of information called *subnet mask* is typically required to figure out what portion of the address is network and what portion is the host.

11.2.1 IP Addressing

The approach used in TCP/IP is to create electronic maps that tie a neighboring node's hardware address to its software address. When a packet is sent from a host, it has to go through a series of translations that takes human-readable names such as *mike@fit.edu* and transforms this name into a software address (an IP address) at the network layer; then with each transfer from point to point (called a hop) along the way to the destination IP address, the packet has to be modified by the networking software at the data link layer to tie the neighbor's hardware address to its software address. In other words, the IP address is known by the source and is used to send data end to end, but hardware addresses are only known by nodes that are connected to each other and must be mapped each time a packet is transferred from one router to the next.

In Focus

A protocol known as ARP—Address Resolution Protocol—is needed to convert hardware addresses (Media Access Control, or MAC) to software-based Internet Protocol (IP) addresses so that networks can be location and device independent.

The *Internet Assigned Numbers Authority* (**IANA**) assigns IP addresses. IP addresses consist of 32 bits and are divided into 4 equal chunks of 8 bits in IPv4. There are two parts in every IP address, a network part and a host part. With 8 bits (0s and 1s), we can represent 256 different addresses within a group of addresses. Using 32 bits for addresses, roughly 4 billion unique addresses can be generated. IP addresses (in *IPv4*) are also grouped into classes, A through E, where in Class A, the first 8 bits represent a network number, and the remainder represent hosts; Class B uses the first 16 bits for network numbers and the remainder for hosts; and Class C uses 24 bits for network numbers and the remaining 8 for hosts. Class D is used for multicasts, and E is reserved for special purposes.

Class A networks are those networks with many hosts. IP addresses with the first group of 8 bits (octet) that range from **1 to 126** are included in this class, and the other three octets are used to identify each host in the network such that the format is NNN.HHH. HHH.HHH, where N represents the network addresses and Hs are the host addresses. Class B addresses reserve the first two set of octets for the network address, and network numbers range from **128 to 191**. The other two sets of octets are used to identify hosts on the network such that the format is NNN.NNN.HHH.HHH.

On the other hand, small- to mid-sized organizations usually have Class C networks. Class C networks reserve the first three sets of octets for IP network addresses and assign the first octet range from **192 to 223**. The last octet is allocated to hosts on the network such that the format is NNN.NNN.NNN.HHH.

Class D networks are available for what is called a multicast. Multicasts are useful for group message distributions, and there are lesser-known Class E networks used for experimentation. Importantly, reserved addresses that begin with *127* are called ***loopback addresses***. These are used for networking on the local host computer typically for testing web applications, interprocess communications, and TCP/IP configurations. A static IP address assigned to an individual computer, called ***localhost***, is 127.0.0.1.

In Focus

Under IPv4, the growth of the Internet was depleting the number of available IP addresses. The IETF development of IPv6 has created 128-bit addresses. The additional 96 bits over the 32-bit IPv4 addresses has made the number of possible combinations of addresses very large. Other benefits of IPv6 include enhanced security, the implementation of the capability to reach a specific group of hosts rather than the IPv4 model of reaching either one host or everyone all at once, and a much more efficient routing capability (for more details, see Forouzan [4] and Comer [5]).

11.2.2 Subnetworks

Subnetworks can be created within a network, and by this we mean that network classes can be subdivided by using a ***subnet mask***. A mask is a way of selecting a group of bits to determine a binary result using the logical AND operator. To determine the mask for dividing up networks into segments, we need to convert binary numbers to decimal numbers and vice versa.

For example, in binary numbers such as 10101010, the zeros do not carry any value and ones carry different values depending on their ordinal positions. The left-most digit is called the most significant bit (MSB) because it has the greatest value. Because we have 8 bits in an octet, the MSB is equal to 128 in decimal. The right-most digit is called the least significant bit (LSB) because its ordinal value is equal to 1 in decimal. See **Table 11.1**.

TABLE 11.1	Base-10 Decimal and Binary for Value 132							
Decimal	128	64	32	16	8	4	2	1
Binary	1	0	0	0	0	1	0	0

TABLE 11.2	Logical AND Operation				
A	&	B	=	C	
0		0		0	
0		1		0	
1		0		0	
1		1		1	

With the logical AND operation, 2 bits are compared and if they both equal 1, then the result is 1, else the result is 0, as illustrated in **Table 11.2**.

If a mask bit is on (1), then the corresponding bit in the address is interpreted as a network bit, whereas if a mask bit is off (0), then the corresponding bit in the address is interpreted as part of the host address. Using this technique, a Class A network can be used to create many Class B or C networks, and a Class B network can be used to create multiple Class C networks. Thus, mask bits establish the pattern for the addresses in a class, such as A, B, or C.

The pattern 255 indicates that all bits in an octet are turned on. The following are default masks by class: Class A: 255. 0. 0. 0, Class B: 255. 255. 0. 0, Class C: 255. 255. 255. 0. There must be at least 2 bits in the mask. If more than 2 bits are used, then the last 2 bits should be 0 [6]. This means that in a given IP address class (A, B, C), each class can use bits as follows: Class A up to 22 bits, Class B up to 14 bits, and Class C up to 6 bits, as illustrated in **Table 11.3**.

As seen from this illustration, we can take a network and host number and subdivide it into subnets. In our example, we had an IP address of 141.70.124.132 (with 124.132

TABLE 11.3	Subnet Mask Operation (Logical AND)			
Decimal	141.	70.	124.	132
IP Binary	10001101	01000110	01111100	10000100
Mask	255.	255.	255.	192
Mask Binary	11111111	11111111	11111111	11000000
Binary AND	10001101	01000110	01111100	10000000
Subnet	141.	70.	124.	128

as the host because this is a Class B network) and we created a subnetted address of 141.70.124.128. Using the mask, if bits are on, that part is applied to the network number, whereas if bits are off, they are applied to the host. Because our original IP address was 141.70.124.132 and applying our mask we created a subnet of 141.70.124.128 by subtracting 128 from 132 which reveals that this subnet address refers to host 4 on subnet 141.70.124.128.

Subnets thus are techniques to allow for the creation of *logical networks* by transforming part of the host portion normally assigned to a network class into a "new" network segment, or subnet. Each subnet communicates with another through its own default gateway (or routers), and this creates a logical separation between networks. Consequently, different departments or facilities may have their own networking infrastructure. A security benefit is that subnets are only known internally, with the original IP address exposed externally; thus, it is a good way to hide internal network and host addresses.

In Focus

A technique to support subnetting is to use network address translation, or NAT. NATs originally were created to extend network addresses in IPv4, but were found also to be quite useful in terms of security for hiding internal network IP addresses from view to the outside—and to help prevent a threat called footprinting, where attackers try to determine and exploit the addresses and services provided by an organization.

11.2.3 IPv4 versus IPv6

So far, we have concentrated mainly on the connection layers and addressing of version 4 of the Internet Protocol (IPv4), which is located at layer 3 of the OSI stack. Although version 6 of the IP standard (RFC 2460) has been around since 1998, it currently represents less than 1% of all Internet traffic [7]. The percentage, however, is expected to steadily increase as recent predictions of IPv4 address exhaustion for IANA is sometime in 2014 [8].

As we move from IPv4 to IPv6, it is important to understand the structural and functional differences between the standards and their impact on security. IPv4, introduced in 1981 as RFC 791, is a connectionless protocol that operates a best-effort delivery service. It specifies a 32-bit address for each host, of which a group of bits represents the network portion of the address, whereas the remaining bits represent the individual host—as we have discussed.

As previously indicated, with a 32-bit address space there can be a maximum of approximately 4.3×10^9 hosts. There are, however, reserved addresses within the address space that include blocks reserved for private addresses (10.0.0.0/8, 172.16.0.0/12, 192.168.0.0/16), local loopback (127.0.0.0/8), future use (240.0.0.0/4), multicasting (224.0.0.0/4), and specific addresses within each network reserved for broadcasting messages to every host on the subnet (host address all 1s), among others which further reduce those available for global routing.

The structure of an IPv4 datagram includes data encapsulated in a variable length header of between 20 and 60 bytes, with the maximum size for the entire datagram, including both the header and the data, being 65536 bytes. Functionally, when passing an IPv4 datagram to a network that has less bandwidth (called a maximum transmission unit, or MTU), IPv4 specifications allow the gateways or routers to fragment the datagram into smaller units. Only the receiving host reassembles the fragments as each fragment can take a different route.

The IPv6 protocol differs structurally from IPv4 in the address space and header, and functionally in how additional headers are added, how fragmentation is handled, and how sending messages to multiple hosts is accomplished. The IPv6 address format consists of 128 bits, of which 64 bits are generally used for the network portion of the address and 64 bits are for the host identification. An address length of 128 bits provides a maximum address space of approximately 3.4×10^{38}. With a world population of approximately 6×10^{10}, this provides the opportunity for assigning multiple addresses for everyone.

11.2.4 IPv6 Address Groupings and Uses

Like IPv4, IPv6 addresses are divided into several groups: Global unicast addresses have globally unique and configurable addresses to be assigned by IANA for use in the Internet. Site-local unicast addresses are IP addresses that are not globally routable, but can be used within an enterprise, similar to the 10.0.0.0/8, 172.16.0.0/12, 192.168.0.0/16 private address space in IPv4. These addresses are in the hexadecimal range designated FC00::/7. There are also link-local unicast addresses—IP addresses that are specific to the physical network segment to which the hosts are attached. These special addresses are in the hexadecimal range designated FE80::/10 and are used for auto-address configuration and neighbor discovery.

Multicast addresses are IP addresses that can be assigned to a group of hosts so that a packet sent to the multicast address will be delivered to all hosts in that group. These addresses are designated FF00::/8. Finally, there are anycast addresses. These are IP addresses that are assigned to a group of hosts, but a packet sent to the anycast address will only be delivered to the nearest host in the anycast group.

Apart from the length of the address, the header structure has been simplified in IPv6 to a fixed-length, 320-bit header with the opportunity to add 6 extension headers that provide path information, quality of service, and security functionality. The fixed-length IPv6 header is faster and easier to route as no calculations with respect to the IP header length must be made. In addition, a functional change from IPv4 to IPv6 is the requirement that the sending hosts handle any required fragmentation of a packet, as opposed to intermediary path routers. If a packet is found to be too large to traverse a network segment, IPv6 specifications instruct the router to drop the packet and send an error report to the host that the packet is too large to transfer, indicating the need for fragmenting.

In Focus

To avoid unnecessary "Packet Too Big" error messages (which are delivered using the protocol ICMP—to be discussed in the next chapter), the standard recommends that any host utilizing IPv6 make use of Path MTU Discovery (RFC 1981), which also relies on ICMPv6 messages to identify the appropriate packet size for the transmission path, and adjusts the sending size accordingly rather than having to fragment the packets. The reliance on ICMPv6 for messaging as a standard part of IPv6 is an important consideration for those transitioning from an IPv4 architecture, where ICMPv4 packets may have been filtered.

An additional functional change important to IPv6 involves how a message is delivered to multiple recipients. As stated earlier, broadcasting to all hosts on a given subnet in IPv4 was accomplished through setting the host part of the address all to 1s. This setting would cause the datagram that was sent to be picked up by all hosts on a given network segment. In IPv6, this method of broadcasting has been eliminated in favor of stronger support for multicasting and anycasting, with a greater variety of uses.

Multicasting is accomplished when a single packet is sent to a group of hosts that are part of a predefined, multicast group, as opposed to broadcasting, which sends the packet to all hosts on a given subnet. Although multicasting was defined in IPv4 with the 224.0.0.0/4 address space, it wasn't often utilized. In IPv6, multicasting is accomplished through addresses that begin with the first byte set to all 1s or, as commonly written in hexadecimal notation, FF00::/8.

The use of multicast addresses in IPv6 takes the place of broadcasting in IPv4, so in addition to the multicasting that was implementable in IPv4, in IPv6 it is used for locating services on the same subnet. Anycasting is similar to multicasting in that a group of hosts will share an IP address; however, rather than all hosts with that IP receiving a packet addressed to it, only the closest host holding the anycast address will receive it. Anycast can be used for load balancing and redundancy in network architecture.

11.2.5 IPv6 Address Configuration

One of the unique benefits of IPv6 is its ability to automatically configure itself with an address (RFC 2462). Autoconfiguration can occur either with a local server, called a **stateful configuration**, or without a local server, called **stateless configuration**, providing the information. In a stateless autoconfiguration, the IPv6-enabled host will first generate a link-local address through appending a variant of their MAC address (or other unique interface identifier) to the link-local prefix (FE80::/10). Once the tentative address is formed, a *Neighbor Solicitation* message using ICMPv6 will be sent to the FF02:0:0:0:0:2:FF00::/104 node information query address.

If the tentative address is in use, a message will be sent back and the autoconfiguration will generally stop. If the address is not in use, the host will use it on the local network and either wait for a local router to send a *Router Advertisement* message that provides configuration information or the host will send a *Router Solicitation* message to the all-routers multicast group, FF02:0:0:0:0:0:0:2. The router will provide the appropriate information required for generating a global unicast address. In a stateful autoconfiguration, either the router will not send a *Router Advertisement* or the *Router Advertisement* will indicate to the host the need to contact a server for stateful configuration.

With the structural and functional changes between IPv4 and IPv6 has also come a change in the security paradigm. Network security management with IPv4 has typically focused on border protection through screening addresses and protocols with perimeter firewalls. The concept of defense in depth adds network and host-based intrusion detection or prevention systems and appropriate architecture design segments networks for operational efficiency and security management. Fundamentally, with IPv4, network security has been about blocking nefarious messages before they pass into the softer network center.

The IPv6 security paradigm is different in that the model has changed from a network segment view to a host-to-host model with a "distributed, identity based security architecture" [9]. What this means is that in IPv6, there are security enhancements defined as IPSec (more later), which makes each globally definable IPv6 address able to authenticate the sender of communications, ensure the integrity of the packets, and, if desired, ensure the confidentiality of the transmitted data through encryption within the protocol rather than separately through differential technologies.

11.3 Network Connections Summarized

Up to this point, we have mainly covered aspects related to the point-to-point level protocols in the TCP/IP stack, such as connections and addressing. In this final section of this chapter, we will encapsulate these ideas in terms of what we might call network architecture. Network architecture reflects the blueprints or frameworks used by a network's physical components and their functional organization, which are often categorized as consisting of network fabric, link-layer connectivity, and communications facilities.

Network fabric usually refers not only to the topology of the network but also to the physical media and the connection methods. Examples of network fabric include physical connectivity such as Ethernet, Token Ring, Asynchronous Transfer Mode (ATM), and Fiber Distributed Data Interchange (FDDI), which we briefly mentioned. Studying each of these types of networks would require considerable work. We will concentrate mainly on Ethernet at the link layer and on the TCP/IP protocol suite at the architecture level in this textbook, but keep in mind that this does not mean that other forms of networks and architecture should be ignored. On the contrary, we point out that, for instance, wireless protocols are rapidly evolving and presenting new protocols and architecture to consider.

As mentioned before, IEEE approved the Ethernet standards. IEEE has had far-reaching influences in the field of electronics, and in the early 1980s, IEEE formed a committee to define and promote industry LAN standards amid competing industry specifications. In the world of networks, we often hear about *IEEE 802.X* standards. The committee was called *Project 802* because it started in February 1980. Subsequently, it formed a subcommittee called 802.3 to focus solely on Ethernet standards. Thus, when we speak of

Ethernet standards, we are talking about a series of standards based on 802.3, whereas the IEEE 802.5 standard deals with Token Ring technologies. Standards play an important role in network fabrics.

Early in its inception, there was only one 802.3 standard, called **10Base5**. 10Base5 was also called **thicknet** because it used thick coaxial cables as a method of implementation similar to the kinds cabling that run into homes for cable TV. The "10" in this designation meant that the maximum bandwidth was 10 megabits per second (Mbps). The "base" meant that it relied on **base-band transmission** rather than **broadband**, and the "5" in the designation meant the network could go up to about 500 meters. Once a particular standard is chosen, one is bound by the given bandwidth, topology, and cable types that are associated with that standard. So, for instance, if we had a network based on 10Base2 and wanted to upgrade to 10BaseT, we would have to change the network topology from a bus to a star and replace all the cables, network interface cards, and other networking equipment.

Also, with the development of fiber optics, the Synchronous Optical Network (SONET) evolved as a standard for optical transport and was popular for some time. However, due to limitations, parallel optical carrier (OC) technologies were developed and have overtaken SONET. It is not uncommon now to find large corporations with fiber optics for link-layers, including OC-192, which has a transmission rate of nearly 1,000 mbits per second, and even faster transmission rates including OC-768 and above.

11.3.1 Data Link Layer Connectivity

IEEE divided the link layer into two sublayers: the logical link control sublayer (LLC) and the MAC sublayer. The LLC sublayer part became official IEEE standard, called 802.2. The rationale was that devices that support the IEEE 802 specifications required a standard MAC sublayer that could receive data packets from multiple network transport protocols such as Token Ring, ATM, FDDI, and Ethernet. The modification also entailed the standard assignment of unique identification numbers to different network interface card manufacturers.

For this, IEEE derived a 48-bit representation, half of which was called the organizationally unique identifier (OUI) and was the unique number assigned to each vendor; the other 24 bits were assigned to the address space that each vendor could use for NICs they manufacture. This scheme tells where each network interface card is manufactured. Thus, the LLC, logical link control, deals with mostly traffic control functions and addressing, and the MAC sublayer communicates with the interface card directly and deals with how the data link layer accesses the network.

If the unit of data at the physical layer is a *bit* (or, more accurately, 8 bits, or an octet), the unit of data at the data link layer is a *frame*. The data link layer looks at every incoming frame to see if it belongs to that computer, which is accomplished by software examining the MAC address that is unique to its NIC card. Once the data link software has determined that the frame is destined for its computer, it will then strip off the frame header and send the payload up to the next layer in the protocol stack. (We will examine this concept of encapsulation in the next chapter.) But what about frames read by the data link layer that are not destined for that computer? These are simply discarded and not passed on to the upper layers.

In Focus

We will later look at how this broadcast feature can be exploited by network monitors (sniffers) to capture unintended information—often called a "man-in-the-middle" attack—and how it can be used for an attack called ARP poisoning.

There are different frame types for different network protocols. Ethernet frames are of variable length, with the data payload ranging from 46 to 1500 bytes. The other fields in the frame are of fixed length. In contrast, there are networking technologies that have fixed data frames such as ATM. Occasionally, there may be a conflict between the frame types configured for a given system, which must be resolved by the link layer software [4].

11.3.2 Communications Facilities

We have already learned that Ethernet resides at the base of the stack and is one of many frame-layer-based media we see today for the transport of data. Ethernet technologies have evolved over the years and provide a high-performance networking infrastructure, especially for local area networks. Each computer's MAC address uniquely identifies the computer on the network, but MAC alone is not a very practical network addressing technique because it creates device dependence; thus, the IP is used between devices to gain device independence—and at this layer, instead of talking about point-to-point communications, we are talking about end-to-end communications.

In Focus

ATM, or Asynchronous Transmission Mode, provides high-speed bandwidth, but there are at least several problems in implementing it. First, the connection cost is much higher with ATM than with Ethernet. That is, ATM is a much costlier way than Ethernet to connect a network host to the network via a network device such as a switch and router. Second, switching to an ATM environment from Ethernet requires the entire existing network infrastructure, including all the devices and cables, to be replaced. And finally, Ethernet technology has evolved quite rapidly and is now reaching through gigabit transmission rates, which surpasses the ATM bandwidth.

As mentioned earlier, in *circuit switching*, network connections are made close to real time, similar to how telephone connections are made. This kind of switching works best for the type of communications that are delay sensitive. An advantage is that parties connected via a switched line have exclusive ownership of the line (channel) for the duration of the connection and have guaranteed bandwidth, but there is a cost: a delay is incurred during connection setup. In circuit-switch technology such as ATM, frames are called cells.

Most circuit-switching technologies are based on the old public switched telephone network (PSTN) carrier services. We still see dial-up connections using modems of various speeds around 50 kbps, and we have switched leased services, T-carrier services, and ISDN (integrated services digital networks). It's hard to imagine in this day and age that these still exist, but there remain many examples of where these services are used, in particular in remote parts of the world. In this light, two protocols have evolved: SLIP, serial line Internet protocol (which is mainly defunct now), and point-to-point protocol (PPP), which enables browser interfaces to surf the Web. The major difference between these is that whereas we can dynamically assign IP addresses within the PPP environment, that was not true in SLIP. In PPP, a user only has to know the *number to call* and his/her user name and password for authentication on the system that provides the services and connection.

In *packet switching*, the type used by TCP/IP does not give ownership of the communications link to anyone. Instead, everyone who can access it shares it, and it has turned out that this method is much more economical for most types of data transmissions. However, packet switching does not guarantee the level of bandwidth you would expect from a circuit-switching method. Nevertheless, packet switching over the years has grown to be quite effective, and we are now seeing applications such as voice and video conferencing deployed on packet-switched networks, especially coinciding with policy-based routing using a protocol conceived by CISCO known as Multiprotocol Label Switching (MPLS), which allows "tagged" packets to gain higher delivery priority.

Finally, circuit- versus packet-switching communications relates to how data are passed through the network fabric. For instance, when systems communicate, it is necessary to have some kind of moderation capability; that is, each computer has to know when to read or stop reading data. The most widely used technique is *synchronous* communications, which operates at the frame level. However, with the introduction of sound and video in digital networks, we have seen the increasing use of *isochronous* communications, which employs a central device to coordinate the traffic to guarantee a certain minimum data transfer rate required for latency-sensitive data.

In Focus

Although isochronous communications is efficient compared to synchronous, it has the risk of a single point of failure [5].

In synchronous communications, the data link layer deals with flow control. Flow control has to do with coordinating the rate at which data are sent. In this case, networked hosts exchange information regarding their capacity to send and receive data. If computer A is sending too much data to computer B, computer B negotiates with computer A to reduce the data sent until further notice. When computer B reaches a point where it can receive more data, it again notifies computer A to increase the transfer rate [5, 8].

CHAPTER SUMMARY

In this chapter, we took a broad survey of link layers of the OSI and TCP/IP protocol stack concepts in preparation for understanding how protocols resolve names and addresses, route traffic, manage the flows of data, and report errors in the next chapter. We introduced the ISO/OSI reference model and contrasted it with the TCP/IP protocol suite, and we covered some of the key differences between IPv4 and IPv6 addressing.

It is important to realize that as 3G and 4G wireless technologies evolve and as communications devices begin to meld with computing devices, there are emerging technologies to consider and new emerging security threats to them. We will address these issues in the last section of this textbook, particularly in regard to peer-to-peer (P2P) networks and multiple ad hoc networks (MANET) and security. For now, we will stick with our introduction of basic concepts, and in the next chapter, we will explore the most important concepts related to routing to provide enough background for our chapter on network security that will follow in the next section.

THINK ABOUT IT

Topic Questions

11.1: What is meant by network architecture?

11.2: Why did TCP/IP become the network implementation of the Internet instead of a purer form of the ISO/OSI?

11.3: In IPv6, autoconfiguration can be either _____ or _____.

11.4: What does a subnet mask do?

11.5: What is the local host loopback address?

11.6: Where does the first octet of Class B networks start?

11.7: Stateful configuration:

_____ Only occurs on IPv4
_____ Is not recommended
_____ Occurs using a local server
_____ Occurs without a local server

11.8: The ability to create subnets was initially done to extend IP addresses in IPv4 because of address depletion.

_____ True
_____ False

11.9: Network address translation (NAT) is a good way to hide internal network and host addresses.

_____ True
_____ False

11.10: Asynchronous transmission mode (ATM) is a packet-switched technology.

_____ True
_____ False

Questions for Further Study

Q11.1: Compare and contrast the functionality and performance (efficiency) of TCP/IP and an implementation of OSI. (Hint: What are some pros and cons of collapsing the session, presentation, and applications layers in TCP/IP?)

Q11.2: Discuss some implications on network security by having multiple layers of protocols that must openly communicate with each other.

Q11.3: Discuss the reasons for having Class A, B, and C networks in IPv4.

Q11.4: Why did the OSI model never materialize as an implementation? Discuss the pros and cons of having the seven distinct layers compared to TCP/IP.

Q11.5: What are metropolitan networks? What protocols do they tend to implement, and why?

KEY CONCEPTS AND TERMS

Internet Engineering Steering Group (IESG) is a subgroup within the Internet Engineering Task Force (IETF), which reviews and selects Internet standards.

NICs carry a media access control (MAC) address hard-coded into them.

Star topology is where a central switch connects the computers.

Transmission Control Protocol/ Internet Protocol (TCP/IP) has been adopted as the de facto standard used in networks ranging from LANs to the Internet.

References

1. Lewis, W. (2000). *Cisco networking academy program*. Indianapolis, IN: Cisco Press.
2. Goldman, J. D. (1995). *Applied data communications*. New York, NY: John Wiley & Sons.
3. Ramteke, T. (1994). *Networks*. Upper Saddle River, NJ: Prentice Hall.
4. Forouzan, B. A. (2010). *TCP/IP protocol suite*. New York, NY: McGraw-Hill.
5. Comer, D. E. (1995). *Internetworking with TCP/IP*. Upper Saddle River, NJ: Prentice Hall.
6. Hunt, C. (1992). *TCP/IP network administration*. Sebastopol, CA: O'Reilly & Associates.
7. Gunderson, S. H. (2008). *Global IPv6 Statistics—Measuring the current state of IPv6 for ordinary users*. Dubai, UAE: RIPE 57.
8. IANA (2010). *IPv4 Address report: Unallocated address pool exhaustion*. Retrieved November 4, 2010, from http://www.potaroo.net/tools/ipv4/index.html
9. Stevens, W. R. (1994). *TCP/IP illustrated: The protocols*. Sebastopol, CA: O'Reilly & Associates.

Protocols and Routing

W E HAVE COVERED NETWORKS AND ADDRESSING, so it's time to consider protocols and how data are routed from one system to another. Routing protocols fall into various types depending on whether they are routing protocols for a wide area network (WAN), a metropolitan area network (MAN), or a local area network (LAN). We will begin with the linkages between networked devices—computers, printers, routers, and so forth, and then work our way through the protocol stack and among various routing stages and techniques.

Chapter 12 Topics

This chapter:

- Covers the concept of encapsulation.
- Discusses address resolution.
- Presents connection-oriented and connectionless networking.
- Explores various routing protocols and types.

Chapter 12 Goals

When you finish this chapter, you should:

- ❑ Have an understanding of the protocol functions that comprise the TCP/IP suite.
- ❑ Know how headers are used by protocols.
- ❑ Know about fragmentation and reassembly of packet fragments.
- ❑ Be able to identify how data are transported end to end over the Internet.
- ❑ Understand how addresses are resolved.
- ❑ Have an understanding of routing.

12.1 Link-Point Networking

When referencing link-point networking, we are referring to the network media and the protocols that deal with the physical connections. Network media include coaxial, shielded twisted pair and fiber-optic cabling, and even airwaves, that connect a network card to the network fabric protocols. The protocols deal with packaging and moving the data from point to point and are part of the data link layer of the OSI model.

In network security, the importance of the distinctions between link-to-link and end-to-end networking will become apparent. In this final chapter of this section, we will explore both link-to-link and end-to-end networks and their respective protocols in sufficient detail so that you will know which countermeasures to use when and where in order to secure a network. We will begin with link-point networking and protocols and work our way up to the applications layer.

12.1.1 Physical Connections

In the previous chapter, we spent considerable time on connectivity and addressing. At this stage, we will cover these concepts less in terms of physical connections and more in terms of protocols for handling the data, with one exception. We will begin with a brief tour of connectivity at the physical layer because at the physical layer, we are talking about hardware. An important consideration in this realm deals with how network interface cards interact with the computer, and vice versa.

To appreciate this issue, we need to reflect on our chapter on computer operating systems and briefly discuss **_device interrupts_**. When devices in a computer have data for the computer's CPU to handle, remember that they send a signal with what is called an interrupt. Because there are many kinds of devices in a computer, devices are assigned an **_interrupt level_**. Most people who have worked with a Microsoft operating system, for example, have become aware of interrupt request (IRQ) levels for devices, which is the mechanism that each computer peripheral device uses to communicate with the CPU. The CPU uses the IRQ levels to figure out where the data are coming from, adjust its internal system clock, and manage the processes accordingly—allocating resources, processing, and computing according to allotted time slices.

With the Window's plug-and-play feature, when devices such as network cards are added, they can experience "contention" with other devices because there may be a conflict on an IRQ. This problem is relatively easy to detect because Microsoft enabled the *right mouse button click* event on the "My Computer" icon to bring up a "Properties" option in a pop-up "Menu." On the resulting tab, the "Device Manager" brings up the list of devices used on the computer. If a problem exists, such as conflicting IRQ, the device is flagged.

In terms of networking, the NICs in a system have a given IRQ. When data arrive from a wire or wireless network, the data are buffered into a queue for processing. When the buffer begins to fill, the NIC generates an interrupt on the bus to signal the CPU (by means of the OS) to gather the data and process them according to what the data contain. In so doing, the OS invokes the TCP/IP software to extract the data from their packaging and pass them up to a given user or an awaiting process.

Thus every communicating device on a network requires at least one NIC, even if they are wireless devices. Considering that more modern systems have more than one network card, we can use this to our (security) advantage. Suppose, for example, that you have a server connected to two different networks; we need two interfaces to do that (in security, we use this approach to create what is called a dual-homed host). Also consider a router that has several Ethernet connections, ATM ports, and several other WAN links. Many different network interface cards are needed in those situations.

When data are sent from a system to a network, the sending NIC converts the parallel data stream received from the computer's CPU and OS into the serial stream of bits carried across the cabling or out over the airwaves. This becomes obvious when you look at the card design and the cables to which cards connect. NICs are connected to computer motherboards using one of several industry standard expansion slots.

However, when the data exit out to the network cable, you can see by the wire that the cable only takes one bit at a time because it has only one line to carry data. Thus the receiving NIC monitors signals transmitted on the cable and picks up the correct data packets sent to the computer. In the opposite way, the serial data from the network cable are converted and packaged to fit the parallel data stream [1, 2].

12.1.2 Carrier Sense Multiple Access with Collision Detection (CSMA/CD)

In the previous chapter, we mentioned that devices must contend with other devices to communicate their messages. Unlike interrupt levels, which were described in the previous section of this chapter as being used to arbitrate communications, networks, especially local area networks, must find another way to signal because there are so many different (unfixed) devices and means for communications that tap into the communications bus or airwaves.

Ethernet is based on the media access method called CSMA/CD, which stands for *Carrier Sense Multiple Access with Collision Detection*. To appreciate this, consider an analogy to a group of people talking in a completely dark room. Each person can hear what another person is saying. This is analogous to the CS part of the carrier sense. Presume that the people in this room are polite and that each person has an equal chance to talk. This is analogous to the multiple access (MA) part, meaning that there is no predetermined order to speak. Anyone who wants to talk can talk.

Nevertheless, what happens when people start to talk at the same time? To be polite, people would stop talking when they would hear something they haven't said. This is analogous to collision detection (CD). When this kind of collision occurs, people would pause a few seconds and resume their conversation (this is indeed what we call a conversational protocol), but there is no rule here about how long to wait before someone begins talking again. Some people would have a longer pause than others.

Using that analogy, we have a good conceptualization of how computers using Ethernet work. When there is a collision of data on the Ethernet bus, the systems stop transmitting and resubmit the message again after a random period of time. Now continuing with this analogy, consider that there are two ways that people address one another. One way is to first call out the name of the person someone wants to talk to and wait for a response from that person. Or, there are cases when a person wants everyone's attention. In that case, people may simply call out what they want to say. In data networking, the analogy of calling out to everyone on the same network is called ***broadcasting***.

In Focus

In the previous chapter, we presented a set of broadcast addresses for a system to use; however, using these represents an intentional broadcast system. Ethernet uses a shared bus/broadcasting system for actions such as address resolutions where systems receive unintentional data (meaning not intended for that system). In other words, all systems that are connected on the network bus receive all traffic, but those who receive unintended communications are supposed to discard the unintended data.

12.1.3 Transiting Data: Egress and Ingress

Until now, we have been primarily describing communications between directly connected systems or systems that share a local area network (LAN), but when data are sent out to a wide area network (WAN), such as the Internet or an extranet that might be shared with trading partners, a variety of protocols must mediate and route the data. A LAN shares a network address with multiple hosts connected to it.

One can think of this as similar to a street where neighbors live, perhaps 1210 through 1505 addresses that reside on Kings Court Lane. LANs are separated from other networks by routers or gateways, which cordon off a local group of networked systems from others, and these are called autonomous systems, or AS. The routers that pass data out of a LAN to a wider area network are called ***egress*** routers, whereas routers that take data from a wider area network into a LAN are called ***ingress*** routers.

In Focus

A network of networks, such as the Internet, is comprised of autonomous networked systems, or AS, including LANs.

Once data packets egress, we are no longer talking about link-to-link connectivity. Although each router in a WAN must have link-to-link connections and protocols, in terms of networking and security, this transit takes on a special meaning. The network layer is responsible for routing information from one location to the next. Not only must this layer translate information that flows between the physical connections, it must also coordinate the data flow (flow control) and report errors that occur, such as data congestion between the data connection points.

Between a sending host computer and a network node or end-point computer, many errors are possible such as a host or network segment that has become unreachable for some reason, or a congested pathway. These are reported back to the source system by the ICMP protocol encapsulated at the network layer. Thus using the ICMP protocol, network devices record and report network errors and conditions back to senders.

12.1.4 Internet Control Message Protocol (ICMP)

The *Internet control message protocol* (**ICMP**) is a complex protocol used for multiple functions such as to manage network congestion, to report errors, such as notifying a host that a destination is unreachable, and in some cases, to update host route tables. ICMP packets are encapsulated in the IP data payload; however, packets are not passed up to the transport layer when they are unpacked. Instead, they are used at the network layer to load status information to report back to the source hosts. This multipurpose function violates the principle of automaticity, a property of good software design. However, because of its flexibility, it has proven very useful in the connectionless environment of the Internet.

One way that you may know ICMP is by means of an "echo request" message, otherwise known as *ping*. Ping creates the ability for IP software on one system to test a connection with IP software on another. A special class of ICMP request message is called a *redirect*, which requests that hosts change routes for passing data. It is this capability that enables systems to learn of new systems and routes that come online via dynamic routing; however, there is the danger that an ICMP *redirect* may be part of a security attack (we will discuss this in more detail later when we get to network security).

In Focus

Even though a useful function, administrators should typically block inbound ICMP messages, especially change route requests if their firewalls allow this fine-grained inspection.

The error handling for ICMP may determine that a router has become congested if a queue has reached a given threshold. It then creates and sends an ICMP *source quench* message to instruct sources to reduce their transmission rates through that router for a period of time. Because ICMP is used to inform a data source, it cannot update intermediate routers about problems. Another issue to consider with ICMP is that because the ICMP messages are encapsulated into an IP packet, as with all IP packets, ICMP messages can be lost or discarded and the source may not receive error information. Also, to prevent further congestion, no ICMP messages are generated about ICMP errors [3].

In Focus

ICMP messages are multipurpose; they are used for both error handling and control of data flow. The device that generates an ICMP message will send it back to the originating source.

12.2 Encapsulation and the TCP/IP Protocol Stack

Now that we have covered most of the basic concepts related to data communications, we need to dig into the idea of encapsulation before we discuss how information is routed through a WAN such as the Internet. Simply put, encapsulation means to put one complete set of information inside another. We will see in this section how encapsulation occurs all the way down the TCP/IP protocol stack from the application layer to the frame layer (referring to the OSI model), and is then undone at the receiving end by stripping off the encapsulation envelopes (**Figure 12.1**).

Recall that network protocols are layered. Each layer of the network protocol stack collects the applicable data for that layer and attaches a header containing control information. The data are encapsulated this way down from the applications layer to the frame layer of the stack, and then transported out of the network interface. When a data packet arrives at a destination, the header portion is inspected and stripped off by the corresponding peer layer at the receiving computer. Thus information in the header attached at each layer on the sending computer will only be recognized and removed by the peer layer on the receiving computer.

This way, when we read an email, for example, our email application displays only our email message, instead of all the extra information added along the way. So the data link layer communicates with the network layer and the physical layer within the OSI protocol stack on the same computer, or in the case of the TCP/IP suite, the data layer and frame layer communicate with both the physical layer and IP at the network layer in the TCP/IP protocol suite.

> **In Focus**
>
> The network layer of the protocol stack deals with how groups of data are routed from place to place based on their addressing scheme. In TCP/IP, it is the Internet Protocol (IP) that is used in this function. The unit of data we deal with at the network layer is called *packet* or *datagram*. At a low-level technical discussion, these differ slightly, but for our purposes (and in most discussions), the terms packet and datagram can be (and are) used interchangeably.

With encapsulation, each layer in the network stack can only communicate with the layer above and below it (they do this through what is called a service access point, or SAP). Thus the network layer receives data from the transport layer, processes the data from the data link layer, and sends it to the transport layer. It only appears that there are parallel communications between the network layer on the sender's machine and the peer network layer on the receiver's machine.

The beauty of the layered approach is that programmers can write applications that work at the application layer without having to worry about the networking underneath. This enables rapid development and deployment of networked applications because the development process is streamlined. However, there is a side effect. When a layer on the protocol stack receives data from the layer above it, it does not recognize the contents in

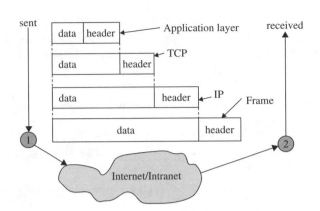

FIGURE 12.1

TCP/IP
encapsulation.

the header data added at the upper layers, and does not know the contents of the data passed down. An analogy to this is a letter sealed in an envelope, which is then placed in a larger envelope for interoffice or for bulk mail transfer. This hides the details of each protocol datum as much as possible unless it is necessary for a software module to have the information. The principle of encapsulation is widely practiced in software development and ensures the flexibility and independence of program modules.

12.2.1 Headers and Name Resolution

As you might have gathered, to completely grasp the concept of encapsulation, you need to know what goes into headers and bodies at each layer. Suppose Mike in Melbourne wrote an email message to his friend Dan in Doha, and sent it. Mike may use an email application such as Microsoft Outlook to construct his message, and supplies *dan@cmu.edu* in the address line to send the message to him. Somehow the user "Dan" must be identified on a given host system to deposit the message into his mailbox, and this must go into an application layer header; but even before that, dan@cmu.edu has to be translated into an IP address because routers have no clue who dan@cmu.edu is, and this data would go into the IP header.

Let's examine this sequence from the user application perspective. First, the human-readable name must be translated to an IP address. In this case, we start at the right-hand side of the address, .edu. As we discovered earlier, the physical layer of networks deal with the mechanical and electrical requirements of network media, and the frame layer deals with the interfaces to the media. The data link layer, using MAC addressing and the ARP protocol to resolve MAC-IP addresses, provides a way to extend networks with equipment such as routers and switches. Now, we must consider how name-to-IP address resolution is done, especially given how the network layer facilitates internetworking. The key to this is the **Domain Name Service** (DNS). The DNS must find an IP address for a given name.

In the early days of the Internet, naming resolution was not a big problem. Systems that ran the UNIX operating system simply shared a common text file called *hosts*. When people added new nodes or changed nodes, they simply updated the *hosts* file on their computer and shared it with other people with whom they wanted to communicate. As the Internet grew, it became evident that a more elaborate system would be needed. The current scheme uses the distributed database DNS. The DNS is used to translate human-readable names into numeric addresses, where human-readable names such as *dan@cmu.edu* are resolved into IP addresses, as well as in the reverse.

In Focus

DNS systems are queried to gather the IP addresses associated with a name, which in turn is used for the IP routing process. The routing of IP packets (datagrams) is done either by direct delivery or indirect routing. Direct delivery is where a datagram is passed from one host across a single physical network to another host.

As seen then, applications use human-readable names. For example, in the network *cob.fit.edu*, the hostname for a system might be *mike*, in which case, we might have an address mikeuser@mike.cob.fit.edu. This complete naming is called a ***fully qualified domain name*** (**FQDN**) because it provides not only the host name but also the domain to which the machine belongs. The FQDN for the host in this example is *mike.cob.fit.edu*. The applications layer protocols distribute the data to the proper user on that FDQN according to the service (e.g., email/SMTP) and the header information provided. Because systems and network routers (and switches) do not understand human-readable names, FQDN are converted into numbers. A system or group of systems is typically assigned an address or a block of addresses by a controlling or "parent" organization.

The domain part of the name such as ".edu" is the top-level (or root-level) access of the DNS, and there are others such as .gov, .com, .int, .mil, and .org. For addresses such as www.fit.cob.edu, the ".fit" part identifies the name of the organization (commonly called OU, for organizational unit). Within the "fit" OU, there are addresses as part of a pool of addresses for departments. Note that there are internal (LAN) and external (WAN) DNS systems used in name resolutions.

Requests to local hosts can be resolved without going out or sending queries to an external DNS system. DNS also caches name resolution information about recently accessed external systems. If a name resolution has not been cached, the name resolution request is sent to the top root domain, and resolved top to bottom. That is, if the top domain of the requested host is edu, it is directed to the edu node and then travels down the domain structure rather than travel horizontally to other .edu domains.

Once the naming is resolved to an IP address, a transport protocol must be determined—either TCP or UDP. If the application requires a reliable connection, a TCP header is created; otherwise a UDP header is created (more about TCP and UDP shortly). Underneath this transport, an IP packet header is formed and the TCP or UDP contents are placed into the body. In other words, once the human-discernable name has been translated to an IP address, a header is created for either TCP or UDP, and then this is placed into the IP body and an IP header is created—in our case for an email message to Dan as the recipient on a given host at a given network using a given application.

Because the IP packet contains all the upper-level data and headers in its payload, the IP layer is responsible for moving the data packet from point to point. Thus the IP header stores source and destination address fields and other information such as whether the packet has been fragmented (along with the segment addresses, or offsets, of the chunks), a time-to-live (TTL) field that informs routers when the packet should be discarded in case it becomes lost, and various options that the protocol needs to properly manipulate and route the data contained in the IP packet. IP addresses consist of both network and computer (host) numbers. **Figure 12.2** shows an illustration of what is contained in an IPv4 header.

12.2.2 Address Resolution Protocol (ARP)

When the IP packet is encapsulated inside the payload of the frame, the frame link-layer attaches a header and a cyclic redundancy check (CRC) bit used for checking the integrity of the data before transporting the information over a medium. Mapping between IP and MAC addresses is done with the *Address Resolution Protocol* (**ARP**), as we have indicated. ARP enables a host to find physical addresses of another system on the same network using only the IP address. Typically, IP addresses are maintained by an accessible physical storage mechanism, but a system that has no physical medium to store this information needs an initial way of getting its address, so the designers of this architecture created *Reverse ARP* (**RARP**), which obtains an initial IP address by doing a request broadcast at boot time.

> **In Focus**
>
> MAC addresses have to be resolved for each IP address, so every time a packet is sent, the ARP table must know the MAC address of the adjacent nodes. As the packet goes from computer to computer (router to router) the software has to reconstruct the frame header with a new destination MAC address. From a command line, arp, a will show ARP table contents.

An ARP exchange between machines results in an entry in each system's ARP cache. Generally, the only time ARP broadcasts are needed is when a machine joins a network, when a system changes its IP address, or when entries expire in the cache. This approach

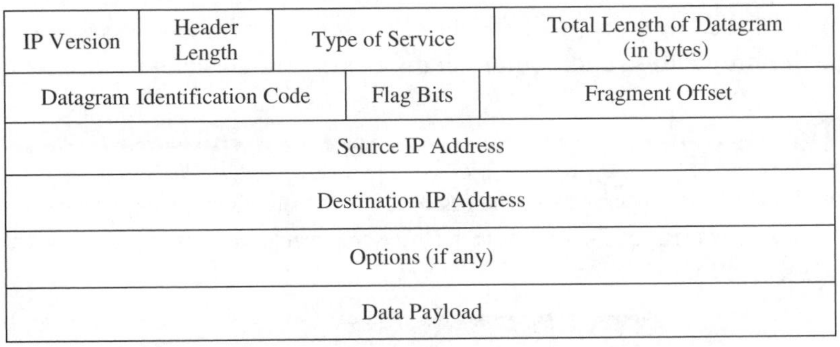

IP Version	Header Length	Type of Service		Total Length of Datagram (in bytes)
Datagram Identification Code			Flag Bits	Fragment Offset
Source IP Address				
Destination IP Address				
Options (if any)				
Data Payload				

FIGURE 12.2

IPv4 header (for more elaborate illustration, see Stevens [4]).

was taken to reduce network traffic. In some cases, a proxy ARP may be used to map an IP network address prefix to multiple physical addresses for administrative convenience.

ARP assumes that systems are trustworthy and typically they will install ARP mappings in their tables without checking their legitimacy. On the one hand, using a proxy ARP exacerbates this problem by making it difficult for network monitors to detect spoofing, where one system purports to be another in order to intercept packets. On the other hand, it helps security defenses by hiding some important networking details from *would-be* attackers.

In Focus

A proxy is a system that acts on behalf of other systems, and a proxy can be hardware, software, or most likely, both—as in the case of a proxy server. Only the proxy server will have the valid, unique IP address that is exposed on a public network.

12.3 End-Point Networking

Now that we have covered a fairly wide range of network concepts from the ground up, at this stage you should have a fairly good conceptual grasp of how networks are addressed and how communications occur from point to point. End-point networking generally refers to the protocols above the network layer in the OSI protocol stack, and also encompasses the higher level protocols that ensure delivery of data to an application or user on a given host system. In this section, we will explore some of the more technical details involved in end-to-end networking so that by the time we arrive at the network security section, the security measures will make sense. We will first discuss services and sockets, and then we will move up to the applications layer.

12.3.1 Services and Sockets

Just as IP is used in the routing among networks, each service on a host implements a given set of functionality that requires protocols to act as a sort of *transport* in conjunction with a service (or session). That is to say, they must have the ability to distinguish among multiple different services or destinations within a given host system. At this layer, the protocols UDP, TCP, and SSL/TLS operate. To distinguish among services, and to queue requests and manage responses, TCP and UDP both use a set of data structures and system calls known collectively as a ***socket***. The combinations of IP addresses and port numbers of the communicating end-point systems identify the socket.

In Focus

Port numbers identify a given service, combined with end-pair IP addresses that sockets use for communications. Thus, ports represent services, or more specifically, servers. In other words, port numbers are queues that servers use to listen for connections.

Services (also called daemons) are provided to clients by means of server programs, data structures, system calls, and queues (called ports). Servers include *httpd* (for Web browsing), *smtpd* (for email), and *ftpd* (for file transfer). Standard port numbers represent well-known queues for services; for example, port 80 is a default port to handle HTTP requests, port 23 is the default for Telnet connections, and port 25 is the default for accepting SMTP email requests. Although systems administrators can assign different port numbers for these types of communications, automatic service discovery relies on these defaults. There are also "free" ports that can be used by software developers to create custom services. The transport layer directs data to appropriate network ports (queues) so that they can be properly processed.

Conceptually then, a server listens on a given port and accepts the connections to a service, which dispatches the communications up through the protocol stack to the appropriate application. As an example, the email service protocol, smtpd, listens by default on port 25 for communications from email clients, and the httpd server listens on port 80 (by default) for communications from browser clients. The important point to note about sockets is that they provide various functions such as the ability to get a hostname by using its IP number, and they enable communications to be established and coordinated between programs that communicate over a network. When communications are established between end-points, a socket is created, and the communications end-points bind to each other, and then send and receive their data by using a series of socket system calls.

At the session layer, the header contains information about "end-points," and end-points are combinations of IP addresses and port numbers, along with a session protocol type. Therefore from a protocol perspective, in TCP/IP, data can be transported either by the **Transmission Control Protocol** (**TCP**) or by **User Datagram Protocol** (**UDP**). All data traffic that requires constant and guaranteed services will pass through the TCP stack, whereas the UDP stack handles the other types of data.

Although there are network applications that are closely associated with either of these transport protocol stacks, sometimes both protocol stacks are utilized to complete a transmission. The main difference between TCP and UDP is that with UDP there is no exchange of acknowledgment packets during or after transmission. In this sense TCP is analogous to certified mail and UDP to regular mail. As with the postal service, both TCP and UDP provide quite reliable and dependable services, but the difference is TCP service has the mechanism in place to ensure this and the notifications that are sent [2].

At its most basic level at the session layer, the communications from one host to another involves a *socket*. If we consider how an operating system processes communications requests, we quickly realize that there are various methods to do these. For example, a pipe is an interprocess communications facility in both UNIX and Windows that forms a communication link between two related processes. Each pipe has a read and write channel: One process reads on the other process write channel. Just as pipes may be used from the command line, they may also be used programmatically with the *pipe* system call. Interprocess communications is only one form of I/O supported by systems.

A "socket," on the other hand, is an IPC in networking vernacular. Sockets utilize data structures similar to file descriptors for a file, and in terms of communications they resemble *pipes*, except unlike pipes, processes need not be related to each other. They use

TABLE 12.1 Socket System Calls	
accept	Accept a connection to a socket
bind	Bind a name to a socket
connect	Initiate a connection to a socket
getsockname	Get a socket name
getsockopt	Get and set options on a socket
ioctl	Get and set data on underlying protocols or devices
listen	Listen for connections on a socket
recv	Receive a message from a socket
select	Allow synchronization of I/O over sockets
send	Send a message from a socket
shutdown	Shut down all or part of a full duplex connection
socketpair	Create a pair of connected sockets

only one channel (full duplex), and they are created with a series of *socket* system calls. There are different socket types: stream, datagram, raw, and sequential packets. The socket types are used to provide for different networking environments. Two environments, called domains, exist for sockets: the UNIX domain and TCP/IP domain. System calls include those seen in **Table 12.1**.

Networking software for both UNIX and Windows is supported at the lowest layers of the networking model. Some utilities exist to help facilitate user communications over networked machines at the higher layers; for example, remote login is accomplished through what has become known as the "r" commands, such as *rlogin*; *rcp*, which performs a remote copy; and *rsh*, which executes a remote shell. The kernel implementation of the network in both Windows and UNIX is structured in three layers: socket, protocol, and network interface.

The socket layer thus provides the interprocess communications facility between network processes. It is configured to the appropriate domain and protocol at creation time, and this allows the underlying kernel structure to be flexible in network interfacing, a primary goal of networking systems. The protocol layer is a table located in kernel memory called the "protocol switch table" (*protosw* table) in UNIX. Each type of protocol is configured into the protosw structures when the system is created. When a socket is created, it scans the *protosw* table for the protocol.

The network interface layer supports the routing of packets from the protocol layer to the device driver, and it also gathers statistics used by the *netstat* command. Once a socket is formed between a client and server, communications commence. As an illustration, once you point your Explorer browser at a URL such as www.bing.com, you (or rather your network system and software) have formed a socket and you (or rather your system) have begun a conversation that you may not even be aware of.

12.3.2 Transport and Sessions

Systems that communicate over a network require an interface to the network protocol stack. Depending on the system and the application, the networking software will make a system-level or privileged system-call to the network operating system and pass its data down through the protocol stack and out the door (so to speak). When the data arrive at their destination, the network software must identify what service is requested.

In Focus

The encapsulation of the data occurs all the way down and is deconstructed all the way up the TCP/IP protocol stack, so that senders encapsulate information down to the frame, where it is sent over a network; once at its host destination, it is deconstructed and the pertinent information is extracted by the software protocol handlers.

Servers enable the information to reach a given application or a specific user of that application on a given host in a particular network. For example, let's say that we wanted to send an email message from our office in Jacksonville, Florida, to our home office in Concord, California. We provide the "To" line and "Subject" and type out a message. When we hit the send button, the message is encapsulated into data payload, and a header is created for this, enabling the application layer at the destination to identify the user to whom we are sending our message.

In Focus

Programs that are executing on the same machine in the same address space can simply make a function call through an application program interface (API) to the other program. Program-to-program communications is called interprocess communications (IPC). If the program interfaces with programs over a network, we need an intermediary—a remote procedure call (RPC).

When data are passed down to the TCP (or UDP) layer, the protocol places both the application layer message and the header contents into the data payload of the TCP (or UDP) data segment. The TCP protocol then creates a header in order to form a sort of "virtual connection" with its peer including source and destination port numbers. Those data are then encapsulated into an IP data payload, and an IP header is then created that contains information about the network and host for which the data are bound. Those data then are encapsulated into a frame, which is given a header before being sent out.

The IP layer is inherently connectionless and unreliable, but a reliable transport service is needed by many applications. TCP compensates for this by forming a full-duplex virtual connection. The connection is initiated by a three-way handshake established with an initial TCP packet in which a SYN (synchronize) bit is set in the header along with a beginning random sequence number. The responding system replies with its own TCP packet, with the SYN bit set, its own beginning random sequence number, and ACK bit set, along with the sender's sequence number plus one.

Once this is received by the originator, the sender replies with a packet in which the SYN bit and ACK bit are set, along with the receiver's sequence number plus one. When the receiver accepts the packet, the handshake is complete and the communication can begin. Each end knows the state of the communications by the increments of the sequence numbers. When communication completes, a close sequence is initiated—similar to the setup handshake, but setting the FIN bits instead.

In Focus

If TCP is used, then a logical connection is formed between two processes at communicating ends—it is a "virtual" connection-oriented protocol. The connection is established with a three-way handshake that synchronizes the exchange with what data to expect. The handshake sends a synchronize packet (syn=1) along with an initial sequence number. The receiving end replies with an acknowledgment of the sender's sequence number +1, along with its own initial sequence number, which is then acknowledged by the originator +1. Then a conversation can begin with each side knowing whether the data are complete by the successive sequence numbers, or whether a retransmission of packets must be requested. This is the TCP three-way handshake, as in the following example:

SYN = 1, initial sequence send = x
SYN = 1, initial sequence receive = y
ACK = initial sequence send x + 1
ACK = initial sequence receive y + 1

In the TCP handshake, if the first message of the handshake sends SYN = 1 and ISN = 1000, then the second handshake message replies with ACK = 1001

For efficiency, TCP transmits data in groups (called a sliding window). Thus the data transmission advances according to a dynamic "window" size. A time-out mechanism allows devices to detect lost packets, and if packets are lost, TCP will ask for retransmission of the batch of packets (*window*) from the last contiguous sequence number packet that was received.

In Focus

If congestion is encountered, TCP will "back off" its data transmission at some multiples less than the previous transmission rate, called a multiplicative decrease. When congestion is relieved, TCP does a slow restart of its transmission rate to minimize future congestion.

UDP, on the other hand, is a connectionless transport layer protocol that provides what is commonly called a *fire-and-forget* type of simple interface. This is because (unlike TCP) UDP does not use acknowledgments to ensure message delivery, nor does it sequence the packets. For these reasons, it is considered an *unreliable* delivery system. However, because UDP has a smaller header than TCP and produces less network chatter, it consumes less bandwidth and so it is considered more "efficient" than TCP.

Because UDP does not require the overhead of the complex handshaking, it is up to the application that uses UDP to handle reliability, including what to do about packet losses or duplications, and out of order packet deliveries, so there may be a performance price to be paid on the receiving end of the processing. Applications that use UDP include the Network File System (NFS), the Simple Network Management Protocol (SNMP), Domain Name Service (DNS), and Trivial File Transfer Protocol (TFTP).

12.3.3 Applications Layer Protocols

When people think of network applications, they most often think of browsers, or more particularly, **HTTP**; however, among the applications layer protocols are the **File Transfer Protocol** (**FTP**), which is an application layer program that enables files to be uploaded from one system to another. FTP uses TCP to create a virtual connection for control information and then creates a separate TCP connection for data transfers. The server for FTP (ftpd), as with most other servers, is a multi-threaded controller. When an FTP connection is made, the main process handles the control while the data transfer connections are handled by separate threads. Generally the FTP protocol provides some security mechanisms such as a login ID and password, but it may permit a dangerous feature called an *anonymous* FTP login, which permits "guest" clients to upload files into a public directory.

The **Simple Mail Transfer Protocol** (**SMTP**) transfers mail messages between systems, and it provides notification regarding incoming mail. SMTP is independent of the particular transmission subsystem, but it does require a reliably ordered data stream channel. Using SMTP, a process can transfer mail to another process on the same network or to some other network via a relay or gateway process accessible to both networks [5]. A gateway is typically a router; however, it might be a host computer that relays network traffic between network segments. In this way, a mail message may pass through a number of intermediate relay or gateway hosts on its route from sender to recipient. The Mail eXchanger mechanisms (called MX records) of the DNS are used to identify the appropriate next-hop destination for a message being transported. SMTP also supports a wide variety of email clients ranging from web-based applications to Microsoft Outlook [6].

In Focus

SMTP was combined with the Multipurpose Internet Mail codE (MIME) for including message types and attachments, although MIME has since been extended into other Internet applications.

The **Post Office Protocol**, or **POP**, can be used for email, but the protocol requires that messages be retrieved from network email servers. The **Internet Message Access Protocol** (**IMAP**) is another option. Both POP and IMAP have evolved through various iterations and versions, but IMAP has become generally preferred over POP for a variety of reasons; in particular, it has both offline and online storage features that go beyond POP. From a security standpoint, let's consider the contents of the sample email header shown in **Table 12.2**.

In Table 12.2, there are many fields that may not make much sense yet, but there are a few that are obvious. Let's mention some of them to illustrate how headers are used. We can see in the table that the header contains a "To" field, which is the destination (in this case, a Yahoo email account), a "Return Path," which was the system that forwarded the message to that account, its "IP address," and several "Received" fields recorded by relays in between the sender and the destination. Much of the information in this header was formed from lower layer protocols; for example, the "To" and "From" IP addresses are kept in the IP header.

A couple of interesting things stand out in the table, such as that petrovs@zumail.ru was the email account that *purportedly* originated the message from Russia, as denoted by the .ru suffix, and that the IP address of the originating host was *purportedly* from 87.174.112.151. Because there was no signature in the "Authentication Results," we know that no authentication that took place in the exchange. This email appears to have come from a scam called ***phishing***, and the email address and even the IP address may have been forged (spoofed). We will explore this kind of header information in more detail later when we cover network security.

Finally, applications layer protocols also include those used in managing networks. Two of the most common network error management protocols in the TCP/IP protocol suite that are used in conjunction with intelligent network switches and routers are the ***Simple Network Management Protocol*** (**SNMP**) and the ***Remote Monitor*** (**RMON**). SNMP is widely used in small- and medium-sized networks, whereas RMON is usually more suitable for larger networks. With these systems, a server monitoring the network sends queries to client machines requesting information, and the results are then stored in a ***management information base*** (**MIB**). Client machines need to have a software component called an *agent* that can correctly respond to the queries. As an example, a threshold for network utilization may be set at 80 percent of the total network capacity (bandwidth), and if the utilization goes above that threshold, either a flag can be set or a network notice can be sent to the system administrators.

Specifically, SNMP is an application layer protocol encapsulated in UDP to allow network managers to store and retrieve information about various network parameters such as throughput and bandwidth stored in MIBs. It relies on three components: **managed devices**, **agents**, and **NMS** (**network-management systems**) (for more details, see Stevens [4], Forouzan [7], Comer [8], and Miller [9]). A managed device is a network node containing an SNMP agent. SNMP devices collect and store management information in MIBs and make the information available to NMSs. Managed devices can be routers, servers, switches, and hosts. On the other hand, some systems are capable of sending out software agents (similar to web search engines) called RMON probes, which collect information and report back to the network management infrastructure. Version 3 of SNMP has new security features over previous versions 1 and 2, including

TABLE 12.2 Email Header Contents

To:	mymail@yahoo.com via 66.196.100.71; Fri, 02 Apr 2010 10:42:27
Return-Path:	<info@javadispatch.org>
Originating-IP:	208.89.132.143
Authentication-Results:	mta1124.mail.mud.yahoo.com from=; domainkeys=neutral (no sig); from=zumail.ru; dkim=neutral (no sig)
Received:	from 127.0.0.1 (EHLO outbound003.roc2.bluetie.com) (208.89.132.143) by mta1124.mail.mud.yahoo.com with SMTP; Fri, 02 Apr 2010 10:42:27 -0700
Received:	from mas002.roc2.bluetie.com ([10.200.3.76]) by outbound003.roc2.bluetie.com with bizsmtp id 0hiS1e0061eQEWa01hiSEt; Fri, 02 Apr 2010 13:42:26 –0400
Received:	by mas002.roc2.bluetie.com (Postfix, from userid 5912881) id B3AF6960CD8; Fri, 2 Apr 2010 13:42:26 -0400 (EDT)
Original-To:	info.rcomehdqvt2812@masc002.roc2.bluetie.com
Delivered-To:	info.rcomehdqvt2812@masc002.roc2.bluetie.com
Received:	from inbound012.roc2.bluetie.com (btroc2-lb.roc2.bluetie.com [10.200.2.8]) by mas002.roc2.bluetie.com (Postfix) with ESMTP id 07980961081 for <info.rcomehdqvt2812@masc002.roc2.bluetie.com>; Fri, 2 Apr 2010 13:42:25 -0400 (EDT)
Received:	from av11-1-sn2.hy.skanova.net ([81.228.8.183]) by inbound012.roc2.bluetie.com with inbound012 id 0hiQ1e00Q3wwjh501hiQgx; Fri, 02 Apr 2010 13:42:24 -0400
Received:	by av11-1-sn2.hy.skanova.net (Postfix, from userid 502) id 6A62B3880A; Fri, 2 Apr 2010 19:42:23 +0200 (CEST)
Received:	from smtp4-1-sn2.hy.skanova.net (smtp4-1-sn2.hy.skanova.net [81.228.8.92]) by av11-1-sn2.hy.skanova.net (Postfix) with ESMTP id 3638B38804; Fri, 2 Apr 2010 19:42:23 +0200 (CEST)
Received:	from dyn-ks-net85-cust13.netit.se (h183n3fls307o1043.telia.com [81.228.58.183]) by smtp4-1-sn2.hy.skanova.net (Postfix) with SMTP id 8AAEF37E47; Fri, 2 Apr 2010 19:42:07 +0200 (CEST)
Message-ID:	<AC4FA9D479F24C92B73A62A6E6A@LOCALHOST>
Date:	Fri, 02 Apr 2010 21:42:02 +030
From:	"Petrov" <petrovs@zumail.ru>
To:	cust.service@hol.gr
Subject:	Co-operation
User-Agent:	Internet Messaging Program (IMP) 2.8.4
Originating-IP:	87.174.112.151
Content-Length:	473

user-based security model (**USM**) for message security, access control module, and remote configuration capabilities [4, 9].

12.4 Routing Data

We have learned that the *Internet Protocol* (IP), which operates at the network layer, contains addressing and control information to enable packets to be routed through a network, and is employed in both LAN and WAN communications. When data are sent or received—for example as an email message or an HTML web page—the messages are divided into packets (datagrams). Each of these packets contains both the sender's Internet address and the receiver's address. Because a message may be divided into a number of packets, each packet can be sent through a different route across the Internet. It is the job of routers to perform this work.

Recall that a message may be segmented into packets, which may be sent through different routes to their destination, but note that packets themselves can be further fragmented into chunks as they traverse the network because network paths may have different *maximum-transmission units* (**MTU**). When they arrive at their destination, the packet must be put back together by a reassembly routine at the destination host. Inside the header of the IP packet are flags that indicate if the packet has been fragmented, along with fragment offsets. Offsets are numbers that the reassembly routine uses to reconstruct the data back into a contiguous packet.

> **In Focus**
>
> Packets are fragmented according to the size restrictions of a network segment (MTU). Fragments have offsets and flags in the header so that when the message reassembly routine on the host runs, it pastes the data together according to size beginning at offset (offset is a location in bytes or octets). All the fragments except the last one have a fragment flag set to 1. Once reassembly has all the data contiguously assembled and the last chunk has a fragment flag set to 0, the reassembly routine knows it is done. If it doesn't have all the data—that is, if all the data fragments are not contiguous—and it receives a fragment with a fragments bit set to 0 (and a timer times out), it sends a request message to the source to retransmit the data.

12.4.1 Routes and Route Tables

As the Internet is currently designed, there are multiple routes that connect points in the vast network. Hence the network layer deals with sending data from one location to another location on the Internet, choosing from multiple delivery routes. However, the bulk of the network layer function has to do with moving data more reliably and hiding the complexities and technical differences of the underlying fabric. This feature is important because data networks are continuing to evolve to support new needs. Voice over IP (VoIP) is a good example that shows this trend.

In Focus

When a network senses many collisions, it decreases the transmission of network packets in what is called multiplicative decrease or back-off, and then it waits for a variable period of time before slowly increasing the transmissions, called a slow restart. A slow restart helps to ensure that a burst of network data does not yet again overwhelm the next node in the data transmission.

Routes are determined by route tables that are maintained by routers. When a router is added to a network, it sends a notification to its router neighbors that it has been activated along with its address. Routers that use dynamic routing will add this router's address to their route tables. Note that some routers are configured to use static routing, which requires an administrator to manually enter IP addresses. Although this is more labor intensive, it is often done for security reasons.

Routing therefore provides a way to move data from one host to another host regardless of their physical locations. A network host only has to know the address of routers to which it is attached if the packets need to be sent outside the local area network. Unlike switching, where network data are simply filtered and forwarded, routing uses more intelligence in the sense that it also determines the best path among available choices. Whereas layer-two connectivity provides the necessary deterministic network data transfer, layer-three routing provides more dynamic data transfer. The IP protocol plays a crucial role in routing, as we have seen.

Each time a packet is received by a router, called a ***hop***, the router must extract the IP header and its payload from the frame and examine the header information. From this, the protocol algorithm determines whether the packet is destined for its local network or if the data should be forwarded. If the information is to be forwarded, then the frame must be rebuilt (using ARP) to map the next logical-to-physical connection for transferring the packet. Thus we can say that routers provide *next hop* information for packets by directing them to the next router. The process continues until the packets reach their destination. To illustrate how this works, let's suppose we used a program called ***traceroute*** (which uses ICMP) to determine how data are passed from our system to our bank. The *traceroute* command is executed from a UNIX shell or DOS command prompt, as in the following example:

```
#> traceroute 171.159.193.173
TraceRoute to 171.159.193.173 [www.bankofamerica.com]
```

Hop	(ms)	IP Address	Host Name
1	0	66.98.244.1	gphou-66-98-244-1.ev1.net
2	0	66.98.241.4	gphou-66-98-241-4.ev1.net
3	1	129.250.10.105	ge-10-50.r0.hstntx01.us.bb.verio.net
4	10	129.250.5.42	p16-1-1.r21.dllstx09.us.bb.verio.net
5	10	129.250.2.195	p16-7-0.r01.dllstx09.us.bb.verio.net
6	11	208.172.129.245	bcr2-so-30.dallas.savvis.net
7	44	206.24.226.99	dc1-loopback.washington.savvis.net
8	56	206.24.227.14	acr2-so-1-0-0.washington.savvis.net
9	58	206.24.225.202	—
10	62	64.241.143.46	s234-1.uswash-j20c.savvis.net
11	49	64.242.6.2	—
12	49	171.159.192.11	—
13	51	171.159.193.173	www.bankofamerica.com

The traceroute program uses ICMP to record hops that packets traverse, and reports that information back to the host. (*Note that not all routers report their routes, so not all hops may be recorded.*) Suppose then that we issue a command called *ping* to see if a destination is reachable—for example: ping www.bankofamerica.com. We may see a response similar to *Reply from 171.159.193.173: bytes=32 time-53ms TTL=224,* along with some statistics that include the number of packets "*Lost.*" Packets may be lost or discarded as they travel through the network, and if they are, they must be retransmitted.

Routers know where to send packets because of their route tables, and as indicated, these contain the addresses for local hosts and for the other routers to which they are connected. As noted, entries in the route tables can be created dynamically or statically. In a dynamic setting, when new routers are connected to the network, the route tables are refreshed with the IP addresses by the network routing protocols. With static routing tables, these must be manually entered. Although dynamic routing is more convenient, in terms of security, routers that serve as gateways may use static routing to prevent a type of attack that attempts to reroute packets [6].

In Focus

As packets traverse from router to router, at the network layer, the routing software (e.g., RIP or OSPF) examines the IP header and compares the destination address with its own address. If it is not a match, it sends it according to its route table. Hosts have a minimal route table that can be examined using the command ifconfig (Unix) or ipconfig (Windows), or with the netstat command. Note that unlike routers, route tables on hosts may be changed by ICMP messages, rather than a routing protocol—this can be a security threat.

12.4.2 Routing Protocols

When discussing protocols, it is important to realize that there are stack protocols and routing protocols (and other types of protocols as well). Stack protocols share network data on a given machine such as in the TCP/IP network stack, whereas routing protocols share information between network devices in a network such as with an exterior gateway protocol.

Routing protocols for the communications on interior networks are called ***Interior Gateway Protocols***, or **IGP**, and these are most often either ***Routing Information Protocol*** (**RIP**) or ***Open Shortest Path First*** (**OSPF**). Because routing must occur between autonomous networks, this is done with a ***Gateway-to-Gateway*** (**GGP**) protocol to connect core networks inside an organization with those that are exterior. Routing protocols to exterior networks are done through ***Exterior Gateway Protocols***, or **EGP**, which like IGP are many and varied. These routing protocols act independently but also must work in cooperative ways, depending on whether they are communicating between routers, between routers and hosts, or host to host, and the degrees of "trust" that may exist between network segments or zones [4].

There are (at least) two ways to implement dynamic routing: ***distance vector routing*** protocol and ***link state routing*** protocol. The most common distance vector routing protocol is the Routing Information Protocol (RIP) mentioned earlier. In RIP, distance is defined by hop counts. The maximum hop count is usually set at 15, and if traffic has to travel more than 15 hops, it is declared unreachable, an error message is generated, and the packet is dropped. One of the drawbacks of distance vector method is that it does not take into consideration important factors that affect network traffic such as the type of link, bandwidth, or reliability. Another drawback of vector distance routing is that it suffers from ***slow convergence***.

Convergence is the point at which all the routers share common routing table information. Distance vector routing relays the entire routing table contents, This can put a significant burden on the network and is a major source of the slow convergence problem. Because of these issues, RIP is usually used for small-scale internetworking. Revisions to RIP are ongoing and some of the drawbacks may disappear in future updates.

Link-state routing protocols allow routers to use information such as status of links and bandwidth to determine the best traffic routes. Hop count is not a factor in deciding network "reachability" in this approach. Because this protocol sends only routing changes and updates to other routers in the same zone, it has much better convergence compared to distance vector routing. Two of the most well-known link state routing protocols are the legacy **NetWare Link Services Protocol** (**NLSP**), which is all but extinct, and the Open Shortest Path First (OSPF) protocol. OSPF has gone through several revisions and is now among the most common link state protocols because it has made it possible to implement policy-based routing both in LAN and WAN environments [4, 8].

Note that we have been describing routing in a rather self-contained environment called an ***autonomous system*** (**AS**). Autonomous systems are networks with routers sharing the same routing policies and protocols governing traffic. This AS uses an Interior Gateway Protocol, or IGP, for routing packets within its network; however, when data are destined outside the AS, there needs to be a translation from one protocol into another—for example, from a LAN protocol into a wireless or WAN protocol. This process is called a **protocol conversion**.

The routing protocols that connect LANs with ISPs or other gateway connections can be quite complex, depending on the IGP used. Thus in addition to sharing routing information between gateways, protocols may also have to perform translations between AS gateways and an Exterior Gateway Protocol, or EGP. An example is the **Border Gateway Protocol (BGP)**. BGP is a protocol within the class of EGP protocols. There are actually many kinds of BGP protocols, each having a different role or function, and each chosen based on requirements of the network such as the levels of interconnectivity and trust needed [8].

CHAPTER SUMMARY

As human activities are increasingly conducted over computer networks, legitimate communications (and the systems that accommodate them) are exposed more often to hostile actions by adversaries that have a variety of motives for their attacks, but still even more common are threats from technological software or hardware failures. Unfortunately, in many cases, the users involved in conducting electronic transactions in these environments only vaguely understand the risks and dangers to which they are being exposed, and some of the users are poorly equipped to deal with these hostile actions. Nevertheless, even an intended use of the network can create problems. When intentional and unintentional problems occur, they must be reported to a system that can either provide alerts to a **human-in-the-loop** or handle the problem on its own.

In this chapter, we gave a high-level overview of networking. We covered the Internet as a vast collection of routers that exchange data packets. In this exchange, there are several levels of organizations or companies that provide routing and other behind-the-scenes operations. Most of us are familiar with our local Internet Service Providers (ISPs). We realize that ISPs provide the links between end users and regional providers, and that regional providers are linked to national providers who have multiple concentrated locations to coordinate data transfers. As data traverse through these organizational systems, routers perform two functions when they receive data packets from local hosts or other routers. First they look up their own routing table to determine the next stop or hop. This has to be done very quickly, in milliseconds. When the next destination is determined, routers modify the data packets so that the next computer or router in the queue can receive them. New frames have to be built with the next hop MAC address and new information is added into the headers.

We now conclude this section by reiterating that within a given IP address class (A, B, and C), we can use subnets to extend the available number of network addresses thereby creating *logical networks*. This is done by using subnet masks and using logical

CHAPTER SUMMARY (CONTINUED)

AND with binary codes. Each subnet represents its own default gateway (or router) to other networks, and this creates a logical separation between the subnets. In this way, different departments or offices may have a layer of security protecting their information from each other. Network address translations (NAT) also help in this regard. As we will discuss later, information systems managers are most concerned with access to their internal networks and those through which employees interact, because these are the assets that belong to the organization and must be properly managed. We will elaborate on these ideas when we get to the chapter on network security.

THINK ABOUT IT

Topic Questions

12.1: What happens when a packet goes from a larger MTU to a smaller one?

12.2: The traceroute command uses what protocol to record the routes?

12.3: TCP creates a session by first creating a

_____ _____ _____.

12.4: The packaging of one protocol layer (body and header) inside the body of another is called _____.

12.5: The protocol that is used when a frame is reconstructed to contain the MAC address of the next hop is:

____ SMTP
____ UDP
____ DHCP
____ ARP

12.6: TCP and UDP both use a set of data structures and system calls known collectively as a socket.

____ True
____ False

12.7: ICMP is encapsulated in what layer:

____ UDP
____ TCP
____ IP
____ Frame

12.8: Packets must be fragmented when they enter a router where the next hop route has a smaller:

____ MTU
____ Route table
____ Network wire
____ DNS

12.9: The _____ field informs routers when the packet should be discarded.

____ Counter
____ Time-to-live (TTL)
____ TOS
____ Version

Questions for Further Study

Q12.1: What are the relationships between ports and services?

Q12.2: Why is a back-off and slow restart strategy important to TCP/IP?

Q12.3: Investigate and describe in detail what is contained in the IP and TCP headers, and how these elements are used by the protocols.

Q12.4: Discuss the major differences between (A) circuit switching and packet switching, and (B) connection-oriented and connectionless communications.

Q12.5: Pick three BGP and/or EGP protocols and briefly describe how they work.

KEY CONCEPTS AND TERMS

ARP enables a host to find physical addresses of another system on the same network using only the IP address.

Carrier Sense Multiple Access with Collision

Detection coordinates LAN communications.

Domain Name Service (DNS) must find an IP address for a given name.

MAC addresses have to be resolved for each IP address.

Interior Gateway Protocols are frequently either RIP or OSPF.

References

1. Goldman, J. D. (1995). *Applied data communication.* New York, NY: John Wiley & Sons.
2. Ramteke, T. (1994). *Networks.* Upper Saddle River, NJ: Prentice Hall.
3. Habracken, J. (1999). *Cisco routers.* Indianapolis, IN: Que Books.
4. Stevens, W. R. (1994). *TCP/IP illustrated: The protocols.* Boston, MA: Addison-Wesley.
5. Rhoton, J. (1997). *X.400 and SMTP: Battle of the e-mail protocols.* Boston, MA: Digital Press.
6. Hunt, C. (1992). *TCP/IP network administration.* Sebastopol, CA: O'Reilly & Associates.
7. Forouzan, B. A. (2010). *TCP/IP protocol suite.* New York, NY: McGraw-Hill.
8. Comer, D. E. (1995). *Internetworking with TCP/IP.* Upper Saddle River, NJ: Prentice Hall.
9. Miller, M. A. (1993). *Managing internetworks with SNMP.* New York, NY: M&T Books.

Computer and Network Security

Information Systems Security

WHEN PEOPLE THINK ABOUT INFORMATION SYSTEMS, most often computers come to mind. However, an information system (IS) extends to all organizational information infrastructure, including networks, databases, hardcopies of documents, computer server rooms, and even physical storage vaults. The primary purpose of an information system is to facilitate the business and its mission; therefore, it is critical to take actions to help protect against threats to IS. In this chapter, we will broadly survey threat categories and provide a few examples. We will take note that employees are on the front lines and need to be trained, made aware, and made vigilant. Technological measures also need to be put into place, and of course, good security defensive postures involve having administrative procedures in place for managing risks.

Chapter 13 Topics

This chapter:

- Explores social media and security.
- Lists attack classifications.
- Describes security measures and unintended consequences.
- Explains security services and technologies.
- Discusses security countermeasures and security management.

Chapter 13 Goals

When you finish this chapter, you should:

- ❑ Understand how interconnectivity gives opportunity for exploitation.

❏ Be able to identify a variety of threats to information and systems as a preview for further exploration in the other chapters in this section.

❏ Know some of the ways that vulnerabilities are exploited.

❏ Have a basic understanding of means by which systems are secured.

❏ Be familiar with the term Infosec, and what it entails, and prepare to understand the countermeasures presented in subsequent chapters in this section.

13.1 Social Interactions and Security Implications

As a result of the Internet and the web phenomena, a wellspring of new terminology has made its way into the common vernacular, such as "blogging," "Tweeting," and "mudding." Many of us have participated online in discussion boards or chat rooms or on social networking sites such as Facebook and YouTube and other virtual communities. Most of us have received some form of viral marketing, and at one time or another, many of us have fallen victim to an email phishing scam, or a Trojan, or had spyware and tracking cookies installed on our computer.

Contemporary societies are being shaped around technologically mediated ways of interacting, and there is a growing number of online transactions in which virtual communities are substituted for in-person (called proximal) exchanges. Some examples include online or distance education, online shopping, online banking, telemedicine, and virtual entertainment. All of these "online" activities create interactions with unknown intermediaries and end-points.

There are many cases where access to virtual communities is useful for business purposes, such as when searching the Microsoft or Oracle websites for answers to technical questions. However, in other cases, virtual communities pose threats—not just in terms of wasting company time, as is often touted—because many virtual communities are sources of Trojans, worms, and the dissemination of misinformation to damage a company or individuals.

13.1.1 Mobility and Threats

Wireless fidelity (wi-fi) involves the means of connecting computers, tablets, and smart phones using infrared or frequency signals, which enable people to "remain connected" to telecommunications and servers when they are on the move. Meanwhile, mobile technologies are becoming more sophisticated, going beyond email, text, and voice communications to include web surfing, running various software applications, and of course taking photographs and movies, as well as downloading and viewing them.

New technologies are constantly burgeoning and their use is outpacing ways to protect users. For example, Bluetooth has expanded from its wireless earpiece to a mobile phone to providing other interesting applications such as its virtual keyboard, which uses a laser to illuminate a surface that mimics a keyboard display. This virtual keyboard can sense where users place their fingers to capture their typing as if on a physical device. Bluetooth is also integral in unconventional technologies; for example, it is increasingly used in automobiles.

One can imagine any number of misuses and potential exploits for these new technologies including capturing wireless communications, filming people's behaviors, or collecting their electronic typing, which may include logging into a system with their user name and password. Most people know the significance of protecting information and assets, and know how to protect their privacy with various technology solutions, although some aspects of security are out of their control.

Basic security technologies such as firewalls, cryptography and authentication software, and virus and spyware scanners are important in the defense arsenal; however, although many security controls exist to help maintain information security, people may not utilize them. For example, although there are certainly measures people can take such as limiting their social media privacy settings or using cryptography, often these features are inconvenient—and are ignored or overlooked.

Also, there remain some "street" threats that are difficult to protect against, such as video or wireless captures of people's typing or online activity. Beyond the "street" threats, corporations may also be gathering information and sharing it with others. Consider, for example, the fairly recent revelation that intelligent phones combined with GPS capabilities and online maps and satellite photographs have enabled people to pinpoint our locations at a given time, which has given rise to a new kind of "peeping Tom" along with even more concerning behaviors such as the combination of cyber stalking with physical stalking.

Mobile devices and social media can become sources of information gathering by social identity thieves. Identity thieves may gain access to personal information not only from what we may post on sites such as Facebook or Twitter, but they may also use genealogy or family history databases. These databases often contain information useful to identity thieves, such as mother's maiden name, names and addresses of relatives, and vocations. An entire package of personal information can be sold anonymously in chat rooms.

13.1.2 Distributed Work and Threats

Many companies employ "teleworkers" and "virtual teams" that span the globe. In many if not most cases, virtual workers are provided with company-owned computer equipment and software, and have in their possession documents and data and other information that may be proprietary or company confidential. As a result, there are important considerations for virtual work that include how to control access to networked resources both resident on virtual workers' machines and those they may access at corporate locations. In addition, many companies are outsourcing parts of their businesses. Information ranging from medical to tax records may flow into foreign countries that may be governed under different laws and practices. The flow of information, as well as the interconnectedness of the sources and storage locations of information, creates many new opportunities for security breaches.

In Focus

In 2008, an FBI computer crime and security survey reported that more than 38 percent of study participants stated that security incidents began from the inside. These malicious insiders misused their access to information for exploitation.

Information is easily disseminated and retrieved over the Internet and the Web, traversing many computers over great distances. Securing information needs to take into account the many machines that intervene between our source and destination systems—for example, between our PC, laptop, tablet, or smart phone and our bank when doing online banking transactions. Even with encrypted passwords using secure sockets and encryption (https/SSL), in some cases information sent over the Internet and using the Web may be intercepted and deciphered using technologies such as Wireshark, ANORT, Achilles, or Cain and Abel.

13.1.3 Interconnectivity and Threats

As illustrated in the last section, if we use the IP address for our bank and type the command *traceroute* from a UNIX/Linux command prompt (or *tracert* in Microsoft Windows), we get some idea of the intervening recipients of information. If we *ping* our bank's system, we may get a reply with the IP address, and number of bytes, time in milliseconds, along with some statistics that include the number of packets "lost." The speed with which those packets travel over the continent is mind-boggling. It may only be a few milliseconds for information to traverse all those systems from ours to its destination through many *hops*. Were the "lost" packets discarded, or were any intercepted?

Web applications—partly owing to their proliferation—are especially tempting targets for attacks, and there are multiple points in a Web application or transaction that can be compromised. The client side of the application is vulnerable to scripting attacks, and particularly if client-side validation is used. The web server may also have vulnerabilities that can be exploited. Different web servers have different vulnerabilities, the transport itself can be vulnerable to attack from eavesdropping (man-in-the-middle) or secure socket layer (SSL) redirection, and the database may be attacked via a web application using SQL injections and query manipulation (and later we will see how).

Many if not most of the network threats we read about discuss access from the Internet. However, a significant threat may exist on the interior LAN. TCP/IP is a broad-casting system, and the technique distributes information to all hosts on the network. Those hosts to which the information is unintended are trusted to be "well-behaved" and to discard unintended information they receive. Consequently, on LANs (just as with WANs), there are many unintended recipients of information. Likewise, technologies such as cable modems allow systems to connect to the Internet via the digital cable, but the cable modem bus is shared across a wide area such as a neighborhood. Because of the shared bus nature of these systems, they too are susceptible to interception from man-in-the-middle attacks or packet sniffing. Also, promiscuous network agents may take advantage of unprotected services such as Windows *shares* [1].

In Focus

Threat potential is exacerbated by security vulnerabilities. Some have defined "threat intensity" as the likelihood that a threat may lead to loss or harm. For instance, a vulnerability for which a known exploit program has been released into the hacker community poses greater threat intensity to a network than another vulnerability for which no such automated attack method is known. Threats also carry with them the degree or severity of harm done that may result from a successful attack.

13.1.4 Security Countermeasures and Complications

Security breaches may result from actions taken contrary to the policies that define legitimate use of assets. The use of cryptography is a primary countermeasure to prevent network security breaches, and is also used in computer security for such things as authentication and protecting data in file systems. Cryptography is the use of secret codes (keys) and obfuscation algorithms (ciphers) to scramble information to help prevent unauthorized information access.

In Focus

From a managerial perspective, network assets derive from the information stored on systems and in transit between systems, but there is also the asset potential of their capabilities such as communications and computation. A network asset may even be its reputation for good service. Liabilities may include downstream attacks (stemming from using a victim's systems and infrastructure to commit attacks on systems external to the organization), and file sharing that violates the DMCA/RIAA policies for hacker attacks. A network security manager imposes restrictions in how assets are to be used according to security policies.

The growing use of cryptographic technology is also essential to protect consumers and businesses against espionage, theft, and fraud committed in electronic commerce. Although cryptography in its various implementations is a primary mechanism to maintain network security, it can pose its own set of problems. Because cryptography obfuscates information, damaging or illicit materials can be encrypted as well, such as child pornography, customs violations, weapons or drug dealings, espionage, embezzlement, obstruction of justice, tax evasion, and terrorism [2].

As a result of this, many governments have placed restrictions on cryptographic strength and on export of certain cryptographic algorithms. Also, the distributed nature of computing can present a variety of problems in terms of cryptographic key management. As we will cover later in the chapter on cryptography, whether using a public or a private key cryptography, the private key for each communicative partner we may share encrypted information with must be kept safe and secure.

Clearly then, we are experiencing exponential increases in complexity with each distributed system. Along with increases in complexity, the number of points of vulnerabilities is growing along with the number of places where systems and applications must be secured. In addition, with distributed networked information systems, not only do they increase security complexity, but they also make it difficult if even possible to find many security vulnerabilities. This is important because a network or system can only be made relatively secure if it has adequate countermeasures for the prevention, detection, and ability to recover from attacks. *Adequate* in this "managerial" context means commensurate with the value of the network's assets and liabilities compared to the perceived threat intensity. Systems must be vigilantly monitored by their custodians—but the more complex these systems are, the more difficult that task.

13.2 Broad Attack Classifications and Examples

Broadly, attacks can be classified into active and passive attacks, although many attacks use both. A typical scenario used by an attacker is to first perform a reconnaissance (or footprint) a potential target. In this stage, the attacker seeks to gain knowledge of the information systems fabric. Next, the attacker may scan the exposed or gateway systems and routers to determine if there are vulnerabilities that can be exploited. The next step might involve enumeration, which is the extraction of information that is exported, such as host information records, or repositories for services and their service descriptions including connection (binding) information. An attacker will then usually try to gain access or pass a malicious program through to a target by exploiting vulnerabilities. If the attacker succeeds, he or she may try to escalate his or her privileges (often using what is called a ***root kit***) to gain administrative control of a system. Once this is done, the attacker may be able to leave open backdoors for future exploits. If the attack was successful, the attacker will attempt to cover his or her tracks to avoid discovery and open the door to future exploits [3, 4].

13.2.1 Information System Attack Examples

Common technologies used for attacks against the confidentiality of information include ***keyloggers***, ***spyware***, and ***eavesdropping*** (sometimes called a ***man-in-the-middle attack***). There are many types of spyware that you may be aware of, but just to mention a common one, a "tracking cookie" is deposited when a user browses the Web. With keyloggers, a malicious hacker may have created a Trojan program that is downloaded (with stealth) onto a computer that logs the keystrokes a user types, and then opens a network connection and transmits this information to the attacker.

In Focus

Attacks that are designed to intercept information without notice are passive attacks. An attack that is designed to damage or disrupt a system or service is an active attack. Passive attacks are often more difficult to detect than active attacks, and sometimes can be more damaging.

Eavesdropping can also take on many forms, but it is typically accomplished by illicitly intercepting traffic on a wireless or wired local area network (LAN) or from a computer system using a monitoring tool that is supposed to be used for intrusion detection and other constructive purposes (e.g., SNORT and Wireshark). It is also possible for eavesdropping to occur over the Web, and it can be used to steal login data to a website or email account using a technology that is typically used for testing systems such as Achilles.

With these kinds of technologies, it is possible to intercept Web client and server communications and modify script code and parameters. This is particularly dangerous if the website uses client-side validation of input. Using HTTP Interceptor, it may even be possible to intercept and modify "secure" https requests and responses. Using a root kit (which contains various technologies depending on the target computer's operating system), a malicious hacker may try to gain access to a system and then escalate the malicious hacker's privileges to a "system administrator" level. By doing this, the attacker may intercept information in transit from one location to another, steal stored information, or destroy or alter information and software.

Attacks against the integrity of information include worms and viruses that destroy files. Also often mentioned about this class of attack are programs that cause "memory buffer overflows," although this is generally reliant on programming languages that use *address pointers* such as "C" or C++, which enable a malicious program to manipulate data in the address space belonging to a different process. The most likely scenarios of information integrity attacks come from executable files passed through web sessions, such as malicious executable code encapsulated in *Microsoft's ActiveX* controls, or malicious scripting (such as written in JavaScript), or from an *SQL injection*, where an attacker is able to intercept the code that stores information in a database, for example, by manipulating parameters passed over a URL during a web session.

Attacks aimed at disrupting the availability of systems or services include *denial of service* (**DoS**) attacks, where an attacker may send large groups of data to a service, or by sending data to a service faster than the service process. To do this, the attacker may generate large volumes of stateless packets using the UDP protocol to consume network bandwidth and interfere with services, or the attacker may try to flood a network with network packets using the ICMP protocol, or generate larger packets than a network router can handle (an example is called the ping of death), or create a problem on a host server called a *half-open connection* by manipulating the TCP three-way handshake such that it cannot close the connections. Although most routers are configured to simply drop these packets and modern servers close half-open connections after a very short interval, sometimes so many of them may occur in succession that on occasion these kinds of attacks succeed.

Another type of DoS attack can come from the *anonymous* use of the File Transfer Protocol (FTP); that is, if anonymous FTPs are allowed on a server, a malicious hacker may upload a program that consumes the computer's disk space. Another approach is the **lockout**. Because many systems utilize a login rule that locks a user out after a certain number of invalid login attempts, an attacker can exploit this security feature by continuously generating bad logins until the victim is "locked out" of his or her account.

Other incidents that have been reported include those by malicious insiders who have conducted corporate espionage, or destroyed equipment, or physically attacked people. There have been incidents involving extortion, where the attacker has threatened to distribute or post in blogs or websites, such as a *Wiki*, damaging or even false information about a company unless some action was done or money paid. In one example, an employee of a major computer hardware and software provider wrote a program to break into management's confidential personnel performance and salary files, and then disclosed the information in an anonymous public discussion forum because he felt *under-rewarded*. Another common threat comes from insiders stealing information or assets such as software they have access to (called **software piracy**, or **softlifting**), breaking product license agreements at the office, or removing products from the office for personal use.

> **In Focus**
>
> An individual incorporated a "consulting" company and created a website and blog. He cross-listed and referenced his website in other frequently visited sites so that it was promoted in search engines such as Google. He then used that forum to post attacks on both companies and people he disliked, blocking and deleting comments and rebuttals from his victims.

13.2.2 Social Engineering Attack Examples

Social engineering has been thought of as a fairly recent phenomenon, but the concepts have been known and used to manipulate people for centuries. One famous study cited in Tom Molloy's *Dress for Success* showed that when a researcher dressed in dirty and raggedy clothing, he was unable to give away free copies of the *Wall Street Journal*, but when he was dressed in an expensive suit, he easily gave them away. The key point is that people who appeared professional were perceived as above reproach. This is often a component of social engineering.

Two of the most frequently encountered forms of social engineering are **phishing** and **pretext**, although increasingly there are attackers who post misinformation in blogs or social media, or distribute misinformation in electronic newsletters to try to damage their targets. Phishing emails often have embedded brands or logos from financial institutions and request banking account information to avoid losing online banking privileges. Phishing emails are often broadcast with an urgent subject line to get the potential victim's attention.

Samples of collected phishing emails have included subject lines: "Alert from Chase Card Services," "Your eBay account will be Suspended!" "Please Update Your Bank of America Profile: Personal Information Error," "Urgent! Invalid information added to your PayPal account," and "Your account has been compromised, reset your login information." There are many other more exotic forms of phishing as well. The best way to combat these kinds of social engineering attacks is to use spam filters, and instruct employees on how to look at the URL without clicking on it, and how to examine the full headers of email addresses. Importantly, employees should be instructed not to respond or click on the links, but rather to report these to the company systems administrator or the service provider.

Pretexts are usually conducted over the telephone or in person rather than in written form such as email because they require the development of the potential victim's trust. A pretext is used most often to gain confidential information that might require some kind of authorization. For example, an employee might receive a phone call from someone pretending to be a customer, asking for copies of his or her records or transactions. The best way to combat these types of social engineering attacks is to make sure the workforce is aware of them, and provide the proper procedures—for example, a series of authentication questions or a script to follow to respond to unverified phone inquiries.

Taking their cues from counter-cyber intelligence operations of disinformation used in military contexts, attackers are now posting false or misinformation in blogs or social media, or distributing so-called *newsletters* electronically to damage their targets. Because people often associate prevalence with truth [5], this kind of attack can be subtle but very damaging. Attackers may link their posts across many high-volume websites to promote the false materials in queries by search engines. This new form of attack needs innovative managerial responses to combat them [6].

In Focus

Disgruntled employees with an axe to grind may leak sensitive company information in blogs or sites such as WikiLeaks.com to get retribution against their employers.

13.2.3 Mobile Device Attack Examples

As mobile devices become more powerful and sophisticated, they are increasingly targets of attacks. Tablet computers, Blackberry, Bluetooth, and Android are all rising on the radar of attackers because they are becoming ubiquitous, and ubiquity plus connectivity provides opportunity. These new devices have large data storage capabilities for text messages, multimedia, and other data along with having diverse wireless LAN connectivity, GPS capabilities, and PC connectivity to transfer files.

Many of these devices lack the firewalls, intrusion detection systems, and virus protections that are common on most PCs. This can make them very vulnerable to attacks. For example, smart phones such as the iPhone may promiscuously connect to an unsecured LAN, which may then be used by attackers to capture packets and send them to an attacker command and control center. Attackers may be able to intercept log file data, personal contact information, and text messages that can be used for blackmail or gathering company confidential information. Also people are conducting more sophisticated financial transactions from their smart phones such as checking bank account balances, transferring funds, and paying bills, they are susceptible to man-in-the-middle attacks, allowing attackers to divert funds or obtain cryptographic keys and credentials.

> **In Focus**
>
> *ABC News* reported on April 23, 2011, that Apple was collecting information (called GEOTAGS) from iPhone and iPad GPS-enabled user devices in which the report stated: "If you've got an iPhone in your pocket, Apple could be recording your every step. Apple iPhone and iPad 3G record the device's geographic position and corresponding time stamp in a hidden file, starting when the company released its latest iOS4 mobile operating system" (see http://abcnews .go.com/Technology/apple-tracks-location-iphone-ipad-data-researchers/story?id=13420041).

Not only are mobile devices themselves targets, but with the increased convenience features, range of applications, increased capabilities and connectivity, they are becoming risk factors for back-end systems or hosting facilities. (Note for example the fairly recent high-profile attacks against Blackberry servers.) When an infected mobile device communicates with corporate hosts, malware and spyware may be spread through uploads into corporate facilities. To help mitigate, managers should perform risk analyses for mobile devices and determine what information should be allowed on them, and enforce governance policies accordingly. For example, policies might dictate what features are permitted on smart phones, or perhaps mandate that users disable multimedia capabilities, and then managers may periodically audit their group members' devices for compliance [7].

13.3 Infosec

Information systems are vulnerable to threats to varying degrees. There are threats to computer hardware, software, operating systems, databases, files, networks, and facilities—all of the systems and infrastructure that support information needed by businesses. The term "Infosec" refers to the policies, procedures, and technological countermeasures used in managing risk, which seeks to protect these resources against threats by mitigating vulnerabilities to the greatest possible extent. There are four important aspects of Infosec: (1) authentication and authorization of users, (2) prevention and resistance against attacks or other threats, (3) detection of attacks or other threats and responding to them, and (4) recovery and resilience in the face of damages. These are planned and executed according to threat risk severities and probabilities weighed against countermeasure costs and benefits. Because threats change constantly, we will begin by pointing out patterns that will help us classify them; thus in this section, we will introduce Infosec in relation to broad classifications of vulnerabilities and threats.

13.3.1 Threat Awareness and Risk Management

As we have previously discussed, threats may result from human error or oversight, deliberate acts, natural disasters, or technology failures. Managers assess and plan for threat risks, but not all threat risks can be foreseen. The ongoing process of uncovering and addressing vulnerabilities and threats to the confidentiality, availability, and integrity of information is part of risk management. Recall that *confidentiality* is the assurance against unauthorized disclosure or unintended release of information or message contents. Threats to confidentiality may come from hackers who bypass a system's access controls, perhaps taking advantage of vulnerabilities in a given operating system, or exploiting file sharing and other convenience features, or hacking in through "back-doors" left by programmers or created with Trojan horse programs [8].

Also, networks allow the flow of data among systems and network nodes; thus data pass through the fabric of a network and among both intended and unintended recipients. For example, the Address Resolution Protocol (ARP) broadcasts requests to all nodes in a network zone to obtain network hardware addresses associated with given Internet Protocol (IP) addresses. The unintended recipient systems are supposed to discard these requests, but because this information can be observed and intercepted, confidentiality can be compromised with the use of *sniffer* (network monitoring) applications, or used in what is known as an ARP poisoning attack. Threats to confidentiality might include the probability that someone may be able to intercept information passed in the clear (called cleartext or plaintext) over a network [9].

Maintaining resource *availability* is the notion that systems must be accessible by authorized users according to their ***service level agreements*** (**SLA**) or expected performance levels [2]. Threats to the availability of information and resources can come from programs that send volumes of large messages in what are called a denial of service (DoS) or distributed denial of service (DDoS) attacks. These types of attacks strive to overwhelm a target with more data than can be logically evaluated or filtered. They can zero in on an intermediate node such as a router or a gateway computer system, or they can be concentrated against an end node system, such as with attempts to try to disrupt a specific web service on a given computer server. Aside from these intentional attacks, the loss of information processing capabilities might result from natural disasters such as fires, floods, hurricanes, lightning strikes, or earthquakes.

Integrity threat risks involve the probability of an unauthorized person gaining access to information in such a way as to alter it. Integrity compromises are particularly severe when they involve controls designed to prevent fraud, abuse, or mission critical operational errors. Threats to the integrity of information include unauthorized changes to unprotected or circumvented protections of data, programs, files, or databases, or from poorly implemented or incomplete controls that are exploited by hackers, Trojans, worms, or viruses [10].

13.3.2 Administrative, Technical, and Physical Controls

Putting controls into place to protect confidentiality, integrity, and availability (CIA) is also part of risk management. Controls are typically divided into administrative, technical, and physical countermeasures. Administrative controls include ensuring that resources are granted to people on a ***need-to-know*** basis, which is premised on the ***principle of least privilege***. The principle of least privilege establishes that personnel should be given access to only those files, programs, and systems that they need in order to perform their job functions [1].

Some functions may also require a ***separation of duties***. With a separation of duties, multiple people are involved in some but not all aspects of sensitive transactions. This is done so that no single individual can perform an important function, such as "payroll" or "bookkeeping." It might be important to use ***job rotation*** not just as a matter of giving employees a variety of work tasks (an important motivational concept in organizational management best practices) but also between functional areas to ensure that different people gain visibility into sensitive operations, making it more difficult for people to collude on fraudulent activity or subvert security processes [2, 10].

Technical controls include technologies and techniques to prevent destruction of or unauthorized access to information resources such as using cryptography and using firewalls to block or prevent attackers from connecting to systems. Technical controls also involve the use of fault-tolerant or fail-over (hot standby) systems, hardware redundancy, disk mirroring, access control software, and antiviral and antispyware software. An example of a combined administrative and technical control is the use of a ***change control system***. Change control systems log user requests and require approvals from authorized agents before granting a requested change. Physical controls include the use of uninterruptible power supply (UPS) systems, off-site operations centers and off-site backup storage facilities, and even physical barriers [8].

> **In Focus**
>
> Although most texts refer to administrative, technical, and physical controls (see for instance Straub, Goodman, and Baskerville [10]), it is also important to security management to address perceptual and behavioral controls.

In determining how to handle risk, managers must know where the information is located, what the classification of the information is, how the information is protected, and who is responsible (the custodian) for the information. Risk matrices are often produced to highlight the greatest risks, and these matrices are often developed using focus groups comprised of security and administrator personnel. The types of questions that are often asked of focus groups include: What is the likelihood that an undetected network monitor could intercept login or other information from authorized users? Or, what is the likelihood that an attacker may be successful in breaking into an email account by running a program such as *Crack*, which tries password combinations from a dictionary or by comparing the results of an encrypted password with results from hashing algorithms?

Sometimes the questions reveal unintended consequences of implementing a counter-measure. For example, a mandatory password change control system tends to generate extremely complex passwords. Although this may help prevent successful password cracking, it can pose its own set of risks because it tempts people to write their passwords down, often on a sheet of paper that accompanies their laptop or is located near their computer [9].

13.4 Managing Organization Members Securely

In addition to technical, physical, and administrative security, managers need to address the human factors that comprise organizational security behaviors [11], and among these factors are control perceptions. Some perceptions can be taught, whereas other perceptual aspects are innate or highly engrained and not easily changed. Security management fundamentally involves managing security behaviors [12]. Albert Bandura [13] defined behavior in terms of reciprocal psychosocial functioning. Psychosocial functioning assumes that people make rational cognitive assessments concerning threats in relation to their social settings. These relationships are triadic, meaning that the way people perceive, conceptualize, and cognitively evaluate information interacts with their social environments, and this influences their behavior, which is either positively or negatively reinforced, ignored (not reinforced), or punished.

13.4.1 Perceptions of Control and Security

From Bandura's [13] social-cognitive theory perspective, there are three types of control perceptions: ***locus of control***, ***self-efficacy***, and ***self-control***. Locus of control is a generalized expectancy that predicts people's behavior across situations and it influences whether people accept or deny responsibility for their actions, uphold the welfare of others, and live up to moral commitments. This is partly because it affects the extent to which people believe they can influence the outcomes. People who have high internal locus of control believe they do control their own destinies and they tend to accept responsibility for their actions, whereas people with low external locus of control believe that outcomes are controlled by fate or more *powerful* others. Nevertheless, people vary along the internal-external continuum, and people develop a greater sense of control as they gain experience.

Self-efficacy is concerned with an individual's skills and abilities that affect his or her perceptions of control over an outcome. High self-efficacy in relation to information security contravention leads people to believe they can both breach a security measure and get away with it as well. On the other hand, high self-efficacy tends to cause people to be proactive in taking security precautions.

In Focus

High self-efficacy can be a double-edged sword. Such confidence may lead people to try to breach a security measure or be more diligent in upholding security responsibilities. Resulting behaviors often rest upon one's attitude toward the law and one's personal set of ethical principles.

Consequently, the issue of contravention of security versus taking security actions is an important aspect for managers to consider, especially in terms of computer self-efficacy [14], which deals specifically with computer technology. This factor interacts with people's attitudes and perceptions such as whether they believe they should uphold the law because it is socially responsible versus those who have poor regard for the law, or who feel they need to obey the law only because they think they might get caught when breaking a law and will be severely punished [15].

Extending the concept of control further is self-control, which is defined as an ability to delay gratification. The lack of self-control acts to grant immediate gratification of desires at the cost of possible long-term negative consequences for the offender whereas high self-control is the tendency to avoid acts whose long-term costs exceed momentary advantages. In terms of information security behaviors, these control constructs may be seen as a hierarchy: first whether control is possible in the first place (locus of control); then whether one has the skills and ability to control a given outcome (self-efficacy), which together form a perception of behavioral control; and then finally, whether one has control over himself or herself in mediating the potential to contravene and impulses to contravene information security measures.

In Focus

Because few aspects of human perceptions can be changed or taught, managers must rely heavily on behaviorally based countermeasures.

13.4.2 Sins of Omission

Research on security behaviors has mainly focused on contravention, although increasingly, the spotlight has been placed on the omission or neglect of countermeasures, such as failures to update or protect passwords or keep security and virus software up to date, ignoring security patches, not using firewalls, failing to back up systems or use surge protectors or paper shredders, or not following due diligence precautions with information marked proprietary and/or confidential. Carelessness with information and the failure to take available security precautions contribute to the loss of information and even to crimes, including corporate espionage and identity theft. This major aspect of the omission problem clearly shows a ***knowing-doing gap*** in information security. By knowing-doing gap, we mean, knowing better, but not doing better.

Suggested behavioral prescriptions to address the omission problem in information security have included levying punishments. However, although this technique has been found to be effective in addressing contravention of information security by insiders, the research [16] shows that it has not been very effective in treating the problem of omission. Also, some people fear their jobs might become more difficult as a result of increased security measures, such as impeding their ability to perform well, or that they might be punished if they make a mistake or forget to implement a security procedure.

Specifically, using a punitive approach to behavior modification imbues a mechanistic organizational environment in which people tend to refuse taking actions not specifically defined for them for fear of punishment [17]. Their focus turns to documented rules and written processes and procedures stipulating how work is to be carried out, and they strive toward risk avoidance, creating a rigid and often ineffective and perhaps even hostile work environment—a work environment where it is often said: "That's not my job."

Raising the level of security awareness and providing security training, along with organizational supports from management, have been shown to reduce security incidents relative to omission [16]. Training on information security comes in many forms, including hybrid collaborative-computer simulation, which may be a viable replacement for the traditional classroom laboratory and workbook forms of instruction employed by organizations. Therefore, the ability to provide training is not difficult because organizations can choose the best approach for their setting and cost structure. The difficulty, relative to omission, is what to train?

There are many underlying factors for the omission problem that may need separate treatments and management training protocols. In cases where people have low computer self-efficacy, skills training is most effective, whereas those low in locus of control are more responsive to visualization and positive-association imagery types of development, and those low in self-control are least affected by training and best respond to behavioral treatments [18]. In nearly all cases, managerial support and ensuring procedural justice is crucial to positive outcomes in dealing with the omission problem.

In Focus

Managers must be concerned with outside attackers, inside attackers, and those who simply do not implement security procedures. The last of these three may be the most difficult to address.

13.4.3 Sins of Commission

It's not practical for managers to try to teach or indoctrinate integrity, ethics, or security conscientiousness to malicious outsiders. However, when it comes to malicious insiders who commit offenses such as maneuvering around security procedures, stealing software, breaking product license agreements, removing products or proprietary information from the office for personal use, and cracking passwords and committing fraudulent acts with the stolen information, research studies have shown that ethics training may be effective in some situations, so long as people are self-principled [19]. Nevertheless, many ethics programs have relied on teaching a particular system of situational ethics for their interventions, and although intuitively appealing, teaching situational ethics has been somewhat ineffectual in practice [20, 21]. This is partly because values and ethical systems are built up over time through learning from family, religious institutions, and peer groups and are not easily changed.

When it comes to contravention from malicious outsiders and insiders, studies [22] have shown that increasing the severity of punishments associated with contravention may reduce their incidence. As we discussed previously, this is consistent with the psychology literature on punishment. However, information security contravention by its very nature relies on stealth, and capturing the perpetrators is difficult. When they do catch perpetrators, in many cases, companies refuse to prosecute for fear of negative publicity. The threat of punishment cannot be solely relied upon as a dissuasive measure [23]. Also keep in mind that deterrence interventions are based on a military frame of reference. Deterrence theory grew out of the notion that imposing costs on a potential enemy greater than the benefits might neutralize the motivation for an act of aggression. This has not always translated well into organizational practice [19].

Given the two postures about security contravention, one punitive and one developmental, managers must consider different underlying factors that account for behaviors in organizations. For example, some studies show that people's varying attitudes about security measures affect whether they adhere to them or not, and that attitudes toward information security affect security-related behaviors. Hence, personal characteristics and perceptions interact with organizational approaches used for gaining compliance with security policies; it is not a "one size fits all" proposition. The bottom line: In terms of applying the theory, managers need to take special care in attending to the needs of individuals under their jurisdictions and apply the most appropriate interventions given their unique personalities, knowledge, and motivational characteristics in combination with the corporate environment.

In Focus

In most states, even those that are employment at will, it is prudent to have a corrective action policy. Unless the offense was intentional and immediately destructive (e.g., threat to others, theft) or in violation of a policy with terminal consequences, then it is generally a good practice to have a standardized approach used consistently and equitably that allows people to be notified, given due process, and permitted to correct their counterproductive behaviors. This protects the company's legal interests and protects valued employees who have made minor mistakes.

13.4.4 Social Influences and Legalistic Perceptions

We have covered individual characteristics that affect how people respond to organizational approaches to security behaviors, and now it is time to consider how these individual factors relate to people's social work environments. **Social identity** develops through the processes of categorization, identification, and comparison of people, which leads to psychological attachments to a collective. In other words, it is how people become connected with their social worlds and distinguish them from "outsider" groups.

Nearly everyone has experienced peer pressures in their social groups, but some people respond more readily to the pressures than others. The need for social conformity is defined by what has been described as the **epistemological weighting hypothesis**. This asserts that the degree to which people conform to peer pressures depends on how closely their own norms match those of their peer groups. More specifically, it postulates that social forces affect behavior only to the extent that people identify with and become *de-individuated* by their peer groups. **De-individuation** is the subordination of one's personal identity and self-interests to that of the groups to which he or she belongs.

As we have indicated before, studies [23] have shown that when people obey the rules out of social conformity or based on observation of their peers, if peers obey the law, they are more likely to be persuaded to obey the law. On the other hand, if peers disobey the law, they are more likely to break the law. In addition, social influences interact with people's attitudes toward the law such that people who follow rules out of a sense of duty or loyalty are more responsive to social influences, whereas people who follow rules to avoid punishment are more responsive to punitive forms of deterrents.

CHAPTER SUMMARY

In this chapter, we reviewed some basic concepts in security. We illustrated how threats are presented to information and systems. We introduced the term Infosec and provided some idea of what Infosec entails. We presented a variety of threats to information and systems and gave some examples of the ways that vulnerabilities can be exploited, and we reviewed some behavioral controls. As you must have gathered, Infosec is a vast and complex arena, ranging from technology to human factors. To try to define dimensions of it, Stanton et al. [23] produced taxonomies of information security behaviors, and their coverage of insider threats ranged from intentional destruction to naïve mistakes. Although their model provided many clues to addressing various forms of failures to implement information security controls, it did not address behaviors related to people who know how to implement security measures but do not follow through. From other research, we have some hints that some of the features in contravention behaviors may also account for omission behaviors as well, and these provide some answers to the question, "What to train?" For example, some research [19] has found relationships between computer self-efficacy and software piracy, and between locus of control and software piracy. In the chapters that follow in this section, we will offer more specifics on each of these areas: administrative, technical (computer and network), physical, and human-based countermeasures. At this point, you should be well prepared to understand the countermeasures presented in the chapters that follow.

THINK ABOUT IT

Topic Questions

13.1: What does the term "Infosec" refer to?

13.2: What is eavesdropping?

13.3: Generally, attacks are divided into what two types?

13.4: What is the idea of knowing better but not doing better called?

13.5: What are the three types of control perceptions?

13.6: The concept of need-to-know is premised on:

_____ Separation of duties
_____ Principle of least privilege
_____ Mandatory Access Control
_____ Discretionary Access Control

13.7: Categorization, identification, and comparison of people is part of:

_____ De-individuation
_____ Social identity
_____ Security contravention
_____ Security omission

13.8: Ethics training is most effective for:

_____ People who are self-principled
_____ Malicious outsiders
_____ Malicious insiders
_____ People who omit security on accident

13.9: People always omit security countermeasures on accident.

_____ True
_____ False

13.10: Deterrents such as threats of punishment are most effective for:

_____ Malicious insiders
_____ Malicious outsiders
_____ People who omit security on accident
_____ People who omit security on purpose

Questions for Further Study

Q13.1: What are some of the differences between DoS and a DDoS?

Q13.2: How has the advent of social media added to or changed security threats?

Q13.3: What are some other forms of social engineering not mentioned in this chapter?

Q13.4: What should managers consider in relation to security about smart phones such as an iPhone or Blackberry and the people in

their organization who use them (including themselves)? How should device selection factor into these considerations?

Q13.5: How does social identity theory explain objectification of others?

KEY CONCEPTS AND TERMS

De-individuation is the subordination of one's personal identity and self-interests to that of the groups to which he or she belongs.

A denial of service attack (DoS) attempts to disrupt a legitimate service.

Epistemological weighting hypothesis explains social conformity.

Infosec refers to the policies, procedures, and technological countermeasures used in managing the risk.

Social identity develops through the processes of categorization, identification, and comparison of people.

References

1. Solomon, M. G., & Chapple, M. (2005). *Information security illuminated*. Sudbury, MA: Jones and Bartlett Publishers.
2. Purser, S. (2004). *A practical guide to managing information security*. Boston, MA: Artech House.
3. Hunt, C. (1992). *TCP/IP network administration*. Sebastapol, CA: O'Reilly & Associates.
4. Thomas, T. (1994). *Network security: First step*. Indianapolis, IN: Cisco Press.
5. Pulton, E. G. (1994). *Behavioral decision theory*. Cambridge, UK: Cambridge University Press.
6. Casarez, N. B. (2002). Dealing with cybersmear: How to protect your organization from online defamation. *Public Relations Quarterly, 47*, 40–45.
7. Kim, D., & Solomon, M. G. (2012). *Fundamentals of information systems security*. Sudbury, MA: Jones & Bartlett Learning.
8. Himma, K. E. (2007). *Internet security: Hacking, counterhacking, and society*. Sudbury, MA: Jones and Bartlett Publishers.
9. Straub, D. W., & Welke, R. J. (1998). Coping with systems risk: Security planning models for management decision making. *MIS Quarterly, 22*, 441–469.
10. Straub, D. W., Goodman, S., & Baskerville, R. L. (2008). *Information security: Policy, processes, and practices*. Armonk, NY: M.E. Sharpe.
11. Fuller, L. L. (1977). Some presuppositions shaping the concept of socialization. In J. L. Tapp & F. J. Levine (Eds.), *Law, justice, and the individual in society: Psychological and legal issues* (pp. 89–105). New York, NY: Holt, Rinehart & Winston.
12. Workman, M. (2009). A field study of corporate employee monitoring: Attitudes, absenteeism, and the moderating influences of procedural justice perceptions. *Journal of Information and Organization, 19*, 218–232.

13. Bandura, A. (1986). *Social foundations of thought and action: A social cognitive theory.* Englewood Cliffs, NJ: Prentice Hall.

14. Compeau, D. R., & Higgins, C. A. (1995). Computer self-efficacy: Development of a measure and initial test. *MIS Quarterly, 19,* 189–211.

15. Sam, H. K., Othman, A. E. A., & Nordin, Z. S. (2005). Computer self-efficacy, computer anxiety, and attitudes toward the Internet. *Educational Technology & Society, 8,* 205–219.

16. Workman, M., Bommer, W., & Straub, D. H. (2008). Security lapses and the omission of information security measures: An empirical test of the threat control model. *Journal of Computers in Human Behavior, 24,* 2799–2816.

17. Sine, W. D., Mitsuahsi, H., & Krisch, D. A. (2006). Revisiting Burns and Stalker: Formal structure and new venture performance in emerging economic sectors. *Academy of Management Journal, 49,* 121–132.

18. Workman, M., Bommer, W., & Straub, D. H. (2009). The amplification effects of procedural justice with a threat control model of information systems security. *Journal of Behavior and Information Technology, 28,* 563–575.

19. Workman, M., & Gathegi, J. (2007). Punishment and ethics deterrents: A comparative study of insider security contravention. *Journal of American Society for Information Science and Technology, 58,* 318–342.

20. Workman, M. (2008). A test of interventions for security threats from social engineering. *Information Management & Computer Security, 16,* 463–483.

21. Workman, M. (2009). How perceptions of justice affect security attitudes: Suggestions for practitioners and researchers. *Information Management & Computer Security, 17,* 341–353.

22. Straub, D. W., Carlson, P. J., & Jones, E. H. (1993). Deterring cheating by student programmers: A field experiment in computer security. *Journal of Management Systems, 5,* 33–48.

23. Stanton, J. M., Stam, K.R., Mastrangelo, P., & Jolton, J. (2005). Analysis of end-user security behaviors. *Computers and Security, 24,* 124–133.

Computer Security

COMPUTER (OR SOMETIMES CALLED HOST) security mainly involves carefully managing computer systems by controlling and monitoring events, services, processes, and configurations. Most operating systems have incorporated mechanisms for identification and authorization of users, but more protections are needed. In addition to these "built-in" security features, systems may require biometric devices, or multiple credentials and other measures and ways of validating those credentials, along with security rights management facilities. They may also require the implementation of security applications such as host-based intrusion detection systems (HIDS), application-layer firewalls, and virus scanners. Equally important but less frequently noted are the procedures used in hardening computer systems and ensuring defensible and auditable characteristics. We will address with these issues in this chapter.

Chapter 14 Topics

This chapter:

- Discusses some examples of built-in host security features, using Windows as a reference.
- Covers host attack architecture, and offer some examples.
- Discusses host-based intrusion detection systems.
- Presents the idea of a reference monitor.
- Conducts an overview of system assessment and elaborate on hardening techniques.
- Covers identification, authentication, and biometrics.

Chapter 14 Goals

When you finish this chapter, you should:

- ❏ Know ways that host security can be undermined.
- ❏ Know how to monitor computer activities using native and layered products.
- ❏ Be able to evaluate host security, and implement basic host security countermeasures to prevent systems from being undermined.
- ❏ Understand configuration management and have knowledge of "host hardening" concepts and the use of biometrics in this endeavor.
- ❏ Have a working knowledge of procedures used to ensure secure software and systems implementation life cycles.

14.1 Hosts and Security—A Windows Example

In this section on computer security, we will quickly survey some of the basic security features that host operating systems implement using Windows as a reference example. It is important to note that implementations are different between operating systems and even between versions of operating systems. Windows in particular has evolved its security mechanisms significantly between Windows 2000 and Windows version 7; thus knowing the internals of a particular version of operating system is important to security. Developers and administrators are constantly striving to improve host security as threats become more sophisticated. The key to maintaining host security is to understand the specific vulnerabilities of a particular operating system, version, and patch levels.

14.1.1 Microsoft Active Directory

Shortly, we will present a more general discussion of attacks and preventive measures that are not computer system specific; however, having some idea of how systems such as Microsoft Windows attempt to prevent attacks is useful in determining how to try to prevent attacks from succeeding. Therefore we will begin with some technical details before moving up to a higher level view.

In many cases, hosts are grouped together into a cooperative collection, or distributed set of systems. Microsoft Windows to date has designed their distributed security services around the ***Active Directory***, which is a directory service that manages objects in a "domain," or "realm." A domain is a logical grouping of "trust" consisting of users, systems, printers, and other resources. For this, Microsoft employs a concept called forest and trees. Trees represent a single domain, whereas multiple domains are called forests.

The Active Directory can be accessed through the lightweight directory service protocol (LDAP).

Besides enabling centralized security controls, the Active Directory can facilitate a capability called ***single sign-on*** (**SSO**), which allows a user to have one password to access disparate resources, simplifying password management. The Active Directory notion of a security realm, domain, or boundary is controlled by administrators who are assigned custody of those resources and objects within their given domain. Domains are stratified by users and groups, and thus users and some groups can be granted permissions for certain access in other domains. Domain data are generally replicated only within a given domain by a domain controller (DC), but data can be exported through a global catalog (GC). A GC is a subclass of domain controller.

In Focus

Using the Active Directory, a security model incorporating a security policy can be applied centrally for maintainability. The Active Directory is a directory service for storing information about users and objects, such as host and client systems, printers, and domains.

14.1.2 Windows Security Access Controls

Realize first that Microsoft Windows continues to evolve. We will present basic security access controls and management in Windows Vista and Version 7 at a high level, but note that Windows continues to adapt its architecture according to needs. Also, because Windows is proprietary, discussions about its internal workings are difficult and always provisional (that is, subject to change).

Consider access control lists as software tables of "who" can do "what." A reference monitor or access control software presents "credentials" to an access control service and receives "permission slips" for what a user can do while on the system. The essence of authentication and authorization is called access management. Important security-related access control and management services in modern versions of Windows have been the ***Winlogon***, ***Session Manager***, ***Local Security Authority*** (**LSA**), ***Security Accounts Manager*** (**SAM**), ***Service Controller***, and ***Event Logger***. The Local Security Authority (LSA) and its ***Local Security Authority Subsystem Service*** (**LSASS**) are invoked at login time. This authenticates the user and grants the user a ***system access token*** (**SAT**). The SAT is needed to start the initial communication, and is inherited by all programs spawned following the login session to allow for auditing user mode functions.

In Focus

Windows can support local security policies such as various access controls according to a user. The Microsoft Management Control (MMC) is an interface that enables administrators to set policies, monitor services and events, and manage the system configuration [1].

FIGURE 14.1

Windows session
privileges.

Winlogon ← → LSA ← → SAM

Security processes are invoked for a user when Windows initiates *Winlogon* and starts the graphical user interface application (GINA) to handle local and remote connection requests via the LSA and SAM. The SAM is a user mode system that maintains the user account database required by the LSA, as seen in **Figure 14.1**. Once a user is authenticated and begins a session, Windows handles access control using ***access control entries*** (**ACE**). The ACE is utilized to determine whether a process is permitted or denied access to a resource or object, and the level of access that is permitted. In other words, ACEs are used by ***access control lists*** (**ACL**) in which permissions are assigned to objects, users, and resources.

In Windows, a security principal is an account to which permissions are assigned, such as a user, a group, or a system account. A ***security identification*** (**SID**) is issued to each principal so that they can be uniquely identified. A ***security descriptor*** refers to data structures associated with an object, and the descriptor is referenced when a user attempts to access an object. More specifically, when a user requests access to an object, the descriptor is checked for its information against the user's SID, and then compares the SID against its ACL permissions. Windows supports two types of ACLs, the ***discretionary access control list*** (**DACL**) for user access, such as allow or deny read access to a given object, and a ***system access control list*** (**SACL**), which is an administrative function that audits and logs in the security event log attempts to access a secured object.

In Focus

ACLs make use of security identifiers (SIDs) to uniquely determine users and their group memberships. Thus users are issued an access token that contains user and group SIDs, along with privilege levels. When a user process requests access (such as write) to a resource or object, the system compares the access token with the permissions in the ACL as whether to grant or deny the requested action on the object.

The Windows operating system assumes that objects are one of two types: (1) containers, such as directories, which may contain other objects, and (2) non-containers, such as files, which cannot contain other objects. Boolean flags are used to control inheritance characteristics of the ACE, which include those in **List 14.1** [2]. For instance, Windows issues both grant and deny access, and if certain ACE flags (Boolean bit masks) are set for a container, the objects within the container also inherit the security permissions of the container.

List 14.1 ACE Security Flags

OBJECT_INHERIT_ACE – This is inherited by objects in a container object.

CONTAINER_INHERIT_ACE – This is inherited by sub-components in a container.

NO_PROPAGATE_INHERIT_ACE – This represents inheritance of control flags that are not propagated in ACEs directly inherited by sub-containers.

INHERIT_ONLY_ACE – This is an ACE that is not used in validating access attempts to the corresponding object, but will be used in those that will be applied to subtype objects as they are created.

The flags in **List 14.2** apply if this ACE is of type SYSTEM_AUDIT_ACE.

List 14.2 System Audit Flags

SUCCESSFUL_ACCESS_ACE_FLAG – This represents audit messages that should be generated for successful accesses.

FAILED_ACCESS_ACE_FLAG – These are audit messages generated for failed accesses.

The masks have different meanings according to type, as seen in **List 14.3**.

List 14.3 ACE Types

ACCESS_ALLOWED_ACE – This represents a binary bitmap *mask* indicating which accesses are granted to a specified security identification (SID) object.

ACCESS_DENIED_ACE – This represents an access mask indicating which accesses are denied to the specified SID.

SID – The security ID to which this ACE applies, and each subject or principal in Windows, has an associated SID.

In Focus

Windows makes it possible to configure a system using what is called a domain controller, which consolidates the security accounts manager (SAM) database into a single server and then allocates access rights accordingly. This approach centralizes the security services and simplifies administration, thereby reducing the possibility of configuration errors that might be exploited. On the other hand, this centralized approach can be a single point of failure.

14.1.3 Windows Service and Process Security

A service, as you have learned, is basically a process (or set of processes) that perform functions for users on behalf of the system. Examples include handling interprocess communications by means of the Component Object Model (COM), or event handling, networking functions, device plug-and-play, and the Windows installer. From a service and process security viewpoint, Windows has four main aspects: (1) executive or kernel mode, (2) protected servers (user mode), (3) network subsystem (both kernel and user modes), and (4) administrator tools (user mode) [3].

For the network subsystems, the ***service control manager*** (**SCM**) in Windows is responsible for service management and provides a ***remote procedure call*** (**RPC**) interface and server for configuration and control. The security context of a process determines the capabilities of the service. Most services run as a local system account that has elevated access rights on the local host, but does not have privileges on a network domain. If a service needs to access network resources, it must run as a domain user with sufficient privileges to fulfill the request [4].

The ***object manager*** controls process access to system resources and objects; and interestingly, processes themselves are objects in the Windows system. Each process is associated with a ***handle***. A handle is a type of pointer or reference to data structures associated with the process (or thread, which is a lightweight process, as you recall). These data structures include virtual addresses, private address space, addresses of data structures in physical memory, and security context, along with a list of threads that belong to the process. Like processes, each thread created by a process has an execution context, including process registers and stack pointers [5].

In Focus

A register is a storage container in memory of operations needed with quick access by the CPU for process execution. A stack pointer is an index (address) into memory containers.

Each process also contains a ***handle table*** that has locations of all of the objects to which a process has access. Being objects, processes can access other processes directly so long as handles to them are available. Because each handle contains information that describes the type of access the process has to another object, such as read and write, the object manager ensures that access is only granted if it is compatible with the handle. When a process requests a new resource or access to an object for the first time, the object manager asks the security reference monitor (SAM) to decide if the process may acquire a handle to it. Subsequent accesses to the same resource will not need to involve the SAM because a handle granting the type of access will already be available in the process handle table [6].

14.1.4 Access Management Framework in Windows

With a centralized policy database, audit log, and SAM database, the various user mode services are conceptually protected from corruption because changes to them are managed through the SAM in Windows. Furthermore, Windows password policies can be established using the User Manager Administration tool, which supports, among other things, password aging, minimum password length, password uniqueness, and account lockout features; however, attackers have found vulnerabilities.

As an augmentation, windows systems use a ***hash-based challenge and response*** mechanism for logins (we will discuss hashing in greater detail in the chapter on cryptography). This implies that although passwords are required for local login, password hashes can be used for remote authentication.

According to de Medeiros [2], early Windows password protection mechanisms were based on the Windows NT password-hashing technique (NTLM). NTLM was vulnerable to dictionary-based attacks such as L0phtrackNTLM because it only used 14 characters in a single hash function. Faster machines have made parsing through the universe of password permutations fairly quick. Newer approaches (beginning with NTLMv2) accept more than 14 characters and encrypt password hashes before storing them in the SAM, which is more secure. However, the old NTLM is still exported in some configurations by default for compatibility with older machines in the same network (that is, placed in the SAM). Nevertheless, unless a user picks an easy-to-guess password, the cryptography used for authentication is quite sophisticated and makes timely session interception very difficult. By the time the credentials have been determined, the session will likely have ended (we will explore this more in the chapter on cryptography).

In Focus

A challenge-response authentication is common for many applications. However, by eavesdropping in a network and capturing challenge and response pairs, an adversary might be able to collect information to perform dictionary and/or brute-force (guessing) attacks on passwords. This was problematic with early Windows systems, but for more modern systems (as long as good passwords are used), this has become impractical because the cryptography used is now so complex.

Still, to mitigate this minor vulnerability, Windows has bundled a technology called ***Kerberos*** for authentication, along with using the ACL techniques described previously. Kerberos is implemented through the Winlogon service. More specifically, the login session of GINA switches the control to the Windows security management system to Kerberos. Kerberos was specifically designed for authenticating users in this way. Recall that authentication is a process of encoding information using digits (keys) to create an encoded ciphertext that is uniquely assigned to a subject (such as a user). Keys are codes distributed by a service running on a secure server, called the ***key distribution center*** (**KDC**), which dispenses cryptographic keys from its database with the account information for all entities in its realm—the equivalent of the old Windows domain.

In Focus

Authentication uses cryptography. Two forms of cryptography are public key (asymmetric) and private key (symmetric) ciphers. In public key cryptography, one key is made available to everyone to encrypt information, where the other is kept secret for decoding. In private key cryptography, both keys must be kept secret. For authentication, a key is used with a cipher to generate code for a legitimate process to use in transacting electronic business.

The KDC consists of two functions: an ***authentication server*** (**AS**) and a ***ticket-granting server*** (**TGS**). The Windows devices on the network share the secret key known only to host and to KDC. In most implementations, this is derived from a user's login password. From that, Kerberos generates a ***session key*** to be used for generating ***tickets*** to secure the exchanges [7].

It is the GINA (Graphical Identification and Authentication) that passes the login information to the LSA for verification and conversion of the plaintext into a secret key that is to be shared between the client and server. It does this by computing and sending a one-way hash, which is a cryptographic technique that transforms plaintext into a jumbled code called a ***message digest*** (**MD**). It is called one-way because the code can only be generated but cannot be decoded by anyone but the server because only the server has a missing piece of information used to verify the code.

The KDC then builds a special session ticket that is called a ***ticket-granting ticket*** (**TGT**). The TGT contains a copy of the session key that a service, such as the KDC, can use for communications. Along with the TGT, the client also receives a copy of the session key communicating with the KDC. The TGT is encrypted, and is retrieved as needed by the TGT for renewal if the session key is about to expire, or for Windows NTLM authentication for servers that are not Kerberos-enabled [7].

The LSA decrypts the session key with the secret key and extracts the authentication code. Then it queries the SAM to determine membership and privileges for the realm. It appends the SIDs gathered from the query to the security data structure that is being assembled, and then uses this information to build an access token. A handle to the token is returned to the Winlogon process, along with an identifier for the session, and confirmation that the login information was valid. Winlogon attaches the access token to the session, which is inherited by applications executed during the session [8].

In Focus

Note that Kerberos is technology independent. It is also implemented with Linux (and other UNIX-based) machines if so desired.

14.1.5 Windows Version Security Differences

There have been many changes to the Windows operating system (OS) over the years, and there seems no end to it. Thus we are only going to raise the issue for awareness, and provide a few examples. Most of us grew familiar with Vista out of necessity after having worked with the relatively functional XP version of Windows. Vista created new paradigms to deal with, and what seemed like a lot of unintuitive behaviors. Windows version 7 attempted to compensate for those quirks and also to attend to some of the more problematic security flaws; but in the process, it grew to resemble a MAC/OS type of operating system to some of us rather than what was familiar to Windows users.

Nevertheless, the underlying architecture has remained quite similar between Vista and Windows 7. This is important because those of us who went through the Windows 2000 to XP transition know only too well what that meant, including that our expensive new laser printer would no longer work after the upgrade, and we found that a printer provider (e.g., Epson) was not inclined to provide a new device driver because the cost was too great to migrate to the new architecture. Furthermore, those who have upgraded to or purchased a new Windows system found that each time it was increasingly bloated, requiring many more gigabytes from the last version to make the new Windows OS version work properly. However, there have been some improvements since then.

In Focus

Consistency in user interaction is important to security. Moving user features or changing them leads to errors.

Security changes in Windows 7 have included improvements to the encryption of Windows disk partitions; indeed, the BitLocker, a disk encryption feature in Windows, has been expanded to include the ability to encrypt complete disk volumes. Windows 7 also includes a new biometric framework that supports various fingerprint readers and recognition facilities. An important aspect of the new biometric framework is that biometric data (called templates) are not accessible directly. Instead, the framework reveals only a handle such as a globally unique identifier (GUID) or a security identifier (SID), which permits applications to access biometric data indirectly and helps preserve the templates from tampering.

Next, Windows 7 has improved upon home-based systems with a new grouping mechanism called *HomeGroup*. Members of a HomeGroup can share files among computers with a special identifier used to authenticate HomeGroup users. The authentication is performed using a public key-based user-to-user protocol (PKu2u). In addition, as we indicated in the previous section, authentication in Windows has been predicated on either Kerberos or on the NTLM challenge-response protocols, but in Windows 7, a new spnego (spnego.dll) protocol extends this not only to the Pku2u, just mentioned, but also to authentication for Windows Live. Windows Live is a collection of services and products accessible from a browser that facilitate game applications (such as for Xbox), web services, and mobile device applications.

When authentication is performed using these technologies, a client (say, using the PKu2u protocol) obtains a certificate from a ***certificate authority*** (**CA**), and that certificate is exchanged with peers at login time for validation. The user's certificate is needed to receive a security access token for the login process. A certificate is a unique encrypted message digest produced using a key. A CA is a recognized entity, such as Verisign, that uses a shared key to compute a message digest, that vouches for the veracity of the client [9].

Windows 7 also has improvements to the user account control (UAC). This facility manages Registry redirection, and application and ActiveX installers. As pointed out on the Microsoft Windows Version 7 upgrades web page: "These features are designed to allow Windows users to run with user accounts that are not members of the Administrators group. These accounts are generally referred to as Standard Users and are broadly described as running with least privilege" (www.microsoft.com/en-us/default.aspx).

In addition to BitLocker changes, there is also an AppLocker control that allows users to have fine-grained control over application access. For example, it provides a "lockdown" policy to facilitate control over what applications can execute and give greater control to users to prevent unauthorized application executions, particularly when one configures features such as "identity level" checks and policy enforcement controls, which help prevent the downloading of potentially dangerous DLLs and software installations, or improper software executions, using an administrator-friendly rules configuration utility.

Still, these changes are not impervious to attacks. For example, although AppLocker checks for executables without enabling the execution of script files, it does little for Trojan-based infiltration. It does not protect the Registry entry in which the AppLocker is stored at the HKLM\Software\Policies\Microsoft\Windows\SrpV2 key, for example, and thus it is subject to a Registry typeset attack.

Finally, Windows 7 has improved on how it handles network domain name service updates using a new validation scheme. Historically, DNS-related exploits have become a significant problem by allowing adversaries to, at a minimum, find mailing systems from MX records to conduct more problematic name spoofing (called a poisoned DNS). In other words, a user may visit a website that may be fashioned to look like a legitimate site, such as Yahoo, but in fact it is a façade.

In Focus

Yahoo, and others, are allowing users to create an image and load it to a secure place on their system so that when they log on, the host (such as Yahoo) reads and renders this visual cue for user identification as being the legitimate host.

In Windows Server 2008 running on Windows 7, a security feature identified as DNSSEC was introduced in compliance with standards RFC 4033, RFC 4034, and RFC 4035. This facility provides origin authority and integrity "proofs" that legitimate hosts establish and publish, so that a server can attach a *digital signature* to a DNS response provided for a DNS query for validation before a name-address resolution is done.

Beyond these features there are other security enhancements such as improvements to distributed SACL controls, and more granulated auditing and reporting. To highlight these, according to Microsoft, before Windows 7, auditing object access was determined by the security descriptor, an object held in its ACE portion of the SACL—specifying what should be audited. The problem this created was that a given Registry key or file could be monitored to see what access was granted. Prior to Windows 7, there was no method to observe what a user was accessing, and thus many "informational" messages were posted in the audit log depending on the log level a user set for his or her system. To overcome this, Windows 7 introduced a Global Object Access Auditing (GOAA) capability that can manage group policies (through the auditpol.exe), which is configurable to needs and levels of detail desired.

Microsoft has also noted that the GOAA "has" a global SACL, which is held in the Registry along with other data related to auditing. In Windows 7, they also added two APIs to manage the SACL, called the Global SACL, identified as the AuditSetGlobalSacl, and the AuditQueryGlobalSacl. Also as noted by Microsoft, updating the Global SACL requires the SeSecurityPrivilege, which protects the Global SACL from being updated by a user without administrator privileges [9].

Finally, there is more detailed reporting of important failures in Windows 7 over previous versions. The global object access auditing features combined with the SeSecurityPrivilege feature (SeAccessCheckEx) helps to determine if consumers of resources using the provisioned API would violate a security policy. For example, it will flag an event if a request from resource managers would violate a rule. More specifically, as stated by Microsoft (*paraphrased*): Windows 7 will assist if an NTFS request conflicts with the Detailed File Share in Windows 7. And when enabled, the API will put information in the audit log about why an access attempt succeeded or failed. Thus these features apply to the file systems and file shares, and can be expanded to other resource managers in future versions of Windows (http://www.microsoft.com/en-us/default.aspx).

In sum, we will take note that there are many other version-specific security changes in Windows from one to the next. Managers need to be aware of these to ensure that all of the staff and administrators are trained before new versions are installed on computer systems, and that they are properly configured, managed, and monitored.

14.2 Getting Past OS Security Features

It should be obvious by now that computer OS providers are striving to build security defenses into their operating systems (think back to the old "Orange Book" classifications of C1, C2, etc.). However, given an attacker, the preventive measures built into systems may be quite easy to figure out, and thus begins the attacker's journey of figuring out how to get around those, and what an attacker might do if he or she encounters an unexpected defensive countermeasure not part of the system's inherent security features. We have presented some insights into how operating systems work (especially in Windows), and discussed some of the key security mechanisms built into the Windows OS. Just how do attackers bypass these preventive measures? Preventive measures can only address attacks at a general level, and attackers are constantly striving for creative ways to take advantage of vulnerabilities in operating systems. Once an attack is formulated, system providers must react after the fact and implement patches to plug the holes.

14.2.1 Circumventing Security (in Windows and Other OS)

Many people rely on their computer manufacturers and operating system providers to protect them from security threats. There are several problems with this: First, system providers want to sell computers and software. They will provide whatever is available *de jure* for the going rate, but they look forward to making more money from consumers with upgrades. Concurrently, providers do not want their name brands tarnished, so they will purport a valiant effort to save consumers from these ever-present threats. Nevertheless, there are at least two problems with this: (1) In the "real world," someone or a group must first be affected before a fix or patch is created and released to others (called a "birthday" or "first day" attack), and (2) not everyone keeps their patches up to date.

Another issue is that some convenience features depend on a certain level of trust in order for them to work properly, or work at all. For example, dynamic link libraries (DLLs) are executable software components that are incorporated into a program at runtime rather than when the program is compiled, and they are used to allow diverse third-party applications to load and run in Windows. When an application loads a DLL without specifying a fully qualified path name, Windows tries to locate the DLL by searching through various directories.

If an attacker can cause a victim to open a file from a certain area such as through a mapped location, USB drive, or a Windows share, Windows may load a malware-infected DLL [10] allowing the attacker to execute malicious code. Microsoft [11] has recommended that administrators disable the loading libraries from current working directories, such as from WebDAV, as well as from remote network shares, to disable the WebClient service, and then block outgoing **Server Message Block** (**SMB**) traffic, which is an application-level network protocol typically used for file and print sharing. Obviously, doing so will curtail some of the conveniences these services and applications provide, not to mention, consider how complicated and time-consuming these activities can be if you manage a large organization!

Applications are often the channel by which vulnerabilities are introduced into host systems. We have discussed some of the threats and vulnerabilities generally, which include the introduction of viruses or Trojans via email in attachments, delivered during web surfing, or executed by means of IPC, but applications often provide the delivery mechanism via distributed objects such as by ActiveX/OLE/COM controls, or from remote procedure calls. Upon execution, an application may call the COM method, *CoCreateInstance*, which is used to construct the component using either the globally unique identifier (GUID) for the object, or a programmatic ID (ProgID). COM then indexes into the server for the object to load it into memory, or it accesses the data structures in memory if the objects are cached and are memory resident, which occurs if they have been recently used. COM then gathers (marshals) the process context if the server is in another memory segment or resides across a network [12, 13]. These types of access present many junctions for malware to strike.

Also, COM objects expose their functionality through well-defined interfaces to the data structures that reside in memory. Thus once the COM component is instantiated it can be queried for a particular interface so that an interprocess communication can take place. Because a GUID uniquely identifies an interface and component, the *QueryInterface* method enables one object to interact with another through the interfaces they expose. As part of this functionality, objects may support the *IUnknown* interface, which enables one object to query another for the methods it supports. This is especially significant given that COM components can be hosted through DLLs, or out of process space through executable files, or in executable files on remote computers [13]. A malicious program may "learn" how to exploit or corrupt programs or their data using there features [14].

In Focus

Although purportedly "sandboxed," the JAVA Reflection capability similar to the IUnknown feature has also caused some of its own security concerns.

One way that such malicious code may be introduced into a system is when users surf the Web. From this, they may become victims of session hijacking, or inadvertently download malicious files or click on links to malicious websites that take advantage of Windows COM/DCOM facilities that underlie many of the Windows mechanisms such as ActiveX and OLE, and other object communications. Given the ubiquitous access to network components by way of Microsoft's .NET component-based framework, it has frequently been targeted by attackers.

For example, although since patched, a few years ago the RealPlayer program was susceptible to a given ActiveX vulnerability because of improper handling of multiple properties by the RealPlayer ActiveX control (rmoc3260.dll). Exploitation of that vulnerability allowed a remote, unauthenticated attacker to execute arbitrary code on the victim's machine [10]. Even though this vulnerability has been patched, it highlights the need to keep patches up-to-date.

Extending from the COM architecture is COM+, previously known as Microsoft Transaction Server, or MTS. COM+ was designed to support distributed transaction services, including two-phased commit with databases. It also extends a message-oriented-model (MOM) for asynchronous message dispatching and management. Where COM was built on synchronous operations, a queued component may produce an asynchronous message that is dispatched by message queuing services through the loosely coupled event management of COM+. COM+ is very flexible in its use of MOM and many applications have used COM+ for role-based security implementations and ACL management; for example, it can be used to authenticate a role prior to the execution of a component. However COM+ itself has been relatively weakly protected, and this same flexibility that has made it useful has also made it vulnerable to exploitation [15].

The connections to databases may also be sources of security breaches. For example, the ADO.NET technology in Windows enables access to distributed information, including Microsoft SQLServer relational databases, Active Directory, and other OLE DB–aware or

Open Database Connectivity (ODBC)–aware databases, along with distributed systems middleware and web applications. These connections may be tapped, and if databases are not password protected or applications send SQL commands in the clear, security is at risk.

The file systems are sources of compromise as well. Windows systems support many file systems, including the file allocation table (FAT), FS, NTFS, CD-ROM FS (CDFS), named pipe file system (NPFS), and the mail slot file system (MSFS). Windows uses abstraction layers for device drivers, and the highest view of a storage or network device is a file system. Currently in Windows, only the NTFS is protected by the access control system. In addition, components and their interfaces are indexed in the Windows *Registry*, which contains references to objects such as hardware and software applications. Although it can be protected with an ACL, the centralized nature of the Windows Registry, and the relatively weak protection (given its critical role) has made it to date a hotbed for host security breaches. Within the Registry, the root stores information about registered applications. Registered objects are indexed by a handle key (HKEY); some categories are seen in **List 14.4**.

List 14.4 Some HKEY Groups

HKEY_CURRENT_USER – This stores settings that are specific to the current user.

HKEY_LOCAL_MACHINE – This stores settings that are general to all users on the system.

HKEY_USERS – This contains subkeys corresponding to the HKEY_CURRENT_USER keys for each user registered on the machine.

HKEY_CURRENT_CONFIG – This contains information gathered at runtime; information stored in this key is not permanently stored on disk, but rather regenerated at boot time.

As seen by the few classes shown in List 14.4, the range of objects managed by the Registry is expansive. File corruption or other damage to the Registry caused by malware can lead to program failures or allow Trojans to corrupt the Windows operating system. Although the security has improved in later versions of Windows such as Vista and Windows 7 to help protect the Registry, malware and Trojans continue to be a threat.

Even though Registry keys may be restricted using access control lists, a way in which malware is often introduced into a victim's machine includes websites that offer Registry cleaners that purport to *mop up* broken or orphaned HKEYs. Although there are legitimate Registry cleaners, such as Norton's WinDoctor, if selected, an attacker website may download a Trojan. WinFixer has been among the more notorious of Registry malware found on the Internet.

A technique used to combat Registry attacks includes Registry virtualization that redirects write operations to more secure locations. An example of this usage is in the case of Internet Explorer (IE) running in "protected mode" that automatically redirects ActiveX Registry writes to a "sandboxed" (meaning bounded) location to prevent some security exploits. Registry monitors are also helpful in that they alert users and system administrators of attempted changes to the Registry.

14.2.2 Host Attack Classifications and Examples

As previously discussed, attacks can be divided into active and passive ones. Examples of active attacks against computer systems consist of contagions and malware, including viruses, Trojans, and denial of service (DoS) or distributed denial of service (DDoS) attacks. Examples of passive attack threats include interception such as from masquerade or spyware, keyloggers, sniffers, and cookie bandits. Active and passive exploits may come through technological enablers including ActiveX, plug-ins, and downloads.

Malware

Malware is designed to damage or disrupt a host system. There are many kinds of malware that use different kinds of attack strategies, which fall largely into categories of destruction and theft. One example is the troj/Cimuz-U, which was also called the Trojan-PSW.Win32.Agent.eo spyware. This malware attacked Windows hosts by loading itself through an infected email or a web page link, and installing itself in the Window's Registry, then it opened ports to transmit information stolen from the victim's system. It was also capable of downloading other malicious applications from the Internet, and leaving other infected files behind on the target host.

Worms

Worms are self-propagating and often do not require interaction with a user to carry out their destruction because a worm copies itself from one computer to another over a network using a victim's system to attack others. Scripts and macros, such as those found in Microsoft's Word application even including its templates (e.g., normal.dot), can be exploited by worms. In one example, the Netsky-PWin32 worm was spread by using Windows networking APIs, MAPI functions, and email clients such as Microsoft Outlook. The worm created malicious code embedded in messages and attached itself to outgoing email.

Viruses

Viruses are malicious code that attaches to executable instructions, for example, Microsoft's Office applications installers. There are various subclasses of viruses, which are typically found in .exe, .dll, or .com files, but they also may be embedded in images, pdf, or zip files. Other viruses infect the Windows Registry and create linkages among various malware executables. Some viruses read email distribution lists (e.g., Microsoft Outlook) and use them to distribute themselves to other machines, as was done by the W95/Babylonia virus. Viruses often have the ability to replicate and spread as a result of interprocess communications. Some viruses become memory resident and infect other programs when they are run, whereas others actively seek out other files to infect.

Buffer Overflow

Buffer overflow is a type of attack where more data are written to a system buffer than it can cache. When a program writes beyond the end of a buffer, the program's memory addressing can be changed. This in and of itself can cause a system to crash, but it can also lead to the insertion of malware that can be used to destroy data or to gain administrative privileges. For example, a program that is a target of such an attack is given more data than the application can store, which then overruns the buffer and forces the system to execute attack code [7].

In Focus

Microsoft's Outlook was once vulnerable to an attack where sending large email messages compromised the integrity of the target system. Unlike most email viruses, users could not avoid the problem by refraining from opening the message. A defect in Outlook's message header made it possible for attackers to overflow the area with data, which allowed them to execute code on the victim's machine. Because the process was activated as soon as the recipient downloaded the message from the server, this type of buffer overflow attack was very difficult to find and defend against. Microsoft has since created a patch to eliminate the vulnerability [16].

Covert Channels

Covert channels are communication channels (or shared storage areas) that allow cooperating processes to transfer information in a way that violates a security policy. Even though protections may be in place, unauthorized information might be exchanged, intentionally or unintentionally, for example by using FTP, or through Microsoft shares, or regular network communications. It was thought that virtual machines such as VMWare were immune from covert channel attacks, but recent research has demonstrated that attacks are possible among virtual machines by using various signaling techniques [17].

Trojans

Trojan horses are programs that may appear to be legitimate but contain malicious code. Many can be spread by means of websites that download the Trojan with the contents of a web page. They may also be used in conjunction with **tracking cookies**, or install themselves on target systems and download other malware, or open up a communications channel and transmit information from the target system to an attacker's system. Some of these may consist of **keyloggers** that send a victim's keystrokes to an attacker. Among these are also remote access Trojans (or RATs) that enable attackers to take remote control of a target computer. Trojans and viruses may also deposit **logic bombs** or **time bombs** hidden within a program and set to activate under some condition, such as a date. When the date or event occurs, the malware attacks its target system.

Remote Control Systems

Remote control systems and root kits are related to Trojan horse and keylogger programs in the sense that they can take administrative control over a computer and network.

Anyone who has experienced having a remote administrator do configuration or repairs on his or her system with a technology such as Netop or Radmin has experienced the power of a remote control system. Although clearly these are useful for benevolent purposes, the potential for misuse is great.

Similarly, **root kits** are a collection of technologies that enable an escallation of privileges. These allow attackers to gain access to system functions changing user level to root (or Administrator on Windows) level, hence the name. Because of the *setuid* capability on UNIX-based systems, these are particularly vulnerable to root kits. Although root kits such as tOrn and Adore are mainly aimed at UNIX-type hosts (Linux and MAC/OS), there are also less common forms of root kits for Windows systems such as NTROOT, NTKap, and Nullsys. Using a root kit, attackers may be able to mask intrusions by overwriting legitimate commands, making it difficult for system and network administrators to detect the attack. In some cases, root kits are used for active attacks, whereas others are used for passive ones.

14.3 Monitoring Attacks—Tools of the Trade

If absolute security were attainable, we would only have to discuss threat prevention techniques. However, because security measures are bound to eventually fail or, more likely, be circumvented, the "remedial" functions of detection and recovery are necessary. Monitoring and auditing are more than a remedial function; they alert security personnel to threats and provide accountability and permit review, maintenance, and planning support. Of course, there are many computer attacks that we have not broached, but now that we have considered some of the more basic classifications of attacks against hosts, let's examine a few specific issues related to monitoring for attacks.

14.3.1 Monitoring Host Attacks

When attacks occur, administrators need to be able to detect them and be prepared to take appropriate actions to stem the damage. Part of these preparations includes having set and enforced security protections, both MAC/DAC, and staying alert to monitoring and intrusion detection systems, checking audit and authentication logs, and examining firewall and virus scanner reports. Administrators need to search systems for unauthorized or modified executable programs, shared files, malicious roaming files, suspicious network connections, and files and executables that might be part of a root kit.

Most modern operating systems have some in-built tools for monitoring system activities. In Windows, basic facilities are provided by the Task Manager. The Task Manager can be invoked by simultaneously pressing the <ctl> <alt> and <del> keys, which will bring up the Task Manager. Selecting the processes tab will show what processes are executing on the system. If any processes are unknown, doing a search of the Microsoft website or using a search engine such as Bing will bring up pages that describe the process and whether it is a potential security threat.

Another useful technique in security monitoring is to determine if there is a conspicuous resource consumption. Resources on a Windows system can be observed by selecting the Performance tab of the Task Manager and examining the resources consumed by processes running. Also looking at the Applications, Networking, and Users tabs will provide an important overview of the system activity. Windows event logs can be inspected for activities that are managed by the OS. This log can be viewed from the Control Panel, choosing Administrative Tools and then Computer Management. The logs will provide information about application and system errors, warnings, and informational events. By clicking on a line in the log, the tool will bring up a detailed record of the selected event.

Security permissions, such password protections, on Windows can be found by going to the Administrator Properties and examining local users and groups. Services and applications can be managed from the Computer Management function. This application will display brief descriptions of what the services do. This is a very important facility because turning off unnecessary services is one of the key aspects of hardening host computers, which we will discuss later. Local Security Policies (on some versions of Windows) can be viewed and created from the Policies application, and these include a password policy and account lockout policy for the machine. Windows has the ability to layer or nest security policies and test them for conflicts, which depends on the version of Windows one uses.

14.3.2 Intrusion Detection Systems

We may consider the anachronistic "Orange Book" approach to determining computer security and monitoring features such as C2 or B2 and so forth, but the practical fact is that the more security work that is done by an operating system, the less functional it tends to be. Most suppliers of OS attempt to reach a straddle point, an optimal compromise, but their main focus is on selling their products. The rest of the security job must be left to other technologies and techniques according to user or organizational needs.

As indicated then, intrusion detection systems (IDS) are extremely important parts of layered defenses. There are host-based and network-based intrusion detection systems as well as hybrids. A network intrusion detection system (NIDS) tries to detect malicious activity such as denial of service attacks, port scans or attempts to crack into computers by monitoring network traffic. We will cover this later in Network Security. On the other hand, a host-based intrusion detection system (HIDS) monitors the internals of a computing system (rather than its external interfaces) for intruders trying to carry out keystroke logging, botnet, or spyware activity. From a host security standpoint, we are interested in HIDS, such as Tripwire or OSSEC. These HIDS are focused on host security issues such as flagging changes in files systems or checksums, peculiar changes to the Windows Registry, and installation of "root kit" components.

In Focus

An IDS may look for anomalies (deviations from normal behavior), examine log files to find attack prototypical behaviors, or use signatures or patterns of previous types of attacks to match or statistically correlate whether a current event is an attack.

Some intrusion IDS use statistics to determine when patterns of activity deviate from a norm. Other IDS use heuristics (rules of thumb) to try to learn from past forms of attacks for making predictions about future attacks, and signature-based IDS rely on discovered attacks that are downloaded into the IDS database from the IDS supplier. Each has some advantages and disadvantages. For example, signature-based IDS are fairly reliable after an attack has been discovered and its patterns disseminated, whereas a heuristic-based IDS is more proactive and better at dealing with first-day attacks, but they also tend to create more false positives. False positives are legitimate activities that an IDS flags as an attack. This creates a situation where activities that should be allowed are prohibited because they "seem" to be like attacks. These "learning" systems typically ask a user (a *human in the loop*) to make a determination for a first instance of a new action; but people who are in a hurry to accomplish a task, or those who have become desensitized by many warnings, often press the "Accept" or "Okay" button, which will allow future similar attacks to be ignored [18] (**Figure 14.2**).

Firewalls have some features in common with IDS. Like IDS, host-based (or computer-based) based firewalls such as TPF (incorporated into the CA Internet Security Suite), Microsoft's embedded Defender firewall, McAfee, Norton, and Zone Alarm, each provide administrative facilities to block certain activities and write to activity logs. Virus scanning systems also create their own logs of threats, infections, and quarantines. For example, Spybot, Ad-Aware, AVG, and Superantispyware (which are freeware in minimal form with commercial-grade products for sale) store signatures of previous attacks in their databases and then search a system for a match. These are very effective in rectifying attacks that have matured somewhat—at least enough to be stored in signature databases.

In Focus

More is not necessarily better. If more than one firewall is installed, some firewall software may defend against other firewall software, allowing "real" threats to escape detection. The best advice for computer security purposes is to choose a single firewall technology carefully depending on needs, and then monitor it carefully.

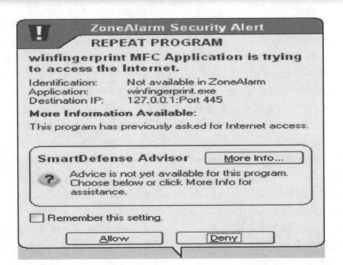

FIGURE 14.2

Security prompt example.

ZoneAlarm® and Check Point are either registered trademarks or trademarks of Check Point Software Technologies, Inc., a wholly owned subsidiary of Check PointSoftware Technologies Ltd., in the United States and/or other countries.

14.4 Assessing Systems Security

The purposes of assessing systems for vulnerabilities are to identify, and mitigate threat risks. Assessing systems involve conducting evaluations, performing testing, and attack modeling. These activities are part of an overall risk management strategy. Several key questions are asked during assessments, such as, what could happen; in other words, what is the threat event? How could it happen, or what is the attack mode? How severe would it be, or what is the threat severity? How possible is it, or what is the likelihood? How frequently might it occur? To accurately answer these assessment questions, managers and administrators must know how systems are configured and what information and software they contain. For instance, on a regular basis an inventory of host contents should be taken, and the materials should be labeled according to the security stance needed based on the sensitivity of the information, software, and the role that the system fulfills, such as whether it is used as a gateway, customer service representative PCs, an account system, a database server, or a general-purpose office computer.

14.4.1 Assessing the Information and System

We have covered some ways to assess computer systems, and in subsequent chapters, we will delve into more detail about how assessments are conducted by audit teams. In the context of computer security, audit teams are primarily interested in four factors: (1) determining the sensitivity of information on the computer, (2) determining the importance of the information, software, or computer, (3) assessing the costs of the assets—both tangible and intangible—and (4) making a determination of the risk potential, such as the visibility of the system to outside attackers and the number of users who have access to the system.

Determining sensitivity and importance of materials on a computer may be (and typically is) a qualitative process, but it can be made more objective by assigning a numeric value based on a set of criteria. For example, suppose we had customer information and product information in our database. On a Likert-type of scale from 1 to 10, with 10 being the most sensitive, we might assign the customer information a 7 (or maybe even 10 if it is HIPAA regulated), and our product information a 5. Or perhaps we might rate lower importance for commercial off-the-shelf (COTS) software if we have the original software distributions versus unique or one-of-a-kind software system.

As an illustration, although MS Office might be crucial to our work, if we have the media (software and documents) to reload in case of a problem, then we might lower the vulnerability assessment number; but if we have files (calculations from a program output) that are hard to reconstruct, then we might assess the information at a higher number. Or we might lower the importance of data if we have a recent backup compared to data that have had significant accumulation in between backups. Finally, the more visible a system, the more vulnerable it is. A back-office computer would probably be less visible than a main corporate system, and a main corporate system is probably less visible than a gateway system into a large corporation network.

One of the ways of determining costs, impacts, and risks to information systems is by using the Common Vulnerability Scoring System (CVSS), which is an open standard for describing the impact of system vulnerabilities [19]. CVSS defines three sets of criteria used in determining vulnerability: (1) base measures, which are the properties associated with a specific threat such as the actual or estimated impact of a confidentiality, integrity, or availability compromise; (2) temporal measures that are associated with how the threat changes over time—in other words, whether the threat increases or decreases with time— and (3) environmental measures associated with the threat such as the conditions under which the threat might be manifested or succeed. The three sets of threat criteria are multiplied to produce an overall vulnerability metric.

Other means of assessments may incorporate "spec sheets" that are issued as part of the ISMS standard BS 7799 Part 2:2002 and ISO/IEC 27001:2005 (the revised version of BS 7799 Part 2:2002) relative to codification of a computer security policy. *Spec sheets* are defined for best practices and certifications of information security management, ISO/IEC 27001 and the supporting family of ISO/IEC 27000 ISMS standards. If the enforcement of the policy in software passes the tests for conformance, managers are more reasonably assured of defensiveness, at least according to what is outlined in the security policies and coded into system controls.

In Focus

A layered defense system takes into account security, both in terms of breadth and depth. More specifically, the core systems are designed to protect the most fundamental and yet basic computing, whereas outer layers strive to filter the most prolific and common attacks.

14.4.2 Vulnerability Testing

Unlike the more static assessment of vulnerabilities using reviews and criteria, vulnerability testing actually involves carrying out attacks to see if a system can be breached. There are different names given to testing systems for vulnerabilities, and they include **red team tests**, **benign hacking**, and **white hat penetration testing**. Nevertheless, they each consist of analyses and tests of security controls to alert security personnel of the techniques that intruders might use and vulnerabilities found, and provide information for corrective measures. These tests among other things attempt to identify weak entry points, unpatched systems, backdoors, effectiveness of access controls, and firewalls. The purpose of vulnerability testing is to produce a thorough and complete set of estimates of threats and concomitant vulnerabilities. When a *red team* tests for vulnerabilities of a system, they often use the same tools hackers would use and follow typical sequences of attack patterns including foot printing, port scanning, and attempts to gain access with root kits, Trojan horses, crack programs, and monitors. For instance, they may begin by foot printing the corporate infrastructure, accumulating data regarding the equipment, and finding ways to intrude without the intrusion detection team detecting the activity (**Figures 14.3** and **14.4**).

The red team may start out with something as simple as the *whois* query to discover what information is provided about domain names and associated networks, and then zero in on specific targets using technologies such as Winfingerprint (see Figure 14.3), Nmap or Asmodeus to determine what services are offered by a system, what ports are

Winfingerprint
scanner example.

winfingerprint by vacuum is an open source project under GNU General Public License (GPL).

exposed, what the patch levels area, and what software is installed on the system. The red team may sift through the organization's website looking for a personnel directory or employee bios, which may prove useful if a hacker chooses to use social engineering to reach the attacker's objective. They may try to alter the URL to determine if error messages are rendered by a server that can be exploited by SQL injection or script attack. They may use crawlers, bots, or software agents to drill into the corporate information bases to obtain confidential information.

In some vulnerability testing, many of the operational personnel are not notified of the test to see whether or not the attacks and intrusions are detected, and whether security personnel are vigilant under normal operations. The red team may try to determine what audit files and system logs security personnel use for tracking activity in a network or on servers. The vulnerability test thus assesses the response effectiveness to determine if and how auditing is done, what forms of intrusion detection is performed, and other operational procedures.

14.4.3 Test Reports and Recommendations

After a system has been assessed and tested, reports of findings are generated for management. Based on what is found, the reports may make recommendations for procedures, policies, and/or technologies. For instance, if a weakness is found in the access controls, the audit team or the red team may suggest the use of a *reference monitor*, which is an access control mechanism that refers to an application that mediates all

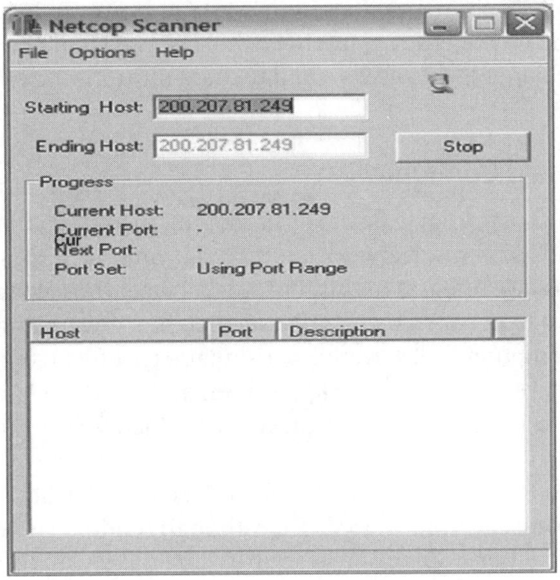

FIGURE 14.4

Netcop example.

accesses to objects by subjects, as noted earlier. That is to say, it is a service feature or technique used to permit or deny use of the components of a system, including the rights of individuals or applications to obtain or inject data into a storage device or transmission. The IBM Tivoli Privacy Manager is an example of a reference monitor. There are also many open source versions freely available.

Because the reports provide an evaluation of the company's security program and define the countermeasures recommended to be implemented to resolve weaknesses, the results of the audits and tests are sensitive and should be controlled so that only those who have a **need to know** can review the evaluation. Then management should assign to the appropriate personnel the responsibility to develop the implementation plan for the corrective measures that address any problems or weaknesses found. Often checklists are used for this to quickly identify the weaknesses to be resolved, and the checklist might serve as a baseline for future evaluations.

In addition to the assessment and test reports, security analysts typically produce a risk mitigation analysis and recommendation report. This report generally involves answering key questions such as, what can be done about the known vulnerabilities, how much will it cost to address the vulnerabilities, how effective are the recommended measures likely to be (estimated response efficacy), and are these measures cost-effective? Countermeasures will then be chosen and implemented to mitigate the risk and meet the company requirements within the cost/benefit framework the company has established.

14.5 Hardening Systems

The term "hardening systems" means *to make systems hard targets*. There are many ways that administrators and security personnel can make systems "hard targets," and how systems are hardened depends on their operating systems, the role or function the system fulfills in the organization, plus vulnerabilities in the system. However, in this section, we will present some of the more common methods that are used to make systems hard targets, such as removing dangerous software and turning off unneeded services (from both hosts and servers).

14.5.1 Ensuring a Trusted Configuration

Limiting or hiding systems is a primary means of hardening them, and therefore making them more trusted by inside systems. Network address translations (NATs) and subnets for hiding internal systems, are integral to this, but we will defer those techniques for hiding systems until we get to network security. Nevertheless, software and services can be hidden even if a host computer is discovered by using proxy software. Proxy software refers to modules that intervene between one application and another. As an example, *smap* and *smapd* are proxies for the UNIX *sendmail* system, which is very vulnerable to exploits.

The sendmail system on UNIX is an email transfer and delivery facility developed around the Simple Mail Transfer Protocol (SMTP). Although sendmail is very flexible, it is a monolithic system that has been prone to security holes and uses the dangerous *setuid* feature. The smap proxy intercepts incoming messages and stores them in a special directory on disk. Although smap must execute in privileged (kernel) mode, it does so only in that confined directory with actions that are profiled and logged. The smapd daemon scans the hidden directory, and after initially filtering the messages, sorts them for delivery to the appropriate accounts through the normal sendmail system, or it can send messages to specific programs or accounts where additional filtering rules are applied and virus scanners are run before delivery.

In addition to proxies for exposed services, such as email, hardening computers includes removing any software that is not required on that computer for the role that it fulfills. For example, there should be no development toolkits on gateway servers. Administrators should remove all *Guest* accounts, change default passwords, change the login ID for the Administrator on Windows systems, ensure that Windows *shares* are constrained, and make sure that the OS and applications patches are installed and kept up to date.

Turning off unneeded services is important to hardening, but the operative word is, *unneeded*. Turning off an important service can render a host inoperative. Needed services should be monitored and any changes or deviations from normal patterns should be investigated. This includes seemingly innocuous anomalies, such as what appear to be legitimate services that perhaps communicate over unconventional ports, or communicating in ways that are unexpected such as consuming large amounts of system resources (disk, processing, and/or network).

Another important hardening feature is to encrypt the data stored on disk. Even though cryptography is readily available and prescribed by companies, people do not always follow these directives. For example, in 2007, a letter was circulated by the Administaff Corporation that read in part: "On October 3, 2007, an Administaff laptop computer containing personal information including social security numbers, names and addresses of current and former Administaff worksite employees was reported missing. . . . The laptop computer is password protected; however, the personal information was not saved in an encrypted location, which is a clear violation of company policies" [20]. Such a violation of policy should never occur on a manager's watch, especially given that cryptographic tools are readily and freely available and easy to use, such as the Cyperix Cryptainer, which encrypts files based on AES (discussed in the chapter on cryptography) to obfuscate files on disk or with Microsoft's "lockers." With Cryptainer, a password is supplied to encrypt a file, and a hint is given in case the password is forgotten. To open a file, the correct password (and hence key) must be supplied.

Next, although some systems administrators purposefully change ports for systems from their defaults, such as web services that might normally be received at port 80 changed to port 8080, these should be known, documented, and monitored. Also, administrators should be aware of what should be running and using which protocol. For example, what might be a legitimate service using a TCP protocol might not be legitimate as a UDP protocol.

If corruption is discovered, the Windows OS offers a restore point for configuration management. Administrators need to review the disk space allocated to the restore and be aware of the consequences of restoration if a system becomes corrupted. The storage for the "change control logs" is set in the Control Panel under System, and then System Properties.

> **In Focus**
>
> If a computer becomes infected by a worm or a Trojan horse, doing a restore may not fix the problem because the worm or Trojan may have spread itself through files that are corrected when a restore is done. Also note that when a restore is done, all legitimate work is lost to the restore point, hence having a current backup is critical.

Services on UNIX-based machines such as Linux or MAC/OS are run as daemons, and many are started using the *cron* scheduling program as defined in the /etc/services file. Running the command *ps* as *root* (superuser) can show these services. On Windows, launching the Task Manager and examining the processes tab will show services. However, in both cases, not all services will be seen; nor will they be easily identified. An Administrator on Windows might be able to better identify services by launching the Services.msc from the start menu's *run* command, but this does not completely solve the problem either. Process monitors may be needed to find all the hidden processes that are running.

14.5.2 Password Protections

There is a cliché about the easiest way into a house is through the front door. The front door of computer systems is the login screen. Simple password protection mechanisms that are built into Windows and UNIX-based systems are often not sufficient to prevent a "crack" utility, or a man-in-the-middle attack, or using a capture and crack tool such as

Cain-and-Abel, from breaching these defense—even though great strides have been made in the Windows password facilities (described earlier) and in using shadow passwords in UNIX-based systems. If a system is exposed to a public interface such as the Internet, something more is needed for host hardening relative to password protection.

Improvements in securing passwords include one-time passwords, tokenized passwords, or various types of challenge-response passwords. A ***one-time password*** system creates a list of passwords in which one copy is stored on the host computer, another copy is given to the user (either electronically or on paper), and each subsequent login uses a different password from the list. One-time passwords generally cannot be guessed if the passwords are chosen at random or from a well-guarded source. The downside of one-time passwords is that they are quite inconvenient because the list must be consulted at each login and the list must be kept secure, and once the list is used up, a new list must be generated.

Leslie Lamport developed an interesting technique, circa 1980, which uses a server to keep a database of user logins. In this approach, the name of the user is used for authentication. An integer is decremented each time the user logs in, and a function is performed that produces a hash value of the password n times. This is called ***repeated hashing***. A simplified description of repeated hashing works as follows: If Mike wants to log in to Dan's machine, he supplies his username to Dan; Dan's machine then sends n to Mike. Mike's computer generates function, $fn-1$ (Mike's password), and sends that to Dan's machine (we will call this x). Dan's machine then computes $f(x)$, which is fn (Mike's password) and compares it to the entry in the database. If the entry in the database matches the result of $f(x)$, Dan allows the login, decrements n, and stores $fn-1$ (Mike's password) in the database.

S/Key is probably the most commonly recognized repeated hash algorithm, which was developed by Phil Karn. Other repeated hash algorithms have been developed using different hash functions, such as Message Digest 5, or MD5 (more about this when we get to ciphers and cryptography later).

In Focus

A one-way hash is a technique where a numeric code is produced using a key and a cipher based on some input—a message or a login. If something is altered in the message or password, it will not match the code that was produced by the original computation, and then the system (and user) will know.

14.5.3 User Authentication

Earlier we presented some aspects of how authentication is done via a native OS, but realize that there are other software add-ons to augment the process. Where user identification codes and passwords are used for identification, to harden a system, the user cannot be taken at his or her word, so the user must be authenticated (are you really who you say you are?). Of course a user in this sense is a process executing on behalf of someone and is not a real person. The electronic tokens in Kerberos (as mentioned earlier) is an example of this. From a Kerberos implementation view, tokens are devices that generate a password for the "real" user. Because an intruder can fake his or her way into a conversation, Kerberos precludes this by synchronizing the token with other computers in the communications, and then changes passwords on the devices at varied intervals measured in seconds. Although this technique makes it quite difficult for an imposter to fake the identity of an authentic user, the security of the system depends on the security of the token; and a lost token equates to a lost password [7].

As noted earlier, Kerberos is a popular method for authentication, but it is not the only one. Other authentication approaches exist including ***challenge-response*** schemes, which as with repeated hashing, the machine that a user attempts to log in to generates some specific information for use in subsequent communications. The information generated is processed as a *token* by the user or the user's system to provide a secret code used between the communicative parties. In that case, the user needs a physical security ID device, such as an RSA token that plugs into the computer. The code is only good to use once, or for only a short period of time (less than a few seconds). We will explore this concept in more detail when we cover cryptography.

14.6 Biometrics

Although biometrics is not strictly a host-only security countermeasure—that is to say, biometrics is also used to protect premises and access to network resources—it is appropriate for our discussion to introduce this topic here. First, however, realize that the term "biometrics" encompasses a huge field, not just what typically comes to mind, such as using fingerprints for authentication to allow entrance into a server room or on to a laptop computer; it also refers to scans and other physical characteristics used for all kinds of access. In this section, we will discuss biometrics as it relates to host computer security and the issues they raise.

14.6.1 Biometrics Acceptance

Many of us are already familiar with cardkeys, smart cards, and access tokens. For example, HDLock from Authenex uses a token, called *A-Key*, that plugs into a USB port on a computer such as laptop or notebook computer to protect it in the same way that a physical key protects a door or file cabinet. Without the A-Key, the computer's hard drive is encrypted and inaccessible. All of the encryption and decryption processes are automated and transparent using an AES-based encryption and two-factor authentication. HDLock is also available for use with a management server for enterprise deployment. This feature allows for greater key recovery options for users in a corporate environment. Although these types of devices are very helpful in protecting assets and access to information resources, keys can be lost or stolen, which makes it possible to duplicate, spoof, or masquerade, regarding encrypted data, so more secure means for authentication and identification have been sought.

Biometrics consists of the techniques used to either identify or authenticate people from a physical or physiological trait, and constitutes one of the many forms of ***strong authentication***. The use of biometrics is growing in both interest and in controversy. Despite some misgivings, biometric systems have the potential to identify and authenticate people with a high degree of certainty. Unlike some other forms of information, their natural representations are often not as readily intelligible as the various text forms of information. The increasing use of DNA as proof of a crime is one example where the public trust is on the increase in terms of confidence in human biometrics.

Identification and authentication in security operates based on (1) **_something you know_**, such as a password, (2) **_something you have_**, perhaps a token or smart card, and/or (3) **_something you are_**, a measurable trait, which might be a fingerprint or eye retinal scan. Biometric security operates on something you are (albeit it is arguable that you *have* a fingerprint rather than you *are* a fingerprint, but the terminology has become engrained in the security literature). In a biometric system, physical traits are recorded in a process known as **_enrollment_**, and these traits are subsequently verified against what is called a **_template_**—a digital representation of traits. The use of these technologies is for providing evidence (called a proof) that individuals are who they say they are, **_authenticity_** or **_identity verification_**, or they are used to identify certain individuals; that is, it means **identification**. The traits that are used can be fingerprints, eye retina, facial scans, gait (the way you walk), or some other unique physical characteristic. These technologies are being used to keep people out of (or permit only certain people into) rooms and to enable only authorized users to access a computer system [21].

14.6.2 Biometric Security Process and Information Protection

When someone is biometrically enrolled into a system, his or her biometric information, known as a template, is usually stored in a relational database and/or smart chip on a smart card. There is a trend, however, to store templates in a directory service such as X.500, LDAP, or Microsoft Active Directory. Thus, some of this information could be made available online and through a network, which elevates privacy concerns, and highlights the need for *securing* the security information. Some ways securing biometric data is done include access control lists (ACL), cryptography, and firewalls. One necessary component in particular is to have a trusted proxy between the storage of templates and the requests for them. Using this, method templates do not leave the trusted server, and on the proxy, ACLs govern the read and write access by authenticated requesters.

As mentioned before, biometric features are generally used for either identification or authentication. When they are used for identification, certain individuals are sought out, such as in the case where the police or intelligence agency might be looking for a particular individual. This is akin to the *black list* concept, where *all except* the identified entity are permitted to enter or access a resource. On the other hand, in biometric terms, authentication is the process of proving an identity. This is akin to the *white list* concept, where *only* identified entities are permitted to enter or access a resource.

The notion of **verification** is also an important part of the biometric usage process. Once someone has been enrolled, the presenter of a biometric credential is verified against a reference template. Performance of a biometric measure is usually referred to in terms of the **_false acceptance rate_** (FAR), **_false rejection_** (non-match) **_rate_** (FRR), and the **_failure to enroll rate_** (FTE or FER). The FAR is a statistical **_type 1 error_**, where the biometric system **_fails to reject a false positive identification_**; that is, it accepts an imposter. The FRR is a **_statistical type II error_**, where the biometric system **_rejects a positive identification_**; that is, it falsely rejects an authentic entity as an imposter [21].

The term biometrics has become most commonly associated with fingerprints and DNA, but biometrics may even range from how one may grip a handle of an object such as a pistol (the touch points) to how one walks (known as one's gait).

14.6.3 Biometrics and Errors

In studies of court testimonies [22], subjects have been shown to be more influenced when a "so-called" expert claims that the "DNA evidence suggests that there is a 90% match of the crime with the suspect" than when an expert states that, "in my expert opinion, I am 90% confident that the suspect did it based on my observations of his tendencies," even though both are dependent on the work of the *so-called expert*, even when the work might be substantially flawed [23, 24]. As with human-induced errors, biometric information technology is not foolproof in either the identification or authentication of people—no matter how much people believe in biometric evidence.

In practice, a biometric system's false acceptance rate (FAR) and false rejection rate (FRR) represent a tradeoff against other parameters. One of the most common of these parameters is the rate at which both acceptance and rejection errors are equal—that is, the **equal error rate** (EER), also known as the **crossover error rate**, or CER. The lower the EER or CER, the more accurate the system is considered to be under most circumstances. Both the enrollment and verification processes represent unique domains of complexity. Any number of problems can arise to compromise the veracity of either the enrollment or verification processes.

It is imperative that FAR, FRR, and in terms of enrollment, FTE, are balanced and within required tolerance levels to meet the objectives of the identification procedures, if the technology is to be effective. For instance, if a biometric system is going to be used to verify an individual (i.e., users will make claims of their identity), it is most important that false rejections (FRR) are minimized to allow the authorized person access to his/her resources, whereas if the biometric system is going to be used for authentications, then false acceptance rates (FAR) become the most important factor for consideration; we don't want to allow an impostor access to secure resources.

Increasingly, biometrics such as fingerprints or eye retina patterns are used for authentication. Biometric data are called a template. Errors in biometric authentication include failure to enroll, or FTE (meaning failure to create a template), false acceptance rate (FAR), and false rejection rate (FRR). In terms of authentication, if an imposter steals an employee's badge and tries to enter a secure area that has a biometric thumbprint system, FAR is most worrisome.

14.6.4 Biometric Errors and Technology

Available biometric technologies vary in terms of techniques and quality. Fingerprints are a common, and in fact the most widely used, biometric to date, especially in regard to computer access. There are many ways in which fingerprints can be analyzed, such as with what are called macro features that include ridge patterns, line types, and ridge count, or by what are called micro features or *minutia* that include spatial frequency of ridges and breaks in them, curvature or arcs of individual ridges, and position of ridges relative to one another.

Optical scanners use cameras and refracted light to detect fingerprint patterns and may be composed of metal-oxide semiconductors (CMOS), which are newer, or the older charge-coupled devices (CCD). Of the CMOS type, there are passive technologies that amplify rows and columns of pixels over an entire scanned image; or active, where each of the pixels implements its own amplification. The active mode is more expensive, but it is more accurate.

In addition to optical scanners, there are also silicon scanners that detect fingerprint patterns using electrostatic discharge. Silicon scanners also come in two forms: capacitive and thermal. Capacitive are the older of the two and use capacitors as sensors to generate signals representing the patterns, whereas thermal sensors do not use external signals. Instead they use body heat as the signal. Other technologies exist as well, such as radio frequency detectors, which use radio waves to image subcutaneous (below the skin surface) features. Some fingerprint scanning devices are better at scanning dry, less defined fingerprints, whereas others are better at greasy fingerprint types. Whether CMOS or CCD, or some other type of scanning, an important factor is the verification objective. Thus relative to fingerprints, for instance, the approach to verification is important [25].

As an example, people who work with their hands tend to have rougher and less defined fingerprints. These factors can influence the effectiveness of the approach to fingerprint verification, especially depending on the technology that the reader uses. Macro-patterns, such as fingerprint ridge patterns, junction areas, delta (difference) points, and other measures compared to micro (or minutia) verification patterns may be processed. However, the conditions of the verification will substantially affect the outcomes [26]. The types of algorithms (e.g., minutia, pattern, or hybrid) used in the verification represent the conditions under which FAR, FRR, and FTE will be manifest. Hence, the conditions and objectives must be carefully considered when choosing a biometric approach.

Next, determining whether a template, related security data, smart chips, networks and systems or their administration, or a given biometric algorithm has been compromised depends on a number of factors that can be assessed. But the assessment has to be balanced against the time-to-verify, FAR, and FFR metrics. In addition, measures must be taken to insulate and protect the various "touch points" of the technologies that can be breached, tampered with or spoofed, exploited, or compromised [21].

To a lesser extent than the use of fingerprints (although on the rise) is the scanning of the eye retina (which is in the back of the eye) and/or the iris (which is in the front of the eye), with the iris being relatively simple to encode (*templatization*) and therefore the more popular. Its uniqueness contributes to a very low FRR and FAR, and so it works quite well for both authentication and identification. Because the iris is behind the cornea and the liquid in the eye (aqueous humor) and located in front of the eye lens, the technology is useful in capturing unique iris patterns. For the most part (as of this writing, although this technology is advancing rapidly), monochromatic CCD, is the most popular. It "photographs" an image of the iris and produces a series of vector points among eye pattern features stored in the template that can be measured and compared.

14.6.5 Biometric Frontiers in Computer Security

In the use of eye-driven (iris or retinal) biometrics, someone looks into a camera and receives feedback on whether to move the camera up, down, left, right, closer, or farther away. Once the camera is appropriately positioned, a frame image is captured and the iris or retina is cast into a template. The image of the iris or retina is then captured in the template where it can be compared to any other using real-time imaging against the template with the commonly applied cryptographic *XOR* logic on the compared values. Then the corresponding mask bit vectors are used in a logical AND operation to verify that there are no differences affecting the comparison. These logical *XOR* and *AND* operations are used to compute a **Hamming distance**, which is a measure of dissimilarity between the two iris (or retinal) templates. The distance is then used to determine whether there is a match or not. Therefore, mathematically this process is both straightforward and relatively simple to compute, but it is not absolute [27].

The greatest resistance to using eye scans so far has been limited public acceptance, driven in particular by irrational fears about damage to the eye and, to a lesser extent, fears about invasion of privacy. There are other biometric techniques and technologies, but most of these others are done in arcane disciplines, and we will defer discussion of them at this point. Suffice it to say that when choosing a biometric, the technology chosen first needs to be accurate, but managers must also consider social and behavioral aspects.

The effectiveness of biometric technology is typically measured along several dimensions: (1) how well it uniquely describes an individual across a population, (2) the maturity of the biometric technology, (3) how easy it is to acquire a biometric for measurement, (4) the performance of the technology indicating the accuracy, speed, and robustness of the system, (5) the acceptance or approval of a biometric technology by the public in everyday life, and (6) how easy it is to bypass or circumvent the biometric system.

One way in which biometrics will likely affect many of us is in the use of biometric or e-passports in regard to giving up physical features for verification—but note that DNA verification is not far off in the future for this purpose. As far as our current systems go, technology will use fingerprints and a digitized picture of the photograph on the passport stored in a *smart chip*. The passport will have a watermarked layer that will destroy the passport if someone tries to tamper with the chip that is embedded in it [21]. Say, for example, when someone is at the airport returning from a trip abroad, in the future, he or she will have to step into a gate, place the passport into a tray that reads the smart chip, and will have to place a randomly selected thumb or other finger onto a reader.

These multiple authentication protocols will compare the digitized fingerprint with the one placed into the reader, and the facial scanner will compare the photographic facial image with the digitized image in the passport. Based on e-passports to date, the passports will probably also employ *radio frequency identification* (**RFID**). RFID is comprised of an antenna and a transceiver, which reads the radio frequency transmissions and relays information to a central processing device based on the emissions from a transponder (tag)—an integrated circuit containing the RF circuitry.

14.7 Secure Software and Systems SDLC

We have surveyed many of the technological issues regarding computer security, but now we need to address the security of the systems produced in the software development life cycle (SDLC) because programmers may introduce vulnerabilities or leave backdoor threats. Among the responsibilities that managers often have in many information or knowledge-based organizations are the development and implementation of software and hardware systems, which have a myriad of implications for information security. No matter the chosen method, if software is developed or systems implemented, there is a life cycle involved; and managers must ensure that there is a *security element* in these SDLC procedures. One of the issues relative to computer security is whether systems and technologies chosen are open source or are proprietary in nature. Open source systems are widely disseminated along with internal workings, such as software source code, which are viewable by the public. Proprietary systems are those in which the internal workings are kept secret. When software systems are proprietary, generally only the compiled executable is delivered to a user. Sometimes hackers use "reverse-engineering" techniques that disassemble the execute code in ways to expose the underlying source code. Programming languages that use intermediate compilers (or interpreters), such as JAVA or C#, are particularly susceptible to this.

14.7.1 Secure Systems Development

Managers need to realize the implications from technologies their programmers use, not just from the traditional points of view of extensibility and productivity, but also in terms of security. When attackers reverse-engineer software, they can steal or modify the code. In open source software, sometimes contributors leave backdoors (as in the case of a fairly recent attack on Linux), or because the inner workings are readily available for examination, hackers may study them to find weaknesses to exploit. Modifications to software may be used to create malware or viruses. In this way, the executing programs may look legitimate but have been modified to do malicious things. The Research into the Security of Operating Systems (RISOS) project found that several areas in common operating systems tend to yield the greatest number of vulnerabilities. Some of their findings included incomplete or inconsistent parameter validation in which interprocess communications between lower privileged processes were allowed to pass parameters to higher privileged processes that may lead to privilege escalation [7].

Other problems that were found included the implicit sharing of privileged data in which a process or user with greater privileges shared information with a process or user with lower privileges. Also, they found asynchronous validation or inadequate serialization of data where there was a violation of the assumption that certain processes would occur in a specified sequence, and thus had missing or inadequate authentication of users and processes, or had violable prohibition logic in which there was the possibility of corrupting the process stack or protected data space; and also exploitable logic errors including incorrect or missing error handling.

In most cases, software applications are developed for hosts. Although there are myriad software applications that can be purchased in the marketplace, our emphasis here is on internally developed or implemented commercial off-the-shelf (COTS) systems. Standards bodies and organizations have sought to create criteria and procedures for development life cycles—the most popular being CMMi, Six Sigma, and ISO900x. As discussed in earlier chapters, most management frameworks require the establishment and management of appropriate configurations to the information system. Conspicuously absent in ISO 27002, ITIL, COBIT, and NIST SP 800-53 is the recognition of the importance of change and configuration management to both the operation and the security management of computer information systems.

Behr, Kim, and Spafford [28] examined high-performing IT organizations that they defined as having high mean time between failures and low mean time to repair, early and consistent integration of security controls into IT operational processes, low numbers of repeat audit findings with less staff time devoted to compliance, and high efficiency related to server to system administrator ratios and low amounts of unplanned work. They found that high-performing organizations consistently supported an organizational mindset of change management and causality.

In subsequent studies benchmarking IT organizations by control use, the key control differentiation between high-performing organizations and others was the high use of change and configuration management controls. From an operational perspective, the high-performing organizations were completing 8 times as many projects as medium and low performers; were managing 6 times as many applications and IT services; were authorizing and implementing 15 times as many changes; when managing IT assets, had server to system administrator ratios 2.5 times higher than medium performers and 5.4 times higher than low performers; and had one-half the change failure rate of medium performers and one-third the change failure rate of low performers.

Based on this research, from a security perspective, breaches that did occur were detected sooner and were significantly less likely to result in financial, reputational, or customer loss. These organizations understood the importance of managing their information systems and the associated risks rather than letting the information system grow and change through a series of *ad hoc* additions and alterations. Although little is often done with respect to the threat environment, organizations should be able to manage the vulnerabilities in their systems. As stated in NIST SP 800-128, "Using configuration management to gain greater control over and ensure the integrity of IT resources facilitates asset management, improves incident response, help desk, disaster recovery and problem solving, aids in software development and release management, enables greater automation of processes, and supports compliance with policies and preparation for audits" [29].

14.7.2 Configuration Management

Configuration management (processes and technology used to cement a known system) is not the sole domain of the information systems department. In the manuscript *Quality Is Free*, Phillip Crosby [30] introduced the importance of management responsibility for the quality of organizational output. Central to this concept is "conformance to requirements" that requires an organization to measure and understand the consistency of its performance. This is also found in many quality improvement methods, including the popular Six Sigma strategy developed by Motorola in 1981 [31]. Let's put this in context with an example. Although our point deals with quality, consider that quality is a buffer for security. As a highlight, let us take for discussion purposes a useful analogy of a systems engineer working for an appliance manufacturer. The engineering team would design an appliance to meet a specific requirement. The prototype would likely be produced and tested to ensure compliance with both functional and safety requirements. Once the design of the system was approved, it would go into production and the engineering team would continue to work on refining the design of existing products or developing new ones. But what if the figures are *fudged*? If the engineer thought a change should be made to the production of an appliance, no one (usually) would run out to the production line and make a change. That is very costly!

Instead, the change was introduced in a test environment, the impact of the change to functional and safety requirements was evaluated, and only once it was approved would a change be made in the production line. One can only imagine the troubles manufacturers might have with their products if every engineer were able to make *ad hoc* changes at the last minute to the production line to an appliance on the assembly line. The same holds true for configuration and change management with respect to a computer system and software.

We can formally define configuration management as ". . . a collection of activities focused on establishing and maintaining the integrity of products and systems, through control of the processes for initializing, changing, and monitoring the configurations of those products and systems. The practice of configuration management is implemented through the establishment of the baseline configuration" [22]. A discrete target of the configuration control process is a configuration item (CI), whereas the formally defined and agreed-upon initial configuration of a CI is called the ***baseline configuration***.

All of these descriptions seem to exist for technical reasons, but they have been instituted for really good reasons. Let's use two examples to highlight, one related to productivity and error, and the other related to security. Suppose programmer *A* wants to insert a bug fix Z by adding the following line (in the programming code written in "C"): `ps->` `amt`, where *ps* is a pointer (an address) to a data structure in memory such that *ps* can store a member of that data structure *amt*, and then in "C" the programmer or attacker might be able to change the amount!

This may seem quite ridiculous as a real-life scenario, but consider that a person who worked at a major banking institution in the 1980s wrote a program that did something just like this by adding rounded fractions (upwards) and deposited those fractions into his own personal bank account. It wasn't until the IRS suddenly noticed (years later) that the programmer was a millionaire without an auditable trail such as paying taxes that the government started to question what had happened.

CHAPTER SUMMARY

Password protection schemes, access controls and control lists, file protections, and other security mechanisms that we have discussed up to this point constitute the basic preventive measures to help protect host computer systems. But we must combine these basic protections using firewalls to build a moat. However, all of these mechanisms must still be maintained, and security administrators and managers must stay vigilant. This typically requires frequent software updating to ensure that systems are running the latest versions of applications and that patches are kept up to date. This occurs both when new exploits are identified, which need to be blocked, and also when problems occur in the interactions between the host and widely deployed applications. Moreover, good anti-virus packages are just as important as firewalls. These too must be updated regularly because new viruses and spyware are constantly emerging.

Important concepts in host computer security involve host hardening and the use of application-layer firewalls. Along with these countermeasures, we find the use of access controls, and increasingly, the use of biometrics in these controls. As information collection about people grows in order to enact the security controls, companies have an ethical responsibility to exercise due care and due diligence in protecting information about employees and consumers. Beyond the organizational security issues raised by these efforts, managers must keep in mind the larger picture. Given recent security breaches at companies such as ChoicePoint and other information repositories, the collection and dissemination of information about individuals carries with it additional security risks. The ***Identity Theft and Assumption Deterrence Act of 1998*** makes the theft of personal information with the intent to commit an unlawful act a federal crime in the United States with penalties of up to 15 years imprisonment and a fine up to $250,000. The act designates the Federal Trade Commission to serve as an advocate for victims of identity fraud. The U.S. Department of Justice estimates that 1 in 3 people will become victims of identity theft at some point in their lifetime, and leakage of personal information from central information repositories continues to exacerbate both the potential and severity of the damage to persons and industry. Managers have a responsibility to their organizations in terms of security, but these larger issues, such as social responsibility, are also very important to consider.

THINK ABOUT IT

Topic Questions

14.1: In Windows, what is responsible for user account databases required by the LSA?

14.2: In Windows, what handles access permissions and denials, and the level of access permitted or denied?

14.3: A class of attack that attempts to keep legitimate users from accessing systems and resources is called what?

14.4: A _____ _____ begins by determining the location and objectives of an attack.

14.5: These enable attackers to gain access to system functions through the escalation of privileges:

_____ Tivoli

_____ Root kit

_____ Nmap

_____ Cookies

14.6: An access control that mediates access to objects by subjects is a:

_____ Software proxy

_____ Biometric token

_____ Transaction manager

_____ Reference monitor

14.7: In biometric access control, FAR means a legitimate user was rejected.

_____ True

_____ False

14.8: Recording physical traits in biometrics is called:

_____ FRR

_____ Enrollment

_____ Template

_____ FTE

14.9: Encoded physical biometric traits are called:

_____ Template

_____ Trait record

_____ Biometric record

_____ Element

14.10: A company may hire a "red team" to try to hack into company systems to test for vulnerabilities.

_____ True

_____ False

14.11: The authentication system that is used by Microsoft (and invented at MIT) is:

_____ CHAP

_____ MD5

_____ Kerberos

_____ IDEA

14.12: Access control in Windows is handled with:

_____ ACE

_____ Active Directory

_____ TPM

_____ Registry

14.13: The Windows object manager controls process access to system resources and objects.

_____ True

_____ False

14.14: Windows login and the SAM are mediated by:

_____ ACE

_____ Registry

_____ MSA

_____ LSA

14.15: Which act makes the theft of personal information with the intent to commit an unlawful act a federal crime in the United States with penalties of up to 15 years imprisonment and a fine up to $250,000?

Questions for Further Study

Q14.1: Write four examples of how biometrics can be used for authentication.

Q14.2: Explain one case where FFR is more severe than FAR, and one where FAR is more severe than FFR.

Q14.3: Discuss host hardening and provide some specific examples of how to harden a system you are familiar with.

Q14.4: Pick one type of attack classification mentioned in this chapter, and give an example of how such an attack is carried out.

Q14.5: For the attack example given in Q14.4, provide an example of how such an attack can be prevented.

KEY CONCEPTS AND TERMS

Attacks can be divided into passive and active.

Authorization is the process of allowing a validated user to perform a function legitimately.

HIDS are systems that detect intrusions into a computer.

Identification is the process of validating a user.

Identification and **authentication** in security operates based on (1) something you know, such as a password, (2) something you have, perhaps

a token or smart card, and/or (3) something you are.

References

1. Solomon, M. G. (2011). *Security strategies in Windows platforms and applications.* Sudbury, MA: Jones & Bartlett Learning.
2. de Medeiros, B. (2005). *Windows security: A synopsis on host protection. A whitepaper.* Tallahassee: Florida State University.
3. Tanenbaum, A. S. (2008). *Modern operating systems.* Upper Saddle River, NJ: Pearson/ Prentice Hall.
4. Silberschatz, A., Galvin, P.B., & Gagne, G. (2007). *Operating system concepts with Java.* New York, NY: John Wiley & Sons.
5. Deitel, H.M., Deitel, P.J., & Choffnes, D. R. (2004). *Operating systems.* Upper Saddle River, NJ: Pearson/Prentice Hall.
6. Elmasri, R., Carrick, G. A., & Levine, D. (2010). *Operating systems: A spiral approach.* Boston, MA: McGraw-Hill.
7. Tjaden, B. C. (2004). *Fundamentals of secure computer systems.* Wilsonville, OR: Franklin, Beedle & Associates.
8. Labmice. (2009). Kerberos in windows authentication. Retrieved September 12, 2009, from http://labmice.techtarget.com/security/kerberos.htm
9. Cooke, P. (2009, March). Windows 7 security enhancements. Retrieved October 29, 2011, from http://technet.microsoft.com/en-us/library/dd560691.aspx
10. CERT. (2010). *Vulnerability note VU# 117394: Buffer overflow in core Microsoft Windows DLL.* Retrieved October 10, 2010, from http://www.kb.cert.org/vuls/id/117394

11. Microsoft. (2010a). *Microsoft security bulletin MS03-007: Unchecked buffer in Windows component could cause server compromise (815021)*. Retrieved October 10, 2010, from http://www.microsoft.com/technet/security/bulletin/ms03-007.mspx

12. Eddon, G., & Eddon, H. (1998). *Inside distributed COM*. Redmond, WA: Microsoft Press.

13. Sessions, R. (1998). *COM and DCOM*. New York, NY: John Wiley & Sons.

14. LaMacchia, B. A., Lange, S., Lyons, M., Martin, R., & Price, K. T. (2002). *.NET framework security*. Boston, MA: Addison-Wesley.

15. Microsoft. (2010b). *COM+ and security*. Retrieved October 10, 2010, from http://msdn.microsoft.com/en-us/library/ms681314(VS.85).aspx

16. Solomon, M. G., & Chapple, M. (2005). *Information security illuminated*. Sudbury, MA: Jones and Bartlett Publishers.

17. Stivers, J. (2009). *Covert channel communications by signaling virtual machines*. Unpublished thesis. Melbourne: Florida Institute of Technology.

18. Workman, M. (2008). A test of interventions for security threats from social engineering. *Information Management & Computer Security, 16*, 463–483.

19. Rasheed, H., & Chow, R. Y. C. (2009). Adaptive risk-aware application-level access control. *International Conference on Security and Management, SAM'09, 1*, 10–16.

20. Workman, M., Bommer, W. H., & Straub, D. H. (2008). Security lapses and the omission of information security measures: An empirical test of the threat control model. *Journal of Computers in Human Behavior, 24*, 2799–2816.

21. Reid, P. (2004). *Biometrics for network security*. Upper Saddle River, NJ: Pearson/Prentice Hall.

22. Tversky, A., & Tuchin, M. (1989). A reconciliation of the evidence on eyewitness testimony: Comments on McCloskey and Zaragoza. *Journal of Experimental Psychology, 118*, 86–91.

23. Ajzen, I. (1977). Intuitive theories of events and the effects of base rate information in prediction. *Journal of Personality and Social Psychology, 35*, 303–314.

24. Tversky, A., & Shafir, E. (1992). Choice under conflict: The dynamics of deferred decision. *Psychological Science, 3*, 305–309.

25. Ohkubo, C., & Muraoka, Y. (2005). *Biometric authentication using PKI* (Vol. 1, pp. 446–450). The proceedings from the Conference on Security and Management, Las Vegas, Nevada.

26. Simms, J., & Butt, L. G. (1996). *Fingerprinting techniques*. Cambridge, MA: Harcourt Press.

27. Wayman, J. L. (2009). Biometrics. In H. Bidgoli (Ed.), *Handbook of computer networks* (pp. 539–552). Hoboken, NJ: John Wiley & Sons.

28. Behr, K., Kim, G., & Spafford, G. (2004). *The visible ops handbook: Starting ITIL in 4 practical steps*. Eugene, OR: IT Process Institute.

29. Johnson, A., Dempsey, K., Ross, R., Gupta, S., & Bailey, D. (2010). *Guide for security configuration management of information systems*. Gaithersburg, MD: Computer Security Division Information Technology Laboratory National Institute of Standards and Technology (NIST), SP 800–128.

30. Crosby, P. (1980). *Quality is free*. New York, NY: Mentor Books.

31. Tennent, G. (2001). *Six Sigma: SPC and TQM in manufacturing and services*. Burlington, MA: Gower Publishing.

Network Security

N OW THAT WE HAVE A FOOTING IN NETWORKS from the previous section, we will discuss key issues in securing them. Network security is one of the primary defenses against an information system (IS) attack. Managers involved with information technology along with network administrators need to understand the kinds of threats that can be posed against network infrastructure and the information assets they interconnect. Important features of a secure network include ensuring redundancies and avoiding single points of failure, creating filters and *choke points* throughout the network fabric, utilizing data hiding techniques such as tunneling and virtual private networks (VPNs), and using cryptography and digital signatures. In this chapter, we will review these techniques for both wired and wireless networking, and we will present how attacks are carried out, and various countermeasures available to help prevent them.

Chapter 15 Topics

This chapter:

- Describes threats to networks and the CIA issues these present.
- Discusses point-to-point versus end-to-end security.
- Examines IPv6 security features, and how some aspects can be retrofit into IPv4.
- Explains security countermeasures for networks.

Chapter 15 Goals

When you finish this chapter, you should:

- ❑ Have an understanding of the relationships between knowing how network technologies work and how to prevent network attacks.
- ❑ Be able to explain link-to-link security compared to end-to-end security.
- ❑ Have an understanding of the main classifications of network attacks, along with some of the technologies and techniques used in carrying out network attacks.
- ❑ Be familiar with and able to explain network security, and what that entails.
- ❑ Be able to describe what a VPN is at a conceptual level.

15.1 Protecting Networks from Being Undermined

The security of information systems depend on defending them from *exterior* and *interior* threats. Interior threats can be more worrisome than exterior ones because attackers from the inside are already past the first line of defenses. Network security deals with all the access points into information systems from inside and out. In this regard, we are interested in what sorts of accesses can take place, by whom, when, and where, and knowing how to implement defensive *countermeasures*.

Wired networks are a little easier to secure than wireless ones [1]. For example, an attacker may go to a public place such as an airport and create a fraudulent "free Wifi hotspot" and wait for victims to connect. Although the victims use the perpetrator's system (sometimes called an evil twin) for their web surfing and accessing their email accounts, the communications are intercepted, including confidential information and perhaps passwords. To help defend against this threat, savvy wireless users ensure the veracity of a service provider before they connect. Also, wireless users are increasingly astute in the use of encryption, although many continue to use the Wireless Equivalent Privacy (WEP), which is fairly easy to break [2], rather than the Wifi Protected Access (WPA) or its successor, WPA2, which are more difficult to break (we will cover encryption later in the chapter on cryptography). At least in a wired environment, company administrators have more control over the access points.

15.1.1 Threats and Network Security

Threats to network security fall into four primary categories: (1) *Masquerade* is where applications are disguised as legitimate applications, or where illegitimate users pretend to be legitimate ones, (2) *interception* is where information is captured in-transit, (3) *modification* is where a hacker may change data values, such as in scripts or data destined for a database, and (4) **interruption** is designed to prevent legitimate user access to resources and information. The objectives of network security countermeasures are (1) to **verify** and **maintain** user **authenticity** to protect from masquerade, (2) to help **maintain** the **privacy** and **integrity** of information from the interception and modification threats, and (3) to **maintain** the **availability** of resources [3].

In considering these threat categories, let's reflect on what we have learned about how networks function; for example, we have covered layering and encapsulation performed by TCP/IP networks. The process of encapsulation is to embed information from one layer into the payload of another layer in the protocol stack. A **staging area of attack** reflects the point at which an attack is launched, which can refer to a computer platform or to a layer in the protocol stack. Recall from our previous chapter on network protocols that a particular network protocol acts upon a given layer, passing its information upwards or downwards through **service access points** (**SAP**). In this scheme, at the application layer, data are placed into a packet and a header appended, which is passed down to the next layer, and the process continues, until at the frame layer, the packet is passed over the network to the destination where the process is reversed.

At each router along the way, the IP header is inspected to see where to route the packet. When a packet arrives at its destined network, the ingress routers look for the applicable host. If subnets are used, a mask is further applied to locate the destination network before locating the appropriate system. Once at the destined host, a connection is established on a given port by means of a socket, which consists of a software mechanism and a set of data structures and system calls that logically ties the communications between two end-points via their IP addresses and port number pairs. As illustrated then, during data communications, there are many layers and staging points where attacks can be launched.

> **In Focus**
>
> The first lines of defense of information security are at the entry points from exterior networks, followed by the protection of information as it traverses over network fabrics. In terms of network security, the two fundamental countermeasures against attacks are **cryptography** and **firewalls**.

Also, attacks can be carried out **passively** or **actively**. Passive types of attack are those designed to be stealthy, and include eavesdropping, whereas active attacks are more like open warfare, and include port flooding or sending a victim malware such as a virus. For obvious reasons, the passive form of attacks are the most difficult to defend against, partly because their stealth makes them hard to detect.

To understand network security, we must distinguish between **link-to-link** and **end-to-end** security. Link-to-link security covers the physical layer through the network layer of the OSI model. This equates to the IP layer of the TCP/IP stack (**Figure 15.1**). End-to-end security extends from the transport layer of the ISO model (which is at the TCP or UDP layer) up to the application layer. Routers can be used to perform both link-to-link and end-to-end security, but hosts generally only perform end-to-end security. Securing

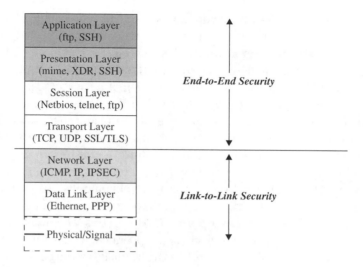

FIGURE 15.1

Security protocol
stack—ISO model.

links means relying on having a secure transmission medium, whereas securing end-points means assuming link levels are insecure and compensating by using layered defenses (such as cryptography) at the source host and destination.

> **In Focus**
>
> The reality is that link-to-link security is not practical outside a physically controlled location. Robust security involves end-to-end mechanisms. This leaves certain aspects of network information exposed to various threats such as traffic analysis where an attacker might be able to infer the types of communications by intercepting and examining the header information in the IP packets, as one example.

15.1.2 Attacks and Tools

There are many available tools that can be used legitimately for network and system analysis and for finding vulnerabilities to patch; however, some can also be used to instigate attacks. Open source tools such Asmodius, Netcop, Nessus, or Winfingerprint are useful for finding vulnerabilities to use in hardening systems against attackers—for example, to scan systems and networks for vulnerabilities attackers might exploit.

A type of network monitor, colloquially called a ***packet sniffer***, has legitimate purposes such as finding sources of LAN congestions, but these can be used for ***interception*** and ***release of message contents*** in which information is covertly captured from packets traveling over a network. Even if encryption is used in the upper layers of the message, these may still be used in ***traffic analysis***, which is a technique used to determine patterns in communications from the kinds of communications and frequency, and based on types and sizes of packets traversing back and forth between particular network end-points or IP addresses.

In Focus

Traffic analysis was one of the techniques the allies used in finding Yamamoto's airplane to shoot it down during World War II [4].

Attacks over the airwaves are becoming more common with the proliferation of wireless networks and sophisticated 3G and 4G smart phones, and new sets of vulnerabilities are being created in devices such as the iPhone, Android, and Blackberry. These are becoming targets for a growing list of viruses and Trojans, and because wireless networks are broadcast systems, just as with a shared LAN network bus, the data are distributed through the air to multiple unintended recipients who have a receiver [5].

Technologies such AirSNORT (SNORT) or Wireshark (formerly Ethereal), or Cain & Abel, which are designed for testing systems for vulnerabilities to create countermeasures, are also capable of gathering broadcast transmissions through the air or over a wire and displaying their contents to unauthorized parties (**Figure 15.2**). Used in this way, we refer to these technologies as **sniffers**. Packets captured by attackers may contain user login names, passwords, and proprietary information transiting the network as **plaintext** or **cleartext**.

In addition to the threats from stealing information as indicated, there is the potential for **destruction** of systems. Destruction may come from viruses and the like, or as a

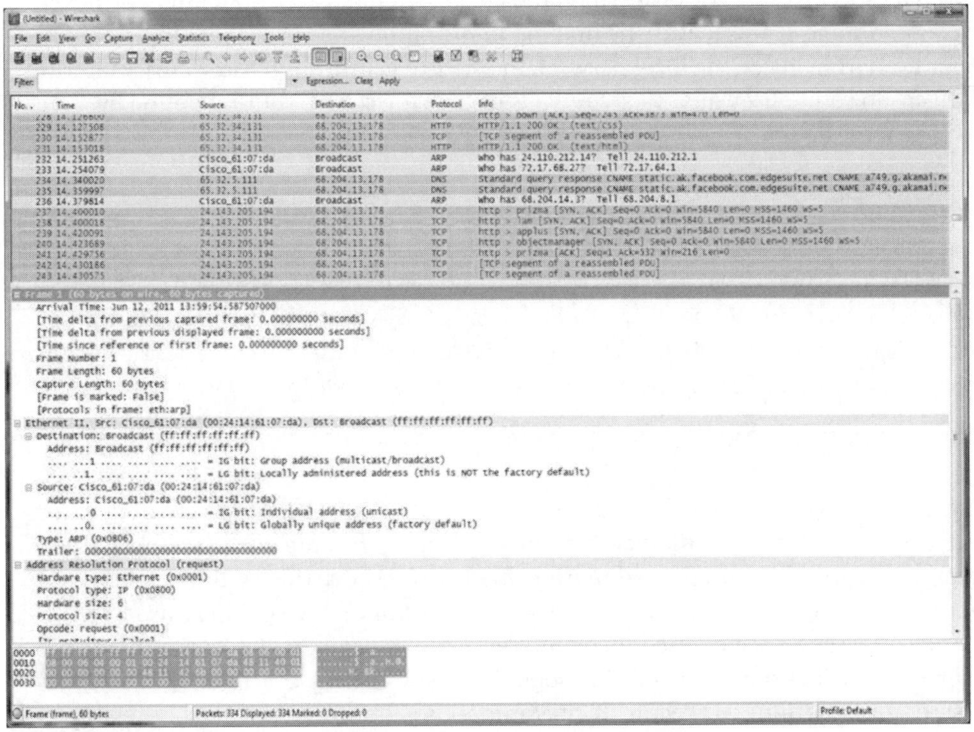

FIGURE 15.2

Wireshark network monitor example.

Wiresharktm® and the "fin" logo are registered trademarks of the Wireshark Foundation. It is an open source project under GNU General Public License (GPL).

denial of service (**DoS**) attack or **distributed denial of service** (**DDoS**) attack. DoS or DDoS can take on many forms, but generally they involve either sending more packets than a system can handle or sending packets that are too large for a system to store or buffer while the system tries to process them, causing an input buffer to overflow with data. In another type of DoS attack, the perpetrator may send a series of requests for a connection to the server from a façade. When the server responds with an acknowledgment and tries to establish a session, it cannot locate the system that made the initial request. By inundating the server with these unanswerable session requests, perpetrators may cause the server to slow down to a crawl or even crash [6].

15.1.3 Some Attack Classifications and Examples

Redirection is a type of attack that comes from the ICMP *Redirect* message in which an ICMP packet is sent to a host causing it to change its route table, redirecting packets to a furtive system. This attack is often used in combination with DoS where a legitimate host is brought down, and traffic is rerouted to a façade before the legitimate host is brought back online. In such cases, the damage is often done before corrective measures can be taken. To prevent this type of attack, in most cases administrators configure routers and firewalls to prevent inbound ICMP packets, but this is not always practical.

Also, in most cases, the paths that packets travel through the Internet (or other network) are determined by route tables in the routers along the paths. However, **source routing** may specify the route over which the packet should travel. Sometimes attackers may take advantage of this feature by making information appear to come from a trusted source or even from inside the local network in order to get through the security filtering mechanisms in router firewalls. Most firewalls disable the source routing option by default, but some do not.

In Focus

The Secure Shell, or SSH, is an example of a countermeasure. SSH works in the topmost three layers of the OSI model. Its encryption services are considered presentation layer protocol entities because they deal with data rendering. The session layer starts and ends connections and maintains synchronization between client and server. Although SSH is one layer of defense against some of the types of threats, it has several weaknesses that can be exploited. One example is for an attacker to modify the SSH packet (called a malformed packet) directed at a system causing it to crash.

IP session hijacking is another technique that enables an attacker to conduct reconnaissance against a target by intercepting and examining the data packets as they traverse a network. In highjacking an IP session, the attacker may force the legitimate user's session to disconnect and then masquerade as (impersonate) the legitimate user. The victim may only see a session disconnect and reattempt to login, which can be denied if the application does not allow multiple logins, or allowed if it does. In either case, the perpetrator may continue to execute illicit commands [7].

Similarly, **HTTP hijacking** (man-in-the-middle attack) can be done using toolkits that are widely available in the open source community such as Achilles. Using these tools, an attacker may change the HTML or script variables during the highjacked session. Web pages that perform client-side validation or other processing in the client are particularly vulnerable to this kind of attack; along with having an increased potential for severe damage caused.

15.2 Know Thy Enemy's *Modus Operandi*

We have provided some general categories with some specific kinds of attacks, and some examples of tools and basic techniques to deter them, but in reality, attacks are often perpetrated in combinations of actions. One general attack sequence assumes a target has already been identified and so the attacker is ready to begin his or her attack as a series of actions. In the most general and usual case, this approach begins with reconnaissance and attack preparations, and then evolves by sorting through vulnerable targets to ultimately carry out an attack on a chosen target.

Oriyano and Gregg [3] described the rationale for such attacks and characterized them as including (1) the *no harm–no foul fallacy*, in which attackers presume that a security breach is okay if no damage is done, (2) *security breach as a game reasoning*, where it is assumed that if a victim did not protect him or herself, then it must be okay to attack, (3) *law-abiding citizen reasoning*, in which attackers assume that which is not illegal is okay (regardless of ethics), (4) *invincibility reasoning*, where attackers presume that because technologies are value neutral and security technologies are freely available through open source, it is up to people to protect themselves; and if they don't, victims assume they are invincible and attackers feel obligated to prove otherwise, (5) *stealing candy from a baby reasoning*, which is where attackers assume that because it is easy for attackers to breach their security, the victims must not care about the consequences, and (6) attacks that are part of an *open information and open source movement* where the culture shares the belief that information should be free and no one should have to pay for it.

15.2.1 Reconnaissance and Attack Preparations

Footprinting and scanning are the sequence of events and actions (reconnaissance) that stem from the identification of the target, such as an organization [6]. At this stage, the attacker will need to gather information about what systems are accessible, the addresses used by those systems, and how those systems are interconnected. In this process, an attacker gathers information about a networked system to determine how to carry out an intrusion. To accomplish this, the attacker will utilize a variety of tools, both active and passive, in an effort to identify vulnerabilities, determine what services are running on systems, and how they are protected. The search for information about the systems can begin with examining company websites to identify names, links, partnerships, and changes that might be useful for carrying out an attack. Standard email address formations give clues as to the username forms whereas links to partnerships on a website can expose possible alternative entry points through exploitation of a trusted relationship.

Organizational changes such as mergers and acquisitions are important indicators of potential disruptions, as the attacker might be able to capitalize on the organizational upheaval. If new personnel are being introduced or significant changes to systems are occurring, the attacker may know that individuals in the organization are likely to assume any new face or name that is related to the change. The attacker can take the opportunity to socially engineer the employees into doing things ranging from releasing confidential information to establishing new accounts for the attacker.

In the case of a technical infrastructure change, if the changes are being made in an uncontrolled and untested manner, the attacker has the opportunity to capitalize on poorly configured systems. A key goal for the attacker at this stage is to gather as much information as possible about the systems, the standards used for the systems, and the individuals who use and manage the systems in order to prepare for subverting authentication mechanisms.

In Focus

We have mentioned poor configurations often. The specifics of configuration are device dependent and detailed. Although we will not enumerate "good" configurations in depth, we will discuss characteristics of "good" configurations versus "poor" ones in the final section of this textbook. For now, realize that poor configurations may mean leaving open ports or servers running for unneeded or unmonitored services, or missing an important filter rule in a router.

In addition to identifying systems, the attacker can begin to utilize the standards inherent in the management of the Internet and networking protocols to derive more information. This *network enumeration* includes getting a list of domain names and addresses assigned to the organization by querying the appropriate regional registrars. Through the Internet Assigned Numbers Authority (IANA) and InterNIC (the Internet's Network Information Center), an attacker can identify which IP blocks have been allocated to the organization, the Domain Name Service used to translate between domain names and IP addresses, and often the name, telephone number, address, and email address of the system administrator responsible for managing the system. This is important because the administrator may not adhere to best practices and utilize the same credentials for privileged access [8].

15.2.2 Enumeration

Once the attacker has information about the IP addresses assigned to the organization and the DNS servers that the organization uses, the attacker can start to query the servers and hosts on the system for more information. As stated previously, in the IPv4 environment and the IPv6 transition environment, the security model has focused on using firewalls to limit network ingress and egress traffic from a network segment. The biggest divide tends to be between the organization's internal network and the systems placed outside the internal network designed to be accessed by the general public.

In Focus

Normally placed between two firewalls controlling server traffic from both the internal network and the public Internet, a special de-militarized zone (DMZ) is usually created where web, DNS, and mail servers are often located. Because they exist in the special place between the internal network and the Internet, they are prime targets for attackers to gain a foothold in the organization's systems and for information gathering.

In general an attacker will attempt to contact all the IP addresses assigned to the organization to see which have hosts that will respond. Once this scanning has produced a group of hosts, the attacker can attempt to scan each host to see what services, if any, it offers. By connecting or attempting to connect to services on a host, the attacker can often determine from how the host responds, which operating system it is running, and which version of the service is currently installed. Through these connections, the attacker can also often enumerate valid resource information and account names. With this information in hand, the attacker is prepared for the next step, identifying vulnerabilities [9].

15.2.3 Sorting Out the Targets and Gaining a Foothold

With the knowledge gained from the footprinting, scanning, and enumeration, the attacker is ready to sort out the most vulnerable targets and modes of attack. The goal at this stage is often to initially gain a foothold in the system, normally unprivileged, and then to elevate these privileges to a superuser or administrator status through additional measures. If the attacker is successful in determining authentication information, or if a resource does not require authentication, the attacker may already have a foothold on the system and will only need to find a way to elevate his or her privileges. If not, the attacker will need to find a way on to the system and to achieve the privilege level necessary to accomplish whatever malicious goal the attacker has in mind.

In Focus

Simply making a connection with a system will yield a significant amount of information about the systems (in both directions) via the header information and any hand shaking that is done. For instance, connecting to a web server will allow that server to collect cookies stored on the client, and the server tells the client what type of server (e.g., Apache) is running, including versions.

Finding a way on to the system will require the attacker to consider what vulnerabilities may exist in the system and how they can be exploited. This may be by way of poor or improper configuration allowing the attacker to gain a list of username/encrypted password pairs that the attacker can then attempt to exploit. The attacker may take advantage of poor password choices by individuals, or may craft packets in such a way as to take advantage of a flaw in the system or application software, forcing the system to execute code of the attacker's choosing. Regardless, at this point the attacker will identify vulnerabilities in the system, develop a plan to exploit those vulnerabilities, and sequence the vulnerability exploitation to achieve the level of access or effect desired.

15.2.4 Target Exploitation

Once the attacker has developed the attack plan, it's time to put it into action. Although it is possible that a system administrator may have identified the attacker earlier, the reality of the Internet environment today is that scans and probes are so ubiquitous due to automated attack code that it is rare that a system administrator will pay much attention to any particular one. This leaves open the possibility that a network or security administrator may miss the trigger of an actual exploitation by pure oversight.

The use of an intrusion detection and prevention systems (IDS/IPS) at both the network and host levels becomes critical to help thwart exploitation. Whereas an automated attack is often indiscriminate, a professional attacker will take a broader view of the target system. In particular, this means that a determined attacker will look at partners and trust relationships and capitalize on them to gain access to the target. As a manager, it becomes important not just to manage the system security within the organization, but also to specify the security requirements for partners before establishing trust relationships.

15.3 Network Security Issues—Link to Link

At this point, we have broadly covered link-to-link and end-to-end security concepts and methods that attackers use to get around these. It is time to dig deeper into the details of attacks before we elaborate on defensive counter measures. In this section, we will step through the layers of the network stack to identify potential vulnerabilities and ways the vulnerability can be exploited. This is not intended to present a comprehensive examination of all vulnerabilities and exploits, but rather to highlight some common ones. To explore these vulnerabilities further, especially as an import into an automated security system, see the Common Vulnerabilities and Exposures (CVE) database hosted by Mitre (http://cve.mitre.org).

15.3.1 Connection Layer Security Issues

The lower layer protocol most often associated with TCP/IP is the IEEE 802.3 standard, commonly known as Ethernet, as we have discussed. Ethernet is typically used to connect computers together in a local area network, originally with coaxial cable directly connected to a single line known as a bus, but more recently through a variety of devices, such as hubs and switches, that can aggregate and direct the traffic. The Ethernet cable connects to a network card on the computer that has a unique, 48-bit address, known as a Media Access Control (MAC) address, assigned at time of manufacture. When a computer needs to send a message to another computer on the network, it first listens on the bus to determine if another system is communicating.

Recall from our chapter on networking that, if there is no other communication on the line, it can send its message. The message propagates along the bus in both directions, and each system attached to that network segment receives the message and determines if it is intended for it by comparing the receiving MAC address with its own. Because there are times when two or more computers transmit at the same time, collisions occur. Under the Ethernet standard, when a collision does occur, both systems will wait a random period of time and begin again by listening to see if someone is transmitting. As the number of hosts attached to a single bus increases so does the chance of collision, which may result in network degradation. The formal name for this scheme is Carrier Sense Multiple Access with Collision Detection, or CSMA/CD.

This feature has implications for shared media. Whereas the original standard utilized a single coaxial cable to connect computers in a bus topology, modern Ethernet architecture usually connects systems through switches in a hierarchical architecture, although some smaller LANs may still use hubs. Both switches and hubs have multiple ports for Ethernet cables to connect. Whereas the hub receives Ethernet frames from a connected device on one port and transmits that frame out all other ports, the switch will consult a table of MAC address/port pairs and re-transmit a received frame only on the port that is associated with the receiving MAC address. This reduces traffic on any given segment, providing operational benefits from decreasing the chance of collision and security benefits from reducing the number of hosts that will receive the frame.

Because switches are most often used to segment network traffic on a LAN, it is important to understand how the MAC address/port table is created. Although it is possible for an administrator in some instances to manually enter the values in the table, that would require a significant amount of time and effort. Rather than manually building the table, the switch has software that can automatically populate the table as it receives broadcasts from various network segments. As it receives a frame on a given port, it will add that port/address pair to the table.

15.3.2 Link Layer Security Issues

Confidentiality is threatened at layers 1 and 2. Ethernet's CSMA/CD design transmits frames on the wire without any consideration of confidentiality. The frames, like any electro-magnetic signal introduced to a conductor, will propagate along the transmission medium in all directions. The frames can be collected by any system connected to the medium, or close enough to the medium to pick up the signal. If the hosts are connected through a bus or hub, then by design all frames are transmitted to all hosts. Rogue users can place their network interface card into promiscuous mode, which will collect and process all frames regardless if the frame is addressed to that host. Without any higher layer protection, this could result in a violation of the confidentiality of the transmitted information. Although switches provide some protection by decreasing the number of hosts receiving the frames, alone they provide no specific protection against violations of information confidentiality.

Integrity likewise is an issue. The Ethernet standard provides basic integrity protection through the use of a checksum. A checksum is a relatively simple computation on a set of data that is attached by the sender and recomputed and compared by the receiver. If the checksum value computed on the data by the receiver does not match what is attached to the frame by the sender, it is determined that an error occurred. The checksum method used by Ethernet is the cyclic redundancy check (CRC). The protection extends only to the frame, and not the information encapsulated in the Ethernet frame.

Availability becomes an issue with the CSMA/CD scheme used by Ethernet because it requires the sending host to wait a random period of time after a collision is detected. As more hosts join a given segment, more traffic is normally sent, and more collisions take place. If a single host floods a segment with traffic, other hosts won't be able to transmit their frames, impending availability of those hosts.

So how could a nefarious user take advantage of the Ethernet standard and architecture devices to violate the confidentiality, integrity, or availability of information? As discussed, the standard by design transmits information without regard for who is listening. Modern switches try to limit frame transmission to only the segments to which the receiving host is attached. This is normally through a dynamically generated table. A malicious user can take advantage of this table in several ways. The simplest is to "lie" to the switch by sending packets with a false MAC address, thereby *poisoning* the information in the table. For example, let's say all the network traffic on our LAN goes to a single system that checks the information before it goes on the Internet. By poisoning (meaning to nefariously change) the switch table in this way to make it think the MAC address of the checking system was on our network segment, an attacker would be able to put the network card in promiscuous mode (meaning the networking is set to seek out a connection) and capture all the traffic bound for the Internet. If poisoning the information in the switch table does not work, another attack option is to overwhelm the switch with so much information that the table becomes too big for the memory on the switch. In some instances, this overflow of the table can cause the switch to transmit information on all segments.

15.3.3 ARP, Neighbor Discovery, and Poisoning

As we move up through the transition from layers 1 and 2 into the network layer, the tie between the MAC address at layer 2 and the IP address at layer 3 is the *Address Resolution Protocol* (ARP) for IPv4 and *Neighbor Discovery* for IPv6. From the IP perspective, when a host desires to send a message to another host on the same Ethernet subnet, it will send a broadcast message to all hosts asking the host with the given IP address to identify its MAC address.

The appropriate host will send back a message to the originating requestor with the information and the sender can then put the IP packet in an Ethernet frame for delivery. The hosts listening on the network will record the IP/MAC association in a table so any future information transfer to the hosts will not require the same IP/MAC association request. Whereas in IPv4 this is accomplished with ARP, IPv6 uses type 135 ICMPv6 messages for neighbor discovery and type 136 ICMPv6 packets for the neighbor advertisement response.

Similar to table poisoning of the switch at the Ethernet layer, ARP and Neighbor Discovery are susceptible to caching false information as well. If a rogue user were to broadcast a false response to the initial request for IP/MAC association that was accepted by the sending host, the traffic would be sent to the rogue user. In both cases, however, the information in the table is not permanent. Because the topology of a network can change over time with the addition or subtraction of hosts and IP addresses, the information in these tables is periodically updated or deleted if not needed. In both IP versions, the administrator can use static entries in the tables to avoid the possibility of cache poisoning, but this would be burdensome. There are tools, such as ARPwatch, that are available to help detect ARP changes.

Layer 3 must also contend with overflow of table memory similar to the ability to overflow the table on a switch. The memory allocated to the association table between MAC and IP can receive more information than it can handle, and when this occurs, an error is usually logged and no new table entries are made. Finally, the ability to affect the relationship between IP address and MAC address opens the possibility for malicious users to inject themselves between two users. This man-in-the-middle (MITM) attack occurs by poisoning the ARP cache of the two communicating hosts to make all traffic go through the nefarious user. For example, if host A with IPv4 address of 192.168.1.2 wants to send traffic to host B with IPv4 address 192.168.1.3, they will each send an ARP request to determine the MAC address associated with each host. If a third host, host C, were to respond to both ARP requests associating host C's MAC address with both IP addresses, then host C will receive all traffic and can forward the traffic on to both host A and host B without either knowing that host C is acting as the *man in the middle.*

15.3.4 Internet Layer Security Issues

At layer 3 of the network stack we have IP addresses, as discussed. However, the address space is significantly different between IPv4 and IPv6. In a generic attack, an attacker will often scan through the subnet address space allocated to an organization to identify which hosts are listening on the network. With IPv4, the address blocks were relatively small, making this feasible. With IPv6, this should be much less of an issue if administrators assign the IP addresses across their allotted spectrum. This, however, can be difficult to manage.

As discussed in RFC 5157, IPv6 Network Scanning, given 8 host bits for the average IPv4 subnet and assuming one probe per second, it would take about 5 minutes to scan the address space. Using the default 64 host bits for an IPv6 subnet and the same probe per second, the scan would take over 5 billion years to accomplish. This assumes, however, that the administrator is assigning the IP addresses across the address space and not sequentially as has often been done with IPv4 addresses. If the hosts are auto-configuring and relying on the MAC addresses, the address space is effectively reduced to 48 bits given the standard transformation.

Additionally, if the attacker assumes the network card was made by a well-known manufacturer, the address space is further reduced to approximately 24 bits. Assuming the same single probe per second, the scan time has been reduced from 5 billion years to approximately 194 days. Although this holds for scanning the address space for unknown hosts, server addresses typically must be available in order to effectively offer any services. These addresses will typically be held by the DNS system, making securing the DNS server particularly important for IPv6.

At the IP layer, we also have to deal with IP address spoofing. Although the switch to IPv6 can have some benefits when it comes to scanning for active hosts, alone it provides no protection again IP address spoofing. To spoof an IP address is to send packets with a source address other than what would normally be assigned to the source host on a given subnet. Though this would mean that any return traffic would be routed to the spoofed IP address, many times the attacker is not concerned with getting replies. This is particularly the case when the goal of the attacker it to overwhelm another system with so much traffic that the attacked system has degraded, if not completely stopped, service. This type of attack, as you know, is a denial of service (DoS) attack, which has become common against many types of organizations [7].

Often, the attacker will make use of many compromised machines to generate traffic in what is known as a distributed denial of service (DDoS). These compromised machines are typically part of a large system of compromised machines known as a **botnet**, and the owners of these machines, whether individuals or organizations, are often not aware that their machines have been compromised and are now under the control of the botnet. The malicious traffic from the hosts could be contained, however, if the managers of the machines had appropriately configured the host-based firewall.

Another use of IP address spoofing is to take advantage of a trust relationship. Many times organizations will allow the use the IP address as a means of authenticating a request for services. In this case, a packet with an IP address that is part of the allowed subnet will be processed. Even though the response might be lost, it may be enough for the attacker to gain access to a host on the network. Many times, however, the border firewall or router will recognize that the packet coming from the public Internet should not have an IP address that should only exist on the internal network, and drop the packet.

15.4 Network Security Issues—End to End

Because one of the first security devices network traffic runs into on its way to compromise a host is a firewall, finding ways to get through the firewall is often an important first step in realizing an attack. One way that firewalls have been thwarted is through fragmentation of the packet in order to make it more difficult for the firewall to identify the payload. By breaking a packet into smaller pieces, a known attack signature can be missed, and the fragments may then bypass the firewall where the fragments may be reconstructed into a whole attack packet. Whereas IPv4 packets can be fragmented anywhere along their path to their destination, IPv6 packets can only be fragmented by the sending host. Where possible, the preventive standard is to use ICMPv6 Path MTU discovery and adjust the size of the packets accordingly. Therefore, with IPv6 it is reasonable to simply block fragmented packets, but there are other end-to-end security issues to contend with.

15.4.1 ICMP Security Issues

ICMP is designed to provide information about the status of the network, and it is a useful tool for administrators to understand and troubleshoot their networks. Although technically the Internet Control Messaging Protocol (ICMP) might be considered part of the link-to-link security layers because it is encapsulated in an IP payload, its considerable number of functions ranging from congestion and error reporting back to host computers to use in gathering connection information (e.g., using ping) makes it more an end-to-end protocol.

For the malicious user, ICMP is often used in the discovery of hosts and network topology. Utilizing ICMP echo request packets (ping), the attacker will send an ICMP echo request to every IP address on a given subnet. An IP address with a host attached will normally respond with an ICMP echo reply. This lets the attacker know that there is a host assigned the given IP address and that that host is active on the network. The attacker can also use the ICMP echo request packets to map the route a packet takes to get to a given host. This is normally done with the Traceroute application that can use the ICMP echo request packets to identify each hop along the way to a given location.

The path is discovered by taking advantage of the standard for sending a message back to the originating host when a packet sent exceeds the number of hops or time-to-live that it was set to allow. By setting the hop count, or time-to-live (TTL) value to 1 at the beginning, the router at the first hop will send a message back to the originating host stating that the packet has reached its limit. The host will then send another ICMP packet with the TTL incremented by one to discover the second hop in the path. This is repeated until the ICMP packet has reached its destination. By understanding the path taken by the ICMP packets, the attacker can derive at least a partial map of the network.

Another use for ICMP packets is to help identify which operating system (OS) a given target is running. This is done by sending a series of ICMP packets, some malformed, others making use of seldom-used options, and examining the responses of the receiver. Because different operating systems will by default respond somewhat differently to these ICMP packets, a reasonable guess of the OS is possible. Finally, like IP packets, ICMP packets can be used to launch DoS attacks against systems, either through resource exhaustion due to the simple volume of traffic, or occasionally by generating oversized ICMP packets that cause some systems to crash.

With all the security issues related to ICMP packets, one might be tempted to turn them off completely. Although ICMP use can introduce potential vulnerabilities and leak information about the network, they also provide an important means for monitoring and troubleshooting the network. ICMPv6 is also fundamental to enabling IPv6 to function properly. The challenge for managers is to help their network and security administrators to be more cognizant of where ICMP should and should not be allowed, and restrict the use appropriately.

15.4.2 Layer 4 (TCP/UDP) Security Issues

Moving up the stack to layer 4, we encounter both the Transmission Control Protocol (TCP) and the User Datagram Protocol (UDP). Whereas TCP is a connection-oriented, reliable transport protocol, UDP offers a connectionless, best-effort delivery service. What this means is that TCP will set up and maintain a connection, tracking the packets sent and received to ensure none are corrupted or missed. In order for TCP to establish the connection, it utilizes a handshake protocol in which a packet is sent from the IP address and port of the sending host to a specific IP address and port on the receiving host.

The handshake protocol is typically known as the "three-way" handshake because it consists of three packets transferred between the hosts. The first packet from the sending to receiving host has a special bit in the header, known as the SYN bit, set and the packet contains a beginning sequence number that is used by the host for the communications. Once sent, the initiating host will go into a wait state waiting for a response or until it times out from waiting too long. Upon receiving the packet on a given port, the receiving host will typically spawn a process to handle the communications and respond with a packet that has the ACK bit set, the beginning sequence number that the receiving host will use, and the sequence number sent by the initiating host incremented by one.

The receiving host will then go into a wait state until it receives the last of the three-way handshake or a certain period of time passes. Once the original sender received the packet with the ACK bit set and the initial sequence number incremented, it will finish the handshake and establish the connection by responding with a packet that has both the SYN and the ACK bit set and the sequence number sent by the receiving host incremented by one. The sequence number is used to ensure that no packets sent between the hosts are lost.

Unlike TCP, UDP, as a connectionless service, will send off the packets without establishing a connection between hosts and trust that the packets arrived as intended. One of the commonalities between TCP and UDP is that each relies on a set of destination ports associated with a given IP address to which either the UDP or TCP packet is addressed. These ports range in number from 0 to 65535, with IANA dividing the ports into three ranges: well-known ports from 0 to 1023, registered ports from 1024 to 49151, and dynamic or private ports from 49152 to 65535 [8].

The well-known ports typically provide network-based services that are executed by privileged users, such as ftp, http, https, smtp, pop, imap, and so on. The registered ports, or user ports, will have services listening as in the well-known ports, but these services are typically executed by non-privileged users. The dynamic or private ports are those that are used to maintain a connection but typically do not have a service listening on them.

15.4.3 Port Attacks and SYN Floods

From the previous section and our previous chapters on networks and about ports being queues and data structures, you have perhaps gathered ways that these could be compromised. We have covered port scanning from a conceptual level earlier and presented some technologies that are often used for such purposes, but the importance of understanding the technical issues in this process cannot be understated. Here, we will elaborate because understanding the basics of TCP and UDP allows us to examine some of the ways in which the protocols can be exploited, subverted, or broken by a malicious user [10].

Much like a malicious user will scan an IPv4 address block to listen for a live host, once the host is located, he or she will scan the ports on the given host to determine what services the host may offer. The most obvious form of scanning is for the attacker to use the full three-way handshake to attempt to make a connection on each port. If the connection is successful, the attacker by default will be greeted with a banner indicating the build of the server software that the user is connected to.

This information is used by the attacker to better understand which operating system is hosting the service, and to research the particular server software associated with the port to determine if it is susceptible to any known attacks. One of the drawbacks for the attacker from this type of port scan, however, is that the completed connection is typically logged by the system and will be examined by security administrators.

Nevertheless, some systems do not log incomplete connections, so an attacker may initiate the connection with the SYN packet and register that the port is active if it receives the ACK response without completing the three-way handshake. In addition to this ***half-open connection*** possibly not being logged, it reduces the time to scan the ports as it does not require the production of the third SYN/ACK packet. Although the half-open SYN scan may not normally be logged, both types of SYN scans may be blocked by an intervening firewall.

A third type of port scan exploits the TCP protocol and attempts to pass through firewalls by not making a true connection at all; rather the malicious user sends a packet with various flags set. If the firewall is just looking at the packet flags to determine if the packet is attempting to initiate a new connection or is part of an already established connection, it may allow such a packet through. Once through, if a server is not listening on a given port, it will typically respond to receiving a packet by responding with the RST bit set. If a server is listening on a given port, it typically will not respond to the packet at all.

If the malicious user does not want to make a connection to the host, and instead has the goal to launch a DoS attack against it, the malicious user can take advantage of the three-way handshake to make multiple, incomplete connections to the server. These open connections will be in a wait state and unable to make a legitimate connection until the connection *times out*. With enough open connections, little to no legitimate traffic can connect [11].

> **In Focus**
>
> The sequence number associated with TCP traffic, as discussed earlier, is designed to ensure a reliable connection. Although RFC 793 (TCP) specifies that the initial sequence number (ISN) comes from a generator that is bound to a 32 bit "clock" that increments every 4 microseconds, many TCP/IP stacks do not follow the specification and have more predictable ISNs. As such, attackers can take advantage of this by guessing the sequence numbers in a given TCP communication and injecting themselves into the communications channel. Normally this also includes flooding the side of the connection that the attacker is taking over to avoid any interfering packets from the original, "true" participant in the communications.

We have covered many representative examples of attacks and vulnerabilities, and many are easily preventable, or their effects can be mitigated through proper configuration of services, vigilant administrators, and good network security architecture. At the service level of a system, the network and systems administrator typically controls the defenses and the information sent to outsiders, such as the banners sent by the server software when a connection is made, or ensuring that the firewalls are properly configured.

15.5 Network Countermeasures

Although we have covered many representative examples of attacks and vulnerabilities, and many are easily preventable, attacks often still succeed for one reason or another, including human failures to implement security measures. Many of the new security technologies built into IPv6, which are collectively called IPSec, can be retrofit into IPv4 to help compensate for these issues.

IPSec is a set of standards protections aimed at securing the IP layer and are described in a set of IETF RFCs. These standards are important because of the vulnerabilities inherent in the IP protocol. For example, an attacker may alter an IP packet header setting the fragment bits and changing the offsets in the packet and sending them to a target computer causing a victim's system to crash when it tries to reassemble the packets. Then using another system, the attacker may spoof the victim's IP address while the system is down. Additionally, the attacker may try to hide the source of the attack by changing the source address in the IP header [12].

Along these lines, because router access filters and access control lists determine what packets may or may not pass through a gateway based on the sender's IP address, this can facilitate the transfer of the attack packets through the gateway while helping to shield the attacker. These types of **IP address spoofing** attacks can occur against hosts or routers. Consequently, security was considered and new mechanisms are being implemented in the design of IPv6 to help preclude many of these issues, and some fall under IPSec.

IPSec is thus a reference to a broad set of facilities being introduced into the network protocols to better secure them. It provides multiple security advantages to IP networks through the use of an **Authentication Header** (**AH**) standard (RFC 4302) and the **Encapsulating Security Payload** (**ESP**) standard (RFC 2406), including, as stated in the RFC, access control, connectionless integrity, data origin authentication, protection against replays (a form of partial sequence integrity), confidentiality (encryption), and limited traffic flow confidentiality (RFC 2410).

The IP AH specifications alone can provide some reasonable assurance of integrity and data origin authentication for IP datagrams, as well as help protect against a replay attack in which previously sent packets are retransmitted in an effort to have the host repeat some function. The ESP standard can also provide protection against replay attacks, and help in data origin authentication, and establish some assurance of integrity, but additionally, the facility provides for the confidentiality of the data and partial confidentiality of the traffic flow.

In Focus

Although the models of security vary, the period of transition from IPv4 to IPv6 will likely bring a hybrid architecture in which both protocols are supported. Although network administrators are generally familiar and comfortable with the security measures and models for IPv4, the transition to IPv6 will certainly introduce unique instances of insecurity from poor configurations by network staff inexperienced with the standards and model. Therefore, appropriately managing the transition is critical.

Many of the security features implemented in IPv6 can be retrofit into IPv4 as earlier indicated. Until the Internet fully transitions to IPv6, network administrators can use a number of facilities [1]: (1) Dual IP protocol stacks can be implemented and translated between external and internal communications, (2) IPv4 and IPv6 address translations back and forth at the gateway junction, (3) tunneling of IPv4 messages inside IPv6 payloads, and (4) network address translations between IPv4 and IPv6 protocols, where an IPv4 internal network can leverage IPv6 IPSec at the egress. In addition to these technologies, there are other important countermeasures needed for network security.

15.5.1 Limiting and Controlling Information Releases

As indicated in the previous section, there is little reason to provide a company's banner information upon connection. Modifying the banner to advertise the expectations for behavior on a given system, noting the level of monitoring a user of the system can expect, and stating penalties for violation of the system policies, would be a useful beginning to securing a network and server.

Next, we discussed how port scanning can be used to carry out attacks, and how ICMP can be manipulated as well as bits in headers for various protocols. Stateful firewalls are helpful in dealing with packet flag manipulation, and most modern IDS/IPS systems can detect such attempts. Still, DoS service attacks remain particularly problematic. Although a simple DoS attack from a single or a few IP addresses can be managed by expanding bandwidth, load balancing and blocking traffic at the firewall and/or upstream router, DDoS are more complicated because they are coming from many addresses. Often this requires blocking traffic from entire sections of the Internet, at least temporarily, to allow legitimate traffic from other areas to connect.

Also, above layer 4, there are numerous application layer protocols that provide various services, such as http, ftp, pop, imap, and smtp. One particular service that has been critical to the success of the Web is the Domain Name Service (DNS). DNS typically operates over UDP on port 53 and provides a mapping between the everyday names we use for sites and the IP numbers that the machines use to connect. Without the DNS directory, finding resources on the Internet would be much more difficult. Unfortunately, as critical as DNS is to our use of the Internet, it has also introduced a significant set of vulnerabilities.

DNS is a hierarchical naming system implemented through a distributed set of servers that provide global resolution to the worldwide domain name space. At the top of the hierarchy are 13 root DNS servers that have a total of 206 instances spread throughout the world (root-servers.org/). These root servers know the IP addresses of all the **top-level domain** (TLD) name servers, such as .com, .org, .net, or .edu. The TLD servers will know the IP addresses of all the second-level domain name servers under their domain, such as the name servers for cmu, fit, gsu, or fsu. The domain name servers at these second-level locations will have the IP address for third-level domain name servers (such as for a department) or the IP address for the hosts themselves (such as www). The resolution of an IP address associated with a given domain name can occur in one of two ways: by successively querying DNS servers until the authoritative record is returned, or by contacting a DNS server and requesting that server to perform the entire look-up.

The former is called an iterative look-up whereas the latter is a recursive look-up. In either case, the DNS client software begins with a query to the local DNS server. If the local DNS server is the authoritative server for the request, or if the server had recently made the request and has the results cached, the server will respond with the appropriate DNS record. If the record is not on the local DNS server, the next request will begin to follow the DNS hierarchy from the root server down until the appropriate record is returned. The record types most often seen in the DNS system are "A" records, which map an IPv4 address to a domain name, "AAAA" records, which map IPv6 addresses to a domain name, "NS" records which specify an authoritative server for a domain, and "MX" records, which specify the mail server for a domain.

15.5.2 Protecting Zone Transfers and Thwarting DNS Spoofing

Where a global DNS allows access to resources worldwide, a local DNS server can be used to map the IP addresses of resources within an organization to more easily remember names. These DNS servers are typically placed behind the internal firewall so that only internal hosts can access them. Problems can occur, however, when the local DNS server sits in the DMZ and acts as the authoritative domain server.

In this case, an attacker can gain a much better understanding of the network infrastructure of an organization by doing a special query of the DNS server known as a zone transfer. A zone transfer is a request for all records held by a given domain name server and was designed to allow a secondary server to receive all the records from a primary server. Once the attacker has all the DNS records from an organization, the attacker will have a much better view of the network architecture.

> **In Focus**
>
> A DNS can act as a proxy inside a firewall to shield the identity of "actual" systems behind the firewall.

In addition to the information that can be collected from an organization by doing a zone transfer of a DNS server, the DNS system itself can be exploited to provide bogus information to a client. The DNS system relies on a series of look-ups to resolve an IP address. At any point along the path of requests, a malicious user could respond to the DNS request with incorrect information that would point the requesting client to a location of the attacker's choosing.

To make matters worse, this information will be cached along the way, so it is possible that injecting false information once into the system can misdirect many hosts. To combat this vulnerability, the IETF has advanced a set of extensions to the DNS protocol known as DNSSEC. These extensions allow for the DNS records to be digitally signed, which will provide origin authentication and record integrity for the client. DNSSEC was implemented on all root servers as of July 2010 [9].

15.5.3 Using Proxies and VPNs

Although many attack perpetrators pick a target to methodically attack, in many cases, attacks are simply opportunistic where an attacker may accidentally stumble onto vulnerability in a system. For example, if someone discovers that a system accepts FTP connections, he or she may seek to find out if it allows anonymous FTP. If not, the attacker may try to use a password "crack" program to furtively login. Attacks also range in their sophistication—some are quite simple and can be executed by mere novices, whereas others are more complex and might require a well-funded specialist as may be found in some criminal syndicates. The use of software and hardware proxies can help shield internal infrastructure from scanning and footprinting, but note that there are also proxy websites that one may access for safe web surfing, such as www.anonymizer .com.

Next, firewalls are important, yet their roles are primarily to screen and filter connections and data, but what about information that must pass out of a trusted setting? A technique that offers substantial insulation is to use a VPN. A VPN, or virtual private network, can mean many things in different contexts, but in general, it is a way to use the public network such as the Internet to provide secure connectivity to private networks. In other words, it is a trusted network that transmits packets across distrusted network infrastructure by using what is called a **tunnel** along with cryptography and authentication techniques [13].

As an introductory idea and prelude to our next chapter for this concept, suppose we dig an underground tunnel between two locations over a public area such as a grassy plane, which in this context is a network, and transmit private data through this secure tunnel. Once the data reaches its destination, the tunnel entrances and exits are buried (closed) until it is needed again. Virtual private networks can be set up in a number of different ways and may be configured in multiple ways. For instance, a VPN can be set up in a site-to-site configuration, or it can be set up so that people, such as traveling salespeople, can call in to the office and get sensitive data without fear of having the data stolen. Other configurations might include site-to-site VPN between the Internet and a local area network depot, this typically being a router that points to an external network.

Choosing a particular VPN technology is not completely straightforward, because there are different protocols, standards, and issues to consider. A common VPN protocol is PPTP (Point-to-Point Tunneling Protocol) developed by Microsoft, and Windows remote access service is based on this methodology. On the other hand, Cisco produced a protocol called L2F, or Layer 2 Forwarding Protocol, and the L2TP, Layer 2 Tunneling Protocol, was issued by the Internet Engineering Task Force and was intended to be an extension of the PPP protocol so that Internet service providers could establish VPN for their services. In terms of technical specifications, L2TP is a combination of PPTP and L2F. Finally as discussed earlier, IPSec has been the candidate of choice for most organization's VPN protocol landscape because IPSec has encryption methods that secure both the data and the header that wraps the data [1].

CHAPTER SUMMARY

In this chapter, we covered, rather broadly, network security concepts. We examined how security is threatened and some techniques that attackers use against networks and network infrastructure. We learned that network security is largely divided between link-to-link and end-to-end security measures, and we learned that relying only on link-to-link security depends on having a secure channel between the communicating systems, but this does not occur in most "real-world" applications, so end-to-end security measures become crucial to maintaining network systems and preventing threats from being realized.

Although we've explored various vulnerabilities and attacks associated with network connectivity, the benefits of easily sharing data and information typically far outweigh the risks. The key to managing the associated risk is to reduce or eliminate it where possible. This is done through a variety of best practices, such as reducing attack surface by turning off unneeded services, protecting hosts from malicious traffic with network and host firewalls, and monitoring network and hosts with intrusion detection and prevention systems. Additionally, risk can be further reduced by designing the network so that a compromise on one segment won't affect other segments. It is important not to lose sight of the fact that the role of the information systems is to provide services that enable the organization to carry out its mission.

We have now provided a conceptual overview of networks and how to secure them. In the next set of chapters, we will explain more specifically how networks and information are secured using cryptography in different modes ranging from obfuscating information in transit to creating message digests to determine if information has been tampered with. Finally, we will delve into firewalls—their types and architecture—before moving on to how systems and networks are monitored for attacks, which will lead into our final section on topics in security operations and management.

THINK ABOUT IT

Topic Questions

15.1: A _____ _____ describes an incomplete three-way handshake.

15.2: Once a successful breach has occurred and the attacker has caused the intended damage, what might the attacker do?

15.3: At the link layer, even if all of the protections available are used by personnel such as cryptography and firewalls (except for if a VPN is used), _____ _____ might still be a potential threat.

THINK ABOUT IT (CONTINUED)

15.4: Issuing a TCP SYN packet without completing the three-way handshake results in a:

_____ Botnet
_____ Half-open connection
_____ Port flood
_____ Virus

15.5: Security of information systems depends on defending them from _____ and _____ threats.

15.6: An attack that attempts to deny company services such as sending a "ping of death" is considered a:

_____ Passive attack
_____ Active attack
_____ Virus
_____ Half-open connection

15.7: Active attacks are more difficult to detect than passive ones.

_____ True
_____ False

15.8: Even with encryption, a traffic analysis attack can still be done.

_____ True
_____ False

15.9: Security provisions built into IPv6 collectively are called:

_____ Karn's algorithm
_____ VPN
_____ IPSec
_____ ESP

Questions for Further Study

Q15.1: Why would anyone use link-to-link layer firewalls at all if they are impractical because they rely on a trusted network?

Q15.2: Explain layered defenses, and investigate other layers that can be used in network security, beyond those described in this chapter.

Q15.3: Describe some of the differences between network architecture and network implementation, and give some examples of their relationships or how they "function" together.

Q15.4: What are some threats to wireless networks that do not apply to wired networks.

Q15.5: Give three recommendations to help prevent successful wardriving and piggybacking.

KEY CONCEPTS AND TERMS

End-to-end security starts at the network layer.

Information sent unencrypted (in the clear) is called plaintext.

IPSec uses an Authentication Header (AH) standard and the

Encapsulating Security Payload (ESP).

Network knowledge can be gained by an attacker from footprinting, scanning, and enumeration.

NIDS is a system that detects intrusions into a network.

References

1. Stewart, M. J. (2011). *Network security, firewalls, and VPNs.* Sudbury, MA: Jones & Bartlett Learning.
2. CERT. (2006). *Using wireless technology security.* Pittsburgh, PA: Carnegie Mellon University, Software Engineering Institute Press.
3. Oriyano, S. P., & Gregg, M. (2011). *Hacker techniques, tools, and incident handling.* Sudbury, MA: Jones & Bartlett Learning.
4. Chen, P. C. (2010). Death of Yamamoto due to "magic" in the Pacific Campaign. *World War II Database Archives of Correspondence. Ref: 18, April, 1943,* 7–12. Retrieved November 14, 2010, from http://ww2db.com/battle_spec.php?battle_id=51
5. Stallings, W. (2003). *Network security essentials: Applications and standards.* Upper Saddle River, NJ: Prentice Hall.
6. Himma, K. E. (2007). *Internet security: Hacking, counterhacking, and society.* Boston, MA: Jones and Bartlett Publishers.
7. Tjaden, B. C. (2004). *Fundamentals of secure computer systems.* Wilsonville, OR: Franklin, Beedle, and Associates.
8. IANA. (2010). *Port numbers.* Retrieved November 25, 2010, from http://www.iana.org/assignments/port-numbers
9. root-servers.org. (n.d.). *Root server technical operation association.* Retrieved September 26, 2010, from www.root-servers.orf
10. Solomon, M. G. (2011). *Security strategies in Windows platforms and applications.* Sudbury, MA: Jones & Bartlett Learning.
11. Solomon, M. G., & Chapple, M. (2005). *Information security illuminated.* Sudbury, MA: Jones and Bartlett Publishers.
12. Doraswamy, N., & Harkins, D. (1999). IPSec: *The new security standard for the Internet, intranets, and virtual private networks.* Upper Saddle River, NJ: Prentice Hall.
13. Kent, S., & Atkinson, R. (1998). *RFC 2401—Security architecture for the Internet protocol.* Internet Engineering Task Force. Retrieved from http://www.ietf.org/rfc/rfc2401.txt

Cryptography Uses and Firewalls

N OW THAT WE HAVE COVERED NETWORK SECURITY and some of the basics of cryptography as ways to defend against threats to information from interception as it transits from point to point, or as it is stored on host platforms or laptops, or even smart phones, we will turn our attention to understanding some other uses of cryptography. Also we will elaborate further on how virtual private networks (VPNs) operate, and we will then cover the vanguard of corporation infrastructure: the firewall, including firewall implementations, configuration, management, and architecture.

Chapter 16 Topics

This chapter:

- Discusses certificates (such as X.509) and certificate authorities.
- Presents internal aspects of IPSec.
- Describes various firewall implementations.
- Covers screened subnet firewall architecture.

Chapter 16 Goals

When you finish this chapter, you should:

- ❑ Understand some of the ways that cryptography is used.
- ❑ Become familiar with how virtual private networks (VPNs) work.
- ❑ Know how routers and hosts implement firewalls, and what they are capable of at the various layers of the network protocol stack where they are implemented.
- ❑ Know the differences between filtering and firewalls.
- ❑ Understand some characteristics of common firewall architectures.

16.1 Cryptography in Use

Earlier, we hinted at cryptography and network security protocols such as IPSec as ways of defending against interception and unauthorized release of message contents. Unauthorized release of message contents is a name for a security breach where someone obtains information for which they are not authorized. These are complicated topics, so we will devote some (incremental) time to them. In this chapter, we are going to elaborate more on cryptography and discuss how it is used in practice. With this basic understanding of how encryption works, we can now turn to the ways in which it is used to secure information assets. Cryptography can appear at many layers of the network stack, depending on what and how much information must be secured. At the network layer, we can use IPSec as mentioned before. At the transport layer, we will discuss Transport Layer Security (TLS), also known as SSL, and at the application layer, we will present S/MIME. Before we begin with an elaboration on those, however, we need to present some more information about digital certificates. Recall that digital certificates and certificate authorities are frequently used to authenticate the entities involved in a communication session and to securely generate and pass symmetric session keys used to encrypt the communication channel for the life of a session.

16.1.1 Who Knows Whom: X.509 Certificates

When someone sends you a message, how do you know that the "someone" is whom he or she purports to be? Mike might have stolen Dan's email login and sends to you a message asking you for the company confidential document we were working on because "I" (Dan) lost mine (but note that I am Mike purporting to be Dan). This question is at the heart of why people use digital certificates. X.509 is a standard issued by the **International Telecommunications Union** (**ITU**), and it defines a mechanism for establishing trust relationships in public key (asymmetric) cryptography (which we will cover later). Although there are other standards, X.509 is among the most widely adopted. The importance of this standard relates to the use of **digital certificates**. We introduced the idea of digital certificates previously when we discussed the web of trust and network security, but now we will expand on the topic.

> **In Focus**
>
> There are public key and private key cryptography, which we will cover in the next chapter. For now, realize that a public key cryptography uses a technique to distribute part of a secret to another it trusts, and retains as private the other part (the secret part) to complete a "puzzle," whereas with private key cryptography, the full secret is shared between the two parties and we must therefore trust that each will keep the full secret safe and secure.

A digital certificate is a verification of an entity by a trusted third party called a **certificate authority** (**CA**). It asserts that the public key bound to a certificate belongs to the entity named in the certificate. This bound identity along with the public key are digitally signed by the CA with its private key. The CA's public key is bound to a special certificate, called a **_root certificate_**, which is distributed to anyone who would need to validate the digital signature.

In addition to the establishment of a CA and a root certificate, the infrastructure to handle digital certificates, often referred to as the public key infrastructure, or PKI, requires that there must be some way to revoke a certificate if it is in some way compromised. Revocation of a digital certificate is accomplished using a certificate revocation list (CRL). This special list, issued by a CA, contains information about all certificates that it has digitally signed that are no longer to be trusted. This can occur if certificates are issued to a party that is later found to be fraudulent or, in the case of expiration, because certificates have a "shelf-life."

In Focus

Microsoft Windows has a set of wizards that facilitate installing certificates from a provider such as VeriSign or Comodo and importing them into applications such as Outlook (email). However, organizations such as Carnegie Mellon University can also set up a "sort of private" CA. The ultimate question is: How much trust does your recipient need regarding your certificate? If we want to sign a document we pass to our colleague, we might just as well use a CMU (or other free trusted intermediary) managed S/MIME certificate, but if we sell products to consumers (who do not know us at all) in the worldwide market, we may want to invest in commercial certificates from VeriSign, Wisekey, or other well-known commercial CA.

16.1.2 IPSec Implementation

As discussed in the network security chapter, IPSec is fundamental to the security paradigm of IPv6 and provides multiple security advantages to IP networks through the use of the Authentication Header (AH) (RFC 4302) and the Encapsulating Security Payload (ESP) (RFC 2406) standards, including "access control, connectionless integrity, data origin authentication, protection against replays (a form of partial sequence integrity), confidentiality (encryption), and limited traffic flow confidentiality" (RFC 2410) [1].

The security architecture document for IPSec is RFC 2401. Both the AH and ESP standards can be used in one of two modes, transport or tunnel. Transport mode is designed to secure communications between a host and another host or gateway, whereas tunnel mode is commonly used to connect two gateways together. In transport mode, the AH or ESP header is inserted after the IP header, providing protection for the data in the packet. In tunnel mode, the entire IP packet to be secured is encapsulated in a new IP packet with AH or ESP headers, providing a means to protect the entire original packet, including the static and non-static fields in the original header.

Whether choosing AH or ESP to provide protection, IPSec requires the use of Security Associations (SA) that specify how the communicating entities will secure the communications between them, with an SA defined for each side of the communication. The SA consists of a 32-bit security parameter index (SPI), the destination address for the traffic, and an indicator of whether the entities will use ESP or AH to secure the communications. The SPI is designed to uniquely identify a given SA between two hosts and is used as an index, along with the destination address and the ESP/AH indicators in a security association database (SAD) for outbound connections, or for a security policy database (SPD) for inbound connections. Minimally, the database must record the authentication mechanism, cryptographic algorithm, algorithm mode, key length, and initialization vector (IV) for each record.

In Focus

Recall that a vector is a value that has both magnitude (displacement) and direction. An initialization vector in the context of IPSec is a block of bits used in a vectoring process by the cipher to produce a unique output from a common encryption key, without having to regenerate the keys.

Whereas ESP provides data confidentiality through payload encryption, AH only provides data integrity, data source authentication, and protection against replay attacks by generating an HMAC (Header Message Authentication) on the packet. The algorithms that are minimally specified for IPSec include DES, HMAC-MD5, and HMAC-SHA, but many implementations also provide support for other cryptographic algorithms such as 3DES and Blowfish. Although it is possible to create all the security associations manually, for a large enterprise, that would require a lot of administrative overhead. To manage the SA (Security Associations) database dynamically, IPSec utilizes the Internet Key Exchange (IKE) specified in RFC 2409.

As stated in RFC 2409, IKE is a hybrid protocol designed "to negotiate, and provide authenticated keying material for, security associations in a protected manner" [2]. IKE accomplishes this through using parts of two key exchange frameworks—Oakley and SKEME—which are used together with the Internet Security Association and Key Management Protocol (ISAKMP). This is a generic key exchange and authentication framework defined in RFC 2408.

16.1.3 IPSec Example

An in-depth examination of cryptographic uses is beyond the scope of this chapter, but it is important to understand the basics of how two entities can negotiate a secure connection, as that is fundamental to most encrypted communications we encounter. There are eight different exchanges that can occur with IKE to authenticate and establish a key exchange, but we will examine the single required one—a shared secret key in *main mode*. In this exchange, two entities we will call Alice and Bob already share a secret key. This may be the case with an employee working from home who needs to establish a secure connection to the company network.

Although there are some issues with this protocol, it still serves as an example of how key exchange can be accomplished. It begins with Alice sending to Bob a message indicating various combinations of cryptographic parameters (CP) she supports. This would include the encryption algorithms (DES, 3DES, IDEA), hash algorithms (SHA, MD5), authentication methods (pre-shared keys, public key encryption, etc.), and Diffie-Hellman parameters (including a prime and primitive root) that she supports. Bob would receive this message and choose from the sets offered by Alice, and respond with his selection. Once Alice receives Bob's selection, she will pass to Bob her computed Diffie-Hellman value and a random bit of information called a ***nonce***.

In Focus

In regard to information security, a nonce is an abbreviation of a "number used once" and is usually a (nearly) random number issued in an authentication protocol to help ensure that old communications are not reused in replay attacks perpetrated by an eavesdropper.

The purpose of the nonce is to add a unique value to the communication session so that it cannot be recorded and played back (called a replay attack) to Alice or Bob in the future in a "new" communication session. Bob will receive the information from Alice and send back his Diffie-Hellman computation and a nonce he creates. Both Bob and Alice can then compute a shared session key utilizing their shared secret key, their computed Diffie-Hellman shared secret, the nonce from Alice, the nonce from Bob, and two unique session cookies that are a function of a secret value and their IP addresses. This key is then used for authentication by Alice for encrypting a message proving she is Alice. She then sends this to Bob, and then asks for Bob to do the same [3]. This process results in a (reasonably) secure exchange.

16.1.4 SSL/TLS

Another common cryptographic implementation that we often encounter is the Transport Layer Security (TLS) protocol specified in RFC 5246, as we mentioned earlier in relation to SSH. As with IKE used in IPSec, TLS is used to negotiate a shared session key that secures the communication channel between two entities. Most modern implementations of the https protocol for secure web traffic, Session Initiation Protocol (SIP) for Voice over IP (VoIP) traffic, and Simple Mail Transfer Protocol (SMTP), each make use of TLS to authenticate and secure the communication.

TLS itself is composed of two layers: the TLS record layer and the TLS handshake layer. The TLS record protocol sits on top of the TCP layer and encapsulates the protocols that are "above it" on the network stack. The record layer protocol ensures that the communications are private, through the use of symmetric encryption algorithms such as AES, and are reliable by using ***message authentication codes*** (**MACs**). The handshake protocol ensures that both entities in the communication can authenticate each other, and securely and reliably negotiate the cryptographic protocols and the shared secret [4].

The TLS record protocol is in charge of doing the encryption and decryption of the information that is passed to it. Once it receives information to encrypt, it compresses the information according to the standards defined in RFC3749. The protocol allows for the compressed data to be encrypted using either a block or a stream cipher, but the session key used for the communication is derived from information provided in the handshake. The master secret passed in the handshake protocol is expanded into client and server MAC keys, and the client and server encryption keys (as well as client and server initialization vectors if required) are used in turn to provide the encryption and authentication credentials [5].

Where the TLS handshake protocols allow the communicating entities to "agree on a protocol version, select cryptographic algorithms, optionally authenticate each other, and use public-key encryption techniques to generate shared secrets" [4], the handshake protocol has the following steps, as specified in the RFC [4]:

1. Exchange hello messages to agree on algorithms, exchange random values, and check for session resumption.
2. Exchange the necessary cryptographic parameters to allow the client and server to agree on a premaster secret.
3. Exchange certificates and cryptographic information to allow the client and server to authenticate each other.
4. Generate a master secret from the premaster secret and exchanged random values.
5. Provide security parameters to the record layer.
6. Allow the client and server to verify that their peer has calculated the same security parameters and that the handshake occurred without tampering by an attacker.

In Focus

Unlike the IKE, TLS specifies a limited set of predefined cipher suites, which are addressed by number. Because the sets are predefined, the selection of what to offer can be simpler.

Finally, there exists a cryptographic standard, Secure/Multipurpose Internet Mail Extension (S/MIME), defined in RFC5751. S/MIME allows a compliant mail user agent to add authentication, confidentiality, integrity and non-repudiation of message content through the use of digital certificates [6]. The benefit of using S/MIME over some other means of encrypting and signing email is that S/MIME certificates are normally X.509 standard complaint, and are sent along with the encrypted email. As long as the certificate was issued by a CA that is trusted by both parties, the transfer of digitally signed and encrypted email is relatively easy.

16.1.5 Virtual Private Networks (VPNs)

There are many kinds of attacks that can take place across a network, as we have learned. Recall that passive attacks consist of unauthorized interception (eavesdropping) of communication that is carried out covertly to steal information. On the other hand, active attacks (using technologies such as *Achilles* or *Cain*) may present attempts to gather information to penetrate defenses or to cause damage, and include protocol (e.g., ARP) poisoning, traffic injection, SQL injection, deletion, delay, and replay, and so forth (**Figures 16.1** through **16.4**). Even though active attacks may be devastating, passive attacks are the most difficult to defend against because in many if not most cases, people are unaware that the attack is taking place. We have discussed that encryption is the most common form of defense against these passive attacks, but even when using encryption, some information may still be vulnerable.

> **In Focus**
>
> Technologies such as Achilles and Cain are designed for legitimate purposes such as vulnerability scanning. Remember our discussion earlier in our textbook that technologies are value neutral. It is up to people as to whether the technologies are used for good or bad purposes.

Moreover, as discussed earlier, in network security, link-to-link security is formed at the connection level (network layer and below), whereas end-to-end security is at the software level (transport and above). One of the main strengths as well as weaknesses of IP security is that network information is encapsulated in each layer's header, but header information is needed for routing other controls.

With link-to-link layer, there is no notion of the associations among network layers and processes. Each node must be secured and trusted, which is of course impractical in the Internet. To help mitigate, the secure shell (SSH) protocol, which uses encryption processes, is often used for Internet and web security purposes, but SSH is an application-layer security protocol. Even when using SSH, data are carried in the payload of a TCP segment, and TCP data are in the payload of an IP segment because various border gateway protocols (BGP) and ARP protocols have to be able to read the header data. Thus headers at the routing layer over a WAN such as the Internet may not be encrypted, and therefore a significant amount of information is exposed for exploitation.

One common exploit at the connection layer is called **_traffic analysis_**, where attackers examine how much information is flowing between end-points by examining the contents in headers. To assist with this problem, we can set up a virtual private network (VPN) inside a network, and in that case, the header information is encrypted and then re-encapsulated using a **_Point-to-Point Protocol_** (**PPP**). This is analogous to hiding a real address inside a proxy address. The packet will cycle through the data link layer twice (_double loop process_), once to encapsulate the VPN address, and once again to encapsulate the BGP address, which allows us to encrypt the VPN address (**Figure 16.5**).

> **In Focus**
>
> There are many types of VPNs, including intranet VPN, extranet VPN, and remote access VPNs. Most have in common the use of a Point-to-Point Tunneling Protocol (PPTP), which is a form of PPP for VPN. (For more specific details, see [7].)

FIGURE 16.1

Achilles man-
in-the-middle
example.

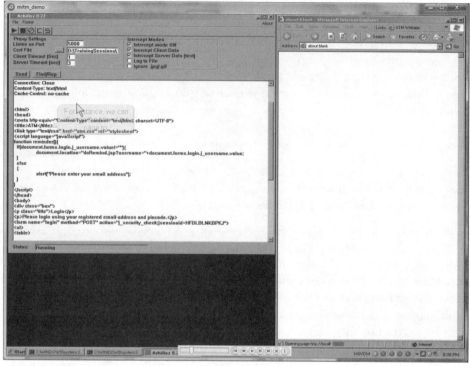

© Massimilian Montoro

FIGURE 16.2

Cain IP/MAC
capture example.

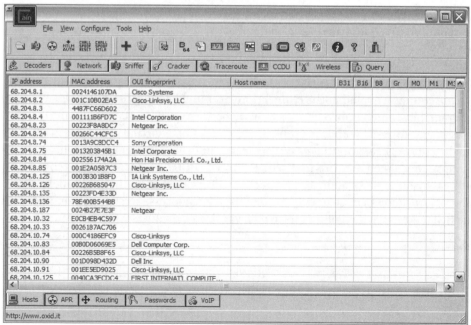

© Massimilian Montoro

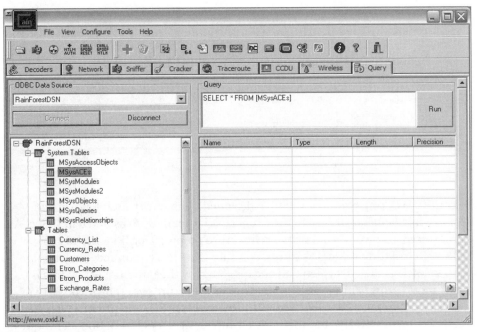

FIGURE 16.3

Cain SQL injection
example part 1.

© Massimilian Montoro

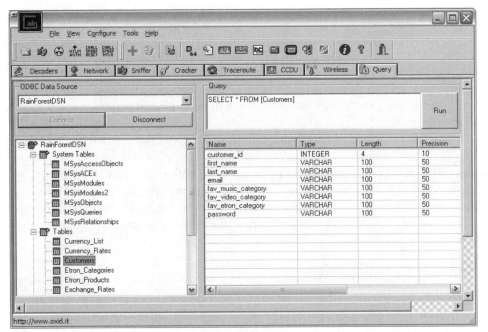

FIGURE 16.4

Cain SQL injection
example part 2.

© Massimilian Montoro

FIGURE 16.5

A VPN encryption
process.

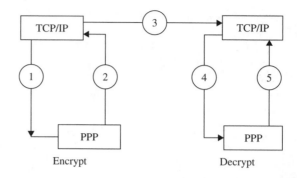

The IP Security Working Group of the IETF designed the security architecture and protocols for cryptographically based security encapsulation in IPv6 as noted in IPSec. As work has progressed, some of the security architecture proposed for IPv6 has also been applied to IPv4. Retrofitting these IPSec protocols into IPv4 has continued in particular where plaintext packets are encrypted and encapsulated by the outer IP packet; this is the essence of most **tunnels** in VPNs. This security architecture generally involves two main protocols: the **Internet Protocol Security Protocol** (**IPSP**) and the **Internet Key Management Protocol** (**IKMP**), but there are a number of IP encapsulation techniques that have emerged such as SwIPe, SP3, NLSP, I-NLSP, and specific implementations of IKMP such as MKMP, SKIP, Photuris, Skeme, ISAKMP, and OAKLEY.

16.2 Firewall Systems

There are many definitions of what constitutes a firewall. Additionally, the term *firewall* is not used consistently; for example, sometimes the term is used in conjunction with intrusion detection systems. We will strive to clarify by presenting an overview of a variety of firewall types, cover briefly how they work in general, and present a few samples of firewall architecture.

Generally speaking, firewalls do not protect information as it traverses a network, but they do help to neutralize some of the threats that come from connections and through the network infrastructure. Firewalls are implemented in both routers and on host computers, and typically, they use filtering and rules to manage the traffic in and out of a network segment [8]. There are also many kinds of firewalls, ranging from basic filtering to inspection of packet contents, as well as layers of the network protocol stack at which firewalls operate.

16.2.1 Stateless Screening Filters

A **screening** filter can operate at the network layer or transport layer by packet filtering in a router or other network device. Network layer packet filtering allows (permits) or disallows (denies) packets through the firewall based on what is contained in the IP header. The rules that determine what actions are allowed or disallowed are defined in the device's security policy and according to access control lists (ACLs). They may also take on one of two **stances**, either **pessimistic** or **optimistic**, in which packets (say, from a particular IP address, port, or protocol type) that are not explicitly permitted are denied (**white list**) or packets that are not explicitly denied are permitted (**black list**); the former being a pessimistic stance and the latter optimistic.

> **In Focus**
>
> Lower layer filtering is more efficient to process than filtering at higher layers, but it is less effective. Managers and administrators have to decide the tradeoff depending on the objectives of the filter and performance requirements depending on what lies behind the firewall.

Accordingly, a network administrator may configure a router's rules to deny any packets that have an internal source address but is coming from the outside (an address spoof), or the administrator may even nest the rules such that any request from an IP address that elicits a response from a router (e.g., a ping) is permitted, but deny any attempt to allow an ICMP redirect from that IP address to a host behind the router [9]. At the transport layer, more information about the data can be inspected by an adversary examining transport protocol header information, such as source and destination port numbers, and in the case of TCP, some information about the connection. As with network layer filtering, transport packet inspection allows the firewall to determine the origin of the packet such as whether it came from the Internet or an internal network, but it also has the ability to determine whether the traffic is a request or a response between a client and a server [10]. However, these stateless types of packet filtering have limitations because they have no "awareness" of upper layer protocols or the exact state of an existing connection. They function simply by applying rules on addressing and protocol types, but many threats are encapsulated at higher layers of the protocol stack that bypass these filters.

The rules utilized in these firewalls are also fairly simplistic, essentially to *permit* or *deny* connections or packets through the filtering router. Consequently, it is impossible at these lower layers to completely filter TCP packets that are not valid, or that do not form a complete active connection. In other words, they cannot determine the type of request or response of a TCP connection, such as if the request–response is part of the three-way handshake that may leave a connection "half-open," which is a particular kind of attack (i.e., *half-open connection denial of service attack*).

16.2.2 Stateful Packet Inspection

Stateful packet inspection is sometimes called *session-level packet filtering*. As indicated, before a packet filter is generally implemented by a router using access control lists (ACLs), and is geared toward inspection of packet headers as they traverse both ingress and egress. On the other hand, many applications such as email depend on the state of the underlying TCP protocol; more specifically, the client and server in a session rely on initiating and acknowledging each other's requests and transfers. Because TCP/IP does not actually implement a session layer as in the OSI model, a stateful packet inspection creates a ***state table*** (more shortly) for each established connection to enable the firewall to filter traffic based on the end-point profiles and state of the type of communications to prevent certain kinds of session layer attacks or highjacking [11].

> **In Focus**
>
> Because UDP is stateless, filtering these kinds packets is more difficult for firewalls to manage than is TCP.

As such, stateful packet inspection firewalls are said to be *connection-aware* and have fine-grained filtering capabilities. The validation in a connection-aware firewall extends up through the three-way handshake of the TCP protocol. As mentioned earlier, TCP synchronizes its session between peer systems by sending a packet with the SYN flag set and a sequence number. The sending system then awaits an acknowledgment from the destination. During the time that a sender awaits an acknowledgment, the connection is "half-open."

The validation is important to prevent a perpetrator from manipulating TCP packets to create many half-open connections. Because most TCP implementations have limits on how many connections they can service in a period of time, a barrage of half-open connections can lead to an attack called a *SYN flood attack*, draining the system's memory and overwhelming the processor trying to service the requests, and this can cause the system to slow down or even crash [10].

To accomplish session-level filtering and monitoring, as noted earlier, stateful packet inspection utilizes a *state table* called a ***virtual circuit table*** that contains connection information for end-point communications. Specifically, when a connection is established, the firewall first records a unique session identifier for the connection that is used for tracking and monitoring purposes. The firewall then records the state of the connection, such as whether it is in the handshake stage, whether the connection has been established, or whether the connection is closing, and it records the sequencing data, the source and destination IP addresses, and the physical network interfaces on which the data arrive and are sent out [11].

Using this virtual table approach, such as with TCP/IP, allows the firewall to perform filtering and sentinel services such that it only allows packets to pass through the firewall when the connection information is consistent with the entries in the virtual circuit table. To ensure this, it checks the header information contained within each packet to determine whether the sender has permissions to send data to the receiver, and whether the receiver has permissions to receive it; when the connection is closed, the entries in the table are removed and that virtual circuit between peer systems is terminated [12].

Although session-level firewalls are an improvement over transport-layer firewalls because they operate on a "session" and therefore they have some capability to monitor connection-oriented protocols such as TCP, they are not a complete solution. Session or connection-oriented firewall security is limited only to the connection. If the connection is allowed, the packets associated with that connection are routed through the firewall according to the routing rules with minimal other security checks [13].

16.2.3 Circuit Gateway Firewalls

In the use of the terms, circuit-level gateways or circuit-level firewalls, it is important to realize that the term "circuit" as used in this context might be a little misleading because technically, there is no "circuit" involved in TCP. The term is applied because TCP is considered a "connection-oriented" protocol because it maintains a session via a setup (three-way handshake) and an exchange of acknowledgments and sequence numbers between client and server. However, to understand a true circuit type of network, we refer back to the asynchronous transmission mode (ATM).

In regard to packet switching networks such as TCP/IP, a circuit-level firewall or gateway is one that validates connections before allowing data to be exchanged. In other words, it uses proxies to broker the "connection" or "circuit" such as with proxy software called *SOCKS*. Therefore, a circuit-layer firewall or gateway is not just a packet filter that allows or denies packets or connections, it determines whether the connection between end-points is valid according to configurable rules, and then permits a session only from the allowed source through the proxy and perhaps only for a limited period of time [12, 13].

The notion of "circuit level" in firewall terms then means that it executes at the transport layer, but it combines with stateful packet inspection such that it can uniquely identify and track connection pairs between client and server processes. In addition, the circuit proxy (such as SOCKS) has the ability to filter input based on its audit logs and previous transactions, and screen the traffic (both inbound and outbound) accordingly. Therefore, a circuit-level firewall has many of the characteristics of an application-layer firewall such as the ability to perform authentication, but it does not filter on payload contents at the application layer [14]. That function is the domain of a host-based application-layer firewall.

16.2.4 Application-Layer Firewall

Although the term "application-layer firewall" is a little misleading in the context of TCP/IP, as one would expect, it is an end-to-end communications firewall and therefore resides on the host computer to provide firewall services up through the application layer. Hence these are sometimes called *application-layer firewall monitors*. They filter the information and connections that are passed up through to the application layer and are able to evaluate network packets for valid data at the application layer before allowing a connection, inbound or outbound, similar to circuit gateways.

In Focus

The two core aspects of the application-layer firewall are the services a host provides and the sockets used in the communications.

Beyond this, most application-layer firewalls are able to disguise hosts from outside the private network infrastructure. Because they operate at the application layer, they can be used by programs such as browsers to block spyware, botnets, and malware from sending information from the host to the Internet. They are also designed to work in conjunction with antivirus software, where each can automatically update the other. In other words, if an antivirus application discovers an infection, it may notify the application-layer firewall to try to prevent its signature from passing through the firewall in the future.

This type of dynamic filtering is especially important for email and Web browsing applications—for example, to prevent an infection delivered via an ActiveX control or JAVA component downloaded during a web browsing session. Moreover, application layer firewalls have monitors and audit logs that allow users to view connections made, what protocols were used, and to what IP addresses, as well as the executables that were run. They also typically show what services were invoked, by which protocol, and on what port [9].

Although the capabilities of application-layer firewalls are not deep, meaning they typically do not inspect lower protocol layers because the data have been stripped off by the time the packet reaches the application layer, they are broad in terms of their protections. With complex rule sets, they can thoroughly analyze packet data to provide close security checks and interact with other security technologies such as virus scanners to provide value-added services, such as email filtering and user authentication [13].

Finally, most application layer firewalls present a dialog to a "human-in-the-loop" for a novel or unusual action, where the user then has the option to permit or deny the action. However, studies involving human-computer interaction (e.g., [15]) have shown that people sometimes do not pay close attention to these dialogs, and furthermore, the option to permanently allow or disallow an action can have harmful side effects. For example, a user may be fooled into permanently allowing harmful processes to run, or permanently block a useful action (such as security patch updates) because people are conditioned to ignore some information, and they are reinforced to avoid annoying cues (such as pop-up dialogs because they interfere with their primary goals). Although application-layer firewalls offer a significant amount of control, these are often negated by human action (or inaction), and therefore the importance of the concept of defense in depth comes into play, which we will explore later using the example of a screened subnet firewall architecture. In any case, it is important for security managers and administrators to regularly examine the firewall logs in case alerts were missed or not reported (**Figure 16.6**).

16.2.5 Bastion Hosts

Given some of the limitations in various firewall technologies and approaches, a bastion host (or gateway) can be a useful complement to them. A bastion host is said to be "hardened" because it serves a specialized purpose, such as to act as a gateway in and out of a protected area known as a DMZ. Therefore, it only exposes specific intended services and has all non-essential software, such as word processing systems, removed from it.

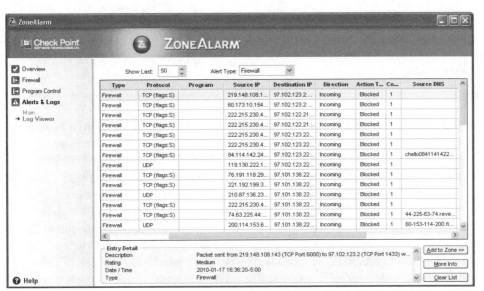

FIGURE 16.6

Example of firewall
log (from zone
alarm).

ZoneAlarm® and Check Point are either registered trademarks or trademarks of Check Point Software Technologies, Inc., a wholly
owned subsidiary of Check PointSoftware Technologies Ltd., in the United States and/or other countries.

As we learned earlier, the Internet enables access to information using a variety
of techniques and technologies. In a typical communication over the Internet or
LAN, a connection is made by means of a socket. A socket, as we learned, represents
a collection of software and data structures and system calls that form end-points
between communicating systems based on their IP addresses and port number pairs,
and the socket API allows for various operations to be executed by software that form
the socket. Port numbers designate various services to which connections are bound.
Server processes "listen" on ports for requests from clients. For example, the *smtpd*
server process listens on port 25 for email messages to arrive, and the *httpd* server listens
on port 80 (by default) for connections from browsers. Once a connection is made,
communication begins.

For protection, bastion hosts often utilize specialized proxy services for those services
they do expose. Proxy services are special-purpose programs that intervene in the communications flow for a given service, such as HTTP or FTP. For example, smap and smapd are
proxies for the UNIX sendmail program. Because sendmail in UNIX is notorious for security
flaws, smap intercepts messages and places them in a special storage area where they
can be electronically or manually inspected before delivery. The smapd scans this storage
area at certain intervals, and when it locates messages that have been marked "clean," it
delivers them to the intended user's email with the regular sendmail system. As seen then,
proxy services can provide increased access control and more carefully inspected checks for
valid data, and they can be equipped to generate audit records about the traffic that they
transfer. Auditing software can be made to trigger alarms, or the administrator can go back
through the audit logs when necessary for conducting a trace in a forensic analysis [16].

> **In Focus**
>
> A bastion host is a system dedicated to providing network services, and is not used for any other purpose such as general-purpose computing.

For additional protection, a bastion host may be configured as a ***dual-homed bastion gateway***. The *dual-home* refers to having two network cards (homes) that divide an external network from the internal one. This division allows further vetting of communications before traffic is allowed into an internal network, and each of the connections and processes that is allowed is carefully monitored and audited [13]. Still, bastion hosts can represent a single point of failure and a single point of compromise, if left on their own. Moreover, these systems require vigilant monitoring by administrators because they tend to bear the brunt of an attack. Although bastion hosts can enforce security rules on network communications that are separated by network interfaces, because of their visibility, these kinds of systems generally require additional layers of protections, such as with other firewalls and intrusion-detection systems [14]. Let's now examine firewall architecture and discuss how bastion hosts can be used as part of various firewall designs.

16.3 Firewall Architecture

Firewall architecture is a layering concept. For example, we can use a packet filtering router to screen connections to a bastion host that is used to inspect whatever gets through the screen before delivering it into an interior network and the systems that reside therein. In many cases, this is a sufficient level of protection, such as for a web server exposed to the Internet that displayed only content. However, if systems are to perform transactions such as those in e-commerce, we need to better protect both the customer information and our internal resources. For that kind of activity, we are likely to need more stringent countermeasures.

16.3.1 "Belt and Braces" Architecture

When a network security policy is implemented, policies must be clear and operationalized, which means that they are determinant and measurable, and the boundaries must be well defined so that the policies can be enforced. The boundaries are called ***perimeter networks***, and to establish a collection of perimeter networks, the collection of systems within each network to be protected must be defined along with the network security mechanisms to protect them. A network security perimeter will implement one or more firewall servers to act as gateways for all communications between trusted networks, and between those and distrusted or unknown networks.

The term *belt and braces* refers to the combination of a screening router and a bastion host with network address translation [11]. The belt portion of this architecture is the screening filter, and the braces involve the NAT and the bastion host. This type of architecture has the following advantages:

1. Filters are generally faster than packet inspection or application-layer firewall technologies because they perform fewer evaluations,
2. A single rule can help protect an entire network by blacklisting (prohibiting) connections between specific network sources such as the Internet and the bastion host, and
3. In conjunction with network address translation and proxy software, we can shield internal IP addresses from exposure to distrusted networks and perform relatively thorough filtering and monitoring. The key here is that it forms a sort of DMZ between the outside world the internal infrastructure.

In Focus

Trusted networks are those that reside inside a bounded security perimeter (such as a DMZ). Distrusted networks are those that reside outside the well-defined security perimeter and are not under control of a network administrator.

If there is an attack, the bastion host will take the brunt of an attack. Thus when monitored closely, it can simplify the administration of the network and its security. Also the bastion host can perform NAT to translate internal and external addresses. This can be done using a static-NAT to map a given private IP address into a given public one on a point-to-point level, which is useful when a system needs access from an outside network such as a web server and also needs accessibility from the Internet.

The bastion host may be configured to use a dynamic-NAT that maps private IP address into public ones that are allocated from a group (which may be assigned using DHCP). In this configuration, there is a point-to-point mapping between public and private addresses, but the assignment of the public IP address is done upon request and released when the connection is closed. This has some administrative advantages, but it is not as secure as static-NAT. The bastion may also use NAT-overloading, which translates multiple private IP addresses into a single public one using different (called rolling) TCP ports. This is useful as a link-to-link filtering technique because the translation hides and also changes the topology and addressing schemes, making it more difficult for an attacker to profile the target network topology and connectivity, or identify the types of host systems and software on the interior network, which helps to reduce IP packet injection, SYN flood DoS attacks, and other similar attacks [10].

In Focus

Firewall architecture, being the blueprints of the network topology and security control infrastructure, must take into account the operational level (technical issues), the tactical level (policies and procedures), and the strategic level (the directives and overall mission) in order to be effective.

16.3.2 Screened Subnet Architecture

As we discussed, screening packet filters are used to separate trusted autonomous networks from each other, such as those that might host DNS that allocates IP addresses for multiple zones, or one that contains an LDAP or Active Directory. They are also used as a choke point at the ingress gateway into a bounded security perimeter called a DMZ from distrusted networks. This approach is used in combination with screened subnet firewall architecture (**Figure 16.7**). Although this less secure filtering approach toward distrusted networks such as the Internet seems counterintuitive, the filtering is efficient in processing packets while allowing some control. The main idea behind a screened subnet is that a network can have multiple perimeters, which can be classified into *outermost perimeter*, *internal perimeters*, and the *innermost perimeter networks*. At the gateways of these networks, the defenses are layered so that if one layer is breached, the threat is met at the next layer.

The *outermost perimeter network* demarcates the separation point between external networks and systems and internal perimeter proxy systems. Here, the filtering firewall assumes a black list (optimistic) stance for efficiency, and yet maintains the ability to block known attacks. Data passed into the internal perimeter network are bounded by the network fabric and systems, which are collectively considered the DMZ. An internal perimeter network typically only exposes the most basic of services such as a hosted web server, and the proxy systems such as bastion hosts and proxy DNS. Because this area is most exposed, it is the most frequently attacked, usually by an attempt to gain access to the internal networks, but also by DoS or defacement.

The screened subnet architecture then uses a white list (pessimistic) firewall to insulate the internal assets of the innermost perimeter network from the internal perimeter network. In other words, traffic intended for a system inside the innermost perimeter network is intercepted by proxy systems in the DMZ before the traffic is relayed to the internal system. Therefore, as seen in the figure, in this configuration at least two sets of

FIGURE 16.7

Screened subnet architecture.

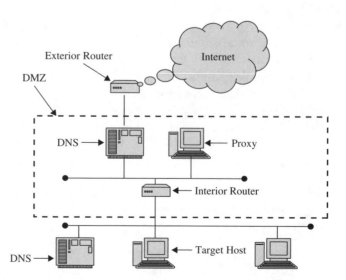

screening routers are used to create the DMZ. The exterior router is set up for an optimistic stance, which is to say, it uses a white list ACL, where all connections are allowed except those that are explicitly denied [8]. The interior router is set up for a pessimistic stance in which all connections are explicitly denied except those that are explicitly permitted. Requests from an exterior connection, such as the Internet, pass through the exterior router destined for a host on an interior network. Within the DMZ, a DNS is set up to return to exterior requests an IP address for a DMZ proxy for the interior host. The proxy is a bastion host that acts as a relay system [16].

When communications are passed from the exterior to the proxy, the proxy can then inspect the content of the communications to ensure that it is conventional and free from viruses or other malware before forwarding it to the target interior host. The forwarding from the proxy relay to the target host is done by a relay query of the interior DNS, which is the only connection permitted by the interior router other than the proxy, and this returns the IP address of the target host to the proxy. The transaction is completed by the proxy passing the data to the target host where it is subject to additional inspection before being delivered to the requested application. As seen, the screened subnet architecture is very secure, but is also complex to manage and requires a great deal of processing overhead.

Therefore, as seen in this configuration at least two sets of screening routers are used to create the DMZ. The exterior router is set up for an optimistic stance, which is to say, it uses a white list ACL, where all connections are allowed except those that are explicitly denied. The interior router is set up for a pessimistic stance in which all connections are explicitly denied except those that are explicitly permitted. Requests from an exterior connection, such as the Internet, pass through the exterior router destined for a host on an interior network. Within the DMZ, a DNS is set up to return to exterior requests an IP address for a DMZ proxy for the interior host. The proxy is a bastion host that acts as a relay system. When a communication is passed from the exterior to the proxy, the proxy can then inspect the contents of the communication to ensure it is conventional and free from viruses or other malware before forwarding it to the target interior host.

The forwarding from the proxy relay to the target host is done by a relay query of the interior DNS, which is the only connection permitted by the interior router other than the proxy, and this returns the IP address of the target host to the proxy. The transaction is completed by the proxy passing the data to the target host where it is subject to additional inspection before being delivered to the requested application. As seen, the screened subnet architecture is very secure, but is also complex to manage.

16.3.3 Ontology-Based Architecture

Although ontology-based defenses are not technically firewalls, they can be used to perform many of the screening and monitoring functions of firewalls. In conventional firewall architecture, security policies are predefined for a given security stance and for a given set of platforms. In other cases, using security policy ontologies have become a popular approach to decouple from some underlying technological interdependencies. In this approach, security policy rules are created with a graphical user interface, and the underlying technology generates the ontology markup (e.g., in OWL).

In their interesting work on security incidents and vulnerabilities, Moreira and his colleagues [17] presented a triple-layered set of ontologies (operational, tactical, and strategic) approach to filtering and monitoring. Because ontologies are comprised of markup documents, they can be easily shared among disparate systems. The operational level is comprised of daily transactions and is governed by the tactical level, which consists of the rules that control access to the resources, the technologies that compose the storage and retrieval methods for information and service resources, the processes used in these activities, and the people who use them.

The strategic level is concerned with directives and governance. Using the Moreira et al. [17] approach, security policy ontologies can draw from the Common Vulnerabilities and Exposures (CVE) ontology, which captures and updates with common vulnerabilities and incidents such as reported by the Software Engineering Institute's CERT. The primary function of the security ontology is to define a set of standards, criteria, and behaviors that direct the efforts of a filtering and monitoring system.

An example of network security policy ontology could consist of threats from remote or local access, the types of vulnerabilities such as SQL injection, buffer overflow, and so forth, and their consequences—including severity and what systems could be affected. The ontology could contain whether a corrective security patch has been released for the vulnerability, and other relevant information. This approach facilitates the automation of the network policy enforcement at a gateway, similar to application-layer firewalls and monitors.

In Focus

Codified into information and communications systems, security policies define the rules and permissions for system operations. For example, a router's security policy may permit only egress ICMP messages and deny those that are ingress, or a host computer's security policy may prohibit files from copying themselves, accessing an email address book, or making modifications to the Microsoft Registry.

A web service, agent framework, or object request broker is then used for policy discovery and enforcement at runtime. In other cases, security policies may be learned and generated by running an application in a controlled environment to discover its normal behavior, and then subsequently monitoring the application to determine whether it deviates from this predefined behavior; and if so, the application execution is intercepted, such as in the case where it attempts to make privileged systems calls that are prohibited [18]. This approach is very flexible, and the flexibility makes the ontology approach to filtering and monitoring attractive for mobile networks and peer-to-peer (P2P) network topologies where devices may join and leave the network unpredictably.

CHAPTER SUMMARY

Just as there are many forms of cryptography, there are many uses beyond creating ciphertext. As we have seen, cryptography is used to create message digests to indicate whether information has been tampered with, and in authentication of users by comparing secret passwords. Still, the concept of defense in depth requires that additional measures be used in combination. A complement to protecting integrity and authenticity of information with cryptography is the use of firewalls that can help control access to services and network components on host computers.

Administrators must carefully watch the access points to "trusted networks," and therefore the term *trusted network* suggests that an administrator has control over it. In some cases, particularly in the government sector, the term trusted network is more specific and refers to a bounded collection of hosts that can only accept packets specifi- cally addressed to them. In this environment, trusted hosts perform extra security checks to ensure that the information contained within the packet is addressed only to and processed only by that host.

A distrusted network might be configured with very tight constraints, and most firewalls allow for a hierarchy in which variable constraints can be placed between zones and on distrusted networks versus unknown networks. Packet filtering is a technique and a set of technologies and not technically a firewall, but the technique is useful for protecting systems and networks from intrusions or to help defend against denial of service attacks from outside the perimeter. Monitoring using security vulnerability ontologies are also not technically firewalls, but are increasingly being used in place of, or complementary to, firewalls, especially for networks comprised of mobile devices.

THINK ABOUT IT

Topic Questions

16.1: Revocation of a digital certificate is accom- plished by using what?

16.2: A "hardened" computer that has at least two LAN cards is called what?

16.3: A combination of exterior filtering routers, proxy systems, network address translation, and interior filtering routers is characteristic of what?

16.4: The RFC 5751 defined:

_____ X.509 certificates

_____ S/MIME

_____ PKI

_____ IPSec

THINK ABOUT IT (CONTINUED)

16.5: A screening filter operates at:

_____ The network layer
_____ The transport layer
_____ Both the network and transport layer
_____ The application layer

16.6: An optimistic stance means:

_____ That which is not explicitly permitted is disallowed.
_____ Everything not explicitly denied is permitted.
_____ No vulnerabilities are expected in a system.
_____ No threats to a system are expected.

16.7: IPv6 IPSec can be retrofit into IPv4.

_____ True
_____ False

16.8: A nonce is:

_____ A tunneling mechanism used in virtual private networks for integrity checks

_____ A secure key cipher that creates a dual-handshake
_____ A symmetric cipher that creates a dual-handshake
_____ A Diffie-Hellman value and random data to create a one-time use element

16.9: A dual-homed host refers to:

_____ Having two network cards
_____ A computer that connects to both a wired and a wireless network
_____ A host that has two servers for redundancy
_____ A host that has two CPUs for redundancy

16.10: Stateful packet inspection uses:

_____ A physical circuit
_____ A virtual circuit table
_____ A cell-switching technology
_____ Only a permit or deny rule

Questions for Further Study

Q16.1: Contrast CHAP with Kerberos for the purpose of authentication.

Q16.2: Distinguish between an application-layer firewall and a filtering technique.

Q16.3: Discuss the concept of false positives in relationship to firewall monitors.

Q16.4: Discuss what the concept of tunneling involves in relation to VPNs.

Q16.5: Explain how to generate a digital signature. Give an example.

KEY CONCEPTS AND TERMS

Ontology-based defenses are not technically firewalls, but they can perform many of the screening and monitoring functions of firewalls.

Perimeter networks are at the boundaries of an internal network.

Screened subnet has multiple perimeters and uses proxy systems inside a trusted zone (DMZ).

Stateful packet inspection is sometimes called session-level packet filtering.

X.509 is a standard issued by the International Telecommunications Union (ITU).

References

1. Kent, S., & Atkinson, R. (1998). *RFC 2401—Security architecture for the Internet protocol*. Internet Engineering Task Force. Retrieved from http://www.ietf.org/rfc/rfc2041.txt

2. Harkins, D., & Carrel, D. (1998). *RFC 2409—The Internet key exchange (IKE)*. Internet Engineering Task Force. Retrieved from http://www.ietf.org/rfc/rfc2049.txt

3. Kaufman, C., Perlman, R., & Speciner, M. (2002). *Network security: Private communication in a public world*. Upper Saddle River, NJ: Prentice Hall.

4. Dierks, T., & Rescorla, E. (2008). RFC 5246—*The Transport Layer Security (TLS) protocol version 1.2*. Internet Engineering Task Force. Security Paradigms Workshop (pp. 48–60). Langdale: ACM.

5. Solomon, M. G., & Chapple, M. (2005). *Information security illuminated*. Sudbury, MA: Jones and Bartlett Publishers.

6. Ramsdell, B., & Turner, S. (2010). *RFC 5751—Secure/Multipurpose Internet Mail Extensions (S/MIME) Version 3.2 Message Specification*. Internet Engineering Task Force. Retrieved from http://tools.ietf.org/html/rfc5751

7. Straub, D. W., Goodman, S., & Baskerville, R. L. (2008). *Information security: Policy, processes, and practices*. Armonk, NY: Sharpe.

8. Stewart, J. M. (2011). *Network security, firewalls, and VPNs*. Sudbury, MA: Jones & Bartlett Learning.

9. Habraken, J. (1999). *Cisco routers*. Indianapolis, IN: Que Books.

10. Thomas, T. (2004). *Network security: First step*. Indianapolis, IN: Cisco Press.

11. Stallings, W. (2003). *Network security essentials: Applications and standards*. Upper Saddle River, NJ: Pearson/Prentice Hall.

12. Tjaden, B. C. (2004). *Fundamentals of secure computer systems*. Wilsonville, OR: Franklin, Beedle & Associates.

13. Chapman, D. B., & Zwicky, E. D. (1995). *Building Internet firewalls*. Sebastopol, CA: O'Reilly & Associates.

14. Goldman, J. E. (2008). Firewalls. In H. Bidgoli (Ed), *Handbook of computer networks* (pp. 553–569). Hoboken, NJ: John Wiley & Sons.

15. Ford, R. (2008). *Conditioned reflex and security oversights*. Unpublished research presentation. Melbourne, FL: Florida Institute of Technology.

16. Zwicky, E. D., Cooper, S., & Chapman, D. B. (2000). *Building Internet firewalls*. Sebastopol, CA: O'Reilly Media.

17. Moreira, E., Martimiano, L., Brandao, A., & Bernardes, M. (2008). Ontologies for information security management and governance. *Information Management & Computer Security, 16*, 150–165.

18. Sterne, D., Balasubramanyam, P., Carman, D., Wilson, B., Talpade, R., Ko, C., . . . Rowe, J. (2005). *A general cooperative intrusion detection architecture for MANETs*, pp. 57–70. Proceedings of the Third IEEE International Workshop on Information Assurance (IWIA). Washington, DC.

Cryptography—And How IT Works

O RGANIZATIONS HAVE A RESPONSIBILITY TO SECURE the information they manage, whether health records, financial records, corporate records, or individually identifiable information, against unauthorized disclosure or alteration. At the same time, this information needs to be stored, transmitted, and processed in order to maintain business operations. To satisfy these security requirements, organizations institute cryptographic protocols and policies designed to ensure the confidentiality and integrity of stored and transmitted data. Cryptography is the process of transforming plaintext into ciphertext and is the primary countermeasure for "unauthorized release of message contents" as well as serves as the basis for authentication systems, for message digests, and in non-repudiation with digital signatures. Thus it is critical to both computer and network security. We will now explore how cryptography works at a conceptual level.

Chapter 17 Topics

This chapter:

- Explains cipher algorithms and the concept of keys.
- Discusses cryptographic concepts used in various means for security.
- Presents public and private key cryptography.
- Describes what block and stream ciphers mean and how they are used.
- Covers transposition and substitution concepts in cipher algorithms.
- Lists key generation and distribution concepts.

Chapter 17 Goals

When you finish this chapter, you should:

- ❏ Have an understanding of how cryptography is used in various facets of security, and understand what threats cryptography helps to prevent.
- ❏ Know the differences between public and private key cryptography, and how (conceptually) keys are used in ciphers to convert plaintext to ciphertext.
- ❏ Understand cryptanalysis and some of the attacks against cryptography.

17.1 Cryptography Overview

Although there are many ways to protect information, by far the most common (and among the most effective) is cryptography. Cryptography is a class of operations that takes human-readable information and encrypts, or scrambles it into an unintelligent form. More precisely, encryption is the process of encoding a message, which we will call plaintext (or cleartext), in such a way that the result, called ciphertext, is undecipherable without knowledge of the information and the process used to encode the message. The process of converting the ciphertext back to plaintext is called decryption.

An important element in encryption is the concept of a key, which is a code that is used within a cryptographic algorithm for generating ciphertext. Although the use of technology has lent itself to more widespread use of these techniques, cryptography has been utilized to protect information assets for millennia. We will explore the main concepts related to cryptography from a conceptual perspective.

17.1.1 Cryptographic Concepts

We have covered potential security violations that may result from active attacks, such as unauthorized modification of information, or from passive attacks, such as the unauthorized interception of messages. In passive attacks, an intruder may intercept information passing over a network without interfering with the data or the data transmission. Valuable information may be captured and the victim may never even realize it. In the most basic form, the purpose of encryption is to be able to exchange messages over a potentially insecure channel. If the encrypted messages are intercepted, the encryption makes it difficult for an eavesdropper to discern the meaning of the message. In addition to its use in exchanging messages, cryptography is also used to secure data on a physical medium such as a disk drive or "flash" drive, as well as in creating passcodes used in authentication, and for message digests and non-repudiation.

It is important to note, however, that encryption is not a "magic bullet." Encryption schemes can sometimes be broken. Even if the information is not decipherable to an intruder, he or she might be able to derive other important information by observing aspects or characteristics of the encrypted information exchange. This type of examination, known as traffic analysis, can still reveal significant information about the type of information that is being passed. To illustrate, port 80 is the well-known port for HTTP traffic. Knowing the http protocol, an intruder can inspect the plaintext control information and compare it with the encrypted ciphertext to try to identify the key used for encryption. Even without breaking the encryption scheme, the attacker can infer that the server accepting connections on port 80 is likely serving information whereas the client with a high-numbered port is likely to be the client.

By examining the amount of traffic flowing to the server, the relative importance of the server can be inferred and potentially targeted if the goal is to disrupt the work of the hosting system. The attacker can use an active attack to intercept and selectively modify, delete, reorder, or duplicate packets and insert them into the communication stream. To help prevent this, header information can be encrypted using a virtual private network (VPN) [1].

Encryption has become so commonplace in many applications that sometimes people are unaware that they are using it. For instance, if we log on to a website using https (which uses secure sockets layer [SSL] or Transport Layer Security [TLS]), as when we are making a purchase online, we notice a "lock" icon in the bottom corner of our browser [2]. Double clicking on that icon may present a certificate digitally signed by a *certificate authority* (**CA**). The certificate contains important information about the owner of the certificate, how long and for what purpose it is valid, and the type of keys it contains. These keys can be used with an appropriate algorithm to exchange encrypted information.

At the heart of cryptography is the cipher algorithm, which is essentially a computation that transforms the plaintext into ciphertext by using a *key* (or sets of keys) where the keys act to seed values for the cipher [3]. With most ciphers, the security of the cryptosystem is not in the secrecy of the algorithm; rather, it is in the secrecy of the auxiliary input used in the encryption process, the key. The key is used with the plaintext and algorithm to create the ciphertext.

There are two primary ciphers: stream ciphers, such as RC4, and block ciphers, such as AES. Most modern ciphers are block ciphers. We will discuss how stream and block ciphers work shortly.

17.1.2 Generating a Simple Cipher Code

As you have probably gathered, modern cryptographic algorithms can be very complex, but conceptually encryption is mainly a matter of permutation, transposition, substitution, or a combination of the three. The best way to understand the basics of how encryption works is to examine some simple ciphers. To begin, let's consider a permutation cipher to the plaintext where all the letters in the original plaintext would be retained, but placed in a different order. We could do this by breaking the message into blocks of six letters and placing them into three rows with three columns. The key in this case is the number and order of the columns. So we can begin with the plaintext message: "MEET ME AT PORTER HALL." By arranging this message to form three rows of six characters, we can create the ciphertext by taking the letters from each column as seen in **Table 17.1**.

Did you notice in Table 17.1 that a "mangler" function [4] has taken various letters and placed them in seemingly odd places? The arrangement is not exactly by random chance because it has to be revised during decryption. Where a permutation cipher scrambles the order of the plaintext symbols, a substitution cipher will map the original symbols to new symbols (making a substitution). An example of a simple substitution cipher using a single alphabet can be seen in **Table 17.2**. The alphabet is scrambled and each letter is mapped to a new letter.

TABLE 17.1 A Simple Permutation
MEETME
ATPORT
ERHALL

Reading down the columns from the permutation table, we end up with a ciphertext of MAEETREPHTOAMRLETL.

TABLE 17.2 A Simple Substitution Cipher
A B C D E F G H I J K L M N O P Q R S T U V W X Y Z = Alphabet
X Y Z A B C D E F G H I J K L M N O P Q R S T U V W = Substitutions
So to encrypt the message, one would use the substituted letters:
Plaintext: MEET ME AT PORTER HALL
Ciphertext: JBBQ JB XQ MLOQBO EXII

One other item to take note of with the substitution cipher is that mapping is on a one-to-one correspondence with the same alphabet, so it makes it relatively easy to decipher the three-letter shift permutation. The benefit of the simple shift like this is that it is easy to encrypt and to decrypt the messages, particularly if the permutation is known beforehand, but it doesn't take long to discover the pattern. To make it a bit more difficult, we could choose a key of some length to begin the mapping and fill in the rest of the alphabet after it.

To illustrate this important point, let's consider a cipher named after the French diplomat and mathematician, Blaise de Vigenere. The Vigenere cipher, which is a substitution cipher that operates on symbols, such as alphabet characters or bytes, by replacing them with other symbols according to a rule and a key [5, 6]. The Vigenere cipher combines the positional value of each character in the alphabetic key with the positional value of a letter in the plaintext message to generate the ciphertext. Because the positional sum of two letters is often greater than the number of letters in the alphabet, it does this using modular arithmetic with, in the case of the English alphabet, modulo 26.

Recall that modular arithmetic operates similar to the numbers on a clock face. Using that analogy, 9 o'clock plus 5 hours is 2 o'clock because once we go past 12 o'clock, we loop back around again. Thus, if we were to project the English alphabet onto the face of a clock, as we pass "Z," we would loop around to "A."

To highlight the Vigenere cipher with an example, we may begin by assigning each letter of the alphabet a value related to the letter's position in the alphabet. Letter "A" would have a value of 0, "B" the value 1, "C" the value 2, "D" the value of 3, and so on until we reach the end of the alphabet "Z" that has the value of 25. By adding the positional value of two letters modulo 26, we will always have a result between 0 and 25, producing a letter equivalent.

In Focus

A modulus is an algebraic function defined by Gauss in which one number is divided by another, and the rounded remainder is taken as a result to "seed" the next sequence in the function. The Vigenere cipher operates on a vector of key (k) values. Remember that a vector is a value that consists of both a magnitude (displacement) and a direction of the displacement.

Let's see an example of the Vigenere cipher that works by choosing an alphabetic key and, for each letter in the plaintext, combining it with a letter in the key to generate a new letter in the ciphertext. If the key is shorter than the plaintext, the key is simply repeated along the length of the entire message. Examine this frequently used example [7, 8] in **Table 17.3** with a key of "CRYPTOGRAPHY." The numeric equivalent, mapping the alphabet A to Z with the numbers 0 to 25, is C=2, R=17, Y=24, P=15, T=19, O=14, G=6, R=17, A=0, P=15, H=7, Y=24. As you can see by this simple example, applying the key to the plaintext message "ATMIDNIGHT" transforms it into "CKKXWBOXHI " in ciphertext.

TABLE 17.3 Vigenere Example									
A	T	M	I	D	N	I	G	H	T
0	19	12	8	3	13	8	6	7	19
2	17	24	15	19	14	6	17	0	15
↓	↓	↓	↓	↓	↓	↓	↓	↓	↓
2	10	10	23	22	1	14	23	7	8
C	K	K	X	W	B	O	X	H	I

17.1.3 Breaking a Simple Cipher Code

Vigenere is a polyalphabetic cipher, meaning that there can be more than one alphabet involved in the encryption process. Notice in our previous English example that both the "T" and the "M" encrypt to "K." This encryption happens because each plaintext letter has its own instance of the 26-letter English alphabet to which it can translate in the ciphertext. However, many traditional substitution ciphers are monoalphabetic, which is to say that there is only one alphabet involved in the encryption. With a given alphabet, the frequency distribution of letters in the ciphertext will match the frequency distribution of letters in the plaintext, albeit with different letters.

Frequency characteristics are an important tool in cryptanalysis of simple ciphers because the frequency distribution of characters in a typical language is not uniform. Note that cryptanalysis refers to "code breaking." A uniform distribution on the 26-character alphabet of the English language would result in all letters having the similar frequency 1/26, or approximately a 3.846% occurrence rate. In contrast, however, the letter "E" actually appears 12.702% of the time, more than three times more frequently than the average. That translates into 1 out of each 8 letters is "E" on average in prose. On the other hand, the letter "Q" appears only 0.095% of the time, or only once every 1052 characters [6]. Thus by knowing the average frequency distribution of letters in the language under observation that the plaintext is written in, given enough ciphertext, cryptanalysts that can make a prediction of the plaintext message based on the letter frequency distribution in the ciphertext. If in the ciphertext message of a monoalphabetic cipher the letter "Y" appears 12.702% of the time, and the known frequency distribution of the letter "E" in the language of the plaintext is close to 12.702%, it may be inferred that the ciphertext letter "Y" maps to the plaintext letter "E" [7, 9]. This is commonly referred to as the "coincidence of determination," and it can be used on any modern language using a simple substitution cipher.

In Focus

Ancient "Caesar" ciphers applied a key with plaintext, and a device called a Wheatstone wheel used to rotate to the ciphertext according to the key.

With a polyalphabetic cipher such as Vigenere, the process of code breaking is a little more complicated than a monoalphabetic cipher, but it can still be done using the same basic statistical techniques. If the key length is smaller than the message length, there will be some degree of repetition in the encryption. Given sufficient ciphertext, this repetition allows for the determination of an index of coincidence on groups of letters that can lead to a prediction of the key length. For example, the letters "THE" are frequently found together in English. Given a sufficiently larger amount of encrypted plaintext, the letters "THE" are bound to be encrypted with the same three-block set of letters in the key.

For example, given our key example of "CRYPTOGRAPHY" from earlier, it is likely that the "CRY" of the key will be used to encrypt the letters "THE" multiple times producing the same ciphertext output. The repetition of blocks of letters in the ciphertext can be used to help determine the possible key length; this is because if the repetition truly represents the encryption of the same letters of plaintext by the same letters of the key, then the repetition occurs as a multiple of the key length. Once the key length is determined, the ciphertext can be arranged so that all letters are together in the ciphertext encrypted with the same letter in the key.

17.1.4 Ciphertext Dissection and "S" Boxes

An "S" box (S-Box) refers to a matrix that is created by a cipher for substituting values. We may treat each group as a monoalphabetic cipher and compare the single letter frequency distribution to determine the plaintext. Let's take a ciphertext that is comprised of the following string of characters:

tigljvtmgbpaaugtigcvrogruefioitignigaugtigcbpdzvhbvwbutigisu

Seeing the repetition of the characters "tig" in the ciphertext and guessing them to be the letters "the" in the plaintext, we can see that they repeat on the boundaries 0, 15, 33, 42, and 57. These all divide evenly by 3, so our guess is that there must be a key length of 3. Then by rearranging the ciphertext into blocks of three and stacking them we can assemble three columns, each column having been encrypted by the character in the key, as seen in **Table 17.4**. Thus we can begin to view the patterns.

Using our example, if we guessed that the ciphertext "tig" equates to plaintext "the," then we can use the frequency characteristics of the English language along with our understanding of the cipher to quickly recognize that the first column represents a shift of 0, the second column a shift of 1, and the third column a shift of 2. Converting back to the plaintext, we can make the associations as seen in **Table 17.5**. By putting this all together, we can see that the plaintext states: "the little boy ate the big cup of pudding then he ate the candy that was theirs" using the key = "abc."

17.1.5 Cryptography and Security Goals

Encryption algorithms, which are the mathematical functions that transform plaintext into ciphertext, as we have noted, generally fall within two categories: symmetric and asymmetric. Symmetric algorithms utilize the same shared secret (key) to both encrypt

TABLE 17.4 Ciphertext Character Stack		
t	i	g
l	j	v
t	m	g
b	p	a
a	u	g
t	i	g
c	v	r
o	g	r
u	e	f
i	o	i
t	i	g
n	i	g
a	u	g
t	i	g
c	b	p
d	z	v
h	b	v
w	b	u
t	i	g
i	s	u

and decrypt a given message. Asymmetric algorithms utilize different, yet related secrets (keys) for the encryption and decryption process. The ultimate goal of a cryptosystem is to have an algorithm that produces ciphertext such that no matter how much ciphertext is available, there is not enough information in it to determine the plaintext that produced it. This is known as an unconditionally secure cryptosystem, and with the exception of a special cipher known as a ***one-time pad***, no other probably unconditionally secure algorithm exists [10]. The reason a one-time pad cryptosystem is unconditionally secure is because the encryption of the plaintext relies on a one-time use, random key that is the length of the plaintext. The resulting ciphertext would contain no information at all about the plaintext that generated it, which means the ciphertext could relate to any set of plaintext.

Central to the one-time pad scheme is the generation of a truly random key that is equal in length to the message and is never reused. If the key were not random, then given enough ciphertext it might be possible to deduce the logic used in the key creation, and by deducing the key be able to reproduce the plaintext. If the key were random, but shorter than the message, then the repetition of the key in the production of the ciphertext could

TABLE 17.5 Plaintext Character Stack

t	h	e
l	i	t
t	l	e
b	o	y
a	t	e
t	h	e
b	i	g
c	u	p
o	f	p
u	d	d
i	n	g
t	h	e
n	h	e
a	t	e
t	h	e
c	a	n
d	y	t
h	a	t
w	a	s
t	h	e
i	r	s

result in determining the key and the resultant plaintext. Such is also the case if the key were to be reused [11].

Although the generation of a random, one-time use key that is equal in length to the message to be encrypted may not seem difficult, the effort required to introduce true randomness and to manage the one-time use keys is substantial. In fact, it is a key distribution and management problem that is at the heart of most difficulties associated with utilizing encryption to secure information assets. One-time pads are used in some highly secure operations where the costs associated with managing the keys are less than the value of the information being processed.

In Focus

Whether private or public, keys (at least the private portion of a public key) must be kept secret and secure. This is called "key management," and the many keys one must manage are called "key rings."

To manage keys in a one-time pad cryptosystem, the keys must be generated with true randomness, often introduced by monitoring some random, natural event. Once the source of randomness is available, the keys must be generated that are longer than any message that may be encrypted with them. Having generated the keys, the messages to be secured are only as secure as the keys used to encrypt them. If the desire is to be able to transmit information securely from one location to another, then both the sender and the receiver of the information must have a copy of the keys in order to encrypt and decrypt the messages. This implies that copies of the keys must have been distributed through a secure channel before any secure communications can commence. Although this may seem trivial, in practice it can be difficult to manage. It also means that before any secure communications can commence, a relationship for key distribution already exists [2].

In Focus

Given the difficulties inherent in the use of a one-time pad encryption scheme, we are forced to utilize encryption algorithms that, although not unconditionally secure, are computationally secure (meaning not practical to break although possible to break eventually).

Although a one-time pad is unconditionally secure, a cryptographic scheme is computationally secure if it takes longer to break the encryption than the useful lifetime of the information that is protected, or the costs more to break the encryption than the value of the information [10]. What provides this security is a combination of the encryption algorithm and the key. The creation of a secure encryption algorithm is incredibly difficult, and most encryption algorithms in use are ones that are considered secure because many people have tried to find ways to subvert their security over a long period of time. For the vast majority of organizations, it is not advisable to try to create a unique encryption algorithm; rather, better security is normally gained by utilizing a standard algorithm.

With a standard algorithm, the computational security then relies on the key. As discussed earlier, if the key is not random, then someone trying to decipher the ciphertext need only discover the pattern used to create the key and he or she will be able to re-create it. A typical example of this is passwords chosen by individuals. Rarely is a truly random password generated; rather, at best it is a pseudorandom password and at worst it is a dictionary word. This reduces the list of all possible keys, known as the ***key space***, significantly and can make it relatively easy to gain access to the protected information. In addition to the key randomness is the key length. The longer the key, the greater the key space and the more possible keys that have to be tried when guessing in the code.

If a password is sufficiently random, then on average, a person trying to gain access to the information protected by the password would have to try at least half the keys (passwords) in the key space. Although we can think of key length in terms of password length, when talking about key size in most modern cryptosystems, the measurement used is the number of bits in a given key. That is, a key might be 56 bits or 128 bits long, meaning that the key space consists of all possible combinations of 2^{56} or 2^{128} bits. Although this might not seem like a lot, the space is actually quite large, but as processing power increases the length of time to search through the key space decreases. Thus, the longer the key, the more computationally secure the information [12].

17.2 Symmetric Cryptography

Modern ciphers can be categorized many ways. One way to separate the ciphers is by whether they use the same key for encryption and decryption (known as **symmetric** or **private key cryptography**). Otherwise they use a different key for encryption and decryption (known as **asymmetric** or **public key cryptography**). Regardless of whether cryptography uses a symmetric or asymmetric key, the key space, which is the range of values available to construct a key, and the key length are important to the impregnability of the cryptography, whether used to digitally sign a document or to encrypt data. Key lengths are measured in terms of the number of bits they contain, which is known as key strength. In this section, we will discuss symmetric cryptography [13].

17.2.1 Symmetric Ciphers and Keys

As indicated, there are many different types of ciphers. Some are considered "classical," such as the Vigenere, the Affine cipher, which uses affine transformation and Euclidean geometry, and the Playfair cipher developed by Charles Wheatstone [14]. "Modern" ciphers include DES and 3DES, which triples the keys and rounds of DES, and although there are others, the most common modern symmetric cipher in use today is AES [14].

> **In Focus**
>
> In addition to categorizing ciphers as symmetric or asymmetric with respect to their key use, they can also be defined by how they process data, whether as chunks of data at a time (block ciphers) or as bits in streams (stream ciphers).

Stream ciphers are **finite state machines** that operate on a few bits at a time, outputting the encrypted values bit by bit. Examples of stream ciphers include RC4, X5/x, Helix, and SEAL. Stream ciphers were popular for a while, but they have been susceptible to corruption, such as through what is called an *insertion* attack. These largely lost favor to block ciphers. The only major stream cipher in much use today is RC4 [6].

Block ciphers are **stateless machines** that replace large blocks of bits at a time (say 64, 128, or 256 bits). Examples of block ciphers are DES, 3DES, Blowfish, and AES; however, note that DES can operate in stream mode, although it does not do so by default. Ciphers also combine substitution with transposition of characters in their algorithms, and this concept goes all the way back to the old German Enigma machine, which was a rotor type of device that used a complex combination of transposition and substitution automated by a mechanical engine. Examine **Figure 17.1**.

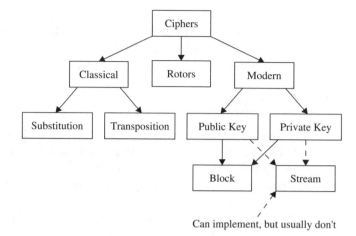

For some time, DES was very popular, but with increases in computational power, DES has been found to be no longer considered secure enough for highly sensitive information [7, 10]. An attempt to strengthen DES was to triple the rounds creating 3DES (and keys), but because 3DES is relatively slow to encipher and decipher compared to other newer ciphers, it is not often used any longer, and it has largely been replaced by AES [9]. Nevertheless, DES serves as a good example of how ciphers work because the basic techniques it uses have been carried over into other ciphers.

In Focus

The DES cipher uses different modes of operation. The electronic codebook (ECB) mode is the simplest, but least secure because it processes plaintext 64 bits at a time and each block is encrypted with the same key. There are other block cipher modes, however, including cipher block chaining (CBC), output feedback mode (OFM), as well as other modes [13].

17.2.2 Substitution, Transposition, and Permutation

To avoid the weaknesses of simple substitution ciphers, the notions of permutation, substitution, and transposition were introduced into modern ciphers. A permutation shuffles the symbols in plaintext by moving them around into other positions according to a rule, and then the codes are split into left and right halves. In the substitution portion of the algorithm, a code or symbol (e.g., groups of bits) is replaced according to a key, as we saw with the Vigenere cipher. A logical XOR (exclusive or) operation is usually used in the substitution process. After the codes are substituted, they are transposed. Transposition swaps the halves. Each time this is done, this is known as a round.

Take for example that characters in an alphabet can be represented as letters or an ASCII decimal or hexadecimal number, but ultimately ciphers use binary representations of these codes (**Figure 17.2**). Because all digital information ultimately ends up as 1s and

Binary	Octal	Decimal	Hex	Symbol
100 0001	101	65	41	A
100 0010	102	66	42	B
100 0011	103	67	43	C
100 0100	104	68	44	D
100 0101	105	69	45	E
100 0110	106	70	46	F
100 0111	107	71	47	G
100 1000	110	72	48	H

FIGURE 17.2

ASCII chart portion.

0s on some level of the programming in a computer, we need to think about cryptography at that level. If we look up an ASCII character set chart (see for instance [8]), we will find that letters, such as "A" and "B" are represented in octal, hexadecimal, and binary forms. For instance, the letter "A" in ASCII is represented in binary code as 1000001, whereas the letter "B" in ASCII is represented in binary as 1000010. When we examine these binary codes, we notice that there are only 7 bits allocated to the binary numbers; this is because 1 bit is reserved for determining the integrity of the data using what is known as a parity bit (we will forgo the discussion of parity bits in this discussion).

To understand substitution and transposition at a binary level, we will illustrate with a modern symmetric key cipher known as Feistel, which is the basis of DES. In reality, the cipher algorithm is quite complex, so we will merely outline the general concept here. In Feistel-based ciphers such as DES, blocks of binary numbers are transformed using a 64-bit key. Note, however, that in DES there are actually only 56 bits available to the actual key because 8 are used as parity bits and are dropped from the cipher algorithm.

Binary data blocks are then split into halves, with each half scrambled independently by the algorithm. One portion of the key (called a subkey) is applied to one half of the split data block, the cipher function is performed, and the two halves are then swapped. If we used the DES as an example of a Feistel-based cipher, this substitution and transposition is done 16 times. Let's further highlight this complex idea by simulating the process and using some very simplified examples with a subset of bits for a message and a key. The steps are as follows [11]:

1. Perform an initial permutation (swap bits around).
2. Divide the bits of the plaintext into left and right halves.
3. Generate subkeys to be used in each iteration or cycle.
4. Mangle the bits. That is, substitute them according to some scheme (function f), apply a rounding function using the logical exclusive OR operator (XOR) to the right-hand set of bits.
5. Shift (transpose) the result of that operation to the left-hand side.

6. Then execute an XOR from the result with the left-hand bits.

7. Then complete the transposition by swapping the halves.

8. Repeat steps 1 through 7 *n* times. (Note that DES does this 16 times; each time is called a round.)

9. Complete a final permutation.

To summarize this complex process, let us say that we have a 64-bit input to encrypt. The input would be divided into 8 inputs that are mangled, which means to place them into a block according to some theorem or function. This is the substitution part of the cipher. In other words, bits are broken up into chunks, and each of the bits is substituted and put into different locations according to the cipher algorithm and S-boxes. An exclusive OR (XOR) is done and then the halves are swapped. This substitution and transposition cipher may be represented in the very simplified illustration in **Figure 17.3**. As seen, the function performs an XOR operation with the right half and subkey, then the halves are swapped. The symbol $\oplus$ means XOR on the data half using the cipher function specified and the key provided.

From our earlier chapters, you are already familiar with how logical operators such as AND, OR, and NOT work. The logical XOR operator converts a result to 1 if only one of either of its two inputs is 1; otherwise the result is 0. We can see how the XOR operator works by viewing the truth table, **Table 17.6**.

FIGURE 17.3

Simplified substitution and permutation.

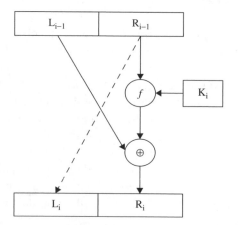

TABLE 17.6 XOR Truth Table		
A	B	A $\oplus$ B
1	1	0
1	0	1
0	1	1
0	0	0

In Focus

Along with XOR, the actions of permutation, substitution, and transposition form the basis of most modern ciphers. A permutation shifts or moves groups of characters or bits from one location to another, and substitution involves exchanging one character (or bit) for another, and transposition trades the halves. The repetition of substitution and transposition processes is performed "n" number of times.

To further illustrate the concept of substitution and transposition, for simplicity, suppose that we have an 8-bit plaintext bit pattern of 11110011 and a subkey of 0110. Using the XOR function and shifting and swapping bits for each round, the cipher algorithm could be computed. This simple cipher divides the bits into left and right halves. Using the subkey of 0110, we perform an XOR logical function to the right half of bits. The product 0101 is then shifted to the left half where the XOR is again applied to the left-hand bits. The product is then swapped, with the initial right half block shifting to the left half, and the left half block to the right (**Figure 17.4**).

We continue this substitution and transposition process multiple times as defined by the cipher algorithm. In this example, we would repeat the next round by shifting bits to the left, which will represent our key function, to generate a subkey for the next round. Thus we begin with the bit pattern beginning from the previous round of 00111010, and we repeat the process as before. To demonstrate this round, let's say that the subkey generated for this next round was 1100. We will use this in this round based on the previous result (**Figure 17.5**). Note that DES uses 64 bits, not 8, as an example.

	L1	L2	L3	L4	R1	R2	R3	R4
Plaintext ASCII character	1	1	1	1	0	0	1	1
Subkey					0	1	1	0
Apply XOR operation					0	1	0	1
Swap right to left	0	1	0	1				
Result of XOR left half	1	0	1	0				
Swap halves	0	0	1	1	1	0	1	0

FIGURE 17.4

Substitution and transposition example 1.

	L1	L2	L3	L4	R1	R2	R3	R4
Plaintext ASCII character	0	0	1	1	1	0	1	0
Subkey					1	1	0	0
Apply XOR function					0	1	1	0
Swap right to left	0	1	1	0				
Result of XOR left half	0	1	0	1				
Swap halves	1	0	1	0	0	1	0	1

FIGURE 17.5

Substitution and transposition example 2.

The theorem used in this simple cipher will continue to repeat these steps *n* more times (in the case of DES, 16 times) until we produce the final ciphertext. Realize that if bits are scrambled in such a way, it needs to be reversed in order to decrypt the ciphertext back into plaintext. That means, in private key cryptography, using the same key and doing the inverse of the encryption (note that public key cryptography is much more complex—and consequently, slower). Because of the nature (and predictability) of substitution and transposition in this simple example, it can be relatively easily "broken" and is not considered secure [4].

17.2.3 Modern Symmetric Ciphers

As a consequence of cipher compromises, modern ciphers have increased the complexity of the ciphering algorithms. For example, the **3DES** carried the DES* concept forward by taking the DES 64-bit keys and tripling the rounds to create an overall key length of 192 bits. (Note that 3DES can be executed in several different ways, or modes, which are beyond the scope of our textbook, but for a more precise and thorough explanation, see [4].) Recall though that DES requires bits for integrity checking and that means some number of bits are siphoned off and the rest are left over for the key. The 3DES breaks the key into three subkeys, padding the keys if necessary so they are each 64 bits long, then the remainder of the encryption process uses the DES algorithm but with 48 rather than 56 bits (for reasons we have explained relative to integrity checking). As described conceptually then in this example, permutation, substitution, and transposition are fairly straightforward in this approach, but the actual computations are much more complex.

> **In Focus**
>
> We often see the International Data Encryption Algorithm (IDEA), which is also a symmetric block cipher that competed to replace DES [15]. It requires a 128-bit key and operates on 64-bit blocks of data through 8 rounds with a final unique output transformation.

Aside from 3DES, we have also seen the popularization of IDEA. With the IDEA algorithm, there are three substitution operations performed on data: (1) a bitwise XOR, (2) addition modulo 2^{16}, and (3) multiplication modulo $2^{16}+1$ where an all-zero block is treated as 2^{16}. IDEA combines 16-bit chunks of keys and data using various substitution functions with a final permutation at the end of each round. The final output transformation consists of repeating the initial substitutions utilizing the same 16-bit key chunks. By these examples, which we have simplified, you can see how difficult it can be to decipher even relatively simple modern ciphers. From an organizational perspective, it would take a really determined attacker and a great deal of time and resources to decipher even relatively simple encryption from modern ciphers, and by then, the information might be obsolete [4].

---

*For a more complete description of DES, see Tjaden, 2004 [11].

In Focus

Emerging ciphers include techniques that range from elliptical (non-linear) calculus to quantum mechanics and inorganic chemistry, where ciphers use physical changes in chemical bonding at the molecular level to determine if information has been tampered with.

The **Advanced Encryption Standard** (**AES**) is described in FIPS PUB 197. AES, like 3DES, is a symmetric cipher that operates on blocks of data rather than a continuous stream. The block size for AES is 128 bits, with the key size being 128, 192, or 256 bits. For clarity, it is recommended that the key size be specified when talking about the algorithm (AES-128, AES-192, AES-256) (FIPS PUB 197). However, AES differs from 3DES in how it handles data blocks. Instead of dividing data blocks in halves, performing the round function and swapping the halves, the Rijndael (named for inventors Vincent Rijmen and Joan Daemen) algorithm on which AES is based creates *parallel* substitution and permutation stages, where for every permutation there are three substitution stages [16]. The basic algorithm for AES is:

1. Take the given key (128, 192, 256 bits) and using the specified key expansion algorithm, generate enough 32-bit chunks (known as words) to cover one more than the number of rounds. A 128-bit key will have 10 rounds, a 192-bit key will have 12 rounds, and a 256-bit key will have 14 rounds.
2. Break the 128-bit block to be encrypted into 8-bit bytes.
3. XOR 128-bit round key with the 128-bit block of data.
4. For all but the last round:
    a. Substitute bytes in the current block according to the substitution table (called an S-box, which is a matrix of values from which to select). This is the first substitution.
    b. Shift the rows in the block cyclically according to the row number. This is the permutation.
    c. Mix the column in the block according to the specified algorithm (for details, see FIPS PUB 197). This is the second substitution.
    d. Add a round key with XOR. This is the third substitution.
5. For all but the last round:
    a. Substitute bytes in the block according to the substitution table (S-box).
    b. Shift the rows in the block according to their row number.
    c. Add the final round key with XOR.

As seen by this simplified description of AES, and more specifically, the Rijndael algorithm, it does not perform a symmetrical substitution (Feistel) as does DES. Instead, using S-boxes (a matrix of values that can be algorithmically vectored and selected), the selections are a multiplicative inverse transformation function for each input value [4]. This is a complicated way of saying simply that the values chosen are not just subdivided, substituted, and swapped as in a permutation, substitution, and transposition. Rather the algorithm has non-linearity properties, making it extremely difficult for a cryptanalyst (a code breaker) to calculate a next iteration result given a known previous iteration result, which otherwise is the case with DES [17].

17.2.4 Key Issues with Symmetric Cryptography

As we have discussed, private key (or symmetric) cryptography uses the same key to encrypt and decrypt a message, and the key must be kept secret. This form of cryptography is quite efficient in terms of encryption and decryption of messages. By simply reversing the process, an encrypted message can be reconstructed because the XOR function reverses bits back in to their original form. To highlight with a simple explanation, if we encode a message segment 1001 with a subkey 1111, the XOR produces 0110. If we XOR 0110 with the subkey 1111, we get 1001. However, relying on one key poses some problems in terms of distributing the keys and keeping them secure.

> ### In Focus
>
> Private-key cryptography (called symmetric) requires that both parties who share a ciphertext keep the key secret, because the same key is used to both encrypt and decrypt the messages. Exchanging keys therefore can be a source of security breach. Private keys can be exchanged over an insecure channel using a Diffie-Hellman technique.

One of the practical problems faced in wide-scale secret key cryptography is how does one exchange a secret key with many others electronically? Whitfield Diffie and Martin Hellman devised a method of using modulo functions with prime numbers to encode the key. Although the "Diffie-Hellman" technique is not technically cryptography, it uses cryptographic techniques to encode keys exchanged by parties. Thus the Diffie-Hellman key exchange protocol allows two users to independently generate a shared secret key utilizing information passed over an insecure communication channel [4]. The key exchange is based on the difficulty of computing discrete logarithms, but for our purposes, it is sufficient to understand how to choose the numbers needed to compute the shared secret. The exchange depends on choosing a prime number, p, and a primitive root of the prime number mod p.

> ### In Focus
>
> A prime number is a number that can only be evenly divided by one and itself—numbers such as 3, 5, 7, 11, and so forth.

A primitive root of a prime number p is one whose powers mod p up to $p - 1$ generates all the integers from 1 to $p - 1$ creating a matrix of primes from which the cryptographic system can choose [10]. As an example, given the prime number 5, the primitive roots are 2 and 3 because each satisfies the requirements:

- $2^1 \bmod 5 = 2$; $2^2 \bmod 5 = 4$; $2^3 \bmod 5 = 3$; $2^4 \bmod 5 = 1$
- $3^1 \bmod 5 = 3$; $3^2 \bmod 5 = 4$; $3^3 \bmod 5 = 2$; $3^4 \bmod 5 = 1$

To generate a shared secret over an insecure communications channel, let's say that two people, Alice and Bob, will choose a prime number, p, and a primitive root of p that we will call r. Alice and Bob can share these values over an insecure channel. Alice and Bob will then each choose a secret value to raise r to mod p. So if Alice chooses a and Bob chooses b, Alice will compute $r^a \bmod p$ and Bob will compute $r^b \bmod p$.

Given our example of choosing 5 as our prime, Alice and Bob could agree to use 2 as their primitive root, giving us $p = 5$ and $r = 2$. Alice then chooses a number $a = 7$ and Bob chooses a number $b = 9$. Alice computes $2^7 \bmod 5 = 3$ and Bob computes $2^9 \bmod 5 = 2$. Alice and Bob share the results of their calculations, 3 and 2, but keep their exponents, 7 and 9, secret. Alice then takes Bob's number 2 and raises it to her secret number 7 and takes the result mod the shared prime, 5. Bob does the same with Alice's 3, raising it to his secret number 9 and taking the result mod the shared prime, 5. The results are the same value that they now share as a shared secret:

- $2^7 \bmod 5 = 3$
- $3^9 \bmod 5 = 3$

An eavesdropper may be able to capture the prime, the primitive root, and results of raising the primitive root to some exponent, but to generate the shared secret between Alice and Bob, the eavesdropper would have to calculate either $2^x \bmod 5 = 3$ or $2^y \bmod 5 = 2$, discrete logarithms. Although with the example using such small numbers it is trivial, when using much larger numbers (as is done in the "real" world) it is impractical [18].

17.3 Asymmetric Cryptography

Public key cryptography, also known as asymmetric key cryptography, is important for widely distributed secure transactions. It enables businesses to conduct e-commerce using trusted messages. An infrastructure used to support asymmetric key cryptography is called PKI (public key infrastructure) and includes (1) certificate authorities who dispense trusted verifications such as X.509 certificates, (2) registration authorities who "log" or register their certificates with a certificate authority, (3) certificate servers that issue digital certificates, (4) certificate revocation where that distributes notifications of revoked, expired, or forged certificates, and (5) key recovery services that allow administrators to recover lost keys, along with others [3]. Public key cryptography relies on special mathematical functions that are very difficult to reverse without a special piece of knowledge that acts in what is called a ***trapdoor*** to the solution. The mathematical problems upon which this type of cryptographic algorithm relies include factoring large prime integer numbers (RSAs), combinatorial optimization (e.g., the knapsack problem), algebraic coding theory, or discrete logarithm problems for finite fields or elliptic curves [19]. In this section, we will discuss the basics of asymmetric cryptography.

17.3.1 Public Keys and Asymmetric Cryptography

What makes asymmetric cryptography particularly unique is that the mathematical functions upon which they are built are designed to be easy to compute but hard to reverse. In fact, they are often called *one-way* functions because like a turnstile, they normally allow travel in one direction only. What makes them useful for cryptography, however, is that with a special piece of knowledge about how and what was computer, the computation can be reversed. This special piece of knowledge acts like a *trapdoor* allowing the function to be reversed and the original input to be determined. The information going into the function and the special information to reverse it are complimentary, and as keys, information encrypted by one can be decrypted by the other. This means that there doesn't have to be a shared secret; any information encrypted with one key can only be decrypted by its complement. One key, known as the public key, can be freely distributed so that anyone can send an encrypted message to the holder of the private key. Only the holder of the private key can then decrypt the message [20].

In Focus

Let's suppose you just got off the train and went through the turnstile to leave. The turnstile only turns one-way to allow you to get off the platform. As soon as you pass through the turnstile, you realize that you dropped your wallet on the other side. The attendant, seeing your distress, walks up to the turnstile and with a special series of movements, is able to pass back through the turnstile to collect your wallet for you. In this case, the turnstile is the one-way function and the special series of movements made by the attendant is the information to activate the trapdoor and reverse the process.

There are many tools and ways to generate keys. One example is that the JAVA programming language extended library javax.crypto can be used to create them. For example, by importing the libraries javax.crypto.KeyGenerator, javax.crypto.SecretKey, and java.security.Key, a secret key can be produced for DES using the generateKey() method. Another technology such as *Putty* can generate asymmetric keys using a variety of algorithms for use with SSH, email, and other uses of public key cryptography.

In Focus

Public and private key pairs are generated so that only a specific part of keys can perform the encryption and another part the decryption functions. Any keys other than the specific pair will not work. A public key is available to everyone. The matching private key must be kept a secret by its owner, just as with private key cryptography—but the private key portion does not have to be distributed.

17.3.2 Beyond Encrypting Messages

In addition to encrypting messages, private key cryptography can be used to ensure non-repudiation of the origins of the message because, presumably, the only one with the private key would be the owner of the key pair. So beyond providing standard encryption benefits of obfuscating messages, asymmetric cryptographic schemes have the additional benefit of being able to capitalize on the public key to provide a means to digitally sign a message. A **_digital signature_** works by using what is known as a hash or message digest (MD). A hash function is a one-way function that takes as its argument a message and outputs a fixed-length block of data that is related to the original message [11].

In Focus

A digital signing certificate is similar to message digests used for documents to determine tampering in the sense that using a key, a cipher code for a digital signature can be generated to ensure that a sender is who he or she purports to be and that a message received is as was sent—called **_non-repudiation_** [18]. There are a variety of ways certificates can be created, but a free certificate can be obtained from Comodo for Outlook. From the www.comodogroup.com website, a user can generate a digital certificate with a passcode, which is downloaded from Comodo in which a user installs into Outlook. When sending signed messages, users merely select the Outlook sign with digital signature option.

The hash is then encrypted with the private key of the signer. The message and encrypted hash can be sent together like a signed document. A recipient of the message and hash pair could retrieve the public key of the signer and decrypt the hash associated with the message. The recipient could then re-create the hash and compare it to the decrypted version sent to him or her. If the two match, then one can be certain that the message was not altered and that the holder of the private key that corresponds to the public key used to decrypt the hash was the originator.

The down side to the use of a hash function is that, because of the fixed-length output, there will be more than one message that can produce the same hash in what is known as a _collision_. Fundamental to a good hash algorithm, however, is that it must be impossible to reproduce the original message from the hash and very difficult to predict, for any given input, what the hash function output will be. This means that it must be nearly impossible to knowingly alter a message in such a way to make the output of the hash function match a predetermined value. If one were able to do so, then it would be possible to create a new message with the same hash and simply attach the digital signature to it.

In Focus

In the use of public keys, keys may be dispensed by a key server, or even included in an email message passed to a recipient. The ciphertext security is not dependent upon secrecy of this public key.

Similar to the digital signature available with public key cryptography, the private or symmetric key cryptography provides message integrity through a message authentication code (MAC). A MAC is similar to a digital signature but a shared key is used in conjunction with a hash algorithm to generate it in a process known as keyed hashing. The shared key is concatenated to the plaintext message and then hashed. The receiver would add the shared key to the plaintext message to generate a hash for comparison. Without the shared key, there is nothing linking the hash to the sender. RFC 2104 specifies a keyed hash called an HMAC that is used in many implementations requiring integrity and data authentication.

17.3.3 Key Distribution and PKI

The term PKI refers to "public key infrastructure" meaning how keys are shared and how those that are not shared are kept secret, and thus PKI shares some of the same issues as symmetric key cryptography. In other words, although the ability to openly publish the public key may seem as though it has many advantages and solves the key distribution problems of symmetric key cryptography, the problem of key authentication exists. Because the public key of the recipient of an encrypted message is used, one must initially have access to that key.

This problem has been partially mitigated through the use of public key servers. If someone wants to send an encrypted message to another person, the person can go to one of the public key servers and look for the appropriate key. A problem arises in ensuring that the public key that is placed in a ***key server*** purporting to belong to a given individual that actually belongs to that person. Yet anyone can generate a key pair and place the public key on the key server. If we were to do so under someone else's name, a person who went to the key server to retrieve the public key would, without some other mechanism, have no way of knowing that the key did not belong to the person under whose name it was listed. The result would be that information intended to be kept secure going to the third party would, in fact, go elsewhere.

As the holder of the reciprocal private key, this "third party" would be able to continue to impersonate the third party for as long as there was trust in that key pair. To reduce the impact of this issue, the notion of a web of trust was established with the implementation of Phil Zimmerman's Pretty Good Privacy (PGP) [21]. The foundation of the *web of trust* is the social network that has built up over time, and the limited number of intermediary nodes necessary to link multiple people. Building on this notion, the owner of a key pair can ask trusted associates to digitally sign their public key with some indication as to the signer's level of trust that the key is valid and the key belongs to the specified owner. Those closest to the owner would place a high degree of trust in the key's providence.

The associates of each of the original signers, if needing to use that public key, would be able to trust the key to the extent that they trust their associate's assertion. If they trust their associate's assertion, they too can sign the public key with a degree of trust. With the more digital signatures attached to a given public key, the easier it is to find a path of trust from the person needing the public key to the individual to whom it purportedly belongs. Because this system is predicated on having another person authenticate a public key and the associative trust through the authentications, to be successful there must be a sufficient number of people involved in the process to make the needed connections. In place of this web of trust, having a single, central third party that is trusted by all parties involved would provide assurance of the authenticity of a key. This is the foundation for digital certificates, dispensed by certificate authorities (CA) such as VeriSign.

> **In Focus**
>
> Public key cryptography (called asymmetric) uses two keys (key pairs), where one is publicly distributed through a key server or in an email message, and the other is kept secret.

With all the advantages of public key cryptographic schemes, you may be inclined to wonder why people bother with symmetric key schemes. Although asymmetric key schemes have a lot of advantages, the processing power required to compute the necessary information can be significant. For that reason, symmetric and asymmetric schemes are often used together, with public key encryption used to securely pass a symmetric key for a given communication session, which is then used to secure the message traffic enroute. We noted this in terms of TLS (SHA) earlier.

> **In Focus**
>
> The secrecy of ciphertext often depends on how and where the secret key is kept, generated, or stored and used by the creator.

17.3.4 Public Key Algorithms: RSA as an Example

As with DES, 3DES, IDEA, and AES for private key cryptography, there are also algorithms for public key cryptography. Two of the most common are RSA and PGP (although note that PGP is sort of a hybrid because it dispenses a public key, but creates a private key that is encoded with a public key cryptography). To explain asymmetric cryptography, we will use RSA to illustrate because it is relatively straightforward. RSA is named for the three individuals responsible for its creation: Ron Rivest, Adi Shamir, and Len Adleman. RSA, like the symmetric algorithms DES, AES, and IDEA, is a block cipher. The block size is variable, but typically around 1024 bits [10].

RSA, unlike most other algorithms we have covered, conceptually works on integers rather than a stream of bits, with a 1024-bit integer being 309 decimal digits. The algorithm relies on the difficulty of factoring large numbers, and generates large number as the product of two prime numbers. The algorithm proceeds as follows beginning with the generation of key pair. We will continue with an illustration using the conventional naming of communicative partners, Alice and Bob, in our scenario (for more detail, see [4]):

1. Alice chooses two, relatively large, unique prime numbers which we will label p, q.
2. The product of the two prime numbers is calculated: $n = p * q$
3. With **Euler's totient function**, denoted ($\Phi(n)$) calculate n. Euler's function returns the number of positive integers less than n that are relatively prime to n. Being

relatively prime means that the greatest common factor between the two numbers is 1. A good way to think of this is to make a fraction and see if you can reduce it. For example, if we chose to calculate $\Phi(10)$, we could create the following fractions: 1/10, 2/10, 3/10, 4/10, 5/10, 6/10, 7/10, 8/10, and 9/10. 1/10 is not reducible, so only 1 and 10 are *relatively prime* to each other. The value 2/10 is reducible to 1/5 as they are both evenly divisible by 2, thus 2 it is not relatively prime to 10. Continuing, we find that 1, 3, 7, and 9 are all relatively prime to 10, so $\Phi(10) = 4$. As it turns out, a quick way to calculate Euler's totient if you already have two factors is just to calculate the product of each factor minus 1. That is, knowing that $2(5) = 10$, if we wanted to compute totient of 10 we could calculate $(2-1)(5-1) = (1)(4) = 4$.

4. An integer is chosen by the algorithm such that it is less than and relatively prime to $\Phi(n)$, which we will call e.

5. An integer, d, is calculated that is congruent to e^{-1} modulo $\Phi(n)$. Remember that two integers are congruent if the modulo value means that they both calculate to the same value, as with $39 \equiv 13$ modulo 26. In this case, we are looking for the value that is congruent to the inverse value chosen in step 4 modulo the value calculated in step 3. Although we can hit on a correct value through trial and error, Euclid's algorithm for finding the greatest common divisor can be used.

The result of these calculations gives the key generator we provide to Alice, which really means a variety of values. Her public key would be the values e, determined in step 4, and n, determined in step 2. Her private key would be the values d, calculated in step 5, and n, from step 2. Alice would publish her public key where people who wanted to establish a secure communication channel with her could find it. If others wanted to send her an encoded message, they would break the message into chunks smaller than the value n in Alice's public key. For each chunk of data smaller than n, the sender would convert it to an integer value and raise it the power e and take the result modulo n. By this we mean the ciphertext would be Message^e modulo n. To decrypt the message, Alice would take the ciphertext value she received, raise it to the power d, and take the result mod n. Let's see an example similar to one given by Stallings [10], except worked all the way through:

1. To generate an RSA public/private key pair, Alice chooses p = 7 and q=11.
2. $n = p * q = 7 * 11 = 77$.
3. $\Phi(77)$ is calculated ($\Phi(77) = (7-1)(11-1) = 60$).
4. A value relatively prime to 60 that we will choose is 17, so $e = 17$.
5. We will calculate $d \equiv e^{-1} \bmod \Phi(n) = 17^{-1} \bmod 60$: Using extended Euclid's algorithm $= -7 \equiv 53$.
6. The public key is then {17, 77} and the private key is {53, 77}.

If we wanted to send the message: "MEET ME AT PORTER HALL" using the method described before, we could use a covert channel for the message with bits using an ASCII table, noted previously for the message. The result would be seen as follows:

01001101	01000101	01000101	01010100	01001101	01000101
M	E	E	T	M	E
01000001	01010100	01010000	01001111	01010010	01010100
A	T	P	O	R	T
01000101	01010010	01001000	01000001	01001100	01001100
E	R	H	A	L	L

Converting that value into an integer would be 6.731217654514961e+42, which if we were using a larger n would be fine, but this is much greater than our n of 77, so we will have to break it into smaller chunks. We will break it into 4-bit chunks, which will give us decimal values of between 0 and 15, and that gives us the values as follows:

0100	1101	0100	0101	0100	0101	0101	0100	0100	1101	0100	0101
0100	0001	0101	0100	0101	0000	0100	1111	0101	0010	0101	0100
0100	0101	0101	0010	0100	1000	0100	0001	0100	1100	0100	1100

Then converting the binary values to integers gives us:

4	13	4	5	4	5	5	4	4	13	4	5
4	1	5	4	5	0	4	15	5	2	5	4
4	5	5	2	4	8	4	1	4	12	4	12

Encrypting the values (X) with the public key would use the equation $X^{17} \bmod 77$, resulting in the values:

16	10	16	3	16	3	3	16	16	10	16	3
16	1	3	16	3	0	16	0	3	18	3	16
16	3	3	18	16	57	16	1	16	45	16	45

To reverse the process, the decryption algorithm would take the values received (X) and compute the plaintext using the equation $X^{53} \bmod 77$. So, for example, to confirm that the equation will yield the values in the previous table, we confirm that $16^{53} \bmod 77 = [(16^{10} \bmod 77) \times (16^{10} \bmod 77) \times (16^{10} \bmod 77) \times (16^{10} \bmod 77) \times (16^{10} \bmod 77) \times (16^{3} \bmod 77)] \bmod 77 = [23 \times 23 \times 23 \times 23 \times 23 \times 15] \bmod 77 = 96545145 \bmod 77 = 4$. As you can see, they are congruent.

CHAPTER SUMMARY

The ability to appropriately utilize cryptography is at the heart of most technical approaches to managing information and computer security. Although cryptography has become ubiquitous with the information age, it has been utilized to secure communications for ages. Ancient classic encryption techniques have operated on the alphabets and relied on a shared key between two communicating parties. Modern cryptography make use of the computational power of computers and modern mathematics to offer both shared key or symmetric cryptography as well as public key or asymmetric cryptography. Modern algorithms can operate on blocks or streams of data, but normally work on the bit level. The choice of cryptographic technique and algorithm will be dependent on the use to which it will be put. Normally, however, asymmetric cryptography with its associated certificates is used to generate and share a new symmetric key that is utilized to secure a particular communication session because the overhead on symmetric encryption is so much less than that for asymmetric cryptography. Even though we covered it somewhat, one doesn't need to know the mathematics behind most of the algorithms and protocols to make use of and derive the benefits from the advances in cryptography. Having an understanding, however, will allow you as a manager to make a more informed decision about which algorithms and protocols to use and how to deploy them.

THINK ABOUT IT

Topic Questions

17.1: Vigenere is a _____ cipher.

17.2: Although DES uses blocks of binary numbers transformed using a 64-bit key, there are only _____ _____ available to the actual key because 8 are used as parity bits and are dropped from the cipher algorithm.

17.3: How many Feistel cipher rounds does DES perform?

17.4: Euler's totient function returns:
____ A public key half
____ Key space from which a key can be chosen
____ Positive integers less than n that are relatively prime to n
____ Large factors of prime numbers

17.5: A key (or sets of keys) acts to seed values for a cipher.
____ True
____ False

17.6: The DES cipher uses a single mode of operation.
____ True
____ False

17.7: With DES, the electronic codebook (ECB) mode is the simplest, but least secure.
____ True
____ False

THINK ABOUT IT (CONTINUED)

17.8: What is a hash function?

17.9: DES/ECB:

_____ Uses 128 bits for a key to process each block of data

_____ Uses 64 bits at a time and each block of data

_____ Uses two keys: one to encrypt and the other to decrypt

_____ Is the strongest of encryption modes for DES

17.10: _____ and _____ are used in modern ciphers.

Questions for Further Study

Q17.1: Write a description of how Kerberos performs authentication, focusing on the cryptography.

Q17.2: Discuss at least three advantages and disadvantages of private versus public key cryptography.

Q17.3: Explain how digital signatures are created and used.

Q17.4: Explain why AES is a preferred cryptography over DES or even 3DES.

Q17.5: Explain how PGP works, and explain why it is considered a hybrid public/private key cryptography.

KEY CONCEPTS AND TERMS

Asymmetric key (public key) cryptography uses two keys, one to encrypt and one to decrypt.

Certificate authorities are organizations that, for a fee, will attest to the authenticity of a third party by means of cryptography.

Digital signatures work by using what is known as a hash or message digest.

Keys need to be generated by a system so that they are random and significantly large.

Public keys are split in half, accompanied by a common

prime. One is distributed as a public key, the other kept secret.

Symmetric key (private key) cryptography uses one key shared between communicative partners.

References

1. Stewart, M. J. (2011). *Network security, firewalls, and VPNs*. Sudbury, MA: Jones & Bartlett Learning.
2. Dierks, T., & Rescorla, E. (2008). *RFC 5246—The Transport Layer Security (TLS) Protocol Version 1.2. Internet Engineering Task Force*. Security Paradigms Workshop (pp. 48–60). Langdale, AL: ACM.

3. Ballad, B., Ballad, T., & Banks, E. K. (2011). *Access control, authentication, and public key infrastructure*. Sudbury, MA: Jones & Bartlett Learning.

4. Kaufman, C., Perlman, R., & Speciner, M. (2002). *Network security: Private communication in a public world*. Upper Saddle River, NJ: Pearson/Prentice Hall.

5. Mao, W. (2004). *Modern cryptography: Theory and practice*. Upper Saddle River, NJ: Pearson/Prentice Hall.

6. Stallings, W. (2011). *Cryptography and network security: Principles and practice*. New York, NY: Pearson/Prentice Hall.

7. de Medeiros, B. (2005). *Windows security: A synopsis on host protection, 59*, 23–30. Tallahassee: Florida State University Press.

8. Lookup Tables (2010). *ASCII in decimal, hex, octal, html, and character*. Retrieved November 16, 2010, from http://asciitable.com/

9. Stallings, W. (2003). *Network security essentials: Applications and standards*. Upper Saddle River, NJ: Pearson/Prentice Hall.

10. Stallings, W. (2004). *Cryptography and network security principles and practices*. Upper Saddle River, NJ: Prentice Hall.

11. Tjaden, B. C. (2004). *Fundamentals of secure computer systems*. Wilsonville, OR: Franklin, Beedle & Associates.

12. Harkins, D., & Carrel, D. (1998). *RFC 2409—The Internet key exchange (IKE)*. Internet Engineering Task Force. Retrieved from http://www.ietf.org/rfc/rfc2409.txt

13. Solomon, M. G., & Chapple, M. (2005). *Information security illuminated*. Sudbury, MA: Jones and Bartlett Publishers.

14. Spillman, R. J. (2005). *Classical and contemporary cryptology*. Upper Saddle River, NJ: Pearson/Prentice Hall.

15. Lai, X., & Massey, J. (1998). *A proposal for a new nlock encryption standard*. Eurocrypt (pp. 389–404). Spring-Verlag.

16. Panko, R. R. (2004). *Corporate computer and network security*. Upper Saddle River, NJ: Pearson/Prentice Hall.

17. Pfleeger, C., & Pfleeger, S. (2003). *Security in computing*. Upper Saddle River, NJ: Prentice Hall.

18. Ramsdell, B., & Turner, S. (2010). *RFC 5751—Secure/Multipurpose Internet Mail Extensions (S/MIME) Version 3.2 Message Specification*. Internet Engineering Task Force. Retrieved from http://tools.ietf.org/html/rfc5751

19. Stinson, D. (1995). *Cryptography Theory and Practice*. Boca Raton, FL: CRC Press.

20. Stewart, J. M. (2009). *Security plus*. New York, NY: John Wiley & Sons.

21. Abdul-Rahman, A., & Hailes, S. (1997). A distributed trust model. *New Security Paradigms Workshop* (pp. 48–60). Langdale, AL: ACM.

Web Applications Security

WHEN WEB APPLICATIONS ARE DISCUSSED, people mainly think of web servers and web pages. Although clearly these are primary web applications, they do not span the range of them. Indeed, many if not most modern applications are at least web-enabled if they are not web-based. We have already covered many of the security issues related to web-enabled applications, but in this final chapter of this section we will narrow in on web-based applications, especially as they relate to web servers and web services. In the process, we will distinguish the present day web 2.0 technologies with their support of rich internet applications (RIA), social media, and streaming video, with the emerging Web 3.0 technologies that are based on what has been called the "semantic web," an effort undertaken by the W3C standards body.

Chapter 18 Topics

This chapter:

- Provides examples of web-based and web-enabled applications.
- Describes service-oriented architecture and cloud computing.
- Explains web security threats and security efforts.

Chapter 18 Goals

When you finish this chapter, you should:

- ☐ Understand what web applications are, as a general category.
- ☐ Be familiar with some of the security threats and attacks against web applications, and how to defend against them.

- ❏ Know about some of the work in major standards bodies to improve web applications security.
- ❏ Know some of the security issues in the context of service-oriented architecture (SOA) and be alerted to security related to software as a service (SaaS).

18.1 Web-Based Versus Web-Enabled Applications

Web applications collectively refer to any application that can use the HTTP protocol for communications [1]. In the most common form, a web application is one that resides in a web server, such as Tomcat, IIS, or Resin, and listens for a connection on a port such as 80 by default, or custom configured on 8080 or some other port. These web applications receive requests from a browser through a URL and dispatch to objects in the application, and provide responses to users. However, systems such as business process management (BPM), decision support systems portals, inventory control systems, accounting systems, sales and customer management, electrical grid management, GPS tracking, and timekeeping systems, are increasingly available through web-based or web-enabled applications [2].

18.1.1 A Definition of Web Applications

Web-based applications are those that use a traditional web server to host an application. In the usual case, people access content or conduct a transaction over the Web with their browser, such as with online banking or purchasing something from an electronic storefront. However, there are many web-enabled applications, such as BridgeGate, that perform applications and data integration using web technologies. Like other such technologies, BridgeGate provides an administrative portal over the Web for application management and administration.

The idea behind web-enabled applications has been to use the HTTP protocol and offer a web interface into a legacy application, some sort of middleware, or a back-end application. Many web-enabled systems are developed using Enterprise Java Beans (EJB) or Microsoft .NET technology, or they are facilitated through a technology such as AquaLogic. Lately, web-enabled applications have come to encompass cloud computing systems, such as Microsoft's Azure, and Software as a Service (SaaS) platforms. These systems have made possible cloud services offered by companies such as Amazon, Google, AppNexus, and GoGrid.

New developments in web technologies have enabled the gathering and sharing of information in virtual environments over existing web infrastructure. For example, it is widely recognized that the technologies on the Web such as *Hypertext Markup Language* (**HTML**) and the *eXtensible Markup Language* (**XML**), along with social media such as Facebook and YouTube, and new search engines such as Bing, have revolutionized information sharing, advertisement, and discovery. These technologies are evolving to support even more active systems. Components that are being developed as part of the W3C standards body toward the next generation "semantic web" (also known as Web 3.0) are increasingly being fashioned into commercial applications to address some aspect of efficient information collaboration, data collection, and dissemination capabilities.

Among these technologies is the ***Resource Description Framework*** (**RDF**) that creates relational linkages among web documents scattered among disparate systems. RDF can be further elaborated using a markup language such as the ***Defense Advanced Research Projects Agency*** (**DARPA**) ***Agent Markup Language*** (**DAML**) or the ***Web Ontology Language*** (**OWL**) to allow the creation of software similar to search engines or bots or crawlers—called ***agents***—that can seek out information encoded with this markup, and then act on instructions, seek goals, and make evaluations as these agents traverse networked computers.

Alternatively, the markup can be persisted in relational databases in what are known as ***triples*** (in the form of subject-predicate-object) using a middleware such as Sesame [3], which can be queried using normal query engines. However, along with these evolutions, as well as others including in ***service-oriented architecture*** (**SOA**), have come new security vulnerabilities and security-related threats.

> **In Focus**
>
> Managers must be mindful of technology employees may have in their work environment. Even cameras on mobile phones may be used to capture company confidential information and that may be displayed on the Web. For example, consider the highly publicized incident where nurses at a hospital in Wisconsin used their mobile phones to take pictures of an embarrassing patient condition and posted the pictures on Facebook in violation of HIPAA laws, which led to a civil lawsuit and federal prosecution [4].

18.1.2 Client-Server Web Applications and Security

One of the things that makes web applications tricky in terms of security is that the HTTP protocol is stateless, and therefore requires careful work to manage sessions and stateful information such as items kept in shopping carts or about stages in a contiguous transaction. Session management refers to logically connecting a series of related interactions between a user and a web application. Two common ways this is done are through the use of hidden form fields, which send parameters over the URL, or session variables (also called session cookies).

The problem with hidden form fields is that they can be viewed in the "view source" option of a browser, and the URL can be manipulated, which in some cases might produce an error page that can provide clues to an attacker. For example, indicating expected syntax for a database in an error page, an attacker may see how to conduct a SQL injection. The problem with session variables is that even though these are non-persistent, meaning that they are not the type of cookie that is stored on a computer but rather kept in memory, browsers often block all cookies to improve security, and the user typically has to specifically and manually set browser security in the advanced options to allow session cookies because using the usual security level slider control tends to disable both persistent and non-persistent cookies.

A second issue has to do with whether to do client-side or server-side input validation. The advantage of client-side validation is that the feedback to the user is more immediate, but this is insecure because client-side validation is susceptible to manipulation by an attacker. The advantage of server-validation is that it is somewhat more secure, but users don't get input error reports until a submission is done to the server to validate and so the user may not find out about a missing field or incorrect input until far into the processing. A defense-in-depth procedure is to use both client-side validation of input but to verify the input on the server side to ensure that the parameters have not been manipulated. Unfortunately, there is additional overhead with this "double duty" [5].

Also, to deal with these and other vulnerabilities, web systems administrators have developed a multiple-layered approach to securing the network infrastructure, the web server systems, and the applications. Securing the network infrastructure includes the use of firewalls and cryptography, as discussed. Protecting the host—in addition to hardening—includes the use of authentication and access controls. There are different ways to authenticate users, as we have already discussed, but one popular mechanism is to use the CHAP protocol, which performs a ***challenge handshake***. A challenge handshake is useful to address at least what is called the "front door" problem where attackers strive to break into a system such as through a password "crack" utility, or to try to prevent man-in-the-middle attacks. Simplistically, CHAP works as follows:

1. A client sends a password to a host.
2. The host sends a random message to the client.
3. Both use the password as the key to compute a message digest (MD) with the CHAP algorithm and additional parameters.
4. The client sends the MD to the host, the host compares the client MD with its own computation, and if they match, the user is authenticated and allowed to log in.

18.1.3 Web Services and Cloud Computing

A form of web application, as indicated before, is called ***cloud computing***, where software systems are "clustered" together in a "virtual" environment, for example, using the open source software called Eucalyptus on Linux Ubuntu. This configuration typically consists of virtual machine (node) controllers, cluster controllers that manage multiple virtual machines across multiple platforms, web service-based storage controllers, and a full cloud infrastructure controller. Collectively, these systems allow web services to interoperate across platforms in a way that they are both contained in a virtual environment (such as VMWare) as well as "virtually" connected together so that the various resources can be dynamically allocated and unallocated on demand. In other words, clouds refer to virtual and dynamic allocation of software, networks, data storage, and platforms that are remotely accessible.

Cloud computing is often divided into three types: infrastructure as a service (IaaS), software as a service (Saas), as indicated earlier, and platforms as a service (PaaS). IaaS allows clients to consume networking services on demand, SaaS allows users to process applications on demand, and PaaS allows users to utilize computing resources on demand. Cloud computing can be done internally within an organization or outsourced to a third party, such as Amazon Web Services (AWS).

An example of security concerns voiced about cloud computing has been that people are often reluctant to turn over mission-critical or proprietary applications and data to a third party—the same concern that led to the death of application service providers (ASPs) by the late 1990s. Moreover, many are concerned about hosting their email by a cloud provider due to concerns over the Electronic Communications Privacy Act, 18 U.S.C. 2510-2521 [6]. However, many companies seem to be willing to allow non-mission-critical applications to be hosted by a trusted third-party cloud (such as Microsoft with Azure) or to allow cloud hosts to provide an email-secure filter to feed a corporate-managed email system.

Furthermore, today's approach to network security is more on par with what might be called enclave security, where inside the security perimeter it is (more or less) a free-for-all. However, in complex networks the security perimeters may be difficult to define. This creates great problems for administrators who are trying to implement trusted versus distrusted network controls, choke points, or other ingress and egress portals. Part of the problem in securing next generation web systems is that in most networks there are security hierarchies, but between them there are interior and exterior routing protocols that operate as peers, making layered defenses difficult at key points in the infrastructure. To deal with these unique problems, there are several organizations focusing on setting security standards for web applications, including the ***Open Web Application Security Project*** (**OWASP**) and the ***Web Application Security Consortium*** (**WASC**).

> **In Focus**
>
> To date, many of the security issues and standards reflect derivatives of previous approaches to security, such as firewalls, but according to Drew Deen (4/29/2011), Program Manager for the Information Innovation Office within DARPA, emerging technologies, especially in the mobile space, will need to radically change to provide adequate protections in the near future.

18.1.4 Securing Web Servers

Previously when introducing web applications we discussed the concept of Model-2 or Model-View-Controller design pattern in web applications, which separates presentation code from server and business processing code, and the data access code. An original aim of this architecture was to improve scalability of systems, but its additional benefit is that it helps to protect web applications by creating partitions between functional subsystems. This is important because web applications need securing at the network, the host server, and the applications and databases levels.

As previously discussed, securing the network involves the use of firewalls and cryptography, and protecting host servers includes authentication and authorization of user access, along with host hardening, such as removal of sensitive data and software and limiting services. Protecting web applications involves techniques for validating input, keeping the system in a known state by managing the configuration, implementing proper error handling (exception management), auditing and logging of activities and services, and implementing security settings for back-end database connectivity used by the web application including ensuring password protections on the database, and prevention of SQL manipulation.

> **In Focus**
>
> Administrators and developers of publicly accessible Web applications often use checklists to help ensure that all of the security bases are covered. As previously described, the checklists are derived from industry standards and best practices. For web applications, these may include the Open Web Application Security Project (OWASP), the Web Application Security Consortium (WASC), SysAdmin, Audit, and Network and Security (SANS) Institute; and for service-oriented architecture (SOA), the NIST SP800-95.

As we have noted, many of the networking and host security measures we have already discussed also apply to web applications. The most unique aspects of security web systems in terms of the technology, however, occur in relation to the stateless nature of HTTP, the scripting, markup, and web application languages, and the need to support a vast array of client software. Specific security issues and approaches for protections depend on whether the application is written in JAVA or C#, or uses scripting such as JavaScript, PHP, Perl, or Python [7].

Regardless of how it is implemented, certain minimum security measures need to be taken regarding transactional systems, which include (1) validation of input, meaning that the input an application receives is valid and has not been manipulated, including filtering and setting criteria for acceptance or rejection of input before processing; (2) authentication, which involves creating an electronic credential that helps to ensure a user who purports to be an authorized user is in fact that user; and (3) authorization, which is the process of determining what a user can do and what an application that a user invokes can legitimately do—such as what data or databases the application may access, and whether it can only read or read and write the data—and of preventing an escalation of privileges beyond those that should be legitimately granted to the user.

18.1.5 Web Application Threats

Web systems administrators must guard against a wide range of threats. Some examples of threats include buffer overflows, cross-site scripting, and SQL injection. Buffer overflows can lead to denial of service attacks or code injection. A denial of service attack causes a process crash, whereas code injection alters the program execution context (data and addressing) to run an attacker's malicious code. Recall that an operating system allocates buffers in memory to store temporary data, such as data coming from a network connection or an input device.

If the application is not properly written or does not have inherent safeguards against buffer or stack overflows, the attacker may be able to "leak" instructions and/or data into adjacent memory locations. In the worst-case scenario, if enough of the malicious code can be leaked into the execution context that is about to be used by another process, it may allow the malicious code to run within the "legitimate" application; otherwise, the code or data will simply "not make sense" and the system may crash.

Buffer overflows usually only occur in older (legacy) types of applications, such as those that used the Common Gateway Interface (CGI) and a language that supported pointers or macros such as "C" or C++. More modern languages geared toward the Web such as JAVA and many of the Microsoft .NET languages are not typically susceptible to buffer overflows because the runtime systems automatically check the boundaries (addressing) that a given application is allowed to occupy; the term for this is often called "sandboxed" or "managed" [5]. However, a weakness in even these more modern systems is in executables or dynamically linked libraries that a rich Internet application (RIA) might call or use to perform some function on the application's behalf. For example, if a .NET application (which is sandboxed, or managed) calls an unmanaged application through an application program interface (API) COM / COM++ / DCOM / OLE / ActiveX objects, then it can still be possible to create a buffer overflow [2].

A cross-site scripting (XSS) attack may cause malicious code to run in a user's browser while the browser is connected to a trusted website, which may occur if, for example, an attacker succeeds in installing an infected "advertisement" or a link on a credible website (or delivered through email), or through a man-in-the-middle attack. XSS targets users of an application and not the application itself, but the application acts as the delivery mechanism for the attack. Because the browser downloads script code unless blocked, the browser does not distinguish whether the code is benign or malicious. In the usual case, the attacker's code uses the trusted site's cookies stored on the user's local computer, and of particular interest to such an attacker are user authentication cookies.

SQL injection is an attack against relational databases. In older systems, an attacker could manipulate the URL string and receive back an error page that would reveal information about the database, such as what type the database was used, e.g., mySQL, Oracle, or SQLServer, and the expected syntax of the SQL. The attacker could then exploit the system using that knowledge by formulating a more focused attack and constructing carefully crafted dynamic SQL statements to access the database. The SQL injection may cause changes to data in a database (an update), deletion of data (delete), or even removal of entire tables. This kind of attack is particularly concerning if the database is distributed across servers, or is part of an application that uses distributed transaction processing, because the corruption can become widespread. Although most systems and web servers have been patched or written in such a way as to prevent such a problem, there are still cases where this occurs, and tools such as Cain and Abel facilitate these types of attacks.

In Focus

To help prevent web application attacks, web systems administrators must ensure that authentication and authorization are used, where appropriate, that input is properly validated, that the applications employ safeguards against manipulation of parameters passed either via the URL or in the body of the HTTP message, that errors (exceptions) are properly handled, that appropriate messages are returned to users and that not too much information about the system is divulged, and that logging and auditing are done and are regularly inspected.

18.2 Protections for Web Servers

Web servers often reside just behind the first lines of defense systems, for instance just within a DMZ, and they often need to provide easily accessible content over the Web. There are a variety of mechanisms that are needed to help prevent attacks from spreading beyond a containment area or the DMZ. If the web server goes beyond simply presenting content and offers logins for conducting transactions or allows employees to enter information, additional countermeasures such as authentication are needed. To help secure web servers, Harwood [2] recommended (1) educating the users, (2) using a combination of policies and procedures to secure sites (as much as possible), (3) using firewalls, and (4) ensuring that users do not select distrusted links in email or on message boards. In addition to these recommendations, we also suggest to post usage policies on websites, make note of copyrights and trademarks, and control input so that posts do not contain malicious code, links, obscene or defamatory comments. We will cover some of these features in the following section.

18.2.1 Authentication

As we explained in previous chapters, authentication is the process of verifying the identity of a purported user through some kind of electronic exchange of a secret. Authentication is important in web-based systems because the authorization of activities relies on assurance of the identity of the authenticated user. An example of a one-way authentication is simply checking the user identification and password supplied at login time. Earlier we mentioned CHAP as a challenge-handshake approach to authentication. CHAP is a two-way authentication, which uses a dual-exchange of identifiable data between a client and a server. A more sophisticated authentication involves three-way authentication (called strong authentication), such as used by **Kerberos**, as presented earlier.

Recall that Kerberos enables users who communicate over an insecure network to purport an identity to another in a secure manner. This helps to prevent eavesdropping and session replay attacks after an initial authentication has taken place. The identification data produced by Kerberos are known as "tickets." Tickets are granted for a given timeframe and they expire, so even if a ticket is intercepted and decoded, by that time the data will be useless. By computing a one-way hash with a symmetric key that has been dispensed by a key distribution center (KDC), Kerberos is able to work in a widely distributed environment, but it requires that at least the key distribution portion come from a trusted domain.

> **In Focus**
>
> Because Kerberos uses a symmetric key, each entity on the network, whether a client or a server, receives the key from KDC. With this, Kerberos generates a session key used to secure the interactions.

As implied, the KDC has two functions: an **authentication service** (**AS**) and a **ticket-granting service** (**TGS**). The AS is used to produce a "master key" computed for the initial authentication, and the TGS is used to dispense session keys (tickets) after the initial authentication has taken place so that the integrity of the communications is maintained after the initial interrogation. Valid tickets are needed for each service requested, from each system, each time it is requested. This "permission slip" is known as a ***service ticket*** [8, 9]. In any case, there are certain critical features important to authentication. It should be used for logins that cross a trusted boundary, such as a host or a DMZ, and once the user is validated, it is generally desirable for subsequent activities to be authorized using an authentication token, such as the "ticket" approach used in Kerberos.

In Focus

An alternative to Kerberos is the CCITT X.509 standard, as we mentioned earlier. X.509 is interesting because unlike Kerberos, it works with asymmetric keys to create strong authentication. However, for this, a distributed directory service is needed for the public key infrastructure, which typically uses RSA.

18.2.2 Password Protections

There is a saying among hackers that the easiest way in is through the front door. Three of the most common (and easiest) ways of getting through the front door are if login pages do not use the secure socket layer (SSL), which is rare but does happen; if login information is stored in a database unencrypted, which happens more often than we'd like to think; and if people use easy-to-guess passwords, such as words in a dictionary that can be "cracked," which happens frequently. Other vulnerabilities exist in the manner in which login information is stored. For instance, in older versions of UNIX, the password (although salted and encrypted) was kept in a publically accessible file, /etc/passwd, easily accessible from the outside. Newer versions of UNIX-based systems use "shadow passwords" in which the passwords are hash indexed into a file that is only readable by means of privileged (root) system calls, and the passwords are stored as a one-way encryption.

In Focus

In cryptography, salt refers to randomly generated bits used as seed input into a key generation function, and the remainder of the input is a password or passphrase, which results in a strongly encrypted password. Salt is similar to the concept of nonce, discussed in the cryptography chapter.

From an administrative point of view, systems should utilize lockout policies in which accounts are disabled after a certain number of failed attempts. However, there is a danger in that this feature may be used in a denial of service attack by going after legitimate user accounts with bad passwords. To help mitigate, the lockout feature should be combined with a filtering technique that blacklists the attacker before too many accounts can be affected.

In addition, the use of authentication such as Windows NT LAN Manager (NTLM) or Kerberos helps to prevent lockout DoS, along with protecting user IDs and utilizing good SPAM filtering that can help prevent ID leakage. Other important security functions are to ensure that accounts are disabled when people leave the company, and ensuring that passwords expire at certain intervals, requiring users to change their passwords—and preventing people from reusing a previous password, if one is chosen rather than generated [10, 11].

18.2.3 Authorization

After a user is authenticated and allowed onto the system, his or her actions need to be controlled—that is, authorized. One method of authorization is called **role-based access control** (RBAC), which assigns permissions to access objects and resources based on a given role that a user fulfills. In other words, a user is identified by his or her username and a role. In most web-based applications, a controller or dispatcher object, such as a JAVA Servlet, collects permissions for an authenticated user, and then when the user attempts to perform an action, the action is compared to the permission list. If authorized, the controller will construct an object to perform the action and hand over control of the action to the user.

A difficulty in this approach is found when a user assumes different roles, which might have different access permissions. For example, a person may normally act as a shift supervisor for *Department A* and should only have access to those items appropriate for *Department A*, but on holidays and emergencies, the person might also serve as a shift supervisor for *Department B*. The controller approach usually does not handle multiple roles and permission conflicts without significant programming logic involved.

As a result, some systems implement trusted kernels, sometimes called profile security managers, which replaces the dispatcher approach. In this manner, resources such as files, folders, Registry keys, and other objects are managed by the profile security manager from an LDAP directory, and access is granted using one of several types of access control lists (ACLs). In this sense, users are authorized to change to certain roles, and in so doing, receive different permissions checked against a different set of ACLs. This approach sometimes offers the benefit of more granularity in the type of access a user may have for a given object or resource. That is, it may allow a user to view a directory and some of its contents, but not certain files within that directory (e.g., hidden files), or use a single sign-on (SSO) for some systems, but not others, and it tends to better address the problem of a user who assumes multiple roles.

18.2.4 Input Validation

Once users are authenticated and authorized, their interactions with the system need to be controlled and validated. Controlling and validating input is an important step in preventing accidental input errors or masquerade attacks that might lead to buffer overflows, XSS, and SQL injections. If input from users is anonymous, such as filling out forms or writing comments, the input is always vulnerable to attack and is therefore suspect. Some of the techniques for controlling input include using drop-down selection lists for expected input rather than having users enter the data, or using a client-side validation for input, such as ensuring that input is of the proper data type and falls within defined boundaries or ranges. The integrity of the client-side input should be checked for conformance to expectancies by the server-side application.

The validation code should also apply to URL and HTML input encoding that encapsulates the data and treats the data as literal text rather than executable scripts. Where users enter information such as phone numbers or zip codes, the patterns can be checked using regular expression examiners. If the application accepts uploaded files, programmers must ensure they are scanned with a virus scanner and that their file name extensions match the file type.

> **In Focus**
>
> Microsoft has an unfortunate characteristic in that it hides final file name extensions, such as Readme.txt.exe, which is viewed instead as Readme.txt.

Once the input has been controlled and validated, if there are errors, the information that is reported back to the client should be screened and sanitized. For instance, if parameters or state information is passed over the URL, an attacker may modify those parameters to receive an error page that may contain clues to expected input or information about the syntax formatting of data for a database in hopes of performing a SQL Injection. Error reports should provide little more than the HTTP error number and message, such as 400 Bad Request, 401 Authentication Required, or 404 File Not Found; and there should be solid error handling internally in the application to notify administrators and software personnel for making corrections.

18.2.5 Session Management

There is always the possibility that someone might intercept a session, known as hijacking or a man-in-the-middle attack. During an exchange among web client and server, much information is exposed in the HTTP header including what file types will be accepted by a client. When a page is downloaded from a server, it may contain an electronic "beacon" that indicates to the server the geographical location of the IP address of the client, or clicks made by the client, pages a client visited, or cookies stored on the client. This information can be used by the server for purposes such marketing in the aggregate or setting preferences for users, but they can also be exploited [7].

There are some basic steps that web users should follow and designers of web applications should take. Web users need to set their browsers to the appropriate level of security for the type of web activity they are performing. Visiting a trusted site is less dangerous than visiting an unknown one. Credentials and certificates should be set to be checked in the security options of the browser, the browser should usually be set to block (or at least ask the user about displaying) images or whether to allow "third-party cookies." Users may even want to consider using a web surfing proxy portal such as *anonymizer.com* to shield them, or *Network-Tools.com* when doing lookups on worrisome or bothersome websites.

> **In Focus**
>
> If you are under an attack, if you ping or do a traceroute of the attacker system, the attacker may be able to "see" your information. It is usually preferable to use a proxy system for these activities.

For server applications designers, if authentication is used, web applications should never pass authentication credentials as cookies through the HTTP protocol. Authentication should occur below the HTTP protocol (e.g., as with Kerberos), or if authentication must be done at the application layer, it should only be done using HTTPS. This is an important first step in preventing a would-be hijacker from taking over a session by first gaining the authentication cookie such as with a technology like Achilles, which is intended for use in development and testing of web applications. However, even using HTTPS, it can be possible for a man-in-the-middle to manipulate HTTPS messages using HTTP Interceptor.

Although they may not be altered, because authentication and session cookies may be intercepted even with HTTPS, they can still be used to impersonate another user, so it is important that web applications limit the lifetime a session remains active and to cause a new set of cookies to be generated and authenticated after a short interval. Although this timeout feature is often annoying to users, it is a necessary evil to prevent severe damage to their information [12].

Another important consideration has to do with the state of the session. Where a session represents the lifetime of a connection, session state indicates where in a transaction a user is—logically, such as browsing a catalog, transitioning from a view state to an input state, selecting items for a shopping cart, checking out, and so on.

In Focus

State and state changes might be thought of as analogous to an automobile driving up to a red light on an infrequently traveled road, and in so doing, driving over a pressure plate in the road triggers a signal changer system to turn the light from red to green in a shorter interval than was programmed into the system.

This state information is likewise critical to manage in a web session. In JAVA, for example, this information is maintained as part of the HttpSession object in a Servlet, which can be retrieved using the client's HttpServletRequest object; for instance: HttpSession session = request.getSession(). Once a reference to the session is obtained, its attributes can be set using a variety of methods. For instance, a Servlet that is associated with a virtual storefront called *eStore* may inject malicious data using session.setAttribute("eStore", badData). Some of the HttpSession methods that are supported in this configuration include setMaxInactiveInterval(int interval), which sets the maximum inactive interval in seconds; getMaxInactiveInterval(), which returns the maximum inactive interval in seconds; and invalidate(), which invalidates a session and removes the session name/value bindings, such as to sign off.

Maintaining session state management is tricky, as we mentioned before. Thus, many JAVA application servers have clustering capabilities that encrypt state information. The information is assigned a globally unique identification (GUID) and is then shared across servers in a secure manner. This allows for processes to be dynamically load-balanced across web servers in large-scale operations in a more secure manner. Microsoft has historically used a more static approach to load balancing with what is called a web farm. Because of this, Microsoft .NET designers and programmers are sometimes tempted to store the session state in the process address space, but this does not scale well. Alternatively, .NET programmers may store the session state "out of process" on a shared server, or on a dedicated one. The shared store is more efficient, but the dedicated one is more secure [12].

18.2.6 Web Services and Security

Up to this point, we have primarily concentrated on web servers (such as Tomcat, Resin, and IIS) and their associated applications, but equally important in security are web services. Web services are loosely coupled applications, increasingly used for data exchange within and among corporate entities and their trading partners, and their distribution channels or retailers. Primary technologies used in web services include XML, SOAP, WSDL, and to a lesser extent, UDDI. However, increasingly, agent frameworks (such as Aglets and Cougaar) are being added into this mix.

Web services allow companies to electronically advertise and connect (bind) systems, such as among service providers, trading partners, and customers. Because of the wide range of possibilities and needs, many web services use a message-oriented approach, such as JAVA Message Service (JMS), along with an enveloped routing mechanism, such as SOAP. Nevertheless, along with this flexibility come new security challenges. To help in this regard, the OASIS Web Services Security (WSS) group is quickly emerging as a leader in defining security standards for web services and SOA. Among the recommendations the WSS group has made is using authentication and cryptography [9].

In addition, just as with web applications and web servers, web services can use authentication, such as for services making queries of the WSDL and the services it describes. Authentication mechanisms previously described can likewise be used by web services, both at the platform and the message level, although there are additional countermeasures available such as ***Security Assertion Markup Language*** (**SAML**). This is because one of the challenges with web services and XML in general is that markup is human-readable plaintext; therefore cryptography is very important in this scheme.

If SOAP is used, it is often necessary to use message digests such as X.509 certificates for authenticating passwords that may be contained in SOAP headers. The bodies of the messages should also be encrypted, which can be done using the same techniques as with other web applications such as SSL. A major difficulty is in the fact that there are many different standards and technologies that have to be agreed upon for parties to interact securely.

In Focus

Because there are so many configurations, new technologies, and a number of standards committees, security for widely distributed and loosely coupled web applications is likely to be challenging for some time to come.

18.2.7 Protecting Web Content

We have covered web systems in this final chapter of this section on security measures, and now we will briefly discuss a framework for protecting web content from attacks such as defacement and information theft. For ease of discovery and access, in most cases, web content servers such as company home pages reside behind only thinly guarded defenses and they are widely advertised; therefore, they are highly exposed. Unless these systems provide a portal into the internal corporate infrastructure, such as an employee login, they typically present less of a risk. Nevertheless, because they are the electronic face of a company, they are crucial to business.

A common website attack is defacement, which can be done in many ways depending on how the website is constructed and the technologies used. Some common ways include injecting code through an open port using a chat or an FTP program. An attacker may try an anonymous login to port 21 (FTP) using a command line interface, or use a browser and replace the default http with FTP. If a login screen is presented, company directory names (and permutations thereof) commonly found on websites may be tried as login IDs along with using password-cracking tools in combination [10].

To protect content, in addition to firewalls, logging and auditing are important to determine origins and types of attacks. Web server administrators must carefully control what services are exposed, what ports are open, and what software resides on the system, and then regularly monitor the logs and the content. They must be prepared with content backups to restore a system if it is changed or disrupted. Along with these basic approaches, which we have already discussed in previous chapters, Wang, Hui, and Yiu [6] presented an interesting method of obfuscating cascading style sheets by "inserting relative noise into web pages and referencing a pool of display policies" (p. 62) to manipulate the display data. They also suggest encoding and encryption in page references.

CHAPTER SUMMARY

In this chapter, we reviewed some of the previously discussed ways of protecting computer systems and networks, but we focused here on the relationship of web-based and web-enabled applications. We presented some of the active standards bodies that are involved in developing security standards and methods for web applications. We also covered some of the threats to web services and service-oriented architecture, along with some countermeasures. We concluded with a brief discussion of how to protect web content. In the next, and final section, we will rely on your knowledge of how systems and networks are designed and secured to understand security operations and present some practical and emerging applications for these measures. As such, we will discuss security modeling and how security is evolving to be more adaptive to threats.

THINK ABOUT IT

Topic Questions

18.1: _____ are similar to search engine bots or crawlers, but besides seeking out information, they are more "intelligent" and can act on instructions, seek goals, and make evaluations.

18.2: What group is quickly emerging as a leader in defining security standards for web services and SOA?

18.3: Name and describe a critical aspect of security for transactional systems that deal with input.

18.4: Name an organization that researches and publishes security threats for web applications and web services, including what they title the "top 10" list.

18.5: Which of the following is NOT recommended for posting on a company website:

____ Copyright
____ Usage policy
____ Navigation cues
____ Employee contact information

18:6: Doing a combination of both client- and server-side validation is a good idea.

____ True
____ False

18.7: The KDC in Kerberos has an authentication service.

____ True
____ False

18.8: Agents are the same as search engine crawlers.

____ True
____ False

18.9: Authorization is the process of:

____ Validating a user's identity
____ Determining what a user can do
____ Granting access to a system
____ A biometric technology

18.10: A URL might be manipulated to cause a web server to give up information that can be exploited.

____ True
____ False

Questions for Further Study

Q18.1: What do managers need to consider in terms of security if they use SaaS?

Q18.2: How do outsourced cloud computing and SaaS differ?

Q18.3: Where web applications are fairly well understood from a web server perspective, how might web applications security change if the technologies proposed for the semantic web are realized at an enterprise level?

Q18.4: What are five security implications for agent frameworks?

Q18.5: Discuss what information should be disclosed on a website and what should be excluded.

KEY CONCEPTS AND TERMS

Agents can seek out information, act on instructions, seek goals, and make evaluations.

Authentication is the process of validating a purported user.

Identification is the process of selecting or singling out an individual from a group.

Kerberos's KDC has two functions: an authentication service (AS)

and a ticket-granting service (TGS).

Resource Description Framework (RDF) creates relational linkages among web documents using URI.

References

1. LaMacchia, B. A., Lange, S., Lyons, M. Martin, R., & Price, K. T. (2002). *.NET framework security*. Boston, MA: Addison-Wesley.
2. Harwood, M. (2011). *Security strategies in Web applications and social networking*. Sudbury, MA: Jones & Bartlett Learning.
3. Aduna, B. V., Sirma Al Ltd. (2006). *User guide for Sesame*. Retrieved July 14, 2011, from http://www.openrdf.org/doc/sesame/users/userguide.html
4. Kaufman, G. (2009). "Nurses fired over cell phone photos of patient: Case referred to FBI for possible HIPAA violation." *Milwaukee News*, p. 1. Retrieved January 14, 2011, from http://www.wisn.com/news/18796315/detail.html
5. Moore, D., Budd, R., & Benson, E. (2007). *Rich Internet applications: AJAX and beyond*. Indianapolis, IN: WROX/Wiley Publishing.
6. Wang, E. K., Hui, L. C. K., & Yiu, S. M. (2009). A new practical scheme for protecting web content. *Proceedings of the 2009 Conference on Security & Management, 1*, 62–66.
7. Scambray, J., & Shema, M. (2002). *Hacking web applications exposed: Web application security secrets & solutions*. New York, NY: McGraw-Hill.
8. Panko, R. R. (2004). *Corporate computer and network security*. Upper Saddle River, NJ: Pearson/Prentice Hall.
9. Reitsma, R. F. (2010). Web services. In H. Bidgoli (Ed.), *The handbook of technology management* (Vol. 3, pp. 578–592). New York, NY: John Wiley & Sons.
10. Tjaden, B. C. (2004). *Fundamentals of secure computer systems*. Wilsonville, OR: Franklin, Beedle & Associates.
11. Meier, J. D., Mackman, A., Vasireddy, S., Dunner, M., Escamilla, R., & Murukan, A. (2003). *Improving web application security: Threats and countermeasures*. Redmond, WA: Microsoft Press.
12. Scambray, J., & Shema, M. (2002). *Hacking web applications exposed: Web application security secrets and solutions*. New York, NY: McGraw-Hill.

Managing Organizations Securely

Configuration Management

ONFIGURATION MANAGEMENT (CM) is a formally defined aspect of management that involves creating and maintaining consistency in systems, keeping services available, and meeting performance objectives. In terms of information security, CM is the protection of the integrity of functions and features by controlling changes made to hardware, software, and information throughout the life of an information system. Primary components in CM include the development and implementation of policies, practices, and processes that ensure conformance and consistency of information and systems through proper governance. The assessment and enforcement of CM is done through compliance auditing procedures.

Chapter 19 Topics

This chapter:

- Presents CM as a framework.
- Describes the main aspects of CM.
- Compares and expands on CM for security configuration management (SeCM).
- Covers some of the criteria and technologies used in SeCM.

Chapter 19 Goals

When you finish this chapter, you should:

- ☐ Have a working knowledge of change and configuration management processes and why they are important.

❑ Understand the planning process associated with change and configuration management.

❑ Understand standards for configuration and how they are applied.

❑ Recognize different operational environments and select appropriate configurations.

❑ Understand how to implement change and configuration management processes.

19.1 CM and Computer Security Procedures

Configuration management (CM) is concerned with performance, and the functional and physical integrity of systems, applications, networks, and information environments relative to a defined "secure state" called a baseline. As an example, a configuration may need a set of policies, models, and defined stances for a gateway that connects a DMZ to the Internet, which must be monitored and audited to ensure that it stays within the guidelines set for it and meets specific measures and metrics outlined by the policies and conformance criteria. As such, many CM aspects are addressed under various compliance criteria, including the Capability Maturity Model Integration (CMMI), the ISO 9000 family of standards, Six Sigma, COBIT, and ITIL, which we covered previously. The key concept in CM is known as **_traceability_**, where a change can be traced through a "chain of custody" back to its source [1].

In the previous sections, we covered key legal, organizational, behavioral, and administrative aspects of security; we introduced how some of the major technologies work; and we covered a broad swatch of how computers, networks, and information security are implemented. In this final section, we are going to discuss security from an operational and managerial standpoint. In this introductory chapter to this section, we will specifically address CM, and review in greater context some of the management procedures and frameworks previously mentioned.

19.1.1 CM and Management Frameworks

The area of CM in security borrows from the software configuration management (SCM) processes defined by Booch and Rumbaugh and others [2]. These processes develop the requirements and attributes for applications and then utilize systematic controls over changes. This is done to maintain software integrity and traceability throughout the software development life cycle. To accomplish this, (1) a configuration's stable base must be determined, (2) a control process must be put into place, (3) an accounting and logging mechanism or mechanisms must be established, and (4) an auditing system must be implemented.

Changes to the configuration must be (1) proposed, (2) reviewed, (3) approved, (4) tracked, and (5) frozen into a new baseline. As indicated, CM is a vast concept that incorporates the facilities used in production, operations, compliance, and auditing. In this context, compliance involves the processes and procedures and rules used to ensure conformance to a security policy or a regulation. Auditing is the evaluation and verification of compliance. In other words, audits assess compliance with rules, regulations, policies, procedures, and laws. To help managers with this expansive responsibility, CM frameworks exist.

As discussed in earlier chapters, most management frameworks require the assessment and oversight of appropriate configurations of the information systems. ITIL, COBIT, and NIST SP 800-53 all recognize the importance of change and CM to both the operational and security management of information systems, although it is conspicuously absent in ISO 27002. Behr, Kim, and Spafford [3], in examining high-performing IT organizations, defined "high-performing" as consisting of the following characteristics:

1. High mean time between failures and low mean time to repair.
2. Early and consistent integration of security controls into IT operational processes.
3. Low numbers of repeat negative audit findings with less staff time devoted to compliance.
4. High efficiency related to server to system administrator ratios and low amounts of unplanned work.

Behr et al. [3] found that high-performing IT organizations consistently supported a culture of change management and causality determination. In subsequent studies that benchmarked IT organizations according to use of controls, the key control differentiator between high-performing organizations and others was the high use of change and CM controls [4]. From an operational perspective, high-performing organizations were completing eight times as many projects compared to medium and low performers, and they were managing six times as many applications and IT services.

They also found that high-performing organizations were authorizing and implementing fifteen times as many changes, and when managing IT assets, had server to system administrator ratios that were 2.5 times higher than medium performers and 5.4 times higher than low performers. Finally, high performers had one-half the change failure rate of medium performers and one-third the change failure rate of low performers. From a security perspective, the research has shown that breaches that did occur were detected sooner and were significantly less likely to result in financial, reputational, or customer loss. Thus high-performing organizations understood the importance of managing their information systems and the associated risks, rather than letting the information system grow and change through a series of ad-hoc additions and alterations.

   Risk management and good governance dictate that, although little can usually be done with respect to the threat environment, organizations can manage the vulnerabilities in their systems. As stated in Johnson, Dempsey, Ross, Gupta, and Bailey [5], "Using configuration management to gain greater control and ensure the integrity of IT resources facilitates asset management, improves incident response, help desk, disaster recovery and problem solving, aids in software development and release management, enables greater automation of processes, and supports compliance with policies and preparation for audits" (chpt. 2, p. 5).

> **In Focus**
>
> There are software applications that can assist with CM. These applications, for example, may restrict who can make what changes and can electronically send notifications to supervisors or administrators to approve a change before it is made.

19.1.2 Managing Configurations

Now that we have presented the concept and importance of CM, let's further define it as a collection of activities focused on establishing and maintaining the integrity of products and systems, through control of the processes for initializing, changing, and monitoring the configurations of those products and systems. Although these may sound like technical functions, CM is not the sole domain of the IT department. In *Quality Is Free*, Phillip Crosby [6] introduced the importance of management responsibility for the quality of organizational output. Central to this is the notion of "conformance to requirements," which requires an organization to measure and understand the consistency of their performance. This is also found in many quality improvement methods, including the popular Six Sigma strategy developed by Motorola in 1981 [7].

   A useful analogy to illustrate is that of an electrical engineer working for an appliance manufacturer. The engineering team designs an appliance to meet specific requirements. A prototype will likely be produced and tested to ensure compliance with both functional and safety requirements. Once the design of the system is approved, it will go into production, and the engineering team will continue to work on refining the design of existing products or developing new products.

   If an engineer thinks a change should be made to the production of an appliance, he or she doesn't run out to the production line and make the change. The change is introduced in a test environment, the impact of the change to functional and safety requirements are evaluated, and only once it is approved will the change be made in production. One can only imagine the troubles a manufacturer might have with their products if every engineer were to make ad-hoc changes to the production of an appliance on the assembly line. The same holds for configuration and change management with respect to information systems.

> **In Focus**
>
> There is a variety of software applications available for both enterprises and individuals to use to help manage the change and CM process. Although many of these may have begun as security products, their value to everyday operations was quickly discovered.

A discrete target of the configuration control process is a *configuration item* (**CI**), and the formally defined and agreed on initial configuration of a CI is called the *baseline configuration*. The practice of CM is implemented through the establishment of the baseline configuration [5], and in addition to managing the baseline configuration, managers develop a *CM plan*. As described by Johnson et al. [5] (p. 12), a CM plan is a comprehensive description of the roles, responsibilities, policies, and procedures that apply when managing the configuration of products and systems. The basic parts of a CM plan include:

1. Instituting a configuration change control board (CCB) with a charter and organizational structure (roles and responsibilities) for the body of personnel responsible for CM.
2. Configuration item identification using methodology for selection and naming of configuration items that need to be placed under CM.
3. Baseline CM, including processes for the establishment and management of the baseline configuration and for the identified configuration items.
4. Configuration change control processes for managing updates to the baselines for the configuration items.
5. Configuration monitoring processes for assessing or testing the level of compliance with the established configuration baseline and mechanisms for reporting the configuration status of items placed under CM.

19.1.3 Security Configuration Management

Although generic change and CM are important to effective IT operations, when addressing change and CM specifically from a security perspective, it becomes *security configuration management* (**SeCM**). More formally, SeCM is the application of CM processes to manage risk and address issues directly related to the security of an information system. Although the goal may be to address security issues, it should not be seen as a completely separate and distinct process from operations. In fact, returning to the work of Behr et al. [3], it is important to "integrate [security] into daily IT operational processes" (p. 19). The four phases of security improvement introduced by Behr are:

1. Phase 1 – Understand the processes of the organization and begin to work with IT operations, particularly with respect to change management, access control, and incident handling, to reduce operational IT risk.
2. Phase 2 – Ensure that security understands the operational needs of the organization and address technology-associated risk by applying appropriate controls.
3. Phase 3 – Implement development and release controls that ensure security and risk objectives are being addressed early in the system development life cycle when it is easiest and least expensive to handle them.
4. Phase 4 – Maintain continual improvement through the selection and monitoring of relevant measures to ensure continuous risk reduction.

It is important to reinforce that these are not static events, but parts of a continuous process of evaluation, design, and implementation that includes vulnerability assessments, threat assessments, and patch management. An automated CM system is an important if not necessary component because of the complex and dynamic nature of these processes and tasks.

19.2 Security Management

As has been discussed throughout this textbook, information system security encompasses the technology and the humans who use the technology. Therefore, technical security management has both organizational and a system aspects component. At the organizational level, we are interested in addressing the organizational concerns presented in the first section of this textbook—policies, law, security behaviors, and the like—whereas the system component is concerned with the technological countermeasures.

At the organizational level, we need to develop and address the items in the CM plan. This includes creating a "culture of change management" through the establishment of an organization-wide SeCM program that centrally manages the policies, procedures, and training related to SeCM and that defines individual roles and responsibilities related to SeCM tasks.

These policies should establish the structures of the SeCM, including the creation of a CI inventory, the use of specified standards and templates, and the specification of any general prohibitions to configuration settings. The procedures should attempt to standardize the SeCM process through delineating what CIs are in scope and should describe "the steps to move a configuration change from its initial request to eventual release into the operational environment" [5]. Specifically, Johnson et al. (p. 23) prescribe that the change control procedures should include:

1. Change request and approval procedures;
2. Criteria to determine the types of changes that are configuration-controlled (e.g., specific criteria in the form of a checklist, or a list of configuration changes that

are preapproved such as updating antivirus signatures, creating or deleting users, changing defective peripherals, motherboard or hard drives);

3. Security impact analysis procedures;
4. Criteria to determine when a change is significant enough to trigger system reauthorization activities;
5. Establishment of a group that approves changes (e.g., a CCB);
6. Requirements for testing of changes for submission to the CCB;
7. Requirements for testing of changes prior to release into the operational environment;
8. Requirements for access restrictions for change (i.e., who can make changes to the information system and under what circumstances);
9. Requirements for rollback of changes in the event that problems occur; and
10. Requirements for management of unscheduled changes (e.g., changes needed for critical flaw remediation) that are tailored to support expedited reviews and approvals.

In addition, consideration should be given to the development of procedures that address SeCM template use; steps for creation and content of baseline configurations; the prioritization, testing, approval, and integration of patches; help desk change request handling; integration of change management throughout the systems development life cycle; the labeling and destruction of media; and how monitoring should be accomplished to track adherence with the configuration and change management process.

19.2.1 Security Management Planning—System Level

At the system level, the CI components involved must be examined individually and as a group in order to develop a specific system SeCM plan. Again, using NIST standards [5] (pp. 25–26), this plan should include the following recommendations:

- Brief description of the target information system(s);
- Information system component inventory;
- Information system configuration items;
- Rigor to be applied to managing changes to configuration items (i.e., based on the impact level of the information system);
- Identification of the roles and responsibilities;
- Identification and composition of the group or individual(s) that consider change requests;
- Configuration change control procedures to be followed (including references to organization-wide procedures);
- Identification of the location where SeCM artifacts (change requests, approvals, etc.) are maintained (e.g., media libraries);
- Overrides of location of SeCM artifacts (if applicable);

- Access controls employed to control changes to configurations;
- Overrides of configuration change control procedures (if applicable);
- SeCM tools that are used;
- Description of secure configuration standards to be used as a basis for establishing approved configuration baselines for the information system;
- Deviations from secure configuration standards for configuration items including justifications; and
- Description of approved baseline configurations for the information system [5].

The baseline configuration will often include:

- Configuration settings (i.e., the set of parameters that can be changed in a hardware or software component of an information system to affect its security posture) including, but not limited to:
  - OS and application features (enabling or disabling depending on the specific feature);
  - Services and ports (e.g., automatic updates, DNS over port 53);
  - Network protocols (e.g., NetBIOS, IPv6) and network interfaces (e.g., Bluetooth, IEEE 802.11, infrared);
  - Methods of remote access (e.g., SSL, VPN, SSH, and IPSec);
  - Access controls (e.g., controlling permissions to files, directories, registry keys, and user activities such as restricting activities like modifying system logs or installing applications);
  - Management of identifiers/accounts (e.g., changing default account names, determining length of time until inactive accounts are disabled, using unique user names, establishing user groups);
  - Authentication controls (e.g., password length, use of special characters, minimum password age, multifactor authentication/use of tokens);
  - Audit settings (e.g., capturing key events such as failures, logons, permission changes, unsuccessful file access, creation of users and objects, deletion and modification of system files, registry key and kernel changes);
  - System settings (e.g., session timeouts, number of remote connections, session lock); and
  - Cryptography (e.g., using FIPS140-2 validated cryptographic protocols and algorithms to protect data in transit and in storage);
- Patch levels—applying vendor-released patches in response to identified vulnerabilities, including software updates;
- Software load and version—using approved, signed software, if supported;
- End-point protection platforms—safeguards implemented through software to protect end-user machines against attack (e.g., antivirus, antispyware, anti-adware, personal firewalls, host-based intrusion detection systems [HIDS]);
- Transport protocol protections (e.g., TLS, IPSec);

- System architecture—where a component physically and logically resides (e.g., behind a firewall, within a DMZ, on a specific subnet); and
- Documentation—supporting documents may include technical specification and design documentation, system security documentation, and system procedures.

19.2.2 Configuring to a Secure State

Once the SeCM planning is complete, it is time to configure the system to a secure state using the system SeCM plan and following the policies and procedures developed. In actuality, a secure state might be thought of as a "known" state, because no system can be completely secure, and sometimes, some vulnerabilities might even be tolerated based on a risk assessment or cost-benefit analysis. Moreover, because there is an incredible diversity of technology components, each with a large number of configuration options, it would be difficult for any individual alone to identify and appropriately specify a baseline configuration that would address the most prevalent vulnerabilities.

Fortunately, there are a variety of community-based, consensus configuration guides that can help. Security checklists—including hardening guides, security technical implementation guides, or benchmarks—provide instructions on how to configure an IT asset to resist threats in a given environment by reducing or eliminating common vulnerabilities, which may exist in the default configuration of the product. Checklists are developed by many different types of organizations, from IT vendors to governments, to consortia of public and private entities. These checklists can vary in their specificity from high-level narratives to low-level, automated scripts that will make the system changes automatically. Included in this collection are Defense Information Systems Agency (DISA), Security Technical Implementation Guides (STIGs), NIST checklists, IT vendor-based standards, and Center for Internet Security Benchmarks.

> **In Focus**
>
> Although one of the advantages of using a checklist is the benefit of receiving advice from a large community of experts and a reduction in configuration time, the specifics of the operating environment in which the asset being configured is to be deployed may not match exactly that of the configuration guide. As such, although the checklist is a great foundation from which to begin your configuration, it needs to be examined and refined for the specific organizational environment.

In partial response to the Cyber Security Research and Development Act of 2002 that promoted the increased investment in cyber-security research, workforce development, and cyber-security–related technology in general, and to the mandate that the NIST develop and disseminate computer security checklists specifically, the NIST created the ***National Checklist Program*** (NCP) for IT products [8]. The NCP, as described in SP

800-70r1, which is the subsection that defines the National Checklist Program for IT Products—Guidelines for Checklist Users and Developers—and is designed to improve the quality, availability, and usability of security checklists. Specifically, the goals of the NCP program [9] (p. 14) are to:

- Facilitate development and sharing of checklists by providing a formal framework for vendors and other checklist developers to submit checklists to NIST.
- Provide guidance to developers to help them create standardized, high-quality check-lists that conform to common operational environments.
- Help developers and users by providing guidelines for making checklists better documented and more usable.
- Encourage software vendors and other parties to develop checklists.
- Provide a managed process for the review, update, and maintenance of checklists.
- Provide an easy-to-use repository of checklists.
- Provide checklist content in a standardized format.
- Encourage the use of automation technologies for checklist application [9].

When deciding on the configuration implementation, again consideration should also be given to the environment in which it will be operating. The NCP outlines two broad categories: standalone and managed. Within the managed environment are three custom or special cases: ***Specialized Security-Limited Functionality*** (SSCF), legacy, and the ***Federal Desktop Core Configuration*** (FDCC). The standalone, or small office/home office (SOHO) environment, is characterized by smaller installations with a low insider threat risk. The specific assumptions of the standalone environment are [9] (p. 18):

- Home users with standalone systems, generally with dial-up or high-speed access to the Internet, possibly using wired or wireless home networks, and possibly sharing resources across the networks.
- Telecommuters using standalone systems who work from a home office.
- Small businesses, typically with small networks of standalone desktop systems and small office servers protected from direct Internet access by a firewall, but possibly including some small centrally managed networks of desktop systems and products, and typically not maintaining publicly accessible servers.
- Other small organizations with similar functions.

The threats assumed in a standalone environment are external, remote threats that typically come from malicious traffic and payloads, such as worms and viruses. The security goals of the standalone environment center on restricting or removing unneeded services and applications and limiting access from outside the local network. NIST [9] (pp. 19–20) specifically provides the following practices for a standalone environment:

- Use of small hardware firewall appliances at Internet connections to block inbound connections and to filter outbound traffic, if feasible.
- Use of personal firewall products on standalone systems.

- Application (e.g., antivirus software, web browser, and email client) and operating system updates.
- Apply patches regularly.
- Web and email clients configured to filter and block traffic/messages that could contain malicious content.
- Unnecessary applications disabled (e.g., personal web servers, Simple Network Management Protocol [SNMP], messaging).
- Encryption used for wireless network traffic and as appropriate for other traffic
- Place restrictions on which systems/users can connect to wired and wireless local area networks (LAN).
- Place restrictions on user privileges.
- Place restrictions on sharing resources such as directories or printers.
- Initiate backup and recovery procedures.
- Implement physical security procedures [9].

19.2.3 Managed Enterprises

The managed or enterprise environment is what one would normally find in a larger organization with a centralized IT staff. Checklists for these environments are designed for advanced end users or IT professionals to use in different enclaves to provide enterprise functionality while typically centrally managing the policies related to the IT assets. Although the typical managed environment tends to be more restrictive than the standalone environment, including the provision of multiple layers of defense known as defense in depth, they also tend to have greater control over and insight into the flow of information in their environment [1]. As specified in Quinn et al. [9] (p. 22), common security practices that relate to the enterprise environment are:

- Segmented internal networks with internal firewalls and other defense-in-depth techniques.
- Centralized management of systems with highly restricted local user access.
- Centralized management of security-related applications such as antivirus software.
- Automated installation of system and application patches and updates.
- Restricted access to printer and multi-function devices and their features.
- Centralized systems for log monitoring.
- Centralized backup and recovery facilities.

The specialized cases of the managed environment—SSLF, legacy, and FDCC—are also covered under the NCP. SSLF custom environments are ones that tend to have security requirements that are more restrictive than those of other systems in the managed environment, causing security to be of a higher concern and to take a priority over functionality in these systems. Examples of SSLF might include highly sensitive and proprietary organizational information, such as geologic surveys for a "gas and oil" company or a "human resources" computer that contains personally identifiable information on the employees of the organization. The impact of a security incident involving these systems would typically be much greater than for that of other systems in the enterprise. The following general security practices and controls are recommended by NIST [9] (p. 23) for these systems:

- Systems should generally process as few types of data as possible (e.g., do not combine multiple server applications on the same system).
- Systems should be stripped of all unnecessary services and applications.
- If possible, host-based firewall applications should be used.
- Systems should have as few users as possible.
- The strongest possible authentication should be used (e.g., authentication token, biometrics, and smart cards).
- Remote administration or access should be restricted; if used, connections should be encrypted.
- Security-related operating system and application patches and updates should be tested and applied as soon as possible.
- Systems should be placed behind firewalls and other network security devices that restrict access and filter unnecessary protocols.
- Intrusion detection logs and other logs should be monitored frequently.
- Vulnerability assessment tools should be run against the systems frequently.
- System administrators should be highly skilled in the appropriate technologies [9].

19.2.4 Checklist Groups

Legacy systems present special configuration challenges, as they often cannot support many advanced or modern security controls. As such, compensating security controls must be identified to account for the current or potential vulnerabilities inherent in the system. An example would be the use of proxies as discussed in the chapter on computer security. The final special case in the NCP is the FDCC. This is a custom desktop environment that is specified by the U.S. **Office of Management and Budget** (OMB) for federal managed desktops.

The checklists that are part of the NCP are specific to a listed IT product and are broadly divided into automated and non-automated groups. An automated checklist is written in such a way that facilitates implementation by a script or other software product. NIST is encouraging the use of the **Security Content Automation Protocol** (SCAP) in developing automated checklists to facilitate a standardized and open means that multiple vendors can use for IT product hardening. The repository (found at http://checklists.nist.gov) can be searched by a variety of fields, including tier, product name, product category, developer (authority), or keyword. Tiers refer to the degree of automation that the checklist provides. Tier I checklists are prose-based, narrative descriptions of how to secure an asset, whereas Tier IV are machine-readable checklists that can be automatically processed and map the low-level configurations to higher level security framework specifications, such as those discussed previously.

19.3 Extended Guidelines

To this point, we have covered a lot of terms in CM and focused on NIST checklists for both government and industry; however, there are some special sets of guidelines specifically designed for the government sector because in many cases, they must conform to very strict and regulated criteria. There are also a vast number of other sets of criteria and checklists that can be used for specialized industries. Some of these include specifications defined by the National Security Agency (NSA) or the Defense Advanced Research Projects Agency (DARPA), or even entities associated with DARPA, such as the Department of Defense (DoD). In other cases, there is a cross-over from government to industry, for example, in the case of government contractors or suppliers.

19.3.1 DISA STIGs

The ***Defense Information Systems Agency*** (DISA), through the Information Assurance Support Environment, provides a series of baseline system configurations known as ***Security Technical Implementation Guides*** (STIGs). These guides are the configuration standards for U.S. Department of Defense (DoD) information systems and together with their security checklists, provide a great foundation for securely configuring systems. Although some of the STIGs and compliance scripts are not available for general public release, most are available from their website. STIGs cover a wide variety of configuration items and provide an auditable means of ensuring systems are minimally protected against the most common threats. In general, STIGs will include an explanation for the guidance as well as the recommended settings, with the vulnerabilities represented in the configuration checklist divided into three categories related to the associated risk.

Category I vulnerabilities are ones "that allow an attacker immediate access into a machine, allow superuser access, or bypass a firewall," Category II vulnerabilities are ones "that provide information that has a high potential of giving access to an intruder," and Category III vulnerabilities "provide information that potentially could lead to compromise" [10]. The checklists that often accompany the STIGs will include more specific information on exactly how to configure the asset, often including specific commands to enter. Even though manually configuring a system to a STIG specification can be done, it is often accomplished through the use of configuration scripts and tools that implement the STIG specifications.

In Focus

Technology companies doing business with a government agency fall under the formal category of government "IT vendor" and are required to comply with the security criteria that the agency defines.

19.3.2 Private Industry Baseline Security

Because there are so many checklists available from government and military organizations, and many of the checklists are also useful on their own merit for enterprises in general, private organizations may have a tough decision to determine which one(s) to use. An important point to know is that checklists are often geared to specific criteria that an agency or an enterprise must meet for compliance with the regulations, policies, rules, and laws set for that entity. In other words, whereas some checklists are generic in nature, some are domain specific. Figuring out which are useful to an organization in and of itself can be a daunting task. Once selected or defined, the baseline needs to be managed accordingly, which, as indicated, can likewise be intimidating. This is especially true for private industry technology vendors.

To assist, technology vendor-based security checklists often include automated tools to help companies assess and configure assets in a more secure manner. Some examples are the Microsoft Baseline Security Analyzer and Microsoft Security Compliance Manager for Microsoft products and Bastille Linux for several variants of Linux. The ***Microsoft Baseline Security Analyzer*** (MBSA) is designed to help an organization "determine their security state in accordance with Microsoft security recommendations and offers specific remediation guidance" [11]. The MBSA is focused on small- to medium-size organizations, similar to the standalone environment described by the National Checklist Program (NCP).

The Microsoft Security Compliance Manager is designed for the larger enterprise and allows an organization to incorporate security guidance recommendations from Microsoft into a baseline configuration that can then be exported in a variety of formats, including SCAP, for use with automated tools to secure Microsoft architecture in the organization. Bastille Linux is a hardening script (available from http://www.bastille-unix.org/) as well as already included with a variety of Linux distributions. The script will provide a series of choices to the administrator from which it will build a policy and configure the system. The script also has a verbose interactive mode designed to teach the user about security and security options.

> **In Focus**
>
> Customers expect that security technology vendors live up to the highest standards of security compliance, which may or may not always be the case.

19.3.3 Center for Internet Security Benchmarks

Recall that CM is concerned with, among other things, performance, and this is crucial to security because a dramatic drain on performance is often an indicator of a security attack. Managers need to also consider system performance benchmarks as a security issue because we need a baseline to determine whether performance degradation is expected due to workload, or an anomaly perhaps induced by a system failure or a security attack. Therefore, we consider performance benchmarks as part of the baseline configuration. Performance benchmarks may also be part of contractual quality and performance commitments to customers, called quality of service (QoS) metrics or parameters.

The *Center for Internet Security* (CISE) is a non-profit organization with a mission to "establish and promote the use of consensus-based standards to raise the level of security and privacy in Internet-connected systems, and to ensure the integrity of the business, government and private Internet-based functions and transactions on which society increasingly depends" [12]. There are at least 52 configuration guides downloadable from the CISE website that cover a variety of IT assets, benchmark audit tools, and 21 security metric definitions for evaluating security process outcomes. The benchmarks often include security profiles that match the NPS specifications of standalone or managed environments.

To partially summarize the Windows 7 benchmark [11]: "Once we have completed configuring the assets to the baseline standard, it's important to test them in an environment reasonably equivalent to the production environment. Testing will highlight the interaction and configuration settings that, in the production environment, may cause significant functional issues." As pointed out, it is much better to discover issues in the testing environment rather than production, but as most organizations don't have the resources to generate a test environment that directly matches the complexity of loads and interactions that occur in the production environment, it is important to understand that some unexpected interactions may occur regardless. Therefore, for any change to the production environment, there should be a clear rollback procedure for how to undo the changes being made.

19.4 Maintaining the Secure State

With the constantly evolving technology landscape uncovering and introducing new threats and vulnerabilities to information systems, changes to the baseline configuration of any asset are inevitable. It is important, however, to clearly and definitively manage the process of making these changes. Much work has highlighted that controlling the change management process is key to having any effective control of our information system and is one of the first steps in any attempt to improve the quality of IT services. In this final section of this chapter, we will cover the main aspects related to maintaining information and systems in a secure state.

19.4.1 Controlling Changes

As previously outlined, fundamental to managing a secure state are controlling the change management process and controlling who is authorized to make changes. NIST recommends a four-phase process to implementing change management: (1) implement access restrictions for changes, (2) implement the configuration change control processes, (3) conduct a security impact analysis, and (4) document and archive the changes [5]. The "implement access restrictions for change" phase will limit who can make changes and begin to enforce the change management process by constraining the types of behavior allowed on the system. The recommended process for initializing change access restrictions is:

1. Identify what types of changes will need to be made to individual IT assets,
2. Identify who will be authorized to make those changes, and
3. Institute appropriate controls restricting changes to only those individuals identified in step 3.

The second phase in implementing change management is introducing the change control process. Although the specifics of the process should be determined in the organizational planning stage of SeCM, it is generally recommended that the process be received, documented, tested, approved, and implemented with a corresponding documented update to the baseline configuration. NIST [5] (p. 36) recommends the following eight steps:

1. Request the change. This occurs when a change is initially conceived. The request may originate from any number of sources including the end user of the information system, a help desk, or management. Changes may also originate from vendor-supplied patches, application updates, and so on.
2. Document the request for the change. A change is formally entered into the configuration change control process when it is documented. Organizations may use paper-based requests, emails, or automated tools to track change requests, route them based on workflow processes, and allow for electronic acknowledgments/ approvals.
3. Determine if the change requires configuration control. Some types of changes may be exempt from configuration change control as defined in the SeCM plan and/or procedures. If the change is exempt, note this on the change request and allow the change to be made without further analysis or approval; however, system documentation may still require updating (e.g., the system security plan, the baseline configuration, and IS component inventory).
4. Analyze the change for its security impact on the information system.
5. Test the proposed change for security and functional impacts. The impacts of the change should be presented to the Change Control Board (CCB).
6. Approve the change. This step is usually performed by the CCB. The CCB may require the implementation of mitigating controls if the change is necessary for mission accomplishment but has a negative impact on the security of the system and organization.
7. Implement the change. Once approved, authorized staff should make the change. Stakeholders (e.g., users, management, help desk) should be notified about the change, especially if the change implementation requires a service interruption or

alters the functionality of the information system. In the latter situation, user and help desk training may be required.

8. Confirm that the change was implemented correctly. Configuration change control is not complete and a change request not closed until it has been confirmed that the change was deployed without issues. Although the initial security impact analysis may reveal no impact from the change, an improperly implemented change can cause its own security issues [5].

19.4.2 Conducting a Security Impact Analysis

Once the controls are in place as recommended by NIST in phases one and two, the purpose of the third phase is to ensure that any changes made to the configuration do not introduce new, unaccounted for vulnerabilities in either the individual IT asset or to the information system as a whole. Although there are numerous guides available for conducting a security analysis, and multiple depths and types of analysis that can be done, the five steps recommended by NIST are:

1. Understand the change for the technical and functional changes that it introduces to the system.
2. Identify potential new vulnerabilities introduced by the change, particularly if this is related to the introduction of new or updated software. The National Vulnerability Database hosted by NIST provides a compendium of vulnerabilities from multiple sources.
3. Assess the risk related to the change against the functionality offered and the risk appetite of the organization.
4. Assess the risk related to the change on the current security controls in place.
5. Plan for and introduce any compensating controls necessary to account for any increased risks introduced by the change.

Once the update has been made to the baseline configuration, it is critical to document the change and update the baseline configuration as suggested by NIST in the final phase. This may also require the organization to reevaluate their overall risk assessment with respect to their information systems and, in some cases, have the systems reevaluated for accreditation. Once a baseline configuration is adopted, whether for a new asset or an update to an existing baseline, monitoring for adherence to the baseline configuration is critical. Identified deviations from the established baseline configuration indicate at best a failure of the change management process and quite possibly a security breach. At a minimum, the identification of a variance from the established baseline should trigger the security and operations teams to begin an investigation into the cause of the variance.

19.4.3 Certification and Accreditation

The CM checklists and procedures are particularly relevant to organizations that require *certification and accreditation* (called **C&A**). C&A may be part of the overall security policy, especially if the organization is a federal agency or is federally regulated. A certification is a comprehensive evaluation of an information system and its infrastructure to ensure that it complies with requirements documented by federal standards, such as the *Federal Information Security Management Act* (FISMA). An accreditation is the result of an audit conducted by an accrediting body, such as NIST, and it is an official decision that authorizes the use of an audited information system. An accreditation represents verification that the current status of the security programs and security controls to protect a system and information processed, stored, or transmitted by the system, meets the certification requirements.

Certifications are conducted by official auditors, which may result in one of four accreditation levels ranging from low security (1) to high security (4). In general, auditors are concerned with whether there are sufficient controls in place in the system. They are interested in which ones are important and which are unnecessary, whether they are properly implemented, and, where applicable, whether there are clear separations of duties among employees. Auditors are also concerned with whether there are procedures to ensure reporting of incidents and corrective actions in case of violations, and if there are controls to contain the problem and help protect from future occurrence [1].

Auditors use different methodologies depending on which agency is doing the certification. As indicated earlier, government agencies are subjected to a particular accrediting body depending on which branch they operate under. It is important to note that audits are not used simply for accreditation. In fact, it is often a good idea for most organizations, and not just federal agencies, to conduct security audits. Internal auditors, or external auditors, or perhaps even both may conduct these informal audits.

CHAPTER SUMMARY

Security is about making sure our systems operate how they are supposed to operate, whereas operations is about providing services, both current and new. The two are complementary. One of the key elements to securing an IT asset is configuration and change management. Once our organization has identified the security requirements for our systems through a risk-based evaluation, it is time to start to secure the assets. Fundamental to securing any computer, whether it is a small "notebook" or critical server, is to configure it appropriately and, once configured, to manage and understand any changes made. From a configuration perspective, one must specify what the system

CHAPTER SUMMARY (CONTINUED)

is to be used for, understand what it requires and doesn't require to accomplish those functions, and apply appropriate controls to reduce associated risks and ensure the system is operating as expected. Once the asset is deployed, any changes to the configuration must be documented and managed carefully, lest you end up with an unmanaged asset that represents a threat to the secure and continued operation of information services.

THINK ABOUT IT

Topic Questions

19.1: What is configuration management (CM)?

19.2: What is a configuration item?

19.3: What is a baseline configuration?

19.4: What is a configuration plan?

19.5: What is security configuration management (SeCM)?

19.6: Give examples of configuration checklists.

19.7: What threats are assumed in a standalone environment?

19.8: What are the differences between a stand-alone or SOHO environment and a managed or enterprise environment?

19.9: A CI is called:

____ The CM

____ The baseline

____ The security initiative

____ Central intelligence station

19.10: Security configuration management borrowed from software configuration management concepts.

____ True

____ False

Questions for Further Study

Q19.1: What happens to an information system if many people make undocumented changes?

Q19.2: What are some advantages/disadvantages of configuration checklists?

Q19.3: What are some problems likely to be initially encountered when introducing a strict change and configuration process?

Q19.4: Describe three frameworks that could be used in SeCM.

Q19.5: How might configuration changes be managed securely in mobile ad-hoc networks?

KEY CONCEPTS AND TERMS

Configuration management (CM) is concerned with performance and the functional and physical integrity of systems, applications, networks, and information environments.

NIST Security Content Automation Protocol (SCAP) involves developing automated checklists to facilitate a standardized and open means that multiple vendors can use for IT product hardening.

Performance expectancies mean that customers expect that security technology vendors live up to the highest standards of security compliance.

SeCM is configuration management specifically from a security perspective.

SeCM planning calls for configuring the system to a secure state.

References

1. Weiss, M. M., & Solomon, M. G. (2011). *Auditing IT infrastructure for compliance.* Sudbury, MA: Jones & Bartlett Learning.
2. Raphael, L., & Delmont, A. (2001). *The Rational Unified Process (RUP): Rational Rose and the merging of the IBM way.* Boston, MA: eAselworx Press.
3. Behr, K., Kim, G., & Spafford, G. (2004). *The visible ops handbook: Starting ITIL in 4 practical steps.* Eugene, OR: IT Process Insitute.
4. Kim, G., Milne, K., & Phelps, D. (2006). *Initial findings from the IT controls benchmarking study.* Eugene, OR: Information Technology Process Institute.
5. Johnson, A., Dempsey, K., Ross, R., Gupta, S., & Bailey, D. (2010). *NIST SP 800-128: Guide for security configuration management of information systems.* Gaithersburg, MD: Computer Security Division, Information Technology Laboratory, National Institute of Standards and Technology.
6. Crosby, P. (1980). *Quality is free.* New York, NY: Mentor.
7. Tennent, G. (2001). *Six Sigma: SPC and TQM in manufacturing and services.* Burlington, VT: Gower Publishing.
8. United States. Congress. House. Committee on Science. (2002). *Cyber Security Research and Development Act: Report to U.S. G.P.O.* Washington, DC: GPO.
9. Quinn, S. D., Scarfone, K., & Souppaya, M. (2009). *NIST SP 800-70r1: National Checklist Program for IT Products—Guidelines for Checklist Users and Developers.* Gaithersburgh, MD: National Institute of Standards and Technology.
10. Defense Information Systems Agency. (2008). *Access control in support of information systems security technical implementation guide*, Version 2, Release 2. Washington, DC: DISA.
11. Microsoft. (n.d.). *Microsoft Baseline Security Analyzer.* Retrieved July 15, 2010, from http://technet.microsoft.com/en-us/security/cc184924.aspx
12. Center for Internet Security. (n.d.). *About.* Retrieved July 15, 2010, from http://cisecurity.org

Operations

O PERATIONS ENCOMPASSES PRODUCT DEVELOPMENT and/or service delivery processes, including implementation, monitoring, auditing, and incident handling; indeed, operations is comprised of the daily activities in an organization. Security operations, more specifically, deals with managing risks and carrying out duties related to security policies. It takes into account technical issues such as using fault-tolerant systems and redundancies, and using administrative facilities such as incorporating oversight of security and quality checking in the systems development or implementation life cycles. Managing operations includes, among other things that we have mentioned, having the "right" people in the "right" places at the "right" time. Thus, managers need to hire, cultivate, and inspire a mix of people with the necessary skill sets within their purview; and this is important in operations to balance out the multiplicity of security and information needs today. In this chapter, we will cover operations from a security point of view.

Chapter 20 Topics

This chapter:

- Describes keeping information systems up and running.
- Explains how to plan and prepare for resilient systems in case of disasters.
- Illustrates how to detect and manage security incidents.
- Considers contingencies and weighs the costs and benefits.

20.1 Maintaining Operations

The term "operations" is used in reference to ensuring that a business or government enterprise is able to conduct business as usual, but this takes planning. In terms of security, when systems are developed or technologies implemented, security features must become a critical factor in the overall schedule and budgeting issues—on par with other quality assurance aspects such as weeding out critical defects from a product, or making sure that technologies are utilized properly, or that systems are implemented as intended. Whether developing a product or implementing a technology or service, it has a life cycle that includes planning; although the exact method used in planning varies from company to company, and even among companies striving to follow a set of guidelines. In any case, security must be part of the checks and balances.

20.1.1 The SDLC and Security

The systems development life cycle (SDLC) represent the collective processes used to introduce a new service or produce software applications, technologies, or conduct integrations of new systems. In the last chapter, we introduced the concept of *security configuration management* (**SeCM**), but here we will address this as a holistic development and production life cycle (as opposed to an implementation cycle). Most SDLCs today use some form of iteration in the processes, such as indicated earlier when we covered object-oriented programming (OOP). To determine the behavior of a system, business analysts, systems architects, designers, and systems developers (called a design team) outline how requirements are determined, the logical and physical designs, the coding, and testing procedures. It is in this phase or iteration of the program design that an understanding of the problem the team wants the application to solve is conceived; in other words, it means gathering requirements and determining potential solutions.

In this phase, the participants define the problem and its solution according to business terms and chart or diagram the solution procedure, typically using the ***Unified Modeling Language*** (**UML**) defined by the ***Object Management Group*** (**OMG**) standards body. This provides a standard way of expressing and understanding the notations and annotations for the solution. Business analysts may use storyboards or story cards that lead to feature statements, or UML Use Cases to describe the business flows and interactions [1].

There are many approaches to how systems are designed and developed, such as IBM's Rational Unified Process (RUP), Agile Unified Process (AUP), eXtreme programming including pair-programming with mentors and mentees [2], and others, but regardless of the terms used, the modern design and development processes are inherently iterative and incremental, meaning that the process is a give-and-take set of stages that leads to what comprises the developments and how components are related and interact [3]. In the Agile method, for example, a team decides what features are included in a cycle (sometimes called a *sprint*) and how long that cycle should last before turning the portion of the development over to a test group or user group to experiment with [2].

In Focus

The description of programming stages may give the impression that the stages are linear and sequential. However, in most modern SDLCs, many of the stages are conducted in parallel, and iteratively.

In more rigid processes, it is sometimes easier for managers to ensure that security has been addressed, such as precluding "backdoors" from being written, or adhering to a set of required standards. In an adaptive and evolutionary method such as Agile, it is up to the team rather than an individual manager to make this determination, and sometimes the only guardians are "product owners" who are supposed to represent the stakeholders, and "scrum masters" who maintain the processes and keep the team focused and moving forward on the tasks at hand. Although sometimes these more flexible methods of developing systems can improve productivity and quality, they tend to be feature-focused and at times may be leaving the "fox in charge of the hen house" for a malicious insider to later exploit, such as through backdoors.

Security features and security consciousness must be emphasized by management to the team. Moreover, in "real life," managers should not abdicate their oversight responsibilities and should remain engaged in the SDLC to ensure that security is implemented and reviewed. There are at least two critical ways that managers need to do this. First, managers should insist on a review cycle specifically for security requirements. Next, managers should review the business requirements, such as ***Use Cases*** or feature statements [3], to ensure that business requirements as well as quality metrics consider security and are met. Managers should review these before the product owner attends a review meeting, and then review the results and decisions after the meeting and ensure an override channel to address any issues.

In Focus

There are many ways to model and conduct OO systems design and development, but two of the more popular approaches have been the Rational Unified Process, or RUP, and Agile.

20.1.2 Planning: Failures Are a Rule, Not an Exception

Even if systems are designed with security in mind, things can and will go wrong with them. Managers develop ***contingency plans*** not because they hope to use them, but because they expect to use them, on occasion. Contingency planning lays out the requirements and steps needed in case a development or implementation or business operation is disrupted by some event or "incident." Contingency planning may use "scenarios" to imagine events that could disrupt the availability of networks and systems, even those that are caused by accident or natural disaster; for example, they address the loss of data processing capabilities that might result from natural disasters such as fires, floods, storms, or earthquakes.

   In actuality then, contingency planning is a rubric under which several other types of planning are done. Where contingency planning is essentially aimed at minimizing the downtime of technology or information resources in the event of natural or man-made disasters or devastating attacks, it also incorporates ***disaster recovery planning***, which provides an alternative means of information processing and recovery in the case of such disasters, and also includes ***facilities management*** that incorporates procedures for dealing with fire, offsite backup storage facilities, and utilizing distributed operations and monitoring centers to prevent single points of failure and support recovery operations. The contingency plans therefore establish ways to deal with threats by planning for and implementing physical, technical, and administrative countermeasures [4].

Physical Countermeasures

Physical countermeasures include having redundant systems, perhaps on "hot standby" in case a system goes down, and using "redundant array of independent disks" (RAID), where data are mirrored in case a disk goes bad, using "uninterruptable power supplies" (UPS) in case the power goes out, using physical barriers and electronic or biometric locks, taking backup media to an offsite storage facility in case a fire or flood destroys the facility, planning for the appropriate fire suppression systems that extinguish fires for a server room with chemical agents that are "less harmful" to equipment than water, or utilizing co-locations where computing facilities reside in different locations and are replicated so that if one facility is affected by an incident, the other can absorb the work in the meantime.

Technical Countermeasures

Technical countermeasures involve those controls that we focused on in Section 3, such as using virus scanners, hardening systems, and using firewalls and cryptography. In other words, technical controls consist of all of the technologies and techniques needed to help prevent unauthorized access to information resources, prevent tampering with programs and data, use intrusion or unauthorized access detection systems, and block or prevent attackers from connecting to systems once they are detected.

Administrative Countermeasures

Administrative countermeasures aim at ensuring that no single person alone can execute a mission-critical function, for example, ensuring that, if a system administrator dies or leaves the company, all of the configurations, passwords, and cryptography can be recovered. It includes ensuring that employees know what to do in case of emergencies or disasters, and it includes having good security policies and ensuring that personnel are not just aware of them but knowledgeable about them, and follow through accordingly.

In Focus

In CMMI and ISO 9000, for example, these criteria explicitly require companies to "document what to do, and ensure that employees do what is documented" in order to become certified.

20.1.3 Maintaining Operational Capabilities

As we discussed before, policies impose restrictions on how networks, nodes, and systems are used. Security breaches (incidents) as we have learned are any actions taken that undermine the policies that define legitimate use of network assets—or that degrade or compromise a system, preventing its intended use. Vulnerabilities as we have also discussed are any characteristics of the network that can lead to either intentional or unintentional circumvention of the policies or defenses put into place. A threat represents a circumstance that has potential to cause loss or harm. An attack is an intentional attempt to exploit vulnerabilities, but a threat may also include natural disasters.

In Focus

One can define the threat intensity as the likelihood or probability that a threat may lead to a specific loss or harm.

Managers and administrators must remain vigilant to exploits by monitoring notifications from organizations such as CERT or SANS because a vulnerability that has a known exploit can be used by hacker communities, and therefore poses a higher threat to a network or system than another vulnerability for which no such known method exists. This idea is at the core of the concept of *threat intensity*. Another element to the threat intensity or threat level is the actual harm that is likely to result from a successful attack. As such, auditing, detection, and recovery are of particular importance to operational security. Audit covers things such as evaluating logs and intelligence gathering. Some audit-based techniques permit detection and recovery from certain network attacks. Recovery usually involves the use of backups. Prevention of attacks, on the other hand, often involves efforts to create a robust and resilient infrastructure, as well as one where assets are carefully monitored [5].

From a security operations standpoint, it is important that when adopting security measures targeted at achieving other goals, such as maintaining confidentiality or integrity, the mechanisms chosen do not make the system more vulnerable to certain other kinds of attacks. For instance, computationally intensive cryptographic operations used to authenticate connections can facilitate DoS attacks by adding to the workload and overwhelming an authentication server. Because prevention against all attacks is unachievable, audit techniques are very important to maintain operational capabilities. Finally, audit data support forensic activities, which are useful to understand weaknesses in advance of future attacks and in recourse against an attacker.

20.2 Operational Continuity

Given good development, planning, and implementation, at a minimum with regard to security operations, managers need to ensure that employees (1) know their roles, duties, and responsibilities, (2) know the bounds of their roles, and consequences for going beyond them, (3) know and understand security policies, (4) are properly trained for their tasks, (5) know how to monitor systems and networks for signs of trouble, and (6) know the proper procedures to follow if called to "battle stations" in the case of security incidents. In the previous sections of this textbook, we devoted a fair amount of time to the first four of these issues—knowing roles and responsibilities, knowing about the law and bounds of authority, training to be competent at one's job, and techniques and issues with awareness about policies—and we presented the concept of security behavior and discussed security standards, criteria, and checklists. These aspects of security are important preventive measures. Now we will cover another important aspect of security "in action," monitoring for signs of trouble.

20.2.1 Monitoring Systems and Networks

Brand [6] pointed out that monitoring systems and networks is a critical element in maintaining operational continuity, and that intrusion detection systems (IDS) are one of the most necessary tools in the monitoring process. Generically, IDSs are technologies that can filter out or stop a known attack, or alert a human-in-the-loop to some anomaly in network or host process activity. Some of the security literature considers firewalls an IDS, whereas others do not. Some of the security literature considers router filter alerts as network-based intrusion detection, whereas others do not. Getting at the heart of what HIDS or NIDS are can be tricky [7]. In general, firewalls have an alert system that may indicate intrusions, but they are general purpose in that regard.

An IDS is specifically geared toward recognizing activities and focusing on attack signatures or correlations with attack behaviors. An HIDS refers to software applications that monitor access to systems and files, and assess configurations. An example of a popular open source HIDS, as mentioned earlier, is the OSSEC (http://www.ossec.net/), which monitors system logs, checks the integrity of files, helps to find root kit components, and alerts to cases of privilege escalations, as well as providing real-time alerting and active configurable responses.

An NIDS aims at detecting anomalies in network activities that may indicate a denial of service attempt, or port scans, or some other illicit network activity. NIDS generally work based on one of two techniques: signatures or anomalies. Signature-based NIDS are similar to some virus scanners in so far as they are "fed" patterns by the NIDS provider on a network intrusion approach for the NIDS to recognize. These have some advantages in that they generate fewer false positives than the other two approaches, which are those cases where the IDS thinks an attack has commenced, but in fact is benign. However, they do not deal well with "novel" attacks and are sometimes more susceptible to false negatives, meaning missing a "real" attack. Anomaly detection scans for differences between an expected behavior and an actual behavior. These systems use heuristics, which are rules of thumb, rather than a signature, or they may use statistical measures of deviations or correlations. Such a system, for example, might be configured to expect the HTTP protocol only on port 80, but if HTTP is attempted on another port, say 8080, it would infer an attack and generate an alert, and possibly work with the firewall to block the attempt.

Many NIDS are embedded into edge or border routers, but there are also hybrid IDSs such as SNORT and Wireshark, which can be loaded onto host computers. These kinds of IDSs monitor network protocol activities, services, network processes, bandwidth utilization, and use of ports for various kinds of activities. Alerts for certain kinds of activities can be set as rules or filters, and if an attack is attempted, the IDS allows the administrator to expand each layer of the protocol stack for each connection to the system, and even read the contents in the payloads at each encapsulated layer. These also write to logs that can be reviewed later.

Although the ability to review or audit the logs is important, it is after the fact. Therefore, system and network administrators must stay vigilant in monitoring real time, but this can be very difficult given three factors: (1) the sheer boredom of that task at times from long periods of examining log files and monitoring dashboard indicators, (2) IDS sometimes and maybe even often giving off false positive intrusion signals, and as a result (3) administrators sometimes becoming conditioned to poor security behaviors from responding to frequent "noise," such as ignoring an alert when there have been many false positives.

Another issue related to monitoring has to do with the fact that passive attacks are generally easier to do and harder to detect than active ones. For instance, in a wireless network, all an attacker needs is an antenna and a receiver, along with a capture application, to read all messages. Similarly, in a wired network in small organizations, an attacker may only have to compromise a single host to have access to all data that traverse the network interfaces.

Even active attacks can be difficult to detect if they have a small footprint or are complex. Packet injection, replay attacks, and impersonation attacks may only require a compromised host, and the footprint of these kinds of attacks might be quite small. Sometimes an impersonation attack of a router or a gateway host will succeed in redirecting traffic to an attacker's machine and the IDS will be "out of the loop." On the other hand, more pronounced attacks such as packet deletion, delay, reordering, or modification may require the attacker to compromise a gateway host, essentially gaining control over the traffic over that link. Although this generates a larger footprint, the root of the problem can be difficult to locate. Although active attacks are easier to detect than passive ones, if an attack requires only a short span of time to be successful, it may not trigger the security mechanisms before the damage has been done [8].

20.2.2 Auditing Systems and Networks

Auditing falls into two major categories and several subcategories. The major categories are **periodic audits** (informal or formal) by an independent internal or external team and **operational audits** by administrators and security personnel. Subcategories of audits include *financial audits* to determine if financial statements are factual and complete and the integrity of the bookkeeping; *compliance audits* to ensure that organizations are adhering to regulations, laws, and other requirements; *technical audits* to ensure that assets are tagged and that all assets are accounted for and configured properly; and *administrative audits* to ensure adherence to procedures and policies, and to ensure that policies are up to date [9].

> **In Focus**
>
> Informal audits are typically those conducted by an organization and may be a regular business process to determine whether assets are accounted for, whether people are following policies and procedures, and so forth, or these may be done when organizations seek financing or are undergoing a merger or acquisition, which is part of a due diligence process called "valuation."

Periodic auditing of systems and networks investigates the administrative and technical implementations according to policies and procedures, such as whether firewall filtering rules are properly set, there are restrictions placed on ports, only necessary protocols are supported, and configurations are implemented as expected. These audits also may involve examination of change control logs and audit files that are created by security technologies. For example, auditors may view data captured from physical entry devices, sensors, or surveillance cameras, such as to see who entered and left a server room and what they did while there.

Operational audits are ongoing; that is, systems and security administrators regularly inspect log files to look for suspicious activity that an IDS or firewall may not have alerted or was missed. For example, auditing should be done across network and system boundaries to ensure that there were no man-in-the-middle attacks. Logs should be inspected for failed login attempts, data accessed and modified, privileged functions and escalation of privileges, and enabling or disabling of functions, including the logging itself, because attackers will sometimes disable logging to cover their tracks.

In some audits, companies may hire an outside firm to try to breach security measures. Operational personnel may not be notified so that management can determine whether or not the attacks and intrusions are detected, and whether security personnel are vigilant under normal operations. These "benign penetration tests" thus assess the response effectiveness of administrators on if and how auditing is done, what methods they use for intrusion detection, and operational procedures they may follow. Auditors will write a confidential report that outlines their findings and present it to management for corrective actions.

In Focus

Not only is auditing important to help prevent or cure a security attack, but log files are often required in legal proceedings and are therefore part of the evidence that might be used in civil or criminal litigation.

Formal audits tend to be more thorough than informal ones, and involve the requirements needed to comply with a regulatory agency or oversight committee. The auditors, called **signatories**, might be the National Security Agency (NSA) or the National Institute of Standards and Technology (NIST), as previously discussed, and use the criteria and checklists as described to determine compliance.

20.2.3 Operations Centers and Contingencies

Operations centers might be thought of as computational and control rooms. Typically operations centers contain all of the computing and technological infrastructure that a company uses to conduct business, along with monitoring facilities. Along with the computing and networking equipment, operations centers power generators or UPSs, they may have mass storage units such as storage area networks (SANs), which are a collection of storage devices attached to a network such that they appear to be one logical unit, they have environmental controls such as heating and air conditioning and fire suppression systems.

Following procedures is very important in operations centers, and procedures again are the step-by-step instructions to help standardize operations, and include steps such as how to configure databases and networks, how to perform backups, and how to install software and how to create system redundancies and fault-tolerance. Procedures may call for how to perform data striping with parity. Striping is the process of spreading data sets across multiple disks to increase performance. A stripe with parity is a logical unit that contains parity data and allows for the restoration of any lost information from a failed disk in the set. Procedures may call for mirroring, where data are replicated on the fly to a secondary storage device. Although redundancy and fault tolerance are important in operations centers, what if a disaster such as an earthquake strikes an operations center; or what if it becomes the target of a devastating distributed denial of service attack?

For these reasons, a contingency operations center is needed. In larger companies, co-locations are maintained. By co-location, we mean that operations and facilities are separated by geography, and have the ability to absorb the work of the other center for a period of time should disaster strike. Smaller companies may opt for a standby site that is used only in case of emergencies. In other words, companies rent space, facilities, and equipment that are on standby, and if a disaster occurs, the company can utilize these resources on an as-needed basis.

In Focus

Because of the importance of the assets in operations centers, there must be strong authentication and access controls in place because these centers often host systems for many organizations and they are often run by third parties who have physical custody of the backup systems.

Two important concepts in relation to operation centers and contingencies are the notions of quality of service (QoS), which is often a contractual commitment to customers, or it can be simply an expectation of a certain level of service, and a service level agreement (SLA), which is a contractual commitment that spells out the QoS. Within the area of QoS, operations are concerned with *mean time between failure* (**MTBF**), and *maximum time to repair* (**MTTR**). MTBF is a mathematical formula that calculates the average time when we expect a system or component to work between failures, and MTTR is a calculation of the maximum amount of time we would expect it take to bring the system or component back on line. We need to compare the MTTR with our maximum allowable downtime according to QoS requirements, which dictate what improvements we need to make. Fault tolerance, resilience, and redundancy (in networks, computers, and facilities), as we have mentioned, are critical to achieving our QoS requirements.

20.2.4 Cloud Computing

An alternative to using co-locations or standby sites is to utilize outsourced computing facilities and operations. In the 1990s, application service providers (ASPs) were popular for this, but due to low trust in transferring mission-critical systems and data to a third party, frequent QoS failures, and other problems, they quickly lost favor and faded from view for the most part. Now, a variation on that theme has again arisen, called cloud computing. One advantage cloud computing has over the old ASP approach is that companies can continue to develop and "operate" their own applications, whereas others maintain the infrastructure.

In Focus

Although most people associate cloud computing with third-party providers, there are many technologies available for companies to implement their own clouds.

Cloud computing is an evolving term because the technologies used for cloud computing are still evolving. The NIST defines cloud computing as a model for enabling convenient, on-demand network access to a shared pool of configurable computing resources (for example, networks, servers, storage, applications, and services) that can be rapidly provisioned and released with minimal management effort or service-provider interaction. The cloud model promotes availability and is composed of five essential characteristics [10]: (1) on-demand services, meaning utilization of the systems and networks, given *as needed*, (2) ubiquitous access in terms of both platform and geography, (3) resource sharing, which allows for more economical delivery of services, (4) elasticity, which means that the computing and communications can scale to the demand, and (5) predictability, meaning that because resources can scale, there is greater predictability in service delivery than when pre-provisioned.

As discussed in Chapter 18, the basic architecture of cloud computing is permitting three fundamental approaches to utilization, or what are called service models [11]: (1) software as a service (SaaS), which enables clients to "rent" infrastructure to run an application, (2) platform as a service (PaaS), which allows clients to deploy their own applications on computing facilities "rented" from a provider, and (3) infrastructure as a service (IaaS), which allows clients to process, store data, provision networks, and deploy and run systems and applications. What distinguishes IaaS from PaaS is that the client has control over the operating systems, storage, and deployed applications, and some limited control over networking components such as host firewalls [12]. In other words, it is hybrid of sorts between SaaS and PaaS [13].

Although using these facilities may improve resource utilization and better support QoS, they come with security and privacy concerns [14]. According to a December 2009 Forrester Research [15] survey, 51 percent of small businesses participants said that security and privacy concerns were their top reasons for not using cloud services. The issue of privacy revolved around ways that a provider might utilize company information. Providers such as Google have stated in their policies that they collect data for consumer profiling and marketing purposes. Next, although providers purport to have higher availability because of resource sharing, managers still worry that providers will not live up to their promises—as was the case with many providers of the old ASP model. Finally, some managers have expressed concerns about data loss or leakage.

20.3 Security Incidents

Despite the best efforts of organizations to anticipate and prevent security lapses or prevent attacks from succeeding, incidents do occur. These may range from a recently fired former employee returning to the workplace with a gun and physically attacking employees, to attacks on the organizational computer systems. According to Oriyano and Gregg [16], an incident involves (1) theft or misuse of sensitive information, (2) an event that negatively affects network or system infrastructure, (3) an unauthorized access, or (4) systems used as a launch pad for staging other attacks, such as being part of a botnet. To deal with incidents, they recommend supplementing policies with procedures and guidelines that include (1) identifying an "owner" or "custodian" who will take responsibility for identifying incidents, (2) determining who (or what department) shall be part of notifying the affected and other applicable parties of the incident such as other employees, the legal department, customers, the press, or law enforcement, and means of notification such as by email or phone calls, (3) designating a lead or single point of contact for follow-up, and (4) implementing the defined response actions to rectify or mitigate the incident. We shall deal with this in this final section of this chapter by presenting responses to attacks, or incidents, on computer systems.

20.3.1 Handling Inevitable Incidents

In the modern environment of interconnected networks, the wonder may not be that there are security attacks, but rather that we haven't seen even more. Some research shows an increasing trend of attacks, whereas other research shows decreasing, a classic Simpson's paradox, but a closer examination indicates that it depends on the type of attack. For instance, social engineering attacks are growing exponentially, whereas viruses are slowing some. As an example, a 2008 survey of computer crime and security found that 1 in 10 organizations had reported a Domain Name Service (DNS) incident, and 27 percent of respondents in organizations reported a "targeted attack" [17]. This is down slightly from research from the 2004–2006 timeframe [18].

Although some attacks on an organization's systems are direct and targeted, increasingly many of the attacks are automated and non-directed. This means efforts to anticipate attacks will not always be successful, given the multiplicity of attack sources. To complicate matters, security personnel in an organization usually face the problem of information overload following an incident, and this makes it difficult to have an initial appropriate response [19]. Attacks often strive to steal trade secrets and other intellectual property, to steal users' identifications, to steal money and other items of value, to cyber stalk and harass others, or are done just out of mischief.

> **In Focus**
>
> Managers must assume that it is not a question of whether but of when they will become victims of a computer attack.

In his teaching about network and systems security, Brand [6] suggested a list of responses to handling security incidents that seems as relevant today as it was more than 20 years ago: "(1) maintain and restore data, (2) maintain and restore service, (3) figure out how it happened, (4) avoid future similar incidents and escalation, (5) avoid looking foolish, (6) find out who did it, and (7) punish the attackers" (p. 22). In maintaining and restoring data, Brand [6] suggested that the computer technician find the most recent backup and restore the data. The next step must be then to fix the problem, and to remove any vulnerability that is present in the system, or that has been added by the attack.

Brand then suggested a corporate image management procedure; that is, management should brief appropriate people so they do not find out the attack information from a reporter and *look foolish*. In finding out who did it, the goal is not necessarily to prosecute (although it might be), but to learn from the attack and discourage future attacks. The organization may find it difficult to punish the attackers through prosecution as enough admissible evidence may not only be difficult to obtain, but the organization may have to wait a long time for law enforcement to give clearance on using certain equipment or techniques in order to gather evidence.

In Section 1, we discussed this topic in terms of forensics and preservation of evidence and we will continue this discussion in more detail shortly; for now we will simply state the need for restoring and maintaining information and services rather than actions that may interfere with the collection and preservation of evidence. To this point, the Open Science Grid [20] noted similarly the following list: (1) Discover and report the incident, (2) conduct an initial analysis and classify the incident by level of severity, (3) contain the situation by preventing further attacks, (4) notify management and update on status, (5) document the response and cost, as this may be important for legal proceedings and the preservation of evidence, and (6) conduct a post-incident analysis of lessons learned.

In Focus

As with security attacks and countermeasures, handling incidents can be proactive or reactive. A pessimistic approach is proactive (such as using video surveillance to monitor someone's movements), whereas an optimistic approach is reactive (such as searching log files for certain activities).

20.3.2 Reporting Security Incidents

Security incidents must be reported in order for an organization to have an effective information security policy [21]. For the federal government and federal civilian agencies, for instance, formal incident responses include "procedures for detecting, reporting, and responding to computer security incidents" as required by the Government Information Security Reform Act (Security Act) [22]. Incidents are to be reported immediately to the Federal Computer Incident Response Center at the General Services Administration.

Some of the factors to consider include the establishment of "call trees" in case of an attack, and approximations of response times required. Call trees represent the chain of command for an escalation, and the time approximation represents the threshold of wait time before escalating the issue. It is also important to determine who makes the final decisions on shut-down or removal of a single attacked computer from the network. Another factor to consider is whether the organization is required to comply with any state or federal reporting requirements. For example, financial institutions and certain entities carrying personal health information (PHI) or personal health records (PHRs) have to follow federal reporting requirements, such as the Gramm-Leach-Bliley Act and the HIPAA (Health Insurance Portability and Accountability Act) compliance requirements.

The organization may also operate in one of many states that have passed a security breach notice law. Such states typically require businesses to notify consumers when their information has been compromised by an attack and may briefly delay that notification to allow law enforcement investigation. As of July 30, 2009, these states included Alaska, Arizona, Arkansas, California, Colorado, Connecticut, Delaware, District of Columbia, Florida, Georgia, Hawaii, Idaho, Illinois, Indiana, Iowa, Kansas, Louisiana, Maine, Maryland, Massachusetts, Michigan, Minnesota, Mississippi, Missouri, Montana, Nebraska, Nevada, New Hampshire, New Jersey, New York, North Carolina, North Dakota, Ohio, Oklahoma, Oregon, Pennsylvania, Puerto Rico, Rhode Island, South Carolina, Tennessee, Texas, Utah, Vermont, Virginia, U.S. Virgin Islands, Washington, West Virginia, Wisconsin, and Wyoming [23, 24].

There is a lot of variation in the states' requirements and foci. Some states only require reporting if the data are personal information that are unencrypted or otherwise unredacted. If there is no reasonable likelihood of consumer harm, no reporting is required. Some states are of the view that if an organization has its own notification procedures to consumers, then it is in compliance. The key then is to have a robust information security policy that includes complying with notification procedures. The notification should include, at a minimum, a notice to each person affected detailing the type of information stolen or compromised, government and organizational numbers to call for assistance, and a recommendation for consumers to alert their credit bureaus.

Congress has tried but thus far been unsuccessful in passing a federal security breach notification law that would preempt the various state laws. The most recent example is the Data Accountability and Trust Act (H.R. 2221) introduced by Bobby Rush (D-Ill) in 2009, affecting businesses engaged in interstate commerce [25]. The closest Congress has come toward this is the passage of the HIPAA and the Gramm-Leach-Bliley Act [26].

In Focus

Every person in the organization must report security incidents. It is important for the organization to have a security policy and established procedures for reporting and responding to computer security incidents. When responding to incidents, a person should take care not to compromise privacy and proprietary information with people outside the response circle.

20.3.3 Collecting and Preserving Evidence

Collecting and preserving evidence of an attack is often called forensics. In reality, forensics is much broader, but these two features do encapsulate the most important aspects. Schultz [27] identified various tell-tale signs that are evidence of an attack, including the obvious ones of whether someone has tried to make unauthorized change to files, passwords, and accounts as well as the now commonplace practice of exploiting system, browser, and applications vulnerabilities. What should managers know about collecting and preserving these indicators as evidence? Sinangin [28] defined computer (or digital) forensics as *the science of recovering lost or hidden data for the purposes of evidence*. Failure to take care in collecting and handling evidence may not only make the evidence worthless, but may open the organization to possible lawsuits of negligence or defamation [29].

To count as evidence, it must meet certain conditions. First, it must be relevant. This relates to the question whether the existence of a fact important to the determination of the action is more or less probable with or without the evidence [30]. Second, it must have been collected through a "scientific method," such as digital forensics, appropriately validated [31]. If the matter gets into the courtroom, the validation may include cross-examination challenges of the computer forensics expert [29]. In addition, Ryan and Shpantzer noted that one of the competency hurdles digital evidence has to overcome may include the processes involved in collecting, storing, processing, and presenting the evidence. They observe that evidence may be altered if it is not immediately frozen or accompanied by a message digest that can be used in non-repudiation, but the very act of opening the files may change them and invalidate the evidence [32].

To address this, Brand [6] suggested making a copy of the entire system after an attack to be able to analyze it later, and to preserve evidence. It is also possible that backup systems may have captured other evidence following an attack. Brand warned, however, that an attacker may return to a computer to destroy evidence, and therefore audit logs must be copied to a secure non-networked area as soon as possible. He also suggested that it is prudent to remove tools used to respond to the incident from the system because an attacker could learn what is being done based on the tools.

Beyond the collection and analysis of evidence, the artifacts need to be preserved. For guidance, we may refer to Schultz's [27] four considerations: (1) authenticity, (2) admissibility, (3) reliability, and (4) completeness. The first consideration, authenticity, has to do with the question of whether the evidence presented is the same as what was collected. The Federal Rules of Evidence require authentication or identification as a condition for admissibility as evidence (FRE 901). Among the pieces of evidence suggested by the federal rules for authenticity is testimony from a witness with knowledge that the matter is what it claims to be (FRE 901(b)(1)) and comparison with specimens that have been authenticated (FRE 901(b)(3)).

The witness with knowledge in computer security incidents will most likely be a computer expert who describes the technological tools used to extract the information, how the information was extracted, how it was stored, who stored it, and the ease or difficulty of inserting false data [33]. Schultz [27] suggested that a video tape with time and date be made of the process of archiving the system audit logs, and as we mentioned earlier, management needs to make sure there is proper documentation of the incident response.

The second consideration, admissibility, has to do with how the evidence was handled from collection to presentation, especially taking care that there is a clearly defined chain of custody and that the data were not contaminated by the system or by the humans using the system. Documentation will be needed on who extracted the evidence; how they extracted it; where they extracted it; who put it together and when; how, when, where, and by whom it was stored; and when and where was it transported, and by whom [34]. It may also be necessary to offer proof of the validity of the extraction method, as well as proof that the extraction tools—for example, the technology used to make an exact copy of the incident data—were functioning as they are supposed to. Showing that a computer industry standard was used in the extraction may be helpful [35]. As Schultz [27] observes, reliability may be the most vexing issue in validating computer forensics. The evidence eventually has to have some relationship to the individual accused. The ***chain of custody*** is also very important here.

Completeness also has to do with documentation, in that it refers to the need for a complete inventory of all the evidence gathered, and that this inventory is verified and reverified. For computer records that are generated in the ordinary course of business to be admissible as evidence, several things need to be shown. First, there has to be a showing that standard equipment was used. Second, it must be shown that when used appropriately, the computer generates accurate records. Next, it must be shown that the computer was used inappropriately. Lastly, it must be shown that the information sources, the method utilized for recording the information and the time of preparation all indicate that the record is trustworthy for admission into evidence [36, 37].

20.3.4 Computer Forensics and the Law

The topic of digital evidence gives us a view into the murky topic of computer security and the law, especially as it relates to computer security incidents [32]. This is murky because there is no single law addressing the subject, but rather a mix of state and federal laws. As we mentioned before, legal action following a security incident may not always be possible or helpful. But there may be situations where you might be forced to pursue legal action, such as when your insurance company requires you to pursue the attackers before paying for the loss. There may be government regulations requiring reporting of security incidents when your organization works with classified data. Managers may also owe a duty of due diligence to report to shareholders regarding a security incident.

Federal legislation includes the Economic Espionage Act (18 USC 1831-39), which was enacted in 1996 to prevent theft of trade secrets by downloading/uploading computer files and is a federal crime punishable by fines and/or imprisonment of up to 10 years. Corporate entities engaging in such behavior risk a fine of up to $5,000,000 (18 USC 1832). Where the theft is intended to benefit a foreign entity, the fine and/or imprisonment may be up to $500,000 and 15 years, and corporate transgressors may face fines up to $10,000,000 (18 USC 1831). The penalties apply not only to acts committed in the United States, but also acts committed outside the United States by U.S. citizens or permanent residents, or by organizations incorporated under the laws of the United States (18 USC 1837).

The Computer Fraud and Abuse Act criminalize certain conduct related to unauthorized access to computer systems. The Act makes it a crime to access any protected computer intentionally, or if authorized, to exceed such authorization (18 USC 1030(a) (2) (C)), especially with intent to defraud. It also makes it a crime if such access recklessly causes damage and loss (18 USC 1030(a) (5) (C)), as well as to extort anything of value on the threat of causing damage to a protected computer (18 USC 1030(a) (7)).

At this point, we should once again point out that the Sarbanes-Oxley Act of 2002 (SOX) was essentially enacted as a response to Enron-type scandals and set standards for how publicly held companies would keep investors informed. Company officers have responsibilities to both disclose certain kinds of information and secure and keep private other kinds of information. If the organization is a publicly held company, it will need to follow SOX's requirements regarding the prohibition against destruction, alteration, or falsification of records (Sec. 802(a)), a 5-year retention period (Sec 802(a)(1)), and include all business records and communications, including electronic communications (Sec 802(a)(2)). Fines and up to 20 years imprisonment can be handed down for altering or destroying records to impede or influence a legal investigation. An attack on the organization's computer system can thus put the organization in severe risk.

The controversial Gramm-Leach-Bliley Act of 1999 also requires financial institutions to establish appropriate standards to safeguard their customer records and information to ensure confidentiality of those records and information, to protect against anticipated threats to the security and integrity of such records, and to protect against harm or inconvenience to the customer that might come about as a result of unauthorized access or use of such information or records (15 USC 6801).

As we mentioned, there are also state laws addressing computer crimes, which vary in their emphases and foci. They variously tackle the subjects of unauthorized computer access, tampering, altering, unauthorized release of proprietary and confidential information, identity theft, cyber stalking, and similar acts. Managers should be familiar with the state's legislation in this area.

> **In Focus**
>
> Computer security is covered by a mixture of federal and state laws. It is important for managers to have familiarity with at least their state laws. Because attacks can originate from anywhere, familiarity with international law is also recommended.

20.3.5 Cyber Stalking and Harassment Incidents

In this final part, we will consider both the situation of cyber stalking and harassment against corporations, as well as against individuals. Bocij [38] defined cyber stalking as *the use of technology as a medium of harassment or in stealthy pursuit of another*, and he argued that organizations can be victims as well as people. Cyber stalking is usually the case of one acting for personal reasons, for example because of a grudge with a coworker or a former coworker. This may include the use of company email to harass. It may also involve posting defamatory information about current or former coworkers (Bocij calls "bashing"), or cyber smearing, where a member or former member of the organization is using the company's technological resources to write or post derogatory information on a website or sent in mass emails. The organization has a duty to rectify the situation and should consider such action a security incident.

However, sometimes an organization as a whole may be involved in cyber stalking, for example, in trying to control the kind of information about the organization that is available on the Internet or in the press. Cases of this include hiring private investigators to pose as a legitimate business entity to determine whether a corporate member or officer is leaking information while "whistle blowing." Some organizations may use SLAPPs (strategic lawsuits against public participation) to try to harass and intimidate critics. Ethical conduct discourages such behavior, and there is a growing number of anti-SLAAP lawsuits and legislations, led largely in California. In other cases, cyber stalking is perpetrated by someone outside the organization, an estranged former spouse or a terminated employee, for example. If not checked, such behavior can escalate into actual violence, as for instance when a stalker shows up at the organization with a weapon.

Parsons-Pollard [39] noted the lack of uniformity in state laws addressing cyber stalking. Some state laws have a threat requirement—that is, the victim must be threatened—whereas other states do not have such a requirement. Some states require that the communications be directly between the offender and the victim, whereas others do not have such a requirement. This means some offenders may go unpunished because of the ways the various laws are written.

Parsons-Pollard [39] also noted three federal laws that try to fill the void created by this lack of uniformity: the Interstate Communications Act (18 USC 875 (c)), the Federal Telephone Harassment Statute (47 USC 223), and the Federal Interstate Stalking Punishment and Prevention Act (18 USC 2261A). Goodno [40], however, criticizes these laws for not offering enough protection to victims of cyber stalking. This is harking back to our discussion on evidence presented earlier. It is important to remember that here too the extraction and preservation of the evidence matters. Extraction should not, for example, consist only of cut and paste of an online chat into a Word document, as a court is likely to rule such documents not sufficiently authenticated [41]. To determine what will likely count as evidence, managers should always consult corporate or private attorneys for guidance.

> **In Focus**
>
> Cyber stalking can create security risks to the organization. Although the laws may not always adequately protect victims, the organization should have a policy in place on how to respond to cyber stalking, and how to protect its organizational members.

CHAPTER SUMMARY

Operations may be thought of as managing or overseeing daily activities, and relative to security, it is the daily regular activities that managers and security personnel take to ensure relative security for systems, personnel, and infrastructure in support of the organization's primary activities and service and/or product delivery. In this chapter, we discussed the need for security oversight in the SDLC or implementation life cycle, and that managers should not abdicate their oversight responsibilities. We discussed operations centers, how to try to eliminate single points of failure, and because of their importance, the use of physical controls, software and hardware access controls, and environmental controls (including heating and air conditioning, generators, UPS, and fire control systems). We suggested that to avoid single points of failure, corporations should consider having a minimum of two co-located operations centers, and potentially utilizing outside services to jointly monitor infrastructure through strategic agreements. We discussed operational procedures, which are step-by-step instructions to help standardize operations, and include steps such as how to configure databases and networks. We discussed monitoring and intrusion detection systems, auditing, and incident handling. In the next chapter, we will pull together in a managerial context many of these previously discussed topics in relation to managing security behaviors.

THINK ABOUT IT

Topic Questions

20.1: At the macro-level, auditing falls into what two categories?

20.2: Asset vulnerability plus visibility are main factors in _____ _____ .

20.3: Beyond the collection and analysis of evidence, preservation should have four considerations:_____, _____, _____, and _____ .

20.4: Chain of custody implies:

_____ One person has control over the evidence.

_____ The evidence is traceable.

_____ The evidence is locked away, such as in a vault.

_____ Managers direct who takes control of evidence.

20.5: Two important aspects of QoS are _____ and _____ .

20.6: Countermeasures fall into three categories: _____ , _____ , and _____ .

THINK ABOUT IT (CONTINUED)

20.7: The standard notation used to create a Use Case is called:

_____ Unified Modeling Language (UML)
_____ Object Modeling Language (OML)
_____ Use Case Notation (UCN)
_____ ASN.1 Notation

20.8: An example of a physical countermeasure is a barricade.

_____ True
_____ False

20.9: Three service models include _____ , _____ , and _____ .

20.10: Two major categories of audits are _____ and _____ .

Questions for Further Study

Q20.1: When you consider security operations, in business terms, this means keeping the computing and applications available to users according to QoS promises; beyond that, list at least five other considerations.

Q20.2: Remembering that managers should not act as lawyers when it comes to security incidents, explain at least five cases where managers need to be aware of laws and regulations.

Q20.3: If an organization posted your company's confidential or secret information on their website (take for example the 2010/2011 WikiLeaks incidents and the subsequent DoS attacks and counterattacks), what would you do? Consider escalation steps, as well as laws, regulations, and ethics.

Q20.4: What countermeasures would be important to control access to a server room? Discuss these in terms of importance, costs, and benefits.

Q20.5: From a security standpoint, what should managers consider regarding using third-party cloud computing facilities?

KEY CONCEPTS AND TERMS

Cyber smearing is where a member or former member of the organization uses the company's technological resources to write or post derogatory information online or in email.

Financial audits determine if financial statements are factual and complete.

Object Management Group (OMG) is an important standards body for notation related to object-oriented software.

Security breach notice means that those states with such laws must notify customers in case of a compromise.

W3C is an important standards body for defining specifications for the Web.

References

1. Booch, G., Jacobson, I., & Rumbaugh, J. (2000). *UML distilled: A brief guide to the standard object modeling language.* Reading, MA: Addison-Wesley.
2. Raphael, L., & Delmont, A. (2001). *The Rational Unified Process (RUP): Rational Rose and the merging of the IBM way.* Boston, MA: eAselworx Press.

3. Booch, G. (1996). *Object solutions: Managing the object-oriented project*. Santa Clara, CA: Addison-Wesley.

4. Valiente, C. (2009). Balancing IT security compliance, complexity, and cost. *The ISSA Journal, 7*(7), 22–28.

5. Gingras, M. (2009). ITS program management: Talking the executive language. *The ISSA Journal, 7*(7), 18–21.

6. Brand, R. L. (1990). *Coping with the threat of computer security incidents: A primer from prevention through recovery*. Berkeley: University of California at Berkeley Press.

7. Thomas, T. (2004). *Network security: First-step*. Indianapolis, IN: Cisco Press.

8. Obimbo, C. (2009). An intrusion detection system for mobile ad-hoc networks. In the *Proceedings of the Conference on Security and Management, SAM'09, 1*, 285–290.

9. Weiss, M. M. (2011). *Auditing IT infrastructure for compliance*. Sudbury, MA: Jones & Bartlett Learning.

10. Mell, P., & Grance, T. (2009). *The NIST definition of cloud computing*. Retrieved November 20, 2010, from http://web.ebscohost.com.portal.lib.fit.edu/ ehost/pdfviewer/pdfviewer?vid=7&hid=17&sid=d7a66a5c-bd63-469d-ba06-69d241f1d6b3%40sessionmgr4

11. NIST. (2009). *Definition of cloud computing*. Retrieved November 20, 2010, from http://csrc.nist.gov/groups/SNS/cloud-computing/

12. Knoit, E., & Groman G. (2009). *What cloud computing really means*. Retrieved November 20, 2010, from http://www.infoworld.com/d/cloud-computing/what-cloud-computing-really-means-031

13. Oltsik, J. (2010). What's needed for cloud computing? *Enterprise Strategy Group ESG*. Retrieved November 20, 2010, from http://www.infoworld.com

14. Martin, J. (2010, April). *Should you move your business to the cloud?* PC World, Vol. 28, 4. Retrieved November 21, 2010, from http://web.ebscohost.com

15. Forrester Research. (2009). *A survey of privacy and security concerns among CIOs*. A white paper. Cambridge, MA: Author. Retrieved from: http://www.forrester.com/rb/research/

16. Oriyano, S-P., & Gregg, M. (2011). *Hacker techniques, tools, and incident handling*. Sudbury, MA: Jones & Bartlett Learning.

17. Richardson, R. (2008). *CSI computer crime & security survey*. Computer Security Institute. Latest survey available at www.GoCSI.com

18. Workman, M., & Gathegi, J. (2007). Punishment and ethics deterrents: A comparative study of insider security contravention. *Journal of American Society for Information Science and Technology, 58*, 318–342.

19. Hertzog, P. (2006). *Visualizations to improve reactivity towards security incidents inside corporate networks*, Proceedings of the 3rd International Workshop on Visualization for Computer Security (pp. 95–102). New York, NY: ACM Digital Library.

20. Open Science Grid. (2004). *Grid security incident handling and response guide*. Retrieved from http://osg-docdb.opensciencegrid.org/cgi-bin/ShowDocument?docid=19

21. Wiant, T. L. (2005). Information security policy's impact on reporting security incidents. *Computers & Security, 24*, 448–459.

22. Forman, M. (2002). *Handling and reporting computer security incidents. Memo to Chief Information Officers*. Retrieved December 2, 2010, from http://georgewbush-whitehouse.archives.gov/omb/inforeg/fedcirc.html

23. Consumer Union (2007). *Notice of security breach state laws.* Retrieved December 2, 2010, from www.consumersunion.org/campaigns/Breach_laws_May05.pdf
24. Proskauer Rose LLP. (2010). *Privacy law blog.* Retrieved December 9, 2010, from http://privacylaw.proskauer.com/articles/security-breach-notification-l/
25. Stevens, G. (2010). *Federal information security and data breach notification laws.* Washington, DC: Congressional Research Service.
26. Chapple, M. J., & Crowell, C. R. (2008). Federal information security law. In M. Quigley (Ed), *Encyclopedia of information and ethics security* (pp. 291–296). Hershey, PA: IGI Global Press.
27. Schultz, E. (2007). Computer forensics challenges in responding to incidents in real-life settings. *Computer Fraud & Security, 12,* 12–16.
28. Sinangin, D. (2002). Computer forensics investigations in a corporate environment. *Computer Fraud & Security, 6,* 11–14.
29. Ryan, D. J., & Shpantzer, G. (n.d.) *Legal aspects of digital forensics.* Retrieved November 22, 2010, from http://euro.ecom.cmu.edu/program/law/08-732/Evidence/RyanShpantzer.pdf
30. Federal Rules of Evidence 401 (1975 and subsequent amendments).
31. *Daubert v. Merrell Dow Pharmaceuticals, Inc.,* 509 U.S. 579 (1993).
32. Vacca, J. R., & Rudolph, K. (2011). *System forensics, investigation, and response.* Sudbury, MA: Jones & Bartlett Learning.
33. Zitter, J. M. (2008). *Authentication of electronically stored evidence, including text messages and e-mail.* 34 A.L.R.6th 253
34. Kizza, J. M. (2010). Ethical and social issues in the information in the information age, In *Texts in computer science.* London, UK: Springer-Verlag.
35. *People v. Shinohara,* 872 N. E. 2d 498 (2007).
36. *People v. Johnson,* 376 Ill. App. 3d 175 (2007).
37. Fischer, R. J., & Green, G. (1992). *Security.* Boston, MA: Butterworth-Heinemann.
38. Bocij, P. (2002). Corporate cyberstalking: An invitation to build theory, *First Monday, 7,* online issue #11. Retrieved December 2, 2010, from http://outreach.lib.uic.edu
39. Parsons-Pollard, N. (2010). Cyberstalking laws in the United States: Is there a need for uniformity? *Criminal Law Bulletin, 46(5),* 954–964.
40. Goodno, N. H. (2006). *Cyberstalking, a new crime: Evaluating the effectiveness of current state and federal laws.* (Bepress Legal Series. Working Paper 1689). Retrieved December 9, 2010, from http://law.bepress.com/expresso/eps/1689
41. *U.S. v. Jackson,* 488 F. Supp. 2d 866 (2007).

Managing Security Behavior

THE FIELD OF BEHAVIORISM IS IMPORTANT to management because it is the basis for most managerial and organizational interventions. In other words, behaviorism is the foundation to address what people do or don't do in an organization. Now that we have covered legal, technical, and administrative aspects of security management so far in our textbook, we are going to incorporate those into behavioral and social science aspects of security. We will draw upon cutting-edge theory and research because theory and research explain phenomena, and we need to understand what the research says in order to develop targeted and effective managerial solutions and programs in such a rapidly advancing field.

Chapter 21 Topics

This chapter

- Presents the relationships between employee behaviors, business environment, and social interaction.
- Discusses the issues of omission of security measures and commission of security breaches.
- Covers the "weakest link" factors, and ways to treat them.
- Gives an overview of behavioral responses to various types of attacks.

Chapter 21 Goals

When you finish this chapter, you should:

- ☐ Understand how the field of "behaviorism" has influenced security management.

❏ Have a working knowledge of security behaviors and their interactions with various personal and interpersonal factors.

❏ Understand what to do about insider versus outsider threats and behaviors.

❏ Be able to explain some of the most important psychosocial and socio-behavioral impacts of security initiatives on employees.

❏ Know how to match positive and negative reinforcement, extinction, and punishments with various types of security and attack behaviors.

21.1 Organizational Behavior

Albert Bandura [1] defined behavioral actions, interactions, and reactions in organizations as "triadic reciprocal determinism." By this term, he meant that behavior does not occur in isolation, but rather it is the product of dynamic interactive forces among people's stable tendencies toward behaving in certain ways (personalities), their situations and environments (including the technologies they use), and whether their resulting behaviors are positively or negatively reinforced, punished, or ignored (**Figure 21.1**). From this point of view, behaviors are shaped and reshaped by many influences on a continual basis. This illustrates the effects of human behavior in relation to the power of structural and environmental—individual and social—forces. In this chapter, we will examine behavior and these triadic relationships in organizations as they relate to security.

21.1.1 Behavior and Control

Consistent with Bandura's view, social psychology research divides behavioral control into three types: (1) locus of control, which is the extent one believes that outcomes in general are controllable or whether outcomes are matters of fate, (2) self-efficacy, which is the degree that people believe they have the skills and capabilities to control an outcome, and (3) self-control, which is the control one exhibits over one's self. Previously we discussed how policies are established to set the boundaries for behaviors and lay down the sanctions for those who disobey. Ironically, when people perceive something as outside their control (high external locus of control), policies and threatened sanctions for disobedience sometimes do not have much effect on their behavioral intentions [2]. In extreme cases, this is called "learned helplessness" [3]. It is important to note, however, that perceptions of control are not static. For example, people gain confidence in their abilities to control outcomes with increased successful experience in similar situations [1].

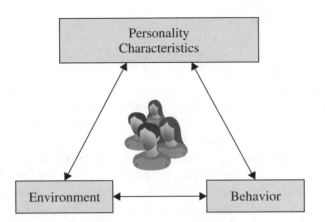

FIGURE 21.1

Triadic reciprocality.

Also, people learn by modeling the behavior of others. More specifically, in addition to one's own experience, a key element in whether someone perceives an event as controllable is whether or not someone observes successes or failures by another person who they perceive to be similar to him or herself. When these "similar others" succeed at something through perseverant effort, then people vicariously develop the perception that the event is controllable and they are likely to try to model the other's behavior. This behavior can be constructive or destructive. Finally, as more people succeed at doing something, even if the behavior is negative or destructive, people—in greater numbers—try to copy the behavior, this is known as a "social contagion" [3].

21.1.2 Behavior Modification

Managers are interested in modifying the behaviors of employees so that they conform to organizational norms and objectives, and behavioral modification is a fundamental part of managerial responsibilities [4]. The term that organizational behaviorists use for this technique is called ***organizational behavior modification*** (**OBMod**), and OBMod is the use of strategic, tactical, and operational interventions to accomplish *a greater good*. Simple examples are levying sanctions on those who do not conform to acceptable behaviors, allocation of rewards for people who meet certain objectives, and terminating the employment of people who do not respond to corrective action directives. Although the idea of behavior modification may seem manipulative, it is (or should be) a process that involves justice and benevolence.

In Focus

Managers strive to ensure that people succeed by helping them to meet organizational objectives.

OBMod incorporates a "carrot and stick" approach to gaining behavioral compliance, but often managers must concern themselves with what are called "antecedents," which are events or conditions that precede a behavior, and in relation to security in particular, the reasons why people may misbehave or fail to live up to expectations. This is important in order to formulate an appropriate reaction to a behavioral problem because something may have triggered a particular behavior that needs to be addressed. Skinner [5] used the term "operant conditioning" to refer to a process of learning, through reinforcement, that links desired consequences to desired behaviors. In other words, once an operant behavior is expressed, it may or may not continue depending on the consequences of the behavior. Consequences that increase the frequency of a behavior are referred to as "reinforcers" [6].

Reinforcers can be positive or negative. Positive reinforcers are those related to rewards, whereas an example of a negative reinforcer may be nagging at a chronically late employee until the employee starts arriving to work on time. Reinforcers may also be intrinsic; for example, people may have strong internal drives to succeed, or they may be extrinsic such as offering company bonuses; whereas functions that decrease the frequency of behavior are either punishments such as "docking pay" for missed work, or extinction—for example, by ignoring an undesirable behavior that leads to its decrease from lack of attention.

21.2 Organizational Security Behaviors

There are many threats to the integrity, confidentiality, and availability of information maintained by organizational systems, as well as many countermeasures such as virus scanners, firewalls, security patches, and password change control systems, along with a range of other technologies and techniques available to improve information and systems security, as we have learned. Also, as we have discussed, security policies are designed to express the governance of acceptable security behaviors, whereas security procedures specify the technologies, steps, and techniques to be used to implement security policies. When considering information and systems security behaviors, there are four categories we can apply: (1) malicious outsiders, (2) malicious insiders, (3) insiders who are not malicious and who unintentionally omit security procedures, and (4) insiders who are not malicious but who intentionally omit security procedures [7].

21.2.1 Malicious Outsiders

By establishing and enforcing security policies, managers hope that the people governed by such policies will take a proactive role in minimizing vulnerabilities. Although security policies help to govern individuals within organizations, they do not directly address the behavior of those who may attack an organization from the "outside." People who attempt to contravene security from outside a company are classified as *malicious outsiders*. The kinds of attacks that malicious outsiders instigate are varied, but they generally fall into three categories: (1) attempts to gather information to which they are not privileged—this is an attack against confidentiality, (2) attempts to destroy or alter information—this is an attack against integrity, or (3) attempts to disrupt the business—this is an attack against service availability [8].

One of the more common malicious outsider attacks comes from ***social engineering***, which is a term that describes furtive actions by con artists for committing fraud and other thefts by gaining information or access to systems using trickery, or by giving incentives so that people willingly give up sensitive information [9]. Social engineering may be used for purposes ranging from identity theft to corporate espionage. Two of the most common forms of social engineering approaches are *phishing* and *pretext*. Both phishing and pretexts are used to gain information, but phishing usually involves using email to elicit passwords or banking account information, where pretext usually involves telephone communications to obtain privileged information under false pretenses.

To do this, social engineers may try to become friendly with a potential victim and gain his or her trust in what is sometimes called a *confidence scheme.* They may prey on someone's loneliness, or create a sense of identity with the potential victim. In other types of social engineering attacks, the perpetrator offers something in exchange for something from the victim. For example, the perpetrator may offer a large sum of money if the intended victim will allow the perpetrator to *park funds* in the intended victim's bank account while performing an international money transfer; or the perpetrator may promise a valuable item in exchange for what appears to be a small financial transaction to cover shipping and handling costs.

With the rise of the social networking phenomenon, another form of social engineering attack has germinated, similar to a denial of service attack in computer security. Companies are increasingly the targets of attacks on social network sites and in blog postings by "trolls" and "cyber bullies." Rather than trying to gain information illicitly, these kinds of attacks disseminate misleading or false information to damage their targets, to interfere with them, or for the purposes of extortion. As a consequence, there might be significant damage to individuals, social relations, and business performance [10, 11]. Accordingly, a new managerial challenge to the security of organizations extends into the social media and virtual realm.

> **In Focus**
>
> A software company had produced new technology and they had begun negotiation for sale of the company. A prospective suitor told the board of directors that the valuation of the company had been diminished because of "attacks" by a single blogger. In those attacks, the blogger distributed false information in a so-called "newsletter" through email distribution lists and posted it on a website with the attacker's stated intention to prevent "the company" from selling its product.

21.2.2 Malicious Insiders

As we have discussed previously, people who attempt to contravene security from inside a company, such as employees or contractors, are classified as *malicious insiders.* Most malicious insiders will not attempt to contravene security in the same manner as malicious outsiders because they may be relatively easy to trace, and most employees today know this. However, some people act rashly or have an overpowering impulse for revenge that may lead them to disregard the risk of getting caught so long as they can inflict damage on their target [12].

To illustrate, a recent and highly publicized incident involved a systems administrator for a state government agency who was fired from his job. Before he was discharged from the building, he managed to lock all of the users out of their accounts and refused to provide the administrator passwords. Although he was prosecuted and eventually the information was obtained, there was a significant disruption to the agency. Thus we can see that although malicious insiders may be easier to identify after the fact, they can at times present a more serious threat than malicious outsiders [13].

21.2.3 Non-Malicious Unintentional Insider Omission

Although many of the security mechanisms available can be automated, and even though the general public has become increasingly aware of pervasive information and security threats, they sometimes do not utilize these technologies even when they are readily, and often freely, available; this results in billions of dollars annually in individual and corporate losses [7]. For instance, there are cases where a "backdoor" may be left open unintentionally because a person may lack the awareness of a threat, or lack awareness of vulnerabilities, lack the knowledge of a security countermeasure, or lack the ability or skill needed to implement a required countermeasure [14].

Also, personnel who are focused on a primary objective, such as delivering a product, may simply overlook a security procedure or countermeasure due to their concentration on their tasks under time pressures [15]. Many software vendors have attempted to intervene in this problem by creating warning dialogs that "pop up" before allowing an ill-advised action, or to negatively reinforce someone into performing an action. Nevertheless, research [16, 17] has shown that when people receive many "reminders," the notification impact tends to "wear off" and users essentially become trained to hit the "okay" button without carefully reading the warnings.

> **In Focus**
>
> Conditioning is a powerful behavior modifier, but aversion is also influential. An example of aversion is that people tend to ignore the fine print in an important contract because it is annoying and hard to read [3].

21.2.4 Non-Malicious Intentional Insider Omission

There are times when people choose to accept a security risk to attend to a higher priority, or to avoid a harsh punishment. For instance, sometimes people will cancel the automatic run of their virus scanner to complete an important task or meet a deadline because the virus scanner is slowing down their computer. This is an example of *non-malicious intentional insider omission*. When it comes to this kind of security behavior, there have been several theoretical frameworks to help explain why, such as illustrated in the threat control model, or TCM [7]. In essence, intentional omissive information systems security behaviors derive from a person's cognitive assessment of a threat versus his or her assessment of coping factors.

Threat assessment factors include (1) the *perceived severity of a threat* such as the assessment of damage a threat might impose, and (2) the *perceived probability* of the occurrence or *vulnerability to a threat*—in other words, the assessment of whether the threat will target them or will succeed if it does.

Coping assessment factors include (1) one's *locus of control*—or whether one believes that a threat is controllable in the first place, (2) the perceived *efficacy of the recommended countermeasures*—for example, will my firewall prevent an intruder from illicitly accessing my computer system? (3) the perceived *self-efficacy* or confidence in one's ability to implement or undertake the recommended preventive actions, and (4) whether the expended effort, time, or money is worth the potential damage if the threatened event succeeds.

Financial Antecedents for Intentional Omission

A primary managerial consideration is how to minimize exposure and manage or contain risk [18]. This is a difficult task because many of the vulnerabilities might not be known, especially in large organizations, and the potential damage can be difficult to quantify. In fact, some aspects of information security can't be quantified; for example, how much is privacy worth? This ambiguity often leads managers toward taking a conservative approach to security. One avenue to address information and systems threats has been to try to automate as many of the security countermeasures as possible, but many companies do not implement mandatory automated controls because some managers believe that the threat level does not warrant such financial investments or the loss of efficiency and productivity [19]. For example, firewall processing and the use of cryptography slow down communications and can negatively affect productivity [20].

When people try to find ways to circumvent security measures, perhaps it is because security measures get in the way of higher priority tasks. This illustrates a tradeoff between security and productivity [21]. When time is money, these concerns are not trivial because as an overhead cost of doing business, security technology and infrastructure doubled between 2001 and 2005—and has grown to more than 8 percent of an average company's budget [22]. Another indication of security conservatism is seen when managers try to create organizational bastions using the military "ISR" approach of intelligence gathering, surveillance, and reconnaissance. ISR infrastructure (and all of its overhead cost) can be very expensive.

Situational Antecedents for Intentional Omission

Studies show that a large number of firms do not have the infrastructure and/or expertise to implement automated information and systems security techniques and thus substantially rely on discretionary controls [23]. In other cases, mandatory controls and automation is simply impossible because of technological and standards incompatibilities. As an example, business *road warriors* sometimes need to reconfigure laptops in the field to allow them access to WiFi network communications. Because of the need for this kind of flexibility, it is not possible to create a centralized automated solution for all possible networks that employees might encounter.

There are also situations that arise through mergers and acquisitions or through global expansion that lead to disparate and even incompatible technologies and approaches across distributed organizational boundaries. In these cases, people often have to remember to adjust their configurable security mechanisms to allow them to access various systems, which often may mean having to configure system security to the lowest common denominator. A simple example is the need to constantly adjust browser privacy settings depending on the type of web access the person requires.

Organizational Culture Antecedents for Intentional Omission

In the study of what has made organizations succeed or fail, the important work of Burns and Stalker [24] described characteristics that define organic and mechanistic organizations. They characterized organic organizations as flexible and adaptive, with organizational decision making delegated to the lowest appropriate levels in the organization. Mechanistic organizations were characterized as having strict inflexible hierarchies of authority. They believed that mechanistic organizations became brittle as they grew and ultimately failed because they were unable to adapt. Consequently, a mechanistic approach to security compliance may be antithetical to some organizational philosophies. In those cases, some managers may not see automation as an optimal solution because it implies a certain degree of centralization; also, if the organizational culture and structure are highly decentralized, single points of control may not be welcome and they can also create single points of failure [20].

Technological Antecedents for Intentional Omission

There are circumstances in which there are good reasons to bypass full-scale automation. In some organizations, systems engineers configure firewalls to prevent promiscuous connections and automatic security updates are prevented; thus individuals must take on the personal responsibility for protecting their own systems [17]. Furthermore, some software requires the use of Microsoft ActiveX controls or other inter-process communications that force security administrators to lower the centralized defensive posture, and although antivirus software might be activated before a server uploads attachments or email, not all systems support this feature and there are many security situations where parameters have to be individualized [19].

In Focus

Threats come from both inside the organization (insiders) and outside. Insiders are probably the most severe form of threat because they have easier access to a wider range of resources. As a consequence, many organizations have different access controls for contractors than for regular employees and conduct background checks prior to employment, sometimes conduct screenings during employment, and utilize employment agreements with clauses such as non-compete and non-disclosure. Beware, however, that non-compete agreements, in some cases, may open the door for countersuits (see Kramer, 2010 [25]).

21.3 Management of Omission Behaviors

Behaviorism focuses on what we observe about people, but the law deals with the concept of "intent" and law enforcement looks at crimes in terms of capability, motive, and opportunity. In organizations, managers must treat people's behavior and not attempt to diagnose or treat psychological factors or they can get into legal trouble. However, behavior is not isolated as we have illustrated, so trying to infer motives or intent as well as antecedents applies to the types of treatments or interventions managers may undertake. For example, a negative behavior that is accidental is generally treated differently than a negative behavior that is intentional. In the previous section, we covered security behaviors and some antecedents for omissions. As seen previously, because people's behaviors are at the core of security breaches people are called the "weakest link" problem. Managers have several behavioral options available to them to address security omissions, but choosing the best option depends on the antecedents—or reasons for the omissions—as well as the type of security omission [26].

21.3.1 Responding to the Unintentional Omission

If employees are not aware of security threats, then they need to be made aware. Although this seems pretty obvious, an abundance of research [11] shows that many company managers fail to accomplish this—partly because there are so many new threats constantly appearing on the horizon. Even if people are made aware of threats, unless people are mobilized against a particular threat, they may become complacent. Sometimes people will even ignore or disable security measures when they are perceived as intrusive or ineffective, unless they are constantly placed in a psychological state of vigilance about severe impending threats [27].

It is important to understand, however, that attempts to make people aware of security threats and heighten their vigilance attenuate and eventually neutralize over time, especially if the attempts are vague. An example is the color-coded threat level technique used by the Department of Homeland Security and whether one will fly on an airplane during a code yellow (elevated) versus code orange (high) versus code red (severe) threat level. Studies [28] have shown that people make no distinction between yellow and orange threat levels, and generally have no idea what to do when a threat level is raised. Just as beyond a certain point people no longer believe in the veracity of the threat appeal and will discount it, even if the threat is real and likely to occur, in addition, when a threat is perceived, people behave according to the amount of risk they are willing to accept, which is known as *risk homeostasis*. Risk homeostasis is a "cognitive equilibrium" that results from the perceived severity of the potential damage, such as financial costs of repairs [29]. Therefore, people tend to adjust their behavior in response to the extent of the damage the threat may cause [30].

The perceived severity of threat and the associated acceptance of risk behavior are based on the premises that (1) people place a certain intangible value on "life," "liberty," and "property"; (2) they have a threshold level of risk they will accept, tolerate, prefer, desire, or choose; (3) this "target level" of risk they will accept before acting depends on the perceived advantages or benefits versus the disadvantages or costs of safe or unsafe behavior alternatives; and (4) this will determine the degree to which people will expose themselves to a threat or hazard before taking precautions or trying to avoid a threat altogether [31].

Perceptual judgments are influenced by these factors and are easily distorted by the tendency to rely on anecdotes, small samples, easily available information, and faulty interpretation of statistical information, among other human cognitive biases. The ways in which managers word or frame threat situations and options presented to employees profoundly influence their perceptions of risks and benefits. Managers must constantly walk a tightrope between trying to alert the workforce against information and systems security threats and desensitizing them.

Finally, Kabay [32] suggested that a difficulty associated with managing and enforcing information security is that the policies run contrary to most people's cultural and behavioral schemas, which includes sharing, trust, and politeness. These same schemas influence what we perceive and remember, compounding the difficulty in identifying potentially insecure behaviors. From this perspective, it is important to implement security policies and procedures that build up a consistent view of information security introduced over a long period of time to allow for the integration of the policy into the "worldview" of those to whom these apply.

21.3.2 Responding to the Intentional Omission

As previously noted, people may intentionally omit security countermeasures for financial reasons, situational reasons, organizational philosophy or cultural reasons, or techno-logical reasons, and managers need to assess what the causes of the omissions are and address them. For example, if the reason for why people fail to take security precautions is that they believe they do not have the skills to implement them, then security-specific training has been shown to be effective [33]. In addition to the technical aspects of security training, educating in the domain of information security must also appeal to people's imagination and emotion (affect) to create the motivation to learn as well as follow through once the skills have been acquired. Depending on the root causes of the omission, managers may also need to utilize techniques to alter the beliefs and attitudes necessary to effectively implement security policies and take responsible and proactive security actions [12].

Situational factors can create resistance toward security technologies and techniques by the fact that people are motivated to take the path of least "punished" resistance [34]. By that we mean people seek to first avoid failure at high-priority tasks before they seek to achieve success at these tasks. McClelland [34] explained this concept as a formula in which people take action when the motivation to achieve success is greater than the motivation to avoid failure. This is determined by whether people have an incentive to take the action, and assess that they have a reasonable probability of success if they try. The behavioral outcomes are moderated by the degree of risk aversion that people have (described as risk homeostasis).

Managers need to ensure that organizational practices are aligned with security goals so that conflicting priorities are minimized. Beyond these recommendations, reducing intentional omission is helped when people perceive high levels of organizational procedural justice. Procedural justice stems from perceptions of equity and fairness in organizational practices. It is perceived when the process used to make the decision was deemed fair. There are a number of conditions that lead people to perceive justice in the process. First, people want to be able to have a say or voice in any decision that might affect them. Furthermore, people want to know that managers and those with power in the organization are suspending their personal biases and motivations from decisions and are relying on objective data, to the greatest possible extent. Finally, procedural justice is perceived when people are presented with a mechanism for correcting perceived errors or poor decisions, such as having an appeal process.

21.3.3 Leading by Example

Not only do managers need to understand and take into account the reasons people may or may not implement security countermeasures in their organizations, an important information security consideration for management is to try to create an ethical work environment where employees know that management cares about security and leads by example using **due care** and **due diligence** [35]. Due care involves taking precautions for the responsible handling of sensitive information, and due diligence is the concept that involves ensuring that the available countermeasures are implemented within the cost/risk parameters, taking into consideration intangible costs such as loss of privacy. Managers must also allow for the impact of security measures on productivity, morale, motivation, and other important human factors, as well as their own practice of good security behaviors. These all form the basis of leading by example.

21.4 Contravention Behaviors, Theory, and Research

To circumvent the "weakest link" problem and prevent attacks from succeeding, managers have been incorporating more automated and mandatory security measures, such as automatically requiring users to periodically change their passwords, and restricting acceptable passwords to a designated range of characters and numeric values including case alterations and special ASCII characters. However, in practice security administrators have found it difficult if even possible to codify every conceivable security behavior in software, scripts, or other automated control mechanisms; and as we have discussed, there are times when people circumvent or neglect to implement automated countermeasures. However, in addition to the insider "weakest link" problem, managers must also deal with outsider attacks and behaviors. For this, understanding attacker motives (and motivations) is helpful in determining appropriate managerial responses.

Knowledge of attacker motives has been gained from work published by those who host **honeynets** and **honeypots**. Honeynets (*networks*) and honeypots (*computer systems*) are traps set by research investigators; they leave open a network or system that investigators expect to be attacked. Once attacked, the investigators may lay traps of their own to record communications or otherwise monitor what the attackers do. A study by the Honeynet Team [36] produced some interesting insights into attack motives, and they identified six, which were: (1) entertainment, (2) status-seeking (including "ego-based" self-promotion and narcissism), (3) cause/ideology (including cyber warfare), (4) social acceptance and need for normative conformance to obtain or retain membership in a group, (5) on impulse (from emotional instability or neuroticism), and (6) from economic motives, such as extortion or monetary gain from theft.

21.4.1 Attacker Motivation, Personality, and Behavior Theory

Social science research [37] has shown that the reasons why people attack information systems also translate well to why people commit other security violations against companies and people. For example, people will write defamatory information (even if they know what they are writing is "not completely true") about a person or company in blogs and other social media for the same reason people attack their computer systems to damage their target. If we take what the Honeynet Team [36] observed during their project from a theoretical standpoint using Rogers' [38] teleological theory of motivation (because theory explains phenomena), managers can create plans to address them using Skinner's [5] operant approach to behavior modification. Assessing the motives of an attacker is an important first step in formulating an appropriate response.

Rogers' [38] theory justifies that (1) human perception of subjective experience forms stable tendencies ("personalities"), which leads to motive consistencies, (2) motives are operants for behavioral responses, and (3) behaviors are environmentally interactive, especially in terms of social relationships; for example, behaviors can be extinguished, reinforced, or punished [5, 39]. For a response, as we explained earlier, people can try to ignore a resulting behavior leading to extinction; that is, the behavior can be ignored with the expectation that the behavior will diminish from a lack of reinforcement, or the behavior can be positively reinforced when the right things are done, or people can be negatively reinforced (such as through reminding) to do the right thing, or they can be punished [5]. Let's examine these features in more detail.

21.4.2 Entertainment and Status

The Honeynet Project [36] identified "entertainment" as a motive for why some people attack computer systems. In one of the intercepted attacker ("blackhat") communication sessions, they showed that what began as a breach of a honeynet's vulnerabilities evolved into an adventure for the attackers. From a theoretical perspective, self-indulgence is a fixation on being entertained. Research has demonstrated that in spite of pop-up warning dialogs in a browser, some people willingly give up personal information in order to continue playing an online game they enjoy [9]. Other research has shown that some give up social security numbers and other personal information to try to win a raffle [40]. Because self-indulgence leads people to focus on entertainment in spite of the risks of negative consequences and because some attackers of systems do so for entertainment, this represents a significant security threat motive.

What the Honeynet Project [36] identified as "status seeking" is defined in Rogers' [38] teleological theory as narcissism. From a psychological point of view, narcissism is defined as *a grandiose perception of self-importance* [41]. This distorted self-perception leads to "grandstanding" behaviors, excessive self-interest, and self-centeredness [42]. A main motive that stems from narcissism is self-gratification [43], and highly narcissistic people have a tendency to be aggressive, antagonistic, unsympathetic, and rude toward others in pursuit of this gratification [44]. For example, studies in this area have shown that there is a significant relationship between high-narcissistic tendencies and both workplace and cyber bullying [45].

21.4.3 Ideology and Social Acceptance

Idealism is the presumption that one's subjective perceptions (the world of ideas) can represent universal standards for others to uphold [46, 47]. Because people often maintain different ethical and moral standards, conflicts emerge when ideals run counter to the viewpoints of others because a highly idealistic person is firm in his or her convictions and concomitantly holds the view that the ends justify the means [48]. From this perspective, the idealistic "cause" is more important to the attacker than any harm he or she may inflict on others [49]. For example, idealism was used as justification by Mao Tse-tung in his oft-quoted statement that change must come from the barrel of a gun [46]. There is evidence to suggest that idealism may lead people to have a greater proclivity toward cyber harassment because of firm convictions and extreme confidence in one's own self-righteousness [50, 51].

Expectancies about punishment are calculated according to the degrees of risk and consequences one perceives for getting caught against perceived rewards, based in large measure from the observation of others. When peers get away with committing unlawful acts, perceptions of consequences are diminished and expectancies for rewards are enhanced. That is, when peers are engaged in deviant behaviors, social norms develop that encourage participation even when the risks of getting caught are substantial and penalties severe. When peers are caught and punished, perceptions of risks and consequences are increased; thus punishment may at times constrain deviant behaviors for some people [52]. Consistent with this, Rogers' [38] teleological theory of motivation explains that, when people are highly socially oriented, they are motivated to strive to gain acceptance into cliques or clubs with greater psychic force (*commitment*) and behavioral accommodation than those who are less socially oriented [53]. This tendency derives from human desires for emotional ties with important others or peer groups and can lead to increased attention-seeking behaviors [54]. If important others or peer groups are involved in dishonest or counterproductive behaviors, people with higher needs for social acceptance are more likely to engage in similar dishonest and counterproductive behaviors than those who score lower on this dimension; conversely, they will have strong tendencies to conform to positive and productive group norms as well [55].

21.4.4 Neuroticism, Impulse, and Exploitation

Neuroticism characterizes emotional instability [56]. When something annoys people who rank high on the neuroticism scale, they show tendencies to be impulsive and overreactive [57]. There are a number of security-related behaviors that are a concern for managers related to this factor. For example, people who rank high in neuroticism (*emotional instability*) have been associated with higher incidents of defacing websites, committing various forms of corporate sabotage, and workplace harassment through the use of degrading sarcasm or insults [36, 57]. Furthermore, because people tend to lose their inhibitions and either "flame" or form qualified intimacies with others they meet online [58, 59], people who show neurotic characteristics also exhibit greater cyber harassment and cyber stalking, and other forms of aggressive online behavior [58].

Finally, in some psychological contexts, an exploitive tendency is a parcel or a component or trait of a narcissistic personality [60, 61]; however, used in the context of a transactional or exchange (as opposed to a communal) relationship, the literature considers exploitation a reflection of an exploitative motive based on the propensity to strive to gain an advantage at someone else's expense. In other words, it is a penchant for engaging in zero-sum games regardless of the cost [62].

A zero-sum game is one where there is a clear winner and a clear loser. As such, people who are exploitive will seek to do things, such as win arguments, just to damage the credibility and value of others to gain some benefit [63]. Stemming from this, people who are exploitive will use threatening, harassing, and aggressive behavior for economic gain [64]. In many of such cases, people who are highly exploitive often set up their own blog websites just to air their gripes against others and then filter the input from blog postings to display only like-minded responses, and they often engage in corporate politicking and sabotage [65].

21.5 Management of Contravention Behaviors

Managers have the responsibility to be proactive in trying to prevent attacks from happening. One main avenue that managers have to be proactive is to ensure that employees do not omit security countermeasures, such as keeping operating system security patches up to date. In the event that an attack does occur, managers must respond quickly—with ***due diligence*** and with ***due care***—and with the guidance of legal counsel and the human resources department. We have already presented that security policies outline what precautions should be taken and the sanctions for violations of these policies or the law, and that procedures should specify the necessary steps to implement the organization's security countermeasures, and that the organization must comply with regulations, laws, and statutes. Given these basic management fundamentals, there are additional considerations relative to responding to attackers. These primarily involve behavior modification techniques.

21.5.1 Responding to the Outside Attacker

When attacked, important actions for management include limiting the exposures, containing the problems, recovering from the problems, and formulating responses. Responses should depend on the kind of attack—for example, whether it is against a computer system or against the company or individuals in the company. Trying to understand the motives of the attacker may help managers to formulate an appropriate response strategy. Thus, managers may need to do "some digging," but it is advisable not to contact an attacker directly to avoid divulging information that could be used in further attacks or as a defense by the attacker should the company pursue legal action. To properly ground the problem and guide managers with an appropriate response, *legal advice should be sought before any response is undertaken.* Some options available to deal with threatening and undesirable behaviors include extinction, which is the decline in a behavior rate because of non-reinforcement [5]. With this, a person or company may decide to ignore the attack in hopes that the attacker will lose interest and move on to another target [51]. This kind of behavior modification is more likely to be effective if the attacker acted *impulsively.*

However, other motives such as from narcissism or self-indulgence may cause the attacker to be relentless, especially if the attacker is an outsider who is difficult to trace or difficult to pursue—for example, if they reside in a foreign country. Moreover, if the attack is against a company via defamatory postings in a blog or other social media, even if the attacker loses interest and decides to move on, the Internet persists or caches information well beyond the date of the initial attack, leaving open the possibility that the attack propaganda may spread among many unintended recipients [47].

A second option is to respond to the attacker in a conciliatory manner to try to handle the problem rationally. This approach may be more successful with those who are *idealistic* or have *high needs for social acceptance.* More often, however, the attacker may perceive this as a weakness, or even sycophancy. This perception may act as positive reinforcement [5], which may only embolden the attacker to continue to victimize the attacked party and others. A third option is to punish the attacker [5] either through established legal means, or through a counterattack. The decision-action regarding punishment depends on the cost-benefit analysis by the victim (e.g., does the perpetrator have deep pockets in which to recover the expensive legal costs), versus a willingness to engage in the behavior in kind (e.g., using a honeynet), which brings about questions of legalities and ethics [11, 48].

In spite of the frequent criticisms in media outlets about the United States, United Kingdom, and European Union being litigious societies, litigation may be among the most effective responses currently available against attackers (so long as it is not merely a SLAPP suit). This bears out in the statistics concerning what companies are choosing to do. Casey Stengel reported on Fox News (November 8, 2009) that there was a 70 percent increase in lawsuits against cyber attackers in 2009 over the previous 2 years. Nevertheless, the punitive approach may be difficult and expensive if even possible to pursue, particularly when the attacks originate from abroad [66]. This must be weighed in determining the appropriate responses.

What else do we suggest that corporate officers, executives, and company managers do when attackers try to destroy or disrupt assets or steal information or disseminate misinformation to try to damage them or their companies? We first suggest that corporations have insurance (including liability insurance) to help defray damages and other legal costs. Next, they should develop an immunization and containment strategy (such as considering reputation management companies for social media attacks) and to quarantine the exposure. They may also consider using companies such as *Bazaarvoice.com* that searches the Internet for defamatory, racist, or other such language posted about their products or services, and then, possibly consider (with the advice of legal counsel), where practical and appropriate, seeking to punish the attackers through legal recourse such as litigation against attackers. Companies such as www.reputation.com may also be employed to help bury a defamatory posting to try to avoid the "Streisand effect"—in other words, drawing attention to the undesirable post [67].

A basic strategy used against social engineering attacks more individually is to freeze one's credit, followed by filing a fraud claim. An immunization and containment strategy for denial of service attacks against a router or computer system is to have a firewall that can filter and then drop the attacking network packets (or utilize hot failover systems depending on the layer of filtering). Legal recourse begins with intrusion or attack detection, identification of the attacker, forensic analysis to assess what was done and preserve evidence, and then possibly the pursuit of the perpetrators through litigation or through state and federal channels such as a state attorney general's office or the Federal Trade Commission (FTC).

21.5.2 Responding to the Inside Attacker

As with the outside attacker, punishment (or the threat of punishment) for the inside attacker can be effective, but it has to be carefully used or productive workers might be negatively affected. Such negative impacts may include decreased motivation or increased worker stress. Companies need to have a corrective action policy in place that dictates what should happen in the case of an offense that does not warrant immediate termination of employment.

A corrective action policy usually dictates a formal written warning, an outline of what needs to be corrected, and how, and what the employee can expect in terms of management support. It should always contain a period of time for the corrective action, a clause that the behavior must not be repeated after the corrective action period, and a clear statement that the employee *WILL* be terminated if the problem is not corrected. In most cases, however, an intentional threat or attack by an employee or other insider will result in immediate termination, and potentially civil litigation and even criminal prosecution.

> **In Focus**
>
> Managers should always include the HR department and legal department before (1) creating any contracts, (2) making any binding commitments, (3) placing people on any form of corrective action, or terminating their employment, (4) administering any psychological or performance assessment or evaluation, or (5) having personal conversations about people's behavior that extend beyond the outlined job performance expectations or written job plans.

21.5.3 Ethics and Employee Attitudes Toward the Law

If the attacker is on the inside, besides punishment, some research [52] has shown that ethics instruction may work to mitigate, but this depends on a person's attitude toward the law. Human factors including risk aversion or sense of control interact with situations and variables such as personal attitudes about the law, which affects security behavior. As we have discussed, one of the law's functions, besides regulating social order and relationships, is to deter crime and prescribe consequences for offenders; and also as we have discussed, laws have been somewhat effective in preventing illegal information security behavior.

Drawing from general deterrence theory, Straub et al. [68] found that deterrent measures, preventive measures, and deterrent severity act as inhibitors to information security breaches and predict information system security effectiveness. Although some studies have introduced various organizational factors that might affect these measures, legal deterrents generally do restrain security contravention; however, studies also show that this effect is partially dependent on one's attitudes toward the law [52].

There are contrasting views about the relationship between law and public attitudes. One view holds that the law has to reflect societal sentiments of justice and morality, whereas another holds that the law is a vehicle to shape those sentiments and bring about a social evolution. Yet another view postulates that individuals also have their own law-consciousness, including conceptions of rights, powers, duties, and related legal interactions. Tapp and Kohlberg [48] studied why people obeyed rules by asking questions such as, "Why should people follow rules?" and "Why do they follow rules?" They found that a person's attitude toward law is largely shaped by the person's legal socialization.

Legal socialization occurs in three main ways: (1) socialization by legal authority—where an individual accepts and understands the norms imposed on him or her through legal constraints (i.e., are motivated by authority), and to avoid negative consequences for misbehavior (i.e., to avoid punishment); (2) socialization by societal normative imposition—where an individual is willing to accept rules to maintain social conformity and to be fair to others who obey the law, and along these lines, the processes involved in learning conforming behavior are also involved in learning deviant behavior; and (3) socialization by human interaction, in which an individual perceives, respects, and participates in the creation of reciprocal expectations that become codified into law. From this frame of reference, people develop their own set of principles they live by. Nevertheless, if a law contradicts an important principle, these people too may deviate from the law.

Finally, research [52] has shown that people who comply with rules to avoid punishment are more likely to be responsive to punitive deterrents, whereas people who comply with rules to be fair to others or who develop their own principles are more likely to be responsive to ethical considerations; consequently, ethics training has been shown to be effective for some organizational members, but not for others. Nevertheless, as with building security defense depth and breadth, using a combination of behavioral modification techniques and training to address security is likely to be most effective.

CHAPTER SUMMARY

We have covered some of the legal aspects of organizations that lead to how organizations are governed. In that process, we highlighted that managers assume certain legal responsibilities. Along with managing security behaviors, management of security must encompass knowledge of employment law, regulations and statutes, and other legal matters, including the protection of company and employee information. As gathered from this chapter, dealing with security behaviors in organizations is complex, and the field of security behaviorism is research-intensive. To fully appreciate the field, one needs to be able to work with abstract ideas and understand how these ideas apply in a practical way to real-life business situations. In this chapter, we surveyed some of the key points about organizational behaviors as they relate to security. We examined behavioral factors involved in security attacks (contravention) and the omission of protective security countermeasures. We also indicted the importance of how people and technology interact, and how these interactions influence behaviors. In the next chapter, we will look at using modeling and reasoning systems for trying to predict security breaches.

THINK ABOUT IT

Topic Questions

21.1: According to social psychology research, what are the three basic types of control, and what does each refer to?

21.2: What are the six factors or motives identified by the Honeynet Team for why people attack computer systems?

21.3: The philosophy that fear of punishment for not obeying the law (or security policy) will help to prevent security violations stems from what theory?

21.4: Self-indulgence is a fixation on:

____ Control over outcomes
____ Financial gain
____ Getting even
____ Being entertained

21.5: Narcissism is defined as:

____ Belief in fate

____ Grandiose perception of self-importance
____ Lack of self-control
____ Need for social acceptance

21.6: A corrective action policy usually dictates what three elements?

21.7: Honeynets are:

____ Subnetworks that are hidden from the outside
____ Exposed gateways that are vulnerable
____ Traps set by investigators that they expect to be attacked
____ Computers that are used heavily

21.8: Leading by example includes using _____ _____ and _____ _____.

THINK ABOUT IT (CONTINUED)

21.9: Procedural justice stems from perceptions of:

_____ Fair distributions of rewards
_____ Equity in organizational practices
_____ Having a court system
_____ Having a legal department

_____ Reinforcement
_____ Carrot-and-stick
_____ Punishment
_____ Legal

21.10: OBMod incorporates a _____ approach to gaining behavioral compliance.

Questions for Further Study

Q21.1: If you had an employee who refused to obey the security policy, what would you do, and why?

Q21.2: Why do managers focus on behaviors and behavior modification in dealing with security problems, and what do self-serving biases have to do with this?

Q21.3: What precautions should managers take before responding to security behavior problems from outsiders, and how might these be similar to or differ from precautions taken before responding to security behavior problems from insiders?

Q21.4: Explain why people seem to be so critical to others when they post or interact online in blogs and other social media.

Q21.5: If someone posts defamatory information about a company management team online, what would be your recommendations to deal with this, and why?

KEY CONCEPTS AND TERMS

Antecedents are events or conditions that precede a behavior.

High external locus of control is where people perceive things generally as being outside their control.

Learned helplessness is the condition in which people feel threatened so often that they quit caring and give up.

Reinforcers are consequences that increase the frequency of a behavior.

Social contagion is where people think: Because others are doing "it," I should do it too.

References

1. Bandura, A. (1986). *Social foundations of thought and action*. Englewood Cliffs, NJ: Prentice-Hall.

2. Ajzen, I. (1991). The theory of planned behavior. *Organizational Behavior and Human Decision Processes, 50*, 179–211.

3. Arkes, H. R., & Garske, J. P. (1982). *Psychological theories of motivation.* Monterey, CA: Brooks/Cole.

4. Baldwin, T. T., Bommer, W. H., & Rubin, R. S. (2008). *Developing management skills: What great managers know and do.* Boston, MA: McGraw-Hill/Irwin.

5. Skinner, B. F. (1960). Are theories of learning necessary? *Psychological Review, 57,* 193–216.

6. Neuringer, A. (2002). Operant variability: Evidence, functions, and theory. *Psychonometric Bulletin & Review, 9,* 672–705.

7. Workman, M., Bommer, W., & Straub, D. (2008). Security lapses and the omission of information security measures: An empirical test of the threat control model, *Journal of Computers in Human Behavior, 24,* 2799–2816.

8. Schifreen, R. (2006). *Defeating the hacker.* New York, NY: John Wiley & Sons.

9. Workman, M. (2008a). A test of interventions for security threats from social engineering. *Information Management & Computer Security, 16,* 463–483.

10. Kerstelica, D., & Baratt-Pugh, L. (2009). Do policies on bullying make a difference? Contrasting strategy regimes within higher education in Australia and Croatia. *International Journal of Management and Decision Making, 10,* 303–320.

11. Lipinski, T. A., Buchanan, E. A., & Britz, J. J. (2002). Sticks and stones and words that harm: Liability vs. responsibility, section 230 and defamatory speech in cyberspace. *Ethics and Information Technology, 4,* 143–158.

12. Workman, M., Workman, J., & Phelps, D. (2008). *The management of infosec.* Boston, MA: eAselworx Press.

13. Solomon, M. G., & Chapple, M. (2005). *Information security illuminated.* Sudbury, MA: Jones and Bartlett Publishers.

14. Bresz, F. P. (2004, July–August). People—Often the weakest link in security, but one of the best places to start. *Journal of Health Care Compliance,* pp. 57–60.

15. Theoharidou, M., Kokolakis, S., Karyda, M., & Kiountouzis, E. (2005). The Insider Threat to Information Systems and the Effectiveness of ISO17799. *Computers & Security, 24,* 472–484.

16. Ryan, J. (2004). Information security tools and practices: What works? *IEEE Transactions on Computers, 53,* 1060–1064.

17. Sherif, J. S., Ayers, R., & Dearmond, T. G. (2003). Intrusion detection: The art and the practice. *Information Management and Computer Security, 11,* 175–186.

18. Straub, D. W., & Welke, R. J. (1998). Coping with systems risk: Security planning models for management decision making. *MIS Quarterly, 22,* 441–469.

19. Ong, T. H., Tan C. P., Tan, Y. T., & Ting, C. (1999). SNMS—Shadow network management system. *Symposium on Network Computing and Management. Singapore, May 21,* 1–9.

20. Ruighaver, A. B., Maynard, S. B., & Chang, S. (2007). Organizational security culture: Extending the end-user perspective. *Computers & Security, 26,* 56–62.

21. Workman, M. (2007). Gaining access with social engineering: An empirical study of the threat. *Information Systems Security Journal, 16,* 315–331.

22. Bartels, A. (2006, November). Global IT spending and investment forecast, 2006 to 2007. *Forrester Research,* pp. 4–31.

23. Post, G. V., & Kagan, A. (2007). Evaluating information security tradeoffs: Restricting access can interfere with user tasks. *Computer & Security, 26*, 229–237.

24. Burns, T., & Stalker, G. (1961). *The management of innovation*. London, UK: Tavistock.

25. Kramer, J. (2010). Non-compete agreements: Are they enforceable? It depends! *US Business, 4*, 82–87.

26. Chapple, M. J., & Crowell, C. R. (2008). Federal information security law. In M. Quigley (Ed), *Encyclopedia of Information and Ethics Security* (pp. 291–296). Hershey, PA: IGI Global Press.

27. Langenderfer, J., & Linnhoff, S. (2005). The emergence of biometrics and its effect on consumers, *Journal of Consumer Affairs, 39*, 314–338.

28. Bragdon, C. R. (2008). *Transportation security*. Amsterdam, the Netherlands: Elsevier/ Butterworth Press.

29. Grothmann, T., & Reussing, F. (2006). People at risk of flooding: Why some residents take precautionary action while others do not. *Natural Hazards, 38*, 101–120.

30. Pyszczynski, T., Greenberg, J., & Solomon, W. (1997). Why do we need what we need? A terror management perspective on the roots of human social motivation, *Psychological Inquiry, 8*, 1–20.

31. Wilde, G. J. S. (2001). *Target risk*. Toronto, Ontario, Canada: PDE Publications.

32. Kabay, M. (2000). Social psychology and infosec. *The Risks Digest, 15*, 1–6.

33. Kankanhalli, A. T,, Tan, B. C. Y., & Wei, K.-K. (2003). An integrative study of information systems security effectiveness. *International Journal of Information Management, 23*, 139–154.

34. McClelland, D. C. (1978). Managing motivation to expand human freedom. *American Psychologist, 33*, 201–210.

35. Calluzzo, V. J., & Cante, C. J. (2004). Ethics in information technology and software use. *Journal of Business Ethics, 51*, 301–312.

36. Honeynet Team. (2004). *The honeynet project: Know your enemy*. New York, NY: Addison-Wesley.

37. Workman, M. (2010). A behaviorist perspective on corporate harassment online: Validation of a theoretical model of psychological motives. *Computers & Security, 29*, 831–839.

38. Rogers, C. R. (1957). The necessary and sufficient conditions of therapeutic personality change. *Journal of Consulting Psychology, 21*, 95–103.

39. Ajzen, I. (2002). Perceived behavioral control, self-efficacy, locus of control, and the theory of planned behavior. *Journal of Applied Social Psychology, 32*, 665–683.

40. Acquisti, A., & Grossklags, J. (2005). Privacy and rationality in individual decision making, *IEEE Security and Privacy, 3*, 26–33.

41. Costa, P. T., Jr., & McCrae, R. R. (1995). Domains and facets: Hierarchical personality assessment using the revised NEO personality inventory. *Journal of Personality Assessment, 64*, 21–50.

42. Rhodewalt, F., & Morf, C. C. (1998). On self-aggrandizement and anger: A temporal analysis of narcissism and affective reactions to success and failure. *Journal of Personality and Social Psychology, 74*, 672–685.

43. Judge, T. A., & Ilies, R. (2002). Relationship of personality to performance motivation: A meta-analytic review. *Journal of Applied Psychology, 87*, 797–807.

44. Neuman, G. A., & Wright, J. (1999). Team effectiveness: Beyond skills and cognitive ability. *Journal of Applied Psychology, 84*, 379–389.

45. Dawn, J., Cowie, H., & Ananiadou, K. (2003). Perceptions and experience of workplace bullying in five different work populations. *Aggressive Behavior, 29*, 489–496.

46. Berkeley, G. (1996). To be is to be perceived. In G. L. Bowie, M. W. Michaels, & R. C. Solomon (Eds.), *Twenty questions: Essays in philosophy.* Orlando, FL: Harcourt & Brace.

47. Crowell, C. R., & Barger, R. N. (2008). Meta view of information ethics. In M. Quigley (Ed.), *Encyclopedia of information and ethics security* (pp. 445–450). Hershey, PA: IGI Global Press.

48. Tapp, J. L., & Kohlberg, L. (1977). Developing senses of law and legal justice. In J. L., Tapp & F. J. Levine (Eds.), *Law, justice, and the individual in society: Psychological and legal issues* (pp. 96–97). New York, NY: Holt, Rinehart & Winston.

49. Kohlberg, L. (1973). The claim to moral adequacy of a highest stage of moral judgment. *Journal of Philosophy, 70*, 630–646.

50. Carroll, A. B. (2009). Business ethics. In H. Bidgoli (Ed.), *The handbook of technology management* (Volume 1, pp. 477–523). New York, NY: John Wiley & Sons.

51. Ford, B. (2009, July). Don't feed the trolls. *Waverider Computer Connection,* pp. 7–11.

52. Workman, M., & Gathegi, J. (2007). Punishment and ethics deterrents: A comparative study of insider security contravention. *Journal of American Society for Information Science and Technology, 58*, 318–342.

53. Tajfel, H. (1982). Social psychology of intergroup relations. *Annual Review of Psychology, 33*, 1–39.

54. Beck, K., & Wilson, C. (2000). Development of affective organizational commitment: A cross-sectional examination of change with tenure. *Journal of Vocational Behavior, 56*, 114–136.

55. Beck, L., & Ajzen, I. (1991) Predicting dishonest actions using the theory of planned behavior, *Journal of Research in Personality, 25*, 285–301.

56. Eysenck, J. J. (1961). *Handbook of abnormal psychology.* New York, NY: Basic Books.

57. Ivancevich, J. M., Konopaske, R., & Matteson, M. T. (2008). *Organizational behavior and management.* Boston, MA: McGraw/Hill.

58. Whitty, M. T. (2008). Liberating or debilitating? An examination of romantic relationships, sexual relationships and friendships on the net. *Computers in Human Behavior, 24*, 1837–1850.

59. Workman, M. (2006). Virtual communities and imaginary friends: Affiliation and affection from afar; the keynote speech. Stowe, VT: *Annual Conference on Technology and Innovation, CTI'06, 1*, 2–12.

60. Burris, C. T. (1999). Stand by your (exploitive) man: Codependency and responses to performance feedback. *Journal of Social and Clinical Psychology, 18*, 277–298.

61. Millon, T., & Grossman, S. (2007). *Overcoming resistant personality disorders: A personalized psychotherapy.* New York, NY: John Wiley & Sons.

62. Clark, M. S., & Waddell, B. (1985). Perceptions of exploitation in communal and exchange relationships. *Journal of Social and Personal Relationships, 2*, 403–418.

63. Swingle, P. G. (1970). Exploitative behavior in non-zero-sum games. *Journal of Personality and Social Psychology, 16*, 121–132.

64. Bond, M. H., & Dutton, D. G. (1975). The effect of interaction anticipation and experience as a victim on aggressive behavior. *Journal of Personality, 43*, 515–527.
65. Casarez, N. B. (2002).Dealing with cybersmear: How to protect your organization from online defamation. *Public Relations Quarterly, 47*, 40–45.
66. Becker, R., Schmidt, M. B., & Johnston, A. C. (2008). Mitigation of identity theft in the information age. In M. Quigley (Ed.), *Encyclopedia of Information and Ethics Security* (pp. 451–456). Hershey, PA: IGI Global Press.
67. Riley, M., & Vance, A. (2011, May). The company that kicked the hornet's nest. *Bloomberg Businessweek*, pp. 35–37.
68. Straub, D. W., Goodman, S., & Baskerville, R. L. (2008). *Information security: Policy, processes, and practices.* Armonk, New York, NY: Sharpe Books.

Modeling and Predicting Attacks

WE HAVE SIGNIFICANTLY COVERED HOW MANAGERS and security personnel work to prevent attacks in both proactive and reactive ways. In this chapter, we will cover some techniques used to predict attacks. Attack modeling techniques are used in determining a wide array of security-related threats, including terrorist attacks. For these purposes, we will introduce stochastic game theory as applied in software applications, which can be used by system and network administrators to predict a set of moves by an adversary in an attack scenario. To begin our discussion, we will present two major approaches to this prediction problem, one called *inductive* and the other called *deductive*. There is even a combination known as "subjective reasoning." These approaches can be used in combination with each other. We will conclude by considering how modeling interacts with human biases, and how these interactions affect security planning and decision making.

Chapter 22 Topics

This chapter:

- Introduces game theory and how it applies to attack modeling.
- Presents the differences among data, information, and intelligence.
- Describes Churchman heuristics and heuristic reasoning.
- Gives an introduction to human biases and how these affect security predictions.

Chapter 22 Goals

When you finish this chapter, you should:

- ☐ Have an understanding of the techniques that can be used to predict attacks.

- ❑ Know the differences between deductive and inductive prediction techniques.
- ❑ Understand basic concepts used in modeling and predicting security events.
- ❑ Know what heuristics are, and how they are involved in security incident modeling and prediction.
- ❑ Be familiar with how human biases interact with scenario generation and security decisions.

22.1 Game Theory and Predictive Models

Game theory is a stream of mathematics and logic in which strategic interactions among "rational" players advance toward a goal or objective. Game theory has been applied in a variety of problems ranging from economic forecasting to nuclear warfare. Also, game theory is amenable to work in combination with a number of common computer algorithms such as stochastic models, finite state machines, and various forms of event chaining such as a continuous-time Markov chain (CTMC). Along with these, a number of formulas have been developed such as the min/max theorem, Nash equilibrium, evolutionary and genetic algorithms, and many others. Game theory has been an important contributor to technologies that model and predict attack episodes, as well as more generally in decision systems used in security planning as done in risk assessments. It turns out that predicting human behavior is incredibly hard; however, game theory has been quite successful on the whole in helping human beings narrow their focus on potential scenarios. In this chapter, we will introduce some of the major theories and concepts that managers may look toward.

22.1.1 Inductive Predictions

Many approaches to attack modeling utilize inductive logic and statistics. Most of us are familiar with statistics, but perhaps less so with inductive logic. Inductive logic essentially relies on the concept that given true premises, the conclusion is likely to be true. An example of an inductive statement is: *Because all previous American presidents have been men, the next American president will probably be a man.* This inductive statement (called an assertion) with its true premise and probably true conclusion is said to be a *cogent inductive argument.* This is because although it is not certain that the next president will be a man, given the samples from the past and the numbers of male versus female presidential candidates in the present, by sheer odds of probability, the conclusion is *likely* to be true.

Inductive arguments are often called hypotheses. In other words, using previous examples and taking samples of data, these "observations" can be computed into a probability. There are several keys to the accuracy of our computation, but two are particularly important. One is ensuring that the samples or observations are chosen at random.

That is, from a data set (called a population), every element in the population must have an equal chance of being selected in the sampling process, such as by using a random number generator to make a selection. The second is that we must select "enough" samples from the population; the concept of "enough" is a calculation based on how large the population is.

The inductive process allows us to make generalizations or to support hypotheses, but anyone who has been exposed to statistics knows that generalizations do not tell us specifics. To illustrate, suppose we had a jar of marbles in which there were four colors of marbles in the jar. If we knew the number of marbles in the jar and the numbers of each color in the jar, we could make a statistical prediction about the probability that the next marble taken from a randomly shaken jar would produce a marble of color X, but it is not guaranteed. More specifically, using this method in predicting security behaviors, we might be able to predict that people with a particular psychological "profile" may generally (probably) take security precautions given proper instructions. However, we cannot say, using this method, that *Bob*, who fits the psychological profile, will certainly take security precautions.

> **In Focus**
>
> Statistics necessarily depend on randomization. Because it involves sampling from a population, if the selections do not have a random (equal) chance of being sampled, the statistics lose their power to make predictions.

Random samples when viewed graphically have a shape, called a distribution. A normal distribution is sometimes called a "bell curve" because the collective samples resemble an inverted U. For us to know how well our sample represents an entire population, we must know or reasonably estimate the size of the population. In other words, if one evening we simply asked people walking down Broadway about their attitudes toward theatrical plays, whether they liked or disliked them, we could not make the generalization that people across the country like or dislike these from this sample because, among other things, our sample is not random. As an example, the people walking down Broadway in the evening are more likely to have attended a theatrical play than the general population, and we have no idea how many people in total walked down Broadway that evening.

For us to know how accurate our sample is, we would need a ***bounded population*** from which to randomly sample. A bounded population is a defined grouping. Again, by way of illustration, if we chose more specifically to sample attitudes toward the Broadway play *Cats*, we could obtain the number of people who attended that play that evening, and then use a fair dice roll to determine which of the people exiting the theater to select. In other words, if we rolled a 3, a 1, a 6, and so forth, we would ask the third person coming out of the door, the next person, and then the sixth one, until the theater was empty. From this, we would run a variety of statistics to tell us how valid and reliable our sample is, and then to tell us the probability that all of the people who attended *Cats* that evening liked the play or not. We can then generalize this to the population who attend the play, but we cannot generalize it to the U.S. population, or even the population of the state of New York, or even Manhattan.

A question might be: Why not simply ask all of the people (the entire population) who came out of the theater their opinions? We could do that in this example, although surely some would refuse to answer our questions, so we would still end up with only a sample and not answers from the entire population. The issue is that gathering opinions from a relatively small group of people is relatively easy, but as our population size increases, so does the difficulty in gathering data from all of the members of the population. An advantage of this approach to making predictions is that even though it cannot say anything about a specific instance, a completely random pattern can be described in a relatively compact manner, namely a statistical distribution, and the distribution can efficiently and effectively be analyzed for making general predictions or presumptions. This is because from a statistical point of view, high complexity is addressed in the same manner as low complexity, and this approach can also accommodate a mixture of regularity and irregularity in the data.

In Focus

Data warehouse data mining applications generally use statistical approaches for pattern identification.

22.1.2 Deductive Predictions

In contrast to using statistics and generalization, a deduction (where logically there are many forms) states facts that if true must lead to an obviously true conclusion, if it is valid. A most simple true deductive statement is that *all circles are round*. This is a true statement because by definition, circles are round. Of course, as ideas and arguments become more complex, the logic likewise grows increasingly complex to prove true or false, but complex true deductive statements must have the same basic properties. An example of a slightly more complex deductive statement is that *because all wines are beverages, and a chardonnay is a wine, then a chardonnay is a beverage*. Complexity therefore might be found in the number of premises used to make an assertion.

As indicated, using deduction we must enumerate all of the elements or events that make up a conclusion so that we can categorically assert something as true or untrue. This ***ideographic*** approach to making predictions uses deductive logic that is often expressed in "set theory." Set theory is a finite state technique that consists of all of the states a set can assume. For example, a traffic light has three states: red (stop), yellow (slow down), and green (go). Likewise, in terms of a security attack, a computer system might be in one of three states: compromised, secure, unknown.

Programmatically, suppose we had the following set of data, {0,1; 1,1; 1,0; 0,0}, and we used a logical AND conditional algorithm as follows: If 0,1 AND 1,1 then 0,1, else if 1,1 AND 0,0 then 0,0. An algorithm such as this could be transformed into a useful program to quickly determine, for example, if computer systems and/or network connections are either up and running or are down. As seen then, the deductive approach to prediction has certain advantages. For one thing, it is algorithmic in nature (rather than probabilistic), and the algorithm can be very short for a regular stable pattern. However, as complexity in a system increases, randomness may also increase, rendering an algorithmic approach impractical. This is because if a completely random pattern is to be described by an algorithm, then this algorithm cannot possibly be shorter than the list of elements (variables) that comprise the pattern. Because identification of all factors in complex systems and for complex problems are usually not computationally practical, just as brute force attacks against a modern cryptography are not computationally practical, it can often be beneficial to combine inductive and deductive techniques, which we will illustrate later.

> **In Focus**
>
> One way induction and deduction may be combined is in "subjective logic," a common form of which is called Bayesian belief.

22.1.3 Game Theory and Attack Modeling

A discussion of game theory is well beyond the scope of our textbook, but we can introduce some basic concepts as they apply to making predictions about security attack episodes and in determining risks and recommended expenditure outlays for future security initiative budgeting. To begin this, picture a game of chess. At the beginning of the game, there are vast numbers of moves we could take; although some moves might be more optimal than others, determining the most optimal move is complex and largely strategic guesswork based on what we think our opponent's next move might be. As the game is played and pieces are removed from the board, the game becomes more finite, and the most optimal moves (given the choices) become clearer. In attack planning, to solve this sort of problem, statistical prediction is best used as the attack game begins, but moving to a deductive approach is best as the attack game becomes more finite.

Many games are predicated on what is known as the "prisoner's dilemma" [1]. To illustrate this concept, Kelly and Thibaut [2] highlighted a classic technique used by law enforcement when two people are arrested for a crime. One is offered "a deal" to "rat" on the other. In the prisoner's dilemma, if the two parties cooperate, which in this case is if they both remain silent, they are both mildly punished. However, if one betrays another, one is severely punished and the other goes free; if they both betray each another, both are moderately punished. This type of game offers the possibility to cooperate, but in most applications of security attack modeling, the game is played as a zero-sum game, where one wins and the other loses, as with the game of chess.

> **In Focus**
>
> Games can be cooperative, non-cooperative, or competitive. A type of game, called a zero-sum game, has a clear winner and loser, which is usually the case when we apply game theory to modeling security threats.

An example implementation of a game regarding the prediction of an attack against (some arbitrary) information systems infrastructure can be illustrated as follows. In logic, the Greek symbol Π is often used to represent an entire attack strategy; for example, reconnaissance/foot printing (node 1), port scanning (node 2), enumeration (node 3), gaining access (node 4), escalating privileges (node 5), creating a backdoor (node 6), and covering tracks (node 7). The Greek symbol $\Gamma(s)$ often represents a phase (or state) of the attack strategy for a given system in the computing infrastructure, for instance port scanning (node 2). Nodes are generally arranged in a directed acyclic graph (DAG), which means that there are certain predicates (things that must be done first) before one can move on to a next probable move among many possible moves.

As an example similar to the IDS stochastic model presented by Shallhammar et al. [3], suppose that our computing infrastructure consisted of a host computer, a public web server, and a private fileserver. To describe the security of the network, we may define the finite state probabilities as: Xi where $\{i = \{x, y, z\} \mid x, y, z \in \{0,1\}\}$. In this formulation, the vertical bar ($|$) represents the logical OR operator, and the symbol $\in$ represents possible states in a ***finite state machine***, such that each state for x, y, and z may be either 0 or 1. In other words, $\in$ denotes membership of a set, which in this case is a set of states that is either 0 or 1.

Now let's suppose "i" is equal to states (1, 0, 1). This represents the states where the host computer (x) and fileserver (z) have been compromised, but the web server (y) has not. The set of actions can be defined as $A = \{a1, a2, a3, \phi\}$, where $a1 = $ "attack host computer," $a2 = $ "attack web server," and $a3 = $ "attack fileserver," and $\phi = $ "do nothing." Given this set and possible states, the attack scenario can be predicted in a continuous time Markov chain (CTMC) among nodes with a finite number of states $i = 1, \ldots n$ [3] (**Figure 22.1**). Each atomic attack action is computed as a probability (or vector or lambda) of the transition from one state to another between nodes, depending on $\Gamma(s)$: Xi; for example, the probability (p) or lambda (λ) that the next move will be $\Gamma(s) = 5$: Xi (0,0,1). This condition represents the state: *privileges escalation on the fileserver*. Each attacker move (φ^n) is met with a countermove (Ψ^n).

The game is played out (modeled) where the attacker's choice of action is based on considerations of the possible consequences. In the context of this example game

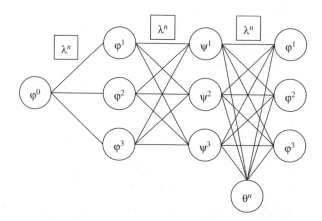

FIGURE 22.1

Action-reaction CTMC.

scenario, the operational security of the computing infrastructure is a two-player, zero-sum, multistage game where, at each stage, the parameters of the game depend on the current state of the CTMC as it transitions from state to state and node to node over time.

> **In Focus**
>
> An example where game theory has been utilized is in some of the commercial intrusion detection systems (IDS) in the marketplace. The interactions between an attacker and the security administrator are modeled as a two-player competitive game for which the best-response strategies (building on the Nash equilibrium theorem) are computed and from which alerts are generated.

22.2 Reasoning and Inference

In the security community, the term *incident* generally represents a state where a system deviates from its security requirements or policies or expectations, as we have previously presented. A security incident might be the result of accident or random failures during normal usage, or may be caused intentionally from attacks upon a system or network, or a combination of these. Such attacks on a system or network often consist of many successive actions and states and a series of state changes leading from an initially secure state or baseline to one of several possible compromised states, which cannot be precisely calculated. For these kinds of problems, heuristic reasoning and inference are very helpful to **humans-in-the-loop**, so long as they conform to the "normative rule" or a "straddle point," which means an optimal solution given the options, or an optimal compromise, respectively. Although there are many different kinds of reasoning and inference systems in the marketplace, we will cover some primary categories and foundations from which many of these are derived.

22.2.1 Reasoning Systems

Developing reasoning systems has been on the minds of computer scientists for quite some time in relation to a number of problems, including prediction about possible future security attack events. Reasoning systems are those that can find patterns in complex information, draw inferences, and make predictions from ill-defined problems and unstructured data. They are a specialized form of **decision support system** or an **expert system**, in which the function of the system is to assist human beings in solving complex problems by going beyond providing information, to also providing recommendations or suggested solutions or outcomes.

> **In Focus**
>
> Expert systems can perform reasoning and inference. They are increasingly used in modern business applications ranging from help desk applications to mortgage loan-processing systems.

Expert decision systems come in many forms. Two of the more common are rule-based and case-based systems, although there are others such as fuzzy logic systems and genetic algorithms. In rule-based systems, rules are defined that enable a deductive form of reasoning, whereas in case-based systems, inferences are drawn from representative samples to suggest conclusions, such as a variety of symptoms may match those associated with a given computer failure. Some interesting technologies have come about, including Norsys Netica, which produces a ***Bayesian belief network*** from semantic concepts, such that it can reason; for example: "If it is raining, then the grass will be wet. If the grass is wet, then there is no need to water the grass." Another interesting technology is Pellet, which can perform reasoning using ontologies (i.e., OWL).

Rather than covering the many types of reasoning and inference expert systems, because these are beyond the scope of our textbook, let's just survey the kinds of problems these systems solve in relation to our topic of interest, predicting information security attacks. To fully appreciate this, we need to touch on the notion of determinism. That is, the question of whether we can accurately make predictions about a future event based on the information we can gather.

> **In Focus**
>
> Probabilistic reasoning involves working from samples, statistics, and logic to assert sets of propositions or make generalizations, such as generating probability scenarios for a range of attack episodes. Ideographic reasoning attempts to enumerate every component in a problem set and uses calculus and deductive logic to draw conclusions about an individual phenomenon, such as calculating an opponent's next move in an attack that has been initiated.

With the advent of expert decision systems, making predictions in complex systems begins by trying to close the gap between the material world of our experience and the conceptual world of ideas, thoughts, models, and theories. Closing the gap requires that computer systems be capable of doing some of the functions that human brains perform, as well as going beyond those by "making sense" out of complexity that human brains perceive as chaos. A useful technique for doing this involves stochastic modeling. A stochastic model computes outcomes with a combination of mathematical calculus with known variables, quantities, or components, and then randomly "seeds" variables that are unknown, or infuses randomization into the calculus for generating probability scenarios.

22.2.2 Ontology and Epistemology

The issue with theory is that it sometimes can be difficult to translate it into practical terms. A challenge is often to "operationalize" concepts so that they are definite enough such that they can be measured. We have been discussing various aspects of making predictions about security incidents. To operationalize these concepts, we need to now include two other important concepts: determining whether enough data exist about a problem (and whether we can collect it), and what the data mean. If we have sufficient data, we can look for possible patterns in the data—say, stored in a data warehouse, for example—which may suggest an attack of some sort is under way, and then we can use these indications to create a set of models for possible attack scenarios, examining them algorithmically.

However, the data gathered may not be sufficient to explain the meaning of the event model. It may appear as merely a random set of unconnected events, even if they are statistically correlated and temporally ordered. We may end up with a model, for example, that shows a person of interest has flown into an airport, a tanker truck was reported missing from a nearby fueling station, and a large quantity of sodium nitrate was purchased from four different locations on the same day in the general vicinity. The meaning of these events must be inferred from their associations and a conclusion, solution, or decision must be heuristically derived. These issues represent the ontological and epistemic levels, as introduced by Scheibe [4].

In Focus

In philosophy, ontology means existence, whereas epistemology refers to meaning. Unfortunately, the term ontology has been misused in the software and security literature (such as in reference to "ontologies").

The ontological level, which means the existence of data, is deterministic; that is, it is possible to identify elements in a data set. In modeling, initially, the ontological level may not be operationally useful because of the complexity in most incident predictions or future security planning problems. In other words, we cannot typically obtain all the data we need in order to ideographically model out a solution or generate a definite scenario, unless it is very simplistic or finite.

Epistemology, on the other hand, deals with the meaning of patterns or relationships we might gather from data. If there are enough data and contexts (known problems, conditions, constraints, and relationships) that can be specified, then meaning may be derived from the data set. As an example, if a possible attack scenario is identified by the evidence of missing materials, such as a missing confidential employee contact list, and subsequent phone calls are made to various employees to gather login information to their computers, then we may conclude that a pretext social engineering attack may be under way. We may then infer that we need to implement countermeasures such as collecting the caller ID and conducting an investigation. For drawing the correct conclusions and making proper inferences, this means that the ontological level, those of facts and elements, must have been sufficiently gathered or determined in order for the meaning of the patterns to be inferred.

To illustrate, we can consider the ontological problem as follows: If someone were to say, "18, 16, 25, 14, 65, 21," we can tell that these data have little to offer us by way of meaning. If we provide some context such as "Age is 21," we can begin to draw conclusions. Nevertheless the conclusions will be based on what we may conjure about people when they reach a certain age. In other words, because we have only limited context, we draw conclusions based on our own cognitive schemas, which are subjective interpretations—that is, what we have learned about being age 21. If, however, we add more context and constraints stating, "The law requires a person to be of age 21 to purchase liquor, but the largest consumer age group of liquor is boys 17 years of age," we can begin to draw meaning (epistemology) about the problem this suggests.

22.2.3 Inference and the Ontological to Epistemic Transformation

The most fundamental problem facing developers of decision and reasoning systems is the transformation of gathering data and churning that into "meaningful" information for making inferences. Even then, many reasoning systems add to the problem of "information overload" because the systems are creating and disseminating more information to human consumers than they can cognitively process. In other words, too much of the "meaning making" is still left up to the human-in-the-loop, and not enough work is being done by the computer beyond collecting and serving up information. By way of example, let us say that we wanted to know if people in a college football stadium were friendly. On the whole, we might be able to say *yes* or *no*, and perhaps we could do that by determining each person's temperament characteristic and having each make their introduction to the others. However, practically speaking, there are too many people to accomplish that, and some people may leave during the game whereas others will show up later.

Perhaps we could run a computer program that samples the temperament of some of the people in the stadium, and then we draw inferences about the rest of the population in attendance. Still, we have no idea if an individual, such as *Bob* in the second row at the 50-yard line, is friendly by nature. To know that, we have to study him, but even then his temperament at that point in time is not necessarily how he tends to be most of the time. If *Bob's* team is losing, perhaps he is not friendly, but otherwise, perhaps he tends to be friendly most of the time.

Using this example, we can see a variety of complications in trying to determine the general patterns in a complex system, such as the football stadium crowd, and then drilling down to determine patterns for a given element, in this case *Bob* in the second row at the 50-yard line at a given point in time. Somehow, enough data, context, and constraints are needed in order to "make sense" of the phenomenon of interest. In other words, trying to predict a security incident, or determine security risks, or make predictions about what a manager may need in justifying his or her security budget in the next years.

In Focus

Many security publications recommend using subjective weights in risk analyses or for computations such as probability or likelihood of a loss. To pick one, we could use annual loss expectancy (ALE) used in risk assessment. However, the sad fact is that depending on the complexity of the organizational infrastructure, many of these estimates are often little more than intuition, gut feeling, or a guess based on past experience, which are often poor predictors of future experiences or expectations [5]. This is one reason why solving the ontological to epistemic transformation is so important.

Given this, it is no wonder then that *plan-to-actual* budgetary expenditures in corporations vary upwards on average by 3 to 1 [6]. Managers often underestimate their expenditures, partially as a matter of pressure from senior management, and when they do fall short, there often follows the typical personnel layoffs, cutbacks, or other austerity plans that can affect organizational and information security. This condition is particularly acute when one considers that security countermeasures and infrastructure are overhead costs of doing business. Said another way, taking security precautions costs money and perhaps adds little or nothing to the bottom line. Managers have to get better at making accurate predictions. That means technologies that managers use have to become better at making predictions.

One solution to this issue was well explained by Bohm [7] in terms of the ontological to epistemic transformation. The transformation may be perceived in the following progression. If we drew a line with equal segments on a piece of paper or a chalkboard, we would in this sense see a line where the segments are similar, yet the segments occupy different places in time on the line; therefore they are also different. They have ***similar differences***. In other words, we have temporally ordered equidistant points on a line (**Figure 22.2**).

Imagine now that there are similar differences among many factors, perhaps a nearly infinite number of factors that interconnect in the overlapping sequences at different times in complex systems. We could think of this as a complex system consisting of the operational activity and the factors that make up this activity going on at any given point in time for all of the components (computers and networks and applications and so on) in a large operation. Then if we were to draw these many factors as lines temporally ordered and equidistant as similar differences (say volumes of activity, bandwidth utilization, compute cycles, latency, and so forth), so that they intersect at a point in time, we would see a representation that could appear to be chaos, but we would know from the first illustration that there are inherent patterns buried in that chaos (**Figure 22.3**).

Similar Differences

FIGURE 22.2

Temporally ordered equidistant points.

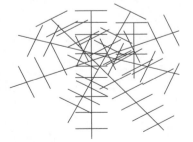

Complex Similar Differences

FIGURE 22.3

Overlapping factorial vicissitudes.

We could represent these lines as natural sine waves and then we might try to reduce them through a ***Fourier analysis***, which is a trigonometric function that reduces a series of wave patterns into a "harmonic" one. In other words, it normalizes or synthesizes the differential patterns into a common (canonical) form. However, as Bohm [7] pointed out, doing so would cause the system to lose many of the features that are expressed in each of the factors that comprise an event (or incident). Bohm refers to these natural features as overlapping factorial vicissitudes, and each added factor, with its own set of patterns, amplifies the complexity in the system by orders of magnitude.

Now consider a practical example in which we ask the question, what will be the stock price for a share of IBM next Wednesday at 10 am? We could deduce the answer to the question if we could discern all of the factors and their similar differences (or vicissitudes) that make up the stock price, such as investor mood, volume of activity, price/earnings ratio, and so forth, which all independently intersect at a given point in time (in our example, Wednesday at 10 am).

If it were possible to know all of the factors that make up such a phenomenon, as well as knowing their individual patterns or vicissitudes, we could predict the phenomenon perfectly. Said differently, if we were able to depict all the similar differences among all of the factors that determine IBM's stock price at a given point in time, we could invest our hard-earned money accordingly with complete confidence (**Figure 22.4**).

Obviously, this is not possible. In fact, this problem is so complicated and so vexing that the military and intelligence communities have been spending vast amounts of money in efforts to move away from the static data warehouse and data mining approaches to analysis and inference and into what is called "semantic intelligence, surveillance, reconnaissance (ISR) fusion." This approach to ontological to epistemic transformation uses multiple levels: a set of conventional data collection facilities such as endpoints and middleware, an "enrichment" capability where the data can be "marked up" or annotated, and organization and storage facilities to categorize the semantically enhanced information into bodies called ontologies. There are also frameworks to advertise and discover these dynamic ontologies, along with reasoning and inference systems "sitting on top" like the proverbial icing on the cake.

FIGURE 22.4

Illustration of a
complexity problem.

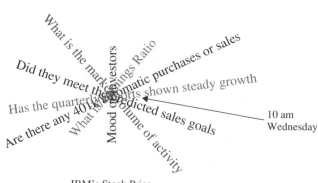

IBM's Stock Price

22.3 Heuristics and Decision Systems

Now that we have covered that patterns can be identified in complex (chaotic) systems using various means, we need to figure out how systems make sense of all this. For this to be possible, the computer system must accomplish an ontological to epistemic transformation, going from determining if data exist to helping humans-in-the-loop determine what the data mean. For this transformation, we must consider whether the questions we ask have a discrete answer or if they pose several possible answers. This is the so-called discrete versus discriminant problem nature. (See for illustration: http://www.dtreg.com.)

22.3.1 Reasoning: Discrete Versus Equivocal Problems

Discrete problems have a single correct solution, such as, how much money do we have left in our security budget at 10 am on July 22? These are discrete because although we may not have all the information we need to know what our budget balance is, there is a single correct answer. The more information we have, such as what monies have we spent this month to date on new security software, the more certain we can be about the correct answer. On the other hand, equivocal problems are those in which there are multiple subjective points of view about a solution or conclusion (although some points of view might be better than others).

Examples of equivocal problems include, should we retaliate against an attacker or seek litigation against a blogger who writes false statements about our company or its managers in order to try to dissuade future attacks? And should private financial institutions receive federal funding to keep them solvent? To resolve the former type of problem, we know that having adequate information will be sufficient to derive the correct solution, but to derive an optimal solution for the latter type of problem, because some solutions tend to be better than others, it requires both context and reasoning in order for us to make inferences or draw appropriate conclusions. Models of reasoning then might be thought of as automated attempts to make a decision or solve an equivocal problem [8].

Reasoning, from a technology perspective, as we have indicated, is a machine that infers about unobservable aspects of a situation based on context and constraints and principles from observed aspects of a situation or condition. For instance, reasoning might be performed to infer a disease or infection from a patient's observable external symptoms, or other information such as X-rays, biopsies, or microbial laboratory studies, or to infer the role of an accused in a crime based on forensic evidence, or to determine the possible intentions of an enemy force based on available intelligence [9, 10].

A number of formalisms for automated reasoning have been developed, ranging from **description logics** to **probability theories**. The choice of the strategy employed is designed to fit the desired outcome or objective. However, the reasoning theorem can be viewed in a general form: Given (1) the context and constraints about an observed phenomenon and (2) some knowledge about the unobserved aspects of the phenomenon, (3) determine conclusions about the unobserved aspects of the phenomenon.

> **In Focus**
>
> Algorithms are a set of rules that are programmed and are inflexible. Objective heuristics are rules of thumb that apply a normative rule (an optimal solution for a given situation), and subjective heuristics are "judgments" people make—right or wrong.

Depending on the nature and type of the observable information, and the objective of the reasoning, the task can be stated in a more refined manner. For example, when *first-order predicate logic* is used for representing the problem, the reasoning may be restated: Given (1) observed aspects of the phenomenon in terms of truth-values (algorithmically) or fuzzy values (probabilistically) for some predicates and (2) domain knowledge in the form of principles using first-order predicate logic, (3) determine truth-values or probabilities for the meaning of the phenomenon.

Many decision-making tasks, particularly those that are of an equivocal nature (where multiple subjective points of view about solutions are involved) demand more than inference about an unobserved aspect of a situation. These tasks demand that the reasoning generate either a hypothesis or an explanation to justify the unobserved events. For example, given some symptoms, a psychological reasoning system may be asked to hypothesize a diagnosis about a patient's psychological disorder, or to propose a stock price for IBM's stock on Wednesday at 10 am for a stock day trader, or suggest parameters of a security attack based on known aspects of common attack architecture. These hypotheses can sometimes be more useful than knowing just the probability of the psychological disorder or the stock price on a given day in the future or the specific nature of a security attack [11].

22.3.2 Synthetic Heuristics

Heuristics are rules of thumb—that is, they are not programmable, but are more educated guesses. Churchman [9] introduced the concept of heuristic reasoning and types of logical inquiry systems important to reasoning models, and he constructed these models based on the viewpoints of various philosophers such as Leibniz, Locke, Kant, Hegel, and Singer. Many information systems have often based their heuristic reasoning on Churchman's framework [12].

When viewed in the context of these models, problems are better framed to provide insight into the reasoning processes. Two primitives Churchman used are the concepts of innate ideas and inputs. Innate ideas are principles or theoretical truths about a phenomenon in which a reasoning machine would assume. The inputs are the experimental observations made by an "observer," which can be either a person or a program. A fact-net is an interconnection of inputs and innate ideas constructed by means of a given set of relations and operators. A fact-net is therefore a network of contingent truths, which are inquired of by an inquirer [13].

The **Leibnizian** heuristic aims at constructing an optimal fact-net for a situation. In this model, optimization means that for any given set of inputs, it can construct any number of correlated fact-nets. In other words, the heuristic develops the relationships and the operators that tie together a result in the form of a fact-net that corresponds to the innate ideas of an inquirer. It is implemented as a *theorem-proving* and *problem-solving* machine, where the primitives, axioms, and inference rules of the logic are the innate ideas, and the various principles form the inputs.

The inquirer (called the theorem prover in this model) creates a network containing consistent "proofs" or assertions, and if there are any conflicts, some sort of "resolver" is needed. In stochastic modeling systems, for example, weighted constraints are often used for this purpose. For instance, if an alternative were chosen based on two opposing constraints (e.g., cost versus quality), the resolver would incorporate a variable weight to resolve the conflict (e.g., weight cost = 0.4 and quality = 0.8). A Leibnizian system thus assumes the existence of a *determinable* optimal solution for a situation, and it attempts to configure its inputs from the situation according to that model.

The **Lockean** heuristic is inductive, in that it builds representations of what is called a "worldview" from shared distributed "observer" systems. Like other heuristics, observers may be human or automated. As an example, suppose a sensor on system A detects anomalous activity compared to what it has observed in the past. System A then shares this information with another trusted observer, System B. If System B observes the same as being an anomaly, they build a shared *worldview* that the sensors have detected unusual activity.

In other words, the heuristic makes elementary observations from input sources and feeds them to an inquirer engine that is shared with each of the observers. The observations have labels and properties that the heuristic assigns to the inputs. The Lockean system is also capable of observing its own process by means of reflection and backward tracing of labels. This *worldview* is therefore developed from shared observations by observers and categorization of learned information from observations, and these collectively create a consensus *worldview* about what has been observed, and then what the affected system should do in response.

The **Kantian** heuristic is a synthesis type of system, building on the Liebnizian system, but it does not presuppose the existence of an *observable* model or situation. The Kantian model uses a clock-event, to enable the inquirer to observe the inputs in its environment. To bootstrap, the Kantian heuristic contains a set of default fact-nets. Each fact-net is an independent set of innate ideas and may contain its primitives, axioms, and rules of inference. An inquirer then selects one from the available set, and then builds a Liebnizian fact-net using the inputs and the innate ideas of this model. The inquirer then determines the extent to which this fact-net is "satisfactory" according to some criterion. The model then generates the most "satisfactory" fact-net, which is proposed as the solution.

Probably the most useful set of heuristics in terms of attack incident prediction is the **Hegelian** approach. This seeks to develop the ability to determine the same inputs from different points of view. The inquirer poses a number of fact-net models, each of which is an independent set of innate ideas and may contain primitives, axioms, and rules of inference. The inquirer selects a thesis for view A from a set, and undertakes to construct a "case" for supporting thesis A, in effect, a defense of thesis A. The next stage of the heuristic seeks to find a thesis for view A that is an antithesis for view B. The inquirer selects a thesis for view B that is the antithesis for view A, and also finds a model that supports B. B does not have to be a logical negation of A. For example, in the context of some battlefield intelligence information, if the thesis is that a "target will be destroyed," the antithesis may be "the attacking army will be destroyed" instead of "target will not be destroyed."

The next action in a Hegelian approach is to observe the two models and the elements that comprise the problem space, examine support for the thesis and the antithesis, and then assess the sources of conflict between them. It is expected that the attempts to understand or resolve these conflicts would lead the heuristic toward the actual (or "real") situation. The larger model of the situation in the context of which the conflict can be understood is called the synthetic model of the situation. Churchman suggested that knowledge does not reside in the collection of information or in the inference done by the system, and underscored the importance of humans-in-the-loop in knowledge and meaning creation.

Churchman's emphasis on the human nature of knowledge and meaning creation is important, but it should not be ignored that systems are capable of dealing with a wide range of potential surprises by eliminating human bias. For example, the "availability bias" [5] is one where human beings overestimate the probability of an event if they frequently read about such an event. Such an environment defeats the traditional organizational response of predicting and reacting to an event based on pre-programmed heuristics. Instead, it demands more anticipatory responses from the organizational members who need to carry out actions faster in advance of possible disastrous episodes.

22.3.3 Issues with Synthetic Heuristic Systems

Many of the systems in place today are based upon heuristics about problems that have well-defined parameters or are amenable to mathematical modeling and programmed logic. They capture "preferred" solutions to the given repertoire of problems that represent well-known situations for which there exists a strong consensual position on the nature of the problem and agreement on the situation, and they rely on well-structured problems for which there exists an analytic formulation with a solution. Types of heuristic systems such as the Leibnizian are closed systems without access to an "external" environment, similar to the problem of how data warehouses work and are confined. That is, they operate based on supplied axioms that may fall into categories based on the system's previous experience or labeling (topic tagging).

In contrast, Lockean systems aim to reduce equivocality embedded in the diverse interpretations of a *worldview*, but there too, success depends on consensus among systems. The convergent and consensus-building emphasis of these kinds of heuristic systems is suited for stable and predictable situations or environments. However, complex systems require variety and agility in the interpretations, which are necessary for deciphering equivocal problems with multiple subjective points of view about an unpredictable future. The Kantian inquiry system attempts to give multiple explicit views of a complementary nature that are best suited for moderate ill-structured problems. However, given that there is no explicit opposition to the multiple views, these systems may also be afflicted by conflicts characterized by plurality of complementary solutions. In contrast, Hegelian inquiry systems are based on a synthesis of multiple synthetic and antithetical representations of conflicts with contrary underlying assumptions. Reasoning systems that model unconventional attack episodes are most suited to analysis with Hegelian inquiry systems, which would facilitate multiple and contradictory interpretations of the focal information. This would help ensure that the focal information is subjected to continual reexamination and modification given a changing reality.

Earlier, we mentioned that reasoning systems may work together to provide a full life cycle modeling technique of information security attacks. The techniques a reasoning system may employ vary from simple, such as the coincidence of determination presented in our discussion about the breaking of the Vigenere cipher to find patterns among various models, to extremely complex such as just described using heuristics. In most cases, reasoning systems produce models that can be rearranged, such as using first-order predicate logic to develop a sequence of probable moves in an attack episode. Next we will examine some ways this might be done.

22.3.4 Combining Techniques

We covered synthetic heuristics and how these can be used for drawing inferences from available data, and we examined stochastic game theory and techniques that can be used by attack modeling and intrusion detection systems to make predictions about an attack. These can be used in combination. Consider a situation where we might want to predict a terror attack episode, and then consider specific various attacks. In such a modeling architecture, we would have two stages that are comprised of multiple steps.

In stage one, we would first choose a probabilistic approach to mine patterns out of mass data. These data may come from many sources, including military or intelligence feeds into a data warehouse or ontology. Consider for example the Common Vulnerabilities and Exposures (CVE) ontology developed and supported by the Mitre Corporation. The CVE is a collection and information store that can be imported into security applications. (We will discuss the CVE in more detail in Chapter 23 when we cover the topic of adaptive security.) Once we have gathered these data, we can use a variety of statistical techniques, such as ***affinity analysis***, to mine out the patterns or correlations. We can parse the constituent elements from these patterns and divide and index them into categories or types. These generally result in an ontology containing subject, object, predicate, and constraints and rules. The ontology would likely consist of a markup language, such as OWL, and contain all the major components to assemble a predictive security game.

A representative example of such an approach is called KAoS [14]. KAoS is an ontology that is used for specifying security policy models. To give a simple example, a partial OWL ontology could include a security `Risk` of which `Intrusion` and `Disaster` are subclasses; the OWL would appear as follows:

```
<owl:Class rdf:ID="Risk">
 <rdfs:subClassOf rdf:resource="Intrusion"/>
 <rdfs:subClassOf rdf:resource="Disaster"/>
</owl:Class>
```

From the ontology, we next may apply heuristics to parse through the ontology to develop various attack scenarios. Using the Hegelian approach, the system would build antithesis fact-nets that would refute attack episodes, and thesis fact-nets that would suggest attack episodes. The fact-nets are analyzed using stochastic algorithms, seeding unknown variables randomly, and producing synthesis fact-nets and scenarios (**Figures 22.5** and **22.6**).

Using the nouns and verbs in subject-object associations assembled into the synthesis fact-nets, we can now build sets of probability-based attack episodes. Episodes may consist of narratives that describe possible causal and inferential relationships along with an overall probability of the episode, and then each attack episode is assembled into a CTMC using the predicates and constraints, and with statistically computed paths through the possible moves. Building such models in this way may help organizations to concentrate their limited resources in the most likely scenarios at the most likely junctures to thwart attacks. These also serve to highlight possible attacks that were not considered because they can neutralize "groupthink" and indicate completely novel approaches. Groupthink

FIGURE 22.5

Pattern detection and ontological indexing.

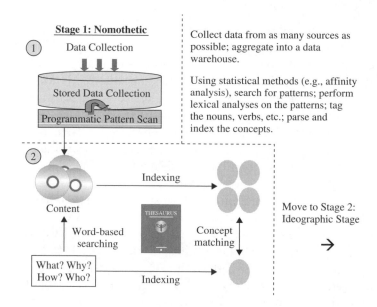

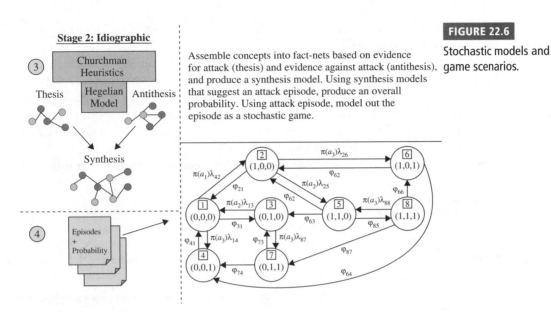

FIGURE 22.6

Stochastic models and
game scenarios.

Assemble concepts into fact-nets based on evidence
for attack (thesis) and evidence against attack (antithesis),
and produce a synthesis model. Using synthesis models
that suggest an attack episode, produce an overall
probability. Using attack episode, model out the
episode as a stochastic game.

is a situation where one goes along with a decision because of peer pressure or because
the "group" thinks it's a good idea.

22.4 Heuristic Biases and Security Planning

As we have presented, managers and other decision-makers typically have at their
disposal decision support and reasoning systems (decision systems) that can generate
probabilistic estimates and provide recommendations for courses of action, yet sometimes
people choose intuition over information and evidence provided by these technologies.
A study by Workman [15], for example, showed that some people ignore the recommendations of decision systems even when the systems are shown to be effective in reducing
the number of human-induced errors. This can lead to unfortunate consequences and
poor decisions.

22.4.1 Decisions, Naïve Theories, and Biases

Using decision systems, managers often follow a set of tasks that include analytical
modeling, generating what-if scenarios, performing sensitivity analyses, conducting goal-
seeking analyses, and doing optimization analyses. In what-if analyses, a person makes
changes to, or relationships among variables and then observes the resulting changes in
the values. With sensitivity analysis, a value of a single variable is changed repeatedly,
and the resulting changes on other variables are observed. Goal-seeking analysis reverses
the direction of what-if analysis. It sets a target value (a goal) for a variable and then
repeatedly changes other variables until the target value is achieved. Finally, optimization
analysis is a complex extension of goal-seeking analysis; however, instead of setting a

specific target value for a variable, it seeks to find the optimum value for one or more target variables given certain constraints [16].

   Decision systems have to date been geared to produce normative recommendations [17] using rational decision-making models [18] such as Bayesian probability trees, or based on economic factors such as estimations of returns on investments and payback periods [19]. Normative rules are those designed to give an optimal solution given a problem and constraints, and the optimal solution may be a straddle point. A straddle point is a mathematical computation that arrives at the best compromise given competing or opposing goals. However, managers sometimes choose to rely on their intuition, which is formally called a naïve theory [20].

> **In Focus**
>
> Naïve theories are normal and necessary. These "theories" are how we conduct our daily lives. For example, we count on the sun rising each morning because it has always been so throughout our lives. Were it not for naïve theories, we could not plan on anything to do anything. However, naïve theories are often wrong about the causal explanation of events.

   The use of the term naïve in this context is not derogatory, nor does it mean irrational, nor does it mean they are necessarily incorrect; rather the term refers to decisions that are not based on scientific or structured decision processes [21, 22]. An example of this was illustrated with a survey by Business Objects [23] in which 43 percent of the respondent managers said they made decisions based on "gut feeling" at least 50 percent of the time. Naïve theories are theories all people have about the workings of activities and events without operationalizing and testing these theories, and they rely on their perceptions and experiences for judgments [24].

   With decision systems and normative, rational models, the probabilities of future outcomes are computed, but managers often do not trust the computations beyond a relatively short horizon, especially when they are under emotional and/or psychological pressure, and under those conditions, people switch to naïve heuristics and may draw wrong conclusions even in the face of disconfirming evidence [15]. Recall that a heuristic is a rule of thumb as opposed to a formal, specified rule. It is an informal strategy or approach that works under some circumstances for some of the time, but is not guaranteed to yield the correct decision. Moreover, this form of *educated guessing* is prone to distortions, inaccuracies, and omissions because of human biases [25].

> **In Focus**
>
> Bias does not necessarily lead to an incorrect decision. In fact, sometimes biased "intuition" can be helpful, such as "sensing" to avoid a dangerous situation without having previously experienced it.

An example of human bias is that people often act as though the uncontrollable is controllable. For instance, people bet more money on games of chance when their opponent seems incompetent because they believe they can take advantage of a weaker opponent [26]. People will wager more money on a fair dice roll if they roll the dice themselves rather than their opponent rolling them [27]. They will gamble more money if the dice have not been rolled than on dice that have been rolled but where the outcome has not been disclosed [28], and they bet more money if they choose the number of the dice that will count to win [27]. A large majority of people feel more certain they will win a lottery if they choose the numbers on their ticket rather than using a machine-generated "quick pick" [26].

Biases also account for why many people will spend more money on gasoline and automobile wear to drive across town to save a small amount on an item on sale, when the normative rule would dictate that it would be cheaper to drive less and pay more for the item. Biases also include the false assumption that past success makes a good predictor of future success [29]. Heuristic bias also explains non-rational financial escalations and over-commitments regardless of "sunk costs" commonly called *pouring good money after bad*, or believing in "shooting streaks" in the game of basketball [30]. Heuristic bias was demonstrated by Kahneman and Tversky [5] in their research in which they established that people often subjectively judge the likelihood of uncertain events based on extemporaneous patterns observed, even if they are aware of how to calculate a statistical probability. As a simple example of this cognitive phenomenon, they showed that some people often judge fair coin tosses with a pattern HHTHTT to be more random than one that is HHHTTT even though the probability for these outcomes is identical. Ajzen [31] showed the impact from these kinds of biases in a study in which base-rate neglect was found to be less likely when the data are seen in a complex causal relationship compared to a simple statistical task. Base rate neglect is the condition where given two relevant but independent probabilities of an event, less weight is given to the first probability, whereas the normative rule is to combine them.

Many methods used in helping organizations make effective security decisions rely on socially constructed and heuristic processes rather than on the use of mathematical technologies and techniques such as decision systems, Bayesian analyses, or stochastic modeling. These more socially and creatively constructed approaches are important to security because security threats are typically not well defined beyond a short horizon, and some security decisions are not very amenable to quantitative approaches, such as whether or not to conduct employee surveillance. However, biases in decision making can have very undesirable consequences.

Thibaut and Kelley's [32] work on prospect theory showed that biases can lead to very strange decisions. This point was illustrated by their description of two suspects of a crime who were offered "deals" if one would testify against the other (the prisoner's dilemma). The mindset was captured by one of the suspects who stated that "I'd rather we both hang than you get off easier than me." In a study by Loewenstein and Prelec [33], they found that when participants were asked if they preferred a job where they earned $30,000 the first year, $40,000 the second year, and $50,000 the third year, or whether they preferred a job that paid $60,000 the first year, then $50,000, then $40,000, the majority of participants picked the first job option even though this yielded less money over 3 years. This bias problem was exacerbated when involving complex decisions, such as security expenditures or threat analyses, that span more than a couple of years.

22.4.2 Interactions of Biases and Framing Effects

We have now studied how decision and reasoning systems may produce scenarios of attack episodes for managers to use in planning. Managers are also taught to use techniques for planning using ideational generation activities such as brainstorming. For example, Tyler [34] described the use of "storytelling" as a method for advancing organizational goals such as in planning security initiatives. Other security planning techniques include developing *affinity diagrams*, which are used to sort ideas or problems into themes or categories, using brainstorming or brain-writing, where participants generate ideas that are shared in a round-robin fashion, and "visioning" in which participants are taught to vicariously experience an event or outcome in order to come up with more realistic responses. It is important to note that the efficacy of these methods depends on how the information is ***framed***. Framing effects [5] are conditions where people's decisions are influenced by how a problem is described, or framed.

Framing of information activates cognitive schema that may have either a positive or negative association [35]. Cognitive schemas are mental scripts based on the association of concepts. As an example, when the word "restaurant" is said, people have a particular script they associate with eating at a restaurant, for instance one is served food in exchange for payment. The cognitive script changes if the modifier "fast food" is used in conjunction with restaurant. Typically people downgrade their assessment of the quality of food served by a restaurant when predicated by "fast" food restaurant. To further illustrate this point, when a scenario is presented to people about a pharmaceutical used to treat a disease, people evoke different cognitive schema depending on how the information is framed; for instance, people have more positive assessments of the pharmaceutical when the term "lives saved" is used than when "lives lost" is used [36].

Research [37] has shown that managers and employees in general tend to rely more on intuition in decision making after having participated in a planning session that used ideational generation techniques such as scenarios and characterizations of problems and solutions. Nevertheless, some people are more prone to framing influences than others. Those that tend to avoid "being biased by the frame can be said to follow the normative rule [and] people who use the frame [either positively or negatively framed] can be said to commit a heuristic bias" [38]. Consequently, the critical issue in using ideational generation techniques in security planning is in the interactions of biases and framing effects, and the implications this has for managers "going with gut instinct" over objective data or following a normative rule.

22.4.3 Biases, Framing Effects, and Security Decisions

Because naïve theories are derived from one's belief system, biases may interfere with judgments and decision making about security issues, including the probability of various attack scenarios [39]. "Belief-consistent hypotheses are constructed with confirmation rather than falsification as the primary goal, and consequently, belief-relevant evidence is interpreted, dismissed, or reinterpreted as a function of consistency of that evidence with the individual's original theory" [40]. As an example, studies [40, 41] have shown that hypothetical arguments are classified as correct or incorrect as a function of the consistency between the arguments' conclusions and the participants' beliefs. Because these biases may create fallibility in judgments, they may be less reliable in terms of solving complex problems using a normative rule.

There are at least four biases that are of particular importance to managers in relation to security attack scenarios, risk analyses, and future security initiative planning: (1) risk tolerance, (2) overconfidence, (3) anchoring and adjustment, and (4) expected utility in forecasting. A risk assessment involves the cognitive evaluation of the risk of a loss one will accept relative to perceived payoffs from success. People differ in their risk tolerance or acceptance; some have low thresholds when there is high uncertainty, but in many cases people experience greater risk tolerance because they underestimate the risks. Overconfidence is based on the false notion that past success makes a good predictor of future success. If one has been successful predicting a security episode in the past, there is an amplified belief that one will be successful in predicting security issues in the future, even though the circumstances may be radically different.

Anchoring involves using a subjective reference point or focusing on one aspect of an event or incident over other important aspects; the adjustment is an evaluative projection of outcomes based on that anchor. It combines with expectancies of an outcome as a pairing of a possible outcome with a plausible causal event (a conjunction) or with under-estimations of the cumulative probabilities of interdependent components of an event (a disjunction). Finally, the expected utility in forecasting is fallacious reasoning about choices involving the prospect of high gains and small losses, regardless of probabilities of the event that would produce gains or losses.

Each of these biases can influence whether managers become too cautionary with security, spending more time and money on security initiatives than is normatively warranted, or are too risky in their behavior, spending less than is normatively warranted. Thus in planning security attack scenarios or in security initiative planning in general, managers need to be mindful of framing effects and biases, and strive to avoid "leading" people into a foregone conclusion; during any modeling or planning sessions or assessments about security, managers should contrast creative ideas with normative rules.

CHAPTER SUMMARY

In this chapter, we covered some reasoning techniques for predicting attack episodes. We considered how models are developed and analyzed by using the ontological to epistemic transformation. We examined a variety of heuristics that can be used to define criteria, draw inferences, and formulate responses related to possible attacks. These techniques narrow the problem space into a manageable set of "possibilities," which can be combined with modeling approaches to develop our contingency plans and actions. Managers in modern organizations have broad responsibilities in terms of defining security policies and managing their organizations securely. Managerial responsibilities include directing and overseeing personnel, administrating security procedures and processes, conducting risk assessments and managing risks, and ensuring that incidents are addressed effectively. The skills to do this will rely on technical knowledge as well. Beyond these fundamentals, managers have a social responsibility, and this means seeing security initiatives with a wider lens than has been required in the past, but managers should be careful about the use of heuristics by taking biases and framing effects into account. In the next chapter, we will discuss how systems themselves are becoming more intelligent, adaptive, and self-organizing: in other words, we will present how systems and security are following the *general systems theory* prescriptions to become more like organic systems.

THINK ABOUT IT

Topic Questions

22.1: Both in reliability analysis and models of attack architecture, the _____ approach is a common and useful way to model possible attack paths through a directed acyclic flow graph.

22.2: A _____ heuristic system builds a synthesis model out of a thesis and antithesis.

22.3: The _____ approach is a statistical method used for identifying patterns and making generalizations.

22.4: A nomothetic method works from general principles to imply specific predictions.

____ True
____ False

22.5: An ideographic method works from general principles to imply specific predictions.

____ True
____ False

THINK ABOUT IT (CONTINUED)

22.6: An ideographic approach to modeling tries to identify all factors in a set and then model them for prediction.

____ True
____ False

22.7: A nomothetic method of prediction can only generalize all factors in a set such that situation X is likely to produce a condition Y.

____ True
____ False

22.8: Deductive logic assumes that an outcome is probably true if premises are assumed true.

____ True
____ False

22.9: Inductive logic assumes that an outcome is probably true if premises are assumed true.

____ True
____ False

22.10: The difference between data and information is:

____ Meaning
____ Context
____ Data mining technology
____ OLAP

Questions for Further Study

Q22.1: Find at least one other example of where game theory is used in a security situation and explain it.

Q22.2: Discuss some of the key differences and strengths and weaknesses of a heuristic approach to making determinations and predictions about some future event versus an algorithmic approach.

Q22.3: Joseph Fourier developed theorems in what are called Fourier analysis. The theorems (especially transformation) have been used widely in computer science for such things as data compression. Discuss some ways that these can be extended to make sense of complex systems.

Q22.4: List two commercially available security modeling technologies, and briefly describe how they work.

Q22.5: What is the difference between a decision and an inference? Explain your answer.

KEY CONCEPTS AND TERMS

Bounded population means a defined grouping by a definable category or characteristic.

Hegelian model builds a synthesis model out of a thesis and an antithesis.

Information richness means the capacity of a medium to carry data, and not how humans interpret what they receive from the medium.

Naïve theories are ideas we all have about the workings of things without scientifically testing them.

Normative rule is a calculated optimal solution to a problem based on the criteria presented and the constraints known.

Statistics can make general claims, but not ones that are specific to individuals.

References

1. Rapoport, A., & Chammah, A. (1965). *Prisoner's dilemma*. Ann Arbor: University of Michigan Press.
2. Kelley, H. H., & Thibaut, J. (1978) *Interpersonal relations: A theory of interdependence*, New York, NY: John Wiley & Sons.
3. Sallhammar, K, Helvik, B. E., & Knapskog, S. J. (2005). *Incorporating attacker behavior in stochastic models of security*. Las Vegas, NV: Proceedings of the World Conference on Security Management and Applied Computing, 122–134.
4. Scheibe, E. (1973). *The logical analysis of quantum mechanics*. Oxford, UK: Pergamon.
5. Kahneman, D., & Tversky, A. (1972). Subjective probability: A judgment of representativeness. *Cognitive Psychology, 3*, 430–454.
6. Meredith, J. R., & Mantel, S. J. (2009). *Project management: A managerial approach*. New York, NY: John Wiley & Sons.
7. Bohm, D. (1990). *Creativity, natural philosophy, and science*. London, UK: New Dimensions.
8. Daft, R. L., Lengel, R. H., & Trevino, L. K. (1987, September). Message equivocality, media selection, and manager performance: Implications for information systems. *MIS Quarterly*, pp. 355–366.
9. Churchman, C. W. (1971). *The design of inquiring systems*. New York, NY: Basic Books.
10. Sikder, I. U. (2008). Discovering decision heuristics in collaborative planning. *International Journal of Management and Decision Making, 9*, 1–15.
11. Workman, M., Bommer, W., & Straub, D. (2008). Security lapses and the omission of information security measures: An empirical test of the threat control model, *Journal of Computers in Human Behavior, 24*, 2799–2816.
12. Linden, L. P., Kuhn, J. R., Parrish, J. L., Richardson, S. M., Adams, L. A., Elgarah, W., & Courtney, J. F. (2007). Churchman's inquiring systems: Kernel theories for knowledge management. *Communications of the Association of Information Systems, 20*, 836–871.
13. Waisel, L. B., Wallace, W. A., & Willemain, T. R. (1999). Visualizing modeling heuristics: An exploratory study. Proceedings of the 20th international conference on Information Systems, ICIS '99.
14. Uszok, A., Bradshaw, J. M., & Jeffers, R. (2004). *KAoS: A policy and domain services framework for grid computing and semantic web services*. In Proceedings of the Second International Conference on Trust Management (iTrust 2004), Springer-Verlag.
15. Workman, M. (2005). Expert decision support system use, disuse, and misuse: A study using the theory of planned behavior. *Journal of Computers in Human Behavior, 21*, 211–231.
16. Workman, M. (2007). Advancements in technology: New opportunities to investigate factors contributing to differential technology and information use. *International Journal of Management and Decision Making, 8*, 221–240.
17. von Neumann, J., & Morgenstern, O. (1947). *Theory of games and economic behavior*. Princeton, NJ: Princeton University Press.

18. Baron, J. (1988). *Thinking and reasoning.* Cambridge, UK: Cambridge University Press.

19. Wijnberg, N. M., van den Ende, J., & de Wit, O. (2002). Decision making at different levels of the organization and the impact of new information technology. *Group & Organization Management, 27,* 408–429.

20. Larrick, R., Morgan, J., & Nisbett, R. (1990). Teaching the use of cost-benefit reasoning in everyday life. *Psychological Science, 1,* 362–370.

21. Bjorklund, D. F. (1995). *Information processing approaches: An introduction to cognitive development.* Washington, DC: Brooks-Cole.

22. Wegener, D. T., & Petty, R. E. (1997). The flexible correction model: The role of naive theories of bias in bias correction. *Advances in Experimental Social Psychology, 29,* 141–208.

23. Business Objects (2004, May). *The fact gap: Disconnect between data and decisions.* Retrieved August 11, 2009, from http://www.bitpipe.com/detail/RES/1090433718_555 .html

24. Kahneman, D., Slovic, P., & Tvsersy, A. (1982). *Judgment under uncertainty: Heuristics and biases.* New York, NY: Cambridge University Press.

25. Pollatsek, A., Konold, C. E., Well, A. D., & Lima, S. D. (1984). Beliefs underlying random sampling. *Memory & Cognition, 12,* 395–401.

26. Langer, E. J. (1975). The illusion of control. *Journal of Personality and Social Psychology, 32,* 311–328.

27. Dunn, D. S., & Wilson, T. D. (1991). When the stakes are high: A limit to the illusion of control effect. *Social Cognition, 8,* 305–323.

28. Strickland, L. H., Lewicki, R. J., & Katz, A. M. (1966). Temporal orientation and perceived control as determinants of risk taking. *Journal of Experimental Social Psychology, 2,* 143–151.

29. Simon, M., & Houghton, S. M. (2003). The relationship between overconfidence and the introduction of risky products: Evidence from a field study. *Academy of Management Journal, 46,* 139–149.

30. Gillovich, T., Vallone, R., & Tversky, A. (1985). The hot hand in basketball: On the misperception of random sequences. *Cognitive Psychology, 17,* 295–314.

31. Ajzen, I. (1977). Intuitive theories of events and the effects of base rate information in prediction. *Journal of Personality and Social Psychology, 35,* 303–314.

32. Thibaut, J., & Kelley, H. (2005). Social exchange theory. In E. Griffin (Ed.), *A first look at communication theory* (pp. 196–206). New York, NY: McGraw-Hill, Inc.

33. Loewenstein, G., & Prelec, D. (1992). Anomalies in intertemporal choice: Evidence and an interpretation. *Quarterly Journal of Economics, 107,* 573–598.

34. Tyler, J. A. (2007). Incorporating storytelling into practice: How HRD practitioners foster strategic story telling. *Human Resource Development Quarterly, 18,* 559–587.

35. Ashcraft, M. H. (1989). *Human memory and cognition.* Boston, MA: Scott, Foresman & Company.

36. Baldwin, W. L., Bowman, J. P., & Courtney, R. (2009). Who will volunteer to be the sacrificial lamb today? The doctrine of economic bailout, the American "tax-poorer"

and fiscal policies from Carter to Obama in the struggle for redistribution of wealth in America. *Contemporary Economics and Socio-Political Policy Issues, Monograph 3,* 122–189.

37. Chermack, T. J., & Nimon, K. (2008). The effects of scenario planning on participant decision-making style. *Human Resource Development Quarterly, 19,* 351–372.

38. Poulton, E. C. (1994). *Behavioral decision theory.* Cambridge, UK: Cambridge University Press.

39. Morris, M. G., & Venkatesh, V. (2000). Age differences in technology adoption decisions: Implications for a changing work force. *Personnel Psychology, 53,* 365–401.

40. Klaczynski, P. A., & Narasimham, G. (1998). Development of scientific reasoning biases: Cognitive versus ego-protective explanations. *Developmental Psychology, 34,* 173–187.

41. Stanovich, K. E., & West, R. F. (1999). Discrepancies between normative and descriptive models of decision making and the understanding/acceptance principle. *Cognitive Psychology, 38,* 349–385.

Adaptive Systems Security

WE HAVE COVERED A BREADTH OF INFORMATION security issues and have done a few "deep dives" into some key topics to give you a good understanding of information security. To become well equipped in the security realm, you will need to continue your study at an even deeper level for each of the four areas we have covered in our textbook. You may want to pick a specialty in one of the four areas and focus on that to help you master it. Or, you may wish to remain a generalist—as is often the case with managers. In this chapter, we will explore adaptive systems and security.

In the past, security defenses have been geared toward building fortified systems, and then focused on detection and recovery from damage. In the previous chapter, we covered some ways that computer scientists are working toward creating systems that can reason and draw inferences about security incidents to make predictions. Deriving from human biology and sociology, newer security systems are aimed at resilience and adaptation. This is called socio-biologically inspired security.

Chapter 23 Topics

This chapter:

- Introduces the "trusted kernel" approach to security.
- Describes how human biology and sociology are influencing security systems of tomorrow.
- Explains ontology and agents for security on the horizon.

Chapter 23 Goals

When you finish this chapter, you should:

- ❏ Have an understanding of some of the ways that biologically inspired security is implemented, particularly with mobile device networks such as those that support laptops and smart phones.
- ❏ Know some differences between trusted security kernels, security ontologies, and agent frameworks.
- ❏ Be familiar with social exchange and agency in resilient security systems.
- ❏ Understand what is meant by socio-biologically inspired adaptive systems.

23.1 Biologically Inspired Security

A new approach to security uses the human body as a metaphor in terms of building more adaptive and resilient systems, particularly in light of the fact that many systems are mobile, such as laptops, smart phones, and other devices that are connected to what is called a mobile ad-hoc network (MANET). These systems are expected to sustain some damage, but they have the ability to recover (recuperate) from infections and develop synthetic immunization. The idea of detecting system damage was developed from danger theory [1], which explains the response of mammalian immune systems when danger such as a virus or bacterium is detected. Using that analogy in computing systems, we can, for example, examine system executable files, and the linkages from one file to another in a calling sequence, along with the change events or state transitions, or code changes, and infer causes [2]. In this section, we will introduce the concept of biologically inspired security, especially as it fits into a cooperative communications infrastructure with mobile devices, peer-to-peer (P2P), and MANETs.

23.1.1 Self-Healing Systems

Traditionally, adaptive systems have meant those systems that have self-healing capabilities. The term "self-healing" means the ability for a system to recover from damage. Just as there are different ways that systems adapt to their environments, there are also many mechanisms systems use for healing or repairing themselves. Many self-healing systems apply a model commonly called *susceptible-infected-susceptible* (SIS). Each node or agent in this model represents a system or device, and each connection is a pathway through which an infection can spread. Individual nodes exist in one of a number of states, as mentioned in the previous chapter, such as "compromised," "secure," "infected," or "susceptible." With each node that becomes compromised or infected, the rate at which other systems become compromised or infected increases dramatically [3].

Until recently, self-healing has relied mainly on traditional security architecture, providing firewalls that can react to attacks and warn of risky behaviors, having built-in redundancies, standby systems, virus scanners, and recovery utilities. However, the term is evolving to represent more "self-correction" methods including the use of genetic algorithms that can propagate information, optimize systems, and instruct changes in a way that resembles how human genetics interact with (or are expressed based on) their environments. Self-healing then relies on the concept of immunology. Immunization has been classified as passive, active, or a hybrid. Passive immunology is the approach previously mentioned, that is, to use firewalls and virus scanning systems that are capable of repairing damage. Active immunization includes using intrusion detection mechanisms that automatically generate an appropriate response to a given signature or type of intrusion or attack.

However, an interesting addition to this concept was described by Toutonji and Yoo [4] in which they defined an "automated method to detect worm attack, analyze the worm's malicious code, and then generate an anti-worm" (p. 252). In this mechanism, the generated anti-worm would reproduce the behavior as the malicious worm and spread through the network until it could overtake the malicious worm and neutralize it. Nevertheless, they acknowledged that the anti-worm could be reengineered to neutralize defensive systems. As implied then, hybrid immunology is a combination of active and passive approaches, which gives better defense in depth than either passive or active immunology alone, but this too, like other systems, is not completely immune to attacks.

Research into self-healing approaches generally involve discovery of spreading damage. By tracing the damage along the paths through which the damage is occurring, the systems involved might (1) begin to predict the trajectory or the pathways most likely to be affected next, (2) trace back to an original source and decouple (block) the source from the infrastructure, and (3) reroute traffic while systems are repaired, for example by having virus scanners quarantine and repair the damage [5].

In Focus

The biological analogy in computing systems isn't a perfect fit. With a virus or injury, for example, the body may rest, or even go into a coma; it can shut down while healing occurs. Solving the problem while coming to a halt is not an option for a network where communication and information must continue. A network must heal while engaged in its mission [5].

23.1.2 Damage and Danger

Systems, especially as they become increasingly mobile and interconnected with other systems, are expected to operate in dangerous conditions and sustain damage from time to time. The concept of allowing systems to operate in dangerous settings with the recognition that systems may suffer some damage goes against the conventional wisdom that tries to establish bastions. However, building fortifications that depend on fixed sites and predictable configurations is becoming a less viable security approach (a fortress is not very mobile). The dynamic and trust-based nature of the network infrastructure, the heterogeneity of systems and applications, and the lack of centralized coordination of components—are just some of the issues that greatly complicate the use of conventional security mechanisms and techniques.

As a result, security systems designers have embarked on new ways to implement artificial immune systems, which allow mobile computing devices and nodes to participate in dangerous environments where they may receive some damage, but will either continue to operate while self-healing or hand off their work to a trusted peer until the system can recuperate. The analog is of a person who becomes ill and his or her immunology produces antibodies to attack the invading "non-self" pathogens [6]. When ill, a person can develop symptoms, such as a fever, and his or her performance may be degraded, but unless the condition is lethal, the person is able to maintain some level of function.

It is not sufficient, however, for systems to simply respond to infections after the fact. Systems need to be able to determine if danger is present and try to avoid it, but if systems become contaminated, they must recognize when damage has occurred and the type of damage that it has sustained in order to initiate the appropriate artificial immunological response [2]. The difficulty this presents is, given that mobile devices are a social collection in which one device may infect another at any time, how can this be done?

In Focus

Where damage in a biologically inspired security design is similar in concept to the human body's immune system, recognizing danger borrows from how humans interact in their social systems.

Some techniques have used self-contained environments called "trusted security kernels" (TSKs). TSKs have a damage detection engine (DDE), a cause analyzer, and an artificial immune response (AIR) activation [7]; other techniques have used security and configuration ontologies for detecting damage and reputation-based systems for determining danger [2].

23.1.3 Trusted Security Kernels

A TSK relies on a general assumption that as a network evolves, machines (i.e., nodes) accrue changes. These changes may or may not introduce security vulnerabilities. A key challenge with mobile devices in particular is that often they are isolated and unable to query any central repository to determine if a change is benign or malicious. Furthermore, as malware can spread rapidly, as with the "*SQL.Slammer*" worm, systems need to be able to respond to threats autonomously and dynamically reconfigure to adapt [8].

To do this, the TSK monitors the behavior and changes to itself and to its peers, constructing *on-the-fly*, dynamic trust estimates for the different tasks. TSKs can also authenticate the communications with peers. Assuming, for instance, an out-of-channel key exchange between TSKs during the pre-configuration phase, communications between kernels may be assumed to be secure and authenticated for the duration of its use.

It is important to note that security measures at this level are no different than any end-to-end security between applications and are still potentially vulnerable to attacks at the network level, both multi-hop transport and routing. Under these assumptions, the main problem consists of building a secure infrastructure that will create and maintain a trusted computation and communications environment from the node perspective, while supporting dynamic changes in configuration, application, and system settings. The goal is to provide needed flexibility for systems, while at the same time ensuring that potential vulnerabilities are properly identified (or inferred) by peer systems for reporting or behavioral adaptation.

The DDE is central in this role because it monitors mission-critical components in the system to identify degradation or security policy violations that should be classified as "damage" to the system. When an event is identified as damage, a trigger is issued to the **artificial immune response** (**AIR**) component that in turn performs a causal analysis using statistical correlation between previous events and current ones to identify the probable cause(s) of the reported damage. A biologically inspired system has no need to find the exact cause, therefore the system uses a probabilistic technique to allow for uncertainty in its conclusions, and consequently is non-linear in creating adaptive immune responses.

AIR is unique also in that it can receive input from a number of different devices. For example, if a system is experiencing a known attack, such as "ping of death" ICMP packets, the system does not need to rely exclusively on damage-based input. As local nodes adapt to varying environmental conditions, the behavior of the AIR component is affected by the collective system. By comparing local conditions with those of similar peers, the adaptive immune response can spread faster through the network than the damage that may be caused.

In Focus

Some conceptualizations of biologically inspired security consider danger equal to damage. In other words, danger is determined when damage is done—but there are other more proactive ways to determine danger as well.

All that said, aside from the differences in scale in relation to human biological systems, computer systems are far more fragile. Unlike in human biology, a single-bit error in a billion-bit program may cause the system to become completely inoperable. By comparison, biological systems generally require far stronger perturbation in order to fail catastrophically; their failure modes are far more flexible and forgiving than synthetic systems.

Small changes in programs lead to dramatic changes in an outcome. Thus it is unreasonable to expect that one can naively copy biology and obtain a workable solution. Beyond these issues, the limitations of such a system are as follows: (1) It relies on an initial trusted configuration that participates in the communications, which may not be the case when new (and uncontrolled) devices join the network (see for instance the problems of security in peer-to-peer networks: Boella, Sauro, & van der Torre [9]). (2) The TSK might have been compromised in any number of ways; and (3) the configuration is not dynamic. These issues leave incomplete the TSK security solution, although it remains a good concept for future security solutions [10].

23.2 Social Systems

In biological terms, organisms can evolve in their social settings by reorienting their behaviors. For example, we learn to adjust our behavior based on the reactions of others. In most TSK configurations, however, a static behavior (configuration) is both assumed and relied upon. Nevertheless, from a biological perspective, basic self-organization capabilities require that systems participate in forming functional security groups and then making socially acceptable adjustments from the feedback they receive; in other words, we trust some friends more than others based on our experience with them. Ultimately, system security must be able to change according to environmental cues.

In this approach, security policies are constructed using a graphical user interface, and the underlying technology generates the ontology markup (e.g., DAML+OIL or OWL). It then performs policy *deconfliction*, which means to resolve conflicts in the rules that govern the decision making. Conflicts may come about often in terms of access controls. For example, *Bob* is a member of *Group A*, which only has read access privileges to *Resource B*; but because *Bob* is also a manager, he has full read and write access privileges to that resource and thus must make an exception for him. Yet as suggested, there are limitations here as well. Something more is needed to take these nominal elements and determine whether there are malevolent deviations for a normative measure.

23.2.1 Socially Inspired Security

To address the problem of resilience, biological mimicry needs to combine with social approaches to learning about danger, adapting to it, and warning others. Modeling human social interactions in cooperative systems involves the concept of "agency" where systems may share information so as to collectively help trusted friends to avoid danger and relieve some of the workload while a damaged node recuperates (self-heals) from the damage or is taken out of service. Socially inspired security complements biologically inspired security in that it shares its symptoms of illness and methods for recovery with others it trusts.

Bandura [11] described human social interaction in terms of agency, and he defined "agentic transactions" as the phenomenon where people are producers as well as products of their social systems. As such, agents act on three levels: (1) direct personal agency in which an agent has goals, makes plans, and takes steps that are governed by certain rules, (2) proxy agency, in which one relies on others to act on his or her behalf to secure desired goals, and (3) collective agency, which is conducted through socially cooperative and interdependent efforts that affect other agents within a social network.

From a synthetic perspective, Sterne et al. [7] suggested the use of a dynamic hierarchical model in which nodes and services are partitioned up through to an authoritative root. In this configuration, the system relies on clustering to enable scalability, resilience (fault-tolerance), and adaptability to the dynamic environments. Each node in the communicative peer group maintains responsibility for its own security (e.g., from an IDS perspective), as well as some limited responsibility for its adjacent peers, which is summarized and propagated up the authoritative chain. Directives, on the other hand, are passed top-downward.

In a biological analog, designers of inorganic systems have relied on lessons from human immunology to develop genetic algorithms and self-healing systems [6]. In a sociological analog, digital sociologists have relied on principles from social networking that have led to developments such as viral marketing and incentive-based cooperative systems [12]. Taken together, these have inspired modeling agentic security transactions in networked systems, especially in highly interdependent and cooperative systems such as cloud computing, grid computing, peer-to-peer (P2P) networks and mobile ad-hoc networks (MANET). As mobile devices become "smarter"—as in 5G—they will come to more resemble MANETs in their need for security.

In these newer configurations, agents behave socially to exchange information, receive instructions, react to the effects of other agent actions, and provide responses in a cooperative fashion to fulfill individual and collective goals in an adaptable and evolutionary way, while simultaneously healing from and warning others of security violations and violators [9]. For agents to take individual and social action, they must rely on the information they have to make predictions about the consequences of their behavior. In other words, to be proactive, agents require an initial set of knowledge from which agents base their assumptions [13].

> **In Focus**
>
> Even though effective ad-hoc networks require the cooperation of all of the systems in the network, just as most people are cautious around those they don't know, systems can also be cautious by monitoring the behaviors of "new" systems.

Security policies may be learned and generated by running an application in a controlled environment to discover its "normal" behavior (a profile). When run subsequently, the security system monitors the application to determine whether it deviates from this predefined behavior; if so, the application execution is intercepted—for example, if it attempts to make systems calls that are prohibited [14].

Another method is to import into the security policy ontology threat and vulnerability information, such as provided by the common vulnerabilities and exposures (CVE) ontology (see Moreira et al., 2008 [15] for a description), which captures and

FIGURE 23.1

Configuration management ontology.

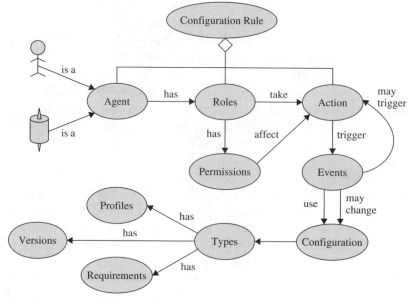

updates with common vulnerabilities and incidents reported by the Software Engineering Institute's CERT and others. Based on these profiles and configuration information, the agent itself may detect damage and then communicate it to an authoritative other (a trusted proxy), or—it may learn of damage or danger by proxy, such as confederated intrusion detection systems [7] that detect changes or monitor events [2] (**Figure 23.1**).

Although proxy agency, such as confederated security, offers some clear benefits, particularly in terms of administration, in highly dynamic and mobile network topologies, this is not always possible. Something more is needed, and to the extent that an agent can understand and manage itself in its environment, the more autonomously it can act (i.e., it relies less on a hierarchy of structures or administrative domains), and when critical information is unknown, it is learned, and this learning is most likely to be derived socially; more specifically, it is learned through collective agency.

23.2.2 Social Systems and Security Adaptation

Although biologically inspired security can be extremely effective in many if not most security systems and network configurations, nodes in a highly interdependent and dynamic configuration create unique challenges that the conventional approach does not address very well in isolation, at least in a static way. For example, in a network that hosts mobile devices, the exchange of information occurs in a flexible topology where devices may join and leave the network in ways that are not predictable.

Paths between any set of communicating devices or nodes may traverse multiple wireless links, which may be comprised of heterogeneous platforms running various applications and consisting of strict limitations, such as in RAM or in network transmission rates. They also vary in their ability to supply underlying security countermeasures such as firewalls, virus scanners, and intrusion detection systems. Eventually, these underlying countermeasures cannot be completely relied upon. Nor is it practical to expect that all nodes will behave in a predictable fashion, or that a centralized or confederated model of security will be able to oversee all of the dynamic activity and respond in an effective and timely manner.

As with human social interaction [16, 17], systems may use the concept of collective agency in which a system assumes certain responsibilities that others rely upon, such as delivering a service at a certain quality of service (QoS) metric. If those responsibilities are not fulfilled, then the agent becomes distrusted by others [12]. It is important to realize that a violation that prohibits a system from living up to a promised QoS metric such as exceeding a latency threshold may not be maliciously caused; it may be a legitimate operation that causes a temporary condition. Nevertheless, a repeated offense would be treated the same as a malicious attack.

Also, in human social systems people tend to trust strangers less than they trust their friends [11]. In making a decision about interacting with a stranger, people often inquire of their friends about the stranger's reputation. In security, this feature is known as a reputation-based system. If friends don't know the stranger, the stranger will not have any reputation. In a highly interdependent network of systems, distrusting systems that have newly joined the network—that is, strangers—can negatively affect the collective performance and availability of information and computing resources because the more systems that cooperate and share the load, the better the performance. Because penalizing a stranger and giving preference to friends discourages participation in a social exchange, an adaptive stranger policy [12] deals with this by requiring each existing peer to compute a ratio of the amount of resources requested by the stranger. If it is less than an established threshold, then the peers will work with the stranger, so long as the stranger does not try to violate a security policy or attempt a known security threat.

In Focus

Damage is not necessarily intentionally caused. Damage may be an unintentional action such as consuming available bandwidth by transferring a large digital file, but doing so degrades system or network performance below an acceptable level. This damages the system or network availability.

If the stranger's request exceeds the threshold, then peers will compute a probability of working with the peer. This probability is used in determining whether the request can be serviced by shared cooperation; throttled back, such as reduced transmission rate, increasing latency, or lowering bandwidth; or deferred to later as a low priority [18]. As devices interact and gain experience with the stranger system, and if the stranger maintains a good reputation over time, the stranger will become a trusted friend—that is unless the stranger inflicts some damage, in which case, the reputation of the stranger will be negatively affected.

Depending on the kind of damage the device inflicts, it may even be labeled an enemy and locked out of the communications. In that case, where a device is determined to be an enemy (an attacker), the enemy may try to rejoin the network as a new stranger—a technique called "white washing." The adaptive stranger policy mitigates this by carefully watching the stranger and sharing reputation experience with trusted "friends." Sometimes trusted friends may try to collude with the attacker by giving the enemy a good reputation, raising the trust of the stranger among the collective nodes. To combat this, each node must carefully watch the resource consumption thresholds and QoS metrics, and only gradually increase trust as a function of the collective experiences of the nodes in the network [2].

23.2.3 Collective Agency, Availability, and Integrity

In the movie *Star Trek*, in "The Wrath of Kahn" episode, Mr. Spock said: "Don't grieve, Admiral. It is logical. The needs of the many outweigh the needs of the few . . . or the one." This is a fitting description of the goal of collective agency. As the designers of the Arpanet envisioned, a survivable network requires the collective effort and redundancy to fulfill an overall objective. In most systems that utilize QoS metrics and local versus remote prioritization, such as scheduling algorithms and routing protocols, a condition known as "selfish link" can occur [19]. A "selfish link" reflects agent actions that lead to a lack of cooperation and undesirable network effects.

Among these issues is "free riding" [2, 19], where an agent disregards its obligations to other agents in favor of self-preservation—for example, to preserve its own compute cycles or communications bandwidth for its own services, such as running local services at the highest priorities and lowering priorities of requests from external nodes. To address these problems, incentive models may be used to encourage more altruistic behaviors—that is, to share resources to better ensure service and resource availability.

To approach the integrity issue, there are three behavioral treatments for collective agency: (1) providing incentives and positive reinforcements for cooperative actions, such as allocating queue preferences to efficient nodes, (2) negative reinforcements, such as sending requests to cause an agent to follow through on an obligation, or to cease malevolent or unintentional damaging behavior, and (3) punishments levied against agents that ignore negative reinforcements or that are violators of a security policy or issue a request that is a known threat. All three approaches are needed to create a resilient environment and preserve the availability and integrity of resources and services [2].

23.3 Socio-Biologically Inspired Security Systems

Adaptive systems security in the future must be able to combine biologically inspired and socially inspired approaches to security, especially given three trends: (1) Computing devices are becoming more compact and mobile, (2) computing devices are increasingly part of sharing resources in a cooperative ad-hoc network, such as in P2P and MANET systems, and (3) computing is becoming more virtual, such as distributed through cloud or grid computing infrastructure, which in many cases may be managed and operated by a third party. Cloud systems may be implemented using Microsoft's Azure or IBM's set of cloud facilities, or used as cloud services provided by Amazon, Google, and others.

Beyond the abilities that system components can monitor themselves and converse with communicative partners, some of which may be considered "close friends," and others acquaintances, and still others strangers, they adjust their behavior accordingly in order to adapt to their environments. At one time an agent may be resident on a familiar "in-house" system, and at another time, it may be distributed to a foreign node in an unfamiliar environment. Security administrators and programmers cannot possibly reconfigure these systems appropriately; the systems must learn their hosted environment and react correctly. With each staging event, such as relocation from one virtual machine to another or from one environment to another, the system (or node) must orient itself to its base configuration; and then it must establish its goals and set its priorities, and begin collecting information about its neighbors.

While making such adjustments, peers may offer incentives for cooperating in a new environment, just as a new employee in the workforce might respond better to a colleague who offers advice rather than one who ignores him or her. Gaining cooperative behavior such as to entice selfish agents to participate is called an *incentive-based security system*, such as giving one node an incentive for routing and forwarding data by giving it preference over others when it makes a request [20, 21]. This method, however, does not discourage malevolent behaviors such as nodes that continue transmissions even after ICMP source quench requests have been made [22]. Still, from this example, danger might be inferred if an agent issues a notification that is subsequently ignored.

In Focus

Rather than waiting for damage to conclude danger, systems can share information to suggest danger, or examine the behavior of other systems in response to a request. A system that continually ignores requests might be considered dangerous.

23.3.1 Novelty as Potential Danger

Given this social interactivity in determining danger and realizing damage to others, the inclusion of a reputation-based system mitigates potential hazards by maintaining and collecting votes from other agents about their favorable or unfavorable history with the requestor. If the requestor has an unfavorable reputation as determined by the agent's local history, an agent may resort to punishing the malevolent requestor by simply adding it to its service prohibitions. On the other hand, if the other agents report an unfavorable reputation, but an agent's local history is favorable, it may choose to allow it, but monitor the behavior of the request, such as its consumption of the agent resources (CPU compute cycles, bandwidth, memory), or attempt to make changes to the configuration, such as copying, modifying, or deleting a file (**Figure 23.2**).

If an agent with a good reputation begins to cause damage to the system, such as through requests of a provider that absorb most or all available resources, the agent may issue negative reinforcement demands that the requester reroute or throttle its requests, and then monitor for compliance and update the reputation history and report to other agents accordingly. If the requestor ignores the demands, the agent may switch to punishments, such as queuing to low priority, for instance, if the request is not a known threat but is exceeding a threshold for some resource such as bandwidth. If a request is

FIGURE 23.2

Reputation management
ontology.

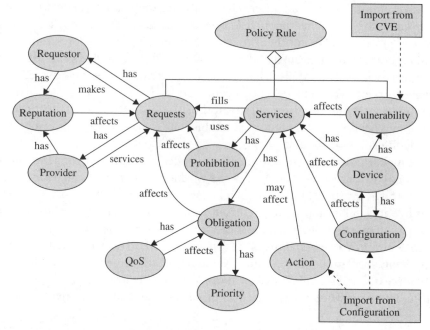

determined to be a threat, then the system would automatically block the attacker agent or drop its packets.

From a security policy perspective, an agent is granted rights according to a given role, but in an ad-hoc communicative environment, rights and roles can be very dynamic. Behavioral role conformance to a well-defined set of behaviors based on allocated rights is the usual case and considered benign. Benign behaviors do not need to consume system resources that need to be closely monitored, because monitoring consumes its own resources. However, when something novel is encountered, it presents potential danger. Novelty may be such that an agent attempts to perform an unauthorized function, or an agent performs an authorized function, but the function attempts to perform some novel behavior. Danger therefore can equate to novelty in terms of security policy enforcement.

From this frame of reference, danger can also be viewed as a continuum on a severe (X coordinate) and imminent (Y coordinate) axis. When danger is encountered, it is monitored according to its coordinates on these axes. A threshold can be set in the continuum in which an intervention may be required to preclude damage from occurring. Damage in this context may be defined as any action that would impinge on mission execution, including negative effects on mission parameters such as exponential consumption of network bandwidth, an application that normally does not copy files tries to copy a file, or negative impact on any QoS parameters needed for successful mission execution.

The structures of the actions could consist of goals, plans, steps, and rules, which are malleable and negotiable. That is, an agent assembles its own set of rules dynamically while reacting to social and environmental events, and selecting appropriate qualifying plans to achieve its current goal. The agent may try other qualifying plans if the initial plan fails, or if events or exceptions cause the agent to change plans. Consequently, agents are adaptive to a given situation in that they select the next plan based on current information that is available, either from the environment or from its local knowledge [13].

23.3.2 Socio-Biological Behavior as Goal-Directed Behavior

The goals at the root of the agent hierarchy consist of the agent's obligations and prohibitions. As a case in point, a goal might be to obligate the agent to provide a web service. Goals consist of plans to execute in order to satisfy the goal; for example, an obligation to provide a web service might require a plan to start httpd on port 8080. Agent behaviors are governed by rules, which might specify that an ActiveX control is not permitted into the web service.

Rules operate on the steps that are part of a plan; thus, if an agent receives an http request containing an ActiveX control, the rule may require steps to discard the request. The choreography of agent actions may be decomposed into three levels: high-level, intermediate, and low-level. Perhaps an agent has multiple goals, and each goal has multiple plans. For example, the goal "maintain current version levels of applications," may have a high-level plan entitled: "Version Updates." For this high-level plan, there are intermediate plans that perform a sequence of steps and tasks, and log data updates, such as, "Automatic Update AcroRd32.exe" may require a network connection to be opened and a file download from the Adobe website over a TCP/IP socket. Low-level plans perform the system tasks and log data updates—for example, open 127.0.0.1:2076, and record the conversation with Adobe.

In Focus

Human beings are called "teleological" in the sense that we seek desired goals, while striving to avoid punishment. Designers of socio-biological security systems strive for this same behavioral set in security systems.

In this way, beginning with an initial set of plans, execution may proceed through paths from one plan to another by the agent, and this allows it to limit the scope of its response to address more localized problems (e.g., provide an http connection for agent X, but not for agent Y). Also, if a goal can be achieved in different ways (for example, manual or automatic update), the three levels of plans allow for this localized ability.

Damages that may occur vary according to the types of activities that an agent attempts. In data sharing, for example, agents need to utilize at least two different forms of resources: storage, in which each agent has to set aside some storage space for files that may be needed by other agents even though these files may not be useful to the agent itself, and bandwidth, where each agent must devote some of its processing and network bandwidth to handling communications requested by other agents. Damage in this specific sense is assessed according to the excess of security policy-defined thresholds.

To illustrate this case scenario, security agents interrogate their configurations and vulnerabilities ontologies against requests for services according to available resources, access and rights, reputations, and "suitable behaviors." According to Provos [14], running initially through applications and generating profiles would create baseline configurations, but this is not always possible. It is more likely in many configurations that agents learn by adding benign behaviors into the agent's ontology. For example, a request may be made for web service on port 8080. When the request is serviced, the agent checks the ontology for the web service to determine what actions are permissible. As long as the requestor behaves properly, no danger is detected, and permissions are granted for using resources according to defined QoS (e.g., memory utilization, network utilization, CPU utilization) and configuration (e.g., file checksums) and plan parameters.

In order for the agent to initiate a self-healing process after servicing a request that causes damage, for instance, if an agent detects violations to QoS mission parameters or a violation of normal behavior, it calculates a vector for the violation and determines damage severity. If severe damage is determined after servicing a request, the damage is flagged as malignant and filtered through a damage controller to determine what part of the agent is malignant and what actions to take, along with gathering data about the agent whose request caused the damage, adding it to the prohibitions, and giving the malevolent agent a low reputation rating.

On the other hand, if a stranger makes a request, or if a requestor with a high reputation makes a novel request, then danger is determined and the request is proactively monitored. That is, in cases of agent or behavior novelty, the request is quarantined and monitored to determine what resources it may utilize and to what extent, according to the obligation QoS parameters, or available resources in lieu of obligations. If a threshold is likely to be exceeded or a resource violation is likely to occur, the agent may notify the requestor, for example, to cease or reroute the request. If the requestor complies, a high reputation is given. On the other hand, if the request represents a known threat, the request is flagged as malignant non-self and is filtered through a damage controller to determine what actions to take, such as to deny the request and issue a low reputation for the requestor.

23.3.3 Adaptive Synthetic Systems

As suggested in our previous scenario about goal-directed agent behavior and how novelty can be optimally treated, agents are permitted to perform actions not explicitly denied them, and dangerous behavior is monitored, but may not be prevented. Because of their nature, MANETs cannot predefine all possible behaviors for agents *a priori*. A baseline can be established, but there may be occasions when agents legitimately need to perform novel behaviors. An agent monitors its environment by acquiring information from other agents, which include reputations of other agents, and monitor self according to QoS metrics, obligations, system resources and utilizations, and so forth. Given a goal and information about its situation, and information about its environment, an agent selects a plan and executes the plan's defined steps.

When an event occurs, depending on the rules governing the behavior, the agent may suspend its current plan and choose a new one. For instance, if an agent has a goal of providing a service and receives an update indicating a poor reputation of a peer, the agent may suspend its planned obligation for providing the agent the service and select a new plan. Thus, an agent selects a plan that fits the goal based on its environment and immediate situation. In summary, although social and cooperative, agent actions work similarly to the body's natural immune system; the idea behind this is to allow for danger and for the potential for some damage to be inflicted, while simultaneously striving to ensure survivability of the agent so that it can continue to provide cooperative support to the collective agency in the network.

As described, then, depending on the flexibility needed for the agent's role, the ability to use and/or make changes to the configuration may be left "wide open," similar to anonymous logins. There are cases in certain field settings where some devices will need to allow anyone who has access to an agent to install software, start services, or otherwise change the configuration. Higher value nodes will not likely permit this, and the graduating agent infrastructure and ontology will allow these types of decisions to be made according to the needs.

An action may lead to other actions depending on the events the actions trigger. Moreover, depending on the authorizations, actions may permit usage of elements in the configuration, or even to change the configuration if authorizations allow it. Configuration types have profiles, which can be as simple as file sizes, access permissions, and checksums—or in the most robust and stringent sense, a profile may consist of all the normal behaviors a given application can perform including the system calls that the application makes (c.f., Provos, 2002 [14]). A type of configuration may also have a version associated with it, as well as requirements, such as the amount of RAM necessary for execution or a set of QoS metrics to fulfill its obligations.

23.3.4 Challenges for Mobile Networks and Adaptive Systems

As we have presented in this chapter, statically defined security policies and configurations are insoluble in dynamic and mobile configurations such as MANET or P2P environments. In this final section, we will summarize and present some key issues that have not been fully resolved. As we pointed out, a more practical solution to the conventional forms of passive security and fortifications is to enable systems to carry out operations in dynamic configurations.

This can be facilitated by direct agency, enabling the flexibility for agent goal-directed autonomous behavior. However, given the nature and limits of the topology, proxy cooperation with other agents is essential [9]. Each agent carries out its own set of goals according to its plans, and makes requests of other agents, which are fulfilled so long as there remains cooperation and "good" behavior. A plan, as we indicated, consists of the sequence of steps associated with the goal, and rules that govern its responses to requests, events, and exceptions. An agent may have multiple plans available for a given goal, and multiple goals to accomplish, which are dynamic and negotiable [13].

Collective agency develops in response to agent reactions to events and other agent requests, and an agent provides services based on its available resources and the agreements the agent forms socially in the mobile network such as a MANET. However, the combined sociability and the *ad-hoc* nature of the MANET create an insecure environment. It must be possible for an agent to have the ability to detect severe impending danger so that some preventive measures can be taken before damage occurs.

Malevolent behavior is collected and reported to other agents by reputation, but some conservatism is built into the immunology by treating strangers cautiously while at the same time not denying them the opportunity to prove themselves as trustworthy.

In Focus

Most networked environments are built around trusted zones and systems; however, this is not practical for mobile networks. Moreover, it impedes the very sociability that makes such a network both effective and resilient. Therefore, an optimistic security stance is essential for mobile and social systems to function.

On some level, danger needs to be monitored, but not necessarily disrupted, unless it presents a severe and imminent threat potential for lethal damage. However, dangerous behaviors by undetected illegitimate agents (or colluders) may involve eavesdropping or interception of communications and may not escalate to disrupting the mission parameters and might not be detected, and thus rely on the typical cryptographic approaches to this problem, which may not be supported by all MANET agents.

Another challenge in MANET applications that needs to be addressed is the establishment and monitoring of QoS parameters. Mission-specific parameters and QoS metrics become crucial in determining the distinction between danger (novel behaviors) and actual impacts (damage) on mission execution. Applications may consist of discrete actions such as file or message exchanges, or involve streaming data such as video or voice. In discrete actions, the entire message or file may need to be received before it can be examined by an agent, causing delay between the time of the service request and the assessment of its quality. In an extreme case, an agent may not discover that a transferred file is valid or is a dangerous file until the file has been completely loaded into the agent. Streamed data, on the other hand, allows an agent to discover if the data are acceptable during points in the transmission.

Additionally, the QoS metrics may be different between discrete and stream data. In cases such as file transfers, metrics are generally download time and integrity of the files transferred. With streaming data, more crucial performance parameters tend to be the degree of jitter, frame rate transfer, and resolution. Danger provokes monitoring and because, in an ad-hoc environment, novel behaviors must be tolerated until it is learned whether the actions are benign or malignant but does not necessarily preclude them, depending on the assessment of the severity and imminent threat assessment. Damage, on the other hand, cannot be tolerated (at least for long). Being able to rapidly assess the QoS, followed by timely actions by an agent, is a critical problem to solve.

Finally, another area that needs exploration is in malevolent agent discovery. Because security policy ontology rules can be structured as subject → event → object, it should be possible to detect collusion issues among both cooperative and non-cooperative agents that may take place—for example, by correlating subjects with events, and events with objects, and subjects with objects to look for collusion patterns. However, by the time this can be done, the colluders may have disappeared from the MANET, or have whitewashed. Research is ongoing into these techniques but remains a yet-to-be conquered challenge [23].

CHAPTER SUMMARY

In this chapter, we introduced the concept of adaptive systems and gave several examples ranging from trusted kernels to agent-based security ontologies. We covered the basic approaches to self-healing systems, and we approached ways that systems can strive to detect danger and avoid damage. These issues are particularly difficult in mobile networks such as P2P or MANETs. With the advent of smart phones, emerging nanotechnologies, and other innovations that include sensors and micro-communications devices, the problems we face will continue to grow and become harder to solve. One of the best hopes for dealing with these issues is in socio-biologically inspired systems security, but accomplishing this necessarily means that systems will have to become more intelligent, and greater communications bandwidth will be needed as applications become richer and devices share more information.

THINK ABOUT IT

Topic Questions

23.1: Contemporary self-healing approaches generally involve what?

23.2: TSK stands for_____ _____, and _____.

23.3: Socially, systems can learn about dangerous nodes by their _____.

23.4: When an agent with a bad reputation leaves an ad-hoc network and rejoins with a different identity, this is called:

_____ Reputation management
_____ Whitewashing
_____ Rebranding
_____ Social contagion

23.5: The three types of agency are _____, _____, and _____.

23.6: What explains the response of mammalian immune systems when danger such as a virus or bacterium is detected:

_____ Damage theory
_____ QoS metrics

_____ Danger theory
_____ Changes to a program

23.7: What ability does the term "self-healing" refer to?

23.8: When an event is identified as damage, a trigger is issued to the:

_____ Damage as danger component
_____ Artificial immune response (AIR) component
_____ Ontology
_____ Hot standby system

23.9: Unintentional damage can lead to a poor reputation.

_____ True
_____ False

23.10: Reputations can be used for:

_____ Determining if damage has occurred
_____ Determining trust levels
_____ Assessing changes to a configuration
_____ Novel behaviors

Questions for Further Study

Q23.1: Biologically inspired security has not been without controversies. What are some of these controversies and what are some alternatives?

Q23.2: How does adding the social exchange component to biologically inspired systems help them detect danger rather than waiting for damage to be detected?

Q23.3: Explain three key reasons that security is moving away from static risk and vulnerability assessments and building fortified systems toward more adaptive systems and policies.

Q23.4: Discuss how closely silicon-based computers can mimic human biology. Is it a realistic goal?

Q23.5: Discuss how "free riding" might be handled in a socio-biological design.

KEY CONCEPTS AND TERMS

Biologically inspired security design is similar in concept to the human body's immune system, recognizing danger borrows from how humans interact in their social systems.

Deconfliction means to resolve conflicts in the rules that govern decision making.

Novelty can be used as a sign of danger.

Proxy agency relies on others to act on his or her behalf to secure desired goals.

Trusted security kernels monitor the behavior and changes to self and to peers, constructing on-the-fly, dynamic trust estimates for the different tasks.

References

1. Iqubal, A., & Maarof, M. A. (2005). Danger theory and intelligent data processing. *World Academy of Science, Engineering and Technology, 3*, 110–113.
2. Workman, M., Ford, R., & Allen, W. (2008). A structuration agency approach to security policy enforcement in mobile ad hoc networks. *Information Security Journal, 17, 267–277.*
3. Wang, A. H., & Yan, S. (1995). A stochastic model of damage propagation in database systems. *Proceedings from the Conference on Security and Management, SAM'09 Las Vegas, NV, 1, 3–9.*
4. Toutonji, O., & Yoo, S. M. (1995). Realistic approach against worm attack on computer networks by emulating human immune system. *Proceedings from the Conference on Security and Management, SAM'09 Las Vegas, NV, 1, 251–257.*
5. Ford, R. (2008). *BITSI.* Unpublished technical whitepaper. Melbourne, FL: Florida Institute of Technology.
6. Aickelin, U., & Cayzer, S. (2002). *The danger theory and its application to artificial immune systems.* University of Kent at Canterbury, doi 10.1.1.11.6815, pp. 141–148.

7. Sterne, D., Balasubramanyam, P., Carman, D., Wilson, B., Talpade, R, Ko, C., . . . Rowe, J. (2005). *A general cooperative intrusion detection architecture for MANETs.* Proceedings of the Third IEEE International Workshop on Information Assurance (IWIA), Washington, DC, pp. 57–70.

8. Ford, R., & Carvalho, M. (2007). *Biologically Inspired Security and BITSI.* A white paper. Melbourne: Florida Institute of Technology.

9. Boella, G., Sauro, L., & van der Torre, L. (2005). *Admissible agreements among goal-directed agents.* Proceedings of the IEEE/WIC/ACM International Conference on Intelligent Agent Technology (IAT'05), Paris.

10. Spector, R. H., & B. Mills. (2009). *Trust, trusted, and trusted kernels: Where are the gaps, and what to do about them?* Proceedings from the Conference of the Centers for Information and National Security, CINSec'09, 2 (1), 122–137.

11. Bandura, A. (2001). Social cognitive theory: An agentic perspective. *Annual Review of Psychology, 52,* 1–26.

12. Feldman, M., Lai, K., Stoica, I., & Chuang, J. (2004). Robust incentive techniques for peer-to-peer networks. *Proceedings of the 5th ACM conference on Electronic Commerce, 102–111.* New York, NY: Communications of the ACM.

13. Dastani, M., van Riemsdijk, M. B., Dignum, F., & Meyer, J. J. (2004). A Programming language for cognitive agents goal directed 3APL. In *Lecture Notes in Computer Science* (pp. 111–130). Heidelberg, Germany: Springer.

14. Provos, N. (2002). Improving host security with system call policies. *Proceedings of the 11th USENIX Security Symposium, 2,* 207–225.

15. Moreira, E., Martimiano, L., Brandao, A., & Bernardes, M. (2008). Ontologies for information security management and governance. *Information Management & Computer Security, 16,* 150–165.

16. Chomsky, N. (1979). Human language and other semiotic systems. *Semiotica, 25,* 31–44.

17. Chomsky, N. (1996). *Language and problems of knowledge.* Mendocino, CA: MIT Press.

18. Sun, O., & Garcia-Molian, H. (2004). *SLIC: A selfish link-based incentive mechanism for unstructured peer to peer networks.* Proceedings of the 34th International Conference on Distributed Computing Systems. Los Alamos, CA: IEEE Computer Society.

19. Feldman, M., & Chuang, J. (2005). Overcoming free-riding behavior in peer-to-peer systems. *ACM SIGccom Exchanges, 5,* 41–50.

20. Kang, S. S., & Mutka, M. W. (2005). A mobile peer to peer approach for multimedia content sharing using 3G/WAN dual mode channels. *Wireless Communications and Mobile Computing, 5,* 633–647.

21. Krishnana, R., Smith, M. D., Telang, R. (2003). The economics of peer to peer neworks. *Journal of Information Technology Theory and Application, 5,* 31–44.

22. Buchegger, S., & Le Boudec, J. Y. (2005, July). Self policing mobile ad hoc networks by reputation systems. *IEEE Communications Magazine,* pp.101–107.

23. Antoniadis, P., Courcoubetis, C., & Mason, R. (2004). Comparing economic incentives in peer-to-peer networks. *The International Journal of Computer and Telecommunications Networking, 46,* 133–146.

Security Horizons: Issues for Managers

WE HAVE COVERED A LOT OF GROUND in this textbook. It has served as an overview of the vast field of information security and has been designed to provide managers with key insights across a broad spectrum of security issues. In this final chapter, we will take some perspectives on information security, followed by presenting some social and cultural issues implied along with implications of information and national security initiatives. We will conclude this chapter with a summary and some resources that you might find helpful for further study.

Chapter 24 Topics

This chapter:

- Introduces some of the security technologies on the horizon.
- Raises some issues for managers to consider about the future of security.
- Provides concluding thoughts and additional recommended reading.

Chapter 24 Goals

When you finish this chapter, you should:

- ❑ Become aware of some of the security threat trends.
- ❑ Be able to discuss some key initiatives now and appearing on the horizon that have implications for organizations.
- ❑ Be able to explain the organizational impacts from global security initiatives.
- ❑ Have familiarity with the theory that influences the systemic relationships between societies, organizational practices, and individual behaviors.

24.1 Localized Security Issues

Before we widen our view to larger issues in security, including societal impacts, let's quickly take stock of some issues that are shaping organizational security practices on a more micro level. One of these issues has been the expansion of security attacks from targeting mainly Microsoft Windows because of their ubiquity, into new and increasingly sophisticated attacks against Linux and Macintosh, smart phones, notebooks, pads, and emerging smart devices. Later in this chapter, we will expand our perspectives on how security initiatives are shaping free societies and discuss what this may mean to organizations and managers in the future.

24.1.1 The Changing Technology, Security, and Attack Landscape

Not long ago, comments in a security blog pointed out vulnerabilities in the Windows Metafile (WMF) and suggested that it exposed weaknesses in Microsoft's operating system architecture. The WMF allows image files to contain code that can be executed when the image is decoded, and hackers have exploited this capability to install root kits, spyware, and other malicious code. Although Microsoft's Vista was purported to solve many of the security problems of earlier versions, it wasn't until the release of Windows 7 that many of those security goals were realized [1]. Although Windows has often received criticism over security, they have had a large footprint, and so by sheer volume, they have been the target of both security attacks and of criticism. However, in more recent years, users of Apple's MAC computers and other devices, who have rarely been affected by viruses, worms, and other malware in the past, have seen numerous security attacks. For example, a flaw in the way Apple software handled downloaded files was a source of attacks by giving attackers backdoor access if malicious files were opened from bogus websites and email.

> **In Focus**
>
> It is important to note that Windows-based systems have felt the brunt of attacks for years because those machines dominate the worldwide PC market. However, Apple users have now joined the ranks of dealing with security "patching" that Microsoft users have had to contend with.

Not long ago, a vulnerability discovered in MAC/OS came just days after the discovery of two other low-level MAC worms, along with the revelation that Linux (and some open source UNIX operating systems) had backdoors left by some of the contributors to its development. As an example, the OSX.Leap.A worm that hit in February 2006 was designed to spread over iChat, Apple's instant messaging system. When launched, it damaged software applications and the OS. The OSX/Ingtana, a worm, also appeared briefly, and according to some reports may have been intentionally created to prove that viruses could be spread across the MAC community.

Another worm attempted to spread via vulnerabilities in the Bluetooth service for MAC/OSX. Bluetooth is a wireless technology that allows devices to communicate at some distance. Likewise, new web exploits are being discovered against Mozilla Firefox, which was previously viewed as a safer alternative to Microsoft's Internet Explorer (IE). These threats usher in a cautionary era for MAC, Linux, and other non-Windows users, who have been unaccustomed to fretting about security patches or about opening unfamiliar email and instant messaging links [2]. However, more importantly, these attacks underscore the idea that no computer system or computing device will be completely safe, and that administrators and managers cannot afford to become complacent or overconfident in their technology.

> **In Focus**
>
> The key point here is that managers cannot rely on history or anecdotes for managing securely. Technologies and threats are constantly changing.

The proliferation of malicious websites is another unfortunate trend on the rise. These websites may contain code that can modify visitors' systems without their knowledge. Many of these attacks come from JavaScript, ActiveX controls, browser flaws, and even images. Multiple attacks may be launched from websites where both web server and browser vulnerabilities are simultaneously exploited. For example, upon visiting a site that executes a dual attack, clients might be covertly redirected to a web server where malicious code such as keyloggers are downloaded and used to track movements through the Web such as banking sites. When a banking site is visited, the keylogger may be used to capture the login information and send it to the attacker. Instant messaging, peer-to-peer (P2P) file exchanges, and chat protocols are becoming common targets because of their propensity to bypass or tunnel through firewalls. Chat protocols are particularly vulnerable to bots because of their tendency to implement Internet relay communications (IRCs) that are susceptible to remote control because an IRC server can connect to other IRC servers to expand its network of connections. Users access IRC networks by connecting from clients to servers in which there can be many, and moreover, they tend to permit server access without requiring users to log in.

24.1.2 Advanced Technologies, Threats, and Attacks

Advanced technologies such as mobile 3G and 4G devices and video teleconferencing are becoming widely available for businesses and for the home user. Video technologies range from sophisticated, multi-user technologies to inexpensive simple, single-user systems such as PC cameras. Rather than using the traditional telephone service, people are frequently turning to voice over IP, or VoIP, and applications such as Skype and Vonage. New VoIP technologies provide a more flexible and easier-to-implement solution than a traditional PBX. With VoIP, virtual offices can be set up with software running on a laptop over a VPN broadband connection. They are also able to carry increasing amounts of data, and along with policy-based routing protocols, are now able to support the nature of voice and video transmission. However, VoIP and technologies are ushering in new forms of voice spam attacks as well as creating some security concerns because VoIP has previously lacked strong encryption capability.

In Focus

Increasingly, devices are transitioning from special purpose such as mobile phones to make phone calls, to general purpose, such as telephony and computing devices that in addition to communications, play music, create and enable viewing videos, play games, allow web access and email, and run other multimedia applications.

Applications in cellular phones commonly support email, web and Internet access, FAX, and other basic services, and palmtop computers, and IP phones are becoming powerful enough that they are able to take the place of laptops for many applications. As third-generation or "3G" cellular phones and WiMAX have taken hold, and "4G" smart phones and notepads are rapidly being adopted, there will be further support for broadband services for mobile phones to enable fast access to the Web, streaming music, on-demand video programming, and videoconferencing.

Along with these capabilities come all kinds of security risks that have affected (and infected) more conventional computer systems for years now. As a result, attacks continue to become more sophisticated and widespread. All organizational members who work with information and systems must be educated in security issues, threats, and technology, and then their level of vigilance must be maintained to guard against new and unforeseen threats. This is requiring investments in areas that managers have previously not been accustomed to making.

24.1.3 Security, Processes, and Priorities

Other managerial issues deal with changing organizational practices and priorities. For example, there has been a strong emphasis on the separation of duties, but is this advice always wise? In July 2008, after receiving a poor performance evaluation, a network administrator in San Francisco reportedly "locked up" the systems used for handling sensitive data such as city payroll files, jail bookings, law enforcement documents, and official email for San Francisco, and refused to provide passwords to unlock the systems. He reportedly also installed and exposed a monitor to allow third parties to view the network traffic and to enable him to trace communications for his personnel case [3].

In Focus

One of the most important skills managers must possess is critical thinking. Many of the solutions that are proposed as gospel need to be critically evaluated to determine whether they make sense in the manager's environment.

Often, systems and networks are allowed to operate with some degree of vulnerability imposed by financial constraints and differences in priorities between technology professionals and organizational leadership. At the root of this issue is that money spent on security is an overhead expense. As the overhead cost of doing business grows and absorbs more of the bottom line in organizations, pressures increase on IT staff to do more with less.

Next, risk assessments and their identified impacts involve some degree of subjectivity, as we have discussed previously, and biases may cause managers to choose poorly. To mitigate this problem, multiple human perspectives along with using sophisticated threat modeling and prediction systems are important to add into important decision making. Also the priorities set by technologists and managers, regarding the capabilities of the security systems have at times been at odds. Risk management strategies have sometimes failed to incorporate overall organizational priorities and vice versa, making matters worse by leading to a lack of cooperation that is crucial to maintaining security.

In Focus

There has been tremendous emphasis in the security literature on security processes and criteria—but what is often lacking is the inclusion of the importance of aligning these with other organizational processes and goals, and aligning all of those with individual employee goals.

24.1.4 Security, Situations, and Behavior

We have discussed that an important organizational issue is to consider the human behavior aspect. Technologists have proposed that the "weakest link" problem should be frequently dealt with using automated and mandatory security measures. However, in practice, we have seen that these approaches alone are not sufficient to cover the range of actions that take place in businesses. Clearly, organizational security policies may require mandatory security measures, but although many security precautions can be automated through security technology by making them mandatory for users, there are many reasons why automation in and of itself will not solve the problem.

One seemingly simple example is automatically requiring users, on a periodic basis, to change their passwords and restricting acceptable passwords to a designated range of characters and numerical values including case alterations and special ASCII characters such as asterisks. On the surface, it would seem that managers would readily accept this because such standards clearly strengthen security. But the reality is not nearly so simple. Because people have trouble remembering these, they often write them down in proximity to the computer they use.

Next, as mentioned previously, other reasons that automated solutions are not universally adopted fall into four categories: (1) financial, (2) situational, (3) cultural, and (4) technological. First, many companies do not implement mandatory automated controls because they believe that the threat level does not warrant such financial investments or the inevitable loss of efficiency and productivity. According to Bartels [4], security technology and process infrastructure, as an overhead cost of doing business, has reached more than 8 percent of a company's average budget. In 2003, private industry spending on information security in the United States was estimated at more than $1 billion, and more than $6.5 billion for the U.S. government, according to the Information Security Oversight Office (2004) of the U.S. National Archives and Records Administration [5].

In addition to the cost of security technologies, firewall processing of communications, encryption, and virus and malware scanning, have a decided impact on productivity. In fact, studies [6] have reported that employees have cancelled their automatic virus scanning because it "slowed down their computer." This is the standard tradeoff of security versus productivity that makes it difficult to dictate an all-or-nothing policy when time is money. As an overhead cost of doing business, security technology and process infrastructure have doubled since 2001, growing to more than 8 percent of an average company's budget, so this limitation will clearly persist beyond whatever new technological improvements appear on the horizon.

Next, although there are innumerable situational factors that could be recounted, among these is the evidence that a large number of firms do not have the infrastructure and/or expertise to implement automatic techniques and so must substantially rely on discretionary controls. Another clear case is that, for business road warriors, it is sometimes necessary to reconfigure laptops in the field to allow them to secure access to WiFi networks. It is not possible to create a monolithic automated solution for all possible networks that employees might encounter.

> **In Focus**
>
> Reasons given by many managers for not implementing some security measures involve disparate and even incompatible approaches across distributed organizational boundaries.

Third, a mechanistic system that enforces security compliance is antithetical to some organizational cultures and, accordingly, will not be seen by managers as a viable approach. Automated solutions imply a certain degree of centralization. If the organizational culture is highly decentralized, single points of control may not be appreciated. In cultures where individualism and entrepreneurialism are valued, stringent security measures may be seen as individual responsibilities that should not be abrogated [7].

Fourth, there are technological conditions that prevent full-scale automation. We have covered many of these issues including disparities in standards and the impacts of mergers and acquisitions (M&A) on technology integrations. Consequently, in some organizations, network engineers configure firewalls to prevent promiscuous connections. In such cases, automatic security updates are precluded and individuals must take on the personal responsibility of protecting their own systems. Also, some software requires the use of ActiveX controls, ORBs that require distributions of "stubs," various scripting, or a variety of interprocess communications that may force security administrators to lower the centralized defensive posture, and although antivirus software might be activated before a server uploads attachments or emails, there are many security situations where parameters have to be individualized. Thus, in review, complete automation of security will likely never be possible and varying levels of human action and decision making will continue to be necessary. User choice and behavior will most likely always play a key role in whether security is implemented, and managers must be well prepared to deal with these technological and personnel issues.

24.1.5 Biometric Trends

The use of biometrics in security is advancing. Biometrics, generally, are measurable biological characteristics that are stored as templates and used for authentication or identification techniques. Fingerprints have been commonly used, but other biometrics are on the rise, including the analysis of facial characteristics in facial recognition, the analysis of hand geometry, which is the shape of the hand and the length of the fingers and even grip (for example, to recognize the owner of a handgun before allowing it to fire), analyses of patterns of veins in the back of the hand and the wrist, and the analysis of voice tone, pitch, cadence, and modulation (frequency) in a person's speech [8].

In Focus

Biometrics is one of the top research areas in both academia and government to solve the "soft" security issues. Eventually, DNA could well become the ultimate globally unique identifier used in security.

Though the field is still evolving, many people believe that biometrics will play a critical role in future computers, and especially in electronic commerce. Personal computers are being designed to include a fingerprint scanner where an index finger or palm print is required for access, and based on the user identity, differential authorization is given for levels of information and functional access. Access levels could include the ability to use credit card information to make electronic purchases.

Biometric passports are also now commonplace. These utilize fingerprints, a digitized image of one's face, and in some countries, radio-frequency identification (RFID) that can be used to track people's movements, such as in and out of a hotel. Key challenges that remain related to these issues include security for RFID, protections of biometric templates, preservation of confidentiality and privacy, and governing laws because much of these data are spread, stored, and used across international borders (as with biometric passport data). Although the use of biometrics is seen in some circles as a panacea, they are not without their own problems. First they are subject to errors, just as any other technology, and second, they are subject to compromises, both in transit to or from an authenticator and in terms of storage of the biometric templates in temporary or permanent storage.

24.2 Political and Behavioral Issues in Security

If we were to view security systemically, we could graph the socio-political aspects of security to socio-cultural aspects of security, and to socio-behavioral aspects of security. By that we mean that governments seek to maintain order and preserve its institutions. In this, deterrence theory has been a focal doctrine—for example, the notion of mutually assured destruction seeks to deter an enemy from committing an act of aggression. The socio-cultural aspects of security have been driven largely by terror management theory, which suggests that governments seek to make their populace vigilant against threats, and cajole them into acceding to approving large military and security expenditures. The socio-behavioral aspects of security have been driven largely by protection motivation theory, which states that people rely on their coping abilities against perceived severity and likelihood of threats.

24.2.1 Legislation and Global Security

First of all, the juxtaposition of globalization and legislation may seem almost an oxymoron. Globalization is fueling network effects and the spread of information, whereas legislation strives to constrain an activity or expression. One thing is clear: there is an inflation of both. Within the United States, laws and legislations frequently vary from state to state, and trying to imagine that legislation may solve global problems seems beyond comprehension. In the minds of many people living in democratic societies, there is little doubt that the nature of intentional threats are changing and that new disasters loom. For example, we have had to come to grips with terms such as ***asymmetrical warfare***. Many people point to the so-called *9-11* terrorist attacks in the United States, or the London Tube bombings, as examples of global threats that have come from perpetrators without association with a geography or national identity.

Also recent events have marked changes where many democratic societies have begun to implement radical constrictions of civil liberties under the banner of such benign sounding names as the *Patriot Act* [9]. For other threats, many have pointed to financial threats from the *greedy unregulated insiders* or *corporate rogues*, or to threats from third-world countries or failed nation states that now have sponsored cyber warfare capabilities and even nuclear weapons. These issues may seem far removed from most managers' concerns about maintaining the security of daily operations, but we might need to weigh threats such as contamination of our headquarter office from a biohazard, or a protracted loss of power from a cyber attack on a power grid or nuclear plant, or devastating natural disasters as with the 2011 tsunami in Japan.

In the United States, and other democratic nations as well, there are sweeping regulations and legislations making it very difficult to keep up with what is required of an individual or organization. Just to name a few in the United States, the Computer Fraud and Abuse Act (Title 18, U.S. Code, 1030) prohibits having knowingly accessed a computer without authorization or exceeding authorized access to commit various crimes; the Economic Espionage Act of 1996 prohibits obtaining trade secrets to benefit a foreign entity; and the Electronic Funds Transfer Act covers use, transport, sale, receipt, or furnishing of counterfeit, altered, lost, stolen, or fraudulently obtained debit instruments in interstate or foreign commerce. The Child Pornography Prevention Act of 1996 (CPPA) prohibits use of computer technology to produce child pornography. The Computer Security Act of 1987 requires Federal Executive agencies to establish computer security programs. The Electronic Communications Privacy Act (ECPA) prohibits unauthorized interception or retrieval of electronic communications, and the Fair Credit Reporting Act governs types of data that companies may collect on private citizens and how it may be used. The Foreign Corrupt Practices Act covers improper foreign operations, but applies to all companies registered with the Security and Exchange Commission (SEC), and requires companies to institute security programs, and the Freedom of Information Act permits public access to information collected by the federal executive branch. There are a myriad of others as well [10].

How can managers keep track of all of these regulations and laws, let alone enforce them in large multinational organizations? The answer seems to require the help from teams of security consultants, security employees, legal teams, and specializations in human resources departments. As both the numbers and the severity of threats increase, societies and organizations especially are going to have to grapple with the levels of security assurance they wish to maintain against the freedoms that are perceived by them as worth preserving. Clearly the answers to the problems will not be easy to come by, but the future of businesses operating in democratic societies might hang in the balance.

Some examples of the yet-to-be fully addressed issues include the fact that companies such as Amazon and online travel agencies examine browser cookies—besides their own—so that they can put together user profiles for marketing purposes. However, what happens when criminals do the same thing for identity theft or other illicit purposes? Can a corporate user's web surfing patterns collected by companies or search engines enhance a threat of *insider trading* from an outside company? What sorts of threats are posed by Google's ads and their ability to tie them to page content? Can individuals behind corporate firewalls unwittingly expose company secrets by their search engine queries?

What about Google maps? Is it a concern that someone can tap into social media such as Facebook or Twitter, say for instance, where someone may announce travel plans or share information while traveling—and then Google maps offers even the most casual observer actual images of the traveler's (vacant) home as well as its location? Will more regulation help to solve these problems? The conception that behavior must be regulated in order for people to comply with established norms is called **deontological behavior**, where ethical behavior and morality are determined to be the results of actions from conformance to rules. However, many people need more than that; they need self-determined principles and feelings of obligations to the broader society at large; these are the notions of self-governance and social responsibility.

In Focus

Web surfing is concomitant with companies that do website analytics. These facilities help companies predict someone's "next move." Although in most cases website analytics are used for marketing purposes, they also offer more opportunities for insidious activities.

24.2.2 Globalization and Information Exposure

Where the standard security data collection efforts tend to assemble information on individuals only after they have been identified as "persons of interest," there is change in posture underfoot by means of non-discriminatory pervasive data collection [9]. The argument for such a collection is to enable earlier detection of criminality by developing full identity profiles much earlier than is possible under the identification scheme. One problem this presents is the combination of data collections with outsourcing of data storage and use. For example, it has become common practice in the United States for many tax processors to outsource tax preparations to workers in foreign countries, and for immigration data used in tracking human flow control to be shared with state visitor bureaus and travel agencies for advertising purposes.

In Focus

With the simultaneous advancements in capabilities and security initiatives, the institutional use of security information has broadened from identifying individuals to authenticating individuals within populations.

Information gathering is potentially ubiquitous and any kind of media or activity can become raw material for production of an information commodity. In this context, both government and private actors conspire to use information gathered about people as well as their communications to maximize economic opportunities. "Meanwhile, government administration and law enforcement agencies follow a desire to extend the traditional state surveillance and investigative power to new digital domains, consider [these data] as merely the translation of existing powers to new mediums. The surveillance extends the logic of power into the mobile arena, but also links up with commercial imperative and characterizes the new communication economy" [11].

These practices are accompanied by a troubled history of both intentional and unintentional information leakage. To highlight this, some have pointed to recent security breaches of information repositories, such as when LexisNexis had 310,000 personal records stolen by hackers in 59 separate incidents. In another instance, ChoicePoint— an affiliate of the Equifax credit bureau—had reportedly maintained more than 17 billion records about individuals and businesses, which ChoicePoint sold to an estimated 100,000 clients, including 7,000 federal, state, and local law enforcement agencies, some of which were later discovered to be fronts for criminal operations.

The high-profile compromises of LexisNexis and of ChoicePoint in 2005, and many others, illustrate that having central repositories containing such sensitive information increases individual vulnerability and fuels public concerns over identity theft, of which the U.S. Department of Justice estimates that 1 in 3 people will become victims at some point in their lifetimes. The obvious technological and procedural issues to be resolved include how to protect the integrity of the devices and data used in the information capture and verification process (e.g., attending to tamper-proof materials and maintaining accurate databases) and also how to secure the information as it is stored and accessed [9].

In Focus

With the broadening of institutional use of information, the frequency and severity of negative impacts on innocent persons and corporations have increased. An example is the growing problem of information leakage by organizations that leads to identity theft.

Beyond these technical issues is cause for alarm over the increased incidence of type-1 errors where the innocent are singled out with potentially devastating and long-term (potentially lifelong) consequences, including arrest records that remain with victims of identity theft by criminals even if victims are later vindicated during adjudication. The concern widens with the consideration that one's sensitive biometric information will be kept in repositories in various countries one visits. Leakage of personal information from these central information repositories continues to exacerbate both the potential and severity of the damage to individuals and industry.

In spite of these concerns, the blending of immigration, intelligence, and commercial data collection and dissemination is gaining traction. An example of this is the e-Passport implementation in some Caribbean islands, which has included provisions for the capture of e-Passport RFID as people visited stores, hotels, and restaurants. It called for the information to be utilized by government law enforcement and intelligence communities, and allowed feeds to information repositories for marketing campaigns and other commercial activities [12].

24.2.3 Security and Ethical Governing

In the foregoing, we have raised some provocative questions that highlight our earlier point: *One of the most important skills managers must possess is critical thinking.* It is unequivocal that security threats are real and that managers and employees in general need to take precautions. Managers in particular are responsible for proactive security measures, and this is undisputed. However, along with the needs for managing securely, managers also hold social responsibility and ethical duties that require more critical thought in order to strike a reasoned balance between the needs for security and the sometimes seemingly endless striving for security assurance. Security issues and initiatives are not isolated. An organizational security enactment is part of a larger set of forces that need to be contemplated in light of organizational and societal justice. The increasing regulations and laws and growing global caches of personal information mentioned in the previous sections are just a couple of examples of this issue.

Commercial enterprises model their practices on the norms and values of the societies in which they are situated. Governmental laws and regulations establish the boundaries and constraints under which capitalism operates, and help shape the forms of commerce, including how businesses conduct themselves as well as their strategic opportunities. Since the 9/11 terrorist attacks in the United States, an entire industry has flourished and coined *fear commerce*. The pervasive effects of these governmental and commercial instrumentalities profoundly shape the psychology and behavior of people. For example, if threats are perceived as severe and imminent, people will often trade their freedom for even the illusion of safety [9]. This has a tangible impact on businesses and managers.

Government, society, and commercial interests and activities are all interrelated where the socio-political, along with the socio-behavioral, dimensions of security shape how governmental policies translate into actions taken in commercial enterprises, and these translate into psychosocial perspectives and behavioral outcomes of employees. With every security initiative, there are concomitant financial and logistical constraints. A simple example can be pointed out in the awkward paradox that mobility and commerce rely on practical levels of safety, and yet the mechanisms required to mitigate security threats, by their nature, may constrain mobility and commerce. Controlling mobility includes the vehicles used for transportation as well as the transactions that people perform—thus security technology controls the things a person does either as physical action or as captured in data, along with movement itself [11, 13]. In addition to the duties of due care and due diligence, managers also carry an ethical responsibility to contemplate how the security actions they take coincide with the core values of society and democracy. We call this the ***duty of social responsibility***.

CHAPTER SUMMARY

As seen throughout our textbook, information security is a significant undertaking in any organization. Beyond the micro-level issues, businesses cannot operate without the national and international infrastructures to support their activities. Maintaining security is a legitimate and critical concern, but the opportunism that tends to arise out of these legitimate concerns winds up helping no one. Managers are on the front lines of many of these decisions, including what opportunities to pursue and at what margin, whether or not to implement organizational surveillance, and with what types and to what extent, and to what degrees they will accept legislation and regulations for information collection and retention of information before banding together and demanding of their elected officials accountability for the fulfillment of their part of the ***Social Contract***. Ethical standards must be established as we are well aware, and managers must lead by example. These larger issues remain some of the most perplexing problems managers must face in a global marketplace to security.

THINK ABOUT IT

There are a number of useful resources on the Web; however, typical of the Web, some resources may come and some may go, and some websites may be credible and others not. We have assembled a few websites you might find useful:

Attack Prevention (www.attackprevention.com). This site is a portal to a very comprehensive set of reading materials and white papers. It also hosts forums, message boards, and email.

Church of the Swimming Elephant (www.cotse .com). This site contains many useful articles and links to a variety of tools such as port scanners, steganography, and cryptographic technology.

Cisco (http://www.cisco.com/en/US/tech/ tk648/tk361/technologies_tech_ note09186a0080120f48.shtml). This page contains some good information about network security.

Insecure (www.insecure.org). This site provides a variety of resources including articles and links to open source technologies useful to information security specialists.

The Security Policy Institute (www .securitypolicyinstitute.org). This is the website for professional training and development, consulting and outsourced security research and development.

CINSec (www.cinsec.org). Training, news, and current events are posted at the CINSec website.

Recommended Additional Reading

Ballad, B., Ballad, T., & Banks, E. K. (2011). *Access control, authentication, and public key infrastructure.* Sudbury, MA: Jones & Bartlett Learning.

Gibson, D. (2011). *Managing risk in information systems.* Sudbury, MA: Jones & Bartlett Learning.

Grama, J. L. (2011). *Legal issues in information security.* Sudbury, MA: Jones & Bartlett Learning.

Harwood, M. (2011). *Security strategies in web applications and social networking.* Sudbury, MA: Jones & Bartlett Learning.

Jang, M. (2011). *Security strategies in Linux platforms and applications.* Sudbury, MA: Jones & Bartlett Learning.

Johnson, R. (2011). *Security policies and implementation issues.* Sudbury, MA: Jones & Bartlett Learning.

Oriyano, S. P., & Gregg, M. (2011). *Hacker techniques, tools, and incident handling.* Sudbury, MA: Jones & Bartlett Learning.

Solomon, M. G. (2011). *Security strategies in Windows platforms and applications.* Sudbury, MA: Jones & Bartlett Learning.

Stewart, M. J. (2011). *Network security, firewalls, and VPNs.* Sudbury, MA: Jones & Bartlett Learning.

Vacca, J. R., & Rudolph, K. (2011). *System forensics, investigation, and response.* Sudbury, MA: Jones & Bartlett Learning.

Weiss, M. M., & Solomon, M. G. (2011). *Auditing IT infrastructures for compliance.* Sudbury, MA: Jones & Bartlett Learning.

KEY CONCEPTS AND TERMS

Deontological behavior is based on the assumption that people are only well behaved because they are driven to conform by rules and laws.

Fear commerce is a term referencing the use of fear to get people to purchase security products or services they may or may not need.

Information caches are information stores kept by many parties (especially on the Web). As a result of increasing information caches, there is a growing risk of leakage.

Regulation refers to governmental actions to control an industry, and regulation is increasing worldwide.

Social responsibility means considering more than one's own business interests, but also how the business affects societies at large. Social responsibility (a macro-concept) will become increasingly important in security management in the future—joining what is now called "business ethics," which is a more micro-level (individual) concept.

References

1. Solomon, M. G. (2011). *Security strategies in Windows platforms and applications.* Sudbury, MA: Jones & Bartlett Learning.
2. Jang, M. (2011). *Security strategies in Linux platforms and applications.* Sudbury, MA: Jones & Bartlett Learning.
3. Lohrmann, D. (2008, July 16). San Francisco network administrator locks everyone out, goes to jail. *Technology and Cyber Security,* pp. 1–4.
4. Bartels, A. (2006, November). Global IT spending and investment forecast, 2006–2007. *Forrester Research,* pp. 4–31.
5. ISOO. (2004). *The report on cost estimates for security classification activities for 2003 from the Information Security Oversight Office (ISOO).* Washington, DC: National Archives and Records Administration.
6. Workman, M., Bommer, W. H., & Straub, D. (2009). The amplification effects of procedural justice with a threat control model of information systems security. *Journal of Behaviour and Information Technology, 28,* 563–575.
7. Workman, M., Bommer, W. H., & Straub, D. (2008). Security lapses and the omission of information security measures: An empirical test of the threat control model. *Journal of Computers in Human Behavior, 24,* 2799–2816.
8. Reid, P. (2004). *Biometrics for network security.* Upper Saddle River, NJ: Prentice Hall.
9. Workman, M. (2008). Fear commerce: Inflationary effects of global security initiatives. *Information Systems Security Journal, 17,* 124–131.
10. Grama, J. L. (2011). *Legal issues in information security.* Sudbury, MA: Jones & Bartlett Learning.
11. Castells, M., Mireia-Fernandez, M., Qiu, J. L., & Sey, A. (2007). *Mobile communication and society.* Cambridge, MA: MIT Press.
12. Bragdon, C. R. (2008). *Transportation security.* Burlington, MA: Elsevier/Butterworth-Heinemann.
13. Canny, J. (2006). The future of human-computer interaction. *The ACM Queue Journal, 4,* 24–32.

Index

Note: Italicized page locators indicate figures; tables are noted with *t*.

INDEX

I

X

Y

Z